The Changing Transitions to Adulthood in Developing Countries

Selected Studies

Cynthia B. Lloyd, Jere R. Behrman, Nelly P. Stromquist, and Barney Cohen, *Editors*

Panel on Transitions to Adulthood in Developing Countries

Committee on Population

Division of Behavioral and Social Sciences and Education

NATIONAL RESEARCH COUNCIL
OF THE NATIONAL ACADEMIES

THE NATIONAL ACADEMIES PRESS
Washington, D.C.
www.nap.edu

THE NATIONAL ACADEMIES PRESS • 500 Fifth Street, N.W. • Washington, D.C. 20001

NOTICE: The project that is the subject of this report was approved by the Governing Board of the National Research Council, whose members are drawn from the councils of the National Academy of Sciences, the National Academy of Engineering, and the Institute of Medicine. The members of the committee responsible for the report were chosen for their special competences and with regard for appropriate balance.

This study was supported by a cooperative agreement between the National Academy of Sciences and the United States Agency for International Development (CCP-3078-A-00-5024) and from grants from the Andrew W. Mellon Foundation, the William and Flora Hewlett Foundation, the David and Lucile Packard Foundation, The John D. and Catherine T. MacArthur Foundation, and the World Bank. Any opinions, findings, conclusions, or recommendations expressed in this publication are those of the authors and do not necessarily reflect the views of the organizations or agencies that provided support for the project.

Library of Congress Cataloging-in-Publication Data

The changing transitions to adulthood in developing countries : selected
  studies / Cynthia B. Lloyd ... [et al.], editors ; Panel on Transitions to
  Adulthood in Developing Countries ; Committee on Population,
  Division of Behavioral and Social Sciences and Education.
    p. cm.
  Includes bibliographical references.
  ISBN 0-309-09680-4 (pbk.) — ISBN 0-309-55130-7 (pdf)
    1. Young adults—Developing countries. 2. Youth—Developing
  countries. 3. Adulthood—Developing countries. 4. School-to-work
  transition—Developing countries.   I. Lloyd, Cynthia B., 1943-   .
  II. National Research Council (U.S.). Panel on Transitions to Adulthood
  in Developing Countries. III. National Research Council (U.S.).
  Committee on Population.
  HQ799.8.D45C43 2005
  305.242′091724—dc22

                                                    2005017524

Additional copies of this report are available from the National Academies Press, 500 Fifth Street, N.W., Lockbox 285, Washington, D.C. 20055; (800) 624-6242 or (202) 334-3313 (in the Washington metropolitan area); http://www.nap.edu.

Printed in the United States of America.

Suggested citation: National Research Council. (2005). *The Changing Transitions to Adulthood in Developing Countries: Selected Studies.* Cynthia B. Lloyd, Jere R. Behrman, Nelly P. Stromquist, and Barney Cohen, eds. Panel on Transitions to Adulthood in Developing Countries. Committee on Population. Division of Behavioral and Social Sciences and Education. Washington, DC: The National Academies Press.

THE NATIONAL ACADEMIES
Advisers to the Nation on Science, Engineering, and Medicine

The **National Academy of Sciences** is a private, nonprofit, self-perpetuating society of distinguished scholars engaged in scientific and engineering research, dedicated to the furtherance of science and technology and to their use for the general welfare. Upon the authority of the charter granted to it by the Congress in 1863, the Academy has a mandate that requires it to advise the federal government on scientific and technical matters. Dr. Ralph J. Cicerone is president of the National Academy of Sciences.

The **National Academy of Engineering** was established in 1964, under the charter of the National Academy of Sciences, as a parallel organization of outstanding engineers. It is autonomous in its administration and in the selection of its members, sharing with the National Academy of Sciences the responsibility for advising the federal government. The National Academy of Engineering also sponsors engineering programs aimed at meeting national needs, encourages education and research, and recognizes the superior achievements of engineers. Dr. Wm. A. Wulf is president of the National Academy of Engineering.

The **Institute of Medicine** was established in 1970 by the National Academy of Sciences to secure the services of eminent members of appropriate professions in the examination of policy matters pertaining to the health of the public. The Institute acts under the responsibility given to the National Academy of Sciences by its congressional charter to be an adviser to the federal government and, upon its own initiative, to identify issues of medical care, research, and education. Dr. Harvey V. Fineberg is president of the Institute of Medicine.

The **National Research Council** was organized by the National Academy of Sciences in 1916 to associate the broad community of science and technology with the Academy's purposes of furthering knowledge and advising the federal government. Functioning in accordance with general policies determined by the Academy, the Council has become the principal operating agency of both the National Academy of Sciences and the National Academy of Engineering in providing services to the government, the public, and the scientific and engineering communities. The Council is administered jointly by both Academies and the Institute of Medicine. Dr. Ralph J. Cicerone and Dr. Wm. A. Wulf are chair and vice chair, respectively, of the National Research Council.

www.national-academies.org

PANEL ON TRANSITIONS TO ADULTHOOD
IN DEVELOPING COUNTRIES

CONTRIBUTORS

JERE R. BEHRMAN, Department of Economics and Population Studies Center, University of Pennsylvania

JOHN B. CASTERLINE, Department of Demography, Pennsylvania State University

BARNEY COHEN, Committee on Population, The National Academies, Washington, DC

MONICA J. GRANT, Policy Research Division, Population Council, New York

SHIVA S. HALLI, Department of Community Health Sciences, University of Manitoba, Winnipeg, Canada

KELLY HALLMAN, Policy Research Division, Population Council, New York

EMILY HANNUM, Department of Sociology, University of Pennsylvania

PAUL C. HEWETT, Policy Research Division, Population Council, New York

SHIREEN J. JEJEEBHOY, Population Council, New Delhi, India

JAMES C. KNOWLES, Independent consultant, Bangkok, Thailand

BARTHÉLÉMY KUATE-DEFO, Department of Demography, University of Montreal, Canada

DAVID A. LAM, Department of Economics and Population Studies Center, University of Michigan, Ann Arbor

JIHONG LIU, Department of Population and International Health, Harvard School of Public Health

CYNTHIA B. LLOYD, Policy Research Division, Population Council, New York

LETÍCIA MARTELETO, Department of Demography, Federal University of Minas Gerais, Brazil

BARBARA S. MENSCH, Policy Research Division, Population Council, New York

AGNES R. QUISUMBING, Consultative Group on International Agricultural Research, Washington, DC

PIYALI SENGUPTA, Independent research consultant, Wilmington, DE

SUSHEELA SINGH, The Alan Guttmacher Institute, New York

NELLY P. STROMQUIST, School of Education, University of Southern California

Acknowledgments

In 2001 the National Research Council (NRC) and the Institute of Medicine convened a multidisciplinary panel of experts to assess how the transition to adulthood is changing in the developing world and what the implications of those changes might be for the design and improvement of programs and policies affecting young people. In December 2004 the panel released its report, *Growing Up Global: The Changing Transitions to Adulthood in Developing Countries*, with the panel's findings, analysis, and conclusions. This companion volume contains the detailed background papers that the panel commissioned to help its work.

The papers in this volume have been reviewed in draft form by individuals chosen for their diverse perspectives and technical expertise, in accordance with procedures approved by the Report Review Committee of the NRC. The purpose of this independent review is to provide candid and critical comments that will assist the institution in making its published volume as sound as possible and to ensure that the volume meets institutional standards for objectivity, evidence, and responsiveness to charge. The review comments remain confidential to protect the integrity of the process.

We thank the following individuals for their review of one or more papers in this volume: Samer Al-Samarrai, Department of Economics, Institute of Development Studies, Sussex, United Kingdom; Mary Arends-Kuenning, Department of Agriculture and Consumer Economics, University of Illinois, Urbana-Champaign; Magali Barbieri, Institut National Etudes Démographiques, France; David Bishai, Department of Population and Family Health Science, Johns Hopkins University; John Bongaarts, Population

Council, New York; Deborah Davis, Department of Sociology, Yale University; Deborah DeGraff, Department of Economics, Bowdoin College, Maine; Anil Deolalikar, Department of Humanities, University of California, Riverside; Andrew Foster, Department of Economics, Brown University; Elizabeth Fussell, Department of Sociology, Tulane University; Paul Glewwe, Department of Economics, University of Minnesota; Daniel Goodkind, U.S. Census Bureau, Washington, DC; Margaret Greene, Center for Global Health, George Washington University; Leah C. Gutierrez, Asian Development Bank, Philippines; John Hobcraft, Department of Social Policy and Social Work, University of York, United Kingdom; Allen Kelley, Department of Economics, Duke University; Reed Larson, Department of Human and Community Development, University of Illinois at Urbana-Champaign; Deborah Levison, Institute of Public Affairs, University of Minnesota; Anju Malhotra, Population and Social Transitions, International Center for Research on Women, Washington, DC; Peter McDonald, Research School of Social Sciences, Australian National University, Australia; Elena Nightingale, Institute of Medicine, Washington, DC; Constantijn W.A. Panis, Center for the Study of Aging, RAND, California; David Post, Department of Education Policy Studies, Pennsylvania State University; Robert Prouty, World Bank, Washington, DC; George Psacharopoulos, State MP, Greece; Vijayendra Rao, Development Research Group, World Bank, Washington, DC; Ronald R. Rindfuss, Carolina Population Center, University of North Carolina at Chapel Hill; Najma Sharif, Department of Economics, Saint Mary's University, Nova Scotia, Canada; Susan Short, Department of Sociology, Brown University; Tom A.B. Snijders, Department of Behavioral and Social Sciences, University of Groningen, The Netherlands; Insan Tunali, Department of Economics, University of Kansas; Etienne van de Walle, Population Studies Center, University of Pennsylvania.

Although the reviewers listed above provided many constructive comments and suggestions, they were not asked to endorse the content of any of the papers nor did they see the final version of any paper before this publication. The review of this volume was overseen by Cynthia B. Lloyd, Population Council; Jere R. Behrman, University of Pennsylvania; and Nelly P. Stromquist, University of Southern California. Appointed by the NRC, they were responsible for making certain that an independent examination of the papers was carried out in accordance with institutional procedures and that all review comments were carefully considered. Responsibility for the final content of this volume rests entirely with the authors.

Contents

xi

1

Introduction

Cynthia B. Lloyd, Jere R. Behrman,
Nelly P. Stromquist, and Barney Cohen

Adolescence is a critical period of human development that sets young people on trajectories that shape their future as adults. Fundamental decisions are made during adolescence relating to transitions out of school, into work, into sexual relations, into marriage, into parenting and, generally, into assuming adult roles in communities in which individuals spend their early adult years. Although these transitions onto various trajectories are not immutable, the transitions in adolescence condition considerably developments over the rest of people's lives and, indeed, the context in which their children are born and raised.

Since the International Conference on Population and Development in Cairo in 1994, young people have been recognized as a critical target group for better health and other social policies and programs. In many countries, the risk of HIV/AIDS and adolescent pregnancy and childbearing are particular sources of social and policy concern, and many international, national, and nongovernment organizations are now focusing more attention on the problems of young people. Increasingly, programs to help young people are being undertaken using broad holistic approaches that incorporate elements of education, livelihood, and citizenship training. This international attention to the situation of young people has been further reinforced in more recent years by the adoption of the United Nations Millennium Development Goals (MDG) by the international community in 2000. The accomplishment of many of these goals, including the reduction in the incidence of extreme poverty, the achievement of universal primary school, gender equity and women's empowerment, reductions in maternal mortality, HIV/AIDS, and the promotion of youth employment, requires a policy emphasis on investments in young people.

1

This growing emphasis on young people in policy and programming arenas has drawn attention to gaps in our knowledge regarding the situation of adolescents in developing countries as well as to how various transitions to adulthood are changing in light of globalization. More young people than ever—more than 1.5 billion youth ages 10 to 24 in developing countries—are experiencing the transition to adulthood during a time of unprecedented global change. Responding to the need for more informed policy making, the National Academies convened a multidisciplinary expert group—the Panel on the Transitions to Adulthood in Developing Countries—to assess how transitions to adulthood are changing for young men and women in developing countries, and what the implications of those changes are for the design of programs that affect young people. Specifically, the panel was asked to:

- document the situation and status of adolescents and young adults in developing countries;
- ascertain the changes that are occurring in the nature, timing, sequencing, and interrelationships of the various transitions to adulthood in developing countries;
- assess the knowledge base regarding the causes and consequences of these changes;
- identify the implications of this knowledge for policy and program interventions affecting adolescent reproductive health; and
- identify research priorities that are scientifically promising and relevant for integrating adolescent research and policy.

In answering these broad questions, the panel was forced to face several difficult theoretical and empirical questions. In part this was inevitable because of the enormity of the subject and the diversity of contexts and experiences of youth in many varied contexts. Where the existing literature was found to be deficient and data to answer particular questions were known to be available, the panel decided to commission a series of background papers to provide more focused treatment of certain issues and greater detail on which the panel report could build. The panel's report entitled *Growing Up Global: The Changing Transitions to Adulthood in Developing Countries* contains its main findings, analyses, and conclusions. This companion volume contains revised versions of the best of these background papers that the panel commissioned along the way.

Because these studies were selected to fill unique gaps in the existing literature, they should not be taken to constitute a comprehensive collection of all potentially relevant topics related to transitions to adulthood in developing countries. In the panel report, many more such topics are indicated at the end of each chapter for which research is still needed. Nevertheless, each paper reproduced here represents a useful scientific contribution in its own right. Collectively, the papers span a broad range of youth issues and cover a wide range of societies both geographically and culturally.

DOCUMENTING THE CHANGING CONTEXTS WITHIN WHICH YOUNG PEOPLE ARE TRANSITIONING TO ADULTHOOD

In Chapter 2, Jere Behrman and Piyali Sengupta describe the extent to which the aggregate contexts in which youth have been making transitions to adulthood in developing countries have been converging toward those in the developed economies. The study finds that the developing countries have tended to converge toward the characteristics of the developed countries in a number of important respects in recent decades. But there also has been significant divergence in some other respects. The tendency for convergence has been considerable for the available indicators of health, education, environment, transportation and communication, and gender differences, but somewhat less for some other indicators. Furthermore, though there has been a tendency for convergence for many aspects of the economy, the pattern is mixed for the important overall economic indicators of economic growth rates and per capita product.

In particular, two of the regions—Latin America and the Caribbean and sub-Saharan Africa—have diverged negatively with regard to economic growth rates, and only two of the regions—East Asia and the Pacific and South Asia—have been converging rather than diverging in terms of per capita real product. Though the majority of youth in the developing world live in the latter two regions, there is a significant minority who live in the other regions for which there has been not only divergence, but decreases in per capita real product in the last two decades. Considering all the indicators, East Asia and the Pacific generally has converged most toward developed economics and sub-Saharan Africa least. The other regions are in between, with Europe and Central Asia in several cases diverging from the developed economies, but converging toward the more developed of the developing regions.

Collectively, these results suggest that the dominant thrust has been toward a more integrated and more similar world in which youth are making transitions to adulthood. This implies many changes for current youth in comparison with previous generations—dependence much more on markets than on family enterprises for jobs, much more on formal schooling than on learning by working with parents and other relatives with regard to education; much more awareness of options and lifestyles from the broader world than just from the local community; longer life expectancies and less susceptibility to infectious diseases with the exception of HIV/AIDS; smaller gender gaps favoring males; and much more mobility in a number of dimensions. But this major thrust should be qualified by some important divergences that have been documented in some regions and with respect to various indicators.

STUDIES ON THE DETERMINANTS AND PATTERNS OF EDUCATION

In Chapter 3, David Lam and Letícia Marteleto focus on the implications for the schooling of youth of trends in family size and in the size of birth cohorts in Brazil, the most populous country in Latin America. One of the important features of the Brazilian demographic transition, as in most other demographic transitions, is that family size and cohort size have moved in opposite directions during much of the transition. Declining fertility rates compete with population momentum to determine the size of birth cohorts, with the increasing numbers of childbearing-age women outpacing the declining fertility rates for many years of the transition. The size of birth cohorts continued growing in Brazil until around 1982, even though fertility rates and family size had been falling since the 1960s. The school-age population continued growing until the early 1990s, with the growth rate dropping sharply in the 1990s. Cohorts born after 1982 are the first cohorts in Brazil to experience both falling cohort size and falling family size relative to previous cohorts, a fact that may have important implications for school outcomes. The peak of Brazil's school-age population coincides with the beginning of a period of rapid improvement in school enrollment and school attainment in Brazil, starting around 1990.

Lam and Marteleto's results indicate that school enrollment is negatively affected by the growth rate of the population ages 7 to 14, with the most negative effects on older males from poorer households, suggesting that school crowding has the biggest impact on students who are closest to the margin of dropping out of school. Counterfactual simulations indicate that enrollment rates would have improved faster in the 1980s if cohort growth rates had not increased, and that enrollment rates were positively affected by the declining growth rates of the 1990s. The number of siblings ages 0 to 6 and 7 to 17 both also had significant negative effects on enrollment. The effect of the number of siblings ages 0 to 6 is much greater than the effect of the number of siblings ages 7 to 17, and is slightly more negative on girls than boys. Simulated counterfactuals suggest that declining family size was one of the factors contributing to the rising school enrollment rates of the 1990s. By far the most important explanatory factor in the analysis is parental schooling, with large positive effects of both mother's and father's schooling on children's school enrollment. Taken in combination, the study results imply that changes in the growth rate of the school-age population, numbers of siblings, and parental education can explain more than 60 percent of the observed increases in school enrollment between 1977 and 1999.

In contrast to the average for the whole developing world, youth in sub-Saharan Africa recently have been transitioning to adulthood in contexts that in some important respects have deteriorated rather than improved. More than 37 million adolescents ages 10 to 14 in sub-Saharan Africa will not even complete primary school. Hence, reducing the number of uneducated African youth is a primary objective of the Education for All (EFA) and the United Nations MDG programs. Achieving these goals will require resources and commitment not previously seen, as well as more effective tools for monitoring progress.

In Chapter 4, Paul Hewett and Cynthia Lloyd assess United Nations Educational, Scientific, and Cultural Organization's (UNESCO) two indicators for monitoring progress toward EFA, and conclude that UNESCO data may provide a potentially misleading picture of current progress. Not only are rates of enrollment significantly higher relative to attendance data from recent nationally representative household surveys, but gender parity ratios as estimated from UNESCO data suggest a greater remaining gap in attendance than do recent comparable household survey data. The authors argue that nationally representative household data provide a useful baseline from which to build. The United Nations Children's Fund's (UNICEF) Multiple Indicator Cluster Survey (MICS) and the Demographic and Health Surveys (DHS), both of which collect information on the educational participation and attainment of household members, are collected in a large enough number of countries for cross-national and regional comparisons of educational progress. Even with the limited education data collected in household surveys such as DHS and MICS, there is much that can be learned about past trends and the current status of schooling in sub-Saharan Africa. The trends in primary schooling completion for sub-Saharan Africa implied by these data raise serious questions about the feasibility of achieving the EFA and MDGs in the foreseeable future. It is even possible some earlier gains could be lost, given recent declines in attendance rates among the youngest boys and the tapering off in attendance rates among the youngest cohort of girls in many countries. It would also appear that the gap between boys and girls is closing rapidly for the region as a whole. These trends in gender parity ratios are occurring despite huge variations in overall levels of educational attainment. Consequently, these findings raise doubts about the likelihood that EFA goals can be achieved with a strategy limited to emphasis on girls' schooling. The largest remaining schooling gap is between the poorest and wealthiest households. This study gives new comparisons of the sizes of gender gaps and wealth gaps across most countries of sub-Saharan Africa using several widely accepted schooling indicators. With the gender gap closing in many cases at levels of educational attainment that fall well short of universal primary schooling, new strategies will need to be devised to reach the poorest parents and their children.

STUDIES ON MARRIAGE

The next three chapters in the volume all deal with various aspects of the transition to marriage, often a sufficient but not a necessary condition for the transition to adulthood. Marriage during the teen years is often perceived to be particularly deleterious (as well as much more common) for women: schooling may be curtailed, autonomy limited—because young brides tend to marry older men—and sexual relations uninformed and perhaps even coercive or dangerous to women's health. Furthermore, the terms and conditions of marriage, including whether or not marriages are arranged, age and education differences between spouses, financial exchanges at the time of marriage, and assets brought into marriage are all important factors in determining young women's bargaining power, scope for action and choice, and life circumstances as adults.

In Chapter 5, Barbara Mensch, Susheela Singh, and John Casterline examine trends in the timing of first marriage among men and women in the developing world. The authors find that during the past 30 years, for most developing country regions substantial declines have occurred in the proportion of young men and women married; the exceptions are South America for men and women, and West and Middle Africa and South and Southeast Asia, for men only. Expansion of schooling for women has had some impact, but there is still a considerable fraction of the reduction in early marriage not explained by changes in education. Other factors that might account for some of the delay in marriage among women include the decline in arranged marriages, the deficit of available older men with increasing cohort size and the concomitant rise in the cost of dowries in South Asia, changes in laws about age of marriage, and a transformation in global norms about the desirability of early marriage of women. Increasing educational attainment of men is also believed to contribute to a delay, but no evidence of this is found for sub-Saharan Africa. In order to better understand the dynamics of union formation, surveys need to collect information on the social, cultural, and economic factors that affect life decisions among young people, including contextual factors that reflect the opportunity structures available. Analyses of such data will permit the development of a more nuanced picture of one of the key transitions in the pathway from adolescence to adulthood.

India, like China, accounts for more than a fifth of youth in the developing world. But within India, perhaps even more than in China, there is considerable variance in the experience of youth. In Chapter 6, Shireen Jejeebhoy and Shiva Halli examine changes in marriage patterns among successive cohorts of women in rural Uttar Pradesh and Tamil Nadu, two culturally distinct social systems. The study finds that marriage age has been increasing moderately and at different paces in the two states. In Uttar Pradesh, among both Muslims and Hindus, early adolescent marriages (under age 15) have declined perceptibly by cohort, yet about two in three recently married women continue to marry by the time they are age 18. Among women in Tamil Nadu in contrast, changes are observed in both early and late adolescence, and the evidence suggests that among both Muslims and Hindus, marriage is increasingly being delayed beyond adolescence. The findings confirm that there are considerable similarities in factors associated with variance in age at marriage across these two cultural settings. Notably, even a primary education is associated with sharply increased marital age, and the association with education remains powerful in both cohorts and settings. Sociocultural context—as measured by religion and setting—suggests that compared to the Muslims of Uttar Pradesh, the Hindus of this state marry significantly earlier, while both Muslim and Hindu women from Tamil Nadu are significantly more likely to delay marriage. Also consistent is the suggestion that women marrying considerably older men (5 years or more) are significantly more likely to marry early than are other women—again there is no significant change in pattern over cohorts in this effect.

Attributes of marriage such as kin marriage, village endogamy and postmarital residence patterns, and spousal age differences continue to be shaped by region and gender systems. The experiences of recently married cohorts remain largely similar to those of older ones in each setting. There are, however, some conditions in which cohort differences have begun to emerge. These include greater autonomy among recently married women in determining the timing of marriage and choice of partner, and a narrowing of the schooling gap between wives and husbands—attributes far more clearly observed in Tamil Nadu than in Uttar Pradesh, and presumably suggestive of more egalitarian relationships among younger cohorts of Tamilian couples. On the other hand, a notable change experienced in Uttar Pradesh is a greater trend toward consumer goods among younger cohorts in dowries even though there is little clear evidence on trends in the total value of dowry per se.

These findings suggest that, by and large, sociocultural setting and individual and marriage-process-related factors are powerfully associated with marriage age and practices. What is not so clear, however, is whether or not these associations have shifted much over successive cohorts of women. Notably, findings suggest that while education is significantly related to enhanced marriage age, and while secondary education is associated with exercise of choice in marriage timing and partner, education is also related to increased dowry payments. Conversely, while premarital economic activity is unrelated to marriage age or marriage-related decision making, it is significantly associated with reduced dowry payments. These kinds of findings argue for further explorations into the causal effects and tentatively suggest that strategies to delay marriage, enhance marriage-related decision making, and counter the practice of dowry may need to expand beyond education and employment. More comprehensive, direct, and context-specific strategies must simultaneously be sought—raising community awareness of the negative effects of early marriage and countering fears of allowing girls to remain single, providing for the acquisition of usable vocational and life skills, and enhancing young women's real access to, and control over, economic resources and decision making relating to their own lives.

The final chapter in this section, by Agnes Quisumbing and Kelly Hallman, contributes to the literature on marriage patterns by analyzing data on husband's and wife's human and physical capital and conditions surrounding marriage based on comparable micro household data from Bangladesh, Ethiopia, Guatemala, Mexico, the Philippines, and South Africa. Though the samples are relatively small and are not nationally representative, the study sites appear to be representative of living conditions for substantial subpopulations within each country and the data sets include recall information on assets brought into marriage, which is fairly unusual information.

In these six cases, age at marriage is increasing for husbands and wives, with the exception of Bangladesh and Ethiopia for men and Ethiopia for women. Schooling at marriage has also been increasing for both men and women, except for men in Bangladesh. There is no clear trend regarding land ownership at marriage, although grooms seem to be bringing more physical assets to marriage in four out of six countries. In the two countries where landholding information is not aggregated with total assets, husbands' land ownership at marriage increases in one case (Philippines) and declines in the other (Mexico). Land ownership at marriage by women is decreasing through time in the Philippines, and remains constant, though very low (less than 1 percent of marriages) in Mexico. Asset values of husbands increase through time in four countries, declining only in Ethiopia, and remaining constant in the Philippines. Asset values of wives increase in two countries (Mexico and Guatemala), remain constant in the Philippines, and decline in Ethiopia and in Bangladesh. In the two countries for which there are data on marriage payments, trends have been in opposite directions: increasing for husbands and decreasing for wives in Bangladesh, and decreasing for both in South Africa.

Differences between husbands and wives, which may affect important intrahousehold allocations of resources and investments in children, have changed in both directions. In four of the countries, age differences have decreased—a move toward increasing equality, given the possibility that greater seniority and experience may give husbands bargaining advantages over their wives. The two countries where differences in age at marriage have not decreased are South Africa and the Philippines, the two countries where women's ages at marriage are the highest among the study countries. In half of the countries, husband-wife gaps in schooling attainment at marriage have also decreased—pointing to an equalization of human capital at marriage. The exceptions are Guatemala and the Philippines, where the difference in years of schooling has not changed over time, and Ethiopia, where the difference is increasing. The trend in Ethiopia contrasts with the results presented above for the reduction of gender gaps in schooling on the average in sub-Saharan Africa. The distribution of assets at marriage continues to favor husbands. In three of the countries, the husband-wife asset difference has not changed through time—and therefore continues to favor husbands—and has even increased in the two Latin American countries. The only country where the gap in assets at marriage has decreased is Ethiopia, probably due to the change in land policies as a result of collectivization. Finally, transfers at marriage are increasingly favoring men in Bangladesh, while the gap in transfers at marriage is decreasing in South Africa. In summary, the reduction of husband-wife gaps in age and schooling indicates potential improvements in the balance of power within the family, but asset ownership continues to favor husbands. It remains to be seen whether the reductions in gender gaps in age and human capital will offset the persistent gender gaps in asset ownership.

THE INTERRELATIONSHIPS BETWEEN VARIOUS TRANSITIONS

The next three chapters in the volume investigate multidimensional aspects of the various transitions to adulthood in different contexts.

In Chapter 8, Emily Hannum and Jihong Liu consider the case of adolescents in China, the most populous country in the world, which alone accounts for more than a fifth of youth currently in the developing world. China is also one of the countries in which economic development and transformation has been occurring most rapidly in recent decades. The chapter traces evidence about changes in adolescents' pathways into adulthood in China over the past two decades of market reforms, focusing on schooling, work, family, and health. On average, the market reform period has benefited many aspects of adolescence. Schooling has increased, and adolescent labor has decreased. The average age at marriage is high, and rose in the 1990s, such that marriage is unlikely to compete directly with educational opportunities except at the very highest levels of education.

Low fertility rates suggest that women's childrearing responsibilities may compete less with other opportunities in China than in many other developing countries.

The benefits of improved standards of living have been shared across social groups, but social and economic inequalities continue to shape the life course of Chinese youth. While wealthier urban youth are beginning to experience problems with overnutrition, some rural youth still face nutritional deprivation. Suicide rates are dramatically higher among rural youth and young adults, especially young rural women. Wealthier adolescents and those in urban areas are more likely to be in school than their poor rural counterparts, and thus enjoy significant advantages in a labor market that increasingly rewards credentials. The mark of rural poverty is clear in the elevated likelihood of rural youth participating in the labor force, in the high percentage of working youth employed in agriculture, and in the large-scale youth and young adult migration into urban settings. Finally, social changes in the reform period raise important concerns about behavioral health issues, especially sexual health and smoking.

In Chapter 9, Cynthia Lloyd and Monica Grant examine another very populous Asian country, Pakistan. The study characterizes Pakistan to be a country of contrasts caught in the conflicting tensions of global political and economic change on the one hand and severe financial duress due to the sluggish economy on the other. While recent decades have brought much social and economic change, many aspects of daily life remain remarkably unchanged. Therefore there are growing contradictions between traditional values and ways of life on the one hand and increasingly accepted global norms and external economic realities on the other. Young people are growing up in the midst of these cross currents, but to a large extent, traditional ways of life prevail. The study emphasizes the fundamental importance of schooling on transitions to adulthood in this context. Without schooling or with very limited schooling, children assume the work burdens of adults prematurely and are deprived of the opportunity for learning in an institutional setting outside the family. Those who attend school eventually do take up very gender-stereotyped roles; however, they do so with some delay, allowing them to enjoy a longer transition to adulthood. For both males and females, there is a large lag between the assumption of adult work roles and the assumption of adult family roles as marked by the transition to marriage. For young males, this is a lag between the timing of first paid work and marriage; for young females, it is the lag between the assumption of heavy domestic responsibilities and marriage and leaving home. The time use of young people varies from community to community according to the array of opportunities available. Current interventions appear, however, to reinforce gender role stereotypes. As the demographic transition continues to progress, family sizes become smaller, and women's time becomes more flexible, there should be opportunities for more transformative interventions to make a difference in the lives of youth, particularly young females.

In Chapter 10, Barthélémy Kuate-Defo builds from the conceptual framework developed for the Panel on Transitions to Adulthood in Developing Countries by formulating and estimating multilevel models of fixed and random influences of competing factors on various transitional events, which are hypothesized to be shaped by the hierarchically clustered contexts in which the individuals' lives are embedded. The author presents the logic and assumptions of multilevel modeling as well as its data requirements, and uses data from Cameroon to illustrate the features of this methodology and to test several assumptions inherent in the macro-micro propositions articulated in the panel's theoretical framework.

By situating the estimated influences on transitions to adulthood within a multilevel framework, this study allows for a more rigorous investigation of the robustness of fixed and random effects at the individual, community, and province levels than conventional statistical methods. The chapter separates the net influences of individual attributes from the fixed and random context-dependent effects, documents the significance of both the fixed and the random effects of the community and the province context, net of the fixed and random effects of individual- and household-level covariates, and assesses their differential implications for young males versus young females given their socioeconomic and demographic backgrounds.

The study finds significant multilevel influences on young people's successful transitions to adulthood including socioeconomic status, ethnic affiliation, community and regional contexts in Cameroon, and these influences operate differently by gender. Furthermore, the estimated parameters suggest that there may be more variation across communities and provinces in the likelihood of some transitional events than standard single-level analyses would have implied. Finally, the study demonstrates the significance of influential unmeasured variables affecting the various transitions of young people during their life course, independently of other covariates. A number of these unobserved influences may be unmeasurable in conventional methods of inquiry and often require a combination of qualitative and quantitative approaches to study.

POLICY STUDIES

In the final chapter in the volume, James Knowles and Jere Behrman argue that better policy choices related to youth would be made if policy makers and analysts were better informed by good estimates of the rates of return or benefit-to-cost ratios for alternative policy options. However, it is

more difficult to make such estimates for possible policy interventions related to youth than for most other interventions because of the multiple
impacts of such interventions (increased by the multiple transitions through
which youth are passing) that may last over decades—in addition to the
usual difficulties of identifying policy impacts as opposed to associations
and in pinning down the true resource costs (as opposed to governmental
budgetary costs) of various policies. Consequently, there are relatively few
good available estimates of the rates of return to alternative policies affecting youth in developing countries. The study combines information from
different sources to provide new estimates of such returns, which in some
cases appear to be quite substantial, particularly related to schooling. Thus,
the chapter elaborates on a procedure for thinking about and evaluating the
relative merits of different policy interventions related to youth in diverse
contexts throughout the developing world.

The studies in this volume served as important inputs in the National
Academies report on the transitions to adulthood in developing countries.
They provide (1) new descriptions of patterns and associations between
various transitions to adulthood both on a comparative level across a numbers of countries and for some particular countries that are of considerable
interest in themselves, (2) methods for analyzing important aspects of those
transitions and how policies might affect them, (3) illustrations of how
existing data and new data enhance our understanding beyond that in the
previous literature, and (4) suggestions of important data and analyses
needed for further understanding. They both complement the report of the
Panel on Transitions to Adulthood in Developing Countries and provide
useful contributions in their own right. Our hope is that these studies will
be useful to those charged with making and implementing public policy as
well as scholars from different disciplines and leaders of civil society organizations wishing to build on the panel's foundation.

2

Changing Contexts in Which Youth Are Transitioning to Adulthood in Developing Countries: Converging Toward Developed Economies?

Jere R. Behrman and Piyali Sengupta

At the start of the twenty-first century, youth in developing countries are making transitions to adulthood in a changing world. Many researchers and other observers suggest, for example, that accelerating globalization is not only changing the world more rapidly than in earlier periods, but is making it more homogeneous, with increasing convergence of developing economies toward the developed economies, in many important dimensions.[1]

The purpose of this chapter is simple: To *describe* to what extent the contexts in which youth have been making transitions to adulthood in developing countries have been converging toward the developed economies. Some aspects of these changing contexts relate to overall economies and societies and affect many outcomes—not only the transitions of youth to adulthood. But the fact that they may have broader effects does not lessen their possible importance for youth in developing economies. Such descriptions do not, of course, tell us anything very persuasive about causality—such as whether globalization or particular components of globalization are causing con(di)vergence. However, they provide useful perspective on many dimensions of the changing contexts in which transitions to adulthood are occurring. They also show to what extent there has been

---

[1]Others, however, suggest that there may be important divergences, or that, whatever the processes, they are in some important respects to the disadvantage of many in the developing world. For discussion of many of these issues in the context of education and gender, for example, see Stromquist and Monkman (2000).

convergence or divergence (or a mixture of both) in a number of important dimensions among countries grouped by geographical region.[2]

The descriptions summarized in this chapter are based on time series of aggregate country-level data for more than 100 selected variables, many of which have been used widely to characterize cross-country patterns.[3] These variables, in turn, are grouped into seven categories that relate to indicators of:

    I. Population
    II. Economy
    III. Labor
    IV. Health
    V. Education
    VI. Environment
    VII. Transportation and Communication

Because of the perceived importance of gender, we include explicit representations of what has happened to gender differentials in those categories in which the data permit such comparisons—namely population, labor, health, and education.

The descriptions presented here focus on the extent to which the selected indicators, in each of these seven categories of variables, have changed in the direction of convergence or divergence, or have shown a mixture of convergence and divergence. For this purpose, developing countries are grouped into six regions (with individual countries weighted by population) as defined by the World Bank.[4] These regions are East Asia and the Pacific,

---

[2]Behrman and Sengupta (2004) also provide similar descriptions for countries grouped by per capita income in 1987.

[3]These data are from the World Bank *World Development Indicators, 2003* CD-ROM, which gives the original sources of the data. These data have limitations that have been discussed extensively elsewhere (e.g., Ahmad, 1994; Behrman and Rosenzweig, 1994; Bouis, 1994; Chamie, 1994; Heston, 1994; Lloyd and Hewett, 2003; Srinivasan, 1994). The interested reader is referred to these discussions. Despite the many limitations in such data, the patterns in them shape considerably what it is thought that we know about cross-country differences and changes in those differences over time at least at a crude level. Therefore, we use these data with this blanket caveat about their limitations—but without repeated qualifications except in occasional cases in which the qualifications seem to enhance understanding of the nature of patterns in the data.

[4]The original source is given in the previous note and Behrman and Sengupta (2004, Appendix B) give the country allocations by these six regions. Some of these geographical regions, of course, include developed as well as developing countries (particularly Europe and Central Asia but also East Asia and the Pacific), but the data summarized for these regions in this chapter refer only to the developing countries in the region (with the developed countries in all regions included in the developed country group with which the developing country groups are compared). Of course, in addition to important patterns on the average for countries grouped by region, there may be important variations within these country groups. But it would be too complicated to attempt to characterize such intracountry group variations in a chapter of this length.

Europe and Central Asia, Latin America and the Caribbean, the Middle East and North Africa, South Asia, and sub-Saharan Africa.

We describe the extent of convergence or divergence by an index that compares in percentage terms the ratio of the developing country to the developed country value in the last year for which data are available (generally 2000 or 2001), with the same ratio for the first year for which data are generally available (generally in the 1960s and 1970s, but some in the 1980s and, for a few variables, data are available only for the 1990s, such as number of Internet users or mobile phones per 100 people, or public expenditure on health).[5] A positive value indicates movement toward convergence and a negative value, divergence. Convergence or divergence is always measured in reference to the paths of the developed country characteristics.[6] However, to shorten the exposition below, we usually summarize the recent history of a variable as having been in the direction of "convergence" or "divergence," without repeatedly stating that the reference group is the developed countries. Because we are focusing on how developing country characteristics compare with the developed country characteristics as the latter change over time, we are assessing "convergence" or "divergence" with respect to a moving target. As we note below, for some of the characteristics we consider, there have been large changes in the developed country characteristics over time so that even if the developing country values have, for example, changed a lot in the direction of the developed country characteristics, they may not have changed enough for there to have been convergence. An important example, to illustrate, is per capita national product. For most (not all) developing country groups, there have been increases in recent decades, but in many cases the increases have not been as great as those for the developed country group—so there has been divergence despite the secular increases.

---

[5]To be more explicit, the index = 100* [(Region value for 2000)/(Developed Country value for 2000) – (Region value for earliest year data available)/(Developed Country value for earliest year data available)] for variables for which (Region value for earliest year data available)/(Developed Country value for earliest year data available) is < 1. This condition holds for most of the variables, but not for some (e.g., exceptions include a number of the population variables such as the dependency ratio and the share of agriculture in production). For the variables for which (Region value for earliest year data available)/(Developed Country value for earliest year data available) is > 1, the index is –100* [(Region value for 2000)/(Developed Country value for 2000) – (Region value for earliest year data available)/(Developed Country value for earliest year data available). The last column in Table 2-1 gives the first and last year used for each of the variables that we consider.

[6]And not, for example, whether there is convergence or divergence among the developing country groups, though, of course, to the extent that for some characteristics the developing country groups converge toward the characteristics of the developed countries, there is also likely (though not with certainty) to be convergence of these characteristics among the developing countries.

The convergence/divergence index that we use gives the change in percentage points over the whole time period considered, relative to developed country values.[7] If, to illustrate, for the earliest year covered a developing country group per capita income were 15 percent of that for the developed country group and for the most recent year the same developing country group per capita income were 18 percent of that for developed countries, the index is 3 percent (18 percent minus 15 percent), indicating convergence with the developing country group; in other words, it represents catching up by 3 percent, relative to the developed country group, over the interim. If, instead, the developing country group per capita income were 15 percent of that of the developed countries in the earliest year covered and fell to 10 percent of that of the developed countries in the most recent year, the index would be –5 percent (10 percent minus 15 percent), indicating divergence by 5 percent from the developed country value over the period considered. Although the index refers to the whole period, of course, there may be combinations of convergence and divergence over the period, even if one or the other dominates. To illustrate, in the first example given in this paragraph, there is convergence of 3 percent over the entire period. However, there may have been divergence for part of the period. For example, suppose the value were 20 percent two thirds of the way through the entire period. That would indicate a divergence of –2 percent for the last third of the period, despite an overall convergence of 3 percent for the entire period.

In the remainder of the chapter we summarize the patterns of convergence and divergence by developing country regional group, on the basis of this index. We consider, in turn, each of the seven variable groups defined above, focusing on the numerical values of our convergence index (shown in Table 2-1) for much of the discussion. For selected variables we also present one of two types of graphs or figures. For most of the variables, the figures give the ratio of the developing country group to the developed country group over time so that the horizontal line at 1.0 in the figures represents the developed country group experience. For a subset of variables, for which the developed country group has very small and varying values over time—such as overall population growth rates on the share of total employment in agriculture—using such values as denominators does not lead to very informative graphs. For this subset of variables, therefore, we present the values for all the country groups (including the developed countries), but NOT relative to the values for the developed countries. (The titles of the figures indicate whether they are "compared to developed countries = 1.0," as they are for the first type of figures.) These figures present more information about the patterns of convergence and divergence

---

[7]If the developed country values are very small (e.g., as for illiteracy rates), this index can have very large values in absolute terms. See the discussion below of the two types of figures we present.

than do the numerical values of the indices because the figures show the paths between the initial values and the end points, while the index just summarizes the changes between the initial values and the end points. The figures also suggest in a number of cases that there are subperiods of convergence and divergence, even though one or the other dominates over the entire period considered. However, the figures take considerable space, so we only present selected ones even though we have generated such figures for all the variables (Behrman and Sengupta, 2004, present a larger set of figures). We indicate in the text explicitly when we include figures because they are included only in selected cases.

POPULATION

We begin with population because aspects of population condition so many of the contexts in which youth make transitions to adulthood. Some of these effects are direct and others work through other groups of variables considered in the sections below.

Population Growth, Fertility Rates, and Mortality Rates

The patterns of the demographic transition, lagged to various degrees in various developing country groups behind that experienced by the developed country group, result in convergence being the dominant feature for population growth rates despite the very low and declining population growth rates for the developed economies (Figure 2-1).[8] However, this pattern is not universal, with both Europe and Central Asia and the Middle East and North Africa diverging from the (declining) population growth rates for the developed countries.

For birth rates and total fertility rates, in contrast, the dominant tendency is for divergence, particularly before 1985. The only exceptions are Europe and Central Asia for birth rates and Latin America and the Caribbean for total fertility rates. The dominance of divergence for fertility rates, however, tends to be offset by considerable convergence for mortality rates so that the overall dominant tendency is for convergence in terms of population growth rates, as noted above.[9] Mortality rates have been converging

---

[8]The low and declining population growth rates in the developed countries also cause the indices for population growth to have large absolute values. This is also the case for other variables discussed below for which the developing country values are relatively small, such as the percentage of value added or workers in agriculture.

[9]Net international migration, in addition to fertility and mortality, also affects population growth rates. We have not been able to find useful data on net international migration. However, although international migration may have considerable impact on population growth of some individual countries, it is not likely to be nearly as important as fertility and mortality for the large aggregates of country groups that we are considering.

TABLE 2-1a Index of Convergence/Divergence by Region

Indicators	East Asia and the Pacific	Europe and Central Asia
POPULATION		
Population Growth, Fertility, and Mortality		
Population growth	64.0	−43.9
Birth rate	−25.3	15.5
Fertility ratio	−19.5	−5.9
Death rate	75.2	−27.6
Age Structure		
Age dependency ratio	4.9	3.5
Population, 0-14 years (% total)	−25.1	−5.6
Female population, 0-14 years (% age group pop.)	0.3	0.2
Male population, 0-14 years (% age group pop.)	0.3	0.2
Population, 65 years and higher (% total)	−3.7	0.2
Population, 15-64 years (% total)	2.7	1.4
Female population, 15-64 years (% age group pop.)	2.4	3.7
Male population, 15-64 years (% age group pop.)	2.3	3.7
Rural-Urban Composition		
Rural population growth	928.1	−77.6
Rural population (% total)	−59.0	−28.4
Urban population growth	−61.6	94.3
Urban population (% total)	17.8	11.2
Female-to-Male Sex Ratio		
Sex ratio	1.6	−3.9
Sex ratio, 0-14 years	−0.6	−0.3
Sex ratio, 15-64 years	4.6	8.7
Sex ratio, 65 years and higher	14.3	−12.8
Other		
Population density	−0.2	−5.7
Female population (% total)	1.0	1.6

[a]Latest year available for high-income countries: 1995; therefore, 1995 was used as the latest year in the convergence index. All other income groups were represented in comparison to the high-income category.

Latin America and the Caribbean	Middle East and North Africa	South Asia	Sub-Saharan Africa	Data Availability: First and Final Years
57.3	−116.4	142.9	150.8	1960/2001
−0.1	−12.1	−54.9	−93.6	1960/2001
14.8	−14.6	−53.4	−100.8	1960/2001
42.3	116.2	97.5	35.4	1960/2001
13.0	−6.5	−27.4	−44.3	1960/2001
−12.0	−35.1	−49.8	−66.3	1960/2001
0.2	−0.3	2.3	−0.8	1960/2001
0.2	−0.3	−2.2	−0.8	1960/2001
−1.4	−14.3	−14.1	−14.5	1960/2001
6.2	1.2	−5.2	−8.9	1960/2001
−1.5	0.2	5.0	−0.5	1960/2001
−1.4	0.2	4.8	−0.4	1960/2001
371.4	410.0	1171.6	979.3	1965/2001
−15.2	32.4	−101.8	−47.2	1960/2001
−55.2	−29.3	−176.2	−126.3	1960/2001
11.9	30.1	11.2	25.8	1960/2001
−1.5	−1.0	5.4	2.2	1960/2001
−0.3	−0.7	4.6	1.6	1960/2001
−3.0	−0.1	−9.3	−1.0	1960/2001
10.5	6.9	3.7	5.7	1960/2001
−3.4	−0.6	4.6	0.9	1965/2001[a]
−1.0	−0.5	3.1	0.9	1960/2001

TABLE 2-1b Index of Convergence/Divergence by Region

Indicators	East Asia and the Pacific	Europe and Central Asia
ECONOMY		
GDP Growth Rates and Levels		
% annual GDP growth	41.2	72.9
Per cap GDP (constant 1995 U.S. dollar)	0.7	−7.6
Per cap GDP (PPP)	2.9	−11.9
Per cap GNI (PPP)	3.6	−12.5
Shares of Production in Major Sectors		
Value added in agriculture	−141.6	−193.1
Value added in industry	45.3	65.4
Value added in services	17.5	−3.8
Openness to International Trade		
Economic openness	−176.7	76.8
Exports (% GDP)	23.6	87.1
Imports (% GDP)	50.9	106.9
Role of Government		
Tax revenue	−11.3	50.8
Health expenditure per capita	1.7	0.6
Public expenditure on health	55.7	63.4
Public expenditure on education	−5.0	29.6
Other		
Wage expenditure	1.0	−4.6
Tourism expenditure	14.5	53.9
Expenditure on goods and services	23.6	54.4

[a]Earliest year available for ECA: 1970.

Latin America and the Caribbean	Middle East and North Africa	South Asia	Sub-Saharan Africa	Data Availability: First and Final Years
−26.6	82.5	81.3	−19.4	1965/2000
−3.0	0.6	0.6	−2.4	1960/2001
−2.1	−9.3	1.8	−3.5	1975/2000
−1.8	−5.7	2.3	−2.9	1975/2000
−23.6	144.4	−168.1	−161.5	1960/2001[a]
95.1	65.4	−7.6	−4.3	1960/2001[a]
30.2	0.3	16.8	16.1	1960/2001[a]
37.8	795.6	−12.5	301.4	1960/2001[a]
−18.0	52.1	−8.3	−17.8	1960/2001[a]
−5.1	42.9	3.0	−6.2	1960/2001[a]
6.7	1.0	−34.5	3.4	1970/2001
3.9	4.0	0.3	−0.6	1990/2000
63.5	50.2	37.2	42.8	1990/2000
11.0	14.9	14.3	35.9	1960/2000
−4.1	0.2	−3.1	−6.4	1970/2001
47.7	−20.9	22.2	−4.1	1980/2001
67.2	14.0	10.8	88.0	1970/2001

TABLE 2-1c Index of Convergence/Divergence by Region

Indicators	East Asia and the Pacific	Europe and Central Asia
LABOR		
Labor Force Activity, Gender and Child Labor		
Female labor force activity rate	62.6	69.9
Female labor force (% total labor force)	36.5	50.1
Male labor force activity rate	3.9	0.4
Child labor, 10-14 years (% age group)	–22705.3	603.6
Sectoral Distribution of Employment		
Employment in agriculture (% total employment)	59.9	–222.4
Employment in industry (% total employment)	29.9	33.5
Employment in services (% total employment)	25.4	15.8
Female agriculture employees (% total female employment)	384.5	–289.6
Male agriculture employees (% total male employment)	504.2	96.7
Female industry employees (% total female employment)	71.0	–15.7
Male industry employees (% total male employment)	47.3	6.3
Female services employees (% total female employment)	44.3	27.4
Male services employees (% total male employment)	46.8	26.4
Unemployment Rates, Gender, and Youth		
Unemployment (% total labor force)	–93.3	12.5
Female unemployment (% female labor force)	77.0	7.4
Male unemployment (% male labor force)	93.1	–68.6
Youth unemployment (% 15-24 years labor force)	–53.6	–65.4
Youth female unemployment (% 15-24 years female labor force)	164.7	–35.9
Youth male unemployment (% 15-24 years male labor force)	–82.1	–6.8

[a]Latest year available for ECA: 1999.
[b]Latest year available for MENA, SA, and SSA: 1999.
[c]Earliest year available for SSA: 1990.

Latin America and the Caribbean	Middle East and North Africa	South Asia	Sub-Saharan Africa	Data Availability: First and Final Years
−1.2	−5.1	70.7	97.4	1960/1999
0.3	1.9	35.6	55.2	1960/2001
4.1	−3.6	7.2	−7.5	1960/1999
−11656.9	−5028.7	−49079.6	−61165.0	1960/2001
−124.6	274.0	−203.2	−456.3	1980/2000
13.2	−70.1	−30.8	−37.1	1980/2000[a]
−2.2	16.0	22.8	52.3	1980/2000
−101.2	−913.9	−304.0	477.9	1980/2000[b]
−7.6	−22.8	78.3	401.2	1980/2000
48.3	67.5	110.1	40.3	1980/2000
7.1	−1.0	18.3	23.7	1980/2000
12.0	−17.3	36.4	62.2	1980/2000
3.2	8.8	32.2	54.3	1980/2000
127.1	23.3	−232.4	−196.7	1980/2000[c]
15.1	−111.0	−91.5	−8.3	1980/2000[d]
40.9	109.5	1.1	4.8	1980/2000[d]
58.7	10.5	392.7	−4857.0	1980/2000[e]
−145.8	−41.6	−36.6	−400.8	1980/2000[e]
−106.4	103.4	6.4	−420.4	1980/2000[e]

[d]Earliest year available for ECA: 1985; for SA: 1990; Latest year available for MENA, SA, and SSA: 1999.
[e]Earliest year available for ECA, MENA, and SSA: 1990; for SA: 1985; Latest year available for MENA and SA: 1995.

TABLE 2-1d Index of Convergence/Divergence by Region

Indicators	East Asia and the Pacific	Europe and Central Asia
HEALTH		
Life Expectancy and Mortality Rates		
Life expectancy (overall)	14.8	−4.9
Life expectancy (female)	14.8	−3.5
Life expectancy (male)	14.8	−6.3
Life expectancy (male-female)	14.4	−33.9
Female mortality	45.6	−82.0
Male mortality	33.2	−94.0
Male-female mortality	25.8	−100.4
Infant mortality	−414.4	−339.1
Under 5 years mortality	−332.3	−291.9
Health Determinants		
Health expenditure per capita	1.7	0.6
Public expenditure on health	55.7	63.4
Incidence of DPT vaccination	13.8	16.2
Incidence of measles vaccination	58.6	17.9
Physicians per 1,000 people	1.8	−52.7
Hospital beds per 1,000 people	7.0	0.3

[a]Latest year available for SA: 2000.
[b]Latest year available for MENA: 1999; for SA and SSA: 1999; for SA: 1999; for SSA: 1995.
[c]Latest year available for MENA: 1999; for SA: 1995; for SSA: 1995.

Latin America and the Caribbean	Middle East and North Africa	South Asia	Sub-Saharan Africa	Data Availability: First and Final Years
7.2	16.9	15.0	3.5	1960/2001
7.9	16.9	16.5	2.7	1960/2001
6.4	16.9	13.3	4.4	1960/2001
28.8	16.3	59.3	−20.8	1960/2001
−11.6	−5.2	35.9	−288.9	1960/2001[a]
−16.3	9.0	19.1	−130.6	1960/2001[a]
40.1	1.4	82.3	12.3	1960/2001[a]
−234.9	−289.7	−860.4	−1284.1	1960/2001
−165.9	−163.4	−820.6	−1446.3	1960/2001
3.9	4.0	0.3	−0.6	1990/2000
63.5	50.2	37.2	42.8	1990/2000
37.0	55.8	64.3	7.8	1980/2001
41.6	59.9	63.0	20.0	1980/2001
9.6	5.0	−7.5	−0.2	1960/2000[b]
−34.3	−18.0	−8.4	−24.4	1960/2000[c]

TABLE 2-1e Index of Convergence/Divergence by Region

Indicators	East Asia and the Pacific	Europe and Central Asia
EDUCATION		
School Enrollment Overall and Gender Differences		
Gross primary enrollment	20.7	6.8
Gross primary enrollment (female)	31.5	5.4
Gross primary enrollment (male)	23.3	−7.2
Gross primary enrollment (male-female)	81.4	81.4
Gross secondary enrollment	21.9	2.5
Gross secondary enrollment (female)	24.6	4.5
Gross secondary enrollment (male)	15.9	−5.1
Gross secondary enrollment (male-female)	120.5	171.9
Ratio, female to male students (primary and secondary)	12.9	−1.5
Years of expected schooling	−0.8	−2.5
Years of expected schooling (female)	23.9	−6.2
Years of expected schooling (male)	18.4	−7.2
Years of expected schooling (male-female)	170.7	171.3
Schooling Inputs		
Pupil-teacher ratio	−68.0	32.3
Public expenditure on education	−5.0	29.6
Years of schooling for adults	27.0	1.4
Years of schooling for adults (female)	33.4	3.6
Years of schooling for adults (male)	21.4	−0.9
Years of schooling for adults (male-female)	18.4	0.0
Adult illiteracy	−34.9	−7.9
Adult illiteracy (female)	−60.1	−0.7
Adult illiteracy (male)	−9.7	−12.5
Adult illiteracy (male-female)	−172.5	38.0
Other		
Youth illiteracy (15-24 years)	−152.6	−2.6
Youth illiteracy (female, 15-24 years)	−350.6	15.4
Youth illiteracy (male, 15-24 years)	−62.9	−4.5
Youth illiteracy (male-female, 15-24 years)	520.7	−108.7

Latin America and the Caribbean	Middle East and North Africa	South Asia	Sub-Saharan Africa	Data Availability: First and Final Years
10.4	15.8	32.1	37.2	1970/2000
9.8	26.3	38.8	40.2	1970/2000
10.9	6.7	26.5	34.1	1970/2000
−231.9	−254.2	−1593.6	−1106.9	1970/2000
18.3	31.9	10.6	20.2	1970/2000
19.1	40.4	14.7	20.9	1970/2000
18.9	20.9	4.8	18.3	1970/2000
103.9	249.5	273.4	−195.0	1970/2000
5.3	36.8	42.1	15.1	1970/2000
−1.5	−0.1	0.0	0.2	1970/2000
4.6	30.1	21.8	18.6	1970/2000
8.2	13.1	12.4	15.0	1970/2000
36.8	381.8	469.2	316.5	1970/2000
−33.7	−33.4	−143.1	−129.4	1970/2000
11.0	14.9	14.3	35.9	1960/2000
12.7	35.6	13.6	15.7	1960/1999
15.2	33.2	13.6	15.6	1960/1999
10.3	38.1	14.7	15.9	1960/1999
−43.6	−158.6	−118.5	−71.3	1960/1999
−37.4	−99.7	−242.1	−209.3	1970/2001
46.4	−184.4	−308.8	−274.8	1970/2001
−26.4	1.7	−161.7	−122.5	1970/2001
29.7	−532.9	−552.6	−472.0	1970/2001
−155.9	−243.6	−911.3	−746.4	1970/2001
−294.4	−827.8	−1990.6	−1631.5	1970/2001
−67.2	26.7	−328.3	−248.1	1970/2001
−74.7	1737.0	2091.3	1609.2	1970/2001

TABLE 2-1f Index of Convergence/Divergence by Region

Indicators	East Asia and the Pacific	Europe and Central Asia
ENVIRONMENT		
CO_2 Emissions (kilo tonnes)	34.9	0.6
CO_2 Emissions (Kg per GDP, 1995 US dollars)	57.0	−246.3
CO_2 Emissions (Kg per GDP, PPP dollars)	29.7	133.1
CO_2 Emissions (metric tonnes per capita)	10.1	−21.9
Electric power consumption (KWH per capita)	11.4	6.9

[a]Earliest year available for ECA: 1960.

Latin America and the Caribbean	Middle East and North Africa	South Asia	Sub-Saharan Africa	Data Availability: First and Final Years
6.6	19.1	30.4	1.4	1960/1999
−134.2	−276.6	−112.2	97.1	1960/1999
57.4	126.6	35.3	16.6	1975/1999
1.0	21.3	1.6	0.0	1960/1999
2.5	13.3	1.1	−3.7	1975/2000[a]

TABLE 2-1g Index of Convergence/Divergence by Region

Indicators	East Asia and the Pacific	Europe and Central Asia
TRANSPORTATION AND COMMUNICATION		
Air Transportation		
Number of airline passengers	15.0	−3.7
Number of aircraft departures	8.4	0.0
Vehicular Transportation		
Vehicles per 1,000 people	26.6	15.1
Vehicles per km of road	41.2	−2.6
Cars per 1,000 people	5.7	17.3
Two wheelers per 1,000 people	0.8	−2.2
Roads paved (% road network)	3.5	−7.2
Communication		
Newspaper circulation per 1,000 people	11.2	−38.6
Radio sets per 1,000 people	−13.9	−8.1
Television sets per 1,000 people	18.6	31.3
Cable TV subscriptions per 1,000 people	19.5	4.4
Phone subscriptions per 100 people (fixed and mobile)	12.6	−0.4
Mobile phones per 1,000 people	12.6	19.9
International Telephone, outgoing (minutes/subscriber)	33.8	151.8
Telephone mainlines per 1,000 people	11.6	25.2
Telephone mainlines per employee	29.0	51.5
Waiting list for telephone mainlines	1802.1	14499.1
Personal computers per 1,000 people	1.8	12.0
Internet users	26.9	1.4

*a*Latest year available for SA and SSA: 1999.
*b*Latest year available for EAP, LAC, and SA: 1999.
*c*Latest year available for EAP: 1999.
*d*Earliest year available for ECA, MENA, and SA: 1995; for EAP: 1990; for LAC and developed countries: 1970; for SSA: 1999.

considerably for all the developing country groups, with the single exception of Europe and Central Asia.

Age Structure

Over the entire period considered, the age dependency ratio has been converging in East Asia and the Pacific, Europe and Central Asia and particularly in Latin America and the Caribbean, but diverging (with some reversal to convergence in the 1990s) in the other three country groups (Figure 2-2). Underlying

Latin America and the Caribbean	Middle East and North Africa	South Asia	Sub-Saharan Africa	Data Availability: First and Final Years
4.7	5.3	0.3	−0.2	1970/2001
8.0	3.7	−3.1	−0.4	1970/2001
3.1	18.6	0.0	12.9	1990/1999
0.4	−6.3	1.7	13.2	1990/2000[a]
−0.6	52.8	0.9	−4.0	1980/2000[a]
−0.7	−0.3	0.0	0.2	1990/2000[a]
1.1	1.2	−8.0	−4.2	1990/2000[b]
−6.6	−10.5	7.1	14.8	1970/2000[c]
−10.6	−28.8	5.5	3.9	1970/2001
20.8	10.4	11.0	10.5	1965/2001
25.7	14.3	6.3	0.7	1970/2001[d]
5.4	12.2	2.4	−12.0	1990/2001[e]
12.2	14.8	1.8	−1.3	1990/2001[e]
47.6	7.2	32.8	92.2	1960/2001[f]
17.4	12.0	3.7	1.0	1960/2001
27.5	33.6	19.0	12.6	1960/2001[g]
1193.1	19731.3	15325.6	1388.0	1965/2000
9.2	4.8	1.3	2.5	1990/2001[b]
5.9	1.7	3.8	−3.0	1995/2001[i]

[e]Earliest year available for EAP and MENA: 1985; for developed countries: 1980.
[f]Earliest year available for EAP and SA: 1975; for LAC and MENA: 1970; for SSA: 1985.
[g]Earliest year available for EAP, LAC, SA, and SSA: 1975; for MENA: 1970.
[h]Earliest year available for developed countries: 1980.
[i]Earliest year available for developed countries: 1990.

these patterns is strong divergence (at least until the 1990s) in the share of population in the 0-14 age range, for although there have been widespread fertility declines in the developing world, they generally have not kept pace with those in the developed world. Another factor is divergence (with the single exception of Europe and Central Asia) in the share of the population in the 65+ age range, though the data show some recent reversal. Although the share of the population in this age range has been increasing rapidly from a small base in developing countries, these increases have not yet been of the magnitude to keep pace with the rapidly aging populations in the developed countries.

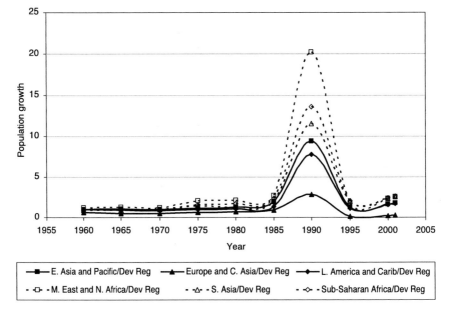

FIGURE 2-1 Population growth (compared to developed countries = 1.0) by region over time.

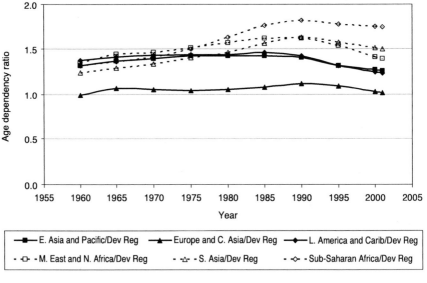

FIGURE 2-2 Age dependency ratio (compared to developed countries = 1.0) by region over time.

In some contrast, the share of the population in the 15-64 age range for four developing country regions—most notably in Latin America and the Caribbean—has been converging, although there has been divergence in South Asia and sub-Saharan Africa. One implication of these patterns is that over the period considered, Latin America and the Caribbean, East Asia and the Pacific, and Europe and Central Asia have had opportunities for exploiting the advantages of the "demographic bonus" part of the demographic transition, with relatively high proportions of working-age population and relatively low proportions of population with the education and health needs of infants and children, and health needs of aged adults. For youth transitioning to adulthood during such a demographic bonus, the lessened dependency ratios potentially offer advantages that may in part offset the competition for work and other options experienced with peers in their relatively large cohorts. Projections are that in the next few decades, Latin America and the Caribbean will continue to have the opportunities related to the demographic bonus and South Asia will have increasingly greater such opportunities, with sub-Saharan Africa lagging somewhat behind (Behrman, Duryea, and Székely, 2003). Rapidly aging populations in developing country regions such as East Asia and the Pacific and Europe and Central Asia, however, imply that opportunities for exploiting this "bonus" are not likely to continue much longer, if at all, in such areas.

Rural-Urban Composition

Rural population growth rates, generally (except in Europe and Central Asia) have been converging toward the very low rates experienced in the developed countries. Despite this convergence in the rural population growth rates, the shares of population in the rural sector generally have been diverging, except in the Middle East and North Africa. The obverse of this is that the growth rates of urban population generally have been diverging despite fairly widespread declines from previous high levels—with the exception of some convergence for Europe and Central Asia, though the shares of urban population have been converging (Figure 2-3). The contrast between the convergence of growth rates and shares is possible because the initial shares (as of the mid-twentieth century) of the population in rural areas were so much larger (and those in urban areas so much smaller) in most developing country regions than in developed countries that convergence in the growth rates will have to continue for some time before the shares, too, start to converge. Associated with the rapid urbanization rates experienced recently in most developing country regions—and projected to continue—are changed opportunities for human capital investments, employment, sexual relations, entertainment, marriage, autonomy, and other related factors for youth.

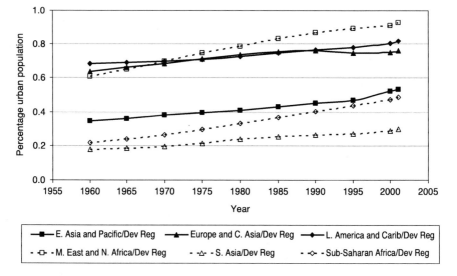

FIGURE 2-3 Urban population (as a percentage of total population) (compared to developed countries = 1.0) by region over time.

Female-to-Male Sex Ratio

The female-to-male sex ratio has tended to converge in the more populous regions of the world, where it previously was relatively low—South Asia and East Asia and the Pacific, as well as in sub-Saharan Africa (Figure 2-4). On the other hand, there has been some divergence in Europe and Central Asia and to a lesser extent in Latin America and the Caribbean and the Middle East and North Africa (the last being a region where the sex ratio was relatively low at the start of the period covered). Thus if historically the relatively low female-to-male sex ratios in parts of Asia and the Middle East and North Africa were caused by more limited access to resources within or outside of the household by females (as claimed, e.g., by Sen, 1990), then in the more populous of these areas (though not in the Middle East and North Africa), apparently, the differential access has been lessened. For two of the regions for which there is divergence (Europe and Central Asia, Latin America and the Caribbean), moreover, the divergence favors females relatively to males because these country groups initially had higher female-to-male sex ratios than did the developed country group. Thus quite broadly in the developing world, with the notable exception of the Middle East and North Africa, sex ratios have shifted toward females. This is consistent with female youth as recently having benefited from more resources and opportunities relative to males on average than was the case

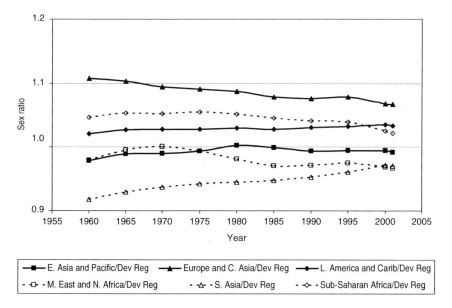

FIGURE 2-4 Sex ratio (compared to developed countries = 1.0) by region over time.

in the past—though the movement toward closing the gender gap favoring males does not mean that it has been closed entirely.

ECONOMY

The nature of the economy has an important effect on the options that youth have through a number of channels, both directly (e.g., in terms of employment options and the returns to different types of human capital investments) and indirectly (e.g., through transfers from family and subsidies from governments for human resource investments). This section explores the impact that some such variables may have on the economic environment that prevails when youth transition into adulthood.

Gross Domestic Product (GDP) Growth Rates and Levels

Rates of growth of gross domestic product (GDP) have varied substantially among regions. Four of the regions—East Asia and the Pacific, Europe and Central Asia, the Middle East and North Africa, and South Asia—have experienced considerable convergence in economic growth rates. The other two—Latin America and the Caribbean and sub-Saharan Africa—have diverged (in a negative direction). Per capita incomes in purchasing power parity (PPP) terms[10] have been converging somewhat on average in East Asia and the Pacific and South Asia, but diverging considerably in Europe and Central Asia and the Middle East and North Africa, and to a lesser extent (but still substantially), in sub-Saharan Africa and Latin America and the Caribbean (Figure 2-5). This suggests that youth in large parts of the developing world are in economies where per capita product/income has been slipping further behind that in the developed world, even if in some cases, such as Europe and Central Asia and the Middle East and North Africa, the growth rates have been converging. On the other hand, the two regions in which the majority of youth live in the developing world—East Asia and the Pacific and South Asia—have been converging somewhat in terms of per capita product/ income level, because their economies on average have grown rapidly enough to offset the momentum of starting from much lower per capita product/ income levels. Different commentators may view this record as more or less positive, or even negative. But it certainly suggests that the overall economic contexts in which most youth in the developing world have been making their transitions to adulthood have changed, and that these changes have varied substantially among regions, with much more positive aggregate economic experiences in Asia, which houses the majority of youth in developing countries, than elsewhere.

Shares of Production in Major Sectors

The shares of production in various sectors may shape substantially the nature of options, particularly employment and human resource-related options, for youth in developing countries. Conventional wisdom is that the share of agriculture in production declines steadily in the process of development—from about half or more at low levels of per capita income to a level of about 5 percent. At the same time, the share of industry increases initially, and then peaks and declines somewhat, and the share of services tends to increase—particularly for per capita income levels above that at which the share of industry starts to fall.[11] The patterns, over time, for most of the developing regions are consistent with these characterizations. The nonlinear

---

[10]"Purchasing power parity" refers to the effort to correct for different price structures (i.e., the prices of services such as haircuts and other items not traded in international markets typically vary a lot across countries with different resources, international trade policies, technology, and income levels). Generally PPP measures are considered to be the best available measures for comparisons among countries, so we concentrate on the GDP PPP measures, but also provide some alternatives in the tables.

[11]Such patterns long have been emphasized in the "patterns of growth" observed by Colin Clark, Simon Kuznets, Hollis Chenery, Moshe Syrquin, and others. See, for example, Chenery and Syrquin (1986).

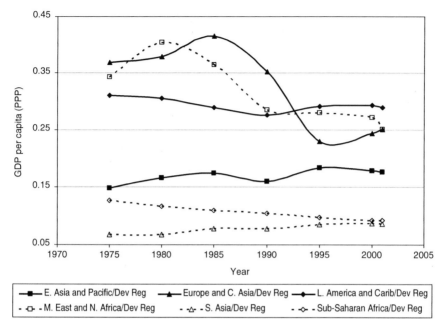

FIGURE 2-5 GDP per capita (compared to developed countries = 1.0) by region over time.

nature of these paths, however, means that what appears to be divergence in the shorter run may be consistent with longer run convergence.

The share of value added in agriculture has been declining fairly steadily in most country groups. The share of value added in industry has been converging rapidly for East Asia and the Pacific, Europe and Central Asia, Latin America and the Caribbean, and the Middle East and North Africa. There has been some smaller divergence, in contrast, for South Asia and sub-Saharan Africa. The share of value added in services has been converging rapidly for Latin America and the Caribbean and East Asia and the Pacific, and somewhat less rapidly for South Asia and sub-Saharan Africa (with a small drop for Europe and Central Asia and almost no change for the Middle East and North Africa). These patterns are roughly consistent with the conventional wisdom sketched out above. However, the relatively large movements toward the developed country shares for Latin America and the Caribbean, South Asia, and sub-Saharan Africa—given their respective levels of development—raise some concerns that the service sectors in these cases may be absorbing labor in low-productive activities because of limited job expansion in goods-production sectors. In any case, youth in the developing countries clearly have faced job options in economies with fairly rapidly changing production structures that probably have changed the returns to different forms of human capital (e.g., increased the returns to formal schooling in comparison with informal learning in family enterprises) and have involved some dislocation (including physical migration) to adjust to the changes—and, once again, with some important differences among regions.

Openness to International Trade

Probably the most prominent conjecture in the development literature about the relation between openness to international trade and levels of development is that exposure to international markets, particularly through having to compete to export in such markets, increases the efficiency of physical and human investments and of technological adoptions, encourages greater national and international investments, and expands markets, and therefore, increases the rate of development. On the other hand, there is a long-standing perception, advocated, for example, by Latin American structuralists and revived recently in a related form by some international economists and other commentators on global changes, that development involves industrialization and high-end services—the domestic expansion of which must be nurtured at least initially by limiting or precluding strong competition from international markets and investors. A related observation is that economies that depend on primary exports of agricultural and mineral products need to be very open, but are not likely to transform themselves into developed economies very rapidly.

Four of the six developing country regions have recently converged toward the developed countries in a standard measure of openness—the share of exports plus imports in national product. The exceptions are East Asia and the Pacific and, to a much lesser extent, South Asia. For East Asia and the Pacific (but not for South Asia), the nature of the divergence has been to *increase* openness more rapidly than the developed countries, which often has been interpreted as being an important causal factor in the relatively successful recent development of this region. In any case, it is clear that openness (and the underlying export and import share components) has changed substantially in the developing world, again with considerable variations among developing country groups. This is likely to have been related to substantial changes in economic structure, and therefore with the opportunities facing youth as they make important transitions to adulthood and consider what time uses are likely to have the highest payoffs for themselves.

Governmental Roles in the Economy

The process of development typically involves an expansion of dependencies on markets and on the government and a reduction of family and kin support (e.g., Ben-Porath, 1980; Pollak, 1985; Chenery and Syrquin, 1986).[12] These changes alter the context in which youth make transitions to adulthood by making those transitions more dependent on markets (e.g., employment opportunities) and governmental services (e.g., publicly subsidized school systems). The expansion of the government, in turn, requires an expansion in governmental revenues, which normally takes primarily the form of expanded tax revenues.

The share of tax revenues in national product has tended to increase and converge for Europe and Central Asia, Latin America and the Caribbean, sub-Saharan Africa, and, barely, the Middle East and North Africa—but to diverge for East Asia and the Pacific and South Asia (though in both of these cases considering a somewhat different time period suggests some convergence). On the governmental expenditure side, we focus on expenditures on human capital because these are among the most relevant expenditures directly affecting youth in transition to adulthood. The shares of public expenditures on health and on education have converged substantially for most of the developing country regions (Figures 2-6 and 2-7). The single exception among the regions is East Asia and the Pacific for education, where public expenditures in recent decades have fluctuated around 4 percent of national product (as compared with about 5 percent in the developed country group). But fragmented evidence for this region suggests a substantially larger role of private financing of education than in most other regions. In summary, generally in developing countries there has been significant convergence regarding governmental roles—that reflect substantial shifts from families to the state for human resource investments.

LABOR

Shifts in the labor force that occur with the process of development are strongly correlated with the shifts described above in population and in the economy, as well as with the concomitant marketization of what formerly were primarily family functions. The latter not only increases adult participation in formal labor markets—particularly by females—but also reduces child and adolescent labor force participation as learning in school tends to replace learning by work experience during childhood and adolescence. The

---

[12]However, in recent years on average there has been somewhat of a reduction in governmental revenues/expenditures relative to total product in the developed country group.

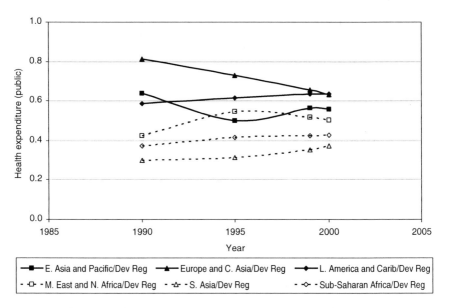

FIGURE 2-6 Share of public expenditure on health (compared to developed countries = 1.0) by region over time.

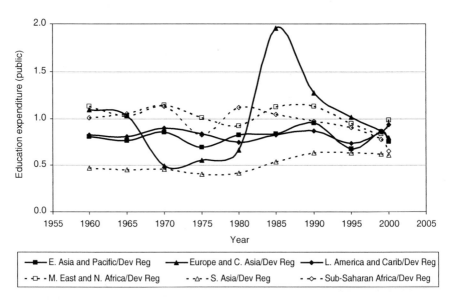

FIGURE 2-7 Share of public expenditure on education (compared to developed countries = 1.0) by region over time.

increased formal labor force participation also results in greater measured unemployment, perhaps in part due to the greater investment in job searches for good matches and in part due to the more rapid changes in the economy.

Labor Force Activity Rates, Gender, and Child Labor

The female labor force activity rates have tended to converge substantially for East Asia and the Pacific, Europe and Central Asia, South Asia, and sub-Saharan Africa, but have diverged slightly for Latin America and the Caribbean and the Middle East and North Africa. In substantial part, this reflects the great change in female labor force participation in the developed countries (nearly doubling between 1960 and 2000), which permitted catch-up with the developing countries in East Asia and the Pacific, Europe and Central Asia, South Asia, and sub-Saharan Africa (in each of which there was much less change), but which increased disparities with Latin America and the Caribbean and the Middle East and North Africa (in which there were increases from lower bases, but not as rapidly as in the developed countries). The male labor force activity rates, on average, in developing countries have changed much less relative to the developed countries than have the female rates—with some convergence in East Asia and the Pacific, Europe and Central Asia, Latin America and the Caribbean, and South Asia and some divergences in the Middle East and North Africa and sub-Saharan Africa. The combination of the patterns for females and males has resulted in substantial convergence in the share of females in the labor force in most regions (much less in Latin America and the Caribbean and the Middle East and North Africa) (Figure 2-8). This is consistent with labor force opportunities by gender shifting (substantially in most regions) toward those in the developed countries. Finally the child (ages 10 to 14) labor force participation rates have dropped considerably in all the developing country regional groups, though the indices generally indicate substantial divergence because of the very low and declining almost to zero rates in the developed countries (Figure 2-9).

Sectoral Distribution of Employment

The shares in industrial and service employment tend to have converged or diverged fairly similarly to those discussed above, with regard to the shares in value added. But the patterns are not exactly the same because of differential average labor productivity changes across group. As a result there is a tendency for somewhat less convergence for labor shares than for production shares, perhaps most strikingly in the case of the industry shares in the Middle East and North Africa. As for the overall labor force activity rates, there is somewhat of a tendency for greater convergence (but somewhat weaker) in the sectoral labor force shares for females than for males.

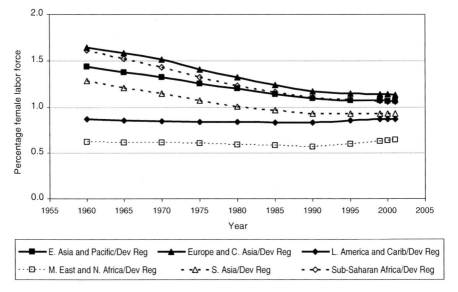

FIGURE 2-8 Female labor force (as a percentage of total population) (compared to developed countries = 1.0) by region over time.

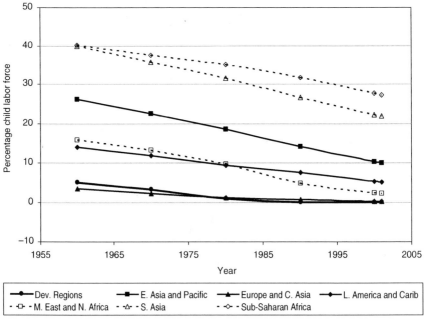

FIGURE 2-9 Child labor, 10-14 years (as a percentage of age group) (compared to developed countries = 1.0) by region over time.

Unemployment Rates, Gender, and Youth

The indices are not very informative for unemployment rates because such rates are rather small with a fair amount of fluctuations in the developed countries. The unemployment rates in the developing country groups also have considerable fluctuations, but in general possibly exhibit some upward trend. Underlying these overall rates tend to be rates that are higher and more volatile for females, including among adolescent and youth ages 15-24 years. The interpretation of trends and relative fluctuations in unemployment rates, however, is not straightforward because there are both demand-side considerations (related to the demand for labor) and supply-side factors (related to more searches for better matches with the marketization of labor and development and a lower dependence on families for absorbing underemployed workers).

HEALTH

Health is of interest in itself because it contributes directly to individual welfare. In addition, improved health has important productivity effects through increased learning and performance directly on the job, with both effects being quite strong in poor populations (e.g., Alderman, Behrman, and Hoddinott, 2005; Behrman, Duryea,and Székely, 2003; Pollitt, 1990; Strauss and Thomas, 1995, 1998). For example, better health not only makes learning easier, but it increases the returns to learning through increasing post-education productivity and higher expected duration of productive years.

Life Expectancies and Gender

Life expectancies and the mortality rates[13] that underlie them refer to fundamental aspects of health as they relate to the duration of life, even though they do not refer to the quality of life or the nature of morbidity.[14]

---

[13]Due to space limitations, we do not discuss the patterns in the underlying mortality rates, but some convergence indices for mortality rates are presented in Table 2-1d for interested readers.

[14]A frequently used measure that refers to the quality of life is Disability Adjusted Life Years (DALYs). We have not included DALYs in this chapter because they are not included in the World Bank database that we use and because estimates are not available for much of the relevant historical period. But analyses of DALYs by types of morbidity indicate considerable recent and predicted convergence, with large shifts from communicable to noncommunicable diseases (despite the spread of HIV/AIDS in the former category). Behrman and Sengupta (2004, Appendix E) summarize some of this information. For discussions of aspects of convergence in the epidemiological and nutritional transitions, also see Omran (1971), Olshansky and Ault (1986), and Popkin (2002).

With the exception of Europe and Central Asia, there has been substantial convergence with regard to overall life expectancies in all the developing country regions (Figure 2-10). This is very impressive because average life expectancy in the developed countries has increased substantially in recent decades, from 66 years in 1960 to 77 years in 2000. The general convergence reflects that in most developing country regions, life expectancy has increased even more than in developed countries. The Europe and Central Asia exception reflects the deceleration and the fall in life expectancies with the deterioration of health services and behaviors in the former Soviet Asia and allied countries. In this case, though there has been divergence from the developed countries, there has been convergence with the other developing countries. Perhaps more troubling is sub-Saharan Africa, for which there has been some convergence over the whole period considered, but divergence since 1990 due in part to the HIV/AIDS pandemic (with a fall in life expectancy at birth from 50.8 years in 1990 to 48.6 in 2001).

Gender differences in life expectancies at birth have converged substantially in most developing country regions, but have diverged in the Middle East and North Africa and sub-Saharan Africa (Figure 2-11). The convergence that is prominent in most parts of the developing world suggests that any differential access to health resources that may have discriminated against females has decreased in recent decades, as is noted above with

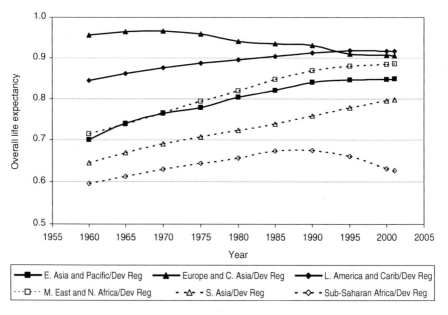

FIGURE 2-10 Overall life expectancy at birth (compared to developed countries = 1.0) by region over time.

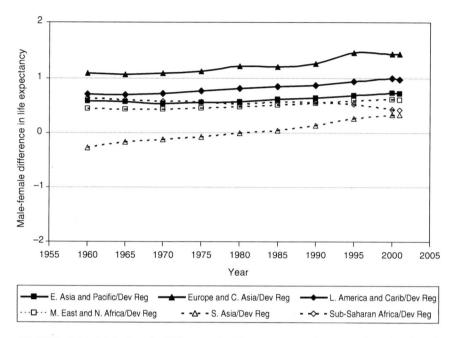

FIGURE 2-11 Male-female difference in life expectancy (compared to developed countries = 1.0) by region over time.

regard to the discussion of population sex ratios. In fact, since 1985 life expectancies for females have exceeded those for males on average in all the developing country regions, as well as the developed country regions. This does not mean that there is discrimination in the distribution of health-related resources against males because some life expectancy differences may be biological rather than behavioral. But apparently even in the developed countries, some of the differences are behavioral (e.g., consumption of tobacco and alcohol products, undertaking risky and stressful activities), with the result that the gender difference in life expectancies favoring females has varied over time (e.g., 4.8 years in 1960, increasing to 6.2 years in 1980, and declining to 5.5 years in 2000). The divergence in gender differences for life expectancies in Europe and Central Asia seems to be part of the convergence to the patterns in other better performing developing country regions that is noted above with respect to overall life expectancies. The divergence in gender differences for life expectancies in sub-Saharan Africa may reflect the feminization of the incidence of HIV/AIDS in that region and possibly that females are more marginalized when economies are stagnant (though the latter factor does not seem to have dominated in Latin America and the Caribbean, which also has been relatively stagnant economically in recent decades).

Health Determinants

Many, and perhaps the most important, health determinants reflect a range of behavioral choices related to nutrition, physical activity, and risky behaviors. Unfortunately we have not been able to locate comparable data on such activities across countries for the time periods covered. But fragmented evidence suggests at least some convergence in such behaviors, including in some behaviors (e.g., smoking, diet) that may be deleterious to health.

What we have been able to compare are a limited set of indicators of curative health. As we note above in the discussion of governmental expenditures in the section on the economy, the share of public health expenditures has converged substantially in all regions. In addition, we consider indices for DPT vaccination, measles vaccination, physicians per 1,000 people, and hospital beds per 1,000 people. The indices suggest that movement toward convergence is predominant for vaccinations. There also has been movement toward convergence in number of physicians per 1,000 people in East Asia and the Pacific, Latin America and the Caribbean, and the Middle East and North Africa, and in the number of hospital beds per 1,000 people in East Asia and the Pacific and in Europe and Central Asia (but only barely).

EDUCATION

Education is widely viewed as critical in improving transitions to adulthood in developing countries, particularly if there are rapidly changing conditions and increased marketization. As noted in Chapter 3 (National Research Council and Institute of Medicine, 2005), the form that education takes generally changes in the development process from learning-by-doing in family-related jobs to formal schooling and subsequent learning-by-doing in wage jobs.

Schooling Enrollments Overall and Gender Differences

Gross primary and secondary schooling enrollments have both converged substantially for all the developing country groups. For primary schooling, this basically represents a catch-up to a stable target, because in the developed countries, gross primary enrollments have been basically 100 percent, at least since 1970. For secondary schooling, the convergence is more impressive because gross secondary school enrollments in the developed countries have increased substantially—from 64 percent in 1970 to 106 percent in 2000.[15] Thus there has been substantial convergence at the

---

[15]Gross enrollments can exceed 100 percent because they are calculated as the number of students attending a school level (of whatever age) relative to the size of the population for the ages for which that school level would be relevant if students entered school at the minimum age and progressed one grade each year, until they graduated from that school level.

secondary level despite a significantly increasing moving target. These relative enrollment increases in the developing countries, together with those at the tertiary level, have implied significant convergence in the expected schooling for synthetic cohorts, as well as the average schooling of adults—changing considerably the educational human capital acquired by youth in developing countries.

There also have been striking changes in gender differences in enrollments. The absolute gender differences favoring males in gross enrollments at both the primary and the secondary levels have fallen substantially for all the country groups that we consider—and in some cases have even been reversed (Figures 2-12 and 2-13).

Schooling Inputs

We have been able to locate little information with which to make comparisons over time regarding schooling inputs. We have already discussed, in the section on the economy, the predominant tendency for the share of public expenditures devoted to education to move toward convergence. One other indicator that we have been able to find pertains to the pupil-teacher ratio. This indicator suggests general divergence, with the

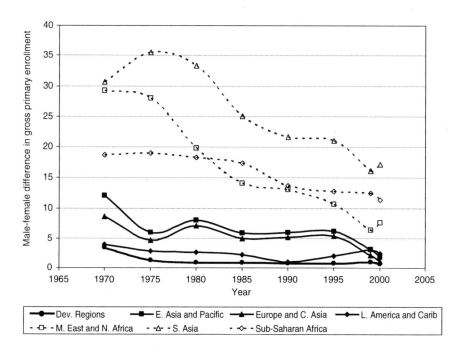

FIGURE 2-12 Male-female difference in gross primary enrollment (compared to developed countries = 1.0) by region over time.

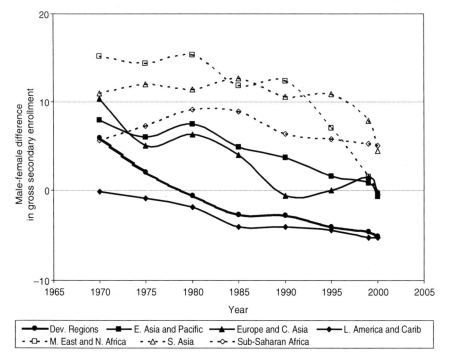

FIGURE 2-13 Male-female difference in gross secondary enrollment (compared to developed countries = 1.0) by region over time.

exception of the Europe and Central Asia region. This is a reflection of the relatively large cohorts of school-age children who have been passing through school systems in developing countries, together with the increasing enrollment rates, during recent decades. Looking forward, however, the combination of more educated adults due to the substantial schooling expansion (the pool from which teachers will be drawn) and the spread to additional developing regions beyond East Asia and the Pacific of the "demographic bonus" is likely to make possible increases in resources (including teachers) per student and in schooling quality more broadly defined.

ENVIRONMENT

We consider carbon dioxide emissions (total, Kg per GDP in PPP dollars, per capita) and electric power per capita in assessing the impact that environmental factors might have on the changing climate in which youth make transitions to adulthood. The predominant tendencies are toward convergence. This is particularly the case for carbon dioxide emissions per

GDP in PPP dollars, which in the case of the developed country measure, declines sharply (to less than a third of its 1975 value by 2000); therefore, the extent of convergence in the developing countries is all the more striking. The convergence by the other measures is less, in part because of the divergence outside of Asia in per capita GDP in PPP terms, noted in the discussion of the section on economy. But generally there is still convergence, though less so in Europe and Central Asia, which (alone among the regions) experienced per capita declines in both carbon dioxide emissions and electric power after 1990 (i.e., after the demise of the Soviet Union). Therefore, while carbon dioxide emissions in general have increased recently (with the exception just noted), suggesting some deterioration in these aspects of the environments in which youth are becoming adults, at the same time the economies in which they live are becoming more like those in the developed countries with falling emissions per unit of real product.

TRANSPORTATION AND COMMUNICATION

Increased transportation and communication, of course, are critical channels through which phenomena such as globalization are often presumed to occur. This suggests that the greater the expansion of transportation and communication (given that the developing countries in most respects are less intensive regarding transportation and communication than the developed countries), the greater the convergence of variables in all the groups that we consider. In most cases, it would seem that the more rapid the expansion of transportation and communication the more the developing countries are converging toward the (changing) developed countries in terms of transportation and communication per se.

Air Transport

The number of air passengers has increased substantially in the developed countries in recent decades—by a factor of about 3.5 between 1970 and 2000. This means that for there to have been some convergence, the number of air passengers in developing countries would have had to increase even more rapidly. In fact, there has been considerable convergence by this measure recently in East Asia and the Pacific, and a somewhat lesser convergence in Latin America and the Caribbean and the Middle East and North Africa—but not much relative change in South Asia and sub-Saharan Africa, and some divergence in Europe and Central Asia (Figure 2-14). For the number of aircraft departures, the patterns are similar, though with about as much convergence in Latin America and the Caribbean as in East Asia and the Pacific and with divergence only in South Asia.

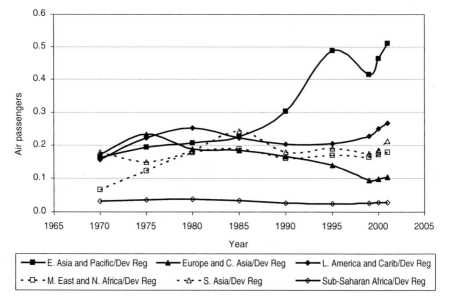

FIGURE 2-14 Number of air passengers (compared to developed countries = 1.0) by region over time.

Vehicular Transport

Convergence has been the primary tendency, though with exceptions. Vehicles per 1,000 people, for example, have tended to converge strongly for East Asia and the Pacific, Europe and Central Asia, the Middle East and North Africa, sub-Saharan Africa, and, to a lesser extent, Latin America and the Caribbean—though not in South Asia. Taking into consideration all the indicators included in the tables, the convergence tends to have been greatest and most consistent in East Asia and the Pacific, and probably least in South Asia, though there are also mixed patterns in the other four regions.

Communication

For most of the available indicators for most regions, a tendency for convergence has been the norm—though with exceptions that tend to be concentrated among older communication media (e.g., radio sets per 1,000 people, newspaper circulation per 1,000 people). Sub-Saharan Africa (all phone and mobile phone subscriptions per 1,000 people and Internet users) also seems to be an exception to this general trend of convergence exhibited by the other developing regions. Some interesting examples for different types of communication are provided by radio sets per 1,000 people, phone subscriptions per 1,000 people, personal computers per 1,000 people, and Internet users (Figures 2-15 through 2-18). There seem to be some weak tendencies for convergence to have been the greatest for Europe and Central Asia, probably with East Asia and the Pacific ranking second, and the least for sub-Saharan Africa.

Thus for both transportation and communication, there has been a much greater tendency for convergence than for divergence for developing country regions. These tendencies have been a little stronger for East Asia and the Pacific in transportation and for Europe and Central Asia in communication, and weakest for South Asia in transportation and sub-Saharan Africa in communication. But generally there have been considerable changes, basically in the direction of the (again, changing) transportation and communication structures of the developed countries in the contexts in which youth in the developing world have been making transitions to adulthood. These changes are associated with greater mobility and greater information about the broader world, both of which would seem to be associated with changed—and probably increased—options and with lessened tendencies to choose traditional options.

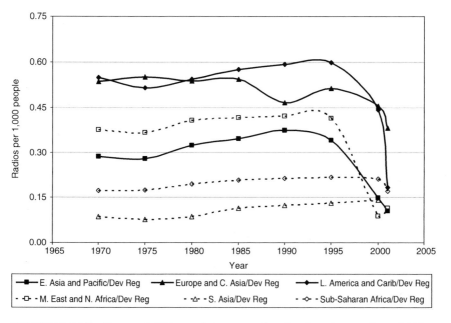

FIGURE 2-15 Radios per 1,000 people (compared to developed countries = 1.0) by region over time.

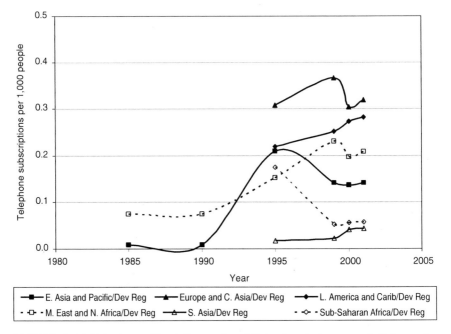

FIGURE 2-16 Telephone (fixed line and mobile) subscriptions per 1,000 people (compared to developed countries = 1.0) by region over time.

CONCLUSIONS

The developing countries have tended to converge toward the characteristics of the developed countries in a number of important respects in recent decades. But there also has been significant divergence in some other respects. Furthermore, there has been considerable variance among the seven groups of indicators considered and among developing country regions. The tendency for convergence has been considerable for the available indicators of health, education, environment, transportation and communication, and gender differences, but somewhat less for the other indicators. Though there has been a tendency for convergence for many aspects of the economy, the pattern is mixed for the important overall indicators of economic growth rates and for per capita product. In particular, two of the regions—Latin America and the Caribbean and sub-Saharan Africa—have diverged negatively with regard to economic growth rates. Only two of the regions—East Asia and the Pacific and South Asia—have been converging rather than diverging in terms of per capita real product. Though the majority of youth in the developing world live in the latter two regions, a significant minority lives in the other regions, for which there has been a

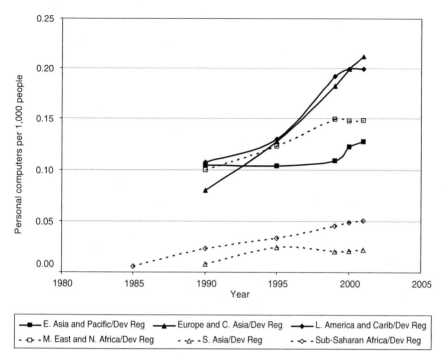

FIGURE 2-17 Personal computers per 1,000 people (compared to developed countries = 1.0) by region over time.

tendency for divergence for per capita real product. Taking into consideration all the indicators, the region of East Asia and the Pacific generally has converged most toward developed economics and sub-Saharan Africa least. The other regions are in between, with Europe and Central Asia in several cases diverging from the developed economies, but converging toward the more developed of the developing regions.

Such results suggest that the dominant thrust, as suggested by many observers of globalization, has been toward a more integrated and more similar world in which youth are making transitions to adulthood. This implies many changes for current youth in comparison with previous generations: much more dependence on markets than on family enterprises for jobs; much more emphasis on formal schooling than on learning by working with parents and other relatives; much more awareness of options and lifestyles from the broader world than just from the local community; longer life expectancies and less susceptibility to infectious diseases; smaller gender gaps favoring males; and much more mobility in a number of dimensions. But this major thrust should be qualified by important nuances that differ importantly among the regions and with respect to various indi-

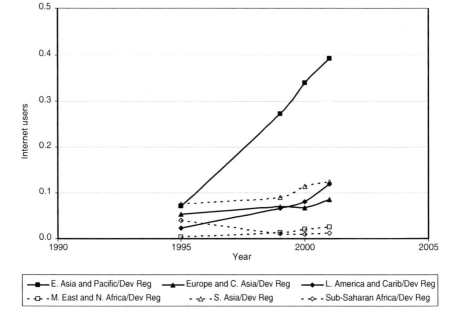

FIGURE 2-18 Internet users (compared to developed countries = 1.0) by region over time.

cators. Opportunities for youth in East Asia and the Pacific have changed differently in important respects from those, for example in sub-Saharan Africa or Europe and Central Asia. Therefore, analysis of changing transitions to adulthood in developing countries needs to be sensitive both to the predominant tendencies toward convergence and to some important tendencies toward divergence.

REFERENCES

Ahmad, S. (1994). Improving inter-spatial and inter-temporal comparability of national accounts. *Journal of Development Economics*, 44(1), 53-76.

Alderman, H., Behrman, J.R., and Hoddinott, J. (2005). Nutrition, malnutrition, and economic growth. In G. López-Casasnovas, B. Rivera, and L. Currais (Eds.), *Health and economic growth: Findings and policy implications.* Cambridge, MA: MIT Press.

Behrman, J.R., and Rosenzweig, M.R. (1994). Caveat emptor: Cross-country data on education and the labor force. *Journal of Development Economics*, 44(1), 147-172.

Behrman, J.R., and Sengupta, P. (2004). *Convergence? Divergence? Or some of both? Major trends in selected indicators among country groups in recent decades.* Philadelphia: University of Pennsylvania.

Behrman, J.R., Duryea, S., and Székely, M. (2003). Aging and economic opportunities: Major world regions around the turn of the century. In O. Attanasio and M. Székely (Eds.), *A dynamic analysis of household decision-making in Latin America.* Washington, DC: Inter-American Development Bank.

Ben-Porath, Y. (1980). The f-connection: Families, friends and firms, and the organization of exchange. *Population and Development Review*, 6(1), 1-30.

Bouis, H.E. (1994). The effect of income on demand for food in poor countries: Are our databases giving us reliable estimates? *Journal of Development Economics*, 44(1), 199-226.

Chamie, J. (1994). Population databases in development analysis. *Journal of Development Economics*, 44(1), 131-146.

Chenery, H.B., and Syrquin, M. (1986). Typical patterns of transformation. In H.B. Chenery, S. Robinson, and M. Syrquin (Eds.), *Industrialization and growth*. New York: Oxford University Press.

Heston, A. (1994). A brief review of some problems in using national accounts data in level comparisons and growth studies. *Journal of Development Economics*, 44(1), 29-52.

Lloyd, C.B., and Hewett, P.C. (2003). *Primary schooling in sub-Saharan Africa: Recent trends and current challenges*. New York: Population Council.

National Research Council and Institute of Medicine. (2005). *Growing up global: The changing transitions to adulthood in developing countries*. Panel on Transitions to Adulthood in Developing Countries. C.B. Lloyd (Ed.). Committee on Population and Board on Children, Youth, and Families. Division of Behavioral and Social Sciences and Education. Washington, DC: The National Academies Press.

Olshansky, S.J., and Ault, A.B. (1986). The fourth stage of the epidemiologic transition: The age of delayed degenerative diseases. *Milbank Quarterly*, 64, 355-390.

Omran, A.R. (1971). The epidemiological transition: A theory of the epidemiology of population change. *Milbank Quarterly*, 49, 509-538.

Pollak, R.A. (1985). A transaction cost approach to families and households. *Journal of Economic Literature*, 23(June), 581-608.

Pollitt, E. (1990). *Malnutrition and infection in the classroom*. Paris, France: UNESCO.

Popkin, B.M. (2002). An overview on the nutrition transition and its health implications: The Bellagio meeting. *Public Health Nutrition*, 5(1A), 93-103.

Sen, A.K. (1990). More than 100 million women are missing. *New York Review of Books*, 37(2), 61-66.

Srinivasan, T.N. (1994). Database for development analysis: An overview. *Journal of Development Economics*, 44(1), 3-26.

Strauss, J., and Thomas, D. (1995). Human resources: Empirical modeling of household and family decisions. In J.R. Behrman and T.N. Srinivasan (Eds.), *Handbook of development economics* (vol. 3A, pp. 1883-2024). Amsterdam, Holland: North Holland.

Strauss, J., and Thomas, D. (1998). Health, nutrition, and economic development. *Journal of Economic Literature*, 36(2), 766-817.

Stromquist, N.P., and Monkman, K. (Eds.). (2000). *Globalization and education: Integration and contestation across cultures*. Lanham, MD: Rowman & Littlefield.

3

Small Families and Large Cohorts: The Impact of the Demographic Transition on Schooling in Brazil

David A. Lam and Letícia Marteleto

The demographic transition that has been observed throughout the developing world is associated with dramatic changes in family size and the size of birth cohorts. During a substantial period of the demographic transition, it is common to observe family size decreasing at the same time that cohort size is increasing. From the standpoint of a child entering school, these changes may imply offsetting effects. Smaller families may mean less competition for resources at the family level, leading to higher school enrollment and better school outcomes. Larger cohorts may mean more competition for resources at the population level, however, leading to more school crowding and worse school outcomes.

This chapter analyzes these issues for the case of Brazil. Brazil provides an interesting case for examining the impact of the changing cohort size and family size on children's school enrollment. During recent decades the country has experienced a large and rapid fertility decline combined with persistent low levels of schooling and high educational inequality. School enrollment improved little in the 1980s, but began to increase rapidly in the 1990s, a period in which the size of the school-age population began to decline. This chapter explores how changing demographics at the family and population levels may help explain the changing patterns in school enrollment in Brazil in recent decades.

We begin by providing an overview of the demographic transition in Brazil and the resulting changes in cohort size, drawing on census data. We focus in particular on the size and growth rate of the population ages 7 to 14. We then describe the annual Pesquisa Nacional de Amostra de Domicílios (PNAD) household survey data from 1977 to 1999 that will be used for most of our analysis. Using these data, we document the decreases in family size and increases in parental education that are observed in Brazil from 1977 to 1999. We then describe the evolution of educational measures over the past three decades, pointing out the improved performance of the 1990s. We then analyze the effect of the growth rate of the school-age population, numbers of siblings, and parental schooling on school enrollment using probit regressions.

We estimate a negative effect of both cohort growth and family size on school enrollment. These effects are statistically significant, but are relatively small in magnitude. Interactions with age, gender, and father's schooling indicate that the group most negatively affected by rapid growth of the school-age population is older boys from poorer households. This supports our theoretical predictions that school enrollment pressures will tend to push out students who are closest to the margin of leaving school. We also estimate positive effects of both mother's and father's schooling on enrollment, effects that are considerably larger in magnitude than the effects of cohort size and family size. Using the coefficients from our regressions, we simulate the impact of macro- and micro-level demographic change on school enrollment during the late 1970s, 1980s, and 1990s. We find that the growth rates of cohort size of the school-age population tended to reduce school enrollment rates in the 1980s and helped increase enrollment in the 1990s. Decreasing family size and increasing parental schooling both tended to increase enrollment in all periods, with parental schooling having the largest impact. Taking all variables together, the combination of our regression coefficients and the observed changes in independent variables explain more than 60 percent of the observed increase in school enrollment between 1977 and 1999.

PREVIOUS RESEARCH ON COHORT SIZE, FAMILY SIZE, AND SCHOOLING

This chapter explores the impact on school enrollments of both cohort size and family size. Both of these variables have been the focus of extensive discussion in previous theoretical and empirical research on the impact of rapid population growth in developing countries. Without attempting to thoroughly review this large literature, we briefly focus on some of the studies that provide a background for this chapter.

The possible negative effect of rapid growth of the school-age population on schooling outcomes has often been raised as one of the potential negative consequences of rapid population growth (Jones, 1971; Knodel, 1992; World Bank, 1984). There has not been strong empirical evidence of a negative impact of the size of the school-age population on school outcomes, however. In one of the most comprehensive analyses of the issue, Schultz (1987) analyzed the economics of school finance in the presence of changing size of the school-age population relative to the adult population. Using aggregate cross-national data on age structure, school enrollments, and school expenditures, Schultz found no significant effect on school enrollment rates of the proportion of the population in school age. He also found no noticeable effect of relative cohort size on the shares of gross national product (GNP) allocated to education, although he did find a negative association between the proportion of the population of school age and public school expenditures per child. Kelley (2001) notes that several other studies based on cross-country data also suggest that there is no impact of relative cohort size on the share of national budgets allocated to schooling. Kelley (1996) updated Schultz's analysis using data from the 1980s and continued to find no significant effect of cohort size on the share of educational spending in GNP, although he did not look directly at the impact on enrollment.

In the case of Brazil, several studies have mentioned the potential benefits generated by lower population growth rates and decreases in the relative and absolute size of the school-age population. Birdsall and Sabot (1996) point to Brazil's rapid increase in the number of children of school age in the 1970s and 1980s as potential cause for the poor educational performance of the 1980s. Rigotti (2001) argues that the decline in the population pressure and resulting smaller cohorts of school-age groups may have helped the performance of the educational system. Along the same lines, Castro (1999) has pointed to the high proportions of the population of school age of north and northeast Brazil as one of the potential reasons for lower enrollment rates in these regions. Although past research has recognized the importance of cohort size on children's schooling in developing countries, this research has typically relied on cross-national regressions using aggregate data. Our analysis will take a different approach, using a combination of time-series and cross-state variation in cohort size, and using household survey data that make it possible to look at the impact of household-level variables as well as aggregate variables.

In addition to the literature on cohort size, there is an even larger literature analyzing the impact of family size on schooling outcomes. As pointed out in the reviews by Lloyd (1994) and Kelley (1996), previous research in this area has produced mixed results, ranging from negative effects to statistically insignificant effects to positive effects. Most empirical studies on educational attainment in developing countries have found that children from large families attain less schooling on average than children with fewer siblings (Anh et al., 1998; Knodel and Wongsith, 1991; Marteleto, 2001; Parish and Willis, 1993; Patrinos and Psacharopoulos, 1997). This is often attributed to a dilution of resources, with a smaller share of financial and interpersonal resources allocated to each child in larger families. Some studies, however, have found a positive association between family size and education (Chernichovsky, 1985; Hossain, 1988; King et al., 1986; Mueller, 1984; Zajonc, 1976), a result that Kelley (1996) argues could be theoretically plausible if there were large economies of scale in the production of human capital within families. Still other studies have found no statistically significant effect of sibship size on children's educational outcomes (Mason, 1993; Shavit and Pierce, 1991). As emphasized in the review by King (1987), whatever the relationship between family size and schooling observed in the data, giving a causal interpretation to the association is difficult, because fertility and children's schooling are choices made jointly by parents.

In the case of Brazil, two studies have examined the role of family size on children's education and have showed an overall negative relationship. Psacharopoulos and Arriagada (1989) found small overall negative impact of number of siblings on school enrollment and attainment, but no effect on school dropout rates. Marteleto (2001) found negative effects of number of siblings on mean years of schooling and school enrollment for cohorts of children born pre- and postdemographic transition. We will include measures of the numbers of siblings in our analysis of schooling outcomes below, and will use the estimated impact of the numbers of siblings to predict how declining family size might be a factor driving the increasing school enrollment rates.

The Demographic Transition and Cohort Size

Brazil's demographic transition is fairly typical of those observed throughout the developing world in recent decades. Table 3-1 provides an overview of Brazil's demographic transition based on census data from 1940 to 2000. As shown in the first row of Table 3-1, the Total Fertility Rate (TFR) for all Brazil was around 6.20 from 1940 to 1960, declining rapidly to 4.35 in 1980, 2.70 in 1991, and 2.31 in 2000. Brazil's rapid fertility decline occurred during a period of far-reaching social change that included periods of both rapid economic growth and economic crisis (Lam and Duryea, 1999; Martine, 1996; Wood and Carvalho, 1988; Potter, Schmertmann, and Cavenaghi, 2002). The precise reasons for Brazil's fertility decline are still subject to debate and are outside the scope of this chapter. For the purpose of this chapter, it is important to note the pace of the decline and the substantial regional differences in the timing of the decline. As Table 3-1 shows, the poorer north and northeast regions have consistently had the highest regional fertility rates and began fertility decline somewhat later than the higher income south and southeast regions. In 1970, the southeast's TFR had fallen to 4.6, while the TFR for the northeast remained at 7.5. In 1991, the regional differences persisted as the southeast showed a TFR of 2.4 and the northeast had a TFR of 4.0. By 2000 the TFR for the southeast had declined to slightly below replacement level at 2.0, with a TFR for the northeast of 2.6. This regional unevenness of demographic indicators mirrors trends and patterns in socioeconomic development. The TFR in the more developed southeast and south regions

TABLE 3-1 Total Fertility Rates by Regions, Total Populations, and
Annual Growth Rates, Brazil, 1940-2000

	Year						
	1940	1950	1960	1970	1980	1991	2000
TOTAL FERTILITY RATES							
Brazil	6.16	6.21	6.28	5.76	4.35	2.70	2.31
North	7.17	7.97	8.56	8.15	6.45	4.00	3.05
Northeast	7.15	7.50	7.39	7.53	6.13	4.00	2.60
Southeast	5.69	5.45	6.34	4.56	3.45	2.40	2.00
South	5.65	5.70	5.89	5.42	3.63	2.30	2.25
Center-West	6.36	6.86	6.74	6.42	4.51	2.90	2.34
Total population (millions)	41.23	51.94	70.07	93.14	119.00	146.83	169.54
Annual intercensal growth rate		2.31	2.99	2.85	2.45	1.91	1.60

SOURCES: Instituto Brasileiro de Geografia e Estatística (1996, 2002); Wong (2000).

is similar to those of high-income countries, while the higher TFR in the
north and northeast regions reflects the lower income, education, and industrialization levels of those regions.

Table 3-1 also shows the population size and annual growth rates for the
country from 1940 to 2000. Brazil experienced rapid population growth
during the second half of the twentieth century, with the annual growth rate
peaking at 3 percent in the 1950-1960 period. This growth was driven primarily by falling mortality, especially infant and child mortality. In the 1970-
1980 period, the growth rate was still about 2.5 percent per year, but had
clearly begun to decline as falling fertility rates began to catch up with falling
mortality. The annual growth rate fell to 1.9 percent in the 1980-1991
intercensal period, and to 1.6 percent in the 1991-2000 period. As the second
to last row of Table 3-1 shows, Brazil more than quadrupled its total population over this period, from 41 million in 1940 to 169 million in 2000.

The dramatic changes in fertility, mortality, and population growth in
Brazil are associated with large changes in the size of birth cohorts. These are
shown graphically in Figure 3-1, which combines the overlapping single-year
age distributions from the censuses of 1970, 1980, 1991, and 2000. The
figure shows the size of the birth cohort as reported in two overlapping
censuses (when possible), without any adjustment for mortality, using the age
distributions from age 0 to age 20 in each census. For example, the two
numbers shown for the 1975 cohort are the number of 5-year-olds in the
1980 census and the number of 16-year-olds in the 1991 census.[1] Because

---

[1]The census is taken in October of each census year. For simplicity we assume that those
reported at age 0 were born in the same year as the census, those age 1 were born in the
previous calendar year, and so on.

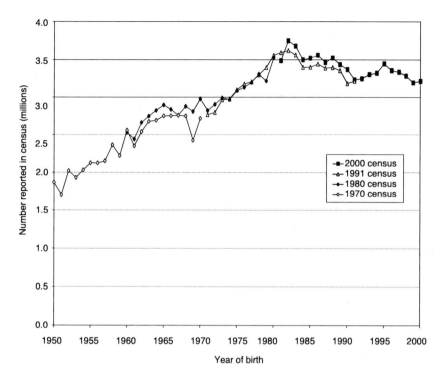

FIGURE 3-1 Size of birth cohorts in Brazilian censuses of 1970, 1980, 1991, and 2000.
SOURCE: Authors' tabulations of Brazilian censuses 1970, 1980, 1991, and 2000.

our interest is in estimating the size of the school-age population, rather than the actual number of births that originally occurred for each cohort, adjustments for mortality will be relatively unimportant to our calculations.

Figure 3-1 shows an increase in cohort size throughout the 1950s, 1960s, and 1970s, peaking around 1982-1983. The rapid increase in cohort size in the 1950s was the result of rapidly falling infant and child mortality. Figure 3-2 makes it clear that the pace of increase varied over time, with much slower growth in the latter half of the 1960s than in the 1970s. These changes in the pace of the increase in cohort size are the result of the complex interaction between falling fertility rates and increasing numbers of women of childbearing age, with the growth of the childbearing population driven by past declines in mortality. The decline in cohort size after the peak in the early 1980s is also uneven, with cohort size actually increasing again during the early 1990s. This is not due to an increase in fertility, which falls rapidly throughout the period, but to an increase in women of childbearing age as an "echo" of the rapid cohort growth of the

FIGURE 3-2 Number and growth rate of population ages 7-14, Brazil, 1965-2000 (number relative to 1965 = 100).
SOURCE: Authors' tabulations of Brazilian censuses 1970, 1980, 1991, and 2000.

1970s. The cohort size changes shown in Figure 3-1 imply that the child-dependency ratio was falling before the peak in cohort size occurred. The ratio of 0- to 14-year-olds to 15- to 59-year-olds fell from 0.8 to 0.7 between the 1970 and 1980 censuses, and continued falling to 0.6 in 1991 and 0.5 in 2000. As pointed out by Carvalho and Wong (1995), the demographic "window of opportunity" created by a rising proportion of the population of working age may have a positive impact on many aspects of Brazilian society.

The changes in cohort size shown in Figure 3-1 translate into large changes in the absolute size and growth of the school-age population. We use the cohort size numbers in Figure 3-1 to generate the number of children ages 7 to 14 and their growth rate for each calendar year. Figure 3-2 shows the absolute size of the population ages 7-14 in each year, using 1965 as a reference year, along with the annual percentage growth rate for that population. As Figure 3-2 shows, the 7-14 age group grew rapidly in the 1965-1975 period, reaching growth rates exceeding 3 percent per year. The age group grew at a much slower rate in the 1975-1980 period, falling to an annual growth rate of approximately 0.5 percent around 1978. The growth rate increased rapidly again in the 1980s, peaking at a growth rate of approximately 2.5 percent around 1988, followed by a rapid decline in the 1990s. The population ages 7 to 14 actually began to decline in absolute numbers around 1995. These rapid changes in the size of that population during the 1980s and 1990s are the result of a complex combination of the pace of fertility decline and the numbers of women entering childbearing age, reflecting past population dynamics. Figures 3-1 and 3-2 demonstrate that both the relative and the absolute size of the school-age population were declining by the mid-1990s.

Brazil's Household Survey Data

Our analysis is based on large household surveys collected by the Instituto Brasileiro de Geografia e Estatística (IBGE), the Brazilian statistical bureau. The PNAD is a nationally representative sample of 80,000 to 100,000 households surveyed collected annually to provide data on employment and earnings. The PNAD contains standard demographic and economic variables such as employment status, occupation, income, and schooling for all members of the household. In this chapter we use the PNAD from 1977 to 1999. There was no survey in 1980 or 1991 because of the censuses conducted in those years, and there was no survey in 1994. The PNAD is appropriate for this study because the repeated cross-sections and comparability of the questionnaires provide us with consistent measures of school enrollment, family composition, and parental characteristics for more than two decades, covering the period in which the school-age population peaked.

To analyze the extent to which changes in population size and family size affected children's school enrollment over the period 1977-1999, the sample will be limited to children ages 7 to 17. This focuses the attention on children at primary and secondary school levels. We will look at the impact of population size using the growth rate of the population ages 7 to 14, estimated using a combination of state population estimates based on census data and single-year age distributions for each state estimated using the PNAD. We take advantage of the rich microdata of the PNAD to generate measures of family size and other characteristics such as age and parents' schooling measured at the household level. To explore the effect of family characteristics such as mother's and father's education, we restrict the sample to children who are classified as children of the household head who have both parents present in the household.

Table 3-2 provides details on our sample selection. The table gives the number of children in the full sample, the number who are children of the household head, and the number who have both parents present at ages 10, 14, and 17. The table demonstrates the large sample sizes we are using. We begin with 187,000 10-year-olds in the pooled PNAD samples. Selecting only those who are children of the household head who have both parents present, this number falls to 149,000, or about 80 percent of the full sample. The size difference between the full and analytical samples increases with age, as more children leave the parental home at older ages. At age 14 and age 17 our analytical sample is 76 percent and 67 percent, respectively, of the full sample. The table also gives two measures that are useful for identifying how our selected sample differs from the sample of all children: mean schooling and the proportion currently enrolled in school. For example, the table shows that 89 percent of all 10-year-olds were enrolled in school, while 90 percent of the 10-year-old children of household head and living with both parents were enrolled. Mean schooling is slightly higher for our selected sample compared to the full sample, as we would expect, but the differences are quite small. The differences between the full and analytical samples increase with age but are never large.

TABLE 3-2 Comparison of Selected Sample with Sample of all Children, Brazil Pesquisa Nacional de Amostra de Domicílios, 1977-1999

	Full Sample	Children of Household Head	Children of Head with Both Parents Present
Age 10			
N	186,943	169,547	149,265
Weighted N	64,310,952	58,464,389	51,717,218
Percentage of full sample	100.0	90.9	80.4
Mean schooling	1.63	1.65	1.66
Enrollment rate (%)	88.9	89.2	89.5
Age 14			
N	181,200	160,860	135,570
Weighted N	62,121,671	55,678,826	47,186,042
Percentage of full sample	100.0	89.6	76.0
Mean schooling	4.03	4.09	4.12
Enrollment rate (%)	75.3	76.4	77.0
Age 17			
N	170,708	138,206	112,039
Weighted N	57,956,268	47,607,592	38,851,303
Percentage of full sample	100.0	82.1	67.0
Mean schooling	5.42	5.58	5.63
Enrollment rate (%)	50.7	54.5	55.5

SOURCES: PNADs 1977-1999.

Changing Family Characteristics

In addition to large changes in cohort size and age structure, the major shifts in the Brazilian demographic and socioeconomic patterns of recent decades have also affected the micro conditions in which children's schooling takes place by changing family size and levels of parents' education. Brazilian families have been changing in recent decades in ways that are similar to trends observed in other developing countries. Children are sharing family resources with fewer siblings as fertility declines. In addition, as a result of steady improvements in schooling, children from recent cohorts have better educated parents than their parents had.

Table 3-3 shows the mean number of siblings ages 0 to 6 and 7 to 17 in the household for children ages 7 to 17, estimated from the annual PNAD surveys. The average number of siblings ages 0 to 6 declined more than 50

TABLE 3-3 Number of Siblings in Household and Schooling of Parents, Brazilian Children Ages 7-17, 1977-1999 Pesquisa Nacional de Amostra de Domicílios

| Year | N | Number of Siblings in Household | | Mother's Schooling | Father's Schooling | Urban % |
		Ages 0-6	Ages 7-17			
1977	107,105	1.17	2.45	2.51	2.75	60.54
1978	110,447	1.15	2.40	2.53	2.77	61.19
1979	90,035	1.11	2.36	2.65	2.88	61.55
1981	97,705	1.05	2.23	2.78	2.98	64.95
1982	102,134	1.03	2.15	2.82	2.98	65.30
1983	102,097	1.00	2.10	2.94	3.12	65.97
1984	100,944	0.97	2.05	3.10	3.24	66.25
1985	101,010	0.94	1.98	3.28	3.38	67.25
1986	56,007	0.90	1.91	3.48	3.58	67.24
1987	58,316	0.87	1.88	3.59	3.67	67.38
1988	58,465	0.80	1.85	3.77	3.77	68.37
1989	59,171	0.77	1.82	3.96	3.96	68.78
1990	60,333	0.73	1.77	4.08	4.05	68.40
1992	58,964	0.64	1.66	4.31	4.30	73.83
1993	60,450	0.61	1.63	4.45	4.38	73.74
1995	61,420	0.55	1.53	4.73	4.59	74.96
1996	59,395	0.52	1.49	4.93	4.80	75.09
1997	60,398	0.52	1.42	5.02	4.84	74.96
1998	58,291	0.50	1.38	5.23	5.02	74.56
1999	57,693	0.49	1.34	5.12	5.07	74.24
TOTALS	1,520,380	0.80	1.85	3.82	3.85	68.98
1999 minus 1977		−0.68	−1.10	2.61	2.32	13.70
Percentage change		−58.10	−45.18	104.11	84.38	22.63

SOURCE: PNADs 1977-1999. Sample is children of household head with both parents present.

percent, from 1.2 to 0.5, from 1977 to 1999. The average number of siblings ages 7 to 17 declined 45 percent, from 2.5 to 1.3 over the same period. As shown by Marteleto (2001), the distribution of children across family sizes has changed considerably over the past three decades, with a large reduction in the number of families with more than four children.

Table 3-3 also shows that the level of parents' education has increased substantially throughout the period studied. The mean years of mother's education nearly doubled over the 22 years covered by our data, from 2.5 years in 1977 to 5.1 years in 1999. Similarly, father's years of schooling increased more than 80 percent throughout this period. This significant improvement in parents' education may have contributed to the substantial increase in children's school enrollment. It may also be that the magnitude of these improvements in educational outcomes is different for specific groups. Table 3-3 also shows the proportion of children in urban areas. In 1977 about 60 percent of children ages 7 to 17 lived in an urban area. By 1999 the urban proportion had increased to 74 percent. In the next section, we show how educational measures for Brazilian children changed during the period of rapid demographic and social changes of the 1970s, 1980s, and 1990s.

Children's Schooling in Brazil

Figure 3-3 shows the mean years of schooling for males and females ages 12, 14, and 16 during the past three decades in Brazil. For consistency with

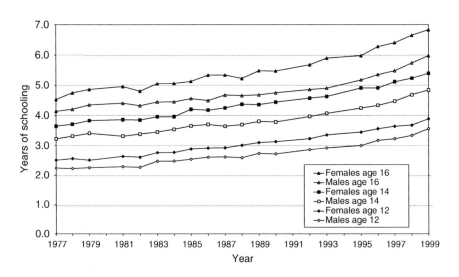

FIGURE 3-3 Mean years of schooling by age, males and females, Brazil, 1977-1999.
NOTE: Sample is children of household head with both parents present.
SOURCE: Authors' tabulations of PNADs 1977-1999.

our later regressions, these figures are based on our sample of children of household heads with both parents present. Although Brazil has lagged behind many developing countries in school performance, Figure 3-3 shows considerable improvements in school attainment for all ages. For example, 16-year-old males had an average of 4.1 years of schooling in 1977, rising to 6 years in 1999. An important feature of Figure 3-3 is that both males and females experienced a more rapid increase in schooling in the 1990s than in the 1980s. For example, from 1981 to 1990, the schooling of 14-year-old males increased by about half a year of schooling: 3.3 in 1981 compared to 3.8 in 1990. In the 1990s, the average schooling of 14-year-old males increased by one full year: from 3.8 in 1990 to 4.8 in 1999. The slower increase in schooling of the 1980s may be related to this period's severe economic conditions, which characterized the 1980s as the "lost" decade. Rapid growth of the school-age population also may have been a factor: we will explore that issue. Figure 3-3 also shows the female schooling advantage in Brazil, an advantage that can be seen already in the late 1970s. The female advantage widens throughout the 1990s for both 14-year-olds and 16-year-olds, reaching nearly one full grade at age 16 in 1999.

Figure 3-4 shows enrollment rates by age over time for the same age groups of males and females shown in Figure 3-3. The figure shows substantial increases in enrollment between 1977 and 1999, with the most rapid improvements occurring in the 1990s. Increases in enrollment rates

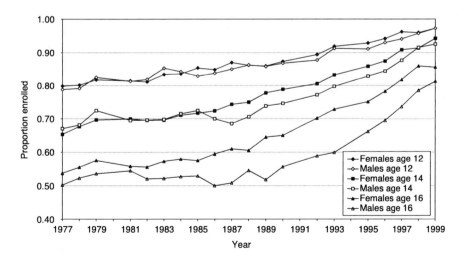

FIGURE 3-4 School enrollment rate by age, males and females, Brazil 1977-1999.
NOTE: Sample is children of household head with both parents present.
SOURCE: Authors' tabulations of PNADs 1977-1999.

are especially large for 16-year-olds. Enrollment rates of 16-year-old boys, for example, grew more than 30 percentage points, from 50 percent in 1977 to over 80 percent in 1999, with nearly all of the increase occurring in the 1990s. The overall pattern shown in Figures 3-3 and 3-4 is one of relatively flat schooling levels and enrollment rates in the 1980s followed by substantial improvements in the 1990s. This pattern of stagnation in educational measures (particularly school enrollment) of the 1980s coincides with periods of the highest absolute and relative sizes of the school-age population. It also coincides with the highest growth rates of the 7 to 14 age group. Conversely, the improvements in education of the 1990s coincide fairly closely with the decline in the growth rate of the school-age population shown in Figure 3-2.

Despite the overall increase in school enrollment and grade attainment shown in Figures 3-3 and 3-4, these numbers also document that schooling levels are still far from the ideal. Brazilian children who have been enrolled continuously in school starting at age 7, as mandated by law, and who have never repeated a grade, should have completed 7 years of education by age 14. The reality is far short of this. Mean schooling of 14-year-olds only reached 5 years in 1999, with significant percentages still more than 3 years behind the target grade attainment for their age. Looking at a birth cohort over time, the average number of grades completed per year of age after age 7 is as low as 0.5 or 0.6, well below the target of 1.0 and well below the percentage enrolled in school (Lam, 2001; Lam and Marteleto, 2000). These patterns are indicative of a high rate of grade repetition among Brazilian children, an important factor to keep in mind in our analysis. Grade repetition is common in Brazil as there is no automatic grade progression, although there have been discussions in implementing a system that automatically promotes children from one grade to the next. The large disparities between age and grade mean that children of widely varying ages are often enrolled in the same grade. An important implication is that it will not be uncommon for 15- or 16-year-olds to be in the same grades as 8- or 9-year-olds. This creates potential competition for school resources between age groups that would not be competing in an educational system such as in the United States, where there is a relatively narrow correspondence between age and grade.

Modeling School Enrollment

As a framework for estimating the impact of cohort size and family characteristics on school enrollment, we assume that the decision to enroll a child in school is based on some evaluation by the family and child of the relative costs and benefits of school enrollment. Although school enrollment is technically mandatory until age 14 in Brazil, we have seen that enrollment below age 14 has been far from universal. While some Brazilian children in rural areas may have no practical access to school at all, we assume that for the great majority there is some option of attending school, with both the costs and benefits of enrollment varying across families. The cost of school enrollment will depend on the distance to potential schools as well as direct costs such as school fees, uniforms, and supplies. We do not have data on any of these variables, and therefore will not be able to include them directly in the analysis below. They are important to keep in mind, however, in interpreting the results. Another important cost is the opportunity cost of school, which will include foregone earnings in the labor market as well as the implicit value of alternative uses of time such as child care and housework. Some of the family size variables we include in our analysis will be related to these issues of opportunity cost. The growth rate of the school-age population may affect the cost of schooling, because school crowding may require some students to travel farther to school or attend school at inconvenient times. Some students may be less encouraged by teachers to continue in school during periods of extreme school crowding, an effect that might be considered an increased cost of enrollment.

Although these cost effects of cohort growth are potentially significant, the most important effects of cohort growth are probably those that affect the benefits that parents and children perceive in attending school. Crowded schools that meet in multiple shifts with inadequate staffing and teaching materials are likely to be less attractive, potentially changing the cost-benefit calculation for some students. The impact of changes in relative costs and benefits will be most important for those closest to the margin of not enrolling. This may mean that the impact of the growth rate of the school-age population is greater for older students than for children just entering school age. Parents are likely to have a strong commitment to enroll their 7- and 8-year-old children in school. The benefits of enrollment in grade 1 will far exceed the costs for most parents, leaving them relatively insensitive to school conditions or other variables that may affect the cost-benefit calculation. Students at older ages, however, are more likely to be at the margin of dropping out of school, either temporarily or permanently, and therefore may be more likely to be affected by factors such as school crowding that lower the benefits of being enrolled. Older students are also more likely to be behind in school, which may make them more likely to be close to the margin of dropping out of school. As noted earlier, Brazil's high rates of grade repetition mean that older students are often in the same grade as children 4 or 5 years younger, making it easy for enrollment pressures at the early grades to spill over to youth as old as 16 or 17. Because these teenagers may be facing cost-benefit calculations for enrollment that are close to the margin, it is plausible that their enrollment will be especially sensitive to the growth rate of the school-age population.

Formalizing these arguments, we assume that we can represent the net value of school enrollment, as perceived by family of the ith child in state s in year t, as:

$$Y_{ist} = \alpha + \delta G_{st} + \gamma \mathbf{Z_{ist}} + u_s + v_t + \varepsilon_{ist} \tag{1}$$

where Y is a latent variable indicating the net payoff to school enrollment, G_{st} is the growth rate of the population ages 7 to 14, Z_{ist} is a vector of characteristics at the family level, including family size and parental schooling, u_s is a fixed effect for the state or region, v_t is a period-specific effect, and ε_{ist} is an idiosyncratic stochastic term that is assumed to be normally distributed and uncorrelated with all of the other right-hand-side variables. The child enrolls in school if $Y > 0$. Given the normality assumption, this implies a standard probit model for the probability that the enrollment indicator $E = 1$:

$$P(E_{ist} = 1) = P(Y_{ist} > 0) = \Phi[\alpha + \delta G_{st} + \gamma \mathbf{Z_{ist}} + u_s + v_t] \tag{2}$$

We use the growth rate of the population ages 7 to 14 as an indicator of the relative number of new school-age children entering the school system in a particular year. Assuming that school capacity is to some degree fixed in the short run, due to limits in both physical facilities and numbers of teachers, a larger number of new students entering the system in a year may be expected to crowd some children out of the system and lower enrollment rates. One might imagine 10 percent more children appearing at school at the start of a new school year. With a fixed capacity, some combination of behaviors by administrators, teachers, parents, and children will lead to lower enrollment than would have occurred the previous year.

Our school-age population growth rate variable must necessarily be measured at the aggregate level. In our regressions we include the growth rate for each state in each year. Because only a complete census could provide accurate estimates of the number of individuals at a given age in a given state in a given year, we do not have accurate data for the age distribution at the state level in every year. We have generated estimates by taking estimated population totals for each state in each year, taken from IBGE (1998, 2002) and combining these with the single-year age distribution estimated in the PNAD for that year. These estimates are likely to have considerable measurement error, a problem that may lead us to underestimate the impact of cohort size. We will discuss this problem further when we interpret our results.

To analyze whether the effect of school crowding is greater on poor families, we include an interaction of the growth rate of 7- to 14-year-olds with the schooling of the father. We also include interactions with the female dummy variable and with age. These two interactions allow us to test whether the impact of school crowding is greater on older youth and whether there is a differential impact on males and females.

We include other variables in our probit regression to pick up factors related to both demand and supply of schooling. We include mother's and father's schooling, entered in quadratic form. These variables, known from previous research to have a large impact on child school enrollment and attainment, pick up a wide variety of effects, including permanent income, household capacity to produce human capital, and inherited ability across generations, factors that will affect the demand for schooling. Parental education may also pick up school supply effects, because better educated parents may live in neighborhoods with better schooling opportunities. We include the number of siblings living in the household separately for ages 0 to 6 and 7 to 17. These variables may reflect competition for resources within the household and demands on the time of children for child care. Unlike younger children ages 0 to 6, older siblings may also contribute resources to the household. To control for regional differences we include dummies for the five major geographic regions, along with a dummy variable for urban.

To control for sectoral changes in enrollment that are driven by variables not accounted for in our regression, we include a dummy variable for each year (with 1978 omitted). Note that this highly flexible treatment of year effects means that we have swept away (and therefore cannot estimate) the effects of variables such as overall macroeconomic conditions that vary over time. We are effectively allocating any variance in school enrollment that is peculiar to a specific year (including any overall time trends) to the year dummies. This means that we are not using the information on the relationship between the overall changes in cohort growth and the overall changes in school enrollment. The identification of any cohort size effect comes from deviations in the rate of cohort growth in particular regions relative to the mean cohort growth for Brazil as a whole.

Regression Results

Table 3-4 provides results of probit regressions for several alternative specifications. All regressions use the sample of children ages 7 to 17 who are classified as the child of the household head and who have both parents present in the household.[2] As noted in Table 3-2, our sample includes

---

[2]More precisely, we require that both the head and spouse of head are present in the household with non-missing values for schooling. The children in the sample are identified as being the child of the head, but we do not have direct reports on whether they are the child of the spouse. The terms "mother" and "father" are used loosely, referring to the man and woman identified as the head and spouse of head.

TABLE 3-4 Probit Regressions for School Enrollment, Brazil PNADs, 1978-1999

Variable	Probit Regression Coefficients and Robust Standard Errors		
	Regression 1	Regression 2	Regression 3
Growth rate of population ages 7-14	−2.181 (0.071)[a]	−1.019 (0.095)[a]	−0.991 (0.095)[a]
Growth rate X female	0.247 (0.095)[a]	0.263 (0.107)[b]	0.281 (0.107)[a]
Growth rate X (age minus 14)	−0.195 (0.014)[a]	−0.174 (0.016)[a]	−0.181 (0.016)[a]
Growth rate X father's schooling		0.231 (0.018)[a]	0.221 (0.018)[a]
No. of siblings ages 0-6			−0.098 (0.006)[a]
No. of siblings ages 7-17			−0.019 (0.001)[a]
No. of siblings 0-6 X female			−0.011 (0.003)[a]
No. of siblings 0-6 X age			0.001 (0.000)
No. of siblings 0-6 X father's schooling			−0.004 (0.001)[a]
Father's schooling		0.098 (0.001)[a]	0.099 (0.001)[a]
Mother's schooling		0.138 (0.001)[a]	0.134 (0.001)[a]
Father's schooling squared		−0.003 (0.000)[a]	−0.003 (0.000)[a]
Mother's schooling squared		−0.005 (0.000)[a]	−0.005 (0.000)[a]
Female	0.107 (0.003)[a]	0.112 (0.003)[a]	0.123 (0.004)[a]
Age 8	0.458 (0.006)[a]	0.574 (0.007)[a]	0.579 (0.007)[a]
Age 9	0.646 (0.006)[a]	0.807 (0.007)[a]	0.803 (0.007)[a]
Age 10	0.747 (0.007)[a]	0.941 (0.007)[a]	0.929 (0.008)[a]
Age 11	0.736 (0.007)[a]	0.929 (0.007)[a]	0.908 (0.008)[a]
Age 12	0.629 (0.006)[a]	0.815 (0.007)[a]	0.783 (0.008)[a]
Age 13	0.441 (0.006)[a]	0.599 (0.007)[a]	0.556 (0.008)[a]
Age 14	0.230 (0.006)[a]	0.348 (0.007)[a]	0.294 (0.008)[a]
Age 15	0.005 (0.006)	0.088 (0.007)[a]	0.025 (0.008)[a]
Age 16	−0.191 (0.006)[a]	−0.144 (0.007)[a]	−0.215 (0.008)[a]
Age 17	−0.374 (0.006)[a]	−0.370 (0.007)[a]	−0.450 (0.008)[a]
Year 1979		0.122 (0.007)[a]	0.120 (0.007)[a]
Year 1981		0.086 (0.007)[a]	0.077 (0.007)[a]
Year 1982		0.139 (0.007)[a]	0.126 (0.007)[a]

Year 1983		0.183 (0.007)[a]	0.167 (0.007)[a]
Year 1984		0.194 (0.007)[a]	0.173 (0.007)[a]
Year 1985		0.203 (0.007)[a]	0.180 (0.007)[a]
Year 1986		0.206 (0.009)[a]	0.178 (0.009)[a]
Year 1987		0.223 (0.009)[a]	0.191 (0.009)[a]
Year 1988		0.254 (0.009)[a]	0.215 (0.009)[a]
Year 1989		0.238 (0.009)[a]	0.195 (0.009)[a]
Year 1990		0.249 (0.009)[a]	0.202 (0.009)[a]
Year 1992		0.122 (0.009)[a]	0.066 (0.009)[a]
Year 1993		0.174 (0.009)[a]	0.115 (0.009)[a]
Year 1995		0.269 (0.009)[a]	0.202 (0.009)[a]
Year 1996		0.321 (0.009)[a]	0.251 (0.009)[a]
Year 1997		0.448 (0.009)[a]	0.377 (0.010)[a]
Year 1998		0.572 (0.010)[a]	0.501 (0.010)[a]
Year 1999		0.676 (0.011)[a]	0.602 (0.011)[a]
Urban		0.406 (0.003)[a]	0.378 (0.003)[a]
North		0.024 (0.007)[a]	0.036 (0.007)[a]
Southeast		0.027 (0.004)[a]	-0.010 (0.004)[b]
South		-0.095 (0.005)[a]	-0.139 (0.005)[a]
Central-West		0.042 (0.005)[a]	0.008 (0.005)
Constant	0.492 (0.004)[a]	-0.665 (0.007)[a]	-0.419 (0.009)[a]
Sample size	1,413,275	1,413,275	1,413,275
Pseudo R-squared	0.150	0.215	0.220
Log likelihood	-617810	-570827	-567072

[a]Significance level = 0.01.
[b]Significance level = 0.05.
NOTES: Robust standard errors in parentheses. Omitted categories: Year 1978, Northeast region, age 7. Sample is children of household head ages 7 to 17 with both parents present.

about 80 percent of 10-year-olds and about 67 percent of 17-year-olds, with most other children classified as "other relative" of the head (including, e.g., stepchildren of the head who are biological children of the mother). We make this sample restriction in order to simplify interpretation of the family variables included in the regression, such as parental schooling and number of siblings. When we use the full sample of age-eligible children, our estimated effects of cohort size growth are quite similar to those reported below. As shown in Table 3-4, we have very large samples in our pooled cross-sections, with more than 1.4 million observations used in each regression.[3]

Regression 1 looks only at the effect of the school-age population growth rate on enrollment, leaving out family-level variables such as number of siblings and parental schooling. Dummy variables are included for single-year age groups and female. The measure of cohort growth is $\log[P_t/P_{t-1}]$, where P_t is the number of children ages 7 to 14 in year t (in the case of a 2-year interval between surveys, the average growth rate over 2 years is used). We also include interactions of the cohort growth rate with both female and age. To simplify interpretation, the age variable in the interaction is defined as age minus 14, meaning that the main effect for cohort growth is measured for 14-year-olds. Regression 1 shows a statistically significant negative effect of the school-age population growth rate on the school enrollment rate, consistent with our expectations. The interaction with the female dummy is positive, indicating that the enrollment rate of girls is less negatively affected by the growth of the school-age population. As discussed further below, we interpret this as evidence that boys are closer to the margin of dropping out of school, perhaps because of a higher tradeoff between school and work. The negative interaction with age indicates that the impact of cohort growth becomes more negative at higher ages. The fact that the effects of cohort growth on enrollment increase with age suggests that a growing school-age population tends to push students out of school at the top of the school-age distribution rather than deterring enrollment by new school entrants. This is also consistent with a view that the children who are closest to the margin of leaving school are the ones affected by enrollment pressures, with older boys being the group most affected.

---

[3]Because the PNAD data are used to construct the estimates of age-specific population totals for each state, and because we use the change in population as an independent variable, we lose the 1977 data in the regressions. We are thus pooling the PNAD data for the years 1978-1979, 1981-1990, 1992-1993, and 1995-1999. When the PNAD surveys are 2 years apart, the growth rate variable is 0.5 times the 2-year growth rate.

Although Regression 1 shows a statistically significant negative effect of the 7-14 growth rate on enrollment, the magnitude of the effect is relatively modest. For a 14-year-old boy, the estimated effect of changing from a zero growth rate to a 3 percent annual growth rate would be a decline in the predicted probability of enrollment from 76.5 percent to 74.4 percent. It is important to recall, however, that this coefficient may be significantly biased downward in absolute value due to measurement error in the cohort size growth rate.

The estimated effect of cohort growth in Regression 1 may be biased due to the correlation of cohort growth with a number of omitted variables. Cohort growth may be correlated with a wide variety of variables, changing across both time and space, that affect school enrollment. One of the most important time-varying covariates is parental schooling, a variable we are also interested in directly. Regression 2 in Table 3-4 adds a number of additional variables to the regression. We include the schooling of the mother and father, the square of these variables, and an interaction between father's schooling and the cohort growth variable. To control for aggregate effects across time and space, we include dummy variables for every year, an urban dummy, and regional dummies for Brazil's five major geographic regions.[4]

The results in Regression 2 indicate that these additional variables reduce the estimated effect of the growth rate of the 7-14 population. The effect continues to be statistically significant and negative, however. We estimate a statistically significant positive interaction with father's education. We interpret this as supporting our hypothesis that children from better-off households are less affected by the growth rate of the school-age population. The interaction with female continues to be positive, and the interaction with age continues to be negative in Regression 2. All of these effects are consistent with our theoretical framework, with older boys from poorer households being the group closest to the margin of dropping out of school.

As in previous research, we estimate large effects of both mother's and father's schooling on school enrollment, with a slightly larger effect of mother's schooling. Effects are largest at low levels of schooling. For a 14-year-old boy in the urban northeast in 1999, an increase in each parent's schooling from 2 to 3 years increases the probability of enrollment from 88.6 percent to 91.9 percent.

Regression 3 adds variables for family size. We use a variable for the number of siblings ages 0 to 6 and the number ages 7 to 17. We also include

---

[4]Results for all variables are very similar if dummy variables are included for every state. The regional dummies are shown here for ease of interpretation.

interactions between the number of siblings ages 0 to 6 and three variables: the female dummy, age, and father's schooling. The results indicate that there is a negative effect of the number of siblings ages 0-6 on enrollment. For an urban 14-year-old girl in the northeast in 1999, going from one to two siblings ages 0 to 6 would lower her probability of school enrollment from 95.0 percent to 93.7 percent. There is also a negative, but much smaller, effect of siblings in the 7-17 age group. The interactions with the number of siblings ages 0 to 6 indicate that preschool siblings have a more negative effect on the enrollment of girls than boys. This result suggests that there is a larger child care role for girls than for boys, as suggested in previous research (Marteleto, 2001). The effect is also slightly more negative when the father is better educated. This result is somewhat counterintuitive, but the magnitude of the interaction is very small. There is no significant interaction with age.

The coefficient on cohort growth changes little between Regression 2 and Regression 3, indicating that controlling for family size has little impact on the estimated effect of cohort growth. Although we estimate a statistically significant negative effect of cohort growth on school enrollment, the magnitude of the effect is relatively small. For a 16-year-old boy in the urban northeast in 1999 with no parental schooling and one sibling in each age group, the impact of an increase in cohort growth from 0 to 3 percent per year would be a decline in the probability of school enrollment from 59.4 percent to 57.8 percent.

The year dummies in Regression 2 and Regression 3 indicate large increases in enrollment over time, even after controlling for parental schooling, cohort growth, and family size. We also estimate significant regional differences in enrollment, some of which may appear surprising. For the full set of independent variables in Regression 3, we estimate that the south and southeast actually have lower enrollment than the northeast, controlling for parental schooling and family size. This is similar to a result observed in Barros and Lam (1996), who found that enrollment rates for 14-year-olds in the northeast and southeast were quite similar, even though children in the poorer northeast region had completed almost two fewer grades of school. Children in the south and southeast are so much farther ahead in school by ages 16 and 17 that their enrollment rates begin to drop below those of other regions, especially when variables such as parental schooling are held constant.

All of the regressions in Table 3-4 indicate a statistically significant enrollment advantage for females, a result that is consistent with previous research on schooling in Brazil. For an urban 14-year-old in 1999 with both parents' schooling at 4 years, the probability of enrollment for a female is about 2 percentage points higher than for a male. This may be another indication that males are more affected than females by a tradeoff between work and school enrollment in Brazil.

Counterfactual Simulations of Enrollment Rates

To analyze the extent to which the variables in our regressions can explain the trends in school enrollment in Brazil during the 1980s and 1990s, it is useful to simulate enrollment under various counterfactual assumptions. Figure 3-5 takes the coefficients from Regression 3 in Table 3-4 and combines them with the actual values for the independent variables for 1977 to 1999. The coefficients are used to predict the probability of school enrollment for a 16-year-old urban male for every year from 1977 to 1999. Calibrating the enrollment rate to the actual 1977 level for 16-year-old males in urban Brazil, the enrollment rate in each subsequent year is simulated using various counterfactual assumptions.

Series 1 in Figure 3-5 simply plots the baseline 1977 enrollment rate of 64 percent as a benchmark for comparison. Series 2 plots the actual school enrollment of 16-year-old boys who are children of the household head for urban Brazil for each year, smoothed as 3-year moving averages.[5] As already shown above, the enrollment rate shows little improvement during the 1980s, actually falling to 62 percent around 1986. The actual enrollment rate turns sharply upward around 1989, and rises steadily to nearly 85 percent by 1999.

Series 3 in Figure 3-5 simulates the school enrollment rate using the coefficients from Regression 3 and the actual changes in the school-age population growth rate, parental schooling, and family size observed over the period (estimated using the sample of 16-year-old urban males). We omit the regional variables from the simulation, implicitly holding the regional distribution constant. We also omit the year dummies because our goal is to see the extent to which the demographic and family changes can explain the observed changes in enrollment.

Series 3, which can be thought of as a baseline for our counterfactual simulations, indicates that the changes in cohort growth, family size, and parental schooling from 1977 to 1999, combined with the coefficients from Regression 3, can explain a significant fraction of the increase in school enrollment over this period, predicting an increase from 64 percent in 1977 to 77 percent in 1999. This is 63 percent of the actual change, suggesting that our variables can explain a high fraction of the observed increase in enrollment. The remaining 37 percent of the increase is presumably due to

---

[5]Although our samples are large, there is still considerable sampling variability when we limit the sample to urban boys age 16. Three-year moving averages are used in Figure 3-5 to reduce the volatility in the series.

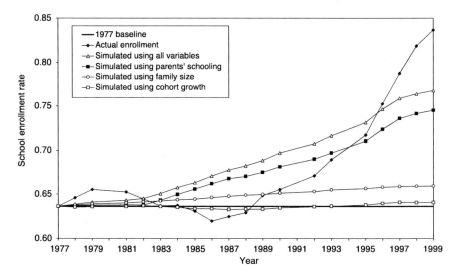

FIGURE 3-5 Actual and simulated school enrollment rates for 16-year-old males, urban Brazil, 1977-1999 (based on Regression 3 in Table 3-4).
SOURCE: Authors' tabulations of PNADs 1977-1999.

other variables for which we have not controlled, such as educational expenditures, school policies, and macroeconomic conditions. The most notable difference between our predicted series and the actual series is that our variables predict relatively steady improvement across both decades, in contrast to the actual pattern of relatively constant enrollment rates in the 1980s and sharper increases in the 1990s. The difficult economic situation of the 1980s, which are swept away in our estimation by the single-year dummies, is one possible reason why enrollment grew more slowly in the 1980s than changes in parental schooling, family size, and cohort growth would have predicted.

Series 4 shows the effect of holding all other variables constant while allowing the parental schooling variables to vary. This simulation indicates that increasing parental schooling can explain a high fraction of the improvements in children's school enrollment. Rising parental schooling alone would have predicted a school enrollment rate for urban boys of about 77 percent in 1999, 52 percent of the actual observed increase. As with Series 3, we see that the changes in parental schooling alone would have caused relatively steady increases in school enrollment over the 1980s and 1990s, in contrast to the declining enrollment observed in the 1980s.

Series 5 shows the effect of holding all other variables constant while allowing the family size variables (numbers of siblings ages 0 to 6 and 7 to

17) to vary. This series rises steadily throughout the 1980s and 1990s, indicating that falling family size contributed to rising school enrollment. The predicted increases are considerably smaller than the effects of parental schooling, however. Falling numbers of siblings alone would have only increased school enrollment to 66 percent, an increase that is 11 percent of the actual observed increase.

Series 6 simulates the effect of changes in the growth rate of the population ages 7 to 14. An important feature of this series is that it is the only simulation that predicts a decline in school enrollment during the 1980s. This is the result of the increase in the growth rate of the population ages 7 to 14 that occurs in the 1980s. Predicted enrollment in Series 6 turns upward in the late 1980s when the cohort growth rate peaks, coinciding closely with the upturn in enrollment observed in the actual data in Series 2. The magnitudes of the changes in enrollment predicted by changes in the school-age population growth rate are quite small, however. Although we are able to predict rising enrollment rates in the 1990s due to the falling rates of cohort growth, the predicted increases in enrollment from this source are only 1 or 2 percentage points. Series 6 shows that we predict a slight fall in enrollment rates after 1997. This is because the growth rate of the school-age population reaches a minimum in 1997, remaining negative but moving toward zero in subsequent years, as shown in Figure 3-2.

Although the role of cohort growth appears relatively modest in these counterfactual simulations, we reiterate the point that there may be substantial measurement error in the cohort growth variables, potentially creating substantial downward bias in the estimated effect. The cohort size variables are the only variables estimated at the state level, and our estimates are necessarily based on indirect methods that may have considerable error as a measure of the true cohort size variables that affect the enrollment of particular children. In contrast, our family-level effects are estimated using cross-section variation across many thousands of household records each year. It is also important to remember that by including a full set of year dummies, we have not used any time-series association between cohort growth and school enrollment to estimate the effect of cohort growth. For example, our estimate is not influenced by the fact that the sharp rise in school enrollment rates around 1990 coincides with sharp declines in the growth rate of the school-age population. If we thought the true coefficient on cohort growth was several times larger than our estimated value, the simulations in Figure 3-5 would begin to much more closely track the actual values. It is especially significant that a large effect of cohort growth leads to predicted enrollment that is much flatter in the 1980s, corresponding closely to the actual pattern. Because both family size and parental schooling grow quite steadily over the 1980s and 1990s, cohort growth is the only variable in our regression with the potential to predict the poor performance of the 1980s combined with large improvements in enrollment in the 1990s. We believe future research using more precise measures of cohort growth may produce results that provide stronger evidence that the rapid growth of the school-age population in the 1980s played a role in Brazil's poor educational performance in that period.

On the other hand, the modest impact we estimate for the effect of cohort growth on enrollment simply may be new evidence in support of the finding in previous literature that the size of the school-age population has little effect on school enrollment rates (Kelley, 1996; Schultz, 1987). Our effects of family size, while they show a statistically significant negative association between numbers of siblings and school enrollment, are also relatively modest in size. This is also consistent with the surveys by Lloyd (1994) and Kelley (1996), who conclude that previous literature does not point to large negative effects of family size on schooling. The biggest effects we estimate are those for parental schooling. Our results indicate that increased schooling of both mothers and fathers plays the largest role by far in explaining the rise in school enrollments in Brazil.

CONCLUSIONS

Brazil's demographic transition, like that of many other developing countries, produced large changes in cohort size and family size during recent decades. In considering the impact of these changes on schooling outcomes, one of the important features of the demographic transition is that family size and cohort size move in opposite directions during much of the transition. Declining fertility rates compete with population momentum to determine the size of birth cohorts, with the increasing numbers of childbearing-age women outpacing the declining fertility rates for many years of the transition. We show that the size of birth cohorts continued growing in Brazil until around 1982, even though fertility rates and family size had been falling since the 1960s. The school-age population continued growing until the early 1990s, with the growth rate of the school-age population dropping sharply in the 1990s. Cohorts born after 1982 are the first cohorts in Brazil to experience both falling cohort size and falling family size relative to previous cohorts, a fact that may have important implications for school outcomes.

The peak of Brazil's school-age population coincides with the beginning of a period of rapid improvement in school enrollment and school attainment in Brazil, beginning around 1990. Although many factors may have affected these improvements in schooling, this chapter has focused on the role of cohort size and family size. Using Brazil's large household surveys to estimate regressions that control for the growth rate of the 7-14 age population, the number of coresident siblings, and parental schooling, we analyze the impact of these variables on school enrollment from 1977 to 1999. Our results indicate that school enrollment is affected negatively by the growth rate of the population ages 7 to 14, with the most negative effects on older males from poorer households. We interpret this result as evidence that school crowding has the biggest impact on students who are closest to the margin of dropping out of school, with older male students from poor households being most sensitive due to the tradeoff between work and school. Our counterfactual predictions indicate that enrollment rates would have improved faster in the 1980s if cohort growth rates had not increased, and that enrollment rates were positively affected by the declining growth rates of the 1990s.

We also estimate significant effects of family size on enrollment, with the number of siblings ages 0 to 6 and 7 to 17 both having a negative effect on enrollment. The effect of siblings ages 0 to 6 is much greater than the effect of siblings ages 7 to 17, and is slightly more negative on girls than boys. Our simulated counterfactuals suggest that declining family size was one of the factors contributing to the rising school enrollment rates of the 1990s. By far the most important explanatory factor in our analysis is parental schooling, with large positive effects of both mother's and father's schooling on children's school enrollment. Our simulated counterfactuals suggest that increases in parental schooling alone can explain a substantial fraction of the increase in school enrollment between 1977 and 1999. Taken in combination, our results imply that changes in the growth rate of the school-age population, number of siblings, and parental education can explain more than 60 percent of the observed increases in school enrollment between 1977 and 1999.

REFERENCES

Anh, T., Knodel, J., Lam, D., and Friedman, J. (1998). Family size and children's education in Vietnam. *Demography, 35,* 57-70.

Barros, R., and Lam, D. (1996). Income and education inequality and children's schooling attainment in Brazil. In N. Birdsall and R. Sabot (Eds.), *Opportunity foregone: Education in Brazil* (pp. 337-366). Washington, DC: Inter-American Development Bank.

Birdsall, N., and Sabot, R. (1996). *Opportunity foregone: Education in Brazil.* Washington, DC: Inter-American Development Bank.

Carvalho, J.A., and Wong, L. (1995). *A window of opportunity: Some demographic and socioeconomic implications of the rapid fertility decline in Brazil.* (Discussion Paper No. 91.) Pampulha, Brazil: CEDEPLAR, Universidade Federal de Minas Gerais.

Castro, M.H.G. (1999). *As desigualdades regionais no sistema educacional Brasileiro.* Paper presented at the Instituto de Pesquisa Economica Aplicada IPEA seminary, May, Rio de Janeiro, Brazil.

Chernichovsky, D. (1985). Socioeconomic and demographic aspects of school enrollment and attendance in rural Botswana. *Economic Development and Cultural Change, 33*, 319-332.

Hossain, M. (1988). *Credit for alleviation of rural poverty: The Grameen Bank in Bangladesh* (IFPRI Research Report No. 65.) Washington, DC: International Food Policy Research Institute.

Instituto Brasileiro de Geografia e Estatística. (1980). *Anuário estatístico do Brasil.* Rio de Janeiro, Brazil: Instituto Brasileiro de Geografia e Estatística.

Instituto Brasileiro de Geografia e Estatística. (1996). *Anuário estatístico do Brasil.* Rio de Janeiro, Brazil: Instituto Brasileiro de Geografia e Estatística.

Instituto Brasileiro de Geografia e Estatística. (1998). *Anuário estatístico do Brasil.* Rio de Janeiro, Brazil: Instituto Brasileiro de Geografia e Estatística.

Instituto Brasileiro de Geografia e Estatística. (2002). *Anuário estatístico do Brasil.* Rio de Janeiro, Brazil: Instituto Brasileiro de Geografia e Estatística.

Jones, G. (1971). *Effects of population growth on the attainment of educational goals in developing countries.* In National Academy of Sciences, *Rapid population growth* (pp. 315-367). Baltimore, MD: Johns Hopkins University Press.

Kelley, A.C. (1996). The consequences of rapid population growth on human resource development: The case of education. In D.A. Ahlburg, A.C. Kelley, and K. Oppenheim Mason (Eds.), *The impact of population growth on well-being in developing countries* (pp. 67-137). Berlin, Germany: Springer.

Kelley, A.C. (2001). The population debate in historical perspective: Revisionism revised. In N. Birdsall, A.C. Kelley, and S.W. Sinding (Eds.), *Population matters: Demographic change, economic growth, and poverty in the developing world* (pp. 24-54). Oxford, England: Oxford University Press.

King, E.M. (1987). The effect of family size on family welfare. In D.G. Johnson and R.D. Lee (Eds.), *Population growth and economic development: Issues and evidence* (pp. 373-411). Madison: University of Wisconsin Press.

King, E.M., Peterson, J.R., Moeriningsih Adioetomo, S., Domingo, L.J., and Syed, S.H. (1986). *Changes in the status of women across generations in Asia.* Santa Monica, CA: RAND.

Knodel, J. (1992). *Fertility decline and children's education in Thailand: Some macro and micro effects.* (Policy Research Division Working Paper No. 40.) New York: Population Council.

Knodel, J., and Wongsith, M. (1991). Family size and children's education in Thailand: Evidence from a national sample. *Demography, 28*, 119-131.

Lam, D. (2001). *Generating extreme inequality: Schooling, earnings, and intergenerational transmission of human capital in South Africa and Brazil.* Paper presented at the annual meeting of the Population Association of America, March, Washington, DC.

Lam, D., and Duryea, S. (1999). Effects of schooling on fertility, labor supply, and investments in children, with evidence from Brazil. *Journal of Human Resources, 341*, 160-192.

Lam, D., and Marteleto, L. (2000). *Grade repetition, school enrollment, and economic shocks in Brazil.* Paper presented at the 2000 meeting of the Population Association of America, March, Los Angeles, CA.

Lam, D., and Schoeni, R. (1993). Effects of family background on earnings and returns to schooling: Evidence from Brazil. *Journal of Political Economy, 101*, 710-740.

Lloyd, C.B. (1994). Investing in the next generation: The implications of high fertility at the level of the family. In R. Cassen (Ed.), *Population and development: Old debates, new conclusions* (pp. 181-202). Washington, DC: Overseas Development Council.

Marteleto, L. (2001). *A cohort analysis of children's schooling in Brazil: Do number and composition of siblings matter?* Paper presented at the 2001 annual meeting of the Population Association of America, March, Washington, DC.

Martine, G. (1996). Brazil's fertility decline, 1965-95: A fresh look at key factors. *Population and Development Review, 22,* 47-75.

Mason, A. (1993). Demographic change, household resources, and schooling decisions. In G. Johnson and R.D. Lee (Eds.), *Human resources in developing countries along the Asia-Pacific rim* (pp. 259-280). Singapore, Thailand: Oxford University Press.

Mueller, E. (1984). The value and allocation of time in rural Botswana. *Journal of Development Economics, 15,* 329-360.

Parish, W., and Willis, R. (1993). Daughters, education, and family budgets: Taiwan experience. *Journal of Human Resources, 28,* 863-898.

Patrinos, H., and Psacharopoulos, G. (1997). Family size, schooling, and child labor in Peru: An empirical analysis. *Journal of Population Economics, 10,* 387-405.

Potter, J., Schmertmann, C., and Cavenaghi, S. (2002). Fertility and development: Evidence from Brazil. *Demography, 39*(4), 739-761.

Psacharopoulos, G., and Arriagada, A.M. (1989). The determinants of early age human capital formation: Evidence from Brazil. *Economic Development and Cultural Change, 37,* 683-708.

Rigotti, I. (2001). *A transição da escolaridade no Brasil e as desigualdades regionais.* Paper presented at the International Union for the Scientific Study of Population conference, August, Salvador, Brazil.

Schultz, T.P. (1987). School expenditures and enrollments, 1960-80: The effects of income, prices, and population growth. In D.G. Johnson and R.L. Madison (Eds.), *Population growth and economic development: Issues and evidence* (pp. 413-476). Madison: University of Wisconsin Press.

Shavit, Y., and Pierce, J.L. (1991). Sibship size and educational attainment in nuclear and extended families: Arabs and Jews in Israel. *American Sociological Review, 56,* 321-330.

Wong, L. (2000). A projeção da fecundidade: Um exercício aplicado ao Brasil para o período 1991-2000. In *Annals of the XII Meeting of the Brazilian Association of Population Studies.* Caxambu, Brazil: Associação Brasileira de Estudos Populacionais.

Wood, C., and Carvalho, J.A.M. (1988). *The demography of inequality in Brazil.* Cambridge, England: Cambridge University Press.

World Bank. (1984). *World development: Report on population change and economic development.* New York: Oxford University Press.

Zajonc, R.B. (1976). Family configuration and intelligence. *Science, 192,* 227-236.

4

Progress Toward Education for All: Trends and Current Challenges for sub-Saharan Africa

Paul C. Hewett and Cynthia B. Lloyd

At the turn of the twenty-first century, significant challenges remain for sub-Saharan African countries attempting to provide universal schooling for their children and youth. We estimate for the region that 20.8 million or 25 percent of young adolescents ages 10 to 14 have never enrolled in school (11.5 million girls and 9.3 million boys). Fully 28.4 million (15.1 million girls and 13.3 million boys) have not completed four grades of schooling. Furthermore, 37.2 million or 45 percent will never complete primary school. This latter number is nearly twice the *entire* population of children ages 10 to 14 in the United States, virtually all of whom will complete a primary education.[1] Indeed, the level of educational participation and attainment in sub-Saharan Africa falls significantly below all other regions in the developing world (Chapter 3). Furthermore, in many countries, rates of growth in primary completion have flattened out or even declined since the mid- to late 1980s.

---

[1] The estimates for sub-Saharan Africa are derived from nationally representative Demographic and Health Surveys (DHS) from 24 countries, collectively representing 81 percent of the total sub-Saharan youth population. The estimates are conservative because they are based on the assumption that the 19 percent of the sub-Saharan African population not represented by our data has the same levels of schooling participation and attainment as the 81 percent of the sub-Saharan population that is represented. Given that much of the missing population lives in countries that are in the midst of armed conflict and civil disruption, it is likely that their schooling performance will be lower than the performance in our sample population. The population estimate for the United States is 20.9 million in July 2001 (Table US-EST2001-ASRO-01, resident population estimates of the United States by age and sex, Population Division, U.S. Census Bureau).

Despite the enormous challenges of overcoming such widespread lack of educational opportunities, the international community remains committed to the goals of providing universal access to, and assuring completion of, a basic level of schooling of good quality. Originally set forth in the "World Declaration on Education for All," signed by more than 150 countries and international organizations in Jomtien, Thailand, in 1990, a target date for achieving universal access to primary schooling was set for 2000. Although this target date was ultimately not met, the international community reaffirmed the Education for All (EFA) framework at the World Education Forum in Dakar, Senegal, in 2000. Specifying six EFA goals, the Dakar conference set a new target date of 2015 for "all children, particularly girls, children in difficult circumstances, and those belonging to ethnic minorities, to have access to and complete free and compulsory primary education of good quality" (Dakar Framework for Action, 2000). Currently, however, only 13 of the 24 sub-Saharan African countries evaluated in this chapter have constitutional guarantees of compulsory schooling and, of these, only 10 guarantee free schooling. The key features of educational systems for 24 sub-Saharan African countries are presented in Table 4-1.

Specific targets for education are also embedded within the Millennium Declaration adopted by the United Nations General Assembly in 2001. The Millennium Declaration set forth eight Millennium Development Goals (MDG) relating to poverty, health, the environment, economic development, and education. The two targets directly related to education state: "by the year 2015, children everywhere, boys and girls alike, will be able to complete a full course of primary schooling and that by 2005 gender disparities in primary and secondary education will be eliminated" (United Nations General Assembly, 2001). The EFA and MDG efforts reflect the fact that investments in basic schooling have received a heightened level of attention from donors, governments, and the media because they are seen as a means of alleviating poverty and jump starting development in many parts of the developing world.

The purposes of the chapter are three-fold: (1) to highlight the value of consistent and comparable population-based data on educational participation and attainment levels for program planning and target setting, (2) to deepen our knowledge of trends in educational participation and achievement among youth in sub-Saharan Africa, and (3) to identify current priorities based on a more in-depth exploration of schooling differentials by gender and household wealth. In the first part of the chapter we review two often-used indicators for monitoring educational progress, the net primary enrollment ratio (NPER) and the survival rate to grade five, and compare them with similar measures from the nationally representative household data generated from the Demographic and Health Surveys (DHS). In the

TABLE 4-1 Key Features of Educational Systems in sub-Saharan Africa, 2000

	Constitutional Guarantee		Age of Entry	Years of Primary
	Compulsory	Free		
Benin			6	6
Burkina Faso			7	6
Cameroon			6	6
Central African Republic			6	6
Chad			6	6
Comoros			6	6
Côte d'Ivoire			6	6
Ethiopia			7	6
Ghana			6	6
Guinea			7	6
Kenya			6	7
Madagascar			6	5
Malawi			6	6
Mali			7	6
Mozambique			6	5
Niger			7	6
Nigeria			6	6
Rwanda			7	6
South Africa			7	7
Tanzania			7	7
Togo	a	a	6	6
Uganda	a		6	7
Zambia			7	7
Zimbabwe	a	a	6	7

aTo be progressively introduced.
SOURCES: UNESCO (2002, 2003) and Tomasevski (2001).

second part of the chapter, we use DHS education data to explore longer term trends in schooling performance. In the final part of the chapter, we evaluate what is likely the biggest challenge for the next 10 years in achieving education for all in sub-Saharan Africa.

MONITORING PROGRESS IN SCHOOLING

International efforts to improve educational participation and attainment have put a premium on the development of indicators to monitor progress and to assess whether countries will meet the targets set by the EFA framework and the MDG. Two principal indicators that have been used by UNESCO and UNICEF to monitor progress toward universal education have been the NPER and the survival rate to grade 5 (UNESCO,

2002, 2003; UNICEF, 2003c).[2] The logic behind the use of these measures is that the attainment of both would imply that the completion of primary school, which typically runs 1 to 3 years beyond grade 4, would shortly follow. In addition, such indicators represent the basic levels of schooling needed for the long-term acquisition of basic literacy and numeracy skills.

The NPER captures, at a moment in time, the percentage of children of primary school age who are currently enrolled in primary school. The NPER is derived from two different statistical sources. The numerator is obtained from beginning of the year registrations as officially reported by schools throughout the country to national ministries of education. These enrollment numbers are then divided by United Nations estimates of the population for the year and ages in question to derive the NPER. An NPER of 100 percent would indicate that all children within the eligible ages of primary school are currently enrolled.

Although often used to monitor progress and trends over time, a variety of limitations are associated with the NPER measure. In a context in which many children start and finish primary school late, it is possible for a country to have achieved universal primary completion while having an NPER below 100. This situation would occur if a significant percentage of students in a particular age cohort completed primary school beyond the standard age of completion.

The NPERs are also not strictly comparable across countries due to variations in the duration of the primary school cycle as defined by UNESCO. Table 4-1 shows that two countries have a primary cycle of 5 years, sixteen have 6 years, and six have 7 years. Countries are free to design their own school systems and international standards have not been established for the length of a primary school cycle. Using the MDG for primary schooling, countries with a longer primary cycle are currently judged by a tougher standard than countries with a shorter primary cycle.

---

[2]The gross primary enrollment ratio (GPER) is a more familiar measure, but its use as a marker for progress is problematic. The GPER includes in the numerator all children enrolled in school regardless of age and, in the denominator, only those in the primary school age range. Thus, it often yields values over 100 percent due to factors such as late entry and grade repetition. Primary completion rates, generated by the World Bank (Bruns, Mingat, and Rakotomalala, 2003), are also now utilized to monitor progress in attainment. Although these statistics benefit from being conceptually closer to the notion of universal primary completion, they are based on the same data sources as the NPER and survival rate to grade 5 and, hence, suffer from some of the same limitations (see also UNESCO, 2003, p. 59 for a critical evaluation). In addition, a proxy-primary completion rate, must be used when end-year enrollment data are not available; in only 7 of the 24 countries in this analysis is an actual primary completion rate available for the most recent period. The proxy indicator requires fairly strong assumptions about repetition and dropout rates that occur from year to year, assumptions that are particularly problematic for sub-Saharan Africa.

This is because the denominator of the ratio is customized to the actual number of years in the primary cycle in each country. The NPER is also set according to the recommended starting ages in each country even if these ages are poorly promoted or enforced. Fifteen of the 24 countries have recommended starting ages of 6, while the other nine have recommended starting ages of 7. Countries with earlier recommended starting ages may have more difficulty achieving a particular NPER than countries with later recommended starting ages.

Furthermore, assessments of UNESCO data have raised questions about their comparability and quality (Behrman and Rosenzweig, 1994; Lloyd, Kaufman, and Hewett, 2000). The enrollment data obtained from the ministries of education vary in quality according to the management information system (MIS) capacity within each country. The development of a good MIS is a continuing challenge in many parts of Africa (Moulton et al., 2001). Where financial flows to schools are a function of the level of enrollment, there is substantial motivation on the part of local education offices to inflate these numbers. Changes in systems of reporting that make current data more accurate, often introduced as part of school reform measures, may compromise comparability over time.

Alternative indicators to monitor progress toward EFA and the MDGs can be developed using data on schooling collected in nationally representative surveys. Data collected since 1995 for 24 sub-Saharan African countries are currently available from the DHS. Based on United Nations population estimates, these surveys represent 81 percent of the population of young people (ages 10 to 24) living in the region.[3] As indicated in Table 4-2, sample sizes in the DHS for the 10- to 24-year age group range from approximately 4,600 to more than 22,000. The median date for these surveys is 1999. In each of these nationally representative surveys, educational participation and attainment information is collected for all household members, while current schooling status is obtained for those ages 5 to 24.[4]

Arguably, the DHS estimate of attendance is likely to be more accurate in assessing actual school participation than the UNESCO NPER estimate, given that the NPER captures those that may have enrolled, but never actually attended school (UNESCO, 2002). Additional benefits of the DHS

---

[3]Data on school participation and attainment of household members is drawn from a household questionnaire, which asks a series of questions of an informed adult, typically the household head, about each household member.

[4]Attendance data from DHS presented in this chapter are from responses to the following question on the household survey: "Is 'name' still in school?" While the UNESCO enrollment ratio measures opening day enrollments, attendance rates from the DHS data will reflect actual school participation during the phase of the school year when the survey was in the field.

TABLE 4-2 Sub-Saharan African Countries Participating in the Demographic and Health Surveys (DHS) Since 1995

Country	Year of Most Recent DHS	DHS Sample Size of Population Ages 10-24	U.N. Estimated Population Ages 10-24 in 2000 (in thousands)
Benin	2001	9,257	2,115
Burkina Faso	1998-1999	10,243	3,976
Cameroon	1998	8,833	4,996
Central African Republic	1994-1995	8,529	1,199
Chad	1996-1997	11,149	2,491
Comoros	1996	4,852	240
Côte d'Ivoire	1998-1999	4,654	5,595
Ethiopia	1999	22,769	19,988
Ghana	1998-1999	6,991	6,581
Guinea	1999	10,097	2,637
Kenya	1998	13,021	11,306
Madagascar	1997	11,080	5,025
Malawi	2000	20,884	3,722
Mali	2001	19,329	3,652
Mozambique	1997	14,730	5,848
Niger	1998	11,052	3,505
Nigeria	1999	11,589	37,637
Rwanda	2000	16,679	2,689
South Africa	1998-2000	17,276	13,715
Tanzania	1999	6,115	11,845
Togo	1998	14,041	1,496
Uganda	2000-2001	12,742	7,757
Zambia	2001-2002	12,788	3,521
Zimbabwe	1999	10,374	4,489

SOURCES: DHS household data, United Nations Population Division estimates, 2000 (United Nations, 2001).

indicator are that the numerator and denominator are derived from the same population base and can be presented for separate sample subpopulations of interest. Furthermore, while UNESCO presents annual data on trends in NPER for those countries reporting enrollment data by age, such data are not available for all countries. In the case of sub-Saharan Africa, only 15 of the 24 countries covered in this chapter have recent net enrollment data as reported by UNESCO. By contrast, attendance rates can be derived for all 24 countries with DHS data.

The DHS does have disadvantages. Because a survey can extend over several months, it may capture some households at different phases of the annual school cycle. Thus, surveys that take place when schools are not in session may lead to an underestimation of current attendance, because some respondents may not report students on vacation as currently attending. Certainly the DHS question wording was intended to capture all who are still enrolled in school, even if they were not currently attending due to illness, school vacation, or other mitigating circumstances. However, to address this concern, the DHS has specifically added a question to their most recent surveys that asks if—during the current school year—the household member attended school at any time.[5]

Table 4-3 presents the most recent UNESCO NPER and attendance rates from the DHS for boys and girls using the same primary school age ranges for each country.[6] Figures 4-1a and 4-1b combine these two indicators in scatter plots, pairing estimates with a 45-degree line representing complete equality between the measures. Although a majority of points are reasonably close to the diagonal line, there is a tendency for the UNESCO estimates to be higher than those of the DHS.[7] This is highlighted in Figures 4-1a and 4-1b by the larger number of cases falling, and sometimes significantly so, below the 45-degree line. These comparisons reinforce suspicions about the inflation of ministry reporting of enrollment and the likelihood that many children are enrolled in, but never actually attend, school (UNESCO, 2002).

Table 4-3 also provides two alternative estimates of the gender parity ratio. By comparing the gender ratios, it is clear that UNESCO estimates are systematically lower than those of the DHS. These results can be explained by the higher reported enrollments for boys in the UNESCO data

---

[5]This question was added to measure enrollment in cases where surveys encompassed more than one school year or encompassed a school year and a vacation period. Note that current attendance rates generated from this question may improperly capture those who have dropped out during the current school year. These changes were initiated so DHS data could become more directly comparable to UNESCO data. The additional question is available for only 9 of the 24 countries. To maintain our comparisons across all 24 countries, we have used the original question wording for attendance: "Is 'name' still in school?" For six of the nine countries, the difference between estimates of attendance generated from the different measures is less than 3 percent. Attendance is 27 percent lower in Rwanda and 12 percent lower in Guinea using only the original question. In Tanzania, attendance is 5 percent higher using only the original question.

[6]Sahn and Stifel (2003) recently assessed progress toward the Millennium Development Goals in Africa during the 1990s using attendance rates among 6- to 14-year-olds. This is problematic because the measure ranges over 9 years of age, whereas the net enrollment rate ranges over 4 to 7 years, depending on the country. Thus, the Sahn and Stifel indicator is, in fact, a much higher standard to meet than is implied by the MDG target.

[7]Similar findings were highlighted in comparisons between UNESCO's NPER and National Attendance Ratios using a smaller selection of the DHS and UNICEF's Multiple Indicator Cluster Surveys (Huebler and Loaizia, 2002, as cited in UNESCO, 2002, p. 49; UNESCO, 2003, Table 2.6). These differences persist if the alternative measure of attendance is used; see footnote 5.

TABLE 4-3 Comparison of NPER (UNESCO) and Primary Attendance Rates (DHS)

Country	Age Ranges	Year of Data		Boys		Girls		Gender Parity Ratio[a]	
		UNESCO	DHS	UNESCO	DHS	UNESCO	DHS	UNESCO	DHS
Benin	6-11	—	2001	79.5	60.5	48.3	46.6	.61	.77
Burkina Faso	7-12	1998	1998-1999	40.2	33.0	27.5	22.8	.68	.69
Cameroon	6-11	—	1998	—	74.7	—	72.8	—	.97
C.A.R.	6-11	—	1994-1995	—	64.0	—	49.5	—	.77
Chad	6-11	1996	1996-1997	59.0	36.7	32.8	24.2	.56	.66
Comoros	6-11	1998	1996	53.7	49.2	45.5	44.6	.85	.91
Côte d'Ivoire	6-11	1998-1999	1998	67.5	58.4	50.8	46.4	.75	.79
Ethiopia	7-12	1998	1999	40.8	32.4	29.8	27.2	.73	.84
Ghana	6-11	—	1998-1999	—	76.8	—	76.1	—	.99
Guinea	7-12	1999-2000	1999	56.4	31.3	41.4	23.9	.73	.76
Kenya	6-12	—	1998	—	87.2	—	86.9	—	.99
Madagascar	6-10	1998	1997	62.1	58.2	63.5	60.2	1.02	1.03
Malawi	6-11	—	2000	—	73.1	—	76.0	—	1.04
Mali	7-12	—	2001	—	45.0	—	33.5	—	.74
Mozambique	6-10	1998	1997	45.2	54.0	36.8	47.1	.81	.87
Niger	7-12	1998	1998	31.9	31.2	20.4	21.1	.64	.68
Nigeria	6-11	—	1999	—	65.5	—	61.3	—	.94
Rwanda	7-12	1999-2000	2000	97.1	43.6	97.5	45.4	1.01	1.04
South Africa	7-13	1997	1998	100.0	88.5	100.0	89.9	1.00	1.02
Tanzania	7-13	1999-2000	1999	45.8	51.6	47.6	56.0	1.04	1.09
Togo	6-11	1998	1998	98.6	74.2	78.3	64.7	.79	.87
Uganda	6-12	—	2000-2001	—	74.2	—	75.8	—	1.02
Zambia	7-13	2000-2001	2001-2002	80.0	65.6	80.0	65.7	1.00	1.00
Zimbabwe	6-12	1999-2000	1999	79.9	80.9	80.4	82.3	1.01	1.02

[a]Calculated as females divided by males.
SOURCES: UNESCO (2002, Table 6), World Bank (2002), and DHS household data.

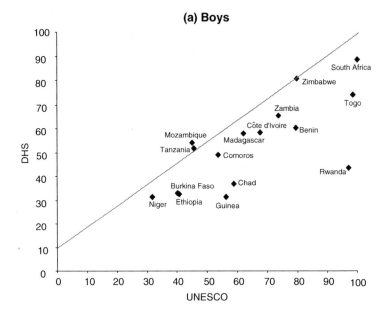

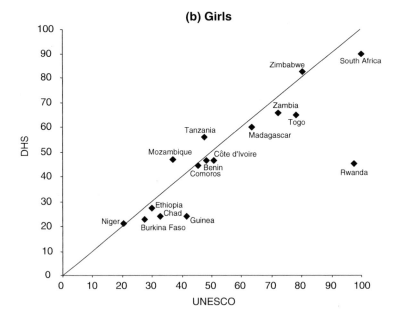

FIGURE 4-1 Comparison of UNESCO NPER and DHS attendance rate.
SOURCE: Table 4-3, this volume.

(Figure 4-1a). These findings suggest the potential for a differential inflation of enrollment by gender, with either structural elements built into some
management information systems that lead to this type of performance
inflation and/or the fact that boys are more likely than girls to be enrolled
in, yet never attend, school. It is possible that while norms about the importance of enrolling boys are pervasive, norms about the enrollment of girls
are less strongly held. As a result, the registration of girls on the first day of
school may reflect a stronger commitment on the part of parents to support
their daughters' regular attendance, whereas, in the case of boys, the act of
first day enrollment may be more routine and therefore less indicative of
parental commitment. Regardless of how we interpret these discrepancies,
UNESCO enrollment data imply much larger gender gaps in schooling in
these countries than DHS attendance data.

Given late starting ages and different lengths of the primary cycle, it is
also interesting to compare UNESCO's survival rate to grade 5 and the
DHS grade 4 completion rate among those ever enrolled, two alternative
indicators of grade progression. UNESCO has developed an indicator of
the survival rate to grade 5 using a ratio of the number of children officially
enrolled in grade 5 in a given year relative to the number of children who
officially enrolled in first grade 4 years earlier. This rate may or may not
capture the actual percentage of any cohort that completes grade 4, because
it does not allow for any repetition or temporary withdrawal and it does
not restrict the measure to children of a common age. In countries with high
repetition or withdrawal, this statistic would underestimate the percentage
of children who would eventually complete grade 4. An alternative measure
to assess progress toward EFA, which can be easily derived from the DHS
and does not have these limitations, is the percentage of 15- to 19-year-olds
who have completed 4 or more years of schooling among those who have
ever attended. This measure accommodates late starters and allows comparisons across age cohorts.

Table 4-4 presents a comparison of estimates of the survival to grade 5
derived from UNESCO and the grade 4 completion rate among those who
ever attended from the DHS, separately for boys and girls. In only 14 of the
24 countries are such data available from UNESCO. Figures 4-2a and 4-2b
present scatter plots of points derived from data in Table 4-4. As can be
seen in the figures, with the exception of Chad and Guinea (for boys) and
Chad (for girls), the UNESCO estimates are lower than the comparable
DHS data. If the UNESCO enrollment numbers are inflated by students
who enroll, but never attend school—as is suggested above—the grade 5
survival rates would be lower than would otherwise be expected. The differences between estimates are also likely a function of the fact that the
grade 4 completion rates calculated from the DHS data are not bounded by
age and include children who spend more than 4 years to complete grade 4.

TABLE 4-4 Comparison of UNESCO Survival Rates to Grade 5 and DHS Grade 4 Completion Rates Given Enrollment

Country	Year of Data		Boys		Girls		Gender Parity Ratio[a]	
	UNESCO	DHS	UNESCO	DHS	UNESCO	DHS	UNESCO	DHS
Benin	—	2001	—	83.2	—	75.5	—	.91
Burkina Faso	1998-1999	1998-1999	66.9	80.3	70.4	84.5	1.05	1.05
Cameroon	—	1998	—	86.8	—	88.0	—	1.01
C.A.R.	—	1994-1995	—	66.7	—	57.1	—	.86
Chad	1997	1996-1997	62.0	57.8	53.0	42.7	.85	.74
Comoros	—	1996	—	75.2	—	74.9	—	.99
Côte d'Ivoire	1997	1998	77.0	87.0	71.0	81.6	.92	.94
Ethiopia	1997	1999	51.0	54.8	50.0	54.3	.98	.99
Ghana	—	1998-1999	—	93.5	—	92.8	—	.99
Guinea	1998-1999	1999	92.5	87.8	79.1	80.7	.86	.92
Kenya	—	1998	—	93.1	—	93.8	—	1.01
Madagascar	1997	1997	49.0	52.0	33.0	55.1	.67	1.06
Malawi	—	2000	—	75.9	—	77.8	—	1.03
Mali	—	2001	—	86.4	—	84.7	—	.98
Mozambique	1997	1997	52.0	64.2	39.0	50.3	.75	.78
Niger	1998-1999	1998	62.1	87.2	60.2	86.0	.97	.99
Nigeria	—	1999	—	96.5	—	95.2	—	.99
Rwanda	1998-1999	2000	47.9	67.0	42.8	66.5	.89	.99
South Africa	1998-1999	1998	75.1	97.4	76.7	98.8	1.02	1.01
Tanzania	1998-1999	1999	78.6	83.0	83.3	88.0	1.06	1.06
Togo	1998-1999	1998	54.2	77.3	48.4	68.0	.89	.88
Uganda	1998-1999	2000-2001	43.9	85.5	45.5	82.3	1.04	.96
Zambia	—	2001-2002	—	84.8	—	84.5	—	1.00
Zimbabwe	1997	1999	78.0	96.3	79.0	97.2	1.01	1.00

[a]Calculated as females divided by males.
SOURCES: UNESCO (2002, Table 10), World Bank (2002), and DHS household data.

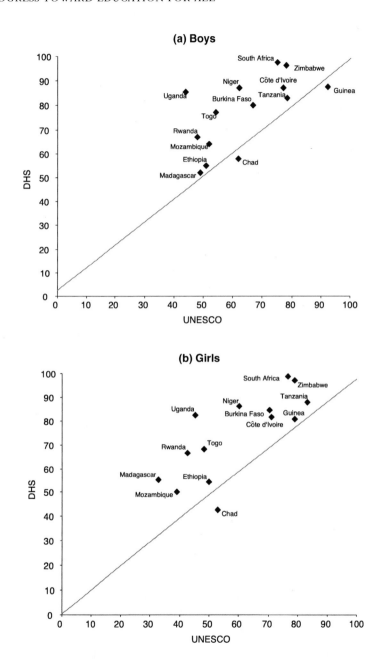

FIGURE 4-2 Comparison of UNESCO survival rate to grade 5 and DHS grade 4 completion rate given enrollment.
SOURCE: Table 4-4, this volume.

In countries with a large percentage of repeaters, the survival to grade 5 statistic would miss those who are ultimately able to complete grade 4, making the achievement of EFA and MDG appear more distant.

The differences between the UNESCO and DHS estimates in Table 4-4 also produce differences in the gender parity ratios. Of the 14 countries where comparisons of alternative indicators of grade progression are possible, nine countries show roughly similar ratios, with four showing an advantage for girls and five an advantage for boys. Although there are substantial differences in five cases, they do not show a consistent pattern; UNESCO gender ratios are substantially higher in two cases and substantially lower in three other cases.

The comparisons between UNESCO and DHS data strongly suggest that monitoring progress toward the EFA and MDGs with the NPERs and survival rates may be problematic and ultimately misleading. By relying on enrollment data from national ministries of education, which are not directly tied to actual attendance, UNESCO appears to overestimate the proportion of children attending school. On the other hand, countries are judged more harshly with regard to grade progression if UNESCO survival ratio estimates are applied. If UNESCO indicators are utilized to monitor progress over time, for example, by comparing estimates at two or more points in time, inaccurate conclusions regarding educational trends and the achievement of EFA goals may be the result.

In the next section of the chapter, we rely entirely on DHS data to derive country-specific, as well as region-wide, trends using alternative indicators that can be obtained from retrospective histories of educational attainment. The results of these analyses give a different, and arguably more accurate, portrayal of past education achievement and current challenges than trend analyses based on UNESCO data.

TRENDS IN SCHOOLING PARTICIPATION AND ATTAINMENT

With so many recent DHS currently available for sub-Saharan Africa, it is now possible to derive estimates of trends over the past 30 years in the school participation and attainment of young people for the region as a whole. These data tell a story of impressive past progress and daunting current challenges. These data also provide a picture of the state of current progress toward the millennium education goal of universal primary completion, a picture that in many ways differs from that portrayed by UNESCO indicators.

Trends in schooling can be derived using the most recent DHS for each country by comparing differences in school participation and attainment across age cohorts. We look at three indicators of progress: (1) the percentage ever attended, (2) the percentage completing four or more grades, and (3) the percentage completing primary.[8] To assure comparability across cohorts, the youngest 5-year age group for each indicator must have reached a sufficient age to be assured of having had the opportunity to achieve the level of schooling captured by that indicator.[9] In the case of the percentage ever attending school, 10 to 14 is the youngest cohort for which we present estimates. Given the variable starting ages (Table 4-1) and late ages of entry—a common practice in sub-Saharan Africa—deriving this indicator for younger children would underestimate the percentage who would eventually attend. For grade 4 completion, the youngest cohort that can be captured accurately is 15 to 19. Again, because of late starting ages, not all children can safely be assumed to complete grade 4 until the age of 15. For completed primary, the base cohort for trend comparisons is 20- to 24-year-olds because in countries with longer primary cycles, students have been known to be still enrolled in primary at the age of 18 or 19 (Lloyd, Mensch, and Clark, 2000).

There are several advantages associated with deriving trends from a single DHS. First, one can compare school trends for a greater range of countries, as only 15 of the 24 countries have had more than one DHS since 1990, when the DHS added education to the household roster questionnaire. Second, with a mean interval of no more than 6 years between surveys, trends can be captured for a longer interval of time using a single survey. Third, there is internal comparability within one sample survey that cannot necessarily be assumed when linking surveys.[10]

On the other hand, there is some loss in comparability when deriving long-term trends from one survey due to the possibility of differential mortality by school attainment. Some of those educated in the past will not be alive at the time of the survey and, therefore, their school attainment will not be reported. Mortality is typically selective of the least educated and is therefore likely to

---

[8]Note that the estimate for grade 4 completion includes in its denominator all children of the age group and is not limited to those ever enrolled. This estimate is therefore different from the grade 4 completion rate used in comparisons with UNESCO data above.

[9]We chose 5-year age cohorts for two reasons: (1) sample sizes are sometimes too small to derive estimates based on single years, and (2) heaping from age misreporting can be smoothed out using a wider age interval.

[10]In an assessment by the authors of education estimates using two or more DHS, it was discovered that although for many countries there is a consistency between estimates of educational achievement across surveys, for those countries with different sampling frames (e.g., Burkina Faso and Nigeria) or differences in the design and implementation between surveys, estimates are sometimes inconsistent. This assessment involved lining up similar age cohorts across both surveys by indicators of achievement. For example, 20- to 24-year-olds in a DHS for a particular country in 2000 should have the same level of achievement in grade 4 completion as the 15- to 19-year-olds in a similar survey in 1995. When these estimates line up, within some confidence interval that accounts for sampling error, for a range of age cohorts and indicators, the data can be considered consistent across surveys. Studies that have used two or more surveys to evaluate trends in education (e.g., Sahn and Stifel, 2003) have been insensitive to the issue of noncomparability in the underlying populations sampled.

lead to an overestimate of education attainment in earlier time periods, thus biasing downward estimated rates of progress. Indicators for the current period will not suffer from this bias. In the context of AIDS, there is some indication that educational differentials in AIDS mortality favor the least educated in the early stages of the epidemic; however, recent evidence suggests that these differentials are disappearing or even being reversed (de Walque, 2002; Glynn et al., 2004; Hargreaves and Glynn, 2002). Unfortunately, we are unaware of data on trends in mortality rates by education for sub-Saharan Africa and therefore cannot assess the extent of the bias or how it might be changing.

Another drawback is that the indicators of progress are less contemporaneous than those generated by UNESCO and others (Bruns, Mingata, and Rakotomalala, 2003; UNESCO, 2002, 2003). For example, because completed primary can only be accurately calculated for those 20 years of age or older, using the most recent DHS such respondents would have passed through primary school some time in the mid- to late 1980s. For completion of 4 or more years of schooling, the most recent estimate can be obtained for the early to mid-1990s.

However, given that the trends for all three indicators track closely together across age cohorts, it is possible to bring grade 4 and primary school completion estimates up to date by projecting rates using simple and plausible assumptions about future trends.[11] Table 4-5 provides an overview of the trends in education for all indicators for boys and girls separately, including estimates for the most recent period. The trends in Table 4-5 are based on weighted averages, using the United Nations estimate of the population ages 10 to 24 in 2000 as the weight for each country.[12] Figures 4-3a, 4-3b, and 4-3c illustrate these trends and place them in a

---

[11]The projections for grade 4 completion and completed primary for the most recent age cohorts (10 to 14 and 15 to 19) are estimated by assuming that the difference between the percentage ever in school and the percent completed 4+ years for each age cohort, and the difference between the percentage completed 4+ years and the percentage completed primary, will be maintained in the near future. The projected estimate for completed 4+ years for 10- to 14-year-olds is obtained by taking the percentage ever in school for that age group and subtracting the average difference between the percentage ever in school and grade 4 completion, which is calculated from the older age cohorts. A similar estimate for 10- to 14- and 15- to 19-year-olds can be obtained for completed primary by subtracting the average difference in completed 4+ years and completed primary from completed 4+ years, which again is calculated from the remaining age cohorts. The differences are weighted to give the more recent age cohorts a greater influence in determining the average difference. The weights for each data point were created by fixing two algebraic conditions, (1) a constant increment between weights, and (2) an average weight equal to one. Thus, the weights for primary completion rounded to two decimals were: .33, .67, 1.0, 1.33, and 1.67, and for grade 4 completion: .29, .57, .86, 1.14, 1.43, and 1.71.

[12]We chose not to vary the population weights for older cohorts. For a large country with a rapid rate of population growth, such as Ethiopia, its weight in the average is higher than it would have been otherwise for the older cohorts. This procedure allows Ethiopia's experience of school progress to be represented on a consistent basis across cohorts.

TABLE 4-5 Trends in Percentage of Education Participation and Attainment for 24 African Countries[a]

Age Groups	Ever Attended School			Completed 4+ Years			Completed Primary		
	Male	Female	Gender Parity Ratio[b]	Male	Female	Gender Parity Ratio[b]	Male	Female	Gender Parity Ratio[b]
10-14	78.3	72.9	.93	68.7[c]	63.8[c]	.93[d]	57.6[c]	53.3[c]	.93[d]
15-19	81.0	71.5	.88	68.9	60.9	.88	57.8[c]	50.5[c]	.87[d]
20-24	78.7	66.8	.85	69.4	58.5	.84	57.8	47.6	.82
25-29	76.9	64.2	.83	68.6	55.7	.81	57.1	44.8	.78
30-34	74.4	58.8	.79	66.2	49.9	.75	55.9	39.8	.71
35-39	72.6	51.8	.71	64.3	43.1	.67	53.9	33.3	.62
40-44	65.8	44.9	.68	56.9	35.4	.62	46.3	26.2	.57

[a]Weighted by population based on United Nations Population Division estimates, 2000 (United Nations, 2001).
[b]Calculated as females divided by males.
[c]Estimates prepared by authors; see footnote 10.
[d]Calculations based on estimates prepared by authors.
SOURCE: DHS household data.

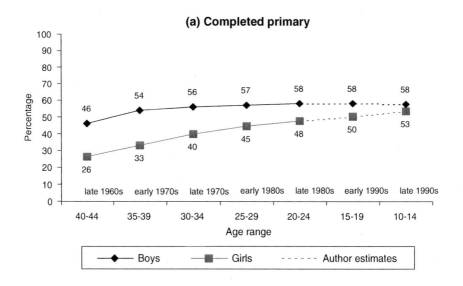

(a) Completed primary

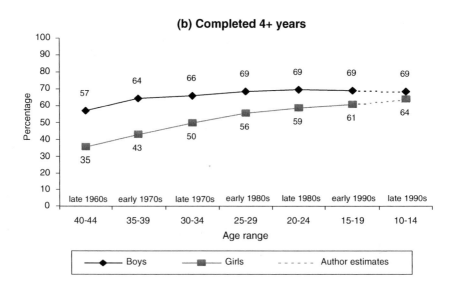

(b) Completed 4+ years

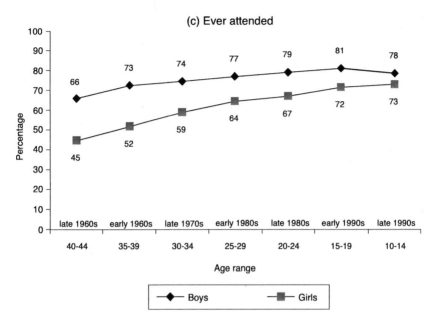

FIGURE 4-3 Trends in completion of primary for 24 African countries (population weighted).
SOURCE: Table 4-5, this volume.

periodic time line when they would have passed through the educational system.

For males, the percentage completing primary is estimated to have risen in sub-Saharan Africa from roughly 46 percent in the late 1960s to roughly 58 percent in the late 1990s. However, primary completion rates have remained at the same level for the past 20 years. Most of the improvement in primary completion for males came a long time ago in the 1960s and 1970s and has stalled since.

In stark contrast, over the same time period, females' primary completion rates have risen steadily from a much lower base of roughly 26 percent in the late 1960s to 53 percent projected for the late 1990s, roughly doubling the level of achievement over this period. The pace of progress for females, which was rapid, has slowed somewhat in the past 10 years. For females, these trends reflect not only more girls enrolling in schooling, but also some small improvement in the grade progression rate once enrolled. With these very different trajectories for males and females, the gender gap that was very wide in the early days of independence has narrowed considerably, with an estimate for sub-Saharan Africa as a whole to be only 5 percentage points in the late 1990s.

Grade 4 completion rates are slightly higher than primary completion rates for both males and females, implying an attrition rate from grade 4 to primary completion of roughly 10 percentage points. In the current period, it is estimated that 64 percent of girls ages 10 to 14 and 69 percent of boys have completed at least 4 grades. Two worrying developments for boys are the stagnation in grade 4 completion for the past 15 to 20 years at 69 percent and the absolute decline in attendance rates for boys in the most recent period. While 81 percent of 15- to 19-year-old boys had ever been to school (Figure 4-3c), the percentage has fallen to 78 percent for the 10- to 14-year-olds. This suggests the possibility of a future erosion in boys' schooling attainment. These weighted regional averages hide the current poor performance of a large number of countries, where boys' attendance rates have shown more dramatic declines.

As with the primary completion rates, grade 4 completion rates for females have increased markedly over time, although it is clear that a large part of the growth was for the older age cohorts. As a result, the estimated gender gap for grade 4 completion has declined to 5 percentage points for the latest time period. With the decline in boys' attendance coupled with increases in girls' enrollment and grade 4 completion, it is likely that girls will meet or surpass boys on this indicator in the near future. However, although grade 4 completion and attendance for girls continues to increase, they are doing so at a much slower rate than in the past. It is possible that the trends in girls' schooling will eventually parallel the flatter trends for boys that have occurred in the past decade or so.

These long-term trends for the region, as a whole, mirror economic and political developments. In the early postcolonial period, the importance accorded to education in national development plans led to a dramatic increase in educational expenditure and a tremendous expansion of the educational infrastructure, irrespective of differing development strategies.[13] These investments were facilitated by strong economic growth rates in the late 1960s and 1970s (Kinyanjui, 1993; World Bank, 1988). Total public expenditure on education in constant dollars grew by roughly seven percent a year between 1970 and 1980 on average across sub-Saharan Africa, with similar average rates of growth in the former British and French colonies, well above rates required to keep pace with the growth in school-age populations (Donors to African Education, 1994). Indeed, growth of educational expenditure exceeded growth in gross national product (GNP) over the decade of the 1970s, resulting in a rising percentage of GNP devoted to educational expenditure.

---

[13]For a more complete discussion of differences in colonial educational regimes, see Lloyd, Kaufman, and Hewett (1999).

The economic, political, and demographic conditions in the 1980s, however, sharply curtailed and often ended the impressive educational gains of the prior two decades. Population continued to grow rapidly, with rates of growth in most countries even higher in the 1980s than in the 1970s (United Nations, 2001). The majority of non-oil exporting African countries were particularly hard hit by increased world prices for oil, decreased export prices, and higher external debt (Hodd, 1989; World Bank, 1988). Additionally, most countries adopted structural adjustment programs that resulted in cutbacks in social-sector spending, including educational expenditures, often leading to the imposition of school fees (Reimers, 1994).[14] The impact of these changes is reflected in declines in the growth rate of educational expenditures in constant dollars, from 6.2 percent on average from 1970 to 1980 to 2.1 percent from 1980 to 1990 (Donors to African Education, 1994).

Since some of the most populous countries in Africa, measured in terms of the absolute size of their youth population in 2000, have achieved higher levels of schooling participation and attainment than their smaller neighbors, weighted averages give a more encouraging picture of the trends in schooling in sub-Saharan Africa than would be the case if we were to give each country the same importance or weight in the analysis.[15] Tables 4-6a, 4-6b, and 4-6c present data on the performance of individual countries for each of the three DHS indicators. As is illustrated in the tables, the most populous countries that have participated in the DHS with relatively strong educational performance include Nigeria with 37.6 million 10- to 24-year-olds, South Africa with 13.7 million, Tanzania with 11.8 million, Kenya with 11.3 million, Uganda with 7.8 million, and Ghana with 6.6 million. Of the populous countries, only Ethiopia with 20 million 10- to 24-year-olds has had relatively poor educational performance. Thus, more than half the countries represented in this analysis with smaller populations of children ages 10 to 24 face even greater challenges in achieving education for all than would be implied by the weighted regional data.

CURRENT CHALLENGES AND FUTURE PROGRESS TOWARD EFA

In the 1990s, qualitative evaluations of the educational situation in the region described a thinning of the provision of education and the inability of countries to maintain current levels of achievement given lagging investment and continuing growth in the size of school-age cohorts (Kinyanjui,

---

[14]Botswana, Cameroon, and South Africa are exceptions.

[15]Another reason that these estimates may be optimistic is that there is evidence for some countries that DHS samples may be overeducated relative to the underlying population (Lloyd, Mensch, and Clark, 2000).

TABLE 4-6a Trends in Percentage Ever Attended School, by Age Group: 24 sub-Saharan African Countries

Country	Survey Date	Ages 10-24	Ages 10-14	
		2000 Population	Boys	Girls
Benin	2001	2,115	.76	.55
Burkina Faso	1998-1999	3,976	.41	.27
Cameroon	1998	4,996	.89	.84
Central African Republic	1994-1995	1,199	.83	.63
Chad	1996-1997	2,491	.55	.35
Comoros	1996	240	.77	.64
Côte d'Ivoire	1998-1999	5,595	.73	.57
Ethiopia	1999	19,988	.50	.40
Ghana	1998-1999	6,581	.87	.86
Guinea	1999	2,637	.58	.40
Kenya	1998	11,306	.96	.95
Madagascar	1997	5,025	.78	.78
Malawi	2000	3,722	.93	.93
Mali	2001	3,652	.51	.36
Mozambique	1997	5,848	.85	.71
Niger	1998	3,505	.41	.27
Nigeria	1999	37,637	.83	.79
Rwanda	2000	2,689	.88	.88
South Africa	1998-2000	13,715	.98	.99
Togo	1998	1,496	.89	.72
Uganda	2000-2001	7,757	.96	.95
United Republic of Tanzania	1999	11,845	.75	.74
Zambia	2001-2002	3,521	.86	.84
Zimbabwe	1999	4,489	.98	.99

SOURCE: United Nations (2001); DHS household data.

Ages 20-24		Ages 30-34		Change for Most Recent Decade		Change for Earlier Decade	
Boys	Girls	Boys	Girls	Boys	Girls	Boys	Girls
.65	.36	.61	.34	16.9	50.1	6.7	8.4
.36	.17	.23	.09	12.7	62.0	58.7	81.1
.91	.78	.85	.67	−2.1	7.8	6.2	15.3
.86	.56	.81	.49	−3.7	11.9	6.6	15.1
.61	.27	.45	.17	−10.6	28.9	35.3	63.0
.78	.64	.62	.35	−1.4	−0.4	26.2	82.4
.63	.53	.52	.38	16.1	7.2	21.6	41.1
.53	.30	.50	.21	−6.7	31.7	6.6	47.0
.87	.75	.83	.65	−0.2	14.4	4.4	14.6
.49	.24	.43	.18	18.7	66.2	12.7	36.5
.97	.95	.96	.91	−0.8	.2	1.5	3.7
.82	.81	.82	.79	−4.9	−4.6	−0.4	3.5
.91	.81	.83	.65	2.2	14.8	8.6	24.0
.34	.20	.33	.19	48.3	81.5	3.7	6.6
.82	.59	.83	.65	3.6	20.7	−1.7	−9.2
.39	.20	.27	.12	4.8	37.6	44.5	62.4
.83	.70	.76	.58	−0.4	13.7	8.8	20.3
.83	.82	.70	.65	5.3	7.4	18.7	25.7
.98	.98	.95	.92	.3	.9	2.5	6.0
.85	.59	.77	.47	4.5	23.0	10.6	26.1
.93	.84	.91	.74	4.2	13.5	2.0	13.7
.89	.83	.91	.79	−15.1	−10.4	−2.2	5.6
.94	.88	.94	.88	−8.4	−4.3	−0.3	−0.1
.99	.98	.97	.94	.0	.6	1.3	4.3

TABLE 4-6b Trends in Percentage Completed 4+ Years, by Age Group: 24 sub-Saharan African Countries

Country	Survey Date	Ages 10-24 2000 Population	Ages 15-19 Boys	Girls
Benin	2001	2,115	.62	.36
Burkina Faso	1998-1999	3,976	.30	.18
Cameroon	1998	4,996	.78	.72
Central African Republic	1994-1995	1,199	.56	.35
Chad	1996-1997	2,491	.36	.14
Comoros	1996	240	.64	.49
Côte d'Ivoire	1998-1999	5,595	.57	.41
Ethiopia	1999	19,988	.31	.21
Ghana	1998-1999	6,581	.85	.79
Guinea	1999	2,637	.49	.25
Kenya	1998	11,306	.91	.91
Madagascar	1997	5,025	.41	.43
Malawi	2000	3,722	.72	.72
Mali	2001	3,652	.35	.23
Mozambique	1997	5,848	.56	.34
Niger	1998	3,505	.36	.18
Nigeria	1999	37,637	.83	.73
Rwanda	2000	2,689	.57	.57
South Africa	1998-2000	13,715	.96	.98
Togo	1998	1,496	.69	.47
Uganda	2000-2001	7,757	.83	.74
United Republic of Tanzania	1999	11,845	.73	.70
Zambia	2001-2002	3,521	.80	.77
Zimbabwe	1999	4,489	.95	.95

SOURCE: United Nations (2001); DHS household data.

Ages 25-29		Ages 35-39		Change for Most Recent Decade		Change for Earlier Decade	
Boys	Girls	Boys	Girls	Boys	Girls	Boys	Girls
.46	.22	.47	.18	34.5	66.0	−1.7	17.5
.21	.10	.13	.08	41.5	84.9	62.7	31.8
.82	.65	.73	.54	−5.2	10.3	13.1	20.9
.58	.32	.52	.18	−3.6	7.9	10.6	82.7
.34	.08	.29	.07	7.4	83.1	16.2	8.9
.63	.44	.35	.15	2.3	12.2	79.3	189.3
.59	.43	.50	.27	−3.2	−5.9	16.9	59.3
.37	.20	.29	.08	−16.1	6.7	24.9	145.9
.84	.62	.77	.60	1.5	26.7	8.7	3.8
.35	.15	.31	.12	38.7	65.9	13.5	25.5
.93	.89	.91	.72	−2.5	2.3	2.3	22.5
.57	.56	.55	.42	−28.1	−22.4	4.4	32.1
.70	.48	.66	.38	3.3	49.2	4.8	25.6
.25	.14	.25	.15	41.1	64.3	−1.2	−5.8
.50	.30	.52	.18	13.0	13.9	−5.0	67.4
.27	.15	.16	.07	33.1	21.1	69.4	108.9
.79	.64	.76	.48	4.9	14.5	5.0	33.5
.65	.62	.52	.37	−12.1	−8.2	25.2	69.0
.93	.91	.89	.84	3.3	6.6	4.7	8.8
.64	.33	.61	.27	7.7	44.3	4.9	22.7
.78	.58	.71	.46	6.1	27.1	9.7	25.6
.83	.78	.85	.54	−10.9	−9.2	−2.7	43.3
.85	.78	.87	.71	−5.5	−1.3	−2.1	10.3
.97	.94	.91	.72	−2.0	1.0	6.7	30.7

TABLE 4-6c Trends in Percentage Completed Primary, by Age Group: 24 sub-Saharan African Countries

Country	Survey Date	Ages 10-24 2000 Population	Ages 20-24 Boys	Girls
Benin	2001	2,115	.38	.17
Burkina Faso	1998-1999	3,976	.25	.12
Cameroon	1998	4,996	.69	.60
Central African Republic	1994-1995	1,199	.40	.22
Chad	1996-1997	2,491	.29	.07
Comoros	1996	240	.51	.41
Côte d'Ivoire	1998-1999	5,595	.46	.34
Ethiopia	1999	19,988	.23	.14
Ghana	1998-1999	6,581	.80	.62
Guinea	1999	2,637	.36	.15
Kenya	1998	11,306	.70	.62
Madagascar	1997	5,025	.31	.32
Malawi	2000	3,722	.44	.26
Mali	2001	3,652	.24	.12
Mozambique	1997	5,848	.18	.08
Niger	1998	3,505	.30	.14
Nigeria	1999	37,637	.79	.65
Rwanda	2000	2,689	.40	.36
South Africa	1998-2000	13,715	.86	.90
Togo	1998	1,496	.50	.22
Uganda	2000-2001	7,757	.47	.32
United Republic of Tanzania	1999	11,845	.71	.67
Zambia	2001-2002	3,521	.68	.54
Zimbabwe	1999	4,489	.88	.86

SOURCE: United Nations (2001); DHS household data.

Ages 30-34		Ages 35-44		Change for Most Recent Decade		Change for Earlier Decade	
Boys	Girls	Boys	Girls	Boys	Girls	Boys	Girls
.34	.16	.26	.10	13.4	5.8	29.2	64.2
.15	.06	.12	.04	72.4	89.2	24.2	61.4
.67	.43	.57	.31	2.9	39.7	17.9	40.5
.38	.18	.26	.06	5.1	24.5	45.6	210.8
.21	.04	.17	.02	40.8	72.2	22.8	123.1
.48	.26	.20	.07	5.3	58.3	140.1	290.0
.44	.27	.37	.28	6.5	27.0	16.8	-3.7
.25	.08	.16	.03	-7.6	75.6	51.7	209.9
.74	.51	.73	.49	7.0	21.8	1.6	5.1
.31	.11	.27	.09	14.4	31.3	14.7	23.3
.81	.65	.73	.41	-13.1	-4.7	10.4	60.5
.45	.39	.30	.22	-30.8	-17.5	47.8	75.4
.37	.15	.33	.11	18.7	69.9	12.9	34.8
.19	.09	.21	.07	27.3	25.6	-12.3	28.1
.20	.08	.13	.02	-6.9	10.8	51.0	309.8
.20	.09	.11	.04	49.9	57.6	79.3	122.7
.72	.52	.60	.31	9.4	24.8	19.0	69.3
.41	.31	.31	.19	-3.4	15.6	35.0	67.4
.78	.73	.65	.61	10.3	22.4	19.8	20.6
.53	.19	.42	.14	-5.0	15.3	27.2	34.8
.44	.24	.44	.21	7.9	34.9	.0	11.4
.75	.62	.51	.30	-5.6	8.7	48.6	108.2
.75	.53	.78	.46	-8.7	1.5	-4.1	15.2
.88	.74	.68	.41	.6	16.4	29.6	79.1

1993; Nieuwenhuis, 1996). The effect of these recent trends are particularly pronounced for the most recent cohort of boys, with a recent drop off in attendance and the projected stagnation in grade 4 and primary completion rates. For girls, these trends are only beginning to be revealed in attendance rates for the youngest cohort.

With continual progress in girls' schooling in the past 10 years and increasing gender parity ratios in levels of attainment, questions remain as to how the international community can focus its limited resources and attention to maximize the possibility of attaining the EFA goals and MDG. Since the Jomtien Conference in 1990, the international community has placed a great degree of weight on investments in girls' schooling, given gender gaps that have historically favored boys in most of the developing world (UNESCO, 2003; UNICEF, 2003a, 2003b, 2003c). The trends in education for girls provide some evidence that those investments have had the intended impact. With the potential closing of the gender gap in sub-Saharan Africa in the near future, albeit at levels significantly below universal primary completion, remaining disadvantaged groups need to be identified, and policies developed, for achieving further progress in educational participation and attainment. Household surveys from the DHS provide an opportunity for focusing attention on the critical remaining challenges in achieving education for all.

Although the UNESCO data do not allow us to explore differential educational attainment by household living standards, this is possible with DHS data. The DHS data are particularly advantageous in this way for EFA monitoring, given that many current reform efforts, in the presence of resource constraints, are attempting to target resources where they are most needed. Based on a methodology for generating a household wealth index utilizing Principal Components analysis (Filmer and Pritchett, 1999)[16] and the indicator of grade 4 completion, we develop an index of educational

---

[16]The living standards or wealth index is generated from the DHS and is based on two sets of indicators, the ownership of a set of consumer durables (e.g., a radio, bike, car) and various quality of housing indicators, including the availability of piped water, electricity, and finished flooring. To generate a single measure of household living standards using these indicators, the individual variables are included in a Principal Components analysis that generates weights for each item that represent the variable's overall importance in capturing household wealth. The score of the first principal component is generated from a linear extrapolation of the weights and the variable score. The scores are then weighted by household size, with somewhat arbitrary percentile cutoffs of 40, 40, and 20 used to delineate low, middle, and high household wealth. This index measures relative inequality, not absolute inequality. Thus, the wealth index is not comparable across countries, and in the poorest countries, many in the middle, or even sometimes the highest wealth category will still be poor in an absolute sense. It should also be noted that the wealth delineations are strongly related to urban or rural residence. The preponderant percentage of the poor live in rural areas while the wealthier most often reside in urban areas.

inequality by household wealth.[17] The inequality index is calculated as 1 minus the ratio of the grade 4 attainment of the poorest 40 percent of households, relative to the wealthiest 20 percent of households. This measure of educational inequality ranges from 0 to 1, with 0 representing complete parity of attainment between the wealthiest 20 percent and the poorest 40 percent in each country and a value of 1 indicating a complete lack of educational opportunities for the poor. A measure of 0.5 implies that the poor have obtained 50 percent of the levels of attainment of the wealthiest.

Figure 4-4 presents the inequality index for grade 4 completion by wealth status and gender. The countries are ordered from low to high inequality using the index for boys. The index varies across the full range of possible values among the 24 countries. Roughly half the countries have indices for both boys and girls that exceed 50 percent, suggesting wide differentials in educational attainment by household socioeconomic status in sub-Saharan Africa. These include Central African Republic, Mozambique, Niger, Chad, Guinea, Benin, Ethiopia, Madagascar, Burkina Faso, and Mali. In many of these countries, the inequality index takes on extreme values ranging from 70 to 90 percent, indicating almost a complete lack of educational opportunities for the poor. A few additional countries have levels of inequality that exceed 50 percent only for girls, including Comoros, Togo, and Côte d'Ivoire. On the other hand, we see that certain countries have achieved near universal schooling even for the poor. These include Kenya, Zimbabwe, and South Africa. Relatively low inequality, in the 0 to 0.25 range, can be seen for both sexes in Ghana and Rwanda and for boys in Tanzania.

In many countries, the index of inequality is substantially higher for girls than boys, supporting the widely held belief that gender inequalities in educational attainment are compounded among the poor. Differences of 10 percentage points or more in the index between boys and girls can be found in 13 of the 24 countries. Such gender differences tend to be greatest in countries where overall wealth inequalities are greatest. It is interesting to note, however, that this pattern is not universal. In a substantial minority of countries, representing the full range in terms of schooling inequalities by household wealth status, we find similar levels of inequality for both boys and girls. These include Kenya, Zimbabwe, South Africa, Ghana, Rwanda, Malawi, Zambia, Cameroon, Madagascar, Burkina Faso, and Mali. We

---

[17]Of the three indicators, grade 4 completion rates were selected because, relative to attendance rates, they provide a measure basic schooling attainment. Also, because grade 4 completion can be calculated for those 15- to 19-year-olds, it is more contemporaneous to current household living standards than primary completion rates for 20- to 24-year-olds.

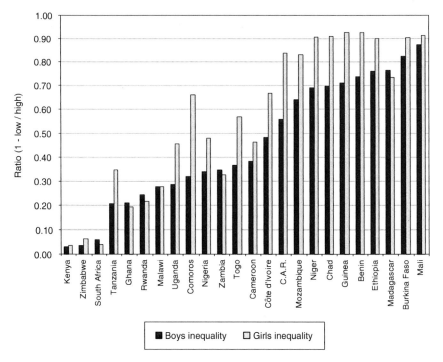

FIGURE 4-4 Index of inequality in grade 4 completion, 15- to 19-year-olds, by household wealth status and gender.
SOURCE: DHS household data.

find a few countries where inequalities for boys are greater than inequalities for girls: South Africa, Ghana, Rwanda, Zambia, and Madagascar.

Figure 4-5 shows levels of grade 4 completion currently achieved by the wealthiest 20 percent of 10- to 14-year-olds in each country, graded from low to high according to the achievement of boys. We see that for many countries at the turn of the century, near universal grade 4 completion has already been achieved for the economically better off. For many others, such an achievement is likely within the next 15 years. For a few countries, however, even the wealthiest 20 percent have a long way to go. This group would include some of the poorest countries: Chad, Ethiopia, Niger, Burkina Faso, and Mali. While in the majority of countries, the gender gap among children from the wealthiest households has narrowed or almost disappeared, this is not the case in much of francophone Africa, including Burkina Faso, Niger, Chad, Mali, Benin, Guinea, Côte d'Ivoire, and Togo. Gender gaps among the wealthy remain large in Ethiopia and Mozambique as well.

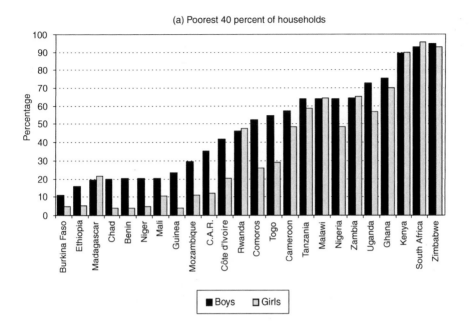

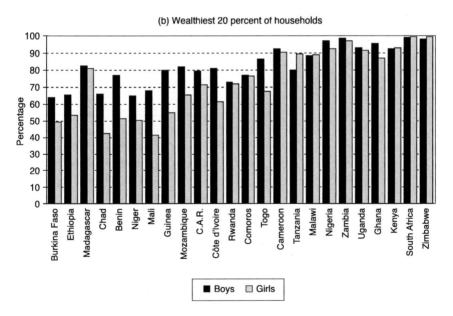

FIGURE 4-5 Grade 4 completion, 15- to 19-year-olds.
SOURCE: DHS household data.

These results suggest that educational reform measures need to be tailored carefully to each country's situation based on recent and accurate measures of the performance of different subgroups of the population. At the country level, DHS data permit other breakdowns as well, including provincial and rural-urban breakdowns. Although many of these breakdowns could be developed within a well-designed MIS, this would not be the case for indicators that require data that are collected at the household level, such as living standards. Given the enormous financial and organizational mobilization that will be required to achieve the millennium goals, resources will need to be targeted to the particular population subgroups that are lagging behind. As is illustrated here, a proper monitoring program will require information on the relative progress of the poor.

CONCLUSIONS

At the turn of the twenty-first century, we estimate that 37.2 million young adolescents ages 10 to 14 in sub-Saharan Africa will not complete primary. Reducing the number of uneducated African youth is a primary objective of signatories of the Education for All framework, as well as the United Nations MDG for education (United Nations, 2001). Achieving these goals in the time frame desired will require a level of resources and commitment not previously seen; it will also require more effective tools for monitoring progress.

We conclude from our assessment of UNESCO's two indicators for monitoring progress toward EFA and the MDG that UNESCO data may provide a potentially misleading picture of current progress. Not only are rates of enrollment significantly higher relative to attendance data from nationally representative DHS surveys, but gender parity ratios suggest a greater remaining gap in attendance than comparable DHS data. Part of the problem arises from UNESCO's reliance on management information systems to make cross-country comparisons. This results in the publication of data of variable quality, with limited comparability across countries and over time. Reliance on such data to track progress toward the millennium goals should be carefully weighed. At a minimum, UNESCO data should be consistently evaluated vis-à-vis alternative data sources and indicators. Although UNESCO will likely remain committed to the net primary enrollment ratio and survival to grade 5 indicators, strides have already been made in utilizing a wider array of attainment data (UNESCO, 2003, Table 2.13).

Nationally representative household data provide a useful baseline from which to build. UNICEF's Multiple Indicator Cluster Survey and the DHS, both of which collect information on the educational participation and attainment of household members, are collected in a large enough number of countries for cross-national and regional comparisons of educational progress. Since 2000, DHS household questionnaires have been expanded to allow the possibility of creating additional schooling indicators, including some which are directly comparable to commonly used UNESCO indicators. This is part of a relatively new project undertaken by the DHS with support from the USAID's Office of Human Capacity Development, which includes the production of country-level fact sheets of education indicators. Furthermore, as part of the same project, the DHS is beginning to launch a series of in-depth surveys on education in sub-Saharan Africa in conjunction with its regular surveys. The first report was recently published on Uganda; results for Malawi and Zambia will follow shortly. This effort would require substantial expansion if it were to take on EFA monitoring throughout the world.

Even with the limited education data already collected in the traditional DHS, much can be learned about past trends and the current status of schooling in sub-Saharan Africa. The trends in primary schooling completion for sub-Saharan Africa implied by these data raise serious questions about the feasibility of achieving the EFA goals and MDG in the foreseeable future. It is even possible that some earlier gains could be lost, given recent declines in attendance rates among the youngest boys and the tapering off in attendance rates among the youngest cohort of girls in many countries. It would also appear that, for the indicators utilized in this chapter, the gap between boys and girls is closing rapidly for the region as a whole. These trends in gender parity ratios are occurring despite huge variations in overall levels of educational attainment. Consequently, these findings raise doubts about the likelihood that EFA goals can be achieved with a strategy limited to an emphasis on girls' schooling.

The education gap between girls and boys has declined largely because of the impressive improvement in schooling for girls in sub-Saharan Africa. Although a large portion of this change occurred decades ago, growth continued in girls' education in the 1980s and 1990s, despite significant economic setbacks. A thorough understanding of the reasons for disparate trends in boys' and girls' education over the past 30 years will require more research. Our data do not allow us to tease out the many possibilities, including rising returns to the education of girls (either market or nonmarket), the diffusion of global cultural values relating to the importance of girls' schooling, and the effects of school reform.

The schooling gap that remains most significant is the gap between the poorest and wealthiest households. Others have also posited the importance of household wealth in relation to schooling. Filmer and Pritchett (1999) provided documentation of the differential in educational attainment by household wealth status using data from many of the DHS available a few years ago. Even earlier, Knodel and Jones (1996), using schooling data from Vietnam and Thailand, raised questions about the heavy emphasis on girls' schooling in the international community given the much wider gaps in schooling by household wealth. This chapter offers a new comparison of the size of gender gaps and wealth gaps across most of the countries of sub-Saharan Africa using several widely accepted schooling indicators. With the gender gap closing in many cases at levels of educational attainment that fall far short of universal primary schooling, new strategies will need to be devised to reach the poorest parents and their children.

REFERENCES

Behrman, J.R., and Rosenzweig, M.R. (1994). Caveat emptor: Cross-country data on education and the labor force. *Journal of Development Economics, 44*(1), 147-171.

Bruns, B., Mingat, A., and Rakotomalala, R. (2003) *Achieving universal primary education by 2015: A chance for every child.* Washington, DC: World Bank.

Dakar Framework for Action. (2000). *Education for all: Meeting our collective commitments.* Text adopted by the World Education Forum, April 26-28, Dakar, Senegal.

de Walque, D. (2002). *How does the impact of an HIV/AIDS information campaign vary with educational attainment? Evidence from rural Uganda.* (Population Research Center, Discussion Paper Series, No. 2002-16.) Chicago, IL: University of Chicago Press.

Donors to African Education. (1994). *A statistical profile of education in sub-Saharan Africa in the 1980s.* Paris, France: Author, International Institute for Education Planning.

Filmer, D., and Pritchett, L. (1999). The effect of household wealth on educational attainment: Evidence from 35 countries. *Population and Development Review, 25*(1), 85-120.

Glynn, J.R., Carael, M., Buve, A., Anagonou, S., Zekeng, L., Kahindo, M., and Musonda, R. (2004). Does increased general schooling protect against HIV infection? A study in four African cities. *Tropical Medicine and International Health, 9*(1), 4-14.

Hargreaves, J.R., and Glynn, J.R. (2002). Educational attainment and HIV-1 infection in developing countries: A systematic review. *Tropical Medicine and International Health, 7*(6), 489-498.

Hodd, M. (1989). A survey of the African economies. In S. Moroney (Ed.), *Handbooks to the modern world: Africa* (pp. 787-809). New York: Oxford University Press.

Kinyanjui, K. (1993). Enhancing women's participation in the science-based curriculum: The case of Kenya. In J. Ker Conway and S.C. Bourque (Eds.), *The politics of women's education: Perspectives from Asia, Africa, and Latin America* (pp. 133-148). Ann Arbor: University of Michigan Press.

Knodel, J., and Jones, G.W. (1996). Post-Cairo population policy: Does promoting girls' schooling miss the mark? *Population and Development Review, 22*(4), 683-702.

Lloyd, C.B., Kaufman, C.E., and Hewett, P.C. (1999). *The spread of primary schooling in sub-Saharan Africa: Implications for fertility change.* (Policy Research Division Working Paper No. 127.) New York: Population Council.

Lloyd, C.B., Kaufman, C.E., and Hewett, P.C. (2000). The spread of primary schooling in sub-Saharan Africa: Implications for fertility change. *Population and Development Review, 26*(3), 483-515.

Lloyd, C.B., Mensch, B.S., and Clark, W.H. (2000). The effects of primary school quality on school dropout among Kenyan girls and boys. *Comparative Education Review, 44*(2), 113-147.

Moulton, J., Mundy, K., Welmond, M., and Williams, J. (2001). Paradigm lost? The implementation of basic education reforms in sub-Saharan Africa. In *SD Publication Series Office of Sustainable Development, Bureau for Africa*. (Technical Paper No. 109.) Washington, DC: U.S. Agency for International Development.

Nieuwenhuis, F.J. (1996). *The development of education systems in postcolonial Africa: A study of a selected number of African countries*. Pretoria, South Africa: Human Sciences Research Council.

Reimers, F. (1994). Education and structural adjustment in Latin America and Sub-Saharan Africa. *International Journal of Educational Development, 14*(2), 119-129.

Sahn, D.E., and Stifel, D.C. (2003). Progress toward the Millennium Development Goals in Africa. *World Development, 31*(1), 23-52.

Tomasevski, K. (2001). *Free and compulsory education for all children: The gap between promise and performance*. (Right to Education Primers No. 2.) Lund and Stockholm, Sweden: Raoul Wallenberg Institute and Swedish International Development Cooperation Agency.

UNESCO. (2002). *Education for all: Is the world on track? EFA global monitoring report 2002*. Paris, France: UNESCO.

UNESCO. (2003). *Education for all global monitoring report 2003/4: Gender and education for all: The leap to equality*. Paris, France: UNESCO.

UNICEF. (2003a). *Accelerating progress in girls' education*. New York: UNICEF.

UNICEF. (2003b). *Making investments in girls' education count*. New York: UNICEF.

UNICEF. (2003c). *The state of the world's children 2004—Girls education and development*. New York: UNICEF.

United Nations. (2001). *World population prospects: The 2000 revision: Comprehensive Tables: Vol. 1*. New York: Author, Department of Economic and Social Affairs, Population Division.

United Nations General Assembly. (2001). Road map towards the implementation of the United Nations Millennium Declaration. In *Report of the Secretary-General*. New York: United Nations, Department of Public Information.

World Bank. (1988). *Education in sub-Saharan Africa: Policies for adjustment, revitalization, and expansion*. Washington, DC: Author.

World Bank. (2002). *World Development Indicators 2002*. Washington, DC: Author.

5

Trends in the Timing of First Marriage Among Men and Women in the Developing World

Barbara S. Mensch, Susheela Singh, and John B. Casterline

For many demographers age at first union is worthy of attention because of the close link between marriage and the onset of childbearing. Thus a number of studies over the years have documented the contribution of changes in the timing of marriage to fertility transitions, both historically in developed countries and currently in developing countries (e.g., Casterline, 1994; Coale and Treadway, 1986; Rosero-Bixby, 1996). It has been argued, however, that "weaknesses in the field of nuptiality research stem from its heavy focus on the fertility implications of nuptiality patterns" (Smith, 1983, p. 510). In charging his fellow demographers to think more broadly about the subject of marriage, van de Walle (1993, p. 118) asserts that we should care about marriage patterns "in their own right" because understanding "nuptiality change could further the understanding of other social change." Indeed, for those interested in family formation, the timing of first union merits investigation not only because it signals the initiation of reproductive life, but also because the marriage process reflects the way family life is organized and functions in a particular culture and because when, who, and how one marries all have implications for gender relations within society (Malhotra, 1997).

The age when men and women form marital unions is influenced by social norms and expectations regarding their roles as spouse and parent—factors that are plausibly changing with globalization, urbanization, and rising educational attainment; as such, the timing of marriage should be of considerable relevance to researchers interested in the transition to adulthood in the developing world. If, for example, men are now postponing marriage because of greater expectations about job status and employment stability and the material possessions needed to form a household, and women are delaying marriage because of shifting gender roles, it is important to document these patterns of behavior and understand what the potential implications are both for the individuals and for the larger society.

In recent years, few demographers have heeded van de Walle's (1993) appeal to explore the process and timing of marriage for its own sake. Yabiku and colleagues' (Yabiku, 2003; Yabiku et al., 2002) analysis of the effect of community variables on the timing of marriage in a region of Nepal experiencing rapid social change is a notable exception.[1] There is, however, a large descriptive literature. Although lacking much in the way of explanatory variables, this research documents trends and differentials in the age of first union among women, with a particular focus on the practice of early marriage in the developing world (see, e.g., Choe, Thapa, and Achmad, 2001; Heaton, Forste, and Otterstrom, 2002; Jejeebhoy, 1995; Rashad and Osman, 2003; Singh and Samara, 1996; Westoff, 2003).

This interest in early marriage reflects the concern of human rights and reproductive health advocates, who in putting "child marriage" on the international agenda have emphasized the potentially harmful consequences for young women of marrying too early. Researchers at the International Center for Research on Women (2004) highlight these possible problems in a rather dramatic fashion:

> Child brides are robbed of the ordinary life experiences other young people take for granted. Many are forced to drop out of school. Their health is at risk because of early sexual activity and childbearing. They cannot take advantage of economic opportunities. Friendships with peers are often restricted. Child marriage deprives girls of basic rights and subjects them to undue disadvantage—and sometimes violence. Countries with a high percentage of child marriage are more likely to experience extreme and persistent poverty, and high levels of maternal and child mortality.

While focus on marriage prior to age 18, the internationally established age of adulthood, has gained prominence, research has yet to establish the

---

[1]There are also several studies that predate van de Walle's call for further research. Fricke, Syed, and Smith's (1986) analysis of marriage timing strategies in Pakistan is noteworthy as is Lesthaeghe, Kaufman, and Meekers (1989) investigation of nuptiality regimes in sub-Saharan Africa, where the timing of marriage and the practice of polygyny were explored in great depth. This latter study was path breaking in linking ethnographic data (including measures of dependence on subsistence agriculture, lineage systems, inheritance, and presence of various types of chiefs) to demographic data. Malhotra and Tsui's (1996) study of the effect of norms about marriage—including the importance of setting up an independent household, the desire to work before marriage, and expectations about arranged marriage—on marriage timing in Sri Lanka is also an important contribution to the literature. To the best of our knowledge, it is the only analysis of marriage that uses panel data; however, while the attitudinal variables included in the event history models are measured prior to marriage, they are still likely to be endogenous to marriage timing.

causal links between early marriage and poor outcomes among women. Is it early marriage in and of itself that is the problem or is it the characteristics of those who marry early?

In contrast to the extensive documentation of female age at marriage, the literature on men is quite sparse (Malhotra, 1997). In part this limited attention to men is because demographic surveys, up until the last decade or so, have been restricted to women. But it is also due to the fact that across a wide spectrum of countries and cultures, relatively few men marry during the teenage years, and it is early marriage that is considered problematic and thus worthy of consideration.

In this chapter we will examine trends in the timing of first marriage or union for men and women. We define marriage broadly to include all socially recognized unions, including legal marriage as well as any other type of union that is recognized and reported in particular countries. The principal focus is on documenting trends in the age at marriage for the major regions of the developing world; however, the chapter also addresses a few subthemes: the current extent of early marriage, differences between men and women in trends in age at marriage, and the association between age at marriage and sociodemographic characteristics, specifically education and rural-urban residence. To the extent that changing patterns of behavior are revealed, we will try to identify to what such transformations might be attributed and draw on the demographic literature to provide insights.

UNDERSTANDING MARRIAGE TIMING

A number of scholars have conducted research on marriage timing. We begin with a brief review of the contributions of various social science disciplines to an understanding of age at marriage.

Historical Demography

Historical demographers have done an admirable job of documenting marriage patterns throughout Europe over the last few hundred years; however, they have fared less well in identifying a particular set of factors that explains trends across cultures. Hajnal (1965) first observed what he called a "European" pattern with late age at marriage and high proportions unmarried. In describing this distinctive pattern that existed from at least as early as the eighteenth century, he hypothesized that an association existed between marriage and household formation, arguing that when marriage involved the establishment of a new household, as it did in much of Western and Northern Europe, resource and skill acquisition were determining factors in the decision to wed. Wrigley and colleagues (1997, p. 122), in their history of English population from the end of the sixteenth century to the beginning of the nineteenth century, supported this view, concluding not only that "the pattern that Hajnal identified was of long standing in England," but also that the decision to marry hinged on the ability to set up an independent household.

While many have noted its "tremendous influence in the historical study of European marriage" (Ehmer, 2002, p. 306), Hajnal's theory of the links between age at marriage and economic self-sufficiency is not without its critics. Watkins (1986, p. 325), in her investigation of marriage in Europe between 1870 and 1960, reveals the inadequacy of Hajnal's explanation, at least in understanding change at the level of geographic aggregates. Examination of provincial data from the late nineteenth century reveals that nuptiality patterns were similar in neighboring provinces, but not necessarily within regions of a particular country. She argues that these contiguous regions shared a common culture and language and not necessarily common occupational structures, suggesting that societal conventions with regard to the timing of marriage existed independent of particular economic conditions. Other studies also suggest that the decision about when to marry may be rooted as much in societal norms as in economic realities. Lynch (1991), examining the experience in cities in Northwest Europe, observed that the pattern of late age at marriage and high rates of celibacy that characterized village society also described more urbanized areas in the nineteenth century. Although she presents herself as an adherent of Hajnal, her argument that the European Marriage Pattern prevailed even as Malthusian constraints weakened with the rise of fertility control is not consistent with a theory that connects age at marriage to economic resources. She claims that late age at marriage represents a set of cultural values, albeit values that emanated, in part, from economic realities of times past.

Individual country studies also reveal the inadequacy of an explanation linking household structure, the economic environment, and age at marriage. For example, an analysis of data from an agricultural region of north-central Italy in the late nineteenth and early twentieth centuries revealed that women married quite late, on average around 24 to 25, despite the fact that multiple-family households were common and patrilocal residence was the norm. Moreover, marriage age did not decline throughout "a period of dramatic social and economic changes," when wage labor supplanted share-cropping (Kertzer and Hogan, 1991, p. 34). In Ireland, even as incomes began to rise in the late nineteenth century, celibacy and late age of marriage continued to prevail (Guinnane, 1991). Proto-industrialization, which provided wage-earning opportunities for young men and women, did not always lead to reduced age at marriage, as Gutmann and Leboutte (1984) demonstrate for Eastern Belgium. They argue that land ownership patterns, the speed with which industrial development takes place, and the nature of that industry all play a role in the timing of marriage. Furthermore, case studies from other areas in Europe do not show a strong association between occupational groups and age at marriage (Kertzer and Hogan, 1991).

These demographic studies of historical Europe are useful for those investigating marriage in the developing world if only to emphasize that nuptiality trends defy easy explanation; while age at marriage is likely to be sensitive to the economic environment, the roots of particular marriage patterns would appear to lie in the distinctiveness of individual family systems.[2]

Social Anthropology

For social anthropologists, kinship systems—which include marriage rules and residential arrangements—have traditionally been a focal, if not *the* focal subject of ethnographic inquiry. While much effort has gone into documenting spouse selection patterns, living arrangements after marriage, and inheritance systems, the subject of age at marriage has been incidental to the larger goal of describing the way in which the overall kinship system and marriage rules function to maintain social order.

The structural-functionalist approach to kinship dominated cultural anthropology throughout much of the twentieth century. Although this paradigm is now considered overly "static" and even "obsolete" (Das Gupta, 1997, p. 36), many anthropologists are still interested in kinship patterns. However, the focus is no longer on delineating complicated marriage rules. Rather, kinship is explored within its broader political and economic context with a view toward understanding social change. Ahearn's (2001) ethnographic study of the way in which increased literacy and exposure to Hindi soap operas has led to a shift away from arranged and capture marriages toward love marriages in a Nepalese village is an example of this new type of kinship research. Yet she pays no attention to whether this transformation in the marriage process has had an effect on the timing of marriage. As was true of earlier kinship studies, no discussion of age at marriage is provided.

A collaborative study between anthropologists and demographers, also conducted in a Nepalese village, does focus explicitly on age at marriage. In the introduction to their chapter, Dahal, Fricke, and Thornton (1993, p. 305) explain why anthropologists should not ignore marriage timing:

---

[2]We thank George Alter for educating us on recent scholarship in historical demography as well as emphasizing the uniqueness of individual family systems and pointing out the danger in generalizing from Europe to the rest of the world (G. Alter, personal communication, April 23, 2004).

If particular marriage forms are evidence of wider strategies of social reproduction . . . then the timing of marriage should itself be seen as a part of that process. Thus marriage timing is no less the proper study of anthropology than any other element of marriage behavior. At the same time, marriage timing should be seen to have implications beyond the merely demographic.

They are critical of even the "most anthropologically informed demographers" who ignore family context in explaining age of marriage, and include only individual factors, such as education, to elucidate behavior change. Indeed, the explanatory variables used in this examination of Nepal set the research apart from conventional survey analyses. In addition to asking the standard demographic questions, information was collected on marriage characteristics of the parental generation, including measures of kin status of parents (cross-cousin or not), the nature of material exchange at their marriage, and the relative land holding of their families. Data were also collected on mothers' characteristics, including the inheritance at marriage and whether Nepali is spoken as well as the local language, all measures that reflect social status. Family context, namely "access to kin and marriage partner networks, intergenerational control and the prestige of natal groups," is found to be significant in explaining marriage timing (Dahal, Fricker, and Thornton, 1993, p. 319).

Sociology

Family sociologists, in contrast to social anthropologists, have not generally considered marriage patterns in developing countries to be within their purview. Goode's classic volume, *World Revolution and Family Patterns,* which is one of the standard textbooks of modernization theory, is the exception. Goode emphasizes the "fit" between the conjugal family and modern industrial society with its need for a geographically and socially mobile population. According to Goode, the ideal type of conjugal family excludes relatives from everyday decision making, establishes a new household at the time of marriage, and because the young person selects his or her own partner, is based on mutual attraction between spouses rather than on an alliance between families.[3] Writing in 1963, Goode (1963, p. 8) noted that in the West, the age of marriage for both men and women dropped during the twentieth century, leading him to conclude that predicting trends in age at marriage as a function of other secular changes in society is problematic:

---

[3]By conjugal, Goode does not mean nuclear. For him a nuclear family system is one where there is no interaction between relatives.

When such a [conjugal] system begins to emerge in a society, the age at marriage is likely to change because the goals of marriage change, but whether it will rise or fall cannot be predicted from the characteristics mentioned so far. In a conjugal system, the youngsters must now be old enough to take care of themselves, i.e., they must be as old as the economic system forces them to be in order to be independent at marriage.

Goode does not argue that industrialization and urbanization "caused" a change in family patterns in the West; rather, he observes that the family has had an independent effect on the development of industrialization in the West. He claims that "no one has yet succeeded in stating the determinate relations between family systems and economic or technological systems" (Goode, 1963, p. 22).

Although Goode was writing 40 years ago, we would argue that success still eludes us. With the exception of the work of Lesthaeghe, Kaufman, and Meekers (1989) on sub-Saharan Africa, and Fricke, Syed, and Smith (1986), Malhotra (1991, 1997), Malhotra and Tsui (1996), and Yabiku (2003; Yabiku et al., 2002) research on South Asia (see footnote 1), few demographic studies explore the timing and process of marriage in developing countries in any depth. In part this is a function of the limited breadth of the typical demographic survey. In contrast, the Asian Marriage Surveys, which were used by Malhotra (1991, 1997) and Fricke, Syed, and Smith (1986), collected extensive data on the marriage process. However, these surveys have limited utility for analyses of marriage timing because of a restriction to those who are married.

Economics

Economists have been less concerned than other social scientists with explaining marital behavior in the developing world. To the extent that they have been interested in marriage, the focus has been on modeling assortative mating (Montgomery and Sulak, 1989) and the increase in dowry payments in South Asia (Rao, 1993a, 1993b). Absent Gary Becker's (1973) seminal article on the theory of marriage, economists have paid much less attention to age at marriage. According to Becker, marriage is yet another manifestation of utility-maximizing behavior; people wed when the utility of being married exceeds that of being single. At the core of his argument is the notion that men and women bring different attributes to marriage and have different roles, such that there is "positive assortative mating of complementary traits" (Boulier and Rosenzweig, 1984, p. 714). As the wage differential between men and women narrows and presumably as women and men begin to substitute for one another, women's incentive to marry decreases. Since publication of Becker's theory, few economists have produced empirical analyses of marriage in the developing world. Using data from the early 1970s in the Philippines, Boulier and Rosenzweig (1984) provide confirmation of Becker's theory of marriage; they demonstrate that while the effect of education on age of marriage is exaggerated in models that treat education as exogenous, additional schooling does lead women to marry later. Brien and Lillard (1994) show that controlling for the effect of delayed marriage on education, that is, for the potential endogeneity of education, later age at marriage among women in Malaysia is explained in large part by increased enrollment and attainment. As Becker would predict, with increased schooling, the opportunity cost of marriage rises for women. However, no explanation is given for the continued significance of ethnicity in models of marriage timing.

With the exception of Becker's work, we have few theories that explicitly address age at marriage, even fewer studies that economists would consider acceptable in addressing the endogeneity problems that arise in studies of the determinants of marriage timing, and still fewer studies that collect the appropriate data to adequately explain when people marry. That said, a considerable literature on the correlates of age at marriage exists, as does speculation about determinants and trends, particularly about reasons for the increase in age of marriage among women. In the next section, we will analyze data on age at marriage from 83 developing countries. We will then return to the demographic literature to help us shed light on the trends we observe.

DATA SOURCES

Data on the age at first marriage are obtained from two sources: (1) a database compiled by the United Nations (UN) Population Division that draws in part from population censuses, and (2) nationally representative DHS.

The UN database provides the percentage of the population married in 5-year age groups for most developing countries (United Nations Population Division, 2000). For this analysis, we consider all countries in Africa, Asia, and Latin America with the exception of those identified by the World Bank as "high income" and those with a population of less than 140,000[4] (World Bank, 2002).[5] Given the chapter's focus on trends, we have identi-

---

[4]If a country had fewer than 140,000 in population, the UN did not provide data.

[5] Income data for all countries but East Timor were obtained from the World Bank's 2002 *World Development Indicators*. For East Timor, the income data were obtained from the World Bank website.

fied 74[6] countries of the 117[7] that meet our criteria for which recent data, that is, data collected in 1990 or later, are available and for which information exists from two censuses or surveys at least 10 years apart. For analyses based on this database, we excluded countries for which a census or survey was not available for both sexes; moreover, we used the same data set for both men and women even if a more recent census or survey was available for women because we wanted to have fully comparable data for both sexes. There are 1.4 billion young people ages 10 to 24 in these 117 countries; 87 percent or 1.2 billion are resident in the 73 countries for which data on trends in proportions married are available. Coverage varies considerably by region.

These data represent approximately 90 percent or more of the population in East and Southern Africa, South Central and Southeast Asia, East Asia, South America and the Caribbean, and Central America, but only 63 percent of the population in the Middle East, 31 percent in West and Middle Africa, and 38 percent in the former Soviet Asia. Note that results for the subregion of East Asia consist entirely of China, as data are unavailable for the two other countries, Mongolia and North Korea. Populous countries for which data are unavailable from the UN database include Afghanistan, Algeria, Democratic Republic of the Congo, Ghana, Iraq, Nigeria, Saudi Arabia, Uzbekistan, and Vietnam.

Survey data come from the DHS carried out by Macro International Inc.[8] The data on age at marriage are obtained in personal interviews with nationally representative samples of individual respondents of reproductive age and are part of an extensive questionnaire covering a full range of sexual and reproductive behaviors. Surveys of women (typically ages 15 to 49) were available for 51 countries in South and Southeast Asia, North

---

[6]Data are not available for 15- to 19-year-olds for Argentina and data are not available for 20- to 29-year-olds for Bahrain due to nonstandard age groups. However, for other age groups, the data for these countries are included.

[7]According to the United Nations (2003), there are a total of 152 countries in Asia, Africa, and Latin America. Thirteen of these contain fewer than 140,000 in population, 16 are listed by the World Bank as high income, and 5 have no World Bank income data. Note that updates of country income groupings on the World Bank website (www.worldbank.org/data/countryclass/classgroups.htm) as of September 30, 2002, led the panel to make a few adjustments to these country groupings including shifting South Korea into the high-income group and therefore out of the developing country group.

[8]The DHS is limited to the household population. Ordinarily they do not survey persons residing in institutions, which may include military personnel and perhaps even students in boarding schools and university dormitories, although this varies by country. The data are also subject to nonresponse error. As compared to rates for surveys in high-income countries, nonresponse rates in the DHS are low. However, the rate can be assumed to be higher for unmarried young adults, especially young adult males, than for older adults.

Africa and the Middle East, sub-Saharan Africa, and Latin America and the Caribbean; surveys of men (ages 15 to 59, in most cases) were available for 32 countries, 29 in sub-Saharan Africa, Latin America, and the Caribbean.[9] Note that unmarried women were not included in the survey of individual women for a number of surveys in Asia and the Middle East. However, unmarried women are listed in the household survey and information on their age, education, and rural-urban location is obtained for these countries, with some exceptions noted in the relevant tables. Using weights provided as part of the microdata files, we adjust for the missing unmarried women by age, place of residence, and education, so that the denominators for the proportion married correctly include all women in the respective subgroups.

The country-specific data are aggregated into averages for subregions (using United Nations geographic groupings[10]), weighting countries according to their population size. For both sets of data, weighted averages are calculated, where the weights are the country's percentage of the region's population or income grouping's population ages 10 to 24 based on UN estimates in 2000.[11]

There are a few countries for which DHS data are available but UN data are not. For example, while there is a DHS for Nigeria, the most populous country in sub-Saharan Africa, the UN does not provide data for the two time periods required for both men and women. Table 5-1 provides a list of the individual countries from each source.

Census data, which are the main source for the database compiled by the UN Population Division, are generally reported by the head of the household, not by individual household members themselves. By comparison, the DHS data on marital status and age at marriage are obtained by personal interviews with the individual respondents themselves with the exception of unmarried women in some Asian and Middle Eastern countries, as mentioned above.

As noted earlier, in this chapter we apply the broad definition of marriage generally used by cross-country comparative studies, that is, marriage is defined to include all of the different forms of socially recognized unions: cohabitation, consensual unions, "free unions," and marriage that is legiti-

---

[9]As we indicated, the analyses based on UN data only include countries where data for both men and women are available. Given that the vast majority of countries have data for both sexes, this restriction is not at all onerous. However, for analyses based on DHS data, we did not limit ourselves to countries where data were available for both sexes because we would be left with too few countries.

[10]The individual country data are available from the authors.

[11]Note that the weights are each country's percentage of the 2000 population ages 10-24 for all countries included in our sample for that region and not for all countries in the region (United Nations Population Division, Department of Economic and Social Affairs, 2001).

TABLE 5-1 Country Lists by Region

United Nations Database on Marriage

Country	Region[a]	Census/Survey Year 1	Census/Survey Year 2
Belize	Carib/CA	1980	1991
Dominican Republic	Carib/CA	1981	1996
El Salvador	Carib/CA	1971	1992
Guatemala	Carib/CA	1973	1990
Haiti	Carib/CA	1989	2000
Mexico	Carib/CA	1980	1990
Nicaragua	Carib/CA	1971	1998
Panama	Carib/CA	1980	1990
Puerto Rico	Carib/CA	1980	1990
Trinidad and Tobago	Carib/CA	1980	1990
Botswana	E/S Africa	1981	1991
Burundi	E/S Africa	1979	1990
Comoros	E/S Africa	1980	1996
Ethiopia	E/S Africa	1984	2000
Kenya	E/S Africa	1969	1998
Malawi	E/S Africa	1987	2000
Mauritius	E/S Africa	1972	1990
Mozambique	E/S Africa	1980	1997
Namibia	E/S Africa	1960	1991
Rwanda	E/S Africa	1978	1996
South Africa	E/S Africa	1985	1996
Tanzania	E/S Africa	1978	1996
Uganda	E/S Africa	1969	1995
Zambia	E/S Africa	1980	1999
Zimbabwe	E/S Africa	1982	1999
China	EA	1987	1999
Bahrain	ME	1981	1991
Egypt	ME	1986	1996
Jordan	ME	1979	1994
Morocco	ME	1982	1994
Occup. Palestinian Territory	ME	1967	1997
Sudan	ME	1983	1993
Tunisia	ME	1984	1994
Turkey	ME	1980	1990
Argentina	SA	1980	1991
Bolivia	SA	1988	1998
Brazil	SA	1980	1996
Chile	SA	1982	1992
Colombia	SA	1973	1993
Ecuador	SA	1974	1990
Guyana	SA	1980	1991
Paraguay	SA	1982	1992
Peru	SA	1981	1996

Demographic and Health Surveys

Country	Region[a]	Most Recent Survey	* = Includes Male Survey
Dominican Republic	Carib/CA	1996	*
Guatemala	Carib/CA	1998-1999	
Haiti	Carib/CA	2000	*
Nicaragua	Carib/CA	1997-1998	*
Comoros	E/S Africa	1996	*
Ethiopia	E/S Africa	1999	*
Kenya	E/S Africa	1998	*
Madagascar	E/S Africa	1997	
Malawi	E/S Africa	2000	*
Mozambique	E/S Africa	1997	*
Namibia	E/S Africa	1992	
Rwanda	E/S Africa	2000	
South Africa	E/S Africa	1998	
Tanzania	E/S Africa	1999	*
Uganda	E/S Africa	2000-2001	*
Zambia	E/S Africa	1996-1997	*
Zimbabwe	E/S Africa	1999	*
Egypt	ME	2000	
Jordan	ME	1997	
Morocco	ME	1992	
Turkey	ME	1998	* [b]
Yemen	ME	1991-1992	
Bolivia	SA	1998	*
Brazil	SA	1996	*
Colombia	SA	2000	
Paraguay	SA	1990	
Peru	SA	2000	*
Bangladesh	SC/SE Asia	1999-2000	
India	SC/SE Asia	1998-2000	
Indonesia	SC/SE Asia	1997	
Nepal	SC/SE Asia	2000-2001	
Pakistan	SC/SE Asia	1990-1991	
Philippines	SC/SE Asia	1998	
Vietnam	SC/SE Asia	1997	
Armenia	Soviet	2000	* [b]
Kazakhstan	Soviet	1999	* [b]
Kyrgyz Republic	Soviet	1997	
Uzbekistan	Soviet	1996	
Benin	W/M Africa	1996	*
Burkina Faso	W/M Africa	1998-1999	*
Cameroon	W/M Africa	1998	*
Central African Republic	W/M Africa	1994-1995	*
Chad	W/M Africa	1996-1997	*

Continued

TABLE 5-1 Continued

United Nations Database on Marriage

Country	Region[a]	Census/Survey Year 1	Census/Survey Year 2
Uruguay	SA	1985	1996
Venezuela	SA	1974	1990
Bangladesh	SC/SE Asia	1981	1991
Cambodia	SC/SE Asia	1962	1998
India	SC/SE Asia	1981	1992-1993
Indonesia	SC/SE Asia	1980	1990
Iran	SC/SE Asia	1986	1996
Malaysia	SC/SE Asia	1980	1991
Maldives	SC/SE Asia	1985	1995
Myanmar	SC/SE Asia	1973	1991
Nepal	SC/SE Asia	1981	1991
Pakistan	SC/SE Asia	1981	1998
Philippines	SC/SE Asia	1980	1995
Thailand	SC/SE Asia	1980	1990
Azerbaijan	Soviet	1989	1999
Kazakhstan	Soviet	1989	1999
Kyrgyz Republic	Soviet	1989	1999
Benin	W/M Africa	1979	1996
Burkina Faso	W/M Africa	1985	1999
Cameroon	W/M Africa	1987	1998
Cape Verde	W/M Africa	1980	1990
Central African Republic	W/M Africa	1975	1994-1995
Chad	W/M Africa	1964	1996
Côte d'Ivoire	W/M Africa	1978	1994
Gabon	W/M Africa	1961	2000
Gambia	W/M Africa	1983	1993
Mali	W/M Africa	1976	1995-1996
Mauritania	W/M Africa	1988	2000-2001
Niger	W/M Africa	1988	1998
Senegal	W/M Africa	1978	1997

[a]Key: Carib/CA (Caribbean and Central America); EA (Eastern Asia); E/S Africa (Eastern and Southern Africa); ME (Middle East [Northern Africa and Western Asia]); SA (South America); SC/SE Asia (South-central and South-eastern Asia); Soviet (Former Soviet Asia); W/M Africa (Western and Middle Africa). Regional groupings based on United Nations World Population Prospects: The 2002 Revision (2003).

Demographic and Health Surveys

Country	Region[a]	Most Recent Survey	* = Includes Male Survey
Côte d'Ivoire	W/M Africa	1998-1999	*
Gabon	W/M Africa	2000	* c
Ghana	W/M Africa	1998-1999	*
Guinea	W/M Africa	1999	*
Mali	W/M Africa	2001	*
Niger	W/M Africa	1998	*
Nigeria	W/M Africa	1999	*
Senegal	W/M Africa	1997	*
Togo	W/M Africa	1998	*

[b]Male survey data are available for these countries, but not in sufficient number to allow aggregation of data to generate regional averages.

[c]Gabon data on women unavailable at time of this analysis; data on men do not include schooling.

NOTE: Middle East, South-central, and South-eastern Asia are excluded from Figure 5-2 and Table 5-9 because the surveys are based on ever-married samples.

mated by custom, religious rites, or civil law. Note, however, that the definition of marriage used in censuses may be more variable than that used in standardized surveys. For the DHS, marriage is a self-defined state. Respondents are coded as married if they say so in response to questions on whether they are currently or ever married or are living with a man. Thus age at first marriage is typically age at first cohabitation with a partner or husband (Kishor, 2003). For censuses, countries typically define marriage to reflect the forms of marriage and union that are generally recognized and accepted, and obtain information accordingly; as a result, for the most part, data on marriage/union status is largely comparable between censuses and surveys. For example, in Latin America, census questions on marital/union status include the category "consensual union" because this is a widely occurring and acknowledged form of union. However, in countries where cohabitation or living together are much less common, "consensual union" may not be explicitly included as a category, with the result that this type of arrangement may be underreported.

Note that the reporting of age and marital status in the censuses and surveys on which our analysis is based is assumed to be accurate. In certain populations, however, this assumption may be questionable particularly when the reporting is retrospective. In Africa, where formation of a marital union has been described as a process that takes place in stages, marriage is not a well-defined event and therefore age at marriage is difficult to establish (van de Walle and Meekers, 1994). To the extent that particular rites and ceremonies have lost significance or been eliminated as the population becomes more urbanized and better educated, comparisons over time are problematic. In countries where, at least officially, early marriage violates newly passed legislation, observed declines in the proportion married at or by a particular age may simply reflect increases in deliberate misreporting. Finally, in countries where age is not reported with a great deal of accuracy, the timing of an event that occurred in the remote past is often estimated to take place closer to the survey than it actually did. Thus in the DHS older women are more likely to report that a marriage took place at a later age (Blanc and Rutenberg, 1990).

TRENDS IN AGE AT MARRIAGE

To what extent has age at marriage changed in recent years? Have the trends for men and women mirrored one another or are they divergent? If men and women are now postponing marriage in increasing numbers, to what can such a transformation in marriage patterns be attributed?

In this section we analyze two different measures of age at marriage to describe trends: (1) the percentage of specific age groups married, based on reports of current status, and (2) the percentage of women married by ages 18, 20, and 25 and the percentage of men married by ages 20, 25, and 30, based on retrospective reports.[12] We include these measures because they are commonly used and we want to determine whether they present a consistent picture of trends in age at marriage in the developing world. Note that there are some differences in extent of geographic coverage of the two measures. The first measure, taken from the UN database, includes 73 countries with information for each of the time periods of interest (1970-1989 and 1990-2000) for men and women, and has some representation of all developing regions. The second measure, the percentage married by specific ages, is based for women on 51 DHS countries with representation from 7 of the 8 developing regions and is based for men on 29 DHS countries with representation from only Latin America and the Caribbean and sub-Saharan Africa.

Note that the United Nations Population Division monitors marriage trends with the singulate mean age at marriage (SMAM), a synthetic cohort measure calculated from census or survey data on the proportions single by 5-year age groups (United Nations, 2003). Although it is referred to as the mean age at marriage, it is actually the mean age at first marriage among those who marry by age 50 or more precisely the average number of years spent single for those who marry before 50 (United Nations Department of International Economic and Social Affairs, 1990).[13] Because the SMAM assumes stability (no change over time in the age-specific incidence of first marriage), it can be misleading when increasing percentages of young people delay marriage and ultimately remain unmarried. If the proportion of young people who ultimately marry is lower than the current proportion aged 50 who have married, the SMAM will be artificially inflated. Preston, Heuveline, and Guillot (2001, p. 89) caution against using the SMAM when nuptiality patterns are changing, noting [the] "SMAM is a hodge-podge of rates in the recent and distant past." However, they do not indicate how and to what extent it is distorted. A comparison of the median age at marriage with the SMAM for women in 118 DHS reveals that for 117 of

---

[12]Note that a substantial decline in the proportion of men and women who marry early may have a small effect on the mean age at marriage for a population. But for those interested in the transition to adulthood, such a decline is of considerable importance because of its potential impact on the lives of young people.

[13]The SMAM, which assumes no marriages before age 15, is computed as follows: (1) sum the proportions single and multiply this sum by 5 (because of the 5-year age groups); (2) subtract the number of years lived by those who do not marry before age 50; (3) divide this total by the proportion who marry by age 50, which is 1 minus the average of the proportion single at ages 45-49 and 50-54; and (4) add 15, which is the number of years lived in the single state before age 15 (see Shryock et al., 1971).

the 118, the SMAM is higher than the median by about 7 years on average, which is to be expected as the distribution of marriage ages is right skewed (analysis conducted by John Bongaarts not shown).[14]

Trend in Percentage Married Among Young People Ages 15 to 29

Tables 5-2 and 5-3 provide data by region on the percentage of women married for three age cohorts, 15 to 19, 20 to 24, and 25 to 29 and for men (for whom marriage during the teenage years is rare) for two age cohorts, 20-24 and 25-29. Given that the interval between censuses or surveys varies by country, an annualized rate of change is computed.

For all regions except the former Soviet Asia, and South America, where early marriage was not that common even 10 to 20 years ago, teenage marriage has declined considerably among women. The reduction in the percent of 15- to 19-year-olds married is particularly striking in Africa. The percentage married among 20- to 24-year-olds has also fallen markedly in most regions, with the exception again of South America. While the majority of developing country women are married by ages 25 to 29, regions where 15 to 25 percent of women are still not married by the late 20s include South America, the Caribbean and Central America, the Middle East, the former Soviet Asia, and East and Southern Africa.

Not only is marriage during the teenage years extremely rare among men, but marriage in the early 20s is also much less common among men than among women and, in some regions, has declined substantially in recent years. For example, in East and Southern Africa, East Asia, the former Soviet Asia, and the Middle East, a large reduction has taken place in the percentage of men married at ages 20 to 24 in the last decade or so.

By ages 25 to 29, sizeable numbers of men in developing countries have wed. However, in certain regions marriage is postponed until the 30s for a large proportion of men. In South America, this pattern is observed in the earlier period and seems to have stabilized. In the Middle East and the former Soviet Asia, there is evidence of increasing delay recently.

In summary, Tables 5-2 and 5-3 reveal declines in the proportion married for both sexes in most regions; the exceptions are South America for men and women, and for men only, West and Middle Africa and South and Southeast Asia. For six of the eight regional groupings, the patterns for men parallel those for women; the exceptions are South and Southeast Asia and West and Middle Africa, where substantial declines are observed in the proportions married for women at ages 15 to 19 and 20 to 24, but little or no change for men at ages 20 to 24 and 25 to 29. While many regions have

---

[14]The median will only be higher than the SMAM in situations where a large fraction of women do not marry.

witnessed declines in the proportions married among young people of both sexes, it is in China and the countries of the Middle East that the change has been most consistent across the three age groups for women and the two age groups for men.

Trends in Percentage of Women Married by Ages 18, 20, and 25: DHS Analysis

The DHS provide additional information to supplement what is available from the United Nations database. Age at first marriage, rather than just current marital status, is obtained on these surveys, enabling the calculation of the proportion of women married by a particular age rather than just the percentage of a particular age group who are married. The one drawback is that the surveys have been conducted in fewer countries than are included in the UN database. To reflect the earlier timing of marriage among women, we examine the proportions married before ages 18, 20, and 25, and for men the proportion married before ages 20, 25, and 30. We compare these proportions across age groups in order to approximately measure trends over time.

The data for women are provided in Table 5-4. The first column indicates the percentage of each region's population that is represented by the DHS. Coverage is highest in East and Southern Africa with approximately 92 percent of the population represented, and lowest in the Caribbean and Central America where, because no recent survey is available for Mexico, by far the largest country, only about one fifth of the population is represented. It is also important to keep in mind that no data are available for East Asia, which includes China. Note, however, there are a few countries for which DHS data are available that are not included in the UN database: Madagascar, Yemen, Vietnam, Ghana, Guinea, Nigeria, Togo, Armenia, and Uzbekistan.

The trends in early marriage revealed by these data are more or less consistent with those shown in Table 5-2, which is reassuring given the difference in the number of countries and the nature of the data—retrospective versus current status. First, the regional rankings essentially follow the same sequence; moreover, the ranking changes little by age group. West and Middle Africa is the region with the greatest percentage of women marrying at young ages, followed by South and Southeast Asia, East and Southern Africa, and the Caribbean and Central America. The Middle East, South America, and the former Soviet Asia have smaller proportions of women who marry early. Second, a comparison of the percentage married across age groups indicates that there has been little change in South America, the Caribbean and Central America, and the former Soviet Asia. Indeed, in the former Soviet Asia, a greater percentage of 20- to 24-year-

TABLE 5-2 Percentage of Women Ever Married, by Age, Time Period, and Region[a] (Weighted[b] Averages)

	% of Region Population Represented	Ages 15-19		
Region		Time 1[c] 1970-1989	Time 2 1990-2000	Annual Change
Africa				
Eastern/Southern Africa	89.8	37.5	24.5	−.75
Western/Middle Africa	30.8	53.0	38.4	−.89
Asia				
Eastern Asia[d]	98.1	4.2	1.3	−.24
South-central/South-eastern Asia	93.3	39.6	32.3	−.64
Former Soviet[e] Asia	37.8	9.4	9.6	.02
Latin America and Caribbean				
Caribbean/Central America	87.5	20.6	18.1	−.27
South America[f]	99.9	14.4	16.3	.12
Middle East[g]				
Western Asia/Northern Africa	62.8	21.0	14.9	−.59
TOTAL	86.5	26.6	20.8	−.48

[a]Regional groupings based on United Nations *World Population Prospects: The 2002 Revision* (2003).

[b]Weighting is based on United Nations population estimates for year 2000 (*World Population Prospects: The 2000 Revision*, POP/DB/WPP/Rev. 2000/3/F1. February 2001).

[c]For the following countries, the first survey/census was before 1970: Cambodia (1962), Chad (1964), Gabon (1961), Kenya (1969), Namibia (1960), Palestine (1967), and Uganda (1969).

olds have married early than 30- to 34-year-olds. Other regions reveal a considerable decline in the percentage married by these ages with a greater decline in the percent married by age 18 than in the percent married by age 20. The decline in early marriage is particularly sizeable in the Middle East, where there is a 49 percent reduction between 20- and 24-year-olds and 40- and 44-year-olds in the percentage married by age 18, and a 38 percent decline in the percentage married by age 20. Note that little change is observed in the percentage married by age 25 among the two age groups for which this can be computed, with the exception of the Middle East and sub-Saharan Africa. Note, also, with the exception of the former Soviet Asia, the regional ranking for age 25 among 30-to 34-year-olds is quite similar to that for age 18. For example, West and Middle Africa and South and Southeast Asia are the regions with the highest percentage of women married by ages 18 and 25.

Ages 20-24			Ages 25-29		
Time 1[c] 1970-1989	Time 2 1990-2000	Annual Change	Time 1[c] 1970-1989	Time 2 1990-2000	Annual Change
77.2	65.6	–.71	89.2	83.4	–.38
85.1	78.6	–.40	93.5	92.3	–.05
60.1	45.9	–1.19	95.9	91.6	–.36
80.6	77.4	–.30	93.7	93.4	–.02
61.2	54.0	–.70	85.0	80.7	–.42
59.4	56.1	–.35	81.0	79.3	–.20
51.1	51.3	.03	75.9	76.0	.00
64.5	54.6	–.95	87.7	81.4	–.58
70.8	63.9	–.56	91.6	89.4	–.18

[d]There are 3 countries in this region, China, North Korea, and Mongolia; data are available only for China, which contains 98 percent of the region's population ages 10 to 24.
[e]Former Soviet Asia includes former Soviet Republics in South-central and Western Asia.
[f]15- to 19-year-old married data not available for Argentina, Survey 1.
[g]Data for Bahrain limited to 15-19 age group, other data in nonstandard age groups.
SOURCE: United Nations Population Division Database on Marriage Patterns (Pop/1/DB/ 2000/3), 73 countries, 1960-2001. See Table 5-1 for list of countries.

In summarizing the data on trends, it needs to be emphasized that while marriage during the teenage years is declining in many regions of the world, substantial proportions of women are still marrying extremely early. Indeed, as Table 5-4 indicates, for the countries where DHS data are available, more than a third of women currently ages 20 to 24 married prior to age 18.

Trends in Percentage of Men in sub-Saharan Africa Married by Ages 20, 25, and 30: DHS Analysis

Recently, Demographic and Health Surveys have been conducted among men in a number of countries in sub-Saharan Africa, Latin America and the Caribbean, and the former Soviet Asia. However, only in sub-Saharan Africa and Latin America and the Caribbean are there a sufficient number of countries with male surveys to aggregate the data and generate

TABLE 5-3 Percentage of Men Ever Married, by Age, Time Period, and Region (Weighted Averages)

Region	% of Region Population Represented	Ages 20-24			Ages 25-29		
		Time 1[a] 1970-1989	Time 2 1990-2000	Annual Change	Time 1[a] 1970-1989	Time 2 1990-2000	Annual Change
Africa							
Eastern/Southern Africa	89.8	36.0	27.8	-.56	71.8	66.5	-.42
Western/Middle Africa	30.8	28.4	26.5	-.10	61.6	60.5	-.04
Asia							
Eastern Asia	98.1	39.0	24.9	-1.17	82.7	77.2	-.46
South-central/South-eastern Asia	93.3	41.6	41.4	-.03	77.5	77.2	-.01
Former Soviet Asia	37.8	31.9	23.9	-.81	78.0	66.0	-1.20
Latin America and Caribbean							
Caribbean/Central America	87.5	38.4	37.5	-.14	72.0	68.8	-.36
South America	99.9	28.3	29.3	.06	65.3	62.8	-.18
Middle East[b]							
Western Asia/Northern Africa	62.6	24.9	16.8	-.78	63.0	53.4	-.91
TOTAL	86.5	37.9	33.0	-.41	76.0	73.1	-.24

[a]For the following countries, the first survey/census was before 1970: Cambodia (1962), Chad (1964), Gabon (1961), Kenya (1969), Namibia (1960), Palestine (1967), and Uganda (1969).

[b]Bahrain excluded; data in nonstandard age groups.

NOTE: For source of regional groupings and population data for weighted averages, see Table 5-2.

SOURCE: United Nations Population Division Database on Marriage Patterns (Pop/1/DB/2000/3), 72 countries, 1960-2001. See Table 5-1 for list of countries.

TABLE 5-4 Percentage of Women Married, by Ages 18, 20, and 25, by Age at Time of Survey and Region (Weighted Averages)

Region	% of Region Population Represented	Age 18			Age 20			Age 25	
		20-24	30-34	40-44	20-24	30-34	0-44	30-34	40-44
Africa									
Eastern/Southern Africa	91.7	36.5	45.7	52.8	54.6	62.9	69.2	83.6	88.2
Western/Middle Africa[a]	75.2	44.8	55.0	57.9	60.1	69.5	73.6	88.7	92.6
Asia									
South-central/South-eastern Asia	86.0	41.5	54.2	57.6	59.5	71.0	74.3	90.4	92.4
Former Soviet Asia	68.4	15.9	10.9	14.2	49.9	39.7	45.9	87.8	87.2
Latin America and the Caribbean									
Caribbean/Central America	21.0	34.9	35.7	38.4	53.3	53.7	58.1	82.3	82.5
South America	74.1	22.7	22.5	21.9	38.0	39.7	39.6	73.1	75.2
Middle East									
Western Asia/Northern Africa	54.8	23.2	35.1	45.5	39.8	52.2	64.2	81.7	87.2
TOTAL	59.8	37.7	48.2	52.0	55.5	65.0	69.1	87.2	89.8

[a]Gabon excluded; data on women unavailable at time of this analysis.
NOTE: For source of regional groupings and population data for weighted averages, see Table 5-2.
SOURCE: DHS tabulations, 51 countries, 1990-2001. See Table 5-1 for list of countries.

regional averages.[15] Table 5-5 provides these data for ages 20, 25, and 30 by age group for 29 countries with surveys between 1994 and 2001; 9 East and Southern African countries, 14 West and Middle African countries, 3 South American countries, and 3 Caribbean and Central American countries.

While this table indicates little consistent change in Latin America and the Caribbean, slight declines in the proportion of men married in both sub-Saharan African regions are observed; however, the declines are considerably smaller than those seen for women. Note that, in comparison to Table 5-3, a smaller decline is observed for East and Southern Africa and a larger decline for West and Middle Africa. These discrepancies arise because of differences in the countries included in the analyses. Nigeria, which constitutes nearly half of the population of West Africa and where there has been a considerable decline in early marriage for young men (10.8 percent married by age 20 among 20- to 24-year-olds, compared with 19.5 percent among 40- to 44-year-olds), is not included in the UN database. Furthermore, DHS data are not available for South Africa, where there has been a large decline in the percentage of men married in their 20s. That a substantial percentage of the male population is not included in our DHS analysis may distort the regional estimates. Indeed, in a recent analysis of DHS data on marriage, it is observed that "the trend toward later ages at marriage for women is not evident for men surveyed in sub-Saharan Africa" (Westoff, 2003, p. 1), an assertion that would likely be modified if data were available for more countries.

DIFFERENTIALS IN AGE AT MARRIAGE

An examination of differentials in the timing of marriage by educational attainment and place of residence, which is possible with DHS data, may provide insights into the forces behind the trends we have observed. Tables 5-6 and 5-7 are limited to women ages 20 to 24 and indicate the percentage married by age 18 by years of schooling attained and by rural-urban residence, respectively. Table 5-8 is limited to men ages 20 to 24 from sub-Saharan Africa, Latin America, and the Caribbean, and indicates the percentage married by age 20 by years of schooling attained and rural-urban residence.

As expected, large differentials by education and residence are observed for both sexes. Women and men with 8 or more years of schooling are much less likely to marry early than are those with 0 to 3 years of schooling.

---

[15]There are an additional 6 countries for which male marriage data are available: Bolivia, Dominican Republic, Haiti, Nicaragua, Peru, and Kazakhstan.

TABLE 5-5 Percentage of Men Married, by Ages 20, 25, and 30, by Age at Time of Survey and Region (Weighted Averages)

Region	% of Region Population Represented	Age 20			Age 25		Age 30	
		20-24	30-34	40-44	30-34	40-44	30-34	40-44
Africa								
Eastern/Southern Africa	69.5	13.8	20.0	21.3	59.3	61.0	86.7	87.7
Western/Middle Africa	75.5	12.0	16.2	17.5	47.7	50.9	77.0	76.5
Latin America and the Caribbean								
Caribbean/Central America	13.7	22.2	20.4	21.9	55.3	58.0	76.0	80.1
South America	60.3	14.0	18.2	10.8	58.7	57.4	80.7	85.6
TOTAL	60.5	13.5	18.1	16.9	54.8	56.2	81.1	82.7

NOTE: For source of regional groupings and population data for weighted averages, see Table 5-2.
SOURCE: DHS tabulations, 29 countries, 1994-2001. See Table 5-1 for list of countries.

TABLE 5-6 Percentage of Women Ages 20 to 24 Married by Age 18, by Years of Schooling and Region[a] (Weighted Averages)

Region	% of Region Population Represented	Years of Schooling		
		0-3	4-7	8+
Africa				
Eastern/Southern Africa	91.7	51.2	38.6	12.6
Western/Middle Africa[b]	75.2	70.5	36.8	14.1
Asia				
South-central/South-eastern Asia[c]	28.0	55.7	44.0	17.3
Latin America and the Caribbean				
Caribbean/Central America	21.0	55.5	43.9	14.7
South America	74.1	41.7	30.3	10.8
Middle East				
Western Asia/Northern Africa[d]	49.6	38.9	25.6	6.4
TOTAL	34.4	53.2	37.6	13.5

[a]Former Soviet Asia excluded; too few women with less than 8+ years of schooling.
[b]Gabon excluded; data on women unavailable at time of this analysis.
[c]India and Pakistan excluded; lack the "all-women" weight.
[d]Yemen excluded; lacks the "all-women" weight.
NOTE: For source of regional groupings and population data for weighted averages, see Table 5-2.
SOURCE: DHS tabulations, 44 countries, 1990-2001. See Table 5-1 for list of countries.

Young people in urban areas are much less likely to marry early than those living in the countryside. While these differentials are considerable, in the regions where data are available for both men and women, greater variability exists in the timing of marriage by education than by residence. For example, in East and Southern Africa, more than four times as many women with 0 to 3 years of schooling marry before age 18 as do women with 8-plus years of schooling, whereas 1.6 times as many women in rural areas marry before age 18 as do women in urban areas.

EXPLAINING TRENDS IN AGE AT MARRIAGE

As we have documented, in most regions of the developing world, young people are delaying marriage by comparison to older generations. Given how widespread this change is, an explanation that spans different cultures would seem warranted. We recognize the specificity of marriage markets and the marital process across time and place. For example, in West Africa, changes in the practice of polygyny, a distinctive feature of that region, may help to explain why age of marriage is increasing for

TABLE 5-7 Percentage of Women Ages 20 to 24 Married by Age 18, by Rural-Urban Residence, and Region (Weighted Averages)

Region	% of Region Population Represented	Residence Rural	Urban
Africa			
Eastern/Southern Africa	91.7	41.0	25.3
Western/Middle Africa[a]	75.2	52.2	30.1
Asia			
South-central/South-eastern Asia	86.0	48.4	24.3
Former Soviet Asia	68.4	17.9	13.9
Latin America/Caribbean			
Caribbean/Central America	21.0	44.5	27.6
South America	74.1	31.4	20.3
Middle East			
Western Asia/Northern Africa	54.8	28.3	16.7
TOTAL	59.8	44.4	23.9

[a]Gabon excluded; data on women unavailable at time of this analysis.
NOTE: For source of regional groupings and population data for weighted averages, see Table 5-2.
SOURCE: DHS tabulations, 51 countries, 1990-2001. See Table 5-1 for list of countries.

TABLE 5-8 Percentage of Men Ages 20 to 24 Married by Age 20, by Years of Schooling, Rural-Urban Residence, and Region (Weighted Averages)

Schooling and Residence	South America	Caribbean/ Central America	Eastern/ Southern Africa	Western/ Middle Africa[a]
Years of schooling				
0-3	20.7	24.6	20.9	21.0
4-7	18.0	30.9	16.7	14.5
8+	10.0	13.9	6.5	6.0
Residence				
Rural	13.4	26.5	15.5	16.0
Urban	14.0	18.2	8.2	5.1
% of region population represented	60.3	13.7	69.5	75.5

[a]Gabon excluded from schooling; missing data on men. Niger excluded from schooling; no respondents ages 20 to 24 are recorded with 8 or more years of schooling.
NOTE: For source of regional groupings and population data for weighted averages, see Table 5-2.
SOURCE: DHS tabulations, 29 countries, 1994-2001. See Table 5-1 for list of countries.

women but not for men in several countries.[16] While acknowledging the unique characteristics of nuptiality in individual countries, a review paper that covers so much territory should seek some general explanations as to why early marriage is less common now than in the past.

Explaining Trends Among Women

The Rise in Educational Attainment

To what can we attribute the rise in age of first marriage among women? Increased schooling is a leading candidate: In all regions of the developing world, save for the countries of the former Soviet Asia, there has been an increase in mean grades of schooling attained among young women in the last few decades (National Research Council and Institute of Medicine, 2005, Chapter 3). This expansion in education, combined with the magnitude in the differentials we observe in Table 5-6 in all regions, has led many to argue that increased schooling is the main force underlying the delay in first marriage among females (United Nations Commission on Population and Development, 2002).

A closer examination of the data raises doubts about the dominant role of educational change as a cause of nuptiality change. For one thing, trends in education and age of marriage are not always closely connected. Indeed, the region with the largest increase in educational attainment among young people—South and Southeast Asia—is not the region with the largest decline in early marriage. (Early marriage among young women has fallen most dramatically in the Middle East.) Moreover, while years of schooling have increased in Latin America in the last few decades, almost no change has occurred in age at marriage. Figure 5-1 plots for 49 DHS countries the association between the absolute intercohort change (the two cohorts are 20 to 24 and 40 to 44) in the percentage of women marrying prior to age 18 and intercohort change in mean grades of schooling.[17] Although an association between changes in schooling and marriage is evident—after all, most developing countries have experienced both a rise in educational attainment and a rise in age of marriage—Figure 5-1 reveals a weaker asso-

---

[16]In Ghana and Togo, for example, a decline has taken place in the percentage of young women in polygynous unions. Such unions are typically characterized by a large age gap between spouses, with women marrying young and men delaying marriage until they are able to acquire bridewealth. Thus it is not surprising to observe a decline in early marriage among women in the two countries, but virtually no change or even a slight increase in marriage among men.

[17]Data on grades of school attained are not available for Paraguay and Yemen; data on women were not available for Gabon at the time of this analysis.

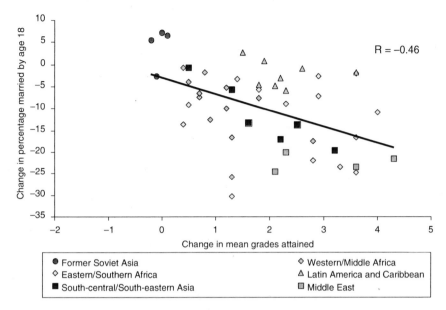

FIGURE 5-1 Association between change in percentage of 20- to 24- and 40- to 44-year-old women married by age 18 and change in grades of school attained.
SOURCE: DHS tabulations, 49 countries, 1990-2001. See Table 5-1 for list of countries. Paraguay and Yemen excluded; missing schooling data. Gabon excluded; data on women unavailable at time of this analysis.

ciation than one might expect, given the determining power often attributed to educational change.

An alternative approach to this question is to take as a starting point the observed individual-level relationship between marriage and educational attainment and to consider, given this individual-level relationship, how much intercohort change in early marriage might be expected to follow from the intercohort change in educational attainment. The individual-level relationship can be obtained by estimating regressions of marriage prior to age 18 on years of schooling. This effect (i.e., the regression coefficients) can then be applied to the observed inter-cohort change in years of schooling to calculate an "expected change" in the probability of early marriage that would be generated by schooling change. The methodology can be briefly described as follows: The observed proportions marrying prior to age 18 can be designated O_1 and O_2, for the older and younger cohorts, respectively, and the observed change in the proportion marrying young is:

$$\Delta O = O_1 - O_2$$

To obtain the "expected change" due to changes in schooling, two regressions are estimated, one for each cohort:

$$p(M_{18})_1 = a_1 + b_1 S_1 \qquad (1)$$

$$p(M_{18})_2 = a_2 + b_2 S_2 \qquad (2)$$

where

$p(M_{18})$ is the probability of marrying prior to age 18;
S is the educational attainment (schooling) of each woman;
a, b are estimated parameters; and
1, 2 are subscripts referring to the older (1) and younger (2) cohorts.

An "expected" proportion marrying before age 18 for the younger cohort is calculated as:

$$E_2 = mean(a_1 + b_1 S_2) \qquad (3)$$

This is the predicted proportion marrying early in the younger cohort given the educational attainment of these women and the association between educational attainment and early marriage observed in the older cohort. That is, this is a hypothetical of the following sort: Suppose the association between schooling and early marriage observed in the older cohort persisted in the younger cohort, along with the increase in educational attainment; if so, what proportion of the younger cohort would be expected to marry young? From this an expected change can be calculated:

$$\Delta E^* = E_2 - O_1 \qquad (4)$$

An equally valid hypothetical can be calculated by reversing the cohorts:

$$E_1 = mean(a_2 + b_2 S_1) \qquad (5)$$

This is the predicted proportion marrying early in the older cohort given the educational attainment of these women and the association between educational attainment and early marriage observed in the younger cohort. From this an alternative expected change can be calculated:

$$\Delta E^+ = E_1 - O_2 \qquad (6)$$

TABLE 5-9 Percentage Distribution of Ratio of Expected[a] to Observed Difference in the Percentage of 25- to 29- and 45- to 49-Year-Old Women Married by Age 18, by Region[b] (Weighted Distribution)

Region	Ratio of Expected[a] to Observed Difference				
	<0.50	0.50-0.99	1.00+[c]	Total	(Number of Countries)
Latin America and Caribbean	0	14	86	100	(9)
Former Soviet Asia	63	0	37	100	(4)
Sub-Saharan Africa[d]	32	26	42	100	(26)
All regions	23	21	56	100	(39)

[a]The expected is derived from individual-level regressions for each cohort. It is the amount of change expected in the proportion marrying before age 18 if the association between early marriage and educational attainment were to remain stable across cohorts while the educational distribution changes across cohorts as observed. See text.

[b]Middle East and South-central/South-eastern Asia are excluded because they are limited to ever-married samples.

[c]Includes those countries where the observed probability of early marriage increased between the two cohorts.

[d]Sub-Saharan Africa combines Western/Middle and Eastern/Southern Africa. Gabon excluded; data on women unavailable at time of this analysis.

NOTE: For source of regional groupings and population data for weighted averages, see Table 5-2.

SOURCE: DHS tabulations, 39 countries, 1990-2001. See Table 5-1 for list of countries.

Either ΔE^* or ΔE^+ are defensible assessments of the amount of change in early marriage expected due to changes in schooling. We therefore simply average the two:

$$\Delta E = (\Delta E^* + \Delta E^+) / 2 \qquad (7)$$

ΔE is the "expected change" in the proportion marrying young in the following discussion and in Table 5-9 and Figure 5-2.[18] This analysis is only conducted in those countries where the DHS interviewed all women, not just ever-married women, because of the difficulty of bringing never-

---

[18]The regressions (1) and (2) are logit regressions. In equations (3) and (5), a predicted logit of early marriage is calculated for each woman and then transformed to a predicted probability, from which a mean is calculated. The logit regressions employ a categorical version of years of schooling (S_1 and S_2), in order to allow for nonlinearities in the effect of schooling on early marriage, with categories 0, 1-3, 4-7, and 8+.

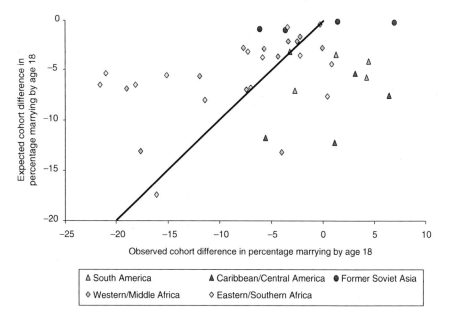

FIGURE 5-2 Association between observed and expected change* in percentage of 25- to 29- and 45- to 49-year-old women married by age 18.

*Expected change = change expected due to cohort difference in educational attainment. See text.

NOTE: The line represents the set of points where the observed equals the expected.

SOURCE: DHS tabulations, 39 countries, 1990-2001. See Table 5-1 for list of countries. Middle East, South-central and South-eastern Asia excluded; limited to ever-married samples. Gabon excluded; data on women unavailable at time of this analysis.

married women into the calculations when estimating individual-level regressions. This exclusion effectively eliminates South and Southeast Asia and the Middle East from this analysis.

The scatter plot of the expected and observed change in early marriage is provided in Figure 5-2, comparing women ages 25 to 29 and 45 to 49 at the time of the survey. The diagonal line in this figure is the point at which the expected equals the observed, that is, the change in schooling would appear to be sufficient to account entirely for the decline in the likelihood of marriage prior to age 18. One striking feature of Figure 5-2 is the large fraction of countries—16 out of 39—where the expected change exceeds the observed change. These are instances where the magnitude of the decline in early marriage between cohorts is less than would be expected given the increase in educational attainment. In roughly half of these 16 countries, the probability of early marriage actually increases between cohorts. Were education the dominant determining factor, such increases would be expected in none of the 39 countries, because schooling increased between these two cohorts everywhere. The pattern in the majority of countries, however, is that the percentage marrying at early ages declined from the older to the younger cohort, and this observed decline exceeds the expected decline; these are countries above the diagonal line in Figure 5-2. Included is a set of countries on the far left of Figure 5-2 where the expected decline in early marriage is substantially less than the observed decline. In these instances, factors other than schooling would appear to be driving the change in the timing of first marriage.

The range of country experiences evident in Figure 5-2 is summarized in Table 5-9, which breaks down the experiences by major region. The regional differences are marked. In Latin America and the Caribbean, the common outcome is that the expected decline in early marriage from increased schooling far exceeds the actual decline. In many of these countries, of course, the probability of early marriage increased rather than declined. By contrast, in about a third of the sub-Saharan African countries, the expected decline (i.e., due to increased schooling) accounts for less than a half of the actual decline. This leaves two thirds of the countries where half or more of the decline in early marriage can be linked to educational increase, an impressive outcome.[19] The four countries in Soviet Asia show both small and large ratios of expected to observed change. In short, increases in schooling hardly appear to be the entire story, although in sub-Saharan Africa there are grounds for attributing a large share of the decline in early marriage to increased schooling.

It should be stressed that the analysis presented in Figure 5-2 and Table 5-9 does not control for the association of schooling with other determinants. The estimated individual-level effect of schooling on early marriage will capture the effects of other variables correlated with schooling. Hence this analysis gives an exaggerated impression of what might be accomplished through changes in schooling alone, that is, in the absence of changes in any other correlated determinants of early marriage.

Even with this likely exaggeration of the impact of schooling change on nuptiality change, the data do not reveal as powerful an association between the two as one might expect. Perhaps this outcome should not come as a total surprise. A critical reading of the existing literature uncovers a

---

[19] If we restrict the analysis to those countries with moderate or substantial decline in the likelihood of marrying by age 18—for example, those countries where the decline in the percentage married by age 18 is three percentage points or greater—the pattern is not markedly different than in Table 5-9. In sub-Saharan Africa, for example, in slightly less than two thirds of the countries in this restricted sample the change in years of schooling can be credited with half or more of the decline in early marriage, an outcome similar to Table 5-9.

number of reasons why the effect of schooling on the timing of marriage might be somewhat weaker than discussions in policy circles imply.

There are good reasons to expect a strong positive association between schooling and the timing of marriage. Some researchers note that in many early-marrying societies, school attendance is incompatible with marriage and childbearing as a matter of practice if not of policy (Lindstrom and Brambila Paz, 2001), resulting in a rather mechanistic positive association between educational attainment and age at marriage. However, for the most part, the countries where sizeable proportions of young women marry very early are the same ones where educational attainment is low, and hence for most women, there is a distinct gap between school leaving and the earliest ages at which marriage might occur. While the autonomy-enhancing effect of school is universally cited, empirical validation of the particular mechanisms is lacking. Education is said to give young women greater influence over the timing of marriage and choice of marriage partners (Jejeebhoy, 1995). Exposure to school is also thought to broaden a girl's perspective on the world, increasing her aspirations; opening up alternative opportunities, for example, to work; and providing her with a more Western outlook on life, which can include wanting to have a greater influence on the choice of her husband (Lloyd and Mensch, 1999). Education also may give parents—because of a daughter's enhanced income-earning potential—a strong rationale for postponement of marriage (Lindstrom and Brambila Paz, 2001). Finally, the marriage search process may be lengthened with more years in school because of a general tendency for women to seek higher status men (Lloyd and Mensch, 1999).

While these are sound reasons for positing that age at first marriage is postponed as years of schooling increase, there are also reasons for concern that empirical estimates of this causal effect will be upwardly biased. For one thing, educational attainment is likely to be endogenous to marriage timing, that is, those who already intend to marry later (for whatever reason) stay in school longer, and those who intend to marry early leave school earlier for this reason. Many researchers disregard this issue (see, e.g., Choe et al., 2001; De Silva, 1997; Islam and Ahmed, 1998); others recognize that educational attainment may be affected by marriage and are very careful about how schooling variables are specified (e.g., Assaad and Zouari, 2002; Malhotra, 1997; Malhotra and Tsui, 1996). But even these researchers ignore the fact that many of the same factors that determine when a girl marries are also likely to affect whether she goes to school and how long she stays, in part because few surveys include questions that would shed light on decision making about schooling and marriage. One notable exception is Yabiku and colleagues' (2002) analysis of school characteristics and the timing of marriage in Nepal, in which attributes of schools—cost, number of female teachers, and teacher credentials—are included as covariates in models of the hazard of marriage. Although separate analyses are not conducted for men and women and no attempt is made to investigate whether changes in the school environment have contributed to a delay in marriage, the study is noteworthy in its attempt to go beyond simple measures of educational attainment.

Finally, there are reasons to question how much of an impact schooling per se should be expected to have on marriage and other aspects of family life. An analysis of the educational literature indicates that schools are not always the progressive force for social change that demographers generally hypothesize them to be (Lloyd and Mensch, 1999; Mensch et al., 2003). Thus a more nuanced analysis of schooling and marriage is required. In particular, measures of the potential factors associated with a rise in schooling, such as changes in adolescent girls' gender role attitudes, in their autonomy, and in norms about the marriage selection process, might prove more illuminating than standard indicators of educational attainment. Data on gender role attitudes of teachers, differences in the curriculum to which boys and girls are exposed, and analyses of the gender content of textbooks would also be useful. The aim would be to distinguish communities with educational systems that reinforce the status quo from communities with educational systems that challenge existing norms.

Growth in Urbanization

At the same time that age of marriage has risen, the percentage of the developing world population living in cities has grown. Beyond the fact that the composition of the population resident in towns and cities differs in ways that would predict a later age at marriage, increasing urbanization is likely to be associated with a delay in marriage because of the very nature of urban life. As Singh and Samara (1996) theorize, women in urban areas are exposed to modern values encouraging later marriage and are less likely to be under the influence of kin who control the timing of marriage and choice of spouse.

While we do not have direct measures of the attributes of urban living that encourage later age at marriage, we can assess the association between changes in age at marriage and changes in the percentage of the population living in urban areas. Moreover, with UN data we can improve on Singh and Samara's analysis (1996) of the cross-sectional correlation between the changes in early marriage among those ages 20 to 24 and 40 to 44 in DHS countries and the increase in the proportion of these cohorts currently living in urban areas. The drawback of their analysis is that women ages 40 to 44 may have migrated since they first married. Figure 5-3 depicts the association between the change in the percentage of women ages 15 to 19

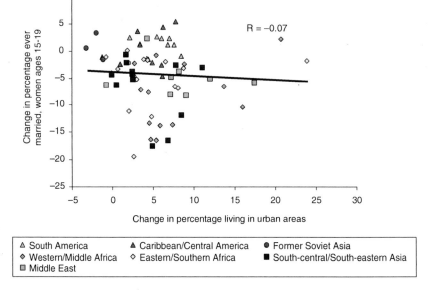

FIGURE 5-3 Association between change in percentage of 15- to 19-year-old women married and change in percentage of population living in urban areas, 1960-2001.
NOTE: Argentina excluded; no Survey 1 marriage data for this age group.
SOURCE: United Nations Population Division data, 72 countries, 1960-2001. See Table 5-1 for list of countries.

married in each of 72 countries and the change in the percentage of the population living in urban areas. Because the time interval in the surveys and censuses from which these data are derived varies, as in Tables 5-2 and 5-3, we computed the annual change.[20] Although we do not have the percentage of the population resident in urban areas at the exact date of each census and survey, we do have the information within 3 years of the marriage data for all countries.

Somewhat surprisingly, Figure 5-3 indicates no association between the increase in urbanization and the decline in the percentage of the female population ages 15 to 19 married. However, we would not want to conclude from this analysis that the theoretical argument relating growing urbanization to a delay in age of marriage is without merit. To actually

---

[20]Here the annual change was multiplied by 10.

assess this relationship, time-series estimates of the social, cultural, ideational, and economic factors associated with city living are required rather than just gross measures of urbanization.

In sum, it is likely that changes in factors other than growth in schooling and urbanization have contributed to observed delays in marriage. With the data at our disposal, we are unable to analyze these other factors. However, a review of individual country studies on age at marriage as well as some of the other literature on social and economic changes taking place in the developing world provides some insight into what these factors might be. It also rules out some factors that might plausibly have been expected to be related to age at marriage.

The Decline in Arranged Marriages

Several demographers who have conducted studies of marriage timing in individual countries in Asia have attributed the increase in women's age at marriage to changes in the marriage process. In particular, the movement away from arranged marriages is considered to contribute to the delay in marriage (Hull, 2002; Malhotra and Tsui, 1996). In Indonesia, according to Hull (2002, p. 8), the rise in the age of marriage "has come about due to the shift of the locus of marriage decision making from parents to children," which, incidentally, he attributes to the expansion in educational attainment among young women. It is generally believed that the process of parental selection is less time consuming than that of individual searching. Furthermore, when parents are involved in spouse selection, daughters are believed to be married off earlier because of a concern with preserving their sexual purity. One frequently cited reason for parental involvement in spouse selection is that in allowing a daughter to explore potential partners for herself, she is more likely to initiate sex premaritally. Another motivation for a parent involved in mate selection to marry off a daughter early is because girls are more likely to be compliant in the choice of spouse when they are young (UNICEF, 2001).

While an association between age of marriage and the spouse selection process seems reasonable, data to test for such a link is lacking. Rarely do surveys include questions that would make possible an investigation of the process of spouse selection. The 1979-1980 Asian Marriage Survey conducted in Indonesia, Pakistan, the Philippines, and Thailand among married women ages 15 to 45 and a sample of their husbands included a question about who chose the spouse, although only in Indonesia, Pakistan, and the Philippines were these data analyzed and only in the first two were there substantial proportions in some form of arranged marriages. Moreover, because of the simple dichotomization of marriages into arranged/not arranged, there is no information on whether the potential groom or bride had any input if the marriage was categorized as arranged or whether the parents had any say if the marriage was categorized as not arranged (Malhotra's 1991 analysis is the exception).

The data that exist on the relative involvement of parents and young people in the selection of marriage partners suggest that in societies where arranged marriage was a common feature of the marriage process, there has been a movement in recent years toward self-choice, as Goode predicted 40 years ago in his discussion of the emergence of the conjugal family with industrialization. This decline in kin control or increase in a young woman's involvement in mate selection has been documented with survey data in Togo (Gage and Meekers, 1995), Indonesia (Malhotra, 1991), and India (Jejeebhoy and Halli, 2002), and in an ethnographic study in Nepal (Ahearn, 2001). It is also asserted to be occurring throughout sub-Saharan Africa (Lesthaeghe, Kaufman and Meekers, 1989; National Research Council, 1993) and Asia (Choe, Westley, and Retherford, 2002). While almost no studies provide data that would permit an analysis of the association between trends in the marriage process and trends in age at marriage, that the two are related seems likely.[21]

The Cost of Marriage: Dowry and Marriage Markets

Researchers interested in age at marriage of women have rarely investigated whether an association exists between the time when women marry and their economic circumstances or those of their family. The study by Abbasi and colleagues (2002, p. 33) in Iran is an exception. They attribute the increase in female age of marriage between 1986 and 1996 to the rise in the cost of living after the revolution and the deteriorating economic situation. They suggest that "young people tend to delay their marriage until they get a job," but they don't indicate whether both young men and young women are entering the labor force or just young men.

One reason that cost may not figure into analyses of female age at marriage is that the groom's family bears the greater financial burden of marriage in most developing countries. To the extent that marriage involves the transfer of gifts, cash, valuables, and consumer goods, by far, the more common form of exchange is from the groom's family to the bride's. Murdock's Ethnographic Atlas, which was initially published in the late 1960s and revised around 1980, indicates that in approximately two thirds of the 1,267 societies catalogued, bridewealth is normative whereas dowry

---

[21]We are aware of one analysis, of Sri Lankan women, where the marriage process was included as a factor in marriage timing. However, contrary to expectations, those who chose their own spouses married earlier than those who had arranged marriages, a pattern that the researchers note is unusual among Asian societies (Malhotra and Tsui, 1996).

is prevalent in just 6 percent, although the South Asian countries where dowry is customary have considerably larger populations (cited in Bhat and Halli, 1999).

To the extent that research has been conducted on the links between the age women marry and the cost of marriage, it has been limited to India and Bangladesh. In their analysis of marriage change in South India in the early 1980s, Caldwell, Reddy, and Caldwell (1983) argued that parents are unwilling to postpone marriage beyond the teenage years because of the increased cost of dowry for older brides, an issue that is also said to be a concern for poor parents in Bangladesh (Amin, Mahmud, and Huq, 2002). Yet there is little quantitative analysis of the association between the costs of dowry and age of marriage of women or, more broadly, on poverty as a factor in the timing of marriage.

On the other hand, there is a considerable body of research that has focused on explaining reasons for the increase, in the second half of the twentieth century, in the prevalence and monetary value of dowry in South Asia. Because of declining infant and child mortality, and because women marry men who are considerably older, a "marriage squeeze" has emerged; in other words, an excess supply of women of marriageable ages now exists. In addition, as maternal mortality began to fall, there are fewer widowers available for women to marry. When too few men of marriageable age are available, families compete for the eligible men by paying higher dowries (Amin and Cain, 1997; Bhat and Halli, 1999; Billig, 1992; Caldwell, Reddy, and Caldwell, 1983; Deolalikar and Rao, 1998; Rao, 1993a, 1993b). Bhat and Halli (1999) argue that the rise in the mean age at first marriage in India is due to the marriage squeeze.[22] They contend that given the low levels of schooling, it is not the increase in educational attainment that has led to a rise in age of marriage, at least not in a mechanical sense. Rather the deficit of eligible men may induce women to stay in school. Caldwell and colleagues (1983) also maintain that the delay in marriage and the decline in age differences between spouses in South India are a function of the marriage squeeze. As do Bhat and Halli (1999), they predict an increase in the education of girls as Indians become more "accustomed to unmarried girls beyond the age of menarche" (Caldwell, Reddy, and Caldwell, 1983, p. 361).

To the degree that an association exists between age of marriage of women and increased schooling in India, these researchers would claim that the delay in marriage, caused by a deficit of eligible men, has been the

---

[22]A marriage squeeze is also believed to be a factor in the increase in age at marriage in Lebanon, where 16 years of civil war and male emigration because of diminished work opportunities have distorted the sex ratios at marriageable ages (Saxena and Kulczycki, 2004).

catalyst for the expansion in female education, rather than the other way around, as is conventionally argued. Whether a marriage squeeze affects age of marriage, age differences between spouses, dowry demands, and educational attainment of young women throughout South Asia clearly merits further investigation. It may well be that the nature of the response to shifts in the sex ratio of eligible men and women varies depending on local traditions surrounding marriage and household formation as well as socioeconomic conditions. Interestingly in rural Nepal, where declines in mortality would also have created a deficit of eligible men of marriageable age, dowry has yet to emerge as a common practice, although it is "increasingly prevalent in Kathmandu" (Ahearn, 2001, p. 89).

Changing Laws, Changing Norms

To the best of our knowledge, no study has investigated the connection between changing laws on age at marriage and trends in age at marriage across countries. That laws are often inconsistently enforced and can vary across states or administrative areas within countries may contribute to the complicated legal situation. A review of policies affecting marriage in seven Anglophone African countries indicates that in some countries, such as Nigeria and Kenya, local and religious laws contradict national laws. In other countries, such as Tanzania, penal codes contradict national laws (Center for Reproductive Law and Policy, 1999). Reproductive rights advocates believe that laws specifying a minimum age at marriage are rarely enforced; rather, customary practice takes precedence over civil law (Boye et al., 1991). The data on marriage would appear to support this view. For example, in Mali the legal age of marriage for women is now 18 and in Uganda it is 21, later than other countries in Africa (see International Planned Parenthood Federation and International Women's Rights Action Watch, 2000), and an increase from 1980 when the legal age was 15 in Mali and 16 in Uganda (National Research Council, 1993). Yet according to DHS data, 65 percent of women ages 20 to 24 married by age 18 in Mali and 54 percent in Uganda, proportions that are among the highest in the developing world. Incidentally, despite the changes in marriage laws in these two countries, comparing the proportions for 20- to 24-year-olds with those for 40- to 44-year-olds reveals only a 1 percent rate of decline in Mali and a 9 percent rate of decline in Uganda, well below the average rates of decline observed for East and Southern Africa (31 percent), and West and Middle Africa (23 percent) (see Table 5-4).

Not only are there countries with laws prohibiting early teen marriage where large proportions of women still marry at very young ages, there are countries with very low legal ages of marriage where the prevalence of early marriage is not nearly as great. For example, the legal age of marriage in

Bolivia and Peru is 14; yet only 21 percent of women married before age 18 in Bolivia and only 19 in Peru.

In some countries the actual age at which many women marry is lower than the legal age (UNICEF, 2001). In the case of Bangladesh, there is even speculation that the rise in age at marriage observed in surveys is not real, but rather a function of an increase in the minimum legal age in 1984 from 16 to 18; adolescent girls who marry are thought to exaggerate their age on surveys (Amin, 2000). In other countries where there has historically been a high prevalence of teen marriage, but where the legal age of marriage is age 18 or later, the declines in age of marriage observed may not be attributable to actual changes in behavior, but rather to some misreporting in age as a result of fear that families may be prosecuted for marrying daughters off at young ages. Many of the Demographic and Health Surveys contain too few 15- to 16-year-olds. The standard explanation for this phenomenon is that interviewers displace 15- to 16-year-olds out of the group eligible for individual interviews. But such a situation could also arise if married 15- to 16-year-olds are reported to be 17 or 18.

Interestingly, the effort to legislate marriage is not only ineffective when the goal is to raise the age, but it also does not appear to be effective on the rare occasions when the goal is to lower the age. In Iran, the legal age at marriage for girls was reduced after the 1979 Islamic revolution from age 16 to age 9, and incentives were provided for couples to marry. Yet, female age of marriage actually increased, albeit slightly, during this period (Abbasi et al., 2002).

Even if laws on age at marriage are not enforced, and little association exists between the legal minimum age at marriage and the percentage of the population that marries early across countries, the reality is that laws on age at marriage have changed in recent years. Indeed, in 55 developing countries for which data on the legal minimum age at marriage are available at two different points in time, 1990 and 2000, the age is now higher in 23 countries for women and 20 for men (see International Planned Parenthood Federation and International Women's Rights Action Watch, 1900, 2000). A change in the legal age of marriage may signal a change in the discourse around marriage that, ultimately, if not in the near term, is likely to lead women and their families to contemplate a change in behavior.[23] The fact that laws have been modified in so many countries suggests that the increased discussion of early marriage among human rights advocates and the publicity generated by various United Nations conferences

---

[23]Of course, in some countries, the increase in the legal age at marriage may simply reflect the fact that women are delaying marriage. In that event, the law is simply catching up with the change in behavior.

have had an impact on global norms governing early marriage of women (UNICEF, 2001). Just as acceptance of the value of girls' schooling has expanded to the poorest countries of the world (see NRC/IOM, 2005, Chapter 3), there would appear to be a growing conviction that marriage should not take place during the teenage years, or at least not before age 18. According to human rights advocates, marriage prior to age 18 contravenes the United Nations Convention on the Rights of the Child, which defines 18 as the end of childhood, and thus marriage before that age as child marriage. In addition, very early marriage is said to undermine other rights guaranteed by the Convention, including the right to be protected from physical abuse and sexual exploitation, and the right not to be separated from parents against one's will (Population Council, 2002).

In theorizing about the increase in the age at first marriage among females in Africa, Hertrich (2002, p. 12) argues that in contrast to earlier generations, "recognition of a social status for women other than that of wife and mother" now exists, although she does not provide data to support this observation. To be fair, such data are hard to come by. Yet changing views about women's roles would seem to be a factor in the rising age at marriage. The growth in indigenous feminist movements, coupled with a more globalized media where women not only feature more prominently than in the past but where more attention is given to the situation of the "girl child," is likely to have undermined traditional norms.

Other social and demographic changes may influence attitudes toward age at marriage. An analysis of DHS data from 21 sub-Saharan African countries found that improvements in child survival are associated with later age at marriage (LeGrand and Barbieri, 2002), suggesting that once awareness about the decline in mortality has spread throughout a population, couples will delay marriage to achieve their family size goals. Indeed, the decline in desired family size, which has occurred throughout much of the developing world[24] (Westoff and Bankole, 2002), might reasonably be thought to affect the timing of marriage because less urgency exists to begin childbearing when fertility goals are reduced. However, analyses of DHS data reveal that even as desired family size has fallen, the interval between marriage and first birth has declined[25] (Mensch, 2003). While some of this narrowing of the interval is likely due to a decline in subfecundity among the newly married who are somewhat older, these data suggest that despite arguments about the improvement of women's status, noted above, considerable pressure still exists for women to prove fecundity.

---

[24]Francophone West Africa is the exception; other than Togo there is little change in reproductive preferences in this region in the past 10 years (Westoff and Bankole, 2002).

[25]This decline occurred among women who gave birth after marriage, suggesting that it is not simply due to an increase in premarital conceptions.

Explaining Trends Among Men

If the increase in educational attainment dominates discussions of the rise in age of marriage of women, what explanation is given for changes in male age at marriage? Some researchers note that, as has been the case for women, the extended educational path taken by men in recent years in many countries may contribute to the rise in their age of marriage (Hertrich, 2002). However, little data are available to assess the association between changes in schooling and age at marriage among men. In our case, we have data on both schooling and marriage only for 22 sub-Saharan African countries, 6 Latin American and Caribbean countries, 2 former Soviet Asia countries, and 1 Middle Eastern country where Demographic and Health Surveys have been conducted among men.[26] Figure 5-4 graphs the absolute change in the percentage of men marrying at age 20 for two cohorts, those 20 to 24 and those 40 to 44 against changes in mean grades of schooling attained by these cohorts. Contrary to Hertrich's (2002) speculation for Africa that increased schooling may have led to a rise in male age of marriage, virtually no association exists between changes in educational attainment and early marriage among men in these countries.

As with women, we consider whether the increase in age of marriage observed among men is linked to urbanization. Figure 5-5 depicts the association between the change over the last 20 years or so in the percentage of men ages 20 to 24 married in each of 72 countries and the change in the percentage of the population living in urban areas. Because the time interval in the surveys and censuses from which these data are derived varies, as in Figure 5-3, we computed the annual change multiplied by 10. The graph indicates that the increase in urbanization and the decline in the percentage of the male population ages 20 to 24 who are married are not correlated.

The economic environment in developing countries is commonly invoked as the primary reason for the delay in marriage of men. For example, in Vietnam, Thailand, and the Philippines, a qualitative study of marriage attitudes revealed that "poverty or lack of financial security, especially among men, was seen as a common (and sound) reason to postpone or avoid marriage" (Williams and Guest, 2002, p. 14). Few quantitative studies have investigated the association between economic conditions and marriage patterns of men; we even lack studies that link employment and wages to age of marriage of men. However, there is some evidence of changes in the economic landscape consistent with postponement of marriage for men.

---

[26]Data on grades of schooling attained are not available for Gabon, although data on marriage are; thus there are 31 countries represented in Figure 5-4, not 32.

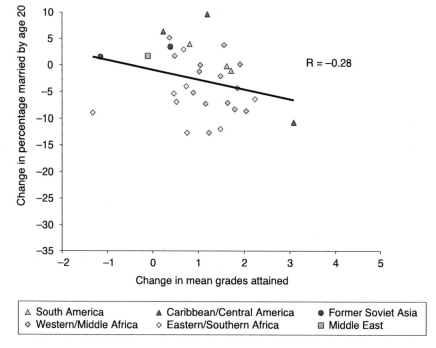

FIGURE 5-4 Association between change in percentage of 20- to 24- and 40- to 44-year-old men married by age 20 and change in grades of school attained.
NOTE: Gabon excluded; missing schooling data.
SOURCE: DHS tabulations, 31 countries, 1994-2001. See Table 5-1 for list of countries.

For rural areas of Asia, there is speculation that a reduction in land holdings may be a factor in delayed marriage. Increasing landlessness has forced young men to move to urban areas as well as to the Middle East in search of employment, leaving women behind (Choe, Westley, and Retherford, 2002).

In African societies the changing nature of bridewealth, with cash payments replacing payments in kind, is said to be a contributing factor in delaying marriage of men because more time is needed to acquire the necessary sums. While there is certainly acknowledgment that the accumulation of a large bridewealth may have led to a delayed marriage in the past (United Nations Department of International Economic and Social Affairs, 1990), the situation is now believed to have altered. Even where traditional bridewealth is no longer part of the marriage process, other costs have emerged for grooms including "future help with food costs, court fees, medical treatment and younger children's school fees" (National Research Council, 1993, p. 51).

More fundamentally, a transformation in the nature of the household economy is said to have occurred. As has been argued for Indonesia, "the assumption in the past that marriage formed a basic productive economic unit for farming or trading, has been modified by the current requirement that basic consumption needs such as capital for a house, or consumer goods, and basic educational attainments must be achieved before a marriage can 'wisely' take place" (Hull, 2002, p. 5).

In countries as diverse as Sri Lanka and Nigeria, researchers have observed that economic considerations apparently factor much more into the decision about the timing of a man's marriage than they did earlier. In Sri Lanka, with increasing industrialization, a man's job status, which was not considered important in the past—particularly where subsistence agriculture was the dominant form of economic life—is now said to be critical in determining when he marries (De Silva, 1997). In Nigeria, where a consid-

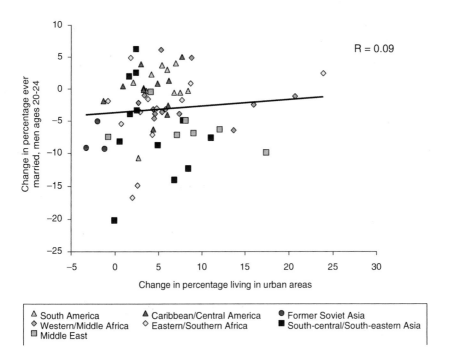

FIGURE 5-5 Association between change in percentage of 20- to 24-year-old men married and change in percentage of population living in urban areas, 1960-2001.
NOTE: Bahrain excluded; nonstandard age grouping.
SOURCE: United Nations Population Division data, 72 countries, 1960-2001. See Table 5-1 for list of countries.

erable decline has taken place in early marriage among men, the oil boom in the 1970s fueled a change in brides' expectations of what purchases grooms needed to marry (National Research Council, 1993).

In Egypt, where housing, furniture, and appliances are considered essential for marriage and "the bulk of financial obligation . . . are still borne . . . by the groom and his family," the cost of marriage is estimated to have increased dramatically in the last 30 years (Singerman and Ibrahim, 2003, p. 97), although it may be the quantity and quality of items that one is expected to acquire that has increased rather than the cost of basic household necessities. A rigorous analysis linking the expense of setting up a household to the timing of marriage in Egypt does not exist. However, the proportion of individuals in the census marriage registration category, *katb al-kitaab*, where the marriage was registered but the couple had yet to establish a marital residence, increased four-fold between 1986 and 1996, while the annual rate of marriage barely changed, indirect evidence that rising costs have led to a delay in the ceremony (Singerman and Ibrahim, 2003). This piece of evidence does not firmly establish a link between the rise in the age of marriage and the costs of marriage. The question is whether the rising cost of establishing a household in Egypt and elsewhere affects the timing of marriage across all segments of society or whether the poorest members have lower expectations, are less constrained financially, and paradoxically have seen less of a delay in age at marriage.

As with women, one also wonders whether some global changes have emerged that are influencing the timing of marriage among men. Increasing exposure to Western media may affect consumer norms and raise expectations such that young men in many societies increasingly feel obligated to postpone marriage until they have acquired the resources that are now expected for the establishment of a household. Given the current size of youth cohorts in the developing world and the difficulty of ensuring adequate employment opportunities for such vast numbers of young people, postponement of marriage among men by several years, possibly until their 30s or beyond may become increasingly common in many societies.

CONSEQUENCES OF CHANGING AGE AT MARRIAGE

Although we have documented and offered explanations for the trends in age of marriage, we have not examined the impact of changing age at marriage on the lives of young people largely because, while speculation abounds, the number of rigorous studies on this topic is extremely limited. Nonetheless, the subject is worth considering, if only to stimulate more research in this area. While separating selection effects from consequences has proven difficult, the assumption is that marriage during the teen years is deleterious for women: Schooling may be curtailed, autonomy limited—because young brides tend to marry older men—and sexual relations uninformed and perhaps even coercive or dangerous to women's health (Clark, 2004; Jejeebhoy, 1995; Mensch, Bruce, and Greene, 1998; Singh and Samara, 1996; UNICEF, 2001). Other than increasing the risk of a premarital pregnancy, delaying marriage into the 20s is generally believed to benefit women.[27]

As for men, although studies are also lacking, it seems reasonable that postponement of marriage, beyond a certain point, may not be considered universally positive, even if rising expectations and not declining economic circumstances are driving the delay. Indeed, a late age of marriage, if it arises from limited resources, may not be viewed as desirable by young men—it may be a source of frustration, particularly where premarital sex is not condoned. Qualitative research would be valuable on the negative psychosocial effects of delaying marriage, particularly in regions, such as the Middle East, where interaction between unmarried men and women is restricted.

Age at Marriage and HIV Risk

In a discussion of consequences of age at marriage, the HIV epidemic brings some new factors into consideration. Given the over-riding importance of reducing HIV, we focus on examining what is known, as well as, plausible hypotheses, about the association between women's age at marriage, the age-gap between partners, and HIV risk. Delaying age at marriage for women, if it delays sex, should reduce the age-specific rate of HIV among young women. In 13 of the 24 sub-Saharan countries where the probability of marrying by age 18 has declined in the last 20 years, the overall proportion of women having sex by age 18 also declined significantly (Mensch et al., 2005). Further, there is evidence that unmarried sexually active adolescents have lower rates of HIV than their married counterparts in sub-Saharan Africa (Clark, 2004). Analysis of DHS data indicates that compared to the unmarried, married adolescents have a higher frequency of sex, are less likely to use condoms, and have older sexual partners, namely their husbands, who are more likely to be HIV positive (Clark, 2004). Thus even if later marriage does not lead to a delay in sexual debut, the argument is that the nature of sexual activity among married women puts them at higher risk of HIV than their unmarried counterparts.

---

[27]In societies where women traditionally marry early and where women's autonomy is severely limited, a delay in age at marriage may have no impact on the lives of young women. Those who marry later may be equally constrained in terms of mobility, household decision making and employment. This observation was made by Nan Astone at a March 2003 meeting of the NRC/IOM panel on Transitions to Adulthood in Developing Countries.

These findings warrant at least four caveats, however. First, the assertion that the level of infection is higher among the married compared to the single is based on prevalence rather than incidence data. Prevalence data obscure the possibility that young married girls may have become infected when single and infected adolescent girls may be more likely to select into early marriage. Second, even if early marriage elevates HIV risk for adolescent girls, in the long run marriage may prove to be more protective than remaining single and sexually active. Data from Rakai, Uganda, indicate that on average across all age groups HIV incidence is higher among the never married than among the currently married and highest among those previously married (Gray et al., 2004). To determine how marital status affects HIV risk it is necessary to conduct epidemiological studies using longitudinal data. Third, the risk of contracting HIV depends not only on one's sexual partner's sero-status, but also, if positive, when the partner became infected. A woman may be more likely to contract HIV if she has sex with a newly infected partner because viral loads, which are estimated to be strongly predictive of the risk of transmission (see Quinn et al., 2000; Gray et al., 2001), are high at the time of infection (see Anderson, 1996). Although infectivity is likely to vary systematically by age of the man, we do not have data on the infectivity rate of partners of married and unmarried adolescent girls to determine which group's partners put them at greater risk of acquiring HIV. Sexually active, never married women are more likely to change partners than currently married women (Alan Guttmacher Institute, 1998; Ferry et al., 2001), which raises the risk of encountering an infected partner. Moreover, the male partners of unmarried women are more apt to be single and, in turn, are more likely to have multiple sexual partners than are men in monogamous unions (Alan Guttmacher Institute, 2003). However, if those in polygamous unions are included, married men may be more likely to have a greater number of sexual partners than single men, as is observed in Rakai (Gray et al., 2004).[28]

With the data currently at hand, definitive statements about the effect of marriage delay on HIV risk canot be made; moreover, the association probably varies by social setting. While later marriage delay may lead to later onset, it may also result in higher lifetime rates of HIV infection. An additional concern is women's HIV status when bearing children. One consequence of delayed marriage may be that women are more likely to be infected during pregnancy, although one study found no evidence to support this speculation (Clark, 2004).

---

[28]This analysis of the consequences of delayed marriage for HIV risk among women also draws on discussions that took place at a November 10, 2004, Population Council workshop on Marriage and HIV/AIDS. For a more detailed discussion of some of these issues see Bongaarts (2005).

As is the case for women, the health consequences of delayed marriage are unknown for men. Although marriage does not impose sexual exclusivity on men, in countries where premarital sex is prevalent, a delay in marriage may increase exposure to HIV and other STDs because, as noted above, compared to married men, a greater percentage of the unmarried have multiple sexual partners (see Appendix Table 3, Alan Guttmacher Institute, 2003). Alternatively, in countries where postpartum abstinence taboos are still present and men marry early, they may be more likely to engage in intercourse with other partners including commercial sex workers during the post-partum period. Clearly more research is needed on the linkages between changing age at marriage, sexual behavior, condom use, and HIV risk among both men and women.

CONCLUSIONS

During the last 30 years, for most developing country regions, substantial declines have occurred in the proportion of young men and women married; the clear exceptions are South America for men and women, and, for men only, South and Southeast Asia.

Given differentials in male and female marriage ages by years of schooling and residence, we assessed whether the decline in the percentage of young people married is related to increases in educational attainment and urbanization. Expansion of schooling for women has had some impact, but there is still a considerable fraction of the increase not explained by changes in education. We asserted that a proper investigation of the association between education and age at marriage would look beyond such factors as years of schooling to what goes on within the school itself, as well as changes in the value of education, which is likely to vary across settings.

In suggesting other factors that might account for some of the increase in age of marriage among women, we reviewed a considerable number of demographic studies. Contributory factors examined in the literature and considered here include the decline in arranged marriages, the deficit of available older men with increasing cohort size and the concomitant rise in the cost of dowries in South Asia, changes in the legal age of marriage, and a transformation in global norms about the desirability of early marriage of women. We noted that there is a much smaller literature on age of marriage of men. While increasing educational attainment of men is also believed to contribute to a delay, we found no evidence of this in sub-Saharan Africa. We suggested that increasing costs of establishing a household may lead men to postpone marriage.

This data analysis and review of the literature revealed that there is much that we do not know about changes in the timing of marriage for men and women and the consequences of these changes for health and other outcomes. To better understand the dynamics of union formation, demographic surveys need to collect information on the social, cultural, and economic factors that affect life decisions among young people, including the contextual factors that reflect the opportunity structures available. Greater attention to the shift in the marriage process including the apparent decline in arranged marriages and the increase in marriages based on mutual attraction would also be useful as both have implications for partner communication and decision-making processes regarding family building. In so doing a more nuanced understanding of marriage, one of the key transitions in the pathway from adolescence to adulthood, can be developed.

REFERENCES

Abbasi, M.J., Mehryar, A., Jones, G., and McDonald, P. (2002). Revolution, war, and modernization: Population policy and fertility change in Iran. *Journal of Population Research, 19*(1), 25-46.

Ahearn, L.M. (2001). *Invitations to love: Literacy, love letters, and social change in Nepal.* Ann Arbor: University of Michigan Press.

Alan Guttmacher Institute. (1998). *Into a new world: Young women's sexual and reproductive lives.* New York: Author.

Alan Guttmacher Institute. (2003). *In their own right: Addressing the sexual and reproductive health needs of men worldwide.* New York: Author

Amin, S. (2000). *Gender, governance, and the making of a new population policy in Bangladesh.* Paper presented at panel discussion on Globalization and Some Aspects of Recent Social Changes in Rural Bangladesh at the annual meeting of the American Rural Sociological Society, August 14, Washington, DC.

Amin, S., and Cain, M. (1997). The rise of dowry in Bangladesh. In G.W. Jones, R.M. Douglas, J.C. Caldwell, and R.M. D'Souza (Eds.), *The continuing demographic transition* (pp. 290-306). Oxford, England: Clarendon Press.

Amin, S., Mahmud, S., and Huq, L. (2002). Marriage. In *Baseline survey report on rural adolescents in Bangladesh: Kishori Abhijan Project.* Dhaka, Bangladesh: UNICEF and Department of Women's Affairs, Ministry of Women and Children Affairs.

Anderson, R.M. (1996). The spread of HIV and sexual mixing patterns. In J. Mann and D. Tarantola (Eds.), *AIDS in the world* (vol. II, pp. 71-86). New York: Oxford University Press.

Anderson, S. (2003). Why dowry payments declined with modernization in Europe but are rising in India. *Journal of Political Economy, 111*(2), 269-310.

Assaad, R., and Zouari, S. (2002). *The timing of marriage, fertility, and female labor force participation in urban Morocco.* Paper presented at the ERF 9th Annual Conference, October 26-28, Sharjah, United Arab Emirates.

Becker, G. (1973). A theory of marriage. In T.W. Schultz (Ed.), *Economics of the family: Marriage, children, and human capital* (pp. 299-344). Chicago, IL: The University of Chicago for the National Bureau of Economic Research.

Bhat, P.N.M., and Halli, S.S. (1999). Demography of brideprice and dowry: Causes and consequences of the Indian marriage squeeze. *Population Studies, 53*(2), 129-148.

Billig, M.S. (1992). The marriage squeeze and the rise of groomprice in India's Kerala State. *Journal of Comparative Family Studies, 23*(2), 197-216.

Blanc, A.K., and Rutenberg, N. (1990). Assessment of the quality of data on age at first sexual intercourse, age at first marriage, and age at first birth in the Demographic and Health Surveys. In *An assessment of DHS-I data quality* (pp. 41-79). Columbia, MD: Institute of Resource Development/Macro Systems.

Bongaarts, J. (2005). *Marriage, sexual behavior, and HIV epidemics in sub-Saharan Africa.* Unpublished document. Population Council, New York.

Boulier, B.L., and Rosenzweig, M.R. (1984). Schooling, search, and spouse selection: Testing economic theories of marriage and household behavior. *Journal of Political Economy, 92*(4), 712-732.

Boye, A.K., Hill, K., Isaacs, S., and Gordis, D. (1991). Marriage law and practice in the Sahel. *Studies in Family Planning, 22*(6), 343-349.

Brien, M.J., and Lillard, L.A. (1994). Education, marriage, and first conception in Malaysia. *Journal of Human Resources, 34*(4), 1167-1204.

Caldwell, J., Reddy, P.H., and Caldwell, P. (1983). The causes of marriage change in South India. *Population Studies, 37*(3), 343-361.

Casterline, J.B. (1994). Fertility transition in Asia. In T. Locoh and V. Hertrich (Eds.), *The onset of fertility transition in sub-Saharan Africa* (pp. 69-86). Liège, Belgium: Derouaux Ordina Editions.

Center for Reproductive Law and Policy. (1999). *Adolescent reproductive rights: Laws and policies to improve their health and lives.* New York: Author.

Choe, M.K., Thapa, S., and Achmad, S. (2001). *Early marriage and childbearing in Indonesia and Nepal.* (East-West Center Working Papers, Population Series No. 108-115.) Honolulu, HI: East-West Center.

Choe, M.K., Westley, S.B., and Retherford, R.D. (2002). *Tradition and change in marriage and family life: The future of population in Asia.* Honolulu, HI: East-West Center.

Clark, S. (2004). Early marriage and HIV risks in sub-Saharan Africa. *Studies in Family Planning, 35*(3), 149-160.

Coale, A.J., and Treadway, R. (1986). A summary of the changing distribution of overall fertility, marital fertility, and the proportion married in the provinces of Europe. In A.J. Coale and S.C. Watkins (Eds.), *The decline of fertility in Europe: The revised proceedings of a conference on the Princeton European Fertility Project* (pp. 31-181). Princeton, NJ: Princeton University Press.

Dahal, D.R., Fricke, T., and Thornton, A. (1993). The family contexts of marriage timing in Nepal. *Ethnology, 32*(4), 305-323.

Das Gupta, M. (1997). Kinship systems and demographic regimes. In D.I. Kertzer and T. Fricke (Eds.), *Anthropological demography: Toward a new synthesis* (pp. 36-52). Chicago, IL: University of Chicago Press.

De Silva, W.I. (1997). The Ireland of Asia: Trends in marriage timing in Sri Lanka. *Asia-Pacific Population Journal, 12*(2), 3-24.

Deolalikar, A.B., and Rao, V. (1998). The demand for dowries and bride characteristics in marriage: Empirical estimates for rural South-Central India. In M. Krishnaraj, R. Sudarshan, and A. Shariff (Eds.), *Gender, population, and development* (pp. 122-140). Oxford, England: Oxford University Press.

Ehmer, J. (2002). Marriage. In D.I. Kertzer and M. Barbagli (Eds.), *Family life in the long nineteenth century 1789-1913, volume two: The history of the European family* (pp. 282-321). New Haven, CT: Yale University Press.

Ferry, B., Caraël, M., Buvé, A., Auvert, B., Laourou, M., Kanhonou, L., de Loenzien, M., Akam, E., Chege, J., and Kaona, F. (2001). Comparison of key parameters of sexual behaviour in four African urban populations with different levels of HIV infection (Study Group on Heterogeneity of HIV Epidemics in African Cities). *AIDS, 15*(suppl 4), S41-S50.

Fricke, T.E., Syed, S.H., and Smith, P.C. (1986). Rural Punjabi social organization and marriage timing strategies in Pakistan. *Demography, 23*(4), 489-508.

Gage, A.J., and Meekers, D. (1995). The changing dynamics of family formation: Women's status and nuptiality in Togo. In P. Makinwa-Adebusoye and A.-M. Jensen (Eds.), *Women and demographic change in sub-Saharan Africa* (pp. 15-38). Liège, Belgium: International Union for the Scientific Study of Population.

Goode, W.J. (1963). *World revolution and family patterns*. New York: Free Press.

Gray, R.H., Nalugoda, F., Serwadda, D., and Wawer, M. (2004). *Marriage and HIV risk: Data from Rakai, Uganda*. Paper presented at Workshop on Marriage and HIV/AIDS, November 10, New York.

Gray, R.H., Wawer, M.J., Brookmeyer, R., Sewankambo, N.K., Serwadda, D., Wabwire-Mangen, F., Lutalo, T., Li, X., vanCott, T., and Quinn, T.C. (2001). Probability of HIV-1 transmission per coital act in monogamous, heterosexual, HIV-1-discordant couples in Rakai, Uganda. *Lancet, 357*(9263), 1149-1153.

Guinnane, T. (1991). Re-thinking the Western European marriage pattern: The decision to marry in Ireland at the turn of the twentieth century. *Journal of Family History, 16*(1), 47-64.

Gutmann, M.P., and Leboutte, R. (1984). Rethinking protoindustrialization and the family. *Journal of Interdisciplinary History, 14*(3), 587-607.

Hajnal, J. (1965). European marriage patterns in perspective. In D.V. Glass and D.E.C. Eversley (Eds.), *Population in history: Essays in historical demography* (pp. 101-143). London, England: Edward Arnold.

Heaton, T.B., Forste, R., and Otterstrom, S.M. (2002). Family transitions in Latin America: First intercourse, first union, and first birth. *International Journal of Population Geography, 8*, 1-15.

Hertrich, V. (2002). *Nuptiality and gender relationships in Africa: An overview of first marriage trends over the past 50 years*. Paper presented at the annual meeting of the Population Association of America, May 9-11, Atlanta, GA.

Hull, T.H. (2002). *The marriage revolution in Indonesia*. Paper presented at the annual meeting of the Population Association of America, May 9-11, Atlanta, GA.

International Center for Research on Women. (2004). *Too young to wed: Child marriage in their own words*. Available: http://www.icrw.org/photoessay/html/intro.htm [accessed August 2004].

International Planned Parenthood Federation and International Women's Rights Action Watch. (1990). *Reproductive rights*. Suffolk, England: Lavenham Press.

International Planned Parenthood Federation and International Women's Rights Action Watch. (2000). *Reproductive rights 2000*. London, England: Terracotta Press.

Islam, M.N., and Ahmed, A.U. (1998). Age at first marriage and its determinants in Bangladesh. *Asia-Pacific Population Journal, 13*(2), 73-92.

Jejeebhoy, S. (1995). Education and women's age at marriage. In S. Jejeebhoy (Ed.), *Women's education, autonomy, and reproductive behaviour: Experience from developing countries* (pp. 60-77). Oxford, England: Clarendon Press.

Jejeebhoy, S.J., and Halli, S.S. (2002). *Marriage patterns in rural India: Influence of sociocultural context*. Unpublished document, Population Council, New Delhi, India.

Kertzer, D.I., and Hogan, D.P. (1991). Reflections on the European marriage pattern: Sharecropping and proletarianization in Casalecchio, Italy, 1861-1921. *Journal of Family History, 16*(1), 31-45.

Kishor, S. (2003). *Uses and limitations of DHS data on age and characteristics of first marriages*. Paper presented at UNICEF Global Consultation on Indicators: Female Genital Mutilation/Cutting and Early Marriage, November 11-13, New York.

LeGrand, T.K., and Barbieri, M. (2002). The possible effects of child survival on women's ages at first union and childbirth in sub-Saharan Africa. *European Journal of Population, 18*, 361-386.

Lesthaeghe, R.J., Kaufman, G., and Meekers, D. (1989). The nuptiality regimes in sub-Saharan Africa. In R.J. Lesthaeghe (Ed.), *Reproduction and social organization in sub-Saharan Africa* (pp. 238-333). Berkeley: University of California Press.

Lindstrom, D.P., and Brambila Paz, C. (2001). Alternative theories of the relationship of schooling and work to family formation: Evidence from Mexico. *Social Biology, 48*(3-4), 278-297.

Lloyd, C.B., and Mensch, B. (1999). Implications of formal schooling for girls' transitions to adulthood in developing countries. In National Research Council, Committee on Population, C.H. Bledsoe, J.B. Casterline, J.A. Johnson-Kuhn, and J.G. Haaga (Eds.), *Critical perspectives on schooling and fertility in the developing world* (pp. 80-104). Washington, DC: National Academy Press.

Lynch, K.A. (1991). The European marriage pattern in the cities: Variations on a theme by Hajnal. *Journal of Family History, 16*(1), 79-96.

Malhotra, A. (1991). Gender and changing generational relations: Spouse choice in Indonesia. *Demography, 28*(4), 549-570.

Malhotra, A. (1997). Gender and the timing of marriage: Rural-urban differences in Java. *Journal of Marriage and the Family, 59*(2), 434-450.

Malhotra, A., and Tsui, A.O. (1996). Marriage timing in Sri Lanka: The role of modern norms and ideas. *Journal of Marriage and the Family, 58*(2), 476-490.

Mensch, B.S. (2003). *Trends in the timing of first marriage.* Presentation at the WHO, UNFPA, Population Council Technical Consultation on Married Adolescents, December 9, Geneva, Switzerland.

Mensch, B.S., Bruce, J., and Greene, M.E. (1998). *The uncharted passage: Girls' adolescence in the developing world.* New York: Population Council.

Mensch, B.S., Ibrahim, B.L., Lee, S.M., and El-Gibaly, O. (2003). Gender role attitudes among Egyptian adolescents. *Studies in Family Planning, 34*(1), 8-18.

Mensch, B.S., Grant, M.J., and Blanc, A.K. (2005). *The changing context of sexual initiation in sub-Saharan Africa.* Paper presented at XXV IUSSP International Population Conference, July 18-23, Tours, France.

Montgomery, M.R., and Sulak, D.B. (1989). Female first marriage in East and Southeast-Asia: A Kiefer-Neumann Model. *Journal of Development Economics, 30*(2), 225-240.

National Research Council. (1993). Marriage: New forms, new ambiguities. In Committee on Population, C.H. Bledsoe and B. Cohen (Eds.), *Social dynamics of adolescent fertility in sub-Saharan Africa* (pp. 37-68). Washington, DC: National Academy Press.

National Research Council and Institute of Medicine. (2005). Schooling. In Committee on Population, Panel on Transitions to Adulthood in Developing Countries, C.B. Lloyd (Ed.), *Growing up global: The changing transitions to adulthood in developing countries* (pp. 67-167). Washington, DC: The National Academies Press.

Population Council. (2002). Unpublished document prepared for Working Group on Girls, United Nations Special Session on Children, May 10, New York.

Preston, S.H., Heuveline, P., and Guillot, M. (2001). *Demography: Measuring and modeling population processes.* Malden, MA: Blackwell.

Quinn, T.C., Wawer, M.J., Sewenkambo, N., Serwadda, D., Li, C., Wabwire-Mangen, F., Meehan, M.O., Lutalo, T., and Gray, R.H. (2000). Viral load and heterosexual transmission of human immunodeficiency virus type 1. *New England Journal of Medicine, 342*(13), 921-929.

Rao, V. (1993a). Dowry "inflation" in rural India: A statistical investigation. *Population Studies, 47,* 283-293.

Rao, V. (1993b). The rising price of husbands: A hedonic analysis of dowry increases in rural India. *Journal of Political Economy, 101*(4), 666-677.

Rashad, H., and Osman, M. (2003). Nuptiality in Arab countries: Changes and implications. In N.S. Hopkins (Ed.), *Cairo papers in social science: The new Arab Family* (pp. 20-50). Cairo, Egypt: The American University in Cairo Press.

Rosero-Bixby, L. (1996). Nuptiality trends and fertility transition in Latin America. In J.M. Guzman, S. Singh, G. Rodriguez, and E.A. Pantelides (Eds.), *The fertility transition in Latin America* (pp. 135-150). Oxford, England: Clarendon Press.

Saxena, P.C., and Kulczycki, A. (2003). Nuptiality transition and marriage squeeze in Lebanon: Consequences of sixteen years of civil war. *Journal of Comparative Family Studies, 35*(2), 241-258.

Shryock, H.S., Siegel, J.S., Stockwell, E., and Swanson, D. (1971). *The methods and materials of demography.* Washington, DC: U.S. Bureau of the Census.

Singerman, D., and Ibrahim, B. (2003). The costs of marriage in Egypt: A hidden dimension in the new Arab demography. In N.S. Hopkins (Ed.), *Cairo papers in social science: The new Arab Family* (pp. 80-116). Cairo, Egypt: The American University in Cairo Press.

Singh, S., and Samara, R. (1996). Early marriage among women in developing countries. *International Family Planning Perspectives, 22*(4), 148-157, 175.

Smith, P.C. (1983). The impact of age at marriage and proportions marrying on fertility. In R.A. Bulatao and R.D. Lee with P.E. Hollerbach and J. Bongaarts (Eds.), *Determinants of fertility in developing countries* (pp. 473-531). New York: Academic Press.

UNICEF. (2001). *Early marriage: Child spouses.* Florence, Italy: United Nations Children's Fund, Innocenti Research Center.

United Nations. (2003). *World population prospects: The 2002 revision, volume 1: Comprehensive tables.* New York: Author.

United Nations Commission on Population and Development. (2002). *Concise report on world population monitoring 2002: Reproductive rights and reproductive health with special reference to human immunodeficiency virus/acquired immunodeficiency syndrome (HIV/AIDS).* Report of the Secretary General (E/CN.9/2002/2). Presented at the Commission on Population and Development, United Nations, April 1-5, New York. Available: http://www.un.org/esa/population/cpd/comm2002.htm [accessed April 2005].

United Nations Department of International Economic and Social Affairs. (1990). *Patterns of first marriage: Timing and prevalence.* New York: Author.

United Nations Population Division. (2000). *Database on marriage patterns (POP/1/DB/2000/3).* New York: Author.

United Nations Population Division, Department of Economic and Social Affairs. (2001). *World population prospects: The 2000 revision* [CD]. File 1: Total population by age group, major area, region, and country, 1950-2050 (in thousands), estimates 1950-2000 (POP/DB/WPP/Rev.2000/3/F1). New York: Author.

United Nations Population Division, Department of Economic and Social Affairs. (2004). *World fertility report: 2003.* New York: Author.

van de Walle, E. (1993). Recent trends in marriage ages. In National Research Council, Committee on Population, Panel on the Population Dynamics of sub-Saharan Africa, K.A. Foote, K.H. Hill, and L.G. Martin (Eds.), *Demographic change in sub-Saharan Africa* (pp. 117-152). Washington, DC: National Academy Press.

van de Walle, E., and Meekers, D. (1994). Marriage drinks and kola nuts. In C. Bledsoe and G. Pison (Eds.), *Nuptiality in sub-Saharan Africa: Contemporary anthropological and demographic perspectives* (pp. 57-73). Oxford, England: Clarendon Press.

Watkins, S.C. (1986). Regional patterns of nuptiality in Western Europe. In A.J. Coale and S.C. Watkins (Eds.), *The decline of fertility in Europe: The revised proceedings of a conference on the Princeton European Fertility Project* (pp. 314-336). Princeton, NJ: Princeton University Press.

Westoff, C.F. (2003). *Trends in marriage and early childbearing in developing countries.* (DHS Comparative Reports No. 5.) Calverton, MD: ORC Macro.

Westoff, C.F., and Bankole, A. (2002). *Reproductive preferences in developing countries at the turn of the century.* (DHS Comparative Reports No. 2.) Calverton, MD: ORC Macro.

Williams, L., and Guest, M.P. (2002). *Why marry? Attitudes of urban middle-class respondents in Vietnam, Thailand, and the Philippines.* (Population and Development Program Working Paper Series No. 01.01.) Ithaca, NY: Cornell University, Department of Rural Sociology.

World Bank. (2002). *Development indicators 2002.* Washington, DC: World Bank.

Wrigley, E.A., Davies, R.S., Oeppen, J.E., and Schofield, R.S. (1997). *English population history from family reconstitution 1580-1837.* Cambridge, England: Cambridge University Press.

Yabiku, S.T. (2003). *Neighbors or neighborhoods? Effects on marriage timing in Nepal.* Paper presented at the annual meeting of the Population Association of America, May 1-3, Minneapolis, MN.

Yabiku, S.T., Axinn, W.G., Ghimire, D.J., and Robinson, K.D. (2002). *School characteristics and marriage timing.* Paper presented at the annual meeting of the Population Association of America, May 9-11, Atlanta, GA.

6

Marriage Patterns in Rural India: Influence of Sociocultural Context

Shireen J. Jejeebhoy and Shiva S. Halli

There is considerable agreement that notable changes have occurred in India in the timing of marriage. For example, the singulate mean age at marriage of females increased from 15.2 in 1951 to 19.0 by 1991 (Bhat and Halli, 1999) and to 19.7 by 1998-1999 (IIPS and ORC Macro, 2000). However, regional variation is quite evident. For example, in 1992-1993 the median age at first marriage was 15.1 among women ages 25 to 49 in Uttar Pradesh in north India, compared to 18.1 in Tamil Nadu in south India (IIPS, 1995).

Less is known about regional differences and trends in marriage patterns, such as endogamy, postmarital residence patterns, spousal age and educational differences, dowry, and the extent to which women have a say in determining timing and partner, on the one hand, and the disbursal of their dowries on the other. Also poorly understood is the extent to which changes in these patterns are conditioned by sociocultural factors such as region and religion and their association with female autonomy. A unique data set provides an opportunity to explore marriage patterns and differences among successive cross-sections of Hindu and Muslim women who were married in the roughly 25 years from 1968 to 1993 in two socioculturally heterogeneous settings, namely rural areas of Uttar Pradesh and Tamil Nadu. The intention of this chapter is to describe differences in marital age and patterns among successive marital age cohorts and explore the extent to which differences emerge by region and religion.

Many arguments have been postulated to explain increases in marital age. Some would attribute the increase as a response to a marriage squeeze rather than as an outcome of increased educational attainment, which they argue is not advanced enough to be incompatible with early marriage (Bhat and Halli, 1999). They argue that India has begun to face an excess supply of women of marriageable ages because of changes such as declining infant and child mortality and the reduction in numbers of widowers available as maternal mortality declined, as well as because women tend to marry men who are older than them. This view would argue that this change resulted in both a longer search for a suitable husband and higher dowries (Amin and Cain, 1997; Bhat and Halli, 1999; Caldwell, Reddy, and Caldwell, 1983; Rao, 1993). Others would argue that increases in marital age may be attributed to shifts in the education of boys and girls and the imposition of a legal minimum age at marriage (Amin and Cain, 1997).

It is well known that marriage patterns reflect a fundamental difference between women from north and south India, and Hindu and Muslim women (see, e.g., Dyson and Moore, 1983; Karve, 1965). However, the extent to which these patterns are changing over time is less well studied. For example, there has been considerable public education on the problems associated with early marriage and laws against marriage to females under 19 and these, along with a growing recognition of the importance of educating females, would argue for an increase in marital age. Legal sanctions exist, at least in theory, against the practice of dowry; yet the consumer culture and the greater education levels of young males are argued to have prompted families to demand larger dowries than before.

In the more patriarchal kinship structure prevailing in the north, and particularly among the Hindus, marriage is regarded as an alliance of two families and involves the incorporation of outsiders as wives into the family. The resulting village exogamy prevailing in the north ensures a break between the natal family and the family into which a woman is married: not only is a woman married off into a distant village, but kinship rules ensure that, by and large, no other women from her natal family, or even village, can be married into the same village (Karve, 1965). The practice of marrying young girls into distant villages and into families with which previous contact has been limited at best and subsequent contacts are usually infrequent heightens women's powerlessness (Committee on the Status of Women in India, 1973). In contrast, north Indian Muslims are much more likely than Hindus to marry kin, and less likely to practice village exogamy. In the south, both Hindu and Muslim women enjoy less alienating marriage ties. Here, marriage is more a means of consolidating existing kinship networks than a political alliance. As a result, there are fewer restrictions on marriage within the village or within easy travelling distance from the woman's natal village.

In Tamil Nadu, marriages often take place among affines. As in the north, the practice of dowry is common. Although in the north the pattern and flow of resources is strictly one way, even after marriage (Das Gupta, 1987), in Tamil Nadu, women themselves appear to have more control over their dowries. Unlike women in the north who are traditionally perceived as temporary members in their natal homes (Dube, 1988), ties between women and their natal families in south India remain close even after marriage; while daughters may continue to receive gifts from their parents and nearest kin even after marriage (see, e.g., Bhat and Halli, 1999), in turn, the daughters provide emotional and sometimes (less frequently) economic support to their parents.

This chapter draws on data from a community-based survey on women's autonomy in two culturally distinct sites: Uttar Pradesh in the north, in which the situation of women is especially poor, and Tamil Nadu in the south, where gender relations are somewhat more balanced, and women are relatively better off. About half the sample in each setting was composed of Hindu women, the other half Muslim women. The survey was conducted in 1993-1994 and included questionnaires for married women ages 15 to 39 and their husbands, if available. Findings presented elsewhere have addressed the measurement of distinct dimensions of autonomy, and have confirmed that social institutions of gender powerfully shape women's autonomy here by region. Findings have not supported, however, the argument that Muslim women are at a disadvantage in terms of women's autonomy, at least when compared to Hindu women from the same region (Jejeebhoy, 2000; Jejeebhoy and Sathar, 2001). Given that household data from this survey suggest that roughly 75 percent of women were already married by age 18, here we explore marriage patterns among those ages 19 to 39 (39 was the cut-off age for this survey).

THE SETTING

Uttar Pradesh and Tamil Nadu lie at two extremes of the social and cultural spectrum in India, although economically they are relatively similar. Both states are poor, with about 37 percent in Uttar Pradesh and 40 percent in Tamil Nadu (and 33 percent in India) living below the poverty level, and both states are largely agricultural (Uttar Pradesh, 72 percent; Tamil Nadu, 61 percent; India, 70 percent). Yet there are huge differences in social development levels. For example, literacy rates are much higher in Tamil Nadu (63 percent) than in Uttar Pradesh (42 percent), and fertility and mortality are much lower. The infant mortality rate is 98 per 1,000 live births in Uttar Pradesh and 58 in Tamil Nadu; the under-5 mortality rate is 141 in Uttar Pradesh and 87 in Tamil Nadu; and the total fertility rate is 5.1 in Uttar Pradesh and 2.2 in Tamil Nadu.

In most of India, both north and south, and among both Hindus and Muslims, the family is mainly patriarchal, patrilocal, and patrilineal, and the region is well known for inegalitarian gender relations (Altekar, 1962; Karve, 1965). Women are defined as inferior; husbands are assumed to "own" women and to have the right to dominate them. Inegalitarian gender relations deny women a decision-making role in family matters, inhibit them from moving about freely, prevent their access to material resources, and expose them to violence in the household. Within this situation of generally limited autonomy, however, there are sharp cultural and regional differences in women's situations and vulnerability (Dyson and Moore, 1983), and these are reflected in available social indicators. For example, in Uttar Pradesh, life expectancy is about 4 years higher for males than for females (54 and 49, respectively); in Tamil Nadu, life expectancy for both females and males is 61 years. Moreover, the maternal mortality ratio is 931 in Uttar Pradesh and 319 in Tamil Nadu. Furthermore, gender disparities in literacy are far wider in Uttar Pradesh (25 percent for females compared to 56 percent for males) than in Tamil Nadu (51 percent for females compared to 74 percent for males).

DATA

The main objectives of the study from which these data are drawn were to operationalize the concept of autonomy, to assess its relationships to reproductive behavior, and to assess the role of context in conditioning both levels of autonomy and its relationship to reproductive behavior. Samples were drawn from north and south Indian women and from Hindu and Muslim women. The survey included a household questionnaire, a questionnaire for eligible women currently married and ages 39 or younger, and a questionnaire for available husbands. Parallel questions were posed to women and their husbands concerning women's autonomy within the home, and gender norms and expectations

Uttar Pradesh in north India and Tamil Nadu in south India were selected deliberately to represent a range of gender and sociocultural conditions. Within each state, similarly, two districts were purposively selected (on the basis of an index of development, measured from indicators such as income, percentage of roads surfaced, and other economic criteria) to maximize differences in socioeconomic conditions, while at the same time allowing for comparisons of Hindu and Muslim women. From each district, one taluka (subdistrict) was similarly selected. The four sites thus selected were as follows: from Tamil Nadu, Pollachi taluka from Coimbatore district (ranked 1 of 21) and Mudukulathur taluka from Ramnathpuram district (ranked 18 of 21); and from Uttar Pradesh, Kunda taluka from Meerut district (ranked 2 of 63) and Baghpat taluka from Pratapgarh district (ranked 51 of 63).

From each of the four sites, a cluster of contiguous villages of roughly 1,000 to 2,000 households was randomly selected, and about 800 currently married women ages 15 to 39 were randomly selected for interview. Husbands who were present were also interviewed. In each setting, on the assumption that sociocultural norms governing female autonomy vary widely among Hindus and Muslims, about half of all respondents selected were Hindu and the other half Muslim. As a result, a total of eight communities are covered: four geographical sites, and within each site, two distinct religious groups, Hindus and Muslims.

A total of 1,842 women constitute the sample: 859 from Uttar Pradesh and 983 from Tamil Nadu. In the course of interviews with women, respondents were asked not only about their education and work status, but also about a variety of dimensions of autonomy within their married lives, including their decision-making authority, personal freedom of movement, control over economic resources, and wife-husband power relations. Also asked were questions relating to marriage age and practices, including the extent to which women had a say in marriage decisions, postmarital residence patterns, the magnitude and content of dowries, and the extent to which women had a say in the use of these valuables. The study was restricted to married women and corresponding data from the unmarried are not available. Ideally speaking, of course, for the study of determinants of age at marriage, unmarried women also must be included in the sample. By performing the analysis on women who are already married by the time of the survey, we allow the sample to be "right-censored"; for example, married women ages 19 to 24 at the time of the survey cannot by definition include women who would be marrying after 24 in the young age cohort, whereas such women would be included in the older age cohorts. The analysis attempts to minimize this limitation as far as possible.

This chapter reports findings from 1,715 currently married women, ages between 19 and 39, and married once. A distribution of all females residing in the selected households suggests that by age 19, three-quarters or more reported themselves to be married; hence, we selected age 19 as the lower cutoff point for this study. Given this age range, and because the objective of this chapter is to explore the marriage experiences over time, we compared the experiences of successive cohorts of women by marital duration. While assessing marriage practices, we compared the experiences of the recently married (0 to 10 years) with those who were married 11 or more years prior to the survey. Similarly, in order to assess marital age, we compared the experiences of successive cross-sections of married women as defined by marriage duration. Only once-married women are included. This chapter compares marriage patterns among Hindus and Muslims from each setting, and explores the extent to which marriage age and patterns have changed in the roughly 25 years separating the marriages of the oldest and youngest women. Clearly, the older women will be subject to significant recall lapses that may limit the reliability of their responses. Data are analyzed separately by region (Uttar Pradesh and Tamil Nadu) and religion (Hindu and Muslim) in order to explore their role in influencing differences in marriage age and patterns.

Table 6-1 highlights background social and economic characteristics of households of the two cohorts of women by marital duration in the four communities. Economic status appears to be relatively similar across sites. For example, per capita annual income varies from Rs 2,600 among Tamilian Muslims married 11 or more years prior to the survey to Rs 5,400 among recently married Hindu women in Uttar Pradesh; households, irrespective of cohort or community, possess an average of two to three consumer goods. By and large, land ownership is more likely to characterize Hindu women residing in Uttar Pradesh than other groups, while household amenities, such as electricity, are more likely to characterize the homes of Tamilian women.

A look at educational profiles of women and their husbands suggests some interesting trends. Although large proportions of women in all communities have never been to school, and few have completed primary school, considerably larger proportions of Tamilian women have ever attended school than have women in Uttar Pradesh, irrespective of religion. Increases in schooling rates appear to have increased most impressively, however, among Hindu women from Uttar Pradesh. While 11 percent of those married 11 or more years prior to the survey had any secondary schooling, this increased to 41 percent among the recently married cohort. Correspondingly, the husbands of Hindu women from Uttar Pradesh have made the most impressive gains in education—from a mean of 7.4 years of schooling among the cohort married 11 or more years prior to the survey to 10 years among the recently married.

Economic activity profiles around the time of marriage differ starkly by region. In general, Hindu women from Tamil Nadu, irrespective of marital duration, are most likely to have worked for wages both before marriage and as newlyweds. Also notable among them is that the more recently married cohort is somewhat more likely than the cohort married 11 or more years prior to the survey to have worked before marriage.

In short and in general, this profile suggests some variation in social and economic conditions across the four communities. Within each community, however, marital duration-specific variation is relatively modest, with some notable exceptions, including educational attainment of women and husbands, especially the Hindus of Uttar Pradesh, and wage work before marriage among Hindus of Tamil Nadu.

AGE AT MARRIAGE

Results presented in Table 6-2 suggest that in general, the familiar north-south dichotomy is reflected in age at marriage patterns; within each region, by religion, differences are modest. Mean and median ages at marriage range between 13 and 17 in Uttar Pradesh and between 17 and 19 in Tamil Nadu. Of interest now are notable changes in marriage age within the four communities studied. Clearly, marriage continues to take place in adolescence for the majority of each cohort under study; however, there is a pronounced shift from early to late adolescence. For example, in Uttar

TABLE 6-1 Profile of Women by Duration of Marriage, Women Married 0-10 and 11 or More Years, Once-Married Women Ages 19-39, Uttar Pradesh and Tamil Nadu

	Uttar Pradesh			
	Muslim		Hindu	
	0-10	11+	0-10	11+
Number	149	221	145	259
Land Ownership Status				
Any land	30.9	33.5	77.2	72.2
6+ acres	2.7	3.6	16.6	13.9
Household Economic Status				
Mean per capita annual income (Rs)	3,182	2,995	5,380	3,942
% with electricity	37.6	38.9	42.1	25.1
Number of consumer durables owned (of 9)	2.5	2.2	2.4	2.2
Schooling Status				
1-6 years	18.8	14.5	20.0	15.8
7+ years	8.7	1.6	40.7	11.2
Mean years	1.6	0.8	4.9	1.7
Schooling of Husband				
Mean years	5.4	3.8	10.0	7.4
Economic Activity				
% worked for wages year 1	2.0	0.9	1.4	0.4
% worked for wages before marriage	5.4	2.7	3.4	4.2

NOTE: Excludes a total of 128 women, including 89 ages 18 or less, and 39 older women married more than once.

Pradesh, among those married 11 years or longer, two-thirds of Muslims and three quarters of Hindus were married by age 15; this proportion fell to around one-third among the youngest. In Tamil Nadu, where marriage by age 15 was relatively uncommon even among the older cohort (27 percent and 20 percent of Muslim and Hindu women were married by age 15), dramatic changes have continued to occur, with fewer than 10 percent of the younger cohort married by age 15.

Marriage by age 18 has also recorded a significant decline in both settings. In Uttar Pradesh, where more than 90 percent of those married 11 years or longer were married by age 18, this proportion has declined to two-thirds among those married more recently. In Tamil Nadu, too, considerable change is apparent: Among Muslims, proportions married by age 18 has declined from 66 percent to 34 percent and among Hindus from 50 percent to 25 percent.

Clearly, a powerful north-south divide remains in marriage age and changes in this age. Although marriage in adolescence has shown remarkable declines in both settings, the large majority of women in Uttar Pradesh

Tamil Nadu			
Muslim		Hindu	
0-10	11+	0-10	11+
230	293	207	211
27.8	33.5	33.3	40.3
2.6	2.4	15.0	11.4
3,292	2,618	4,203	3,587
63.5	64.5	46.9	40.3
3.0	3.0	2.6	2.5
56.5	56.0	40.6	31.3
21.7	7.8	20.8	15.2
4.2	2.8	3.6	2.6
5.7	5.0	4.9	4.6
7.8	12.6	39.1	39.8
21.7	17.4	61.4	55.4

continue to marry in adolescence. In Tamil Nadu in contrast, it appears that marriage is increasingly postponed beyond the adolescent years.

MARRIAGE PATTERNS

Arranged marriage and extensive dowries continue to characterize marriage in much of India, both north and south. Here we explore the extent to which these traditional patterns are changing over the lives of the two marriage cohorts. Available data enable us to piece together a substantial profile of marriage-related decision making, the extent of arranged marriage and premarital acquaintance between spouses, postmarital residence patterns and extent of endogamy, spousal age and educational disparities, and the size and content of dowry and the extent of female control of its disbursal. Findings suggest that marriage patterns are by and large stable over time, but that practices are far less alienating or likely to limit exercise of autonomy among south Indian women, irrespective of age or religion, than among northern women.

TABLE 6-2 Marriage Age Among Women by Duration of Marriage, Women Married 0-10 and 11 or More Years, Once-Married Women Ages 19-39, Uttar Pradesh and Tamil Nadu

	Uttar Pradesh			
	Muslim		Hindu	
	0-10	11+	0-10	11+
Number	149	221	145	259
% married by age 15	34.9	67.4	36.6	76.8
% married by age 18	63.1	93.7	65.5	95.4
Mean age at marriage (women aged 20+)	16.6	14.5	16.7	13.0
Median age at marriage	16	15	17	14

NOTE: Excludes a total of 128 women, including 89 ages 18 or less, and 39 older women married more than once.

Marriage-Related Decision Making

Marrying off a daughter is regarded as one of the most important duties of a father in both north and south India. Findings presented in Table 6-3 confirm that in neither Uttar Pradesh nor Tamil Nadu are marriage negotiations left entirely to the daughter. Women were asked whether they had selected their own spouses or participated in the decision on when and whom to marry. Responses suggest that for the overwhelming majority, irrespective of marital duration, region, or religion, marriages were arranged either by parents alone or with relatives and matchmakers. Yet subtle differences do emerge, and substantial minorities of women reported having a say, or being consulted in these decisions. While the familiar regional disparities persist, with Tamilian women exerting far more autonomy in these decisions than north Indian women, marital duration-specific differences are also evident within each setting. Recently married cohorts exerted considerably more of a voice than older cohorts in marriage-related decision making. For example, among Hindu and Muslim women from Tamil Nadu, proportions reporting a say in marriage decisions increased from 37 and 29 percent, respectively, among the longer married cohort to 45 and 35 percent, respectively, among the recently married ones. In contrast, among women from Uttar Pradesh, although increases are reported by both Muslim and Hindu women, no more than a handful of even the recently married—about one in six in both groups—had any say or veto powers in this decision.

Tamil Nadu			
Muslim		Hindu	
0-10	11+	0-10	11+
230	293	207	211
7.0	26.6	4.3	19.9
34.3	66.2	25.1	50.2
18.1	16.8	19.2	17.5
18	17	19	17

Kin Marriage and Premarital Acquaintance with Husband

Regional differences in kin marriage and village exogamy have been extensively documented in the literature. In the north, and particularly among Hindus, the practice is to marry young girls into families with which previous contact has been limited and kin marriage is rare—both features that heighten women's powerlessness (Committee on the Status of Women in India, 1973). In the south, in contrast, both Hindu and Muslim women enjoy less alienating marriage ties. Here, marriage is more a means of consolidating existing kinship networks than a political alliance, and as a result they are both more likely to be married within the wider kin network and to be acquainted with their husbands prior to marriage. Results presented in Table 6-3 bear out these conclusions. Among north Indian Hindus, for example, only 1 to 2 percent were married within the kin network and an equal percentage were acquainted with their husbands prior to marriage. Among south Indians and to a lesser extent north Indian Muslims, kin marriage and premarital acquaintance with husband are far more prevalent. What is particularly interesting from these findings is the suggestion that these are cultural practices that are deeply embedded; there is no convincing evidence, for example, of change over time in either the extent of marriage within kin networks or of premarital acquaintance in all four communities.

TABLE 6-3 Marriage Practices by Duration of Marriage, Women Married 0-10 and 11 or More Years, Once-Married Women Ages 19-39, Uttar Pradesh and Tamil Nadu

	Uttar Pradesh			
	Muslim		Hindu	
	0-10	11+	0-10	11+
Number	149	221	145	259
Autonomy in marriage decisions: % had say in marriage decision	14.8	10.0	15.9	6.6
Age difference with husband (mean)	4.6	5.7	4.0	5.0
% husband 10+ years older	5.4	9.5	0.0	3.9
Education difference with husband (mean)	3.8	3.1	5.1	5.6
Husband is 2+ levels better educated than wife	47.7	35.7	57.9	63.3
Husband is as or less educated than wife	42.3	54.3	21.4	25.9
% living in natal family area	16.1	13.6	1.4	1.9
% in polygamous unions	0.7	1.4	1.4	0.4
% married to relative	27.5	23.5	1.4	2.3
% knowing husband before marriage	28.2	19.5	1.4	0.8
% residing with husband's family after marriage	92.6	83.3	97.9	90.7

NOTE: Excludes a total of 128 women, including 89 ages 18 or less, and 39 older women married more than once.

Village Endogamy and Postmarital Residence

In the more patriarchal kinship structure prevailing in the north, particularly among Hindus, marriage involves the incorporation of outsiders as wives into the family and the resulting village exogamy ensures a break between the natal family and the family into which a woman is married. In the south, in contrast, marriage is perceived as a means of strengthening existing community-level bonds, and this is ensured through village endogamy (Karve, 1965). Corresponding with findings concerning kin marriage, results suggest wide regional, and to a lesser extent religion-wise, disparities in the practice of village endogamy, measured here by the proportion of women who currently reside in villages in which they were born or spent their childhood. Village endogamy is rarely reported among Hindu women in Uttar Pradesh (1 to 2 percent), is reported by about one-sixth of Muslim women in that setting, and increases to about one-third and one-half among Hindu and Muslim women in Tamil Nadu. Again, marital duration-specific changes are imperceptible, suggesting again that this traditional practice remains the norm.

Postmarital residence patterns remain uniform over all communities:

Tamil Nadu			
Muslim		Hindu	
0-10	11+	0-10	11+
230	293	207	211
35.2	28.7	45.4	37.4
5.6	6.8	5.9	6.2
8.2	16.7	11.6	16.1
1.6	2.2	1.3	2.0
24.7	29.7	24.2	27.0
49.1	40.6	56.0	48.3
48.3	54.9	33.8	33.6
0.4	1.4	1.9	3.3
60.4	66.6	51.2	59.7
48.7	56.3	45.4	46.4
77.0	79.9	78.3	73.9

The overwhelming majority of women coresided with their husbands' families immediately following marriage, although again, women from Tamil Nadu were somewhat less likely than those from Uttar Pradesh to have done so. Although in Tamil Nadu, this proportion has remained virtually unchanged over the two marriage cohorts studied, in Uttar Pradesh there is some evidence of increasing postmarital joint family residence over time, perhaps the result of improvements in mortality among the parental generation.

Spousal Imbalances in Age and Education: Extent of Polygamy

It is hypothesized that characteristics of the husband such as his age and education and particularly wide spousal age and educational disparities can further limit the autonomy of young married women. Spousal age differences are, in general, considerably wider in Tamil Nadu than in Uttar Pradesh, and these disparities persist even among younger cohorts. Even so, the evidence suggests a considerable narrowing of age differences among successive cohorts of Muslim women in both settings. For example, while 16 percent of both Hindu and Muslim women in the older cohort in Tamil

Nadu were married to men 10 or more years older, this proportion fell to 12 percent and 8 percent, respectively, among the recently married cohort, and in Uttar Pradesh, from 4 percent and 10 percent to 0 percent and 5 percent, respectively.

Educational differences are, in contrast, considerably more inegalitarian in Uttar Pradesh than in Tamil Nadu. More interesting for purposes of this chapter, is evidence that educational disparities are narrowing rapidly over time among Hindu and Muslim women in Tamil Nadu and more gradually among Hindu women in Uttar Pradesh, and are actually increasing among Muslim women in Uttar Pradesh. For example, in Uttar Pradesh, among the cohort married 11 or more years prior to the survey, 54 percent of Muslim women and 26 percent of Hindu women reported educational levels that equalled or exceeded those of their husbands; this proportion falls to 42 percent and 21 percent, respectively, among the recently married cohort. In Tamil Nadu in contrast, the proportion reporting equal or better education levels increased significantly for both Hindus and Muslims: from 48 percent to 56 percent among Hindus and from 41 percent to 49 percent among Muslims. Mean differences in educational attainment levels tell a similar story.

Contrary to public opinion, the incidence of polygamy—that is, proportions reporting that their husbands have two or more wives—is very low. An insignificant 1 percent of the sample was in polygamous unions. There is no contextual variation: Hindus and Muslims are about as likely to be in polygamous unions as those from Uttar Pradesh and Tamil Nadu. While not entirely comparable (because recently married women are more likely to be at an early age of their married lives), there is no evidence of marriage duration-specific differences in polygamous unions.

Dowry

In both Uttar Pradesh and Tamil Nadu, marrying a daughter is expensive, and by far the greatest expense is dowry. Fewer than 10 percent of all respondents were married without some kind of dowry.[1] The financial implications of dowry are recognized by all respondents, irrespective of region and level of education. Daughters are clearly perceived by educated

---

[1]Women sometimes preferred to use the word "gifts" for the substantial jewelry, money, and consumer goods that were given to the husband's family at the time of marriage. Even among women who labeled the wealth that accompanied their marriages as gifts, the majority indicated that the content and amount of these gifts were negotiated between the families prior to marriage. Hence the distinction between "dowry" and gifts becomes blurred.

and uneducated women alike as a drain on family resources, as observed in focus group discussions:

> To have a daughter is necessary except for the expense. (Gounder,[2] Coimbatore)

Moreover, insufficient dowry can threaten the physical security of women, particularly in Uttar Pradesh. For example, in focus group discussions on domestic violence, women suggested that not only was insufficient dowry a common reason for wife beating, but a cause of death as well:

> You talk only of beating; they even kill her if dowry is insufficient. (Brahmin,[3] Pratapgarh)

There is a clear positive association between the level of education of a young man and the dowry he is able to command in each of the four communities studied. This was substantiated by participants of focus group discussions:

> If the boy is well educated and from a good family, they [the bride's family] may have to pay a higher dowry. According to today's times, if we have to fix a marriage in a family like ours, we would have to spend Rs 10 lakh [US$32,000] on the entire marriage. (Jat,[4] Meerut)

In an attempt to estimate the size of the dowry, and capture wide regional disparities in its content, the survey asked a battery of questions on particular items included in the dowry. These included jewelry or gold, cash, land and livestock, and a variety of consumer goods ranging from furniture and cooking utensils to stereos, TVs and refrigerators, and bicycles, motorcycles, and cars. From responses, we imputed a rupee value to items in 1993 rupee terms (except in the case of cash transfers) and the approximate rupee value of the dowry was thus assessed.

In both settings, dowry amounts can be crippling and well out of proportion with the household's income. Rupee values of dowry ranged from 0 for those whose marriages involved no dowry to Rs 110,000. Although dowries were large in every setting, their content varied. Gold and jewelry were the dominant form of dowry among Tamilian women, whereas the focus in Uttar Pradesh was on consumer goods. To explore the extent to which dowry patterns have changed over time, Table 6-4 presents dowry transfers reported by successive marriage cohorts of women married 11 or more years and 0 to

---

[2]Prominent caste, Coimbatore site.
[3]Prominent caste, Pratapgarh site.
[4]Prominent caste, Meerut site.

TABLE 6-4 Dowry Practices by Duration of Marriage, Women Married 0-10 and 11 or More Years, Once-Married Women Ages 19-39, Uttar Pradesh and Tamil Nadu

| | Uttar Pradesh | | | |
| | Muslim | | Hindu | |
	0-10	11+	0-10	11+
Number	149	221	145	259
Dowry Amount (equivalent Rs)[a]	22,849	21,172	36,835	28,639
CONTENT				
Jewelry				
Any	77.2	71.0	87.6	79.2
Large amount	14.1	12.2	33.1	21.2
Cash	8.7	3.6	31.0	21.2
Other:				
Furniture	34.3	25.1	60.8	39.2
Stereo sets	32.9	16.1	47.6	44.5
TV set	1.3	1.4	15.9	3.1
Bicycle	37.9	19.60	38.5	44.5
Car, vehicle	0.7	1.8	2.8	2.3
Refrigerator, other goods	0.7	0.5	7.6	0.4
Livestock	2.1	6.0	27.3	32.2
Say in Dowry				
Any	44.3	37.6	52.4	37.5
Major	28.2	19.9	22.8	16.2

NOTE: Excludes a total of 128 women, including 89 ages 18 or less, and 39 older women married more than once.

10 years ago (ages 19 to 39). Findings suggest that dowry expenses have actually recorded moderate increases in all communities in recent years, and increases are particularly striking among younger marriage cohorts among the Hindus of Uttar Pradesh and the Muslims of Tamil Nadu.

Changes in the content of dowry are more evident in Uttar Pradesh than in Tamil Nadu. In both states, jewelry continues to dominate. However, it is in Tamil Nadu that jewelery is the main item in the dowry, and rupee values of the dowry are largely shaped by jewelry payments; this trend has hardly changed over the two marriage cohorts under study. It is notable that dowries have not included, for the most part, consumer goods, even among the younger marriage cohort. The item most likely to be included in dowries of Tamilian women is furniture, usually comprising no more than a steel cupboard, and proportions reporting that their dowries included furniture have increased modestly among the more recent mar-

Tamil Nadu			
Muslim		Hindu	
0-10	11+	0-10	11+
230	293	207	211
42,272	38,666	34,645	33,296
96.5	93.2	92.8	89.1
67.0	60.4	48.3	47.4
47.0	10.6	13.0	2.4
25.0	15.7	21.6	15.4
4.5	3.9	5.0	4.1
0.0	0.0	0.5	1.0
0.9	0.4	1.0	0.0
0.0	0.3	1.4	1.4
2.2	0.6	5.8	2.8
1.8	2.8	9.5	8.7
86.1	90.4	89.9	93.4
58.7	67.9	59.9	64.9

[a]Imputing Rs amounts: furniture Rs 2,000; stereo Rs 1,000; TV Rs 10,000; bicycle Rs 1,000; vehicle Rs 30,000; refrigerator/other Rs 10,000; livestock Rs 7,000; land Rs 25,000; cash Rs 500, 1,000, 2,000; jewelry/gold Rs 5,000, 15,000, 50,000.

riage cohort. There is a significant increase, however, in cash transfers over the two cohorts, particularly among Muslims (from 11 to 47 percent in contrast to an increase from 2 to 13 percent among Hindus).

In Uttar Pradesh, in contrast, along with increases in jewelry and cash transfers, come increases over cohorts in the transfer of major consumer goods, including bicycles, furniture, stereos, and TV sets. Thus there is evidence from Uttar Pradesh, but not Tamil Nadu, of an expansion of dowry to include major consumer goods along with gold and jewelry.

Another significant difference is evident in trends pertaining to the control of jewelery and cash transfers included in dowries. Our data suggest that the overwhelming majority of women in Tamil Nadu (86 to 90 percent among Muslims and 90 to 93 percent among Hindus) report that they had some say in how these items were used, and between half and two-thirds reported that they had the major control over them. In contrast, it is clear that dowry transfers in Uttar Pradesh are more likely to be made to the groom's family rather than for the use of the woman herself. In Uttar Pradesh, for example, half or fewer women report having any say in the use of these valuables, and far fewer than one third report the major say. In Uttar Pradesh, moreover, there are signs that the more recently married cohort of women exert considerably greater control over their dowries than do women married 11 or more years; in Tamil Nadu, women in the recently married cohort have about as much control over these valuables as does the cohort married 11 or more years. In general, however, the major divide continues to be regional rather than religion or marital duration.

Several hypotheses may be raised for this regional divide in dowry payments. For one, as Srinivas (1989) has suggested, there are two types of dowry, traditional and modern. In Tamil Nadu, where dowry transfers traditionally have been accepted, dowry transfers and content remain essentially traditional—payments include predominantly jewelry and gold along with some household gifts, and are generally regarded as the property of women. On the other hand, in Uttar Pradesh, where dowry transfers are of more recent origin, dowry transfers follow the modern type, comprising a lump sum of money along with the "many and much desired of products of modern technologies" (Srinivas, 1989, p. 14). Srinivas argues that the practice of modern dowry is a comparatively new phenomenon and this practice has become more ingrained in recent years in order to attract better qualified and hence more desirable grooms in the marriage market.

A second hypothesis relates to differences in marriage practices themselves. This quest for a suitably qualified groom is further exacerbated in Uttar Pradesh by its hypergamous tradition, argued to create stronger demands for cash and consumer goods. With modernization, the hierarchical class structure that made hypergamy possible in the first place has strengthened the practice and, along with it, adherence to groomprice in the north (Bhat and Halli, 1999). Tamil Nadu, in contrast, is characterized by caste endogamy in which postmarital residence is often the natal village or vicinity. In this environment, the young woman has greater social and natal family support to maintain control of her property and valuables than in Uttar Pradesh, where she has no close allies. Finally, as we have maintained, women in Tamil Nadu have more autonomy in every sphere of their lives than do women in Uttar Pradesh, and control over dowry is no exception (see, e.g., Jejeebhoy, 2000; Jejeebhoy and Sathar, 2001).

Factors Contributing to Delayed Marriage

Marriage patterns have been argued to influence age at marriage in several ways. A number of factors have been observed to delay age at marriage among women. For example, parents' quest for a mutually acceptable husband is inevitably prolonged when women have a say in whom and when to marry (or at least veto rights) (see, e.g., Dixon, 1975; Mason, 1984). Similarly, where employment opportunities are available for unmarried girls, and work outside the home is socially acceptable and available, women or their parents may defer early marriage in favor of participation in the labor force (Dyson and Moore, 1983; Standing, 1983). Others have argued that the marriage squeeze or relative paucity of males are the factors that have led to an increase both in marital age and education levels of females (Bhat and Halli, 1999; Rao, 1993). In fact, women's economic independence has been hypothesized as the leading reason for delayed marriage in gender-stratified settings where families stand to gain from the employment of their uneducated daughters, but especially in more equal settings where the woman herself stands to gain (Caldwell, Reddy, and Caldwell, 1983; Jain and Nag, 1986; Mason, 1993; Salaff and Wong, 1977).

Others have argued differently, placing education more at the center of the force for change. Factors that enhance age at marriage are said to be related more to reducing the marriageability of females than increasing the autonomy of young women. Even in settings where traditional attitudes and norms persist, the demand for educated wives by "eligible" men has made female education an asset in arranging a good marriage (Minturn, 1984, for Rajasthan; Caldwell, Reddy, and Caldwell, 1982, for Karnataka; Caldwell, Reddy, and Caldwell, 1983, for Karnataka; Vlassoff, 1996, for rural Maharashtra). However, the longer a young girl is kept in school, the longer she will remain out of the net of marriage negotiations. Because the pool of available, better educated potential husbands is smaller, negotiations for the marriage of an educated daughter are, in all likelihood, even more time consuming than for an uneducated one (see Caldwell et al., 1989). This pursuit of an education may deter parents from postponing the search for a husband.

To address the limitation associated with the lack of corresponding data on unmarried women, we restrict our multivariate analyses of factors influencing marital age to women ages 19 and above, among whom the overwhelming percentage (more than 95 percent) have made the transition into marriage. To understand the correlates of age at marriage for the two age groups, data were subjected to ordinary least-squares regressions with the age at marriage as the dependent variable. Several dummy variables have been constructed for nominal and ordinal variables; the excluded category is designed to be the reference category by which the effects of other dummy variables can be compared.

Table 6-5 presents the results of regression analyses (OLS), which regress age at marriage on various individual-, family-, and community-level

TABLE 6-5 Correlates of Marriage Age Among Women Ages 19-39, Married 0-10 and 11+ Years, Uttar Pradesh and Tamil Nadu: OLS Regression Coefficients, by Site

	Total	
	Married 0-10 Years	Married 11+ Years
INDIVIDUAL LEVEL		
Education		
Primary	0.986[c]	1.088[c]
Secondary	2.585[c]	2.723[c]
Economic activity for wages before marriage	−0.222	−0.015
Participation in marriage decisions	0.008	0.218
Marriage Practice and Partner Level		
Spousal age difference >5 years	−0.469[b]	−0.398[b]
Spousal educational difference >5 classes	0.235	0.230
Endogamy: resides in natal village or vicinity	−0.099	0.274
Kin marriage: married to relative	−0.452[b]	−0.154
Dowry payments >Rs 50,000	−0.008	0.248
NATAL FAMILY LEVEL		
Father's Education Level		
Primary	0.310[a]	0.138
Secondary	−0.048	0.266
Sociocultural Context		
Uttar Pradesh Hindu	−0.892[c]	−2.017[c]
Tamil Nadu Muslim	1.161[c]	1.481[c]
Tamil Nadu Hindu	2.442[c]	2.338[c]
Constant	16.244[c]	14.461[c]
R squared	0.377	0.426
Number	731	984

[a]Equals .000.
[b]Equals .001-.05.
[c]Equals .051-.099.

factors assumed from the above discussion to influence it. Among individual woman-level factors are education, premarital employment, and say in choice of husband. Among marriage practice and partner-level factors are age and educational differences between women and husbands, endogamy, and dowry payments. Natal family factors are represented by father's education levels, and sociocultural context by state and religion. Results are presented for all women married 0 to 10 years and 11 or more years in Uttar Pradesh and Tamil Nadu, respectively.

Findings suggest that not all blocks, and not all indicators within each block, play a role in influencing marriage age. Among individual-level factors, the role of education is prominent. In both settings and in both co-

Uttar Pradesh		Tamil Nadu	
Married 0-10 Years	Married 11+ Years	Married 0-10 Years	Married 11+ Years
1.309^b	1.574^b	0.992^c	0.831^c
1.784^c	2.812^c	3.027^c	2.579^c
-0.027	0.411	-0.074	-0.094
0.337	0.951^a	-0.159	-0.058
-0.438^a	-0.017	-0.607^c	-0.757^c
-0.207	0.317	0.418^a	0.141
0.471	0.006	-0.052	0.100
-0.061	-0.093	-0.517^b	-0.175
0.068	0.026	-0.163	0.395^b
0.090	-0.288	0.436^b	0.367^b
-0.711	0.114	0.747^b	0.476^a
-0.248	-1.962^c	1.212^c	0.884^c
16.308^c	14.140^c	17.320^c	16.270^c
0.140	0.150	0.393	0.295
294	480	437	504

horts, even a primary school education has a significant effect on delaying marriage; there is some evidence that in Tamil Nadu, the influence of both a primary and a secondary education on delaying marriage has become stronger among the recently married cohort. At the same time, the effect of a secondary education is clearly far more pronounced in each group. In contrast, economic activity prior to marriage is unrelated to marriage age in each setting and cohort. Thus, having a say in marriage decisions does not appear to delay marriage.

Few marriage practice and partner-level factors are uniformly significant. For example, recently married women with considerably better educated husbands are significantly more likely to delay marriage in Tamil

Nadu, but not in Uttar Pradesh. There is no evidence that those marrying within or in the vicinity of the natal village marry any later than other women. In contrast, among both cohorts in Tamil Nadu, and to a lesser extent among the recently married cohort in Uttar Pradesh, findings suggest that women marrying considerably older men (5 years or more) are significantly more likely to marry early than are other women. Among older women—but not younger—in Tamil Nadu (but not Uttar Pradesh), there is evidence that large dowry payments tended to delay marriage.

Among natal family factors, there is evidence that natal family socioeconomic status, as measured by father's education, does influence marriage age, but this effect is statistically significant only in Tamil Nadu.

Finally, the evidence suggests that sociocultural context—as measured by religion and setting—exerts a powerful influence on marriage age. A look at findings for the two states combined suggests that compared to the Muslims of Uttar Pradesh, the Hindus of this state marry significantly earlier, but both Muslims and Hindus from Tamil Nadu are significantly more likely to delay marriage. As shown in earlier tables, state rather than religion plays the more prominent role in explaining variation in age at marriage.

FACTORS INFLUENCING THE MARRIAGE EXPERIENCE: DOWRY PAYMENTS

The literature tends to agree that dowries have become more entrenched in marriage negotiations. One of the arguments posed in the literature is that because there are too few men of marriageable age, families compete for the eligible men by paying higher dowries. A second argument is that a "qualified" man demands a larger dowry or economic contribution from a bride or her family (Jain and Nag, 1986; Kasarda, Billy, and West, 1986), that education has actually strengthened the dowry system (Kapadia, 1958), and that educated women routinely must pay larger dowries than uneducated women (Goldstein, 1970, for Bangalore; Minturn, 1984, for Rajasthan; Seetharamu and Ushadevi, 1985, for Karnataka).

In the multivariate analysis of dowry practice, the more conventional logistic regression model is employed, in which the parameter represents the increment or decrement in log odds associated with reports of a large dowry (with rupee values of Rs 50,000 or more), as opposed to small or no dowries (with rupee values of less than 50,000). It is assumed that large dowry payments occur at discrete intervals of time and the odds of conditional probability experiencing the payment of large dowries are small. The analysis is performed separately for women married for 0 to 10 and 11 or more years (ages 19 to 39 and once married). In this way, not only is the censoring effect reduced, but also we are able to assess changes in covariate effects over two marriage cohorts.

Table 6-6 presents the results of logistic regression analyses, which regress payment of a large dowry (equivalent of Rs 50,000 or more) on various factors assumed from the above discussion to influence it. Individual woman-level factors, again, include education, premarital employment, and say in choice of husband. Among marriage practice and partner-level factors are age and educational differences between women and husbands, endogamy, and kin relationship. Natal family factors, as before, are represented by father's education levels, and sociocultural context by state and religion. Results are now presented for all women by marital duration, on the assumption that marriage practices, if changing, will be reflected among recently married (and not necessarily younger) women. Hence findings are presented for women married 0 to 10 and 11 or more years preceding the survey in Uttar Pradesh and Tamil Nadu, respectively.

Findings suggest that individual-level factors play a significant role in influencing dowry payments. As others have noted, dowry payments increase systematically and dramatically by woman's education level, and especially a secondary school education. What is notable is that the influence of education in one state—Tamil Nadu—has become considerably stronger among women marrying in the recent past than among women who married earlier. For example, compared to uneducated women, seven times as many secondary schooled women who married more than ten years before the survey had paid dowries in excess of Rs 50,000; this ratio increased to 13 times as many among women marrying more recently. A similar trend is observed in Uttar Pradesh, but differences over time and by educational status are more modest.

In contrast to the effect of education, premarital economic activity appears to reduce dowry payments for all women, but again, more significantly among Tamilian women, here there is little evidence of change over cohorts. Finally, the results suggest that while participation in marriage-related decisions did not have a significant influence on dowry payments, the direction of the relationship hints that, with the exception of young women in Uttar Pradesh, involvement in marriage-related decisions is consistently inversely related with the magnitude of dowry payments.

Marriage practice and partner-level factors also influence dowry payments. For one, findings confirm that a well and better educated husband is more likely to command large dowries than others, although the magnitude of this influence appears to be weakening in both settings. Kin marriages, particularly in Tamil Nadu where they are more prevalent, and notably among the recent cohort, are associated with lower dowry payments.

As far as natal family socioeconomic status is concerned, it is clear that father's education—and particularly a secondary school education—pow-

TABLE 6-6 Results of Logit Analysis of Large Dowry Payments
(Rs 50,000 and above) Among Women Ages 19-39, Married 0-10 and
11+ Years, Uttar Pradesh and Tamil Nadu: Odds Ratios

	Total	
	Married 0-10 Years	Married 11+ Years
INDIVIDUAL LEVEL		
Education		
None	1.000	1.000
Primary	3.536^c	2.800^c
Secondary	8.986^c	6.235^c
Economic Activity for Wages Before Marriage		
No	1.000	1.000
Yes	0.397^c	0.408^c
Participation in Marriage Decisions		
No	1.000	1.000
Yes	0.949	0.834
Marriage Practice and Partner Level		
Spousal age difference 5 years	1.000	1.000
Spousal age difference > 5 years	0.945	1.041
Spousal educational difference 5 classes	1.000	1.000
Spousal educational difference > 5 classes	1.511^a	1.971^c
Exogamy: does not reside in natal village or vicinity	1.000	1.000
Endogamy: resides in natal village or vicinity	1.264	0.578^b
Not married to relative	1.000	1.000
Kin marriage: married to relative	0.512^b	0.668^a
NATAL FAMILY LEVEL		
Father's Education Level		
None	1.000	1.000
Primary	1.301	1.494^b
Secondary	3.456^c	1.596^a
Sociocultural Context		
Uttar Pradesh Muslim	1.000	1.000
Uttar Pradesh Hindu	0.954	1.421
Tamil Nadu Muslim	7.874^c	9.711^c
Tamil Nadu Hindu	4.432^c	3.329^c
Pseudo R Squared	0.26	0.21
Number	731	984

^{a}Equals .000.
^{b}Equals .001-.05.
^{c}Equals .051-.099.

Uttar Pradesh		Tamil Nadu	
Married 0-10 Years	Married 11+ Years	Married 0-10 Years	Married 11+ Years
1.000	1.000	1.000	1.000
2.515[a]	1.832[c]	4.047[c]	2.370[c]
5.644[c]	5.584[c]	12.669[c]	7.177[c]
			0.371[c]
1.000	1.000	1.000	
0.738[a]	0.420	0.376[c]	
1.000	1.000	1.000	1.000
1.029	0.830	0.843	0.812
1.000	1.000	1.000	1.000
1.287	1.065	0.737	1.003
1.000	1.000	1.000	1.000
1.452	2.638[b]	1.451	1.606[a]
1.000	1.000	1.000	1.000
1.342	1.589	1.384	0.484[b]
1.000	1.000	1.000	1.000
2.442[a]	1.314	0.357[c]	0.599[b]
1.000	1.000	1.000	1.000
1.322	3.473[c]	1.268	0.933
3.307[b]	2.051[b]	3.884[b]	1.156
1.000	1.000		
2.005	1.995[b]	1.000	1.000
		0.541[b]	0.305[c]
0.21	0.182	0.271	0.192
294	480	437	504

erfully influences dowry payments, and this is even after the influence of the woman's own education and work status have been controlled.

Finally, the influence of sociocultural context—as measured by religion and setting—varies considerably by state. In Uttar Pradesh, the marriages of Hindu women, irrespective of cohort, were considerably more likely to attract a large dowry than were the marriages of Muslim women, although the effect was not significant among the younger cohort. In Tamil Nadu, in contrast, Muslim women are more likely to report large dowries, though there is some indication that differences may be narrowing among the recent cohort.

SUMMARY AND CONCLUSIONS

The objective of this chapter was to explore marriage patterns and changes in marriage patterns among successive cohorts of women in rural Uttar Pradesh and Tamil Nadu, two culturally distinct social systems. In doing so, it aimed to explore the extent to which marriage age, practices, and factors underlying these had changed in the experiences of successive marriage cohorts. Several conclusions can be drawn from this study, some very clear, and others tentative and suggestive.

First, findings confirm that marriage has been increasing moderately and at different paces in the two states. In Uttar Pradesh, among both Muslims and Hindus, early adolescent marriages (under age 15) have declined perceptibly by cohort, yet about two in three recently married women continue to marry by the time they are 18. Among women in Tamil Nadu, in contrast, changes are observed in both early and late adolescence and the evidence suggests that among both Muslims and Hindus, marriage is increasingly being delayed beyond adolescence. This is consistent with other studies (Bhat and Halli, 1999).

Second, a review of marriage practices suggests that practices are largely context dependent. Such attributes of marriage as kin marriage, village endogamy and postmarital residence patterns, and spousal age differences, for example, continue to be shaped by region and gender systems. The experiences of recently married cohorts remain largely similar to those of older ones in each setting. However, there are some conditions in which cohort differences have begun to emerge. These include greater autonomy among recently married women in determining the timing of marriage and choice of partner, and greater egalitarianism among these women in terms of educational differences with husband—attributes far more clearly observed in Tamil Nadu than in Uttar Pradesh, and presumably suggestive of more egalitarian relationships among younger cohorts of Tamilian women. On the other hand, a notable change experienced in Uttar Pradesh is in the content of dowry and specifically a greater trend toward consumer goods among younger cohorts. Data provide little clear evidence on trends in dowry per se—there is a tentative suggestion that it may have increased over time in all four groups, but particularly among the Muslims of Tamil Nadu and the Hindus of Uttar Pradesh.

Third, findings confirm considerable similarity in determinants of marriage age in this region, though the magnitude of certain effects may vary. Clearly the most powerful and consistent factors shaping marriage age are woman's education and sociocultural setting—notably, even the influence of a primary education sharply increases marital age, and the influence of education remains powerful in both cohorts and settings. Sociocultural context—as measured by religion and setting—suggests that compared to the Muslims of Uttar Pradesh, the Hindus of this state marry significantly earlier, while both Muslim and Hindu women from Tamil Nadu are significantly more likely to delay marriage. Also consistent is the suggestion that women marrying considerably older men (5 years or more) are significantly more likely to marry early than are other women; again there is no significant change in pattern over cohorts in this effect. In contrast, few other factors are uniformly significant: Only among the cohort married 11 years or longer—but not the recently married cohort—is there evidence that large dowry payments may have resulted in delaying marriage, and only in Tamil Nadu is there evidence that natal family socioeconomic status has a significant influence on delaying marriage age.

Fourth, in contrast, findings suggest considerable heterogeneity in factors influencing dowry payments in the two settings. Findings confirm, for most groups, a strong positive association between payment of large dowries and natal family socioeconomic status, woman's education, as well as suitability of the husband, measured in terms of his relative superiority in education. The influence of a secondary education appears to have become stronger in the case of recently married women, particularly in Tamil Nadu. In contrast to this effect, premarital economic activity appears to reduce dowry payments for all women irrespective of timing of marriage, but significantly among Tamilian women. Finally, sociocultural context exerts a strong effect on dowry payments. In Uttar Pradesh, Hindus are significantly more likely to report large dowry transfers, and this effect is consistent over cohorts. In Tamil Nadu, in contrast, Muslim women, irrespective of cohort, report significantly larger dowry transfers than do Hindu women.

These findings suggest that by and large, sociocultural setting and individual and marriage process-related factors have a powerful effect on determining marriage age and practices. What is not as clear is that these determinants have shifted over successive cohorts of women. Notably, findings suggest that although education plays a significant role in enhancing marriage age, it also tends to raise dowry payments. Conversely, although premarital economic activity is unrelated to marriage age, it plays a significant role in reducing dowry payments. These kinds of findings suggest that strategies to delay marriage and counter the practice of dowry need to expand beyond education or employment. More comprehensive, direct, and context specific strategies must be sought simultaneously—raising community awareness of the negative effects of early marriage and countering fears of allowing girls to remain single; providing for the acquisition of usable vocational and life skills; and enhancing young women's real access to and control over economic resources and decision making relating to their own lives.

REFERENCES

Altekar, A.S. (1962). *The position of women in Hindu civilization.* Delhi, India: Motilal Banarasidas.

Amin, S., and Cain, M. (1997). The rise of dowry in Bangladesh. In G.W. Jones, R.M. Douglas, J.C. Caldwell, and R.M. D'Souza (Eds.), *The continuing demographic transition* (pp. 209-306). Oxford, England: Clarendon Press.

Bhat, P.N.M., and Halli, S.S. (1999). Demography of brideprice and dowry: Causes and consequences of the Indian marriage squeeze. *Population Studies, 53*(2), 129-148.

Caldwell, J.C., Reddy, P.H., and Caldwell, P. (1982). The causes of demographic change in rural South India: A micro approach. *Population and Development Review, 8*(4), 689-727.

Caldwell, J.C., Reddy, P.H., and Caldwell, P. (1983). The causes of marriage change in South India. *Population Studies, 37*(3), 343-361.

Caldwell, J.C., Gajanayake, I., Caldwell, B., and Caldwell, P. (1989). Is marriage delay a multiphasic response to pressures for fertility decline? The case of Sri Lanka. *Journal of Marriage & the Family, 51*(2), 337-351.

Committee on the Status of Women in India. (1973). *India: Towards equality.* New Delhi: Government of India.

Das Gupta, M. (1987). Selective discrimination against female children in rural Punjab, India. *Population and Development Review, 13*(1), 77-100.

Dixon, R.B. (1975). Women's rights and fertility. *Reports on Population/Family Planning, 17,* 20.

Dube, L. (1988). On the construction of gender: Hindu girls in patrilineal India. *Economic and Political Weekly, 23*(18), WS11-WS19.

Dyson, T., and Moore, M. (1983). On kinship structure, female autonomy, and demographic behavior in India. *Population and Development Review, 9*(1), 35-60.

Goldstein, R.L. (1970). Students in saris: College education in the lives of young Indian women. *Journal of Asian and African Studies, 5*(3), 192-201.

International Institute for Population Sciences. (1995). *National Family Health Survey: India 1992-93.* Bombay, India: Author.

International Institute for Population Sciences and ORC Macro. (2000). *National Family Health Survey: India 1998-99.* Mumbai, India: Author.

Jain, A., and Nag, M. (1986). Importance of female primary education for fertility reduction in India. *Economic and Political Weekly, 21*(36), 1602-1608.

Jejeebhoy, S. (2000). Women's autonomy in rural India: Its dimensions, determinants, and the influence of context. In H. Presser and G. Sen (Eds.), *Female empowerment and demographic processes* (pp. 204-238). Oxford, England: Clarendon Press.

Jejeebhoy, S., and Sathar, Z. (2001). Women's autonomy in India and Pakistan: The influence of religion and region. *Population and Development Review, 27*(4), 687-712.

Kapadia, K.M. (1958). *Marriage and family in India*. Oxford, England: Oxford University Press.

Karve, I. (1965). *Kinship organization in India*. Bombay, India: Asia Publishing House.

Kasarda, J.D., Billy, J.O., and West, K. (1986). *Status enhancement and fertility: Reproductive responses to social mobility and educational opportunity*. New York: Academic Press.

Mason, K.O. (1984). *The status of women: A review of its relationships to fertility and mortality*. New York: The Rockefeller Foundation.

Mason, K.O. (1993). The impact of women's position on demographic change during the course of development: What do we know? In N. Federici, K.O. Mason, and S. Sogner (Eds.), *Women's position and demographic change*. Oxford, England: Oxford University Press.

Minturn, L. (1984). Changes in the differential treatment of Rajput girls in Khalapur: 1955-1975. *Medical Anthropology, 8*(2), 127-132.

Rao, V. (1993). Dowry "inflation" in rural India: A statistical investigation. *Population Studies, 47*(2), 283-293.

Salaff, J.W., and Wong, A.K. (1977). Chinese women at work: Work commitment and fertility in the Asian setting. In S. Kupinsky (Ed.), *The fertility of working women* (pp. 81-145). New York: Praeger.

Seetharamu, A.S., and Ushadevi, M.D. (1985). *Education in rural areas*. New Delhi, India: Ashish Publishing House.

Srinivas, M.N. (1989). *The cohesive role of Sankritization and other essays*. Oxford, England: Oxford University Press.

Standing, G. (1983). Women's work activity and fertility. In R.A. Bulatao and R.D. Lee (Eds.), *Determinants of fertility in developing countries* (pp. 517-546). New York: Academic Press.

Vlassoff, C. (1996). Against the odds: The changing impact of education on female autonomy and fertility in an Indian village. In R. Jeffery and A.M. Basu (Eds.), *Girls' schooling, women's autonomy, and fertility change in South Asia* (pp. 218-234). New Delhi, India: Sage Publications.

7

Marriage in Transition: Evidence on Age, Education, and Assets from Six Developing Countries

Agnes R. Quisumbing and Kelly Hallman

Marriage is an event of great social and economic significance in most societies. It is a rite of passage that marks the beginning of an individual's separation from the parental unit, even if families continue to be socially and economically interdependent. In many developing countries, it represents the union not only of two individuals, but also of two families or kinship groups. In many societies, it also entails a substantial transfer of assets from the parent to the child generation.

Assets brought to marriage are more than a form of intergenerational transfer—they may affect the distribution of bargaining power and resources within the marriage itself. Recent work testing the collective versus the unitary model of household behavior suggests that conditions at the time of marriage may affect the distribution of welfare within marriage. In particular, it has been shown that the distribution of assets between spouses at the time of marriage is a possible determinant of bargaining power within marriage (Quisumbing and de la Brière, 2000; Quisumbing and Maluccio, 2003; Thomas, Contreras, and Frankenberg, 2002). Assets at marriage confer bargaining power because they influence the exit options available to spouses. Although assets at marriage may not completely determine the distribution of assets upon divorce (Fafchamps and Quisumbing, 2002), these measures are, in themselves, worth investigating because they shed light on the institution of marriage and inheritance.

Given the centrality of marriage in an individual's life history, surprisingly little has been written regarding trends in marriage patterns. Because the timing of first marriage critically influences subsequent life events for women, most of the analyses have focused on the female mean singulate age at marriage (e.g., United Nations, 1990) and its determinants. Singh and Samara (1996), using data from 40 Demographic and Health Surveys (DHS) in developing countries, found that, although age at marriage is increasing, a substantial proportion of women in developing countries continue to marry as adolescents. Increases in age at marriage are associated with major social-structural changes such as increases in educational attainment, urbanization, and the emergence of new roles for single women. Jejeebhoy (1995), analyzing 51 studies based on a number of data sources, mostly the World Fertility Survey and the DHS, found that education is the single factor most strongly related to the postponement of marriage, but the relationship may be subject to threshold effects. In many countries, the tendency for education to raise marriage age becomes universal only after a few years of primary education. However, because the results of the few studies available are contradictory, little can be said about trends in the relationship between education and age at marriage over time (Jejeebhoy, 1995, p. 66).

Because research on marriage timing has been motivated largely by a demographic interest in the initiation of reproduction (Malhotra, 1997), and because few fertility surveys collect marriage data for men, most of the studies on age at marriage have been limited to women's experiences (Singh and Samara, 1996). As Malhotra (1997) argues, the focus on women neglects the fact that entry into marriage is also an important life course transition for men, which reflects family structure, gender relations, and social change. Malhotra's own work in Indonesia is one of a few recent studies that examines the determinants of marriage timing for both men and women. Although not examining determinants, Hertrich (2002) documents trends in marriage age for men and women in Africa. (Earlier studies include Dixon, [1971], and Smith, [1980].)

In addition, the literature on marriage rarely pays attention to the resources that men and women bring to marriage. This is a serious gap because empirical work on intrahousehold behavior suggests that the distribution of resources at marriage may affect bargaining power within marriage. Part of this gap is because of data limitations.

Anthropological studies are detailed and informative, but only for a small set of people in a particular setting, and they rarely follow the same group through time. However, anthropological techniques have been used innovatively to study changes in marriage patterns. For example, Caldwell, Reddy, and Caldwell (1983) combine data collected using quasi-anthropological approaches and small-scale surveys in a rural area of the south Indian state of Karnataka to examine the changing nature of marriage. Economic analyses have focused mainly on transfers at marriage such as dowries and brideprice (Rao, 1993b; Zhang and Chan, 1999), and not the **totality of assets** that spouses bring to marriage. Even if dowries or brideprice have great social and cultural significance, there is evidence that they account for only a small proportion of assets brought to marriage, at least in rural Ethiopia (Fafchamps and Quisumbing, 2002), and none at all in countries that do not practice either dowry or brideprice. In general, there are little quantitative data that capture both cross-sectional and longitudinal variation with enough detail to capture the significance of marriage conditions in different cultures. Thus, work analyzing marriage patterns and resources at marriage in a number of countries, using comparable data collection methodologies and empirical analyses, has been scarce.

This chapter contributes to the literature on marriage patterns by analyzing data on husband's and wife's human and physical capital and conditions surrounding marriage; the data were collected by the International Food Policy Research Institute (IFPRI) in six developing countries.[1] Four data sets—Bangladesh, Ethiopia, Guatemala, and South Africa—were collected as part of a larger research program on gender and development policy at IFPRI (Bouis et al., 1998; Fafchamps and Quisumbing, 2002; Hallman, 2000; Hallman et al., 2005; Maluccio, Haddad, and May, 2000; Ruel et al., 2002; Quisumbing and de la Brière, 2000); the Mexico data were collected for the evaluation of PROGRESA (Programa Nacional de Educación, Salud, y Alimentación), a nationwide conditional transfer program (de la Brière and Quisumbing, 2000; Skoufias, 2001); and the Philippines data were part of an earlier study on gender difference in intergenerational transfers (Quisumbing, 1994).[2] The data sets in all six countries used comparable data collection methodologies, drew from qualitative studies or the anthropological literature to formulate quantitative survey modules, and contain retrospective data on family background and physical and human capital at marriage for both husbands and wives. The IFPRI study countries were also chosen to capture geographic and cultural variation, as well as to focus on specific policy issues related to gender. Assets at marriage are deflated using the appropriate consumer price index (CPI) to make the real value of assets from earlier and later marriages comparable. Unlike the DHS, the samples are relatively small and are not nationally representative; the study sites are not, however, outliers relative to living conditions within each country (see Table 7-1). Moreover, because the surveys were not designed to

---

[1]In this chapter, we use "union" and "marriage" interchangeably, although for most of our countries, the data refer to actual marriages. The exception is urban Guatemala, which has a high percentage of consensual unions (40 percent of unions in our sample).

[2]The first author directed the overall research program at IFPRI while the second author worked intensively on the Bangladesh and Guatemala studies. The modules on assets at marriage were similar to those used in the Philippine study (Quisumbing, 1994), but were adapted for specific country conditions.

examine demographic variables (e.g., fertility histories, age at marriage), it is possible that these aspects of the data are less reliable than the economic modules. These caveats need to be borne in mind when interpreting some of the regression results, particularly those on age at marriage.

We use these data to estimate similar regressions for all countries: (1) regressions on *levels* of human capital (education), age at marriage, and assets at marriage, separately for husband and wife, as a function of parental background for each spouse, the population sex ratio (ratio of females to males of mean sample marriageable age, an indicator of the "marriage market squeeze") in the 5-calendar-year interval during which the marriage took place, and the year of marriage; and (2) regressions on *differences* in age, human capital, and assets at marriage between husband and wife, as a function of the year of marriage, the sex ratio when the marriage took place, and differences in the corresponding parental background variables. The second set of regressions enables us to examine whether schooling differences, age differences, and asset differences are changing through time, controlling for parental background effects.

Our results show that both husbands and wives are more educated and older in more recent marriages. Although husbands bring more physical assets to marriage than wives, trends in physical assets at marriage are less clear cut. Asset values of husbands increase through time in four countries, and remain constant in the Philippines and Ethiopia. Asset values of wives increase in three countries (South Africa, Mexico, and Guatemala), remain constant in the Philippines and Ethiopia, and decline in Bangladesh. In terms of differences between spouses, in four out of six countries, age differences between husband and wife have decreased; the exceptions are the Philippines and South Africa where females marry relatively later. In three out of six countries, husband-wife gaps in schooling attainment at marriage have also decreased. Despite trends toward equality in education and age, the distribution of assets at marriage continues to favor husbands. In three out of six countries, the husband-wife asset difference has not changed through time—and therefore continues to favor husbands—and has increased in the other three countries. The reduction of husband-wife gaps in schooling and age argue well for an improvement in the balance of power within the family, but asset ownership continues to favor husbands. Persistent differences in assets in favor of men have important implications for household well-being and the welfare of future generations, given recent findings which show that increasing women's status and control of assets has favorable effects on a number of human capital outcomes, particularly of the next generation.

TABLE 7-1 Description of Data Sets

Country	Description of Data	Country-Level Descriptors	
Bangladesh	Project title: Commercial Vegetable and Polyculture Fish Production in Bangladesh: Their Impacts on Income, Household Resource Allocation and Nutrition	% urban[a]	23.9
	Survey coverage and dates: 955 rural households; 4 rounds of data collection from June 1996 to September 1997	% literate[b] Female:	29.3
	Study sites: The data were collected as part of an impact evaluation of vegetable and fish pond technologies being disseminated in rural areas through nongovernmental organizations (NGOs). The survey sites were areas where new Consultative Group for International Agricultural Research (CGIAR) technologies had been introduced but their impact not yet evaluated. CGIAR technology is highly prevalent in rural Bangladesh. These areas are in no way unusual relative to others in rural Bangladesh.	Male: Estimated earned income[c] Female:	51.7 1,076[d]
	Sampling design and notes: In each of the 3 survey sites (47 villages total), 3 types of households were identified: A households—NGO member adopting households in villages where the technology has been disseminated (A villages); B households—NGO member likely adopter households in villages where the technology has not been introduced (B villages); and C households—a sampling of all other households in both types of villages (C villages). The general sampling approach involved a multistage design using unique sampling methodologies in each site that randomly selected the A, B, and C villages followed by the A, B, and C households.	Male:	1,866[d]
	Collaborator: Data Analysis and Technical Assistance, Dhaka, Bangladesh		
Philippines	Project title: Gender Differences in Schooling and Land Inheritance	% urban[a]	57.7
	Survey coverage and dates: 275 rural households; Round 1 – 1989, Round 2 – 1996-1998	% literate[b] Female:	94.9

South Africa

Study sites: The five survey sites are rice-growing villages that were surveyed by the International Rice Research Institute for a study on the differential impact of modern rice technology (1985-1986). These are typical rice-growing villages that span the range of environmental conditions, from fully irrigated to rainfed.

Sampling design and notes: For this survey, the data came from two retrospective surveys conducted in 1989 covering 339 households and a resurvey in 1997 covering 275 of the same sample households in 1989.

Collaborators: Tokyo Metropolitan University and International Rice Research Institute

Male:	95.3
Estimated earned income[c]	
Female:	2,684
Male:	4,910

Ethiopia

Project title: Gender and Intrahousehold Resource Allocation

Survey coverage and dates: 1399 rural households; 4th-round data were collected from May to December 1997

Survey sites: This survey added a 4th-round to a panel collected by IFPRI, the Centre for the Study of African Economies, and Addis Ababa University (CSAE/AAU) in 1994-1995. Six of the 15 village sites were originally surveyed by IFPRI in 1989 for the Ethiopia Famine Project. IFPRI added 3 villages to the sample in 1994 for a study assessing vulnerability to droughts. The rest of the other villages represent different ecological zones. Although not nationally representative, the sample is representative of the country's agroecological zones.

Sampling design and notes: The original sample size of 1,500 households was decided jointly by IFPRI and CSAE/AAU. The sample was to be allocated based on the wereda (the level of administration next to region) population of each site, with a minimum of 60 households per site.

Collaborators: CSAE/AAU[a]

% urban[a]	17.2
% literate[b]	
Female:	31.8
Male:	42.8
Estimated earned income[c]	
Female:	414[d]
Male:	844[d]

continued

TABLE 7-1 Continued

Country	Description of Data	Country-Level Descriptors	
	Project title: KwaZulu-Natal Income Dynamics Study	% urban[a]	50.1
	Survey coverage and dates: 1,200 rural and urban households; Round 1 – August-November 1993, Round 2 – March-June 1998	% literate[b] Female:	84.2
	Survey sites: This was a resurvey of households in the KwaZulu-Natal area that were part of the 1993 national survey of South Africa. IFPRI has access to the 1993 data set. KwaZulu-Natal is 43% urban and has a slightly higher proportion of inhabitants of Indian descent than other provinces. Its poverty, education, unemployment, and infrastructure indicators are just slightly worse than the country average, but the majority of these differences are not statistically significant. It has a higher than average HIV/AIDS prevalence (South Africa Department of Social Development, 2000).	Male: Estimated earned income[c] Female:	85.7 5,473[d]
	Sampling design and notes: The sampling design was a two-stage, self-weighting procedure. In the first stage, clusters were chosen proportional to population size from census enumeration areas or approximate equivalents where not available. In the second stage, all households in each chosen cluster were enumerated and then a random sample of them selected. In 1998, only African and Indian households were targeted. Sample is representative at the province level.	Male:	12,452[d]
	Collaborators: University of Natal-Durban and University of Wisconsin		

continued

% urban[a]		74.2
% literate[b] Female:		89.1
Male:		93.1
Estimated earned income[c] Female:		4,486
Male:		12,184

Mexico

Project title: Evaluation of the National Program for Education, Health, and Nutrition (Programa Nacional de Educación, Salud, y Alimentación [PROGRESA])

Survey coverage and dates: 24,000 households in rural Mexico; census survey in November 1997 (ENCASEH) to select beneficiary households; evaluation surveys (Encuesta Evaluation de los Hogares or ENCEL) in March 1998 (prior to distribution of benefits); October/November 1998 (ENCEL98O), June 1999 (ENCEL98M), and November 1999 (ENCEL99N). The module on family background and assets at marriage was fielded as a part of the June-July 1999 round (ENCEL99M).

Survey sites: 506 localities in the seven states of Guerrero, Hidalgo, Michoacan, Puebla, Queretaro, San Luis Potosi, and Veracruz. Of the 506 localities, 320 localities were assigned to the treatment group ($T=1$) and 186 localities were assigned as controls ($T=0$).

Sampling design and notes: The 320 treatment localities were randomly selected using probabilities proportional to size from a universe of 4,546 localities that were covered by phase II of the program in the 7 states mentioned above. Using the same method, the 186 control localities were selected from a universe of 1,850 localities in these 7 states that were to be covered by PROGRESA in later phases. The coverage of the program in its final phase constitutes around 40% of all rural families and one ninth of all families in Mexico.

Collaborators: Programa Nacional de Educación, Salud, y Alimentación, Mexico; University of Pennsylvania; Yale University and University of California

Guatemala

TABLE 7-1 Continued

Country	Description of Data	Country-Level Descriptors	
	Project title: Strengthening and Evaluation of the Hogares Comunitarios Program in Guatemala City	% urban[a]	39.4
	Survey coverage and dates: 1,340 urban households in Guatemala City, surveyed in 1999	% literate[b]	
		Female:	60.5
	Survey site: Site was one of three areas where the Hogares Comunitarios Program was operating in Guatemala City at the time of the survey. Characteristics of this area did not differ from other two program areas. All program areas were among the lower half of the urban socioeconomic strata. The study site is representative of urban poor areas of the country.	Male:	75.6
		Estimated earned income[c]	
	Sampling design and notes: This survey was designed to provide a qualitative and quantitative assessment of the operations and impact of the Hogares Comunitarios Program, a day care program under the auspices of the office of the First Lady of Guatemala. Two surveys were carried out: a random sample of 1,340 households with preschool children, and an impact evaluation sample of 550 households with preschool children divided into participating and control households. The current manuscript uses the random sample data.	Female:	1.691[d]
		Male:	5,622[d]
	Collaborator: Staff from the Programa de Hogares Comunitarios		

[a]United Nations, Human Development Report 2001. Rates as of 1999.

[b]United Nations, Human Development Report 2001. Age 15 and above in 1999.

[c]United Nations, Human Development Report 2001. Figures are PPP US$ (Purchasing Power Parity—see technical note 1 in HDR 2001 report).

Note: Because of the lack of gender-disaggregated income data, female and male earned income are crudely estimated on the basis of data on the ratio of the female nonagricultural wage to the male nonagricultural wage, the female and male shares of the economically active population, the total female and male population and GDP per capita (PPP US$) (see technical note 1 in HDR 2001 report). Unless otherwise specified, estimates are based on data for the latest year available during 1994-1999.

[d]United Nations, Human Development Report 2001. Note: No wage data available. For purposes of calculating the estimated female and male earned income, an estimate of 75 percent, the unweighted average for the countries with available data, was used for the ratio of the female non-agricultural wage to the male non-agricultural wage.

BACKGROUND AND METHODS

Assets at Marriage and Bargaining Power

The IFPRI studies collected data on assets at marriage and conditions surrounding marriage in order to arrive at quantifiable indicators of bargaining power within marriage that are exogenous to current marital decisions. While data on human capital at marriage, such as schooling, have been collected in numerous surveys, data on assets at marriage are relatively rare. This data collection effort was motivated largely by the desire to test the collective model of the household, which predicts that one's share of resources received within a relationship will be determined by one's bargaining power within that relationship.[3] Because bargaining power is an elusive concept, candidate proxies for bargaining power have included: (1) public provision of resources to specific household members and exogenous policy changes that affect the intrahousehold distribution thereof (Lundberg, Pollak, and Wales, 1997; Rubalcava and Thomas, 2002); (2) shares of income earned by women (Hoddinott and Haddad, 1995); (3) unearned income (Schultz, 1990; Thomas, 1990); (4) current assets (Doss, 1999); (5) inherited assets (Quisumbing, 1994); and (6) assets at marriage (Thomas et al., 2002). Of course, none of these measures is perfect. In most contexts there is no public program that can serve as a natural experiment. Labor income, typically included in the calculation of income shares, is problematic because it reflects time allocation and labor force participation decisions that are likely to have been the *result* of some bargaining process within the marriage. Several studies use nonlabor income, either directly, or as an instrument for total income (Thomas, 1993). However, the assumption that nonlabor income is independent of tastes and labor market conditions may not be true if much of it comes from pensions, unemployment benefits, or earnings from assets accumulated over the lifecycle.

Current asset holdings, used by Doss (1999) in her study of Ghanaian households, also may be affected by asset accumulation decisions made within marriage. Depending on provisions of marriage laws, assets acquired within marriage may be considered joint property and will not be easily assignable to husband or wife. The validity of inherited assets as an indicator of bargaining power may be conditional on the receipt of assets prior to marriage, unless bargaining power also depends on the expected value of inheritance. Inherited assets could also be correlated with individual unobservables, such as previous investments in the individual during

---

[3]For a discussion of tests of the collective versus the unitary model of the household, see Haddad, Hoddinott, and Alderman (1997); Quisumbing and Maluccio (2003); Thomas and Chen (1994).

childhood (Strauss and Thomas, 1995). Assets brought to marriage, however, are plausible indicators of bargaining power that are not affected by the decisions made within the marriage—that is, they are exogenous to those decisions, although assets of husband and wife could be correlated if the marriage market is characterized by assortative matching.

Differences in Other Husband-Wife Characteristics and Their Implications

Although a clear body of evidence has begun to emerge on how husband versus wife assets affect various human capital investments and outcomes within the household, assets at marriage are only one aspect of the conditions surrounding marriage and later bargaining power within the union. Husband age and education seniority also have been used to connote male control over women (e.g., Cain, 1984; Miller, 1981). Education differences can be viewed as a proxy for differences in earning power, which carries bargaining power (e.g., Sen, 1989). For example, Smith and colleagues (2003) measure of women's decision-making power relative to their male partners (usually their husbands) is based on four underlying indicators: whether a woman works for cash; her age at first marriage; the age difference between her and her husband; and the education difference between her and her husband.

Aside from their use as proxies for differential economic resources, the effects of spouse age differences on power imbalances have not been well studied. One issue has to do with measurement error: Measurement error in the age variable is likely in low-literacy populations with unreliable civil registration systems. Another issue is the difficulty of predicting the effect of age differences outside a particular social and cultural context.

Recent studies from sub-Saharan Africa, for example, show that wider age differences between sexual partners confer greater HIV vulnerability to young women (e.g., Gregson et al., 2002; Kelly et al., 2001), presumably via greater male sexual experience and their correlation with male wealth advantage in sexual relationships. However, the reverse effect could also be true if women, especially in patriarchal settings, derive status from their husband's characteristics. This would imply that having a husband who is senior in age, education, or economic means would impart well-being (e.g, Kishor, 1995).

The fact is that only a handful of studies have even documented the extent of such spouse differences. Notable exceptions include Luke and Kurz (2002), who in reviewing literature on the extent of age mixing in sexual relationships in sub-Saharan Africa find that a sizable proportion of sexual partners of adolescent girls are at least 6 to 10 years older. Hertrich (2002) documents trends in age at first marriage for men and women in

African countries where survey or census information are available for at least two points in time; she finds women's marriage age is increasing, the trend for men is mixed, and spouse age differences are declining. Mensch, Bruce, and Greene (1998), using DHS data from Colombia, Egypt, and Turkey to document spouse age differences by a woman's age at marriage, find that even after controlling for female education, spouse age differences are larger among women who marry before age 20. Kishor and Neitzel (1996), also using DHS data, report spouse education differences for 25 countries: husbands are likely to have more education in 16 countries; in 7 countries education levels are likely to be equal; only in Brazil and the Philippines are women more likely to be more educated than their husbands. Casterline, Williams, and McDonald (1986) examine spouse age differences in 28 developing countries using World Fertility Survey data; they find that age differences are generally largest in societies which are patriarchal and have patrilineal kinship organization (much of sub-Saharan Africa and the Middle East Crescent, and some of South Asia), and smallest in settings where the traditional social structure allows for more equal status of spouses and/or where processes of modernization have improved the status of women (many in Southeast and East Asia, Latin America, and the Caribbean).

Data Collection Methodology

Separate qualitative studies on different aspects of gender, including marriage customs, informed the design of surveys in Bangladesh, Ethiopia, Guatemala, and South Africa. For the Philippines and Mexico, an extensive review of the anthropological literature and interviews with anthropologists and researchers who had worked on marriage customs in those areas influenced questionnaire design. The authors and their colleagues participated in intensive pretests of the survey modules in all countries except Mexico.

Because each data set has specific features related to the purpose of the survey, we discuss only the common features of the data in this section, and leave the country-specific details for later. All the modules on assets at marriage include information on the premarital human and physical capital of each spouse (e.g., age, education, work experience, land, livestock, other assets), year of marriage, and parental background. A variety of assets brought to the marriage were recorded, as well as all transfers made at the time of marriage (gifts, brideprice, and dowries), where applicable. Some of the surveys also collected information on marriage histories of each spouse (Ethiopia), the circumstances surrounding the marriage (e.g., type of marriage contract, involvement in the choice of a spouse, relative ranking of parents' social status) (Bangladesh, Ethiopia); social networks of the wife (Bangladesh, South Africa, Guatemala); inheritance by siblings (Philippines);

and gender-specific information on income streams and control and owner-ship of land and livestock; and other assets (Bangladesh, Ethiopia, Philip-pines). In all the surveys (except Mexico and South Africa), the reported values of assets at the time of marriage have been converted to survey year values using the national CPI and the year of marriage. For Mexico, we used an asset index, and for South Africa, a count of assets at marriage. Details regarding the construction of the asset measures are found in the country-specific sections.

Empirical Methodology

We first estimate a series of levels regressions on husband's and wife's human capital (education), age at marriage, and assets at marriage using the general form:

$$A_i = \alpha + \beta(\text{Year of marriage}) + \gamma_1(\text{Sex ratio})$$
$$+ \gamma_2(\text{Human capital of parents})_i$$
$$+ \gamma_3(\text{Physical capital of parents})_i$$
$$+ \delta(\text{Other family background variables})_I + \varepsilon_i \qquad (1)$$

where A is a vector consisting of outcomes such as human capital, age at marriage, and assets, all evaluated at the time of marriage for each i, i = h, w (for husband and wife, respectively); year of marriage is the reported year of marriage, which is the same for husband and wife; the sex ratio is the ratio of females to males of marriageable age in the 5-calendar-year interval when the marriage took place; human capital of parents is an indicator of the parents' educational attainment (usually years of schooling); physical capital of parents includes land holdings of parents (in some cases, disag-gregated for fathers and mothers); family background variables include other indicators of parental status, number of male and female siblings, birth order, and other factors; and ε is an error term. We estimate (1) separately for husbands and wives.

With the exception of the sex ratio, all the explanatory variables were obtained from the household surveys. The sex ratio is defined as the ratio of females in the age category corresponding to the mean marriage age of fe-males to that of males in the corresponding mean marriage age category, and was obtained from United Nations country-level population statistics. Al-though it would have been desirable to have district- or village-level sex ratios corresponding to the marriage year, historical data at this level of disaggrega-tion for each study site were not available. Therefore, we used the country-level figures instead. Because this variable is defined at the country level, it masks the possibility that some areas within the same country (e.g., rural areas with high rates of male outmigration) may have a relative surplus of marriageable wives, while other areas may have a deficit. It also does not capture possible differences in the supply of marriageable individuals of a specific caste or race, if interracial or intercaste marriages are rare. Thus, the coefficients on the sex ratio variable should be interpreted with caution because it is a highly imperfect measure of the "marriage squeeze." We use year of marriage rather than year of birth as an explanatory variable because of difficulties in recalling birth year; because marriage is a more recent event, respondents were better able to recall the year of marriage, or the number of years they had been married. We do not include education as a regressor in the age at marriage equation because the same variables that determine age at marriage may also influence educational attainment, especially in societies where young women leave school to get married. Although one approach could have been to estimate an age at marriage equation with education treated as endogenous, in practice it is difficult to find instrumental variables which would affect only education, but not age at marriage.

To ascertain whether differences between husbands and wives are narrowing across time, we also estimate a version of (1) in difference form:

$$
\begin{aligned}
dA = {} & \alpha' + \beta'(\text{Year of marriage}) + \gamma_1' \text{ (Sex ratio)} \\
& + \gamma_2' \, d(\text{Human capital of parents}) \\
& + \gamma_3' d(\text{Physical capital of parents}) \\
& + \delta' d(\text{Other family background variables}) + \eta \quad (2)
\end{aligned}
$$

where d is the difference between husband's and wife's variables, and all lefthand-side and righthand-side variables (except year of marriage and the sex ratio) are in difference form and η is the error term in this equation.

MARRIAGE PATTERNS IN ASIA, AFRICA, AND LATIN AMERICA: AN OVERVIEW

In this section we present a descriptive overview of marriage trends in our six study countries, characterizing the societies in which the data were gathered, describing the samples, and examining trends in spousal characteristics and assortative mating over time. Our sample consists of two countries each in Asia, sub-Saharan Africa, and Latin America. Although partly motivated by reasons of data availability, we also chose countries that were different rather than similar within each geographical region to highlight the role of cultural differences and to see whether, despite these differences, there are common emerging trends.[4]

---

[4]As discussed above, the IFPRI study countries were also chosen to capture geographic and cultural variation, as well as to focus on specific policy issues related to gender.

Country Overviews

Table 7-2 consists of means and standard deviations of spouses' characteristics at marriage (age, schooling, and assets), while Table 7-3 presents trends in these variables through time for all six study countries.

Bangladesh[5]

Similar to other societies in South Asia, Bangladeshi society is dominated by a patrilineal and patrilocal kinship system. Despite Islamic law, which in principle applies to 85 percent of the population and allows women to own property, the practices of *benami*, where husbands acquire property in their wives' name, and *naior*, where daughters are encouraged to relinquish their inheritance claims to their brothers, illustrate some of the limitations that rural women face in exercising their property rights (Subramanian, 1998).

The survey was conducted in 47 villages from 3 sites in rural Bangladesh, each chosen as part of an impact evaluation for 2 agricultural technology dissemination programs (IFPRI-BIDS-IFNS, 1998). In two of the sites (Saturia and Jessore), NGO programs targeting only women promoted vegetable gardening and group-based fishponds, respectively, providing training and credit. In the third site (Mymensingh), project and Department of Fisheries extension agents provided training in fishpond cultivation to relatively well-off households and the same training, combined with credit, to relatively poorer households. This program was intended for both men and women, though in practice there were more male beneficiaries. The four-round survey, conducted every 4 months from June 1996 to September 1997, collected information on household expenditures on various food, health, and other items in each round; information on parental and sibling background for both the husband and wife; and in the last survey round, information on premarriage assets, transfers at marriage, inheritance, and indicators of women's mobility and empowerment. In particular, respondents were asked to recall the assets they owned before their wedding (land, cattle, housing, food items, and "durables"—jewelry, clothes, and household utensils), the questions were designed based on the findings of a qualitative study conducted in two villages from each of the three sites (Naved, 2000). The reported values of these assets at the time of marriage have been converted to current values using the national consumer price index.

The first notable finding is that Bangladeshi wives bring far less to the marriage than do their husbands, as measured by the value of premarital

---

[5]This section draws from Quisumbing and de la Brière (2000).

assets (in 1996 taka) and years of schooling (Table 7-2). Indeed, the value of female assets seems to have decreased through time, while those of males has increased (Table 7-3). Female assets typically consist of food items and durable goods. In addition, a specific module about gifts and transfers at marriage was administered to the female respondents. The transfers to the bride and groom include assets and cash and were computed by summing up all transfers to each individual and assigning to each individual half of the transfers reported "to the couple." Data presented in Table 7-2 show an average net transfer to the bride at the time of marriage, although more recent weddings exhibit a net transfer to the groom (Table 7-3). This is consistent with the shift from brideprice to dowry reported in Naved (2000).[6] In no case are the transfers at marriage enough to overcome the value of the other resources including cattle and housing, that men bring to the union, however, as indicated by the husband's advantage in the sum total of prewedding assets and marriage transfer payments.

Bangladeshi women have the youngest age of marriage across the six studies (Table 7-2), although age at marriage has been increasing through time (Table 7-3). Men's age at marriage is at par with men from the Philippines and Latin America. There is also a gender gap in education of spouses. However, with the introduction in the past decade of "Food for Education" and other female education subsidy programs (Ahmed and del Ninno, 2002), spouse education gaps are narrowing (see Table 7-3; discussed more below). Indeed, the higher levels of schooling reported by wives in the last 5-year period may be due to such programs that link receipt of food and other assistance to attendance in secondary school.

Philippines

Unlike Bangladesh, the other Asian country in our sample, the Philippines is characterized by bilateral kinship and bilateral inheritance patterns, and both anthropological studies (e.g., Medina, 1991) and studies on intrahousehold allocation support the notion that society is basically egalitarian (Estudillo, Quisumbing, and Otsuka, 2001a, 2001b). For example, the word for "child" in Tagalog does not distinguish between "son" or "daughter"; in some Philippine languages, there is no distinction between "husband" and "wife." Egalitarian distribution does not necessarily mean that men and women within the same household receive the same transfers from parents. In the lowland Philippines, for example, parental preferences in land inheritance may favor male children in communities where farming is intensive in male

---

[6]This phenomenon is also widely reported in India. See Rao (1997) and Bloch and Rao (2002).

TABLE 7-2 Assets at Marriage and Human Capital of Husband and Wife

Assets and Human Capital
ASIA
Bangladesh
Age at marriage (years)
Years of schooling
Value of assets + transfers at marriage (1996 taka)
Value of assets at marriage (1996 taka)
Value of transfers at marriage to each (1996 taka)
Philippines
Age at marriage (years)
Years of schooling
Land area at marriage
Value of nonland assets (1989 pesos)
AFRICA
Ethiopia
Age at marriage (years)
Years of schooling
Value of assets at marriage (1997 birr)
South Africa
Age at marriage (years)
Years of schooling
Count of assets at marriage
Value of transfers from this family at marriage (1998 Rand)
LATIN AMERICA
Mexico
Age at marriage (years)
Years of schooling
Owned land at marriage (1 if yes)
Asset score
Guatemala
Age at marriage (years)
Years of schooling
Value of assets at marriage (1999 Quetzales)

labor (Estudillo, Quisumbing, and Otsuka, 2001a, 2001b). Among the Ilocanos of the northern Philippines, for example, parents traditionally give a portion of their land holdings to a newly married son as a gift. Some writers (e.g., MacArthur, 1977, cited in Caldwell et al., 1998) term this as bride-wealth; the local term (*sabong*) means male land dowry (Anderson, 1962). Both primogeniture and ultimogeniture—inheritance by the first and last born, respectively—are practiced among the Ilocanos depending on the availability of land. Among the Ilonggos of Panay Island in the middle Philippines,

Husband		Wife	
Mean	Standard Deviation	Mean	Standard Deviation
23.8	5.7	15.0	3.8
3.2	4.0	1.7	2.8
36,428.5	150,560.2	12,950.1	20,139.5
32,146.0	148,767.9	2,542.9	10,477.0
4,258.7	15,116.7	10,333.5	16,339.0
25.1	5.7	22.2	5.1
6.3	3.1	6.3	3.0
0.5	0.9	0.2	0.6
761.8	769.3	463.3	473.2
26.3	7.6	17.9	6.0
1.7	2.3	0.7	1.6
4,584.0	8,340.3	1,918.0	3,744.4
28.5	8.4	23.2	7.1
5.2	3.8	5.1	3.6
2.1	1.6	0.7	1.0
36,272.4	50,740.4	6,435.4	22,680.6
23.3	6.3	18.4	4.0
3.2	2.9	3.0	2.8
0.13	0.34	0.00	0.06
0.02	0.08	0.01	0.06
22.6	5.1	19.9	3.7
7.2	3.5	6.0	3.7
5,226.8	12,013.8	727.4	1,684.5

daughters and sons may receive land rights more equally and independently than the Ilocanos, although for land-constrained households, children who help the parents in farming receive more land than do their siblings.

Preferential land inheritance in favor of males is balanced by higher educational attainment of females, at least since the expansion of public education in the 1960s. An ethnographic study by Bouis et al. (1998) indicates that parental decisions regarding schooling depend on the inherent attitudes of the child. According to this study, Filipino parents invest in

TABLE 7-3 Trends in Husband and Wife Characteristics at Marriage, by 5-Year Marriage Intervals

ASIA	No.	Years of Schooling		Age at Marriage		Marriage Assets + Transfers	
		Husband	Wife	Husband	Wife	Husband	Wife
Bangladesh							
1930-1934	1	0.00	0.00	27.00	9.00	0.00	0.00
1935-1939	2	0.00	0.00	28.19	12.50	0.00	0.00
1940-1944	3	5.00	1.67	19.42	11.33	0.00	0.00
1945-1949	16	2.31	0.88	20.84	11.32	0.00	0.00
1950-1954	34	2.82	0.82	22.93	13.05	8,621.90	21,507.74
1955-1959	50	2.64	0.86	22.47	13.62	40,355.99	19,638.39
1960-1964	62	2.44	0.97	22.40	12.70	33,399.62	23,142.25
1965-1969	94	3.86	1.77	24.39	14.45	37,466.66	20,959.34
1970-1974	120	3.54	1.42	22.92	14.16	65,319.44	18,201.53
1975-1979	121	4.38	2.15	23.22	14.98	44,708.19	11,703.86
1980-1984	141	2.76	1.46	24.09	16.01	28,593.82	6,524.70
1985-1989	108	2.42	1.44	24.64	16.28	27,741.57	6,919.89
1990-1994	83	3.13	3.39	26.26	17.45	27,482.85	5,679.25
1995-1999	6	3.33	5.17	26.54	16.00	30,184.62	3,228.01

Philippines	No.	Years of Schooling		Age at Marriage		Land at Marriage	
		Husband	Wife	Husband	Wife	Husband	Wife
Philippines							
1925-1929	2	5.50	9.50	16.00	22.00	0.00	0.50
1930-1934	4	4.75	3.25	23.25	19.75	0.25	0.67
1935-1939	8	2.75	3.63	21.50	23.50	0.10	0.24
1940-1944	12	4.08	4.08	24.17	19.75	0.18	0.50
1945-1949	14	4.64	4.86	25.21	22.14	0.02	0.52
1950-1954	29	4.34	5.24	24.45	22.45	0.27	0.40
1955-1959	28	7.32	5.46	25.75	22.25	0.89	0.26
1960-1964	27	5.93	6.63	24.04	21.30	0.48	0.39
1965-1969	33	6.61	6.15	24.45	21.97	0.66	0.11
1970-1974	34	6.85	6.74	25.29	21.38	0.72	0.12
1975-1979	38	7.37	7.58	27.71	24.13	0.37	0.00
1980-1984	30	7.87	7.73	24.20	21.80	0.52	0.03
1985-1989	3	10.00	10.00	34.00	31.00	0.00	0.64

| Assets at Marriage | | Transfers to | | Sex Ratio |
Husband	Wife	Husband	Wife	
0.00	0.00	0.00	0.00	1.02
0.00	0.00	0.00	0.00	1.02
0.00	0.00	0.00	0.00	1.02
0.00	0.00	0.00	0.00	1.02
5,679.54	5,335.48	2,770.26	19,021.64	1.02
28,739.80	19,257.46	9,955.70	15,727.31	1.06
27,329.91	11,918.45	5,621.68	19,977.07	1.12
32,792.70	7,388.71	4,673.96	18,009.26	1.11
58,167.31	5,800.13	5,442.83	15,576.75	1.31
39,691.58	16,617.34	4,355.09	7,400.15	1.10
28,571.70	3,468.11	3,243.71	4,995.88	1.11
24,637.40	13,602.81	2,400.25	4,085.83	1.08
24,900.69	1,885.30	3,547.63	4,703.04	1.07
26,947.19	1,334.24	3,237.43	2,548.52	1.06

| Assets at Marriage | | Sex Ratio |
Husband	Wife	
407.64	472.45	1.15
693.72	299.84	1.15
723.82	413.82	1.15
888.83	442.27	1.15
704.53	435.28	1.15
902.62	506.99	1.15
790.80	582.67	1.29
516.27	434.45	1.15
757.92	490.17	1.17
595.65	388.06	1.13
868.60	449.85	1.26
847.86	440.84	1.17
1,243.85	700.34	1.16

continued

TABLE 7-3 Continued

AFRICA	No.	Years of Schooling Husband	Wife	Age at Marriage Husband	Wife
Ethiopia					
1955-1959	144	0.69	0.08	31.68	20.11
1960-1964	56	0.67	0.09	25.52	16.44
1965-1969	84	1.20	0.36	23.76	15.72
1970-1974	62	2.29	1.00	23.65	16.32
1975-1979	72	2.31	1.03	24.08	17.01
1980-1984	99	2.86	1.52	24.17	17.98
1985-1989	53	3.29	1.24	26.29	19.43
1990-1995	1	5.00	0.00	50.25	46.25

	No.	Years of Schooling Husband	Wife	Age at Marriage Husband	Wife	Asset at Marriage Husband	Wife
South Africa							
1950-1954	7	2.57	2.14	17.86	11.57	1.14	0.00
1955-1959	14	3.36	2.50	25.36	17.93	2.00	0.36
1960-1964	30	3.30	3.00	24.03	18.17	1.60	0.63
1965-1969	66	4.15	3.62	26.03	21.42	1.89	0.53
1970-1974	67	5.51	4.69	26.55	21.82	1.96	0.55
1975-1979	92	5.39	5.30	26.08	20.75	2.20	0.77
1980-1984	83	6.00	6.04	30.13	24.18	2.22	0.80
1985-1989	72	5.75	5.57	31.92	26.19	2.47	0.82
1990-1995	47	5.68	6.38	34.04	28.87	2.40	1.04
1995-1999	14	6.29	7.43	39.00	35.93	1.93	1.57

LATIN AMERICA	No.	Years of Schooling Husband	Wife	Age at Marriage Husband	Wife
Mexico					
1920-1924	1	0.00	0.00	17.00	16.00
1925-1929	1	1.00	0.00	23.00	17.00
1930-1934	17	0.76	0.39	22.24	17.00
1935-1939	52	0.73	0.58	21.79	17.00
1940-1944	128	0.84	0.54	22.41	17.00
1945-1949	215	0.97	0.75	22.37	18.00
1950-1954	421	1.33	0.83	23.15	18.00
1955-1959	665	1.47	1.04	23.06	18.00
1960-1964	889	1.56	1.26	23.24	18.00
1965-1969	1,210	1.86	1.46	23.44	18.00
1970-1974	1,457	2.23	1.87	23.45	18.00
1975-1979	1,854	2.88	2.51	23.42	18.00
1980-1984	2,008	3.44	3.09	23.25	18.00
1985-1989	2,165	4.27	4.08	23.04	19.00
1990-1994	2,047	4.94	4.92	22.99	19.00
1995-1999	1,038	5.36	5.34	24.05	20.00

Assets at Marriage		Sex Ratio
Husband	Wife	
6,664.50	2,360.70	1.37
6,661.85	3,450.78	1.38
4,964.11	1,789.68	1.39
3,818.32	2,548.83	1.39
2,925.50	1,233.61	1.39
2,873.41	1,059.34	1.45
2,565.61	1,133.21	1.47
1,605.21	500.00	1.45

Transfers From		Sex Ratio
Husband	Wife	
17,477.13	7,413.69	1.06
44,270.71	6,480.63	1.07
51,014.27	8,110.00	1.12
46,676.74	8,617.73	1.18
46,719.09	15,143.04	1.17
55,176.04	7,624.90	1.20
29,727.18	3,713.56	1.12
16,419.83	1,792.36	1.17
11,608.50	937.60	1.19
6,517.53	1,007.00	1.11

Land		Assets		Sex Ratio
Husband	Wife	Husband	Wife	
0.00	0.00	0.00	0.00	1.15
0.00	0.00	0.00	0.00	1.15
0.21	0.00	0.01	0.01	1.15
0.23	0.00	0.02	0.02	1.15
0.16	0.01	0.01	0.02	1.15
0.15	0.00	0.01	0.01	1.15
0.15	0.01	0.02	0.01	1.15
0.15	0.00	0.01	0.01	1.14
0.15	0.01	0.02	0.01	1.20
0.14	0.00	0.02	0.01	1.19
0.14	0.00	0.02	0.01	1.24
0.14	0.01	0.02	0.01	1.24
0.13	0.01	0.02	0.01	1.22
0.12	0.01	0.03	0.01	1.26
0.11	0.00	0.03	0.01	1.24
0.13	0.00	0.04	0.02	1.10

continued

TABLE 7-3 Continued

	No.	Years of Schooling		Age at Marriage	
		Husband	Wife	Husband	Wife
Guatemala					
1945-1949	2		1.00		20.00
1950-1954	3	4.00	0.00	18.00	22.00
1955-1959	1	3.00	7.00	24.00	16.00
1960-1964	4	5.33	7.00	21.33	17.75
1965-1969	7	1.50	2.00	20.50	18.00
1970-1974	18	5.53	3.00	26.33	19.83
1975-1979	55	5.75	4.00	22.34	19.58
1980-1984	117	6.09	4.00	22.90	19.73
1985-1989	224	6.83	6.00	23.45	20.61
1990-1994	424	7.13	6.00	23.24	20.53
1995-1999	435	7.60	6.00	23.35	21.10

the schooling of girls because they are "more studious," "patient," "willing to sacrifice," and "interested in their studies," which are traits that would make them succeed in school. On the other hand, boys are more prone to vices (e.g., drinking), fond of "roaming around" and "playing with their *barkada*" (peer group) and have to be "reminded" and "scolded" to do their schoolwork.

The data used for this analysis come from a retrospective survey of 344 households—in five rice-growing villages in the Philippines with different agroecological characteristics—conducted from June to October 1989. Two villages are in Central Luzon, and three are in Panay Island. The retrospective survey in 1989 included questions on the parents, siblings, and children of the respondents, yielding information on three generations called the grandparents', parents' (respondents and siblings), and (grand)children's generations. The respondents were asked about premarriage wealth (education and land ownership) of their parents and in-laws, their own and their spouses' education and inheritance, and schooling and proposed bequests to their children. Spouses were present during most of the interviews, facilitating collection of data on spouses' family background.[7] The respondents were also asked about the transfers of land and assets received by each sibling regardless of whether the individual lived in the survey area or had migrated.[8]

---

[7]Wives of the predominantly male respondents usually answered the fertility and child schooling questions; questions on proposed bequests were answered jointly by husband and wife.

[8]Nonland assets are valued in 1989 prices. For assets whose present values were declared by the respondents, these present values were used. Asset values for which only values at

Assets at Marriage		Sex Ratio
Husband	Wife	
16,075.40	700.50	1.14
167.79	773.91	1.14
0.00	0.00	1.07
374.50	375.75	1.13
306.25	932.53	1.20
900.50	141.61	1.25
1,818.03	204.96	1.17
5,224.25	525.46	1.22
3,876.46	469.78	1.21
5,476.17	728.64	1.23
6,288.56	1,236.61	1.21

Compared with Bangladesh, Filipino women marry at later ages (Table 7-2), although, in this rural sample, there is no clear trend toward rising marriage age (Table 7-3). Although Filipino men bring more land and assets to marriage, there is no gender gap in education in this generation of respondents.

Ethiopia

Ethiopia is characterized by substantial ethnic and religious diversity; more than 85 ethnic groups and most major world and animist religions are represented, making generalizations about gender roles difficult (Webb and von Braun, 1994). The ethnographic literature does suggest, however, that women's status is relatively higher in the north, but declines as one goes south. The diversity within Ethiopia extends beyond the people and their cultures to its environment; agroecological zones, and consequently farming systems, vary substantially around the country. Currently, Ethiopia ranks as one of the poorest countries in the world, in part a reflection of its tumultuous recent history; over the past decade, it has experienced drought, famine, civil war, and the demise of a military government.

bestowal were available were inflated to 1989 values using the farm gate rice price index for farm animals, farm assets, on-farm residential house and lot, or a region-specific CPI for readily tradeable consumer durables. Because mobility and fungibility of farm assets is limited, and the value of farm property is linked to returns on rice production, the rice price index may be a better adjustment factor than the CPI.

The 1997 Ethiopian Rural Household Survey (ERHS) interviewed approximately 1,500 households in 15 villages across Ethiopia, thus capturing much of the diversity described above.[9] Although sample households within villages were randomly selected, the choice of the villages themselves was purposive to ensure that the major farming systems were represented. Thus the sample cannot be taken as representative of rural Ethiopia as a whole, but it does capture much of the country's diversity.

The survey collected information from ever-married individuals regarding their circumstances at the time of marriage (e.g., age, education, experience, family background, and assets) as well as the circumstances surrounding the marriage itself (e.g., type of marriage contract used, if any; decision maker regarding the choice of a spouse). A variety of assets brought to the marriage and transfers made at the time of the marriage were recorded. The value of assets at the time of marriage is inflated to current value based on the date of marriage and a national consumer price index. Only households with a partnership are considered, yielding a sample of 1,347 households, of which this chapter examines approximately 550 first marriages.[10] Marriage is a fluid state in Ethiopia; divorce is frequent and serial marriages are common (Pankhurst, 1992). We focus on the first marriage because of its significance in Ethiopian society. This is due to the economic value put on virginity and the greater likelihood that the marriage involved a bond between households, rather than a personal arrangement by the bride and groom (Pankhurst, 1992, p. 122).

Given the difficulties inherent in a long recall period and choice of inflation factor for these items, it is hard to measure premarital assets precisely. Nonetheless, clear patterns emerge. On average men bring substantially more physical and human capital to the marriage than do women (Table 7-2). Contrary to expectations, ritual gifts—such as, dowry or brideprice—account for only a small proportion of the transfers of ownership that take place at the time of marriage (Fafchamps and Quisumbing, 2002). On average, the groom's family spends three times as much as the bride's family on gifts to the bride's family or to the bride and groom. The

---

[9]The 1997 ERHS was undertaken by the Department of Economics, Addis Ababa University (AAU), in collaboration with IFPRI and the Centre for the Study of African Economies (CSAE), Oxford University. The 1997 survey built on a panel survey conducted by AAU and CSAE in 1994-1995, but these earlier rounds are not used in the present analysis.

[10]The number of observations varies across regressions because of missing information for some unions. We chose to use the greatest number of valid observations to preserve sample size. For a more thorough analysis of marriage patterns in Ethiopia, see Fafchamps and Quisumbing (2003a, 2003b).

amounts involved are quite small, on average, however, and the median is always zero; hence they are not analyzed separately in this chapter.

The great majority of the new couple's assets are brought by the newly-weds themselves, with grooms bringing substantially more start-up capital than brides. Assets brought to marriage vary dramatically among couples, with a median of zero for most asset categories except livestock and jewelry/clothing/linen. Contrary to the preconception that marriage is the time at which parents endow their offspring with farmland, most of the land brought in by grooms was already theirs prior to marriage. This finding may be specific to Ethiopia, given that the state nominally owns all land (e.g., Gavian and Ehui, 1999; Gavian and Teklu, 1996). User rights over land are supposed to be allocated by Peasant Associations (PAs), the local administrative units in rural areas, although many regions of the country have not experienced land reallocations in recent years. Many young men may wait until the PA allocates them land before deciding to marry. In recent years, marriages have been delayed both because of poverty and as an indirect effect of state policies due to new rigidities in land allocation, labor mobility, and house construction. Pankhurst (1992) notes that given chronic land shortages, a growing population, and increasing corruption, most young households had to wait before being allocated their own plot of land. The sale of labor within the community and seasonal labor migration were restricted, and after villagization, even building a new hut became problematic. This is reflected in lower values of assets at marriage through time, for both husbands and wives, but particularly so for husbands (Table 7-3). Whether these time trends are significant needs to be confirmed by the regressions that control for other confounding variables. Although both husbands and wives appear to be obtaining more schooling through time, the improvement in schooling attainment seems to be greater for husbands.

South Africa

KwaZulu-Natal, South Africa's most populated province, is ethnically diverse, although not to the extent of Ethiopia. More than three quarters of its people are African (nearly all of these Zulu), 10 percent Indian, 7 percent white, and 1 percent colored (mixed race). Ethnographic evidence on marriage contracts and other relations between men and women indicate large differences in the African versus Indian cultural traditions. The marriage agreement in the Zulu tradition, as is common in many other African cultures, involves a bridewealth payment, or *lobola*, from the groom and his family to the bride's family before the couple can marry. Among Indians, the more common traditional scenario is dowry, with the majority of payments being made from the bride's to the groom's family.

The survey, the KwaZulu-Natal Income Dynamics Study (KIDS), includes Africans and Indians in both rural and urban areas.[11] Aside from the Guatemala sample, this is the only other country in this study that includes urban areas. Despite the fact that South Africa is an upper middle-income country with 1997 per capita gross national product (GNP) of approximately $3,000, it is a highly unequal society and the majority of the population lives in poverty (Carter and May, 1998). The survey site, though not the poorest province, is relatively poor despite being relatively urban. In addition to being culturally different, Africans and Indians also differ economically. For example, annual per capita expenditures for Africans average just under $500, while for Indians they are nearly four times as large. It should be noted that Africans and rural residents have relatively low educational attainment, reflecting historical disparities in access to education.

For couples, information was collected on whether each partner owned a variety of assets before marriage, including cattle, other livestock, land, a house, and jewelry, among other things. The simple count of the number of assets owned by each partner is used as a proxy for assets owned at marriage (see Table 7-2). Although this measure obviates the need for respondents to impute values of items owned in the distant past, it suffers from the same concerns for assets at marriage described in detail above, that is, it is imprecise. Due to sensitivities in the reporting of asset ownership (stemming from apartheid-era abuses), information on family background wealth was not collected. However, given the combination of late age at marriage and short life expectancy of parental generations, parent survival to a child's marriage year is not always the rule (approximately 80 percent of mothers and 65 percent of fathers are living at the time of the child's marriage), and therefore is used as an indicator of parental social and economic resources available to a bride or groom.

As in the other countries, men bring far more assets to the marriage. They do not, however, have more schooling than women, reflecting historic and current trends in gender equity in educational attainment within traditional race categories (Statistics South Africa, 2001; United Nations Development Program, 2000). Both men's and women's schooling levels have risen through time as well (Table 7-3). Compared with Ethiopia, South African men and women marry late (Table 7-2), with age at marriage rising in recent years as well (Table 7-3). Because of the dominance of the Zulu population in our sample, we see large mean marriage payments from the groom's side to the bride's side. However, marriage payments from each

---

[11]The first South African national household survey, the Project for Statistics on Living Standards and Development (PSLSD), was undertaken in the last half of 1993 (PSLSD, 1994). KwaZulu-Natal province, on the east coast, was resurveyed from March to June 1998 for KIDS (May et al., 2000).

side have fallen with time, reflecting the modernization that has come with the opening of up of former African homelands and with later generations of Indians becoming more distanced from the dowry customs of South Asian society (Table 7-3). Africans have higher marriage transfer payments than Indians, with amounts coming from the husband's side being more than double those from the wife's side, consistent with the Zulu tradition of *lobola* (75 percent of couples are African; 25 percent are Indian). Over time, differences in spouse education and marriage payments from each side have narrowed. Disparities in age and assets brought to marriage appear not to have changed, although the mean differences here are not large anyway. For Africans, however, there are statistically significant spousal differences in each outcome. Being African means that relative to their wife, men are one year older, have one less year of schooling, bring more assets to marriage, and have families that make more marriage payments.

Mexico

Data on assets at marriage in rural Mexico were collected as part of the evaluation of the impact of PROGRESA on women's status and intrahousehold decision making (Adato et al., 2000; de la Brière and Quisumbing, 2000). The IFPRI and PROGRESA teams jointly designed a module to collect information on family background and the human and physical capital of the husband and wife (assets at marriage).[12] Previous work on marriage patterns in Mesoamerica (e.g., Robicheaux, 1997) was instrumental in the design of this module, which was first administered to a group of *promotoras* (community organizers) in February 1999 as a pilot. Based on the results of the pilot and further discussion with PROGRESA staff, a module on family background was fielded as a part of the June-July 1999 evaluation survey round.[13]

The module on family background and assets at marriage asked the wife to report whether or not she and her husband owned land, farm assets, farm animals, a house, or consumer durables at the time of marriage. The question was asked separately regarding the husband's and wife's assets,

---

[12]Patricia Muñiz, Ana Núñez, and Gabriela Vázquez were instrumental in designing and fielding the pilot survey among the *promotoras*.

[13]Note also that because this module was administered in the third round of the evaluation surveys, sample attrition implies that we do not have this information for all households that were originally included in the baseline. Because we wanted to examine the effects of bargaining power variables on outcomes over time, and because we are interested in the bargaining power of husband and wife, the analysis in this chapter is restricted to intact couples who were interviewed in all three survey rounds (98M, 98O, and 99M).

but neither the quantity in each category nor the value of each asset was asked. We used a modification of a procedure employed by Morris et al. (1999) to arrive at an aggregate asset index for each spouse.[14] The asset score for each spouse was computed by assigning to each item on the list of assets (g) a weight equal to the reciprocal of the proportion of husbands and wives that reported owning the item at the time of marriage (w_g), multiplying that weight by the indicator (0 or 1) that the spouse owned the particular asset g (f_g), and summing the product over all possible assets:

$$\text{spouse's asset score} = 100 \ (\Sigma \ f_g \bullet w_g \ ) \ \text{for } g = 1, ..., G. \qquad (3)$$

The choice of the weighting system is based on the assumption that households would be progressively less likely to own a particular item the higher its monetary value. Morris et al. (1999) find that the log of the asset score is highly correlated with the log of the household asset value (computed by summing the reported value of assets) and thus is a good proxy indicator of household wealth.[15] We did not include land in the asset score; rather, we have two dummy variables indicating whether the husband and the wife had land at the time of marriage.

Husbands enter marriage with more physical capital than their wives: husbands' asset scores were twice those of wives (Table 7-2). Thirteen percent of husbands had land at the time of marriage, compared to less than 1 percent of wives. Table 7-2 also indicates that husbands have more years of schooling than wives, suggesting that they enter a union with significantly more human capital as well. If, as the literature suggests, human and physical capital significantly influence bargaining power within marriage, rural Mexican husbands wield more power within their households than their wives. However, Table 7-3 indicates that women's schooling levels have increased through time, although the asset index continues to favor males. The age at marriage has also increased for women, with no clear trends for males. This suggests that for some measure of resources at marriage—those related to human capital—gaps between husband and wife may be decreasing.

---

[14]The assets included in the asset score were blender, gas stove, traditional stove, television set, jewelry, clock, agricultural equipment, chicken, pig, goat, and cow.

[15]The asset score in Morris et al. (1999) is slightly different: the weight is multiplied by the number of the units of asset "g" owned by the household rather than the indicator that the household owns the asset. We used the indicator because the survey module did not ask how many of the assets each spouse owned, but only whether or not they owned at least one of each item. We also multiply our asset score by 100.

Guatemala

The Guatemala data were collected as part of an impact evaluation of the Hogares Comunitarios government-sponsored day care program by the International Food Policy Research Institute.[16] It included a random sample of 1,363 women with a child ages 0 to 7 years located in Mixco, one of the three urban zones of Guatemala City where the Hogares Comunitarios government-sponsored day care program was operating in 1999.

The household survey collected data on household demographic and socioeconomic characteristics, maternal characteristics and employment, child care arrangements, maternal family background and social networks, and maternal and child anthropometry. Among the family background variables of interest are factors that may have shaped a woman's labor force behavior during adolescence and early adulthood, such as the composition of her natal household and her mother's work behavior and child care utilization patterns when the woman was a child, as well as the value of nine major categories of assets that the woman or her husband brought to her most recent marriage (or union): house, land, furniture, vehicle, stove, sewing machine, linens and bedding, savings, and other assets.

Because the purpose of the original study was to evaluate the benefits children and their mothers received from the Hogares Comunitarios day care program, family background information was not collected for husbands. Human capital information is available, however, for current husbands. In this sample 1,290 women have ever been married; 1,136 are currently married; 997 of the current marriages are first marriages, of which 976 have complete background information on the wife.

Husbands have completed more years of schooling than wives (Table 7-2), and husbands bring more assets to marriage as well. Both husbands' and wives' years of schooling have increased through time (Table 7-3), along with wives' age at marriage. Although both husbands and wives also bring more assets to marriage through time, the relative percentage that wives bring is increasing slightly with time.

Trends in Assortative Matching Through Time

One way of characterizing the marriage process is to examine the criteria through which spouses are matched. Are spouses matched randomly, or is marriage characterized by assortative mating? Although a thorough analysis of assortative mating—the tendency of individuals to select partners

---

[16]See Ruel et al. (2002) for a fuller description of the study and Hallman et al. (2005) for a related paper on women's work and child care arrangements.

who are most similar to them—is outside the scope of this chapter (see Fafchamps and Quisumbing, 2003b), we can examine the degree to which the socioeconomic characteristics of spouses are correlated, and whether this correlation has changed through time. We examine patterns in the correlation between personal characteristics of husbands and wives, and between their parental characteristics, to indicate whether personal characteristics are more or less important than familial characteristics in one's choice of a spouse, and whether the importance of personal versus parental characteristics has changed through time.

Table 7-4 presents simple correlation coefficients between husbands' and wives' personal and parental characteristics, for 5-calendar-year periods corresponding to the year of marriage, for all our study countries. To avoid "noise" due to excessively small cell sizes, we report only those correlation coefficients for samples with at least 14 observations. Not surprisingly, age at marriage of both husband and wife are highly correlated in all time periods, with no discernable time trend in the correlation coefficients. In Bangladesh, positive assortative mating based on schooling appears to be stronger than matching based on assets or parental characteristics. Matching based on wedding transfer payments is greater than that on assets brought to marriage, while the correlation between parental land of spouses is higher than that with parental schooling. The strength of sorting based on personal versus parental characteristics is a possible indication of individual choice, as individuals—particularly girls—become more educated and exercise a stronger role in the choice of a spouse, even if marriages are still arranged by parents.

In the Philippines, positive assortative mating is evident in nonland assets at marriage in addition to sorting on age and schooling. Correlations between spousal characteristics are larger than those on parental characteristics, with the exception of maternal schooling. In the Philippines, marriages are no longer arranged by parents, although young people are reluctant to marry without parental approval (MacArthur, 1977). Surprisingly, the correlation between mothers' schooling of both spouses is higher than that for fathers' schooling, or even parental land, probably indicating the importance that mothers play in the choice or approval of a future spouse. An interesting feature is the low, and often negative, correlation between spouses' land at marriage. Although the groom's parents will typically give their son land to farm, if a groom enters marriage without land, the bride's parents will provide land. Thus, land bestowal behavior tends to be compensatory rather than strategic in Philippine marriages.

In Ethiopia, the highest correlation is between spouses' age at marriage, followed by years of schooling. Sorting based on assets at marriage is evident as well, indicating the presence of assortative mating, although it operates on a variety of levels that cannot be summarized into a single additive index (Fafchamps and Quisumbing, 2003b). In South Africa, the strongest correlations are between age at marriage and schooling; assortative mating based on assets appears to be weaker. Interestingly enough, the correlation between marriage payments is weak, and is turning negative, indicating both that traditional marriage systems are weakening, and that, instead of competing to bestow their children with assets, families of the bride and groom may "trade off" or compensate transfers from each side. While we have limited information on family background in the South Africa survey, the available data show that sorting along paternal education exists, and is stronger than that along maternal education. The correlation between maternal education of both spouses has decreased through time.

In both Latin American countries, the strongest correlations are between spousal age and years of schooling. In Mexico, correlation between spouses' land brought to marriage is weak, probably because women rarely, if ever, bring land to marriage. Correlation among parental characteristics—father's schooling, mother's schooling, and land—is positive, but not as strong as the correlation with spouse's schooling. Indeed, the correlations among father's schooling, mother's schooling, and parental land seem to have decreased through time. This is consistent with evidence that personal characteristics of spouses have become more important in the choice of a marriage partner; younger Mexican women emphasize trust, intimacy, and communication more than women of their mothers' generation, who put greater importance on marrying someone from a good family (Hirsch, 2003). Although we cannot perform the same extent of analysis for the Guatemala data because of limited information on the family background of husbands, we find that spousal correlations between age at marriage and years of schooling are high—higher than that between assets at marriage for both spouses.

REGRESSION RESULTS

Bangladesh

Table 7-5 presents regressions on years of schooling, age at marriage, and value of assets at marriage for husbands and wives. Findings show that although both spouses are more educated in more recent marriages, the gains for women are larger. This finding is consistent with recent shifts in education finance policies designed to close the male-female schooling gap. Despite this trend toward more gender equity in education, changes over time in the value of assets brought to marriage (defined here as the sum of premarital assets and payments made at the time of marriage) show distinct

TABLE 7-4 Trends in Assortative Matching at Marriage, by 5-Year
Marriage Year Intervals

| ASIA | Correlation Coefficients Between Husband and Wife | | | |
	No. of Marriages	Age at Marriage	Years of Schooling	Land at Marriage[a]
Bangladesh				
1945-1949	16	0.69	0.78	—[c]
1950-1954	34	0.49	0.57	—
1955-1959	50	0.71	0.80	—
1960-1964	62	0.27	0.62	—
1965-1969	95	0.58	0.72	—
1970-1974	121	0.58	0.68	—
1975-1979	122	0.56	0.68	—
1980-1984	144	0.63	0.54	—
1985-1989	108	0.63	0.49	—
1990-1994	83	0.81	0.58	—

| | Correlation Coefficients Between Husband and Wife | | | |
	No. of Marriages	Age at Marriage	Years of Schooling	Land at Marriage
Philippines				
1930-1934	4	—	—	—
1935-1939	8	—	—	—
1940-1944	12	—	—	—
1945-1949	14	0.73	0.51	−0.10
1950-1954	29	0.86	0.37	−0.09
1955-1959	28	0.78	0.05	−0.10
1960-1964	27	0.64	0.54	−0.30
1965-1969	33	0.75	0.53	0.48
1970-1974	34	0.18	0.44	0.02
1975-1979	38	0.70	0.63	−0.03
1980-1984	30	0.59	0.13	−0.20
1985-1989	3	—	—	—

| AFRICA | Correlation Coefficients Between Husband and Wife | | | |
	No. of Marriages	Age at Marriage	Years of Schooling	Land at Marriage[a]
Ethiopia				
1955-1959	144	0.75	0.37	—
1960-1964	56	0.54	0.52	—
1965-1969	85	0.63	0.44	—
1970-1974	62	0.78	0.34	—
1975-1979	72	0.48	0.38	—
1980-1984	99	0.75	0.39	—
1985-1989	53	0.60	0.34	—
1990-1995	1	—	—	—

Assets + Transfers[b]	Assets to Marriage	Transfers to Marriage	Father's Schooling
—	—	—	—
0.32	0.09	0.45	-0.02
0.34	0.03	0.07	0.30
-0.03	0.05	0.52	0.01
-0.12	-0.08	0.22	0.14
0.08	0.01	0.28	0.30
0.00	-0.02	0.43	0.13
0.03	-0.04	0.47	0.17
0.20	0.00	0.18	0.12
0.10	0.02	0.39	0.22

Assets at Marriage[d]	Father's Schooling	Mother's Schooling	Parents' Land
—	—	—	—
—	—	—	—
—	—	—	—
0.80	0.27	0.44	0.37
0.91	0.12	0.22	-0.02
0.58	0.13	0.50	0.25
0.57	0.07	0.11	0.15
0.79	0.38	0.65	0.24
0.76	0.25	0.56	0.20
0.90	0.29	0.25	-0.12
0.80	0.41	0.04	0.09
—	—	—	—

Assets at Marriage[b]	Father's Schooling	Mother's Schooling	Parents' Land
0.20	-0.02	—	0.00
0.37	-0.03	-0.03	0.29
0.37	0.26	—	0.46
-0.01	0.28	—	-0.06
0.25	0.27	0.70	0.41
0.45	0.06	0.29	-0.01
0.54	-0.07	0.43	0.32
—	—	—	—

continued

TABLE 7-4 Continued

| South Africa | Correlation Coefficients Between Husband and Wife | | | |
	No. of Marriages	Age at Marriage	Years of Schooling	Marriage Payments From This Side
1955-1959	14	0.51	0.85	0.87
1960-1964	30	0.70	0.65	0.47
1965-1969	66	0.74	0.68	0.13
1970-1974	67	0.66	0.84	0.35
1975-1979	92	0.65	0.72	0.05
1980-1984	83	0.82	0.79	0.13
1985-1989	72	0.60	0.61	0.07
1990-1994	47	0.90	0.66	−0.02
1995-1999	14	0.55	0.60	−0.14

| Latin America | Correlation Coefficients Between Husband and Wife | | | |
	No. of Marriages	Age at Marriage	Years of Schooling	Land at Marriage[a]
Mexico				
1930-1934	19	−0.28	−0.01	—
1935-1939	53	0.36	0.58	—
1940-1944	134	0.10	0.24	−0.04
1945-1949	220	0.25	0.57	—
1950-1954	437	0.25	0.30	0.09
1955-1959	679	0.35	0.30	−0.02
1960-1964	904	0.33	0.39	0.04
1965-1969	1,233	0.37	0.38	—
1970-1974	1,484	0.42	0.44	0.00
1975-1979	1,899	0.39	0.45	0.01
1980-1984	2,038	0.47	0.45	0.03
1985-1989	2,198	0.45	0.41	−0.03
1990-1994	2,075	0.49	0.42	0.05
1995-1999	1,086	0.49	0.44	−0.03

| Guatemala | Correlation Coefficients Between Husband and Wife | | | |
	No. of Marriages	Age at Marriage	Years of Schooling	Assets at Marriage
1970-1974	18	0.14	0.58	−0.13
1975-1979	55	0.52	0.46	−0.07
1980-1984	117	0.42	0.60	0.07
1985-1989	224	0.33	0.53	0.10
1990-1994	424	0.50	0.51	0.07
1995-1999	435	0.55	0.49	0.22

[a]Land is included with assets.
[b]Value of assets plus transfers to and from both families.
[c]Nonland assets only.

Assets at Marriage[e]	Father Has Any Education[f]	Mother Has Any Education[f]
0.37	0.15	−0.21
0.52	0.43	0.39
0.47	0.54	0.53
0.41	0.65	0.36
0.47	0.49	0.35
0.33	0.42	0.39
0.39	0.55	0.39
0.39	0.50	0.27
0.63	0.28	−0.03

Assets at Marriage[b]	Father's Schooling	Mother's Schooling	Parents' Land
0.14	—	—	0.14
0.44	—	—	0.65
0.71	—	—	0.16
0.29	0.50	0.71	0.43
0.19	0.40	0.58	0.55
0.21	0.00	0.00	0.30
0.25	0.39	0.77	0.24
0.16	0.44	0.38	0.37
0.23	0.36	0.23	0.29
0.19	0.23	0.23	0.31
0.18	0.31	0.23	0.27
0.19	0.30	0.16	0.27
0.24	0.17	0.23	0.25
0.18	0.30	0.13	0.34

[d]Correlation coefficients not reported for cell sizes less than 14.
[e]Count of assets.
[f]1 = yes; 0 = no.

TABLE 7-5   Determinants of Years of Schooling, Age at Marriage, and Assets at Marriage (Assets Include Marriage Payments), Bangladesh

	Years of Schooling				Age at Marriage OLS with Robust SEs	
	Tobit Husband		Wife		Husband	
Variance Name	Coeff	t	Coeff	t	Coeff	t
Year of marriage	0.04	**1.88**	0.10	**4.54**	0.09	**4.10**
Sex ratio	3.89	1.17	–6.78	**–1.98**	–3.94	–1.61
Own birth order	–0.04	0.27	–0.15	–1.17	–0.20	**–1.87**
No. of brothers	–0.03	–0.17	0.16	1.05	–0.03	–0.22
No. of sisters	0.07	0.39	0.25	**1.71**	–0.08	–0.56
Value of parents' land	0.00	**6.78**	0.00	**3.89**	0.00	0.60
Father's schooling	1.31	**5.98**	1.19	**5.95**	–0.24	–1.58
Mother's schooling	1.77	**4.14**	1.60	**5.97**	–0.15	–0.45
Site 2	2.98	**4.52**	3.36	**5.22**	1.37	**2.66**
Site 3	1.04	1.59	1.49	**2.33**	0.32	0.65
Constant	–98.47	**–2.10**	–201.37	**–4.49**	–142.94	**–3.41**
No. of observations					779.00	
F–statistic					3.09	
Prob > F					0.00	
R–squared					0.05	
Chi–squared	775		778.00			
LR chi^2	171.82		240.44			
Prob > chi^2	0.00		0.00			
Pseudo R^2	0.06		0.11			

NOTE: t–statistics in bold are significant at 10 percent or better.

patterns favoring men.[17] Age at marriage has been rising for both sexes over time, but more so for women. Rising education and age at marriage, especially for females, reflect overall changes in the economy of Bangladesh. Severe declines in the average size of land holding of rural households due

---

[17]The values of premarital assets and transfers received at the time of marriage are aggregated here because in South Asia they may constitute the same types of goods and because marriage transfer payments often come not only from the spouse's family, but from one's own family as well (see, e.g., Edlund, 1997, 2000; Gardner, 1995). In an earlier version of the paper with regressions for premarital assets and transfers run separately, it was found that premarital asset holdings of men rise with later marriage dates while women's show no change over time; on the other hand, marriage transfer payments to men increase with time, while transfers to women fall over time—a confirmation of the trend toward dowry payments found in the literature cited above.

		Value of Assets at Marriage			
Wife Coeff	t	Husband Coeff	t	Tobit Wife Coeff	T
0.12	10.43	827.53	2.60	–318.18	–5.19
–3.12	–1.96	13,5290.20	3.08	37,851.37	4.27
–0.08	–1.30	9456.12	4.98	771.82	2.16
–0.03	–0.47	–417.54	–0.18	–197.34	–0.45
0.12	1.40	–5,606.05	–2.44	–343.39	–0.81
0.00	–2.31	34.00	3.66	4.69	4.79
0.18	1.70	–1,699.95	–0.57	1,630.56	2.79
–0.41	–2.69	4,379.91	0.69	1,826.25	2.05
0.67	2.16	17,002.77	1.97	–5,672.38	–3.27
–0.11	–0.35	–1,2291.70	–1.49	–5,470.40	–3.26
–217.81	–9.57	–178,8906.00	–2.80	59,3495.00	4.83
786.00					
14.54					
0.00					
0.17					
		755		766.00	
		67.27		103.63	
		0.00		0.00	
		0.00		0.01	

to population growth may encourage parents to invest in the education of their children in the hope that they will be better equipped to obtain non-farm jobs in the emerging market-based economy (Caldwell et al., 1998).

The female-to-male marriageable age population sex ratio at the time of the marriage has the effect of reducing women's schooling and age at marriage, consistent with a female competition for scarce males hypothesis. Increases in this ratio also raise the total wealth (assets plus transfers) that both men and women bring to marriage, but the effect for males is much greater.

Parental characteristics are important determinants of education, age, and assets at marriage. Value of own parents' land, the major form of wealth holding in rural Bangladesh, increases levels of schooling and the value of assets brought to marriage of both husbands and wives. This is consistent with better resourced parents investing in and passing on resources to the

TABLE 7-6 Determinants of (Husband-Wife) Differences in Years of Schooling, Age at Marriage, and Assets at Marriage, Bangladesh, OLS with Robust Standard Errors

Variance Name	Years of Schooling		Age at Marriage		Value of Assets at Marriage	
	Coeff.	t	Coeff.	t	Coeff.	t
Year of marriage	-0.03	-3.20	-0.04	-2.98	386.16	1.80
Sex ratio	2.31	1.72	-0.51	-0.23	48,648.66	1.04
Differences in:						
No. of brothers	-0.03	-0.52	0.03	0.44	3,278.32	1.60
No. of sisters	-0.02	-0.30	0.00	0.06	1,304.91	0.87
Value of parents' land	0.00	-1.25	0.00	2.09	11.04	2.17
Father's schooling	0.02	0.25	-0.10	-0.95	-472.77	-0.19
Mother's schooling	0.12	0.88	-0.16	-1.14	-215.10	-0.07
Constant	57.43	3.13	96.34	3.26	-79,4488.00	-1.86
No. of observations	724.00		729.00		710.00	
F-statistic	2.67		2.50		2.34	
Prob > F	0.01		0.02		0.02	
R-squared	0.03		0.02		0.02	

NOTE: t-statistics in bold are significant at 10 percent or better

next generation regardless of sex (Edlund, 1997, 2000; Gardner, 1995). Higher parental land holding, however, reduces age at marriage for women, consistent with the notion that wealthier parents do not have to save for long periods of time to accumulate sufficient dowry to marry off their daughters. Young marriage age for women traditionally has been highly valued in Bangladeshi society. Goody (1976, cited in Caldwell et al., 1998) argues that this is based on the notion that girls can better marry into "good" families if they are virgins and hence bring no possibility of "other" descendents (through past sexual relations or pregnancy) who may attempt to claim entitlement to inheritance or property. Higher birth-order children bring more assets to marriage, although after controlling for birth order, additional siblings reduce the marriage assets of husbands. Parental schooling increases the educational attainment of both husbands and wives. For wives, paternal and maternal education each increase the value of total assets she brings to marriage, but have opposing effects on her marriage age, possibly reflecting differences in parental preferences for daughter's marriage age.

Turning to differences between husbands and wives, we observe in Table 7-6 that the husband's age and schooling seniority are decreasing over time, but the husband's asset advantage is getting larger. In an earlier specification with assets and transfer payments entered separately, not reported here, it was found that net wedding transfer payments are made increasingly to husbands, consistent with evidence of dowry inflation in South Asia. The sex ratio significantly increases husband's schooling advantage. The only family background difference variable that is statistically significant is the difference between parents' land values, and the magnitude of the effect is not large. The greater the difference is between land owned by the husband's and the wife's family, the greater the difference is between the husband's and wife's age and assets brought to marriage.

Philippines

Table 7-7 presents regressions on years of schooling, age at marriage, land area, and nonland assets at marriage of husband and wife. Reflecting the expansion of public education in the 1960s, both husbands and wives are more educated in more recent marriages. In line with rising levels of education, age at marriage also has been rising for both men and women. However, while husband's land area at marriage has remained constant, the trend is distinctly negative for women, probably due to increased land scarcity and the increasing tendency of Filipino parents to give land to sons and schooling to daughters (Estudillo et al., 2001b). There are no clear time trends in nonland assets.

Parental characteristics are important determinants of both age at marriage and human and physical capital brought to marriage. Father's land, a

TABLE 7-7 Determinants of Years of Schooling, Age at Marriage, and Assets at Marriage, Philippines

Variance Name	Years of Schooling OLS with Robust Standard Errors				Age at Marriage OLS with Robust Standard Errors			
	Husband Coeff	t	Wife Coeff	t	Husband Coeff	t	Wife Coeff	t
Year of marriage	0.08	5.55	0.07	5.28	0.12	3.79	0.08	2.51
Sex ratio	0.71	0.21	−0.99	−0.28	5.32	0.76	8.40	1.24
Father's schooling	0.09	1.42	−0.01	−0.09	−0.09	−0.72	−0.13	−1.12
Mother's schooling	0.10	1.22	0.27	3.13	−0.49	−3.03	−0.20	−1.32
Father's land	0.06	0.96	0.09	1.29	0.17	2.29	0.35	2.02
Mother's land	0.13	1.12	0.09	0.83	0.05	0.44	0.03	0.15
Village dummies								
P2 dummy	0.82	1.22	0.71	1.12	0.00	0.00	0.70	0.63
P3 dummy	−0.97	−2.02	−1.25	−2.80	0.38	0.34	1.80	1.57
CL1 dummy	0.44	0.80	−0.77	−1.54	−2.97	−3.10	−1.40	−1.43
CL2 dummy	−0.35	−0.75	−1.02	−2.04	−3.69	−3.68	−1.21	−1.27
Constant	−143.77	−5.39	−134.16	−5.13	−214.95	−3.49	−139.10	−2.26
No. of observations	259		259		259		259	
F–statistic	9.27		10.43		4.50		2.88	
Prob > F	0.00		0.00		0.00		0.00	
R–squared	0.24		0.28		0.18		0.11	
Chi–squared								
Prob > chi^2								
Pseudo R^2								

NOTE: t-statistics in bold indicate significance at 10 percent or better.

proxy for parental wealth, increases age at marriage and land area for both husband and wife. In Ilocano-speaking areas such as our Central Luzon sites, land from the groom's parents is considered essential to the start of the new family unit. Mother's land increases land that wives bring to marriage, as well as husband's nonland assets. Father's schooling increases nonland assets of the wife, but has a slight negative effect on husband's land, probably because fathers with more schooling are likely to be working in nonagricultural occupations and may have less land. Mother's schooling has a positive and significant effect on wife's schooling, which is larger than the effect of father's schooling, and a negative (but only weakly significant) effect on husband's nonland assets. Unlike in Bangladesh, the sex

Land Area Tobit				Nonland assets Tobit			
Husband Coeff	t	Wife Coeff	t	Husband Coeff	t	Wife Coeff	t
0.02	1.55	-0.04	-3.20	2.79	0.85	-2.24	-1.04
-0.61	-0.23	-0.09	-0.03	1,391.35	1.86	655.98	1.32
-0.10	-1.72	-0.01	-0.09	9.44	0.62	26.45	2.38
0.04	0.63	-0.01	-0.20	-34.48	-1.87	-12.92	-0.99
0.09	2.17	0.20	3.76	12.87	1.08	8.72	0.77
-0.01	-0.23	0.19	2.21	51.98	3.11	3.68	0.19
0.31	0.63	-0.33	-0.65	699.73	5.28	368.56	4.10
1.09	2.43	0.64	1.50	166.05	1.32	136.21	1.63
1.14	2.59	0.75	1.87	1,404.18	11.80	927.27	12.10
0.68	1.54	-0.84	-1.68	353.81	2.94	515.60	6.49
-37.08	-1.58	72.14	3.15	-6,948.45	-1.09	3,544.47	0.84
259		259		259		259	
16.71		57.82		164.52		148.14	
0.08		0.00		0.00		0.00	
0.03		0.15		0.04		0.04	

ratio does not affect either years of schooling, age at marriage, or land area, and has only a weak positive effect on husband's nonland assets.

Turning to changes in the difference between men and women over time, we find that neither age, schooling, nor asset differences change through time (Table 7-8). This is not surprising given the underlying egalitarian social structure of Philippine society. The only gap that seems to be increasing through time is that in land area: husbands are bringing more land to marriage than their wives. Although this may seem to increase the bargaining power of men within the household, it is offset by women's rising education levels and their increasing propensity to be employed in nonfarm jobs, which have higher returns to schooling (Estudillo et al.,

TABLE 7-8 Determinants of (Husband-Wife) Differences in Age, Years of Schooling, and Assets at Marriage, Philippines, OLS with Robust Standard Errors

Variance name	Age		Years of Schooling		Land Area		Nonland Assets	
	Coeff	t	Coeff	t	Coeff	t	Coeff	t
Year of marriage	0.02	0.79	0.00	0.22	0.02	3.83	1.97	0.81
Sex ratio	-0.71	-0.12	1.28	0.31	0.00	0.00	755.26	1.15
Differences in:								
Father's schooling	-0.06	-0.80	0.02	0.42	0.01	0.30	-16.17	-1.37
Mother's schooling	-0.10	-0.92	-0.01	-0.20	0.01	0.20	-13.36	-0.91
Father's land	0.06	1.05	0.02	0.47	0.05	2.54	0.99	0.13
Mother's land	0.00	-0.03	0.22	1.62	0.03	1.11	24.11	1.66
Constant	-36.43	-0.71	-7.05	-0.29	-33.61	-3.87	-4,459.98	-0.95
No. of observations	259		259		259		259	
F-statistic	0.88		0.70		4.49		1.31	
Prob > F	0.51		0.65		0.00		0.25	
R-squared	0.01		0.04		0.08		0.04	

NOTE: t-statistics in bold indicate significance at 10 percent or better.

2001b). The only parental background variable that is significant in the entire set of regressions is the difference between husband's and wife's fathers' land, which is positive and significant. That is, the greater the difference is between land owned by the husband's father and the wife's father, the greater the difference is between husband's and wife's land area at marriage. Similar to the levels results, the sex ratio or "marriage squeeze" factor does not affect the gap between the resources that each spouse brings to marriage.

Ethiopia

Similar to the Philippines and Bangladesh, more recent marriages are characterized by husbands and wives with more schooling (Table 7-9). Father's schooling has a strong positive influence on husband's schooling, but none of the parental background variables significantly affect wife's schooling. Trends in age at marriage in Ethiopia appear counterintuitive: Age at first marriage seems to be declining for both men and women. This could be due to reporting error in the age variable and thus should be taken with caution. Evidence from Hertrich (2002) and the National Family Fertility Survey (NFFS) (Central Statistical Authority, 1993), for example, suggest that women's age at marriage, though still quite low, has increased over time (World Bank, 1998).[18] Husbands whose parents have more land appear to marry later, while those with more brothers marry earlier, perhaps because of the availability of substitutes for male labor on the family farm. Although human capital has been increasing at marriage, however, the real value of physical capital brought to marriage has not changed appreciably through time, contrary to the descriptive results.[19] Parental land increases the value of assets that husbands bring to marriage, while mother's schooling increases the assets that wives bring. Probably due to sibling competition effects, wives with more sisters bring fewer assets to marriage.

The ratio of women to men of marriageable age affects neither schooling nor assets brought to marriage, but increases marriage age for both men and women. This may reflect longer waiting time for women, due to the

---

[18]According to the NFFS, mean age of women who married before 1966 was 14.9 years, compared to 15.5 for those who married between 1966 and 1970 and 15.8 and 17.1 for those who married between 1971 and 1975 and after 1976, respectively.

[19]Fafchamps and Quisumbing (2003a), using a different specification, find that the value of grooms' assets at marriage do not increase through time, but for first marriages, the value of brides' assets at marriage posts a secular increase. There is no secular trend in the value of brides' assets at marriage for subsequent marriages.

TABLE 7-9 Determinants of Years of Schooling, Age at Marriage, and Assets at Marriage, Ethiopia, First Marriages Only

	Years of Schooling Tobit				Age at Marriage OLS with Robust Standard Errors			
	Husband Coeff	t	Wife Coeff	t	Husband Coeff	t	Wife Coeff	t
Year of marriage	0.19	**3.74**	0.31	**3.36**	−0.34	**−4.42**	−0.18	**−2.74**
Sex ratio	−0.92	−0.07	−9.65	−0.44	53.05	**2.89**	51.40	**3.42**
Father's schooling	2.27	**2.77**	1.81	1.43	1.13	0.72	0.08	0.11
Mother's schooling	0.80	0.38	−0.18	−0.08	1.12	0.42	−0.01	−0.01
Parents' land	0.00	0.65	−0.04	−0.53	0.01	**4.74**	0.01	0.13
No. of brothers	0.14	1.22	0.17	0.98	−0.51	**−3.63**	0.01	0.10
No. of sisters	0.08	0.64	0.25	1.32	−0.18	−1.00	−0.14	−0.99
Region (Tigray excluded)								
Amhara	−0.51	−0.61	2.64	1.48	−2.55	**−2.13**	−1.23	−1.19
Oromo	1.02	1.29	4.16	**2.39**	−4.48	**−4.01**	−1.64	**−1.75**
South-Central	1.37	**1.84**	4.03	**2.39**	−2.05	**−1.84**	−0.18	−0.20
Constant	−374.06	**−4.52**	−603.02	**−3.89**	626.59	**4.88**	305.47	**2.73**
No. of observations	546		532.0		554		554	
F-statistic					22.7		2.37	
Prob > chi^2					0.00		0.01	
R-squared					0.16		0.03	
Chi-squared	122.83		92.75					
Prob > chi^2	0.00		0.00					
Pseudo R^2	0.07		0.10					

NOTE: t-statistics in bold indicate significance at 10 percent or better.

larger supply of marriageable women. Facing a market where there are fewer males per marriageable woman, males may also feel no pressure to accelerate marriage.

How have differences between husbands and wives changed over time? Age differences between husbands and wives have declined (Table 7-10). A marriage in which the husband's mother is better educated than the wife's mother is associated with a smaller age difference between husband and wife. The increasing gender gap in schooling attainment at marriage is more surprising, although this effect is only weakly significant. While overall schooling levels of husband and wives have increased, the difference between husbands and wives is also increasing. Differences in father's schooling increase the gap between husband's and wife's schooling, but differences in parental land in favor of the husband's parents reduce the schooling gap between husband and wife. It is possible that fathers who are better

Value of Assets at Marriage Tobit			
Husband Coeff	t	Wife Coeff	t
−132.24	−1.59	4.23	0.10
−3,458.13	−0.15	−14,842.62	−1.27
757.76	0.52	−842.93	−1.13
5,649.13	1.61	2,278.18	1.95
17.23	4.90	−9.78	−0.54
−248.52	−1.32	102.06	1.08
−16.75	−0.08	−204.45	−1.98
−701.44	−0.54	−3,017.56	−4.73
−376.69	−0.31	−4,682.03	−7.58
−904.75	−0.77	−4,045.30	−6.99
270,900.40	2.02	17,929.32	0.27
558.0		555.0	
65.94		85.51	
0.00		0.00	
0.01		0.00	

educated invest more in their sons' education, but families who have more land are less likely to do so, given the heavy involvement of males in Ethiopian agriculture. Husbands also tend to bring more assets than their wives to marriage if their families have more land, although the trend shows no narrowing in asset gaps over time. In contrast to its effects on levels, the sex ratio does not affect age differences between spouses nor differences in the resources that they bring to marriage.

South Africa

Table 7-11 presents regressions on years of schooling, age, asset counts, and transfers made at marriage of husband and wife. Here the values of prewedding assets and marriage transfers could not be combined because the assets are merely counted and values not imputed.

TABLE 7-10 Determinants of (Husband-Wife) Differences in Age, Years of Schooling, and Assets at Marriage, Ethiopia, First Marriages Only

	Age		Years of Schooling		Value of Assets at Marriage	
	Coeff	t	Coeff	t	Coeff	t
Year of marriage	-0.18	-3.45	0.04	1.72	-124.89	-1.52
Sex ratio	-3.59	-0.27	-0.55	-0.08	8,407.69	0.47
Differences in:						
Father's schooling	-0.31	-0.45	1.26	3.82	-750.54	-1.53
Mother's schooling	-2.48	-1.90	-0.01	-0.01	2,982.81	1.57
Parents' land	0.00	1.31	0.00	-4.62	19.17	13.11
No. of brothers	0.03	0.38	-0.05	-1.29	-155.96	-1.40
No. of sisters	-0.10	-1.10	0.00	0.04	-152.99	-1.57
Constant	368.26	4.27	-76.84	-2.10	236,732.10	1.69
No. of observations	548		525		552	
F-statistic	12.52		11.81		43.47	
Prob > F	0.00		0.00		0.00	
R-squared	0.139		0.07		0.09	

NOTE: t-statistics in bold indicate significance at 10 percent or better.

Unlike the South Asian case where payments may come from one's own family, most payments were transferred across families. Regression results show that education, age, and assets at marriage have been rising over time for both men and women. Across our six study countries, both schooling and age at marriage are rising for both sexes at an average rate of about 0.10 units per year (with the exception of Ethiopia, where education is rising at more than twice the average rate and age at marriage is falling). While time trends in educational advances in South Africa are around this average, age at marriage is rising at three times the rate of the other countries. Observing marriage patterns before independence, Schapera (1933, quoted in Caldwell et al., 1998) describes rising age at marriage across southern African countries and attributes the change to the church and state largely suppressing polygyny in combination with the high value of cattle needed for bridewealth payment: Older men no longer legally take younger second and third wives, but young men may have to delay marriage because they have not yet accumulated sufficient resources for payment of bridewealth. Although this is no doubt a factor, it does not explain the major increases observed in the 1980s and 1990s. The later increases are likely due to two primary causes: (1) the opening of the economy and associated structural adjustment and capital intensification, which have raised unemployment to astronomical levels, and (2) increases in HIV prevalence and deaths due to AIDS. Both factors may delay marriage, in part by reducing family resources available for marriage ceremonies and bridewealth payments. Marginal increases in the female-to-male population sex ratio raise the value of bridewealth payments. This result was unexpected, but needs to be taken with caution given the level of aggregation of the "marriage squeeze" variable.

Background and parental characteristics are important determinants of all three marriage outcomes. Parental survival to child marriage, a proxy for access to parental resources and support, reduces age at marriage, especially for men. Parental education, particularly the father's, has a similar effect. These two factors may help ensure availability of bridewealth payment, thus hastening the marriage of young men. Mothers' and fathers' educations increase the education of children at marriage regardless of sex. Fathers' education increases the assets that husband and wife bring to marriage; this may reflect paternal earning power and hence unmeasured parental wealth. Marriage payments from each side have fallen with time, reflecting the modernization that has come with the opening up of former African homelands and with later generations of Indians becoming more distanced from the dowry customs of South Asian society. Africans have higher marriage transfer payments than Indians, with amounts coming from the husband's side being more than double those from the wife's side,

TABLE 7-11 Determinants of Years of Schooling, Age at Marriage, Assets at Marriage, and Marriage Payments, South Africa

	Years of Schooling Tobit				Age at Marriage OLS with Robust SEs			
	Husband		Wife		Husband		Wife	
Variance Name	Coeff	t	Coeff	t	Coeff	t	Coeff	t
Year of marriage	0.10	**6.15**	0.13	**8.85**	0.33	**10.28**	0.35	**11.73**
Sex ratio	−4.27	−0.94	−4.64	−1.08	0.61	0.07	8.07	0.98
African race	−2.06	**−4.20**	−0.99	**−2.14**	1.42	**1.66**	0.28	0.35
Urban resident	2.79	**6.32**	2.02	**4.87**	−0.85	−0.97	−0.20	−0.25
Mother alive at wedding	0.49	1.19	0.12	0.29	−4.50	**−4.23**	−1.85	**−2.15**
Father alive at wedding	0.22	0.64	−0.02	−0.07	−1.63	**−2.56**	−0.66	−1.13
Mother any education	1.59	**4.24**	1.55	**4.30**	−1.47	**−2.08**	−0.99	−1.35
Father any education	1.20	**3.09**	1.39	**3.63**	−1.34	**−1.89**	−1.69	**−2.45**
Constant	−182.99	**−5.89**	−247.80	**−8.58**	−624.85	**−9.86**	−679.10	**−11.61**
No. of observations					492.00		492.00	
F-statistic					20.42		19.48	
Prob > F					0.00		0.00	
R-squared					0.30		0.30	
Chi-squared	492.00		492.00					
LR chi^2	275.98		242.77					
Prob > chi^2	0.00		0.00					
Pseudo R^2	0.11		0.10					

NOTE: t-statistics in bold are significant at 10 percent or better.

consistent with the Zulu tradition of *lobola* (75 percent of study couples are African and 25 percent are Indian).

Over time, differences in spouse education and marriage payments from each side have narrowed (Table 7-12). Disparities in age and assets brought to marriage appear not to have changed with time, although the mean differences here are not large anyway. A higher female-to-male marriageable age population ratio at the time of the wedding increases the marriage payments made by husbands. This result runs contrary to a "scarce husband hypothesis" and the same caveat as above applies. Being African means that relative to his wife, a man is one year older, has one less year of schooling, brings more assets to marriage, and has a family that makes more marriage payments. In urban areas, husband-wife asset

Count of Assets at Marriage Tobit				Value of Marriage Payments from Family Tobit			
Husband Coeff	t	Wife Coeff	t	Husband's Coeff	t	Wife's Coeff	t
0.02	2.44	0.04	4.71	−1545.46	−6.08	−500.31	−2.83
2.29	0.96	0.02	0.01	18,2234.20	2.52	−18,834.74	−0.37
1.55	5.84	0.20	0.72	52,227.22	6.27	20,263.96	3.46
−0.35	−1.50	0.39	1.55	−9,897.23	−1.40	6,362.25	1.30
0.18	0.81	−0.47	−1.92	1,655.72	0.25	9,310.94	1.79
−0.05	−0.26	0.06	0.29	1,674.52	0.31	−3,962.29	−1.03
−0.24	−1.20	−0.30	−1.36	2,139.56	0.34	12,130.33	2.73
0.44	2.12	0.61	2.60	12,145.61	1.89	1,378.11	0.29
−41.86	−2.57	−85.02	−4.69	2,831,604.00	5.69	973,536.40	2.83
492.00		492.00		492.00		492.00	
92.64		41.02		110.35		35.36	
0.00		0.00		0.00		0.00	
0.05		0.03		0.01		0.01	

disparities are smaller. A husband's mother surviving to his marriage results in a smaller spouse age difference. If a husband's mother has more schooling than his wife's mother, he will be closer to his wife in age and in the number of assets at marriage. If, on the other hand, his father is more educated than his father-in-law, he will have more assets at marriage than his wife.

Mexico

Table 7-13 presents regressions of the effects of parental characteristics on husband's and wife's schooling, age, land ownership, and asset scores. For both husband and wife, years of schooling increase with later marriage

TABLE 7-12 Determinants of (Husband-Wife) Differences in Years of Schooling, Age at Marriage, Assets at Marriage, and Marriage Payments, South Africa, OLS with Robust Standard Errors

	Years of Schooling		Age at Marriage		Count of Assets at Marriage		Value of Marriage Payments	
	Coeff	t	Coeff	t	Coeff	t	Coeff	t
Year of marriage	-0.03	**-2.59**	-0.02	-0.99	0.00	-0.66	-1015.40	**-4.85**
Sex ratio	0.94	0.26	-4.67	-0.71	2.36	1.37	155,126.70	**2.37**
African Race	-0.98	**-2.49**	1.08	**1.81**	0.92	**5.19**	23,929.24	**3.02**
Urban	0.50	1.46	-0.76	-1.29	-0.55	**-3.13**	-10,446.60	-1.39
Wife's mother alive at wedding	0.30	0.79	-0.09	-0.13	0.20	1.26	-2,248.93	-0.38
Wife's father alive at wedding	0.18	0.62	0.84	**1.65**	0.08	0.53	9,275.94	**1.86**
Husband's mother alive at wedding	0.18	0.55	-3.65	**-4.82**	0.17	1.02	3,613.20	0.60
Husband's father alive at wedding	-0.05	-0.19	-0.85	**-1.85**	-0.14	-1.03	-1,001.00	-0.21
Differences in:								
Mother's schooling	0.04	0.72	-0.26	**-2.77**	-0.08	**-2.65**	845.10	1.03
Father's schooling	0.04	0.77	0.02	0.25	0.05	**2.30**	-769.80	-1.03
Constant	60.61	**2.61**	57.10	1.30	5.95	0.49	1,837,739.00	**4.50**
No. of observations	492.00		492.00		492.00		492.00	
F-statistic	3.87		5.47		15.18		7.04	
Prob > F	0.00		0.00		0.00		0.00	
R-squared	0.08		0.14		0.19		0.12	

NOTE: t-statistics in bold are significant at 10 percent or better.

years. More years of schooling are also associated with literate parents (both father and mother), and primary school attendance and completion of both parents. Although social status variables of the father—proxied by the father's wearing shoes—have a positive and significant effect on both husband's and wife's schooling, the corresponding social status variable for the mother only affects wife's schooling. Lastly, parental land holdings also positively influence the number of years completed in school. A larger supply of women relative to men of marriageable age is associated with fewer years of schooling for both men and women. If women stop schooling to get married, the potential of increased competition for mates may induce them to marry earlier and thus stop schooling.

Similar to the other countries in our study, both spouses are older in more recent marriages. Whether the husband's father wore shoes while the husband was a child—an indicator of parental status—seems to decrease husband's age at marriage, but the mother's wearing shoes has an opposite effect on husband's age. Wives whose parents owned more land tend to marry late, but primary school completion by the father reduces wife's age at marriage. The sex ratio has opposite effects for husbands and wives. A larger supply of women of marriageable age exerts downward pressure on women's age at marriage and increases men's age at marriage.

How do time trends and parental background affect the assets that each spouse brings to marriage? Land ownership by husbands at the time of marriage has declined through time, possibly reflecting land scarcity and population pressure. Land ownership by wives, which is minimal, has not been affected by secular trends. For both husband and wife, parental land holdings are the most important determinant of land ownership at marriage, although the size of the marginal effects is small. In contrast, over time, new husbands and wives seem to be bringing more durable assets to marriage. Husbands whose fathers have completed primary school, and whose parents wore shoes in the husband's childhood, bring more assets to the marriage. Wives whose mothers wore shoes, and whose parents owned larger land areas, bring more assets to the marriage. A larger supply of marriageable women seems to decrease the durable assets that both spouses bring to marriage, but the reason behind this is not clear.

Turning now to differences over time, we find that schooling, age, and land ownership differences have declined in more recent marriages (Table 7-14). However, asset differences have increased. Thus, it seems that while gaps in human capital at marriage are decreasing, gender differences in durable asset ownership are increasing. Differences in parental literacy and schooling (in favor of the husband) are reflected in larger educational differences between husband and wife. Parental land holding inequalities also contribute to age differences. None of the differences in parental background variables are significant determinants of gender differences in asset

TABLE 7-13 Determinants of Years of Schooling, Age at Marriage, and
Assets at Marriage, Mexico

| | Years of Schooling Tobit | | | |
| | Husband | | Wife | |
	Coeff	t	Coeff	t
Year of marriage	0.12	**46.48**	0.13	**54.19**
Sex ratio	−1.21	**−2.05**	−1.29	**−2.27**
Father is literate	0.76	**5.64**	0.76	**5.89**
Mother is literate	0.54	**3.72**	0.49	**3.79**
Father has some primary schooling	0.23	**1.72**	0.33	**2.52**
Mother has some primary schooling	0.17	1.18	0.43	**3.38**
Father completed primary	0.98	**3.06**	0.80	**2.95**
Mother completed primary	0.83	**2.13**	0.65	**1.99**
Father wore shoes	0.21	**1.79**	0.23	**2.06**
Mother wore shoes	0.04	0.36	0.39	**3.57**
Parents' landholdings	0.02	**3.07**	0.03	**4.14**
State dummies (Guerrero excluded)				
Hidalgo	0.73	**4.66**	1.43	**9.06**
Michoacan	0.09	0.53	1.61	**9.67**
Puebla	0.58	**3.70**	1.12	**7.02**
Queretaro	0.96	**4.90**	1.56	**8.04**
San Luis Potosi	0.74	**4.68**	1.98	**12.37**
Veracruz	1.04	**6.98**	1.49	**9.91**
Constant	−225.59	**−45.77**	−265.20	**−53.41**
Selection term	3.09		3.06	
No. of observations	11,488		12,218	
F-statistic				
Prob > F				
R-squared				
Chi−squared	3,275.3		4,765.6	
Prob > chi^2	0.00		0.00	
Pseudo R^2	0.06		0.09	

NOTES: t-statistics in bold indicate significance at 10 percent or better. Marginal effects
reported for probit estimates.

scores. Note, however, that because our land ownership measure is only a
dummy variable for whether the husband or wife owned land at the time of
marriage, this measure is more imprecise relative to the other measures of
physical and human capital. The sex ratio affects years of schooling and
asset score differences in opposite ways: A larger supply of females of
marriageable age increases the schooling gap between husbands and wives,
while it reduces the gap between husband and wife asset scores. It is pos-

Age at Marriage
OLS with Robust Standard Errors

Husband Coeff	t	Wife Coeff	t
0.02	4.70	0.04	14.10
-3.09	-2.58	-3.94	-5.37
-0.32	-1.30	0.11	0.71
0.00	-0.02	-0.16	-1.21
-0.31	-1.25	-0.02	-0.10
-0.29	-1.14	0.02	0.14
0.71	1.00	-0.50	-1.73
-0.89	-1.48	0.23	0.63
-0.70	-3.24	-0.08	-0.61
0.20	0.96	0.16	1.30
0.01	0.91	0.03	3.44
1.46	5.14	0.55	3.69
1.04	3.54	0.65	4.10
1.25	4.33	0.13	0.83
0.67	2.03	0.80	4.21
2.08	7.05	0.80	5.02
0.74	2.75	0.08	0.57
-15.80	-1.81	-50.46	-10.10
11,506		12,279	
7		18.96	
0.00		0.00	
0.01		0.03	

continued

sible that, facing competition from other women, women leave school early in order to marry. If most assets that couples bring to marriage are their own, as this is not a dowry nor a brideprice society, the main asset that would come from parents would be land. It is then possible that, facing a larger supply of marriageable females, prospective grooms do not feel they need to accumulate more assets to be worthy candidates in the marriage market.

TABLE 7-13 Continued

	Land Ownership Probit with Robust Standard Errors			
	Husband Coeff	t	Wife Coeff	t
Year of marriage	0.00	**-4.55**	0.00	1.06
Sex ratio	-0.08	-1.30	0.00	0.67
Father is literate	-0.01	-0.44	0.00	-0.13
Mother is literate	-0.01	-0.74	0.00	-0.76
Father has some primary schooling	-0.01	-0.52	0.00	-1.45
Mother has some primary schooling	0.01	0.71	0.00	0.91
Father completed primary	0.00	-0.09	dropped	0.07
Mother completed primary	-0.03	-0.84	0.00	0.84
Father wore shoes	0.01	0.97	0.00	0.06
Mother wore shoes	0.02	**1.79**	0.00	0.86
Parents' landholdings	0.00	**4.74**	0.00	**2.76**
State dummies (Guerrero excluded)				
Hidalgo	0.15	7.37	0.63	0.54
Michoacan	0.03	**1.73**	0.76	0.57
Puebla	-0.01	-0.58	0.54	0.48
Queretaro	0.00	-0.03	dropped	0.04
San Luis Potosi	0.04	2.20	0.60	0.52
Veracruz	0.05	**3.00**	0.49	0.54
Constant				-1.82
Selection term				0.20
No. of observations	11,675		11,556	
F-statistic				
R-squared				
Chi-squared	275.38		not computed	349.43
Prob > chi^2	0.00		not computed	0.00
Pseudo R^2	0.03		0.05	

NOTES: t-statistics in bold indicate significance at 10 percent or better. Marginal effects reported for probit estimates.

Guatemala

Levels regressions are presented in Table 7-15. Here age of marriage (or, more accurately, age at first union) is increasing over time for wives but not husbands. Years of schooling and assets at marriage have each increased over time for both husbands and wives in the slums of Guatemala City. A higher female-to-male marriageable age population ratio at the time of the wedding decreases the assets wives bring to marriage, perhaps be-

Asset Score Tobit			
Husband Coeff	t	Wife Coeff	t
0.00	4.44	0.00	3.18
−0.14	−2.98	−0.21	−2.33
0.01	0.45	−0.01	−0.37
0.01	1.21	0.03	1.23
0.01	0.49	0.00	−0.06
−0.01	−0.92	−0.01	−0.39
2.86	0.00	0.02	
0.05	1.66	0.09	1.81
0.02	1.69	0.01	0.29
0.02	2.06	0.05	2.50
0.00	2.32	0.00	2.14
0.03	2.12	0.15	4.24
0.12	8.03	0.30	8.11
0.05	3.57	0.09	2.57
2.28	0.05	1.20	
0.02	1.25	0.16	4.29
0.05	3.77	0.18	5.23
−4.60	−2.82	−3.63	
	0.30		
11,675		12,279	
	331.63		
	0.00		
0.06		0.07	

cause, facing competition, women who are poor migrants from the countryside more readily enter a consensual union. Similar to Mexico, it is likely that the assets spouses bring to marriage are their own, because dowry and brideprice are not common, and land transfers would not be relevant to most couples because the sample is entirely urban. Indigenous ethnicity is associated with low levels of human capital (education) for both sexes, younger marriage age for men, and fewer assets brought to marriage by females.

TABLE 7-14 Determinants of (Husband-Wife) Differences in Age, Years of Schooling, Land Ownership, and Assets at Marriage, Mexico

	Age OLS with Robust SE		Years of Schooling OLS with Robust SE	
	Coeff	t	Coeff	t
Year of marriage	–0.03	**–8.88**	–0.01	**–4.57**
Sex ratio	1.39	1.55	1.28	**2.34**
Differences in:				
Father is literate	–0.12	–0.76	0.25	**2.76**
Mother is literate	0.10	0.58	0.31	**3.20**
Father has some primary schooling	0.09	0.56	0.10	1.05
Mother has some primary schooling	–0.16	–0.97	–0.06	–0.63
Father completed primary	0.21	0.56	0.42	**1.95**
Mother completed primary	–0.26	–0.63	0.05	0.18
Father wore shoes	–0.22	–1.33	0.08	0.91
Mother wore shoes	–0.26	–1.39	0.16	**1.70**
Parents' landholdings	0.02	**2.31**	0.01	1.43
Constant	6,5.91	**9.25**	15.06	**4.39**
No. of observations	1,1177		11,072	
F-statistic	8.19		1,1.28	
Prob > F	0.00		0.00	
R-squared	0.01		0.01	
Chi–squared				
Prob > chi^2				
Pseudo R^2				

NOTES: t-statistics in bold indicate significance at 10 percent or better. Marginal effects reported for probit estimates.

Family background characteristics are important for the timing and the human and physical capital brought to marriage by women. Having been raised in a rural area and migrated to the city as an adult is associated with younger age and less education at marriage for women. Rural areas in Guatemala historically have been characterized by scarcity of infrastructure and services, particularly for education and health (Brush et al., 2002). Having additional brothers slightly increases a woman's marriage age, while additional sisters reduces the value of assets a woman brings to her marriage, possibly because of competition for parental resources. If a woman's mother worked for pay (an indicator of economic need in her natal household), her marriage age and level of education is reduced. Her mother being literate has opposite effects, increasing her education and assets brought to marriage.

Land Ownership Ordered Probit, Robust SE		Asset Score OLS with Robust SE	
Coeff	z	Coeff	t
−0.01	−4.96	0.00	5.63
−0.20	−0.69	−0.06	−3.02
0.01	0.11	0.00	−0.60
−0.05	−1.00	0.00	0.77
0.01	0.10	0.00	0.83
0.06	1.09	0.00	−1.22
−0.03	−0.25	0.01	1.29
−0.21	−1.62	0.00	0.03
−0.06	−1.25	0.00	−1.18
0.06	0.99	0.00	−0.54
0.00	0.78	0.00	0.75
		−0.56	−5.44
11,177		11,177	
		3.34	
		0.00	
		0.00	
36.93			
0.00			
0.00			

Spouse difference regression results are presented in Table 7-16. Because background data are not available for husbands, family of origin difference variables could not be constructed. Therefore, two versions of the difference results are presented: one with only year of marriage, population sex ratio, and ethnicity, and a second that also includes levels of family background characteristics for women. In the first specification, spouse age differences are declining over time, but male advantage in the value of assets brought to marriage is rising. Indigenous ethnicity is associated with larger husband education advantage. In the second version of the regressions, spouse schooling differences are now found to decline over time, and male advantage in the assets brought to marriage is still rising. Further, if a woman was raised in a rural area, her husband will be relatively older and more educated. If her mother was a single mother, her husband is likely to

TABLE 7-15 Determinants of Years of Schooling, Age at Marriage, and Assets at Marriage, Guatemala, First Marriages

| | Years of Schooling Tobit | | | | Age at Marriage OLS with Robust SEs | | | |
| | Husband | | Wife | | Husband | | Wife | |
	Coeff	t	Coeff	t	Coeff	t	Coeff	t
Year of marriage	0.09	4.95	0.09	5.23	−0.03	−0.91	0.08	4.82
Sex ratio	7.44	1.44	8.06	1.62	−7.36	−0.92	2.74	0.52
Indigenous ethnicity	−2.23	−6.11	−2.52	−6.54	−1.06	−2.46	−0.41	−1.05
Rural upbringing			−2.41	−9.86			−0.70	−2.67
Mother a single mom		0.58	1.32			−0.54	−1.19	
No. of brothers			−0.05	−0.72			0.18	2.64
No. of sisters			0.00	−0.04			0.04	0.52
Mom worked for pay		−0.58	−2.58			−0.46	−1.91	
Mother literate			2.17	9.60			0.09	0.38
Constant	−181.22	−4.78	−189.53	−5.10	84.36	1.37	−137.26	−4.17
No. of observations					976.00		976.00	
F-statistic					2.37		5.31	
Prob > F					0.07		0.00	
R-squared					0.01		0.04	
Chi–squared	976.00		976.00					
Prob > chi^2	63.38		356.58					
P-value	0.00		0.00					
Pseudo R^2	0.01		0.07					

NOTE: t-statistics in bold are significant at 10 percent or better.

be younger. Women with more brothers bring fewer assets to marriage relative to their husbands; those with more sisters marry men with education levels similar to their own. Women whose mothers worked for pay marry men who are slightly older, while those whose mothers are literate are closer in age and educational attainment to their spouses. The population sex ratio variable does not have any effect on spouse differences.

SUMMARY AND CONCLUSIONS

Table 7-17 presents a summary of trends in schooling, age, and assets at marriage, based on the regression coefficients on the year of marriage.

Value of Assets at Marriage
Tobit

Husband Coeff	t	Wife Coeff	t
310.33	**3.59**	47.37	**3.19**
−23,718.53	−0.99	−11,101.02	**−2.70**
−337.09	−0.20	−561.59	**−1.74**
		−321.77	−1.59
	−155.87	−0.42	
		56.87	1.07
		−118.10	**−2.16**
	−79.13	−0.43	
		611.11	**3.27**
−587,440.60	**−3.25**	−81,150.60	**−2.62**
976.00		976.00	
16.42		57.45	
0.00		0.00	
0.00		0.01	

Human capital at marriage has been increasing for both men and women in the majority of our study countries. In all six countries, years of schooling at marriage have increased for husbands and wives.

Consistent with rising educational attainment, age at marriage is increasing for husbands and wives in the majority of countries; that is, men and women are marrying at later ages in more recent marriages. This upward trend can be observed for husbands in five out of six countries. Age at marriage for men is decreasing in Ethiopia, although the latter could reflect measurement error in the age variable. Women are also marrying at later ages in five out of six countries. In Ethiopia, age at marriage is decreasing, possibly reflecting both measurement error and isolation from outside forces

TABLE 7-16 Determinants of (Husband-Wife) Differences in Years of Schooling, Age at Marriage, and Assets at Marriage, Guatemala, First Marriages, OLS with Robust Standard Errors

Variance Name	Years of Schooling				Age at Marriage			
	Coeff	t	Coeff	t	Coeff	t	Coeff	t
Year of marriage	−0.02	−1.10	−0.10	**−3.54**	−0.10	**−3.68**	−0.01	−0.47
Sex ratio	−0.06	−0.01	−9.07	−1.18	−9.17	−1.20	0.55	0.11
Indigenous ethnicity	1.51	**4.05**	−0.94	**−1.93**	−0.44	−1.03	0.78	**1.95**
Rural upbringing			0.88	**2.43**			1.13	**4.56**
Mother a single mom	−0.01	−0.02			−0.86	**−2.53**		
No. of brothers			−0.01	−0.11			0.06	0.90
No. of sisters			−0.18	**−1.96**			−0.01	−0.21
Mom worked for pay	0.18	0.58			0.46	**2.03**		
Mother literate	−0.56	**−1.71**			−0.73	**−3.19**		
Constant	40.93	1.07	211.21	**3.61**	221.43	**3.74**	17.19	0.45
No. of observations	976.00		976.00		976.00		976.00	
F-statistic	6.20		2.51		4.80		7.67	
Prob > F	0.00		0.01		0.00		0.00	
R-squared	0.02		0.03		0.02		0.06	

NOTE: t-statistics in bold are significant at 10 percent or better.

in these rural villages. In spite of considerable political turmoil over the past decades, local traditions regarding marriage and inheritance have remained relatively untouched, given the lack of roads and the relative isolation of the countryside.[20]

There is no clear trend regarding land ownership at marriage, although grooms seem to be bringing more physical assets to marriage in four out of six countries. In the two countries where land holding information is not aggregated with total assets, husbands' land ownership at marriage remains constant in one case (Philippines) and declines in the other (Mexico). Land ownership at marriage by women is decreasing through time in the Philip-

---

[20]This is not to say that local traditions have not changed at all—they have, especially in areas influenced by urbanization and labor migrations. But, in our opinion, they have changed much less than in African countries previously colonized by Europe.

Value of Assets at Marriage			
Coeff	t	Coeff	t
134.66	2.79	146.06	3.05
−12,030.85	−0.74	−8,569.73	−0.54
314.44	0.27	−39.64	−0.03
		1,171.24	1.31
	−987.86	−1.08	
		525.09	1.89
		99.04	0.46
	356.19	0.45	
	658.89	0.84	
−24,9076.30	−2.60	−27,7950.70	−2.91
976.00		976.00	
2.69		1.94	
0.05		0.04	
0.01		0.02	

pines, and remains constant, though very low (less than 1 percent of marriages) in Mexico. Asset values of husbands increase through time in four countries, remaining constant in the Philippines and Ethiopia. Asset values of wives increase in three countries (South Africa, Mexico, and Guatemala), remain constant in the Philippines and Ethiopia, and decline in Bangladesh. (In the two countries for which we have data on marriage payments, trends have been in opposite directions: increasing for husbands and decreasing for wives in Bangladesh, and decreasing for both in South Africa.)

We now turn to how differences in human capital, age, and assets at marriage between husband and wife have changed through time. In three out of six countries, husband-wife gaps in schooling attainment at marriage have decreased—pointing to an equalization of human capital at marriage. The exceptions are the Philippines, where the difference in years of schooling has not changed over time; Guatemala, where the evidence is mixed as to whether the difference is stable or falling; and Ethiopia, where the differ-

TABLE 7-17 Trends by Marriage Year in Age, Human Capital, and Assets at Marriage

Trends	Husband	Wife	Difference (Husband-Wife)
ASIA			
Bangladesh			
Years of schooling	Increasing	Increasing	Decreasing
Age at marriage	Increasing	Increasing	Decreasing
Value of assets + transfers at marriage (1996 taka)	Increasing	Decreasing	Increasing
Philippines			
Years of schooling	Increasing	Increasing	Constant
Age at marriage	Increasing	Increasing	Constant[a]
Land area at marriage	Constant	Decreasing	Increasing
Value of nonland assets (1989 pesos)	Constant	Constant	Constant
AFRICA			
Ethiopia			
Years of schooling	Increasing	Increasing	Increasing
Age at marriage	Decreasing	Decreasing	Decreasing
Value of assets at marriage (1997 birr)	Constant	Constant	Constant
South Africa			
Years of schooling	Increasing	Increasing	Decreasing
Age at marriage	Increasing	Increasing	Constant
Count of assets at marriage	Increasing	Increasing	Constant
Value of transfers from family at marriage (1998 Rand)	Decreasing	Decreasing	Decreasing
LATIN AMERICA			
Mexico			
Years of schooling	Increasing	Increasing	Decreasing
Age at marriage	Increasing	Increasing	Decreasing
Owned land at marriage (1 if yes)	Decreasing	Constant	Decreasing
Asset score	Increasing	Increasing	Increasing
Guatemala[b]			
Years of schooling	Increasing	Increasing	Constant
Age at marriage	Constant	Increasing	Decreasing
Value of assets at marriage (1999 Quetzales)	Increasing	Increasing	Increasing

[a]"Constant" implies that t-statistic on the marriage year variable is not significant at 10 percent or better, regardless of the magnitude of the coefficient.
[b]Guatemala difference results are for the first specification reported in Table 7-16, without female family background variables.

ence is increasing. In the Philippines, there is no gender gap in schooling in current marriages (see Table 7-2), however, in urban Guatemala the difference is still greater than one year. The disturbing trend in Ethiopia is consistent with a leveling off of enrollment rates for girls and persistent through diminishing gender gaps in education in sub-Saharan Africa, a consequence of lack of improvement in public education facilities and high opportunity costs of education for girls.[21]

In line with the closing of the education gap, in four out of six countries, age differences between husband and wife have decreased—a move toward increasing equality, given the possibility that seniority and experience may give husbands a bargaining advantage over their wives. The two countries where the difference in age at marriage has not decreased are South Africa and the Philippines, the two countries where women's age at marriage is the highest among our study countries.

The distribution of assets at marriage continues to favor husbands. In three out of six countries, the husband-wife asset difference has not changed through time—and therefore continues to favor husbands—and has even increased in the two Latin American countries. Finally, transfers at marriage are increasingly favoring men in Bangladesh, while the gap in transfers at marriage is decreasing in South Africa.

What do these trends imply for the distribution of power within marriage? The reduction of husband-wife gaps in age and schooling indicates a potential improvement in the balance of power within the family, but asset ownership continues to favor husbands. These findings from our data mirror changes in investment in human capital and asset ownership worldwide (Quisumbing and Meinzen-Dick, 2001). In general, investment in women's human capital has improved markedly in the past 25 years: Life expectancy has increased 20 percent faster for females than for males, fertility rates have declined, and gaps in educational attainment have begun to close. However, gender gaps in physical assets and resources that women can command through available legal means continue to persist. In large part this is due to social and legal mechanisms that do not give women equal rights to own and inherit property, particularly land (Crowley, 2001; Gopal, 2001). Persistent differences in assets in favor of men have important implications for household well-being and the welfare of future generations, given recent findings that increasing women's status and control of assets

---

[21]Although the gender gap in schooling worldwide has decreased over time, girls' primary enrollment rates have leveled off in sub-Saharan Africa at around 54 percent. Absolute levels of female enrollment and schooling remain lower in sub-Saharan Africa than in other developing regions, with female secondary enrollment rates of 14 percent in 1995 (World Bank, 2001).

has favorable effects on child nutrition and education (Hallman, 2000; Quisumbing and Maluccio; 2003; Smith et al., 2003).

These trends do not only affect the distribution of power within marriage, but also the role that marriage plays in the transition to adulthood. Rising education levels, particularly of women, increase the role of individual choice rather than parental choice of a spouse or partner. Indeed, the increasing importance of personal rather than parental characteristics in characterizing matches in the marriage market point to increased individual choice. At the same time, globalizing and modernizing economies raise the expectations of young people beyond traditional roles. Young people delay marriage in the hopes of getting payoffs for their educational investments in the form of secure and well-paying jobs (Caldwell et al., 1998). However, structural adjustment programs have altered the employment structure of many developing economies; with the contraction of the public sector, there are now fewer government and other types of jobs historically considered "good." Transition to paid work, especially for adult males, often precedes the transition to marriage and adulthood; rising youth unemployment is associated with the feeling of frustration with the inability to move on in life. If marriage marks the transition to adulthood in most societies, this transition is being delayed, either due to the desire to stay in school or capture returns to schooling through employment, or to the inability to find gainful employment. The impact of this delayed transition on the institution of marriage itself deserves further investigation.

REFERENCES

Adato, M., de la Brière, B., Mindek, D., and Quisumbing, A. (2000). *Final report: The impact of PROGRESA on women's status and intrahousehold relations.* Washington, DC: International Food Policy Research Institute.

Ahmed, A., and del Ninno, C. (2002). *The food for education program in Bangladesh: An evaluation of its impact on educational attainment and food security.* (Food Consumption and Nutrition Division Discussion Paper No. 138.) Washington, DC: International Food Policy Research Institute.

Anderson, J.N. (1962). Some aspects of land and society in a Pangasinan community. *Philippine Sociological Review, 19,* 41-58.

Bloch, F., and Rao, V. (2002). Terror as a bargaining instrument: A case study of dowry violence in rural India. *American Economic Review, 92,* 1029-1043.

Bouis, H.E., Palabrica-Costello, M., Solon, O., Westbrook, D., and Limbo, A.B. (1998). *Gender equality and investments in adolescents in the rural Philippines.* (Research Report No. 108.) Washington, DC: International Food Policy Research Institute.

Brush, L., Heyman, C., Provasnik, S., Fanning, M., Lent, D., and De Wilde, J. (2002). *Description and analysis of the USAID girls' education activity in Guatemala, Morocco, and Peru.* Report produced for the Bureau for Economic Growth, Agriculture, and Trade, Office of Women in Development, U.S. Agency for International Development.

Cain, M.T. (1984). *Women's status and fertility in developing countries: Son preference and economic security.* (World Bank Staff Working Paper No. 682.) Washington, DC: World Bank.

Caldwell, J.C., Reddy, P.H., and Caldwell, P. (1983). The causes of marriage change in south India. *Population Studies, 37*(3), 343-361.

Caldwell, J.C., Caldwell, P., Caldwell, B.K., and Pieris, I. (1998). The construction of adolescence in a changing world: Implications for sexuality, reproduction, and marriage. *Studies in Family Planning, 29*(2), 137-153.

Carter, M.R., and May, J. (1998). Poverty, livelihood, and class in rural South Africa. *World Development, 27,* 1-20.

Casterline, J., Williams, L., and McDonald, P. (1986). The age difference between spouses: Variations among developing countries. *Population Studies, 40*(3), 353-374.

Central Statistical Authority. (1993). *Report on the National Rural Nutrition Survey, Core Module.* (Statistical Bulletin 113.) Addis Ababa, Ethiopia: Author.

Crowley, E. (2001). Land rights. In A.R. Quisumbing and R.S. Meinzen-Dick (Eds.), *Empowering women to achieve food security* (2020 FOCUS 6). Washington, DC: International Food Policy Research Institute.

de la Brière, B., and Quisumbing, A.R. (2000). The impact of PROGRESA on intrahousehold decision making and relative schooling achievements of boys and girls. In M. Adato, B. de la Brière, D. Mindek, and A.R. Quisumbing (Eds.), *The impact of PROGRESA on women's status and intrahousehold relations: A final report* (pp. 1-45). Washington, DC: International Food Policy Research Institute.

Dixon, R.B. (1971). Explaining cross-cultural variations in age at marriage and proportions never marrying. *Population Studies, 25*(2), 215-234.

Doss, C.R. (1999). Intrahousehold resource allocation in Ghana: The impact of the distribution of asset ownership within the household. In G.H. Peters and J. von Braun (Eds.), *Food security, diversification, and resource management: Refocusing the role of agriculture?* (pp. 309-316). Aldershot, England: Dartmouth.

Edlund, L. (1997). *Dowry to daughters: Theory and evidence.* New York: Columbia University Press.

Edlund, L. (2000). The marriage squeeze interpretation of dowry inflation: A comment. *Journal of Political Economy, 108*(6), 1327-1333.

Estudillo, J., Quisumbing, A.R., and Otsuka, K. (2001a). Gender differences in land inheritance, schooling, and lifetime income: Evidence from the rural Philippines. *Journal of Development Studies, 37*(4), 23-48.

Estudillo, J., Quisumbing, A.R., and Otsuka, K. (2001b). Gender differences in schooling and land inheritance in the rural Philippines. *Land Economics, 77*(1), 130-143.

Fafchamps, M., and Quisumbing, A.R. (2002). Control and ownership of assets within rural Ethiopian households. *Journal of Development Studies, 38,* 47-82.

Fafchamps, M., and Quisumbing, A.R. (2003a). *Assets at marriage in rural Ethiopia.* (Working Papers Series No. 2000-28.) Oxford, England: University of Oxford and International Food Policy Research Institute, Centre for the Study of African Economies.

Fafchamps, M., and Quisumbing, A.R. (2003b). *Marriage and assortative matching in rural Ethiopia.* (Development and Comp. Systems Working Papers Series No. 0409023.) Oxford, England: University of Oxford and International Food Policy Research Institute, Centre for the Study of African Economies. Available: http://econwpa.wustl.edu:80/eps/dev/papers/0409/0409023.pdf [accessed June 2005].

Gardner, K. (1995). *Global migrants, local hires: Travel and transformation in rural Bangladesh.* Oxford, England: Oxford University Press.

Gavian, S., and Teklu, A. (1996). *Land tenure and farming practices: The case of Tiyo Woreda, Arsi, Ethiopia.* Paper presented to the annual conference, Agricultural Economics Society of Ethiopia, International Livestock Research Institute, Addis Ababa.

Gavian, S., and Ehui, S. (1999). Measuring the production efficiency of alternative land tenure contracts in a mixed crop-livestock system in Ethiopia. *Agricultural Economics, 20,* 37-49.

Goody, J.R. (1976). *Production and reproduction: A comparative study of the domestic domain.* Cambridge, England: Cambridge University Press.

Gopal, G. (2001). Law and legal reform. In A.R. Quisumbing and R.S. Meinzen-Dick (Eds.), *Empowering women to achieve food security* (2020 FOCUS 6). Washington, DC: International Food Policy Research Institute.

Gregson, S., Nyamukapa, C.A., Garnett, G.P., Mason, P.R., Zhuwau, T., Carael, M., Chandiwana, S.K., and Anderson, R.M. (2002). Sexual mixing patterns and sex-differentials in teenage exposure to HIV infection in rural Zimbabwe. *Lancet, 359,* 1896-1903.

Haddad, L., Hoddinott, J., and Alderman, H. (1997). *Intrahousehold resource allocation in developing countries: Models, methods, and policy.* Baltimore, MD: Johns Hopkins University Press.

Hallman, K. (2000). *Mother-father resource control, marriage payments, and girl-boy health in rural Bangladesh.* (Food Consumption and Nutrition Division Discussion Paper No. 93.) Washington, DC: International Food Policy Research Institute.

Hallman, K., Quisumbing, A.R., Ruel, M., and de la Brière, B. (2005). Mothers work and child care: Findings from the urban slums of Guatemala city. *Economic Development and Cultural Change, 53*(4), 855-886.

Hertrich, V. (2002, May 9-11). *Nuptiality and gender relationships in Africa: An overview of first marriage trends over the past 50 years.* Session on Family Change in Africa and Latin America, Population Association of America 2002 annual meeting, Atlanta, GA.

Hirsch, J.S. (2003). *A courtship after marriage: Sexuality and love in Mexican transnational families.* Los Angeles: University of California Press.

Hoddinott, J., and Haddad, L. (1995). Does female income share influence household expenditures? Evidence from Côte D'Ivoire. *Oxford Bulletin of Economics and Statistics, 57,* 77-95.

International Food Policy Research Institute, Bangladesh Institute of Development Studies, Institute of Food and Nutrition Science. (1998). *Commercial vegetable and polyculture fish production in Bangladesh: Their impacts on income, household resource allocation, and nutrition* (Donor Report). Washington, DC: International Food Policy Research Institute.

Jejeebhoy, S.J. (1995). *Women's education, autonomy, and reproductive behavior: Experience from developing countries.* Oxford, England: Clarendon Press.

Kelly, R.J., Gray, R.H., Sewankambo, N.K., Serwadda, D., Wabwire-Mangen, F., Lutalo, T., and Wawer, M.J. (2001). *Age differences in sexual partners and risk of HIV-1 infection in rural Uganda.* Baltimore, MD: Johns Hopkins University School of Hygiene and Public Health.

Kishor, S. (1995). *Autonomy and Egyptian women: Findings from the 1988 Egypt Demographic and Health Survey.* (DHS Occasional Papers No. 2.) Calverton, MD: Macro International.

Kishor, S., and Neitzel, K. (1996). *The status of women: Indicators for twenty-five countries.* (DHS Surveys Comparative Studies No. 21.) Calverton, MD: Macro International.

Luke, N., and Kurz, K.M. (2002). *Cross-generational and transactional sexual relationships in Sub-Saharan Africa: Prevalence of behavior and implications for negotiating safer sexual practices.* Washington, DC: International Center for Research on Women and Population Services International.

Lundberg, S., Pollak, R., and Wales, T.J. (1997). Do husbands and wives pool their resources? Evidence from the United Kingdom child benefit. *Journal of Human Resources, 32*, 463-480.

MacArthur, H. J. (1977). *Adolescent peer groups and socialization in the rural Philippines: A socioecological perspective.* Ph.D. dissertation, University of Hawaii.

Malhotra, A. (1997). Gender and the timing of marriage: Rural-urban differences in Java. *Journal of Marriage and the Family, 59*(2), 434-450.

Maluccio, J., Haddad, L., and May, J. (2000). Social capital and income generation in South Africa, 1993-98. *Journal of Development Studies, 36*(6), 54-81.

May, J., Carter, M.R., Haddad, L., and Maluccio, J.A. (2000). KwaZulu-Natal income dynamics study (KIDS) 1993-1998: A longitudinal household database for South African policy analysis. *Development Southern Africa, 17*, 567-581.

Medina, B.T.G. (1991). *The Filipino family: A text with selected readings.* Diliman, Quezon City: University of the Philippines Press.

Mensch, B., Bruce, J., and Greene, M.E. (1998). *The uncharted passage: Girls' adolescence in the developing world.* New York: Population Council.

Miller, B.D. (1981). *The endangered sex: Neglect of female children in rural North India.* Ithaca, NY: Cornell University Press.

Morris, S., Carletto, C., Hoddinott, J., and Christiaensen, L.J.M. (1999). *Validity of rapid estimates of household wealth and income for health surveys in rural Africa.* (Food Consumption and Nutrition Division Discussion Paper No. 72.) Washington, DC: International Food Policy Research Institute.

Naved, R.T. (2000). *Intrahousehold impact of transfer of modern agricultural technology: A gender perspective.* (Food Consumption and Nutrition Division Discussion Paper No. 85.) Washington, DC: International Food Policy Research Institute.

Pankhurst, H. (1992). *Gender, development, and identity: An Ethiopian study.* London, England: Zed Books.

Project for Statistics on Living Standards and Development. (1994). *Project for statistics on living standards and development. South Africans rich and poor: Baseline household statistics.* Cape Town: University of Cape Town, South African Labour and Development Research Unit.

Quisumbing, A.R. (1994). Intergenerational transfers in Philippine rice villages: Gender differences in traditional inheritance customs. *Journal of Development Economics, 43,* 167-195.

Quisumbing, A.R., and de la Brière, B. (2000). *Women's assets and intrahousehold allocation in rural Bangladesh: Testing measures of bargaining power.* (Food Consumption and Nutrition Division Discussion Paper No. 86.) Washington, DC: International Food Policy Research Institute.

Quisumbing, A.R., and Maluccio, J.A. (2003). Resources at marriage and intrahousehold allocation: Empirical evidence from Bangladesh, Ethiopia, Indonesia, and South Africa. *Oxford Bulletin of Economics and Statistics, 65*(3), 283-328.

Quisumbing, A.R., and Meinzen-Dick, R.S. (2001). Overview. In A.R. Quisumbing and R.S. Meinzen-Dick (Eds.), *Empowering women to achieve food security* (2020 FOCUS 6). Washington, DC: International Food Policy Research Institute.

Rao, V. (1993a). Dowry "inflation" in rural India: A statistical investigation. *Population Studies, 47,* 283-293.

Rao, V. (1993b). The rising price of husbands: A hedonic analysis of dowry increases in rural India. *Journal of Political Economy, 101*(4), 666-677.

Rao, V. (1997). Wife-beating in rural South India: A qualitative and econometric analysis. *Social Science and Medicine, 44,* 1169-1180.

Robicheaux, D.L. (1997). Residence rules and ultimogeniture in Tlaxcala and Mesoamerica. *Ethnology*, 36(2), 149-171.

Rubalcava, L., and Thomas, D. (2002). *Family bargaining and welfare*. Santa Monica, CA: RAND.

Ruel, M.T., de la Brière, B., Hallman, K., Quisumbing, A.R., and Coj, N. (2002). *Does subsidized childcare help poor working women in urban areas? Evaluation of a government-sponsored program in Guatemala City*. (Food Consumption and Nutrition Division Discussion Paper No. 131.) Washington, DC: International Food Policy Research Institute.

Schapera, I. (1933). Premarital pregnancy and native opinion: A note on social change. *Africa*, 6(1), 59-89.

Schultz, T.P. (1990). Testing the neoclassical model of family labor supply and fertility. *Journal of Human Resources*, 25, 599-634.

Sen, A.K. (1989). Cooperation, inequality, and the family. *Population and Development Review*, 15(Suppl.), 61-76.

Singh, S., and Samara, R. (1996). Early marriage among women in developing countries. *International Family Planning Perspectives*, 22(4), 148-157, 175.

Skoufias, E. (2001, July). PROGRESA and its impacts on the human capital and welfare of households in rural Mexico: A synthesis of the results of an evaluation by IFPRI (Research Report). Available: http://www.ifpri.org/themes/progresa.htm.

Smith, L.C., Ramakrishnan, U., Ndiaye, A., Haddad, L., and Martorell, R. (2003). *The importance of women's status for child nutrition in developing countries*. (Research Report No. 131.) Washington, DC: International Food Policy Research Institute.

Smith, P.C. (1980). Asian marriage patterns in transition. *Journal of Family History*, 5(1), 58-96.

South Africa Department of Social Development. (2000). *The state of South Africa's population report 2000: Population poverty and vulnerability*. Pretoria, South Africa: Department of Social Development, National Population Unit.

Statistics South Africa. (2001). *South Africa in transition: Selected findings from the October household survey of 1999 and changes that have occurred between 1995 and 1999*. Pali Lehohla, Pretoria, South Africa: Office of Statistician General.

Strauss, J., and Thomas, D. (1995). Human resources: Empirical modeling of household and family decisions. In T.N. Srinivasan and J. Behrman (Eds.), *Handbook of development economics* (pp. 1883-2023). Amsterdam, The Netherlands: Elsevier.

Subramanian, J. (1998). *Rural women's rights to property: A Bangladesh case study*. Madison: University of Wisconsin-Madison, Land Tenure Center.

Thomas, D. (1990). Intrahousehold resource allocation: An inferential approach. *Journal of Human Resources*, 25, 635-664.

Thomas, D. (1993). The distribution of income and expenditure within the household. *Annales de Economie et de Statistiques*, 29, 109-136.

Thomas, D., and Chen, C. (1994). *Income shares and shares of income*. (Labor and Population Working Paper 94-08.) Santa Monica, CA: RAND.

Thomas, D., Contreras, D., and Frankenberg, E. (2002). *Distribution of power within the household and child health* (mimeo). Santa Monica, CA: RAND.

United Nations. (1990). *Patterns of first marriage: Timing and prevalence*. New York: United Nations, Department of International Economic and Social Affairs.

United Nations Development Program. (2000). *Human development report 2000*. Oxford, England: Oxford University Press.

Webb, P., and von Braun, J. (1994). *Famine and food security in Ethiopia: Lessons for Africa*. Chichester, England: John Wiley and Sons.

World Bank. (1998). *Ethiopia: Social sector note.* (Report No. 16860-ET.) Washington, DC: Author.

World Bank. (2001). *Engendering development through gender equality in rights, resources, and voice.* (World Bank Policy Research Report.) Washington, DC: Author.

Zhang, J., and Chan, W. (1999). Dowry and wife's welfare: A theoretical and empirical analysis. *Journal of Political Economy, 107*(4), 786-808.

8

Adolescent Transitions to Adulthood in Reform-Era China

Emily Hannum and Jihong Liu

This chapter traces evidence about adolescents' pathways into adulthood in China over the past two decades of market reforms, focusing on the realms of education, work, family, and health. We draw together information from policy documents, reports, secondary research, and aggregate and individual-level data from a variety of sources. Evidence shows that on average, the market reform period has benefited many aspects of adolescent and young adult life. Education has increased and adolescent labor has decreased in the reform period. The average age at marriage is high, and rose in the 1990s, enough that marriage is unlikely to compete directly with educational opportunities except at the highest levels of education. Low fertility rates suggest that women's childrearing responsibilities may compete less with other opportunities in China than in many less developed countries.

The benefits of improved standards of living have been shared across social groups, but social and economic inequalities continue to mark the youth life course. While wealthier urban youth are beginning to experience problems with overnutrition, some rural youth still face nutritional deprivation. Suicide rates are dramatically higher among rural youth and young adults, especially young rural women. Wealthier adolescents and those in urban areas are more likely to be in school than their poor rural counterparts, and thus enjoy significant advantages in a labor market that increasingly rewards credentials. The mark of rural poverty is clear in the elevated likelihood of rural youth participating in the labor force, in the high percentage of working youth employed in agriculture, and in the large-scale youth and young adult migration into urban settings. Finally, social changes in the reform period raise important concerns about behavioral health issues, especially sexual health and smoking.

THE CHANGING CONTEXT OF ADOLESCENCE IN CHINA

The transition to markets in China in the late 1970s marked the beginning of a political focus on promoting economic modernization and growth. In rural areas, the transition meant decollectivization of agriculture and implementation of the household responsibility system, in which farmland and resources were contracted to individual households whose earnings were linked to output.[1] In urban settings, the privatization of state-owned enterprises and the emergence of a labor market were important elements of growth-promoting reforms. Reforms brought unprecedented growth and poverty reduction, but also rising economic inequality and a deteriorating social safety net.[2] Reforms in the education and health sectors decentralized administration and finance, increasing the diversity of services and the costs to individuals. Layoffs and unemployment heightened the economic insecurity of urban residents in the wake of labor reforms. Rural residents faced rising costs for education and health in the context of new pressures for self-sufficiency in agriculture.

These changes have dramatically modified the context of adolescence over the past two decades. For many of China's youth, the market reform period has improved living standards and increased life choices in education, work, and family formation. However, adolescents and young adults face new risks as a result of diversified choices, and disadvantaged groups continue to experience problems characteristic of youth in developing countries, such as difficulty obtaining access to basic nutrition, health, and education. The experiences of China's youth are significant in the global context, as 18 percent of the world's 15- to 24-year-old youth reside in China, as do 21 percent of the total youth population in developing countries (see Table 8-1).

This chapter outlines major reform-era patterns and trends in adolescents' pathways into adulthood, focusing on the realms of education, work, family, and health. The chapter is structured as follows: after briefly intro-

---

[1]Experiments with such contracting began in 1978, and by 1983 nearly all of China's farmers had adopted the responsibility system (Lin, 1988; Powell, 1992).

[2]For example, World Bank estimates indicate that the number of people living in poverty declined from 398.3 million in 1985 to 269.3 million in 1995; the head-count index for the same period fell from 37.9 to 22.2 percent (World Bank, 1997). At the same time, recent household income surveys indicate that interprovincial income inequality increased markedly between 1988 and 1995; the urban-rural gap in income and living standards remains large, by some estimates wider than anywhere in the developing world (Carter, 1997; Khan and Riskin, 1998).

TABLE 8-1 Population of 15- to 24-Year-Olds, 2002

	Total	World Total	Percentage of: Less Developed Country Total
World	1,112,549,895	—	—
More developed countries	164,122,595	15	—
Less developed countries	948,427,300	85	—
China	202,484,007	18	21

NOTE: Census Bureau definitions of "More Developed" and "Less Developed" are employed here.
SOURCE: U.S. Bureau of the Census (2002).

ducing data sources, we discuss educational policies and the changing educational opportunities available to adolescents. Next, we discuss youth employment and the changing economic backdrop in which employment occurs. We then provide an overview of family formation changes, considering marriage and childbearing. Finally, we consider persisting and new health issues facing adolescents. We close the chapter by synthesizing patterns and trends in each of these domains, placing them in the context of broader social changes in reform-era China.

DATA SOURCES

We draw on a variety of sources of information. To document policies, we employ reports and policy documents issued by Chinese government offices and a variety of secondary sources, including English- and Chinese-language analyses of economic and social policy problems in the reform era. To trace patterns and changes empirically, we draw on several sources of aggregate data, including census data from the National Statistical Bureau of China, demographic data from the U.S. Census Bureau International Data Base, education data from the United Nations Educational, Scientific, and Cultural Organization (UNESCO) Institute for Statistics, and education, marriage, and health data from the United Nations Millennium Indicators and the United Nations Common Database. To investigate attitudes about sexuality, we employ tabulated survey data from the 1997 National Reproductive Health Survey (Jiang, 2000). Finally, where possible, we complement aggregate data with our own tabulations of individual-level data on education, employment, and marriage from adolescent and young adult cohorts in the 1989 and 1997 waves of the China Health and Nutrition Survey (CHNS), a multipurpose panel survey conducted by the Chinese Academy of Preventive Medicine and the Institute of Nutrition and Food Hygiene, in collaboration with the Carolina Population Center at the University of North Carolina.[3]

EDUCATION

For adolescents, some of the most fundamental shifts in the reform period have occurred in the realm of education. On the eve of market transition in the late 1970s, China's education system was oriented around the political goal of eliminating class differences in society. With the transition to markets in the late 1970s and early 1980s, the focus shifted to economic modernization, and this new orientation was clearly reflected in educational reforms aimed at efficiently producing an appropriately skilled labor force.[4] A complex hierarchy of programs varying in length, quality, curriculum, and financial base supplanted the egalitarian structure of the Cultural Revolution education system. Classrooms moved away from a focus on egalitarianism and class struggle, instead emphasizing quality, competition, individual talents, and the mastery of concepts and skills important in the development of science and technology (Broaded, 1983; Kwong, 1985; Lin, 1993). Vocational education was reinstated, with the intention of making education provide labor market skills and skills relevant to rural living circumstances (Tsang, 2000; UNESCO, 1998). Higher education, shut down completely for 6 years at the start of the Cultural Revolution, was reinvigorated due to recognition of its critical role in supplying the high-level personnel and scientific expertise needed for national development (Tsang, 2000).

Most recently, attention has turned to molding the education system to better stimulate critical thinking and creativity perceived to be necessary for the new economy. Learner-centered teaching approaches and the so-called "quality education" *(suzhi jiaoyu)* reforms are intended to develop the abilities of the

---

[3]The CHNS used a multistage, random cluster process to draw a sample from eight geographically diverse provinces, which differ by level of economic development, public resources, and health indicators. The provinces covered were Liaoning, Jiangsu, Shandong, Henan, Hubei, Hunan, Guangxi, and Guizhou in 1989. Liaoning was replaced by Heilongjiang in 1997. Counties in each of these eight provinces were stratified by income level and randomly selected based on a weighted sampling scheme. In addition, the provincial capital and a lower income city were selected. Villages and townships within the counties and urban and suburban neighborhoods within the cities were selected randomly. Overall, the sample consisted of 32 urban neighborhoods, 30 suburban neighborhoods, 32 towns, and 96 villages. For more details, see http://www.cpc.unc.edu/projects/china/. In this study, we excluded Liaoning (in 1989) and Heilongjiang (in 1997) from the analysis.

[4]Education laws continue to exhibit this orientation. The Education Law of 1995 and the Education Plan for the 21st Century of 1999 confirmed the priority placed on education as a strategic area for social and economic development (UNESCO, 1998; Ministry of Education, 1999).

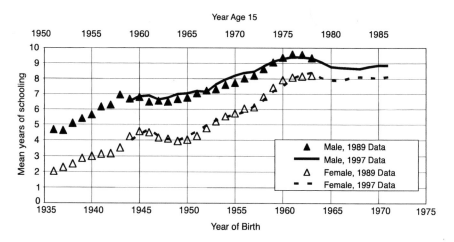

FIGURE 8-1 Mean years of schooling by birth year, 25- to 54-year-olds, China Health and Nutrition Survey, 1989 and 1997.

whole child, and to stimulate critical learning (Tsang, 2000). Additional reforms designed to develop locally relevant curriculum are also under way.

Educational opportunities have increased dramatically in the years since the establishment of the People's Republic in 1949. Using data from the 1989 and 1997 China Health and Nutrition Surveys, Figure 8-1 shows mean years of education by birth year for men and women ages 25 to 54 in both years.[5] The year that each cohort would have reached age 15 is also labeled on the graph. The figure shows dramatic increases in mean years of schooling for men and women reaching age 15 through the latter years of the Cultural Revolution in the mid- to late 1970s. For example, mean years of schooling for women rose from about 2 years for women age 15 in 1951 to more than 8 years for those age 15 in 1978. Cohorts coming of age in the early years of market transition experienced slight dropoffs in years of schooling. This downturn is not fully understood, but often attributed to some combination of push factors—shutdowns of low-quality rural junior high schools as part of the upgrading that occurred in the early reform years and rising educational costs—and pull factors—the new economic opportunities that followed agricultural decollectivization in the reform period (see Hannum, 1999a and 1999b, for discussion).

Following the downturn in the early 1980s, the reform period has seen an expansion of educational access. Table 8-2 shows aggregate educational

---

[5]Data points shown in Figures 8-1, 8-2, 8-4a, and 8-4b are based on 3-year moving averages.

indicators that extend further into the reform period. Panel A shows gross enrollment ratios, or total enrollment in a level of education, regardless of age, expressed as a percentage of children in the officially-designated age range corresponding to that level of education in a given school year. At the primary level, gross enrollment ratios are over 100 throughout the reform period for girls and boys. At the secondary level, enrollment ratios were around 54 for boys and 37 for girls in 1980, around the time of the start of reforms. Consistent with Figure 8-1, ratios dropped through the mid-1980s. However, by the mid-1980s, the downturn ended. By 1997, enrollment ratios were 74 percent for boys and 66 percent for girls. Tertiary enrollment ratios have expanded since 1980, from 2.5 percent for boys and 0.8 percent for girls in 1980, to 7.3 percent for boys and 3.9 percent for girls in 1996.

Although gross enrollment ratios are useful for temporal and gender comparisons, they do not have clear implications regarding levels of education, because of the lack of consistence of numerators and denominators.[6] Other measures not plagued by this problem similarly show rising access to education for adolescents after the mid-1980s. From 1988 to 1995, primary to secondary transition ratios rose from 62 percent to 88 percent, with girls only about 3 to 4 percentage points behind boys (see Table 8-2, Panel B). In 1987, only 3 percent of male youth ages 15 to 24 were illiterate, compared to nearly 1 in 10 female youth. By 2001, only 0.8 percent of male youth and 3.3 percent of female youth remained illiterate (see Table 8-2, Panel C).

Data from the China Health and Nutrition Survey also indicate improvements in the 1990s in adolescents' access to schooling. Focusing on CHNS adolescents, among those who were 12 to 18 years old in 1989, 61.0 percent of males and 55.9 percent of females were enrolled in school (see Table 8-3). By 1997, the figures were 74.6 percent for males and 74.2 percent for females. Average years of school completed were also greater in the 1997 sample cohorts than in the 1989 sample cohorts (see Table 8-4). In 1989, mean years completed were 7.0 for boys and 6.8 for girls. By 1997, corresponding figures were 8.0 and 8.0.

While the long-term trend has been expansion of access, certain concerns have arisen about social disparities in access, especially to a

---

[6]Gross enrollment ratios often overestimate enrollment rates due to enrollments of children outside of official age ranges. They are also affected by repetition rates. They are commonly employed, however, because they are much more widely available than other, preferable measures such as net enrollment ratios. Net enrollment ratios, which have age-eligible children in both the numerators and denominators, are available for China only at the primary level, for the years 1988 to 1996. These ratios are above 90 percent throughout the period. A gender gap that favored boys by about 6 percentage points in 1988 diminished to zero by 1995 (see UNESCO, 2002).

TABLE 8-2   Selected National Education Indicators, 1980-2001

| | A. Gross Enrollment Ratios[a] | | | | | | B. Transition Ratios[a] | | |
| | Primary | | Secondary | | Tertiary | | Primary-Secondary | | |
Year	Male	Fem.	Male	Fem.	Male	Fem.	Tot.	Male	Fem.
1980	121.0	103.7	53.9	37.4	2.5	0.8	—	—	—
1981	122.5	102.4	46.7	31.7	2.7	0.9	—	—	—
1982	124.2	102.5	42.7	29.3	—	—	—	—	—
1983	125.6	103.9	41.9	29.1	2.7	1.0	—	—	—
1984	130.8	108.5	43.6	30.9	3.2	1.3	—	—	—
1985	132.0	113.9	46.3	32.6	3.9	1.7	—	—	—
1986	134.0	117.5	48.8	35.9	4.1	1.9	—	—	—
1987	134.0	118.9	51.3	37.9	4.0	2.0	—	—	—
1988	133.3	119.8	52.0	38.8	3.9	2.0	62.3	—	—
1989	132.2	120.7	52.8	39.0	3.9	2.0	67.8	—	—
1990	129.6	120.3	55.3	41.7	3.9	2.0	70.2	—	—
1991	125.7	118.5	58.1	45.2	3.8	2.0	75.3	—	—
1992	121.9	115.8	61.1	48.5	4.0	2.1	74.2	—	—
1993	119.1	114.5	61.6	51.7	5.0	2.6	78.8	80.4	76.9
1994	118.3	115.2	65.2	56.4	—	—	87.6	89.0	86.0
1995	118.3	116.6	69.5	61.8	—	—	87.9	89.4	86.3
1996	120.0	119.6	72.5	65.1	7.3	3.9	—	—	—
1997	122.5	123.0	73.7	66.2	—	—	—	—	—
1998	—	—	—	—	—	—	—	—	—
1999	—	—	—	—	—	—	—	—	—
2000	—	—	—	—	—	—	—	—	—
2001	—	—	—	—	—	—	—	—	—

[a]UNESCO, Institute of Statistics (2002).
[b]United Nations Millennium Indicators (2002).
[c]UNESCO, Institute of Statistics (2002).

high-quality education. These concerns are in large part attributable to changes in education finance in the reform period. Major components of reform era education policy were the decentralization of the administration and finance of primary, secondary, and tertiary education and the privatization of costs (Lofstedt, 1990; Tsang, 2000). Currently, the central government runs and finances certain institutions of higher education; more typically, provincial, county, township, and village governments respectively take responsibility for schools at the tertiary, upper secondary, lower secondary, and primary levels (Tsang, 2000, p. 13). This finance structure has increased the regional disparities in funding

C. Literacy Rates[b]		D. Program Type[c]						
Ages 15-24		Secondary: % in:	Tertiary: % in:					
Male	Fem.	Gen. Educ.	Educ.	Humanities	Soc. Sci.	Nat. Sci.	Med. Sci.	Other
—	—	97.0	29.3	5.7	3.7	48.2	12.3	0.8
—	—	96.9	24.9	6.0	4.5	51.2	12.4	0.9
—	—	96.3	24.6	5.8	6.1	48.5	14.2	0.8
—	—	93.8	25.4	6.2	7.4	48.6	11.6	0.8
—	—	92.5	25.1	7.0	8.8	48.0	10.3	0.8
—	—	91.1	23.8	8.2	10.6	46.7	9.3	1.4
—	—	90.4	24.4	7.7	11.2	46.8	9.2	0.7
97.0	90.2	89.9	24.7	6.7	11.2	47.3	9.4	0.7
97.2	90.8	88.8	24.6	6.4	12.0	46.9	9.4	0.7
97.3	91.3	87.9	24.6	6.1	12.4	46.5	9.7	0.7
97.4	91.9	87.5	24.3	5.8	12.6	46.8	9.9	0.7
97.6	92.4	87.2	24.5	5.6	12.5	46.8	10.0	0.6
97.8	92.9	86.6	24.2	5.7	13.1	46.6	9.8	0.6
98.0	93.4	85.3	22.8	7.5	25.1	36.9	7.1	0.6
98.2	94.0	84.5	16.4	6.4	9.4	53.2	8.9	5.6
98.4	94.5	84.2	—	—	—	—	—	—
98.5	94.9	84.1	—	—	—	—	—	—
98.7	95.3	83.7	—	—	—	—	—	—
98.8	95.7	—	—	—	—	—	—	—
99.0	96.1	—	—	—	—	—	—	—
99.1	96.5	—	—	—	—	—	—	—
99.2	96.7	—	—	—	—	—	—	—

for schools, and has increased family educational expenditures needed even for compulsory education.[7]

Government concerns about these problems are evident in equity-oriented policies instigated throughout the reform period. For example, although implementation was tied to regional economic development levels, the Law on Compulsory Education of 1986 designated 9 years of education—6 years of primary

[7]In poor areas, the lack of government resources has strained the ability of local communities to finance high-quality public education. In general, the government budget finances only teachers' wages. Other costs must be covered from local resources, including specially raised earmarked funds collected from households, collective contributions, school-generated revenues, or fees charged directly to students (Hannum and Park, 2002).

TABLE 8-3 Enrollment Rates,[a] Youth Ages 12-18

Characteristic	1989				1997			
	N	Male	Female	P-Value	N	Male	Female	P-Value
Total	1,991	61.0	55.9	0.02	1,494	74.6	74.2	NS
Age								
12-13	522	93.1	92.7	NS	413	96.2	96.0	NS
14-15	582	77.4	68.9	0.02	442	85.9	83.5	NS
16-17	581	38.3	31.3	NS	407	64.7	58.9	NS
18	306	17.2	16.1	NS	232	33.9	42.9	NS
P-value		0.00	0.00			0.00	0.00	
Urban-rural residence								
Urban	465	68.5	62.6	NS	406	84.1	82.8	NS
Rural	1,525	58.7	53.9	NS	1,088	71.0	71.1	NS
P-value		0.01	0.02			0.00	0.00	
Household head's education								
None	374	51.1	43.6	NS	134	63.4	59.6	NS
Primary	940	58.5	55.2	NS	511	70.6	68.2	NS
Junior high	509	67.9	61.1	NS	544	75.8	78.4	NS
Senior high+	160	74.7	75.4	NS	285	88.7	83.3	NS
P-value		0.00	0.00			0.00	0.00	
Number of consumer items owned[b]								
Missing	54	83.3	58.3	0.04	40	88.0	80.0	NS
Lowest quartile	409	54.4	49.7	NS	338	69.1	60.5	NS
2nd quartile	665	56.7	50.2	NS	480	70.6	69.4	NS
3rd quartile	588	64.8	60.6	NS	281	74.8	81.5	NS
Highest quartile	275	70.3	67.2	NS	355	83.3	87.2	NS
P-value		0.00	0.00			0.01	0.00	

	N			P-value	N			P-value
School-age children in household[c]								
One	361	44.4	48.7	NS	468	71.4	74.5	NS
Two	795	65.0	54.9	0.004	654	76.0	74.2	NS
Three or more	835	65.5	59.3	NS	372	77.1	73.9	NS
P-value		0.00	NS			NS	NS	
Province								
Jiangsu	205	62.8	61.3	NS	145	75.0	81.5	NS
Shandong	218	63.1	51.3	NS	185	81.4	68.2	0.04
Henan	321	58.7	45.6	0.02	202	67.6	77.3	NS
Hubei	249	67.7	52.8	0.02	231	71.8	72.9	NS
Hunan	249	62.9	66.7	NS	232	77.9	75.2	NS
Guangxi	310	55.9	55.0	NS	264	75.7	74.2	NS
Guizhou	438	59.8	59.8	NS	235	73.2	72.2	NS
P-value		NS	0.01			NS	NS	
Relationship to household head								
Own child	1,858	60.9	55.7	0.02	1,382	73.7	73.8	NS
Other[d]	133	62.9	59.2	NS	106	86.4	80.9	NS
P-value		NS	NS			0.03	NS	

[a]Calculations were based on the question, "Are you currently in school?"

[b]Both the 1989 and 1997 surveys asked, "Does your household or do any household members own the following electrical appliances or other goods?" To reflect economic changes over time in China, several new items were added in the 1997 survey. Regardless of small differences in the lists of consumer items in the two waves, we summed up the ownership of all items for each household, then grouped all households into quartiles.

[c]This refers to the number of children who are under 18 years old at survey date in each household.

[d]Others include grandchildren, siblings, other relatives, and other nonrelatives (one "spouse" was included in 1989).

NOTE: NS: P-values are not significant at 0.05 level. P-values are results from chi-squared tests of independence. P-values listed to the right of enrollment rates result from tests of gender by enrollment (within categories of the listed characteristic, if applicable). P-values listed below enrollment rates are within-gender chi-square tests of enrollment by the listed characteristic.

SOURCE: China Health and Nutrition Survey.

TABLE 8-4 Average Years of School Completed,[a] Youth Ages 12-18

Characteristic	1989					1997				
	Male		Female			Male		Female		
	Mean	SD	Mean	SD	P-Value	Mean	SD	Mean	SD	P-Value
Total	7.0	2.2	6.8	2.6	0.01	8.0	2.2	8.0	2.2	NS
Age										
12-13	5.4	1.6	5.6	1.7	NS	6.2	1.4	6.3	1.4	NS
14-15	7.1	1.7	6.6	2.5	0.01	8.1	1.4	7.9	1.7	NS
16-17	7.9	2.2	7.6	2.5	NS	9.1	1.9	9.0	1.9	NS
18	7.9	2.5	7.4	3.2	NS	9.3	2.7	9.4	2.4	NS
P-value		0.00		0.00			0.00		0.00	
Urban-rural residence										
Urban	7.9	2.1	8.2	2.1	NS	8.4	2.3	8.7	2.2	NS
Rural	6.7	2.1	6.3	2.5	0.00	7.9	2.2	7.8	2.1	NS
P-value		0.00		0.00			0.00		0.00	
Household head's education										
None	6.5	2.4	6.2	2.9	NS	7.6	2.7	7.2	2.5	NS
Primary	6.8	2.1	6.6	2.4	NS	8.0	2.1	7.8	2.2	NS
Junior high	7.3	2.0	6.9	2.5	NS	8.0	2.2	8.2	2.0	NS
Senior high+	8.3	2.1	8.2	2.3	NS	8.3	2.1	8.5	2.1	NS
P-value		0.00		0.00			NS		0.00	
Number of consumer items owned										
Missing	6.8	2.3	6.4	2.2	NS	7.2	2.2	8.7	3.3	NS
Lowest quartile	6.2	2.2	5.2	2.7	0.00	7.4	2.3	6.9	2.1	NS
2nd quartile	6.8	2.0	6.3	2.5	0.00	7.9	2.1	7.8	2.0	NS
3rd quartile	7.5	2.0	7.5	2.2	NS	8.3	2.0	8.5	2.0	NS
Highest quartile	8.2	2.1	8.3	2.0	NS	8.7	2.3	8.9	1.9	NS
P-value		0.00		0.00			0.00		0.00	

School-age children in household										
One	7.8	2.3	7.5	2.7	NS	8.9	2.1	8.7	2.1	NS
Two	7.1	2.1	7.1	2.4	NS	7.8	2.1	8.1	2.1	0.03
Three or more	6.6	2.1	6.2	2.6	0.02	7.1	2.0	7.3	2.1	NS
P-value	0.00		0.00			0.00		0.00		
Province										
Jiangsu	7.8	2.3	7.3	2.8	NS	8.5	2.9	8.1	2.2	NS
Shandong	7.0	2.2	6.4	2.9	NS	8.6	1.9	8.1	2.3	NS
Henan	7.1	1.9	6.8	2.5	NS	8.1	1.8	8.3	2.1	NS
Hubei	7.2	1.9	6.9	2.3	NS	8.4	2.1	8.3	2.1	NS
Hunan	7.2	1.9	7.3	1.8	NS	8.6	2.1	8.6	2.2	NS
Guangxi	7.1	2.3	6.9	2.4	NS	7.4	1.9	7.6	1.9	NS
Guizhou	6.4	2.4	6.1	2.7	NS	7.1	2.3	7.4	2.2	NS
P-value	0.00		0.00			0.00		0.00		
Relationship to household head										
Own child	7.0	2.2	6.7	2.6	NS	8.0	2.2	8.2	2.2	NS
Other	7.2	1.9	7.2	2.3	NS	8.2	2.2	7.6	2.0	NS
P-value	NS		NS			NS		NS		

[a]Calculations were based on the question, "How many years of formal education have you completed in a regular school?" We used a system of 6 years for primary school, 3 years for lower middle school, and 3 years for upper middle school to obtain the total number of years of education for each person. Technical school was treated as being at the same level as upper middle school and all college/university education was assumed to start after graduation from upper middle school.

NOTE: SD = Standard deviation. NS = Not statistically significant at 0.05 level. P-values are results from t-tests or ANOVA tests, in the case of characteristics with more than two categories. P-values listed to the right of years of schooling measures are results from t-tests of gender differences (within categories of the listed characteristic, if applicable). P-values listed below years of schooling measures are within-gender tests of difference (t-tests or ANOVA tests) by the listed characteristic.

SOURCE: China Health and Nutrition Survey.

and 6 years of lower secondary—as compulsory for all children (Ministry of Education, 1986). The 1999 Action Plan for Revitalizing Education in the 21st Century confirmed a commitment to implementing compulsory education across the country (Ministry of Education, 1999). A more recent campaign to pour development money into the western interior part of the country, where poverty is concentrated, took education as an important element (State Council, 2000).

What does evidence suggest about the effectiveness of reform-era policies designed to help education reach disadvantaged members of society? On the one hand, the rising enrollments and increasing rates of primary-secondary transition presented in Table 8-2 suggest, with the exception of the early 1980s, an overall trend of increasing inclusiveness. However, certain caveats to this conclusion exist. Earlier research indicates that significant gaps in access to schooling persisted through the early 1990s across lines of socioeconomic status, gender, and urban-rural residence status (Hannum, 1999a, 2002a, 2002b, 2003).

More recent data from the China Health and Nutrition Survey suggest that some of these disparities persisted through the 1990s, while others narrowed. For example, while enrollment rates have risen for both urban and rural residents, the premium on urban residence persists. Urban-rural differences in enrollment were statistically significant in both years: in 1989, 53.9 percent of rural girls were enrolled, compared to 62.6 percent of urban girls. In 1997, figures were 71.1 and 82.8 (see Table 8-3). For boys, the rural enrollment rate in 1989 was 58.7 percent, compared to 68.5 percent for urban boys; in 1997, rural and urban enrollment rates were 71.0 and 84.1 percent. Bivariate tests also showed significant urban-rural differences in average years of schooling in both years (see Table 8-4). Multivariate analyses controlling for demographic and family background factors and province of residence confirm the premium on urban residence for enrollment in both years (see Table 8-5). Multivariate analyses indicated no change in the enrollment advantage associated with urban residence, but offered evidence of a diminished years-of-schooling advantage for urban residents, once other socioeconomic background characteristics were taken into account.

Socioeconomic differences in enrollment are striking. Tables 8-3 and 8-4 illustrate socioeconomic gaps with a possession index and with parent's level of education.[8] For boys, the possession index measure shows differ-

---

[8]Income or wealth measures would be preferable as more standard measures of socioeconomic status. Comparable income measures calculated by CHNS staff were produced for waves of the survey prior to 1997. However, documentation on those calculations is not available, and no income measures have been made available to the public for 1997. We checked enrollment rates and years of schooling for boys and girls by income quartile for 1989 and 1993, and compared results to our possession index quartile results. Socioeconomic gaps in enrollment and years of schooling were similar for both socioeconomic status measures, though the possession index measure appears somewhat more sensitive than the income measure in terms of differentiating school enrollment and years of schooling.

TABLE 8-5 Logistic Regressions of Enrollment and Linear Regressions of Years of Education, China Health and Nutrition Survey, 1989 and 1997 Samples

	Enrollment			Years of Education		
	1989	1997	Combined	1989	1997	Combined
Age, in years	-1.452	-0.871	-1.381	3.136	3.546	3.394
	$(2.24)^a$	(1.11)	$(2.69)^b$	$(7.90)^b$	$(9.43)^b$	$(12.21)^b$
Age squared	0.020	0.004	0.019	-0.090	-0.098	-0.096
	(0.96)	(0.16)	(1.14)	$(6.72)^b$	$(7.67)^b$	$(10.22)^b$
Year indicator (ref.: 1989) 1997			0.460			1.203
			(1.35)			$(4.35)^b$
Female (ref.: male)	-0.299	-0.056	-0.295	-0.262	0.065	-0.263
	$(2.51)^a$	(0.36)	$(2.55)^a$	$(2.78)^b$	(0.78)	$(2.77)^b$
Year female			0.213			0.318
			(1.08)			$(2.50)^a$
Urban (ref.: rural)	0.458	0.507	0.388	0.795	0.186	0.731
	$(2.48)^a$	$(2.60)^b$	$(2.25)^a$	$(6.15)^b$	(1.77)	$(5.77)^b$
Year urban			0.179			-0.533
			(0.70)			$(3.28)^b$
Household head's education (ref.: none)						
Primary	0.329	0.649	0.366	0.437	0.499	0.499
	(1.88)	$(2.24)^a$	$(2.14)^a$	$(2.75)^b$	$(2.22)^a$	$(3.11)^b$
Junior high	0.628	0.782	0.647	0.722	0.793	0.810
	$(2.95)^b$	$(2.58)^b$	$(3.11)^b$	$(4.12)^b$	$(3.46)^b$	$(4.60)^b$
Senior high+	1.132	1.178	1.137	1.089	0.828	1.159
	$(4.04)^b$	$(3.50)^b$	$(4.13)^b$	$(5.23)^b$	$(3.51)^b$	$(5.56)^b$

continued

TABLE 8-5 Continued

	Enrollment			Years of Education		
	1989	1997	Combined	1989	1997	Combined
Interaction terms between year and household head's education						
Year primary			0.168			-0.120
			(0.52)			(0.47)
Year junior high			-0.001			-0.194
			(0.00)			(0.73)
Year senior high			-0.102			-0.499
						(1.70)
Number of consumer items owned (ref.: lowest quartile)						
Second quartile	0.104	0.462	0.122	0.551	0.554	0.532
	(0.53)	(2.21)[a]	(0.65)	(3.47)[b]	(3.57)[b]	(3.32)[b]
Third quartile	0.517	0.810	0.529	1.210	0.915	1.200
	(2.41)[a]	(3.25)[b]	(2.57)[a]	(7.15)[b]	(5.70)[b]	(7.10)[b]
Highest quartile	0.785	1.183	0.755	1.685	1.125	1.633
	(2.88)[b]	(4.30)[b]	(2.87)[b]	(8.48)[b]	(6.56)[b]	(8.33)[b]
Interaction terms between year and number of consumer items owned						
Year second			0.316			0.042
			(1.17)			(0.20)
Year third			0.277			-0.254
			(0.90)			(1.16)
Year highest			0.471			-0.430
			(1.33)			(1.77)
School-age children in household (ref.: one)						
Two	0.172	-0.094	0.029	-0.001	-0.361	-0.189
	(1.01)	(0.52)	(0.24)	(0.01)	(3.17)[b]	(2.10)[a]

Three or more	0.276	−0.065	0.116	−0.405[a]	−0.641[b]	−0.540[b]
	(1.47)	(0.27)	(0.80)	(2.54)	(4.24)	(4.79)
Relationship to household head (ref.: other)						
Own child	0.095	−0.479	−0.094	0.093	−0.400[a]	−0.088
	(0.36)	(1.24)	(0.44)	(0.53)	(2.21)	(0.66)
Province (ref.: Jiangsu)						
Shandong	−0.407	−0.367	−0.359	−0.707[b]	0.242	−0.280
	(1.50)	(1.07)	(1.72)	(2.98)	(1.10)	(1.59)
Henan	−0.378	−0.588	−0.446[a]	−0.284	0.273	−0.079
	(1.66)	(1.84)	(2.44)	(1.43)	(1.28)	(0.51)
Hubei	−0.221	−0.463	−0.304	−0.143	0.397	0.097
	(0.88)	(1.47)	(1.57)	(0.72)	(1.90)	(0.63)
Hunan	0.015	−0.521	−0.197	−0.008	0.307	0.108
	(0.06)	(1.70)	(1.04)	(0.04)	(1.47)	(0.72)
Guangxi	−0.362	−0.818[a]	−0.533[b]	−0.161	−0.254	−0.245
	(1.46)	(2.54)	(2.75)	(0.75)	(1.32)	(1.58)
Guizhou	−0.049	−0.093	−0.062	−0.547[b]	−0.199	−0.405[a]
	(0.21)	(0.28)	(0.32)	(2.65)	(0.85)	(2.41)
Constant	17.125[b]	13.282[a]	16.688[b]	−20.540[b]	−23.487[b]	−22.895[b]
	(3.44)	(2.18)	(4.19)	(7.06)	(8.45)	(11.14)
Observations	1,929	1,428	3,357	1,924	1,488	3,412
R-square				0.32	0.45	0.40

[a] p < 0.05.
[b] p < 0.01.
NOTE: Z-statistics in parentheses.

ences in enrollment rates between those in the bottom and top quartiles of about 16 percentage points in 1989 and 14 points in 1997. For girls, the difference was about 18 percent in 1989 and about 27 percentage points in 1997. Similarly striking were enrollment gaps between children of parents with a high school or better educational attainment and children of parents with less than a primary school educational attainment. For boys, these gaps were 24 percent in 1989 and 25 percent in 1997; for girls, corresponding figures were 32 percent and 24 percent. The gap between wealthiest and poorest youth in mean years of schooling is also highly significant in both waves of the survey, with a gap between lowest and highest quartiles of 1.3 years for boys and a full 2 years for girls in 1997. Differences in mean years of schooling by parental education were significant for both genders in 1989 and for girls in 1997.

Multivariate analyses indicate that both socioeconomic status measures significantly predict enrollment and years of school completed in both survey years, net of other child and family background factors and provincial controls (see Tables 8-4 and 8-5). A lack of significant interactions between the possession index and time, or the parental education variables and time, suggests that there was not a marked weakening of the relationship between socioeconomic status and enrollment or years of schooling between 1989 and 1997.[9]

Finally, an overall male advantage in enrollment and years of schooling, significant for youth cohorts in 1989, was insignificant among youth cohorts in 1997 (see Tables 8-3 and 8-4). Multivariate analyses confirm these results (see Table 8-5). Specifically, for enrollment and years of schooling, models using 1989 data alone showed gender differences, while the model using 1997 data alone failed to show significant gender effects. The combined model testing interactions between gender and time indicated a significant narrowing of the gender gap for years of schooling; in the enrollment models, the coefficient marking the interaction of gender and time was in the same direction, but failed to achieve significance.

In interpreting these results, it is important to recognize that past studies using nationally representative samples have suggested that gender inequalities in access to schooling are tied to region and poverty in China, and thus the CHNS data cannot be regarded as fully representative of the scope of gender disparities in China as a whole. Lack of coverage of the impoverished and culturally distinct northwest may influence the portrait of gender

---

[9]To be precise, for the years of schooling models, marginally significant (p < .1) negative coefficients for year interactions are observed for dummy variables representing the wealthiest and best educated parents. These results are suggestive of some weakening of the socioeconomic advantage of the wealthiest youth in terms of years of schooling. However, as the within-year models indicate, parental education and the possession index remain highly significant predictors of years of schooling in both years.

disparities. However, the declining gender gap is consistent with the national data presented in Table 8-2 and with other national data showing rising female participation in primary, secondary, and tertiary education, and a long-term decline in the gender gap, especially after the mid-1980s (Hannum, 1999b, 2002b).

It is important to note that although access is improving as more youth enter secondary school, they face an increasingly diverse mix of experiences within the school system. One reason is rising quality differences associated with the new diversity in finance discussed above. However, diversification has emerged in other ways. For example, at the secondary level, vocationalization is evident in the declining proportion of secondary students in general education, from 97 percent of secondary students in 1980 to 84 percent of secondary students in 1997 (see Table 8-2, Panel D). The current rounds of curriculum reforms, aimed at making curriculum more locally relevant and stimulating discussion and critical thinking in the classroom, are likely to further diversify the experiences of children in the classroom, albeit in ways that are difficult to empirically evaluate (Cheng, 2003).

For those youth who make it to the tertiary level, some aspects of opportunity have remained stable, at least through the mid-1990s.[10] In terms of the broad fields of study, students are most likely to enroll in natural sciences (53.2 percent of tertiary students in 1994), followed by education (16.4 percent of tertiary students in 1994); the predominance of these two fields has not changed over the course of the reform period (see Table 8-2, Panel D). Social sciences, which were reinstated only in the reform period, have attracted increasing numbers of students in recent years.

However, opportunity structures in higher education are changing in ways that parallel the discussion above for secondary schooling. On the one hand, overall access to higher education is expanding (see Table 8-2, Panel A). This expansion can be attributed in part to government policies expanding public university slots, and in part to the proliferation of private tertiary-level institutions (Cheng, 2003; Lin, 2003). Yet, although overall access is rising, it is likely that the social composition of those who can avail themselves of higher education is changing. Increasing private costs associated with higher education, in both the public and growing private sectors, give an increasing edge at the margins to those who can pay. Furthermore, the diversification of higher education finance also implies increasing diversity of educational quality among tertiary-level students. This issue is present even within the public sector, where recent policy initiatives have targeted a

---

[10]Unfortunately, the Ministry of Education categories for reporting tertiary fields were redesigned after 1994, and thus comparisons with subsequent years are not possible.

select few leading universities in China for dramatic increases in funding,[11] with an eye to creating world-class universities (Cheng, 2003).

Overall, adolescents and youth in China have seen a general increase in educational opportunity since the mid-1980s. Evidence suggests that all social groups are benefiting from educational expansions, though important social differences in access persist. At the same time, new qualitative differences in the school system mean that experiences in school, and their implications for labor market opportunities, are increasingly diverging.[12]

ECONOMY AND LABOR

Linked to educational changes are changes in youth labor force participation. Little information is available about the nature of youth labor force participation prior to market transition. However, it is clear that many economic policies associated with market transition have direct implications for the choices that adolescents make about economic activities. First, market reforms themselves dramatically changed the economic context in which youth function. In rural areas, widespread adoption of the household responsibility system in the early 1980s improved the wealth of the agricultural population. Similarly, privatization of state-owned enterprises, the rise of township and village enterprises, and the emergence of private enterprise have contributed to a reduction in poverty.

Yet, the new economic opportunities that contributed to poverty reduction were also thought to compete with education, as youth and their families faced higher direct and opportunity costs for schooling in the 1980s. In the 1990s, several regulations were passed that specified regulations on minors and the special protections to be afforded them in the workforce (Regulations on Ending the Use of Child Labor, 1991; Communiqué, 1994; Rules and Regulations Related to the Protection of Children, n.d.).[13] Most notably, child labor was mentioned in China's

---

[11]These initiatives include the Millennium Project and Project 211. See Cheng (2003) for descriptions of these projects.

[12]One important caveat to this discussion is that a dimension of inequality that is not well addressed by the CHNS or by aggregate data is that of minority access to schooling. Ethnic differences in education in China are closely tied to location of residence, and substantial disadvantages for particular minority groups persisted through the early 1990s (Hannum, 2002a). Although aggregate data show a promising trend of increases in the minority percentage in total enrollment at all levels of schooling through the 1990s (Hannum, 1999b), this trend represents a very imprecise indicator of changes in access, and says nothing about access for particular ethnic groups. Ethnic differences in the CHNS sample are likely to understate the scope of ethnic differences in the country as a whole. Most of China's minorities live in the impoverished western part of the country, represented in this sample by two southwestern provinces and none in the northwest.

[13]Unfortunately, we found little documentation of youth and child labor problems or policies that predated the information cited in this section.

National Labor Law, which went into effect in 1995 (SCENPC, 1995, Article 15). The law prohibits employers from hiring workers under 16 years of age and specifies sanctions such as fines and revocation of business licenses for those businesses that hire minors. Laborers between the ages 16 and 18 are barred from engaging in certain forms of physical work, including labor in mines. Ironically, with the abolishment of the job placement system for college graduates in the early 1990s, the gradual emergence of a labor market, the large-scale layoffs that have accompanied market reforms, and the underemployment of the rural workforce, policies that have emerged to protect against the employment of underage youth have coincided with rising government concerns about providing enough employment for working-age adolescents and young adults.

Changes in youth and young adult employment in the 1990s are the mirror image of changes in education. Focusing on respondents ages 16 to 25, employment rates for CHNS cohorts dropped from about 81 percent for males and females in 1989 to about 69 percent for males and 72 percent for females in 1997 (see Table 8-6). Gender differences in the overall rate of employment were not significant in either year. In 1989, employment rates were higher among rural youth and among poorer households. In 1997, significant urban-rural differences were present for males, but not females. Socioeconomic disparities remained stark. For example, in 1989, about 16 percentage points separated the employment rates of girls in the lowest and highest possession index quartiles. By 1997, the gap was nearly 22 percentage points.[14]

The broad categories of work in which youth and young adults were involved did not change dramatically over time, at least through the early reform years (see Table 8-7). Many of the educational improvements appear to have contributed to credential upgrading within broad occupational categories, rather than to major shifts in the youth and young adult labor force across broad occupational categories. For example, census data from 1982 indicate that the majority of youth who were working in the early years of reform were doing so in agricultural occupations. Nearly 82 percent of 15- to 19-year-old workers, 66 percent of 20- to 24-year-old workers, and 68 percent of 25- to 29-year-old workers were in agricultural jobs. In 1990, percentages were similar. Labor was the second most common type of work. In 1982, 14 percent of 15- to 19-year-old workers were laborers, compared to 23 percent of 20- to 24-year-olds and 20 percent of

---

[14]We only describe employment patterns and do not attempt a multivariate analysis of employment. Given the older age group needed for this analysis, some percentage of individuals are likely to have separated from natal homes, and thus causal interpretations of family background characteristics are complicated. We were particularly concerned about causal (rather than descriptive) interpretations given dual directions of causation between employment status and family background characteristics for older youth and young adults.

TABLE 8-6 Employment Rates,[a] Ages 16 to 25

Employment Rates	1989				1997			
	N	Male	Female	P-Value	N	Male	Female	P-Value
Total	2,840	80.6	80.9	NS	2,104	68.9	71.8	NS
Age, in years								
16	290	43.5	55.2	0.05	195	20.4	24.1	NS
17	287	63.6	61.1	NS	195	31.3	55.6	0.00
18	305	75.2	76.3	NS	246	59.7	52.7	NS
19	293	79.6	80.9	NS	173	70.1	66.3	NS
20	296	90.4	86.4	NS	195	72.3	79.2	NS
21	303	87.5	86.2	NS	226	79.2	85.4	NS
22	255	94.1	87.5	NS	215	80.0	83.3	NS
23	251	93.5	87.5	NS	237	89.6	86.6	NS
24	266	94.4	93.6	NS	197	86.8	89.0	NS
25	294	92.4	93.9	NS	225	91.5	89.1	NS
P-value		0.00	0.00			0.00	0.00	
Urban-rural residence								
Urban	804	71.1	69.5	NS	574	59.9	67.7	NS
Rural	2,036	84.2	85.6	NS	1,530	72.0	73.4	NS
P-value		0.00	0.00			0.00	NS	
Number of consumer items owned								
Missing	62	67.9	70.6	NS	64	63.6	61.3	NS
Lowest quartile	504	88.9	90.9	NS	489	77.5	82.5	NS
2nd quartile	893	80.3	86.4	0.01	618	72.3	72.4	NS
3rd quartile	879	79.4	75.1	NS	442	67.3	74.8	NS
Highest quartile	502	75.4	74.8	NS	491	56.5	60.9	NS
P-value		0.00	0.00			0.00	0.00	

[a]In the 1989 wave, the question, "are you presently working?" was asked of all members in the household. We used an additional question, "What is your primary occupation?", to eliminate adolescents who answered "yes" to the occupation question but stated their primary occupation as student.

NOTE: NS = not statistically significant at 0.05 level. P-values are results from chi-squared tests of independence. P-values listed to the right of employment rates result from tests of gender by employment (within categories of the listed characteristic, if applicable). P-values listed below employment rates are within-gender chi-square tests of employment by the listed characteristic.

SOURCE: China Health and Nutrition Survey.

25- to 29-year-olds; percentages were similar in 1990. However, proportionally, sales workers increased between the censuses, from 2 percent to nearly 4 percent of 25- to 29-year-olds.

Of course, there may be significant shifts in the structure of labor within these broad categories. Furthermore, we note that the stability shown here has emerged together with several important labor changes. First, the criteria for obtaining and keeping jobs and for being rewarded within the workplace are different for youth entering the labor force now, compared to earlier cohorts. Studies of career mobility and income determination trends suggest that human capital, as a marker of abilities, is becoming increasingly important for these aspects of the occupational attainment process (e.g., Zhang and Zhao, 2003; Zhao and Zhou, 2003; Maurer-Fazio, 2003; De Brauw and Rozelle, 2003; see Bian, 2002, for a review). Scholars attribute these changes to the emergence of labor markets and to new incentives in the workplace for productivity.

A second important change lies in the welfare implications of securing a job. Work units traditionally have provided a broad variety of social welfare services. However, this pattern is rapidly dissipating. For example, work units have been a primary provider of urban residents' housing, but waves of reforms starting from the late 1980s have raised rents, detached housing from work units, and commodified and privatized housing (Bian, 2002, p. 101; Wu, 2002).[15] Furthermore, emerging private-sector jobs may offer high incomes, but do not typically offer the other benefits historically associated with state-sector jobs. Finally, jobs in either sector are much more unstable under market reforms, placing incumbents at higher risk of losing whatever benefits are associated with those jobs. Compared to their earlier counterparts, youth entering the workplace now enjoy higher incomes, on average, but they face fewer benefits and reduced job security.

Finally, an important trend that is not easily traceable in available statistics on youth labor in China is the rise in population movement, and especially the "floating population" or unregistered, temporary labor migrants. Enabled by a convergence of different reform-era policies,[16] the floating population is largely a new phenomenon in China. Floaters largely consist of rural laborers moving from central and western regions to east coast regions for work in township and village enterprises and unskilled urban jobs (Goodkind and West, 2002). Estimates of the size of China's floating population vary widely, but recent official estimates indicate that the population has increased steadily from the early 1980s and is projected to increase to 160 million, or more than 10 percent of China's entire

---

[15]Bian (2002, p.101) cites the 1998 State Council Housing Reform Directive as requiring that all new housing units be sold and purchased at market prices.

[16]A convergence of reform-era policy shifts has created the circumstances under which the floating migration has grown. These include the following: (1) the loosening of migration restrictions; (2) tremendous requirements for manpower in the cities in low-level construction and manufacturing jobs, and more recently, in household service and related jobs, associated with urban market reforms; (3) the eradication of food coupon systems and the emergence of private housing and labor markets in cities; and (4) the creation of a huge surplus labor force without means of sustenance in rural areas created by decollectivization of agriculture (see, e.g., Poston and Duan, 1999, or Liang, 2001).

TABLE 8-7 Occupational Distribution of Economically Active Youth by Gender and Census Year

	Age Group	Scientists: Technical, Professional, and Related Workers	Administrative and Managerial Workers	Clerical and Related Workers
1982				
Total	15-19	1.42	0.01	0.39
	20-24	5.06	0.11	1.20
	25-29	6.03	0.44	1.35
Male	15-19	1.35	0.01	0.56
	20-24	4.92	0.15	1.57
	25-29	6.21	0.64	1.69
Female	15-19	1.48	0.01	0.23
	20-24	5.21	0.06	0.79
	25-29	5.80	0.20	0.96
1990				
Total	15-19	1.12	0.01	0.61
	20-24	4.51	0.15	1.31
	25-29	7.23	0.71	1.94
Male	15-19	0.81	0.02	0.97
	20-24	4.12	0.22	1.75
	25-29	7.10	1.16	2.58
Female	15-19	1.41	0.01	0.28
	20-24	4.92	0.07	0.83
	25-29	7.38	0.20	1.21

NOTE: Data on armed service personnel were unavailable for 1990, so this category was removed from calculations for both years.
SOURCE: Calculated from China census data posted to the U.S. Census Bureau International Database (2002).

population, by 2010 (Liang, 2001; Goodkind and West, 2002, p. 2242). The floating population is young, tends to be more male than female, and tends to be either single or married but without accompanying spouses (Poston and Duan, 1999; Goodkind and West, 2002; Roberts, 2002; Wang, 2002). In some ways analogous to undocumented workers in the United States, floaters in China enjoy few labor rights and limited access to social services (Goodkind and West, 2002; Wu, 2002). Youth among this population are vulnerable to exploitation and labor abuses, but the scope of such problems is unclear.

Sales Workers	Agriculture, Animal Husbandry, Forestry, Fishing and Hunting	Production and Related, Transport Equipment, and Laborers	Service Workers	Unknown
1.21	81.64	13.89	1.28	0.16
2.26	66.17	22.93	2.12	0.16
2.00	68.01	20.15	1.94	0.08
1.05	79.81	15.74	1.30	0.18
1.89	63.27	26.19	1.84	0.17
1.83	63.60	24.29	1.66	0.08
1.36	83.36	12.16	1.26	0.15
2.68	69.37	19.33	2.42	0.14
2.21	73.24	15.24	2.27	0.08
1.39	81.69	13.49	1.61	0.08
2.62	70.51	18.78	2.03	0.10
3.91	64.71	19.23	2.22	0.05
1.26	80.93	14.56	1.37	0.09
2.42	67.44	22.17	1.76	0.12
3.74	60.20	23.34	1.84	0.04
1.52	82.42	12.47	1.83	0.06
2.84	73.83	15.12	2.32	0.08
4.10	69.82	14.56	2.65	0.06

In summary, as can be anticipated from rising rates of educational attainment described in the previous section, youth are joining the workforce at increasingly late ages. Those who do enter the workforce, especially those who enter in their teens, are overwhelmingly likely to be working in rural, agricultural jobs. This finding reflects the concentration of the population in rural areas, and the persisting educational disadvantage of rural youth. Rising numbers of these rural youth are moving in search of employment in cities, and are at risk of exploitation in the workplace. More broadly, the jobs that youth obtain offer greater economic remuneration than in the past, but fewer benefits and less security, and access to good jobs is increasingly conditioned by education.

FAMILY, MARRIAGE, AND CHILDBEARING

Beyond education and the transition into the workforce, family formation is an activity crucial to the transition to adulthood. From the inception of the People's Republic of China, the marriage and childbearing choices of adolescents and young adults have been constrained by explicit laws. The Marriage Law of 1950 specified that the minimum legal age for marriage was 20 for males and 18 for females; these ages were revised upward by the new Marriage Law (1980), to 22 for males and 20 for females (Zeng, 2002). The 1950 and 1980 Marriage Laws advocated legal marriage based on the free choice of marriage partners, monogamy, and equal rights for both sexes and outlawed arranged marriage (Arnold and Liu, 1986). Under the influence of such decrees and other social and economic changes, a major shift away from arranged marriage has occurred in China over the past four decades (see Xu and Whyte, 1990, for evidence in Chengdu; see Riley, 1994, for evidence in six provinces of China). Family planning policies have also had important implications for the family formation. China initiated its first official national family planning policy, the *wan-xi-shao* (later-longer-fewer) policy, in 1970 (Tien, 1980). The later-longer-fewer policy advocated later marriage and childbearing, longer birth intervals, and fewer births. Although no unified standard existed, the lower limits on age at marriage were set as high as the mid-20s for females and late 20s for males in parts of China (Zeng, 2002). The later-longer-fewer policy also slowed the pace of childbearing by promoting a two-child norm and recommending at least 3 years of spacing between births. Signaling a dramatic change in the lives of reproductive-aged women, the policy coincided with a drop in total fertility rates from 5.8 in 1970 to 2.2 in 1980 (Zhang, 2000).

Around the time of market reforms, in 1979, the Chinese government issued the more restrictive one-child policy. Banister (1987) summarized the new policy as promoting late marriage, late childbearing, and few and healthy children, and encouraging one child per family. However, it met strong resistance and many violations took place. In 1984, the policy was revised to allow exemptions for having a second child for rural couples under certain circumstances.[17] In the late 1980s, policy loosened further

---

[17]For example, in some areas, rural couples were permitted to have a second child with a birth interval of 4 years, if their first child was a daughter. Some ethnic minority couples were permitted to have three children, but in no cases were fourth births to be allowed. The other exceptions include: (1) the first child is disabled; (2) the couple are both only children; and (3) the couple both have other special occupations (Short and Zhai, 1998).

and took son preference into greater account (Zeng, 1989). In most rural areas, daughter-only families were allowed a second child (Croll, 2000, p. 22).[18]

In the early 1990s, the Chinese government introduced the family planning responsibility system[19] to strengthen political and financial support from leaders at all levels (Xie, 2000). Overall, instead of enforcing a single state-derived, one-child policy, local governments were allowed to adapt national policy to take local socioeconomic circumstances, culture, and ethnic composition into consideration. Croll (2000, p. 22) observes that by the late 1990s "rigorous application" of the one-child rule occurred almost exclusively among urban residents, and then only very stringently in a select group of municipalities and high-population density provinces. According to Croll (2000, p. 22), in many provinces, general regulations now allow a second child for couples whose first child is a daughter, and some allow two children in most rural areas, regardless of the gender of the first child.

Furthermore, since the mid-1990s, new strategies for implementation have emerged, with particular relevance to adolescents. These strategies put more emphasis on quality of care, on informed contraceptive choices, on integrating family planning programs with economic activities, and on the improvement of women's status. It is important to note that because family planning services had long been organized to serve married women, unmarried adolescents were not always able to access services (Gu, Xie, and Hardee, 1998). The new service-oriented approaches have started to target reproductive health issues for adolescents. Examples of youth-oriented initiatives include offering new sex education programs in schools and communities,[20] increasing the retail sales of condoms, and addressing problems of unwanted pregnancies among adolescents, especially college students, in urban areas.

What are the trends in family formation in the reform period? Evidence indicates that rates of marriage are high in China, but the age at marriage is also high, with few adolescents among the married. Table 8-8 shows estimates of the singulate mean age at marriage (SMAM) and marital status for cohorts ages 15 to 19 years, 20 to 24 years, and 25 to 29 years for select years. The SMAM is a proxy for the mean age at marriage calculated from

---

[18]Rural fertility increased during this period (Zeng, 1989).

[19]The responsibility system requires that the head of the Communist Party and governments at all levels should take full responsibility for implementing the local population plans and give priority to the family planning program. Failure to meet the population targets may lead to some penalties for the leaders, such as withholding bonus, demotion, or dismissal.

[20]See, for example, no author (2002) for a description of one program in Changsha.

TABLE 8-8 Singulate Mean Age at Marriage and Percentage Married
Among 15- to 29-Year-Olds, Select Years

	1982		1987	
	M	F	M	F
N				
15-19 years	63,705,558	61,462,900	65,186,200	62,885,400
20-24 years	37,800,462	36,403,280	60,813,900	60,700,100
25-29 years	47,676,631	44,750,195	38,036,500	36,328,000
Percentage that are:				
Single				
15-19 years	99.1	95.6	98.6	95.8
20-24 years	72.0	46.5	61.0	39.9
25-29 years	23.6	5.3	17.3	4.1
Married				
15-19 years	0.9	4.3	1.4	4.2
20-24 years	27.8	53.3	38.7	59.8
25-29 years	75.7	94.3	81.9	95.4
Divorced				
15-19 years	0.0	0.0	0.0	0.0
20-24 years	0.2	0.2	0.2	0.2
25-29 years	0.5	0.2	0.5	0.3
Widowed				
15-19 years	0.0	0.0	0.0	0.0
20-24 years	0.0	0.1	0.1	0.1
25-29 years	0.2	0.2	0.2	0.2
SMAM[a]	24.9	22.4	23.9	22.0

[a]Singulate mean age at marriage (SMAM) is the average number of years lived in the single
state by those who marry prior to 50 years. For 1982, data for ages 50 to 54 were not
available. Reported SMAM substitutes 1987 data for percentage married at ages 50 to 54.
The United Nations Common Database (code 1030) offers ready-made estimates of SMAM

current status data, and represents the average number of years lived in the
single state by those who marry prior to age 50.

   Rates of singlehood were stable and nearly universal among teenagers,
ranging between 98.2 and 99.5 percent among males and between 95.3 and
98.4 percent for females for the years for which data are available. However, between 1982 and 1987, the singulate mean age at marriage dropped
from 24.9 to 23.9 for men and from 22.4 to 22.0 for women. In the 1990s,
the age rose again to 24.5 for men and 22.8 for women. Similarly, marital
status data for youth and young adult cohorts reveal that rates of singlehood among 20- to 30-year-old cohorts of men and women dropped in the
1980s, then rose thereafter (see Coale, Feng, Riley, and Lin, 1991 and

1990		1996		1997	
M	F	M	F	M	F
61,650,589	58,507,832	46,193,000	43,330,000	47,912,000	43,829,000
64,233,023	61,528,151	51,449,000	52,289,000	47,711,000	48,643,000
53,512,983	50,754,542	63,325,000	64,106,000	64,203,000	64,597,000
98.2	95.3	99.5	98.4	99.0	98.3
62.5	41.4	71.3	49.6	72.4	50.8
16.7	4.3	20.3	6.8	20.9	7.4
1.8	4.6	0.5	1.6	0.9	1.7
37.3	58.3	28.4	50.1	27.2	48.8
82.4	95.1	78.5	92.4	77.9	91.8
0.0	0.0	0.0	0.0	0.0	0.0
0.2	0.2	0.0	0.1	0.3	0.3
0.6	0.5	0.3	0.2	0.9	0.6
		0.0	0.0		
0.0	0.0	0.0	0.0	0.0	0.0
0.1	0.1	0.2	0.3	0.1	0.1
0.2	0.2	0.9	0.6	0.3	0.2
23.8	22.1	24.5	22.8	24.5	22.8

for the census years 1982 and 1990 from WESTAT. For 1982, estimates were 25.1 for men and 22.4 for women. For 1990, estimates were 23.8 for men and 22.1 for women.
SOURCE: United Nations (2002).

Zeng, 2002, for confirmatory evidence on the drop in age at marriage in the early 1980s, and Zeng, 2002, for rising trends in the 1990s). In Figure 8-2, the percentage married among 15- to 29-year-old cohorts in the CHNS confirm a substantial delaying tendency between 1989 and 1997.

The drop in age at marriage in the 1980s is commonly attributed to the 1980 Marriage Law, which in theory lifted the national legal age at marriage, but in fact loosened the age restrictions that had been in practice in some regions during the 1970s as part of the *wan-xi-shao* family planning policy (Zeng, 2002, p. 94). Zeng (2002, p. 95) credits rapid economic development with contributing to the more recent recovery in age at first marriage: With the emergence of the labor market and new employment

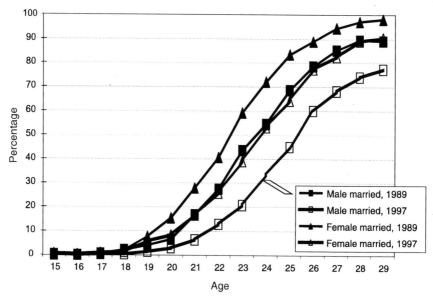

FIGURE 8-2 Marriage rates, 15- to 29-year-olds, China Health and Nutrition Survey, 1989 and 1997.

opportunities in cities, many young people delayed marriage. A strong population program that advocated late marriage may also have contributed to this delay. Finally, increased market access to contraceptives has allowed young people to engage in sexual activity with less worry about unwanted pregnancy, further delaying incentives for marriage.[21]

Given low marriage rates at young ages, and low rates of out-of-wedlock childbearing in China, it is not surprising that adolescent fertility rates are also low. Figure 8-3 shows total fertility rates and age-specific fertility rates for cohorts of young adults ages 15 to 19, 20 to 24, and 25 to 29. The total fertility rate is very low in China, having dropped from 2.2 in 1990 to about 1.8 by 1992 and 1.7 by 2000, where it remained stable through 2003. Age-specific fertility rates dropped for each of the three youth and young adult cohorts,[22] suggesting a shift toward later childbearing.

---

[21]The percentage of young people facing divorce remains very low, although overall divorce rates appear to be rising very quickly in China (Zeng and Wu, 2000).

[22]Rates among 15- to 19-year-olds dropped from 21 in 1990 to 11 in 2003; rates for 20- to 24-year-olds dropped from 197 to 164; and rates for 25- to 29-year-olds dropped from 150 to 107.

ASFR: TFR:

Births/1,000 women   **Births/woman**

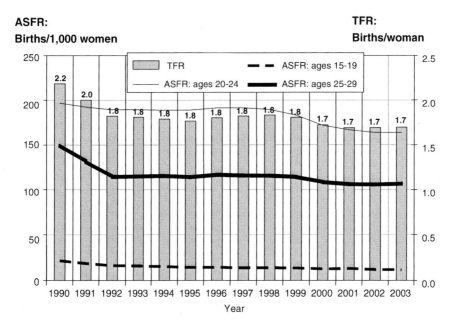

FIGURE 8-3 Total fertility rates and youth age-specific fertility rates.
NOTE: ASFR = age-specific fertility rate; TFR = total fertility rate.
SOURCE: Calculated from U.S. Bureau of the Census (2002), Table 028. International Database. Available: http://www.census.gov/ipc/www/idbnew.html.

HEALTH

In China, many of the reform-era changes in the education sector have parallels in the health-sector reforms. On the eve of market reforms, health care access was widespread, if not high quality. Public health institutions were financed by the government, and public health services were provided to users at no cost (Liu and Mills, 2002). Hsiao and colleagues (1997) state that by 1975, insurance coverage provided by the government and state enterprises and the rural cooperative medical system had reached nearly to 90 percent of the population. This coverage included nearly all of the urban population and 85 percent of the rural population. It provided access to cost-effective preventive and curative health care services (Hsiao et al., 1997, pp. 1-2).

As we discussed in the context of education, beginning in 1978, the Chinese government introduced radical economic policy shifts that moved China away from a centrally planned economy and toward a competitive market system (Hsiao et al., 1997). In the health-sector, fiscal decentralization and the diminishing role of rural collectives resulted in an increasing private share in health expenditures and growing inequities in access to health services (Bloom and Gu, 1997; Yu, Cao, and Lucas, 1997). Beginning in the early 1980s, public health institutions were no longer seen as pure welfare entities, but rather as economic bodies, and charges were introduced as an important source of income (Liu and Mills, 2002). Government spending on health increased during the early reform years, but private health spending increased even faster, transforming the financial base of health care (Hsiao et al., 1997).

The most dramatic change in health financing in the early reform years was the decline of the rural cooperative medical system; the financing gap that resulted was filled mainly by private out-of-pocket spending (Hsiao et al., 1997). Even within urban areas, however, some evidence suggests increases in out-of-pocket payments and a decline in the population covered by government insurance (Gao et al., 2001). Overall, out-of-pocket payments rose from 20 percent of the health-sector's revenue in 1978, to 26 percent in 1986, to 42 percent in 1993 (Hsiao et al., 1997). In the 1990s, some evidence suggests that preventive health care services declined as costs for those services rose. For example, immunization rates appear to have dropped as fees for immunizations have increased (Gu et al., 1995; Hsiao et al., 1997; UNMI, 2002). Evidence suggests that access to health insurance among children and youth was extremely limited through the 1990s. For example, just 16 to 17 percent of children under age 16 in the 1989, 1993, or 1997 waves of the CHNS had access to health insurance (Adams and Hannum, 2005).

Against a backdrop of rising disparities in availability of high-quality services, China faces the challenge of new health problems common to developed countries and persistent problems more characteristic of those facing developing countries. One general problem facing children and youth in China is nutrition, as a dual pattern of overnutrition and nutritional deprivation is emerging (Hesketh, Ding, and Tomkins, 2002). Child malnutrition declined in rural areas in the late 1980s and early 1990s, but dramatic regional variations exist and physical stunting remains common in some poor rural areas (Chen, 2002; Park and Zhang, 2000). Using longitudinal data from the China Health and Nutrition Survey in 1991 and 1993, Wang, Popkin, and Zhai (1998) found that among children ages 10 to 18, the prevalence of stunting declined from 23 percent in 1991 to 19 percent in 1993, but that undernutrition was still a problem among 13 percent of adolescents.

Wang et al. (1998) note that overweight status is emerging as a problem associated with high-income and urban adolescents, though the overall prevalence is low, at 4 percent.[23] Other studies focusing on urban popula-

---

[23]Wang et al. (1998) defined undernutrition as an age- and gender-specific body mass index (BMI) less than the 5th percentile of the National Center for Health Statistics/World Health Organization (NCHS/WHO) reference; they defined overweight status as a BMI at or above the 85th percentile of the NCHS/WHO reference.

tions have similarly begun to track an emerging problem of obesity among urban youth (Hesketh, Ding, and Tomkins, 2002). Wang and colleagues' (1998) review of smaller studies suggests that the prevalence of overweight status may have reached 6 to 9 percent in several coastal provinces and in north China by the early 1990s. Although problems of overnutrition have yet to reach the proportions seen in the United States,[24] they illustrate new health issues emerging as a direct result of the wealth brought by market reforms.

Another adolescent health issue that the market reform era may have exacerbated is smoking. Although smoking is a major health problem in China across age groups, the majority of smokers begin as adolescents (Cheng, 1999). A national prevalence survey conducted in 1996 showed that the steepest rise in smoking occurs between the ages of 15 and 20, and that the majority of teen smokers and nonsmokers were unaware of the health risks of smoking (Cheng, 1999, pp. 608-611). Two studies conducted in Beijing, in 1991 and 1997, found that the prevalence of teenage smoking ranged from 15 percent to 25 percent (Li, Fang, and Stanton, 1996, 1999). Hesketh, Ding, and Tomkins' (2001) survey of 6,674 13- to 18-year-old students in Zhejiang province indicated that 25.7 percent of boys and 5.4 percent of girls has ever smoked. Among ever-smokers, 41.9 percent had smoked before age 10, and 7.9 percent before age 5.[25]

Furthermore, the problem appears to be growing. Analysis of a national survey of smoking prevalence conducted in 1996 suggested that the age of smoking initiation fell by approximately 3 years for both men and women between 1984 and 1996 (Yang et al., 1999). Beyond long-term health implications, smoking among Chinese adolescents is associated with poor school performance and problem behaviors such as truancy from school, running away from home, destructiveness, and fighting (Li et al., 1996, 1999). A tobacco advertising ban was enacted in 1995, and through the 1990s, smoking bans were passed in some cities and some school-based campaigns emerged. However, the scope of implementation of these strategies remains unclear (Cheng, 1999; Unger et al., 2001).

A third health concern that is looming large for adolescents in the reform period is reproductive health. Recent delays in the age at marriage

---

[24]In the United States, 26.5 percent of adolescents were overweight, defined using a cutoff point of the 85th percentile based on the smoothed version of the National Health and Nutrition Examination Survey (NHANES I). The number was estimated using a sample of 13,783 adolescents from the National Longitudinal Study of Adolescent Health (Popkin and Udry, 1998).

[25]Unger et al. (2001, p. 162) report that studies in various parts of mainland China have reported adolescent smoking prevalence rates of 28 to 43 percent for boys and 1 to 11 percent for girls, with results dependent on the age of respondents and the specific measures of smoking employed.

and an increasingly early age of menarche[26] leave young adults with a long period of sexual maturity before marriage. Concerns have been raised about premarital sex, lack of knowledge of and access to contraceptives (Gao, Tu, and Yuan, 1997; Zhang, 1997), a rise in abortions due to unwanted pregnancies (Luo et al., 1995; Wu et al., 1992), and increasing vulnerability to HIV and other sexually transmitted diseases among adolescents (Xiao, 1996; Qi and Tang, 2000).

Empirical estimates of trends in premarital sex are difficult to come by, due to the still-sensitive nature of the topic. Wang and Yang (1996) indirectly examined the incidence of premarital sex using data from the 1988 China's Two-Per-Thousand Fertility and Birth Control Survey. The authors defined premarital conceptions as intervals of 8 months or less between the date of first marriage and first birth. They found that premarital conceptions rose from 1.5 percent in the 1950s, to 3.0 percent in the late 1970s, to 5.0 percent in the mid-1980s. The percentages of premarital conception were twice as high for urban residents as rural residents (5 percent versus 2.5 percent). There was no significant difference by ethnicity, but women with secondary schooling or more had higher percentages of premarital conceptions (4.4 percent) than women who were illiterate or semiliterate (1.4 percent). Professional couples were more likely, and farming couples less likely, to have a premarital conception. These findings suggest that the incidence of premarital sex has increased over time, and increases with higher social status. However, these figures are likely to underrepresent actual premarital sexual activities due to the rising availability of contraceptives and the use of abortions to prevent unwanted births.

National studies of abortion are unavailable, but smaller scale studies suggest that nontrivial numbers of young, single women do experience abortion. For example, one study of five districts in Shanghai indicated that the abortion rate among single women in 1988 was 56 abortions per 1,000 15- to 19-year-olds, 159 per 1,000 20- to 24-year-olds, and 94 per 1,000 25- to 29-year-olds (Wu et al., 1992). The figure for 15- to 19-year-olds represented a dramatic increase from 5 per 1,000 in 1982. In the same period of time, abortion rates increased nearly fourfold for single women ages 20 to 24 and 30 to 34, and more than doubled among women ages 25 to 29. Furthermore, the proportion of abortions obtained by single women increased from 14 percent in 1982 to 28 percent in 1986, then decreased slightly to 25 percent in 1988 (Wu et al., 1992, p. 51). A study of abortions conducted between August and November 1999 in four hospitals in Beijing indicated that 40 percent of the procedures were for unmarried women (no

---

[26]Wu, Gao, and Zhang (2000) reported that due to improved health conditions and nutrition, age at menarche in China dropped from 16.5 years for women born in 1947-1949 to 13.9 years for women born in 1980-1982.

author, 2001). A survey of 457 unmarried women undergoing first-trimester abortions in six Sichuan counties between July 1990 and June 1991 found that 28.2 percent of them were under 20 years old and 64.8 percent were 20 to 24 years of age. The vast majority (92.6 percent) were not using any form of contraception when the pregnancy occurred, and 35 percent reported at least one previous abortion (Luo et al., 1995).

The use of abortion by young women is itself a significant health issue, but it also suggests that methods other than indirect estimation from first birth intervals are needed to determine the sexual activity of adolescents. The National Reproductive Health Survey, conducted in 1997, inquired indirectly among reproductive-aged women about premarital sex, asking, "To your knowledge, among the people you know, are there any people having sex before their marriage? If yes, how widespread is this behavior?" (see Table 8-9). Overall, about 30.9 percent of respondents stated that premarital sex was nonexistent among those around them, 35.1 percent said there were occasional or some cases, and 14.5 percent said it was relatively widespread.[27] Interestingly, the youngest cohorts—15 to 19 and 20 to 24—were less likely to perceive widespread premarital sex than their older counterparts. Perceptions of widespread premarital sex were greatest among women in the middle of the reproductive-age range. Less educated women respondents perceived less widespread premarital sex than more educated women, and rural women were less likely to perceive widespread premarital sex than urban women.

The current prevalence of premarital sex is linked in the popular press to more permissive social attitudes. However, evidence about trends in attitudes is hard to come by. The 1997 National Reproductive Health Survey suggests that the vast majority of people continue to express attitudes unfavorable to premarital sex (see Table 8-10). The survey asked a relatively conservative question: "Nowadays some people think, as long as two people plan to get married, they can have sex before marriage. Do you agree with this view?" Overall, 80.3 percent of people disagreed with this statement; only 12.6 percent agreed. For young age cohorts, ages 15 to 19, rates of agreement were even lower, at 6.2 percent. The rate of agreement rises with the 20- and 30-year-old cohorts, then drops among the oldest cohorts. The highest agreement rates emerged among urban women ages 20 to 34, where 17 to 20 percent of women agreed. The least educated women tended to have somewhat lower agreement rates.

---

[27]In the survey, 19.2 percent gave a response of "don't know" and 0.2 percent refused to answer the question.

TABLE 8-9 Distribution of Responses to the Questions: "To your knowledge, among the people you know, are there any people having sex before marriage? If yes, how widespread is this behavior?"

	N	No	Occasional Cases	Some Cases	Relatively Widespread	Don't Know	Refuse to Answer
Total	15,213	30.87	23.42	11.73	14.50	19.25	0.24
By age							
N							
All women	15,213						
15-19	1,620	37.90	19.94	8.83	4.38	28.40	0.56
20-24	1,944	30.71	27.73	13.43	12.29	15.53	0.31
25-29	2,881	27.91	25.27	13.16	17.49	16.00	0.17
30-34	2,776	29.90	21.90	12.21	17.44	18.37	0.18
35-39	1,840	29.40	22.55	11.74	15.43	20.76	0.11
40-44	2,223	30.95	23.48	10.93	15.38	19.03	0.22
45-49	1,929	32.24	22.19	10.52	14.62	20.22	0.21
Rural women							
N	11,668						
15-19	1,284	40.50	19.00	8.18	4.28	27.49	0.55
20-24	1,498	34.78	27.70	11.82	9.81	15.55	0.33
25-29	2,253	33.07	25.83	10.52	13.76	16.69	0.13
30-34	2,184	34.80	21.89	10.44	14.10	18.64	0.14
35-39	1,316	35.18	22.11	9.73	12.54	20.36	0.08
40-44	1,652	37.23	22.82	9.26	11.92	18.58	0.18
45-49	1,481	37.00	22.15	9.12	11.34	20.12	0.27
Urban women							
N	3,545						
15-19	336	27.98	23.51	11.31	4.76	31.85	0.60
20-24	446	17.04	27.80	18.83	20.63	15.47	0.22
25-29	628	9.39	23.25	22.61	30.89	13.54	0.32
30-34	592	11.82	21.96	18.75	29.73	17.40	0.34
35-39	524	14.89	23.66	16.79	22.71	21.76	0.19

						N
40-44	0.35	20.32	25.39	15.76	25.39	12.78	571
45-49	0.00	20.54	25.45	15.18	22.32	16.52	448

By education

N

All women 15,213

						N
Illiterate and semiliterate	0.43	22.19	8.65	8.59	20.62	39.52	3,249
Primary schooling	0.15	17.64	12.41	10.49	22.64	36.67	4,546
Junior middle schooling	0.20	18.85	16.54	12.53	24.61	27.27	4,892
Senior middle schooling	0.21	19.80	23.64	14.09	24.62	17.64	1,434
Secondary technical schooling	0.00	17.63	19.29	16.88	28.20	18.00	539
College and over	0.36	18.81	19.71	22.06	28.03	11.03	553

Rural women 11,668

N

						N
Illiterate and semiliterate	0.42	22.08	8.20	8.39	20.60	40.31	3,121
Primary schooling	0.14	17.66	11.58	9.77	22.75	38.10	4,207
Junior middle schooling	0.19	18.57	13.58	11.31	25.06	31.29	3,624
Senior middle schooling	0.00	19.60	16.91	10.43	28.06	25.00	556
Secondary technical schooling	0.00	17.99	13.67	15.11	28.06	25.18	139
College and over	0.00	14.29	9.52	4.76	57.14	14.29	21

Urban women 3,545

N

						N
Illiterate and semiliterate	0.78	25.00	19.53	13.28	21.09	20.31	128
Primary schooling	0.29	17.40	22.71	19.47	21.24	18.88	339
Junior middle schooling	0.24	19.64	25.00	16.01	23.34	15.77	1,268
Senior middle schooling	0.34	19.93	27.90	16.40	22.44	12.98	878
Secondary technical schooling	0.00	17.50	21.25	17.50	28.25	15.50	400
College and over	0.38	18.98	20.11	22.74	26.88	10.90	532

SOURCE: Jiang (2000).

TABLE 8-10 Distribution of Responses to the Questions: "Nowadays some people think, as long as two people plan to get married, they can have sex before marriage. Do you agree with this view?"

	N	Agree	Disagree	Don't Know	Refuse to Answer
Total	15,213	12.61	80.30	6.43	0.66
By age					
N	15,213				
All women	15,213				
15-19	1,620	6.17	82.35	9.69	1.79
20-24	1,944	13.07	79.32	6.89	0.72
25-29	2,881	15.41	76.92	7.08	0.59
30-34	2,776	16.17	78.06	5.44	0.32
35-39	1,840	12.39	81.25	5.87	0.49
40-44	2,223	11.11	83.67	4.59	0.63
45-49	1,929	10.16	83.05	6.32	0.47
N	Rural women 11,668				
15-19	1,284	6.15	81.78	10.20	1.87
20-24	1,498	11.88	80.91	6.34	0.87
25-29	2,253	14.25	79.23	5.99	0.53
30-34	2,184	15.34	79.40	4.99	0.27
35-39	1,316	12.31	81.31	6.16	0.23
40-44	1,652	10.96	84.56	4.12	0.36
45-49	1,481	10.20	82.31	6.89	0.61
N	Urban women 3,545				
15-19	336	6.25	84.52	7.74	1.49
20-24	446	17.04	73.99	8.74	0.22
25-29	628	19.59	68.63	10.99	0.80
30-34	592	19.26	73.14	7.09	0.51
35-39	524	12.60	81.11	5.15	1.15
40-44	571	11.56	81.09	5.95	1.40
45-49	448	10.04	85.49	4.46	0.00

By education	N				
N	15,213				
Illiterate and semiliterate	3,249	10.80	80.39	7.94	0.86
Primary schooling	4,546	12.65	80.55	6.25	0.55
Junior middle schooling	4,892	13.41	80.78	5.19	0.61
Senior middle schooling	1,434	12.97	79.85	6.35	0.84
Secondary technical schooling	539	12.06	79.59	7.98	0.37
College and over	553	15.37	75.23	8.68	0.72
Rural women					
N	11,668				
Illiterate and semiliterate	3,121	10.99	80.26	7.88	0.87
Primary schooling	4,207	12.79	80.48	6.16	0.57
Junior middle schooling	3,624	12.06	82.53	4.86	0.55
Senior middle schooling	556	12.77	82.01	5.04	0.18
Secondary technical schooling	139	11.51	79.86	7.91	0.72
College and over	21	9.52	85.71	4.76	0.00
Urban women					
N	3,545				
Illiterate and semiliterate	128	6.25	83.59	9.38	0.78
Primary schooling	339	10.91	81.42	7.37	0.29
Junior middle schooling	1,268	17.27	75.79	6.15	0.79
Senior middle schooling	878	13.10	78.47	7.18	1.25
Secondary technical schooling	400	12.25	79.50	8.00	0.25
College and over	532	15.60	74.81	8.83	0.75

SOURCE: Jiang (2000).

These patterns provide some hints of likely trajectories of change, though they do not speak directly to change. The fact that agreement rates tend to be higher in urban areas and among the somewhat better educated suggests that the segments of society that have greatest exposure to the forces of development are also those with more permissive attitudes, and those perceiving more sexual activity outside of the context of marriage.

Indications of rising premarital sexual activity, in the context of increases in the age at marriage (except in the early 1980s), suggest the possibility that what is changing may not be youth sexual behaviors per se, but the link between these behaviors and marriage. Yet, adolescent and young adult nonmarital sexual activity carries numerous public health concerns not implied by sexual activity within the context of marriage. Importantly, public health concerns about the prevalence of premarital sex in China are made urgent by the rapid increase in HIV prevalence. Overall estimates of the impact of HIV in China are regularly shifted upward, with recent estimates suggesting that more than a million people carry HIV (United Nations Theme Group on HIV/AIDS in China, 2002). Trend data for youth are not available. However, among youth ages 15 to 24, United Nations estimates for 2001 suggest that the prevalence is between 0.11 percent and 0.2 percent for males and between 0.06 percent and 0.11 percent for females (United Nations Millennium Indicators, 2002). In a recent speech, the Minister of the State Population and Family Planning Commission suggested that more than 60 percent of China's HIV cases were among people ages 15 to 29 (Zhang, 2003).[28]

Knowledge of AIDS remains limited. A Centers for Disease Control and Prevention report on a survey of 7,000 randomly selected individuals ages 15 to 49 in seven counties showed that nearly 17 percent had never heard of AIDS, and more than half did not know the cause of the disease (CDC, 2002). Among those who had heard about AIDS, about 90 percent knew that it could be transmitted person to person, but 85 percent were unaware it could be passed from mother to child. Eighty-one percent did not know it could be acquired by sharing needles, and 52 percent were unaware that it could be transmitted by unsafe blood transfusions. More than 75 percent were unaware that proper use of condoms could prevent infection (Brown, 2002).

Adolescent sexual behavior is a concern that the public health system is struggling to address, despite China's extensive family planning system and its recent shifts toward a reproductive health services orientation (Gu, 2000; Simmons et al., 2000). To address concerns about adolescents, in recent years, numerous reproductive health programs have been implemented that target reproductive health services for youth and adolescents.[29] Adolescent

---

[28]However, the speech acknowledged that statistics were "incomplete."

[29]These include programs such as the China Family Planning Association's recent project on adolescents' sexual health (China Family Planning Association, 2001).

reproductive health issues are recognized as being an important element in the mid- to long-term plan for AIDS control in China (Zhang, 2003). The challenges are exacerbated by ever-increasing numbers of unattached youth and young adults migrating to cities for work; these youth often remain excluded from urban welfare services, such as reproductive health services.

A fourth public health problem facing adolescents and young adults that has gained considerable public attention in recent years is suicide. Table 8-11 shows two recently published estimates of adolescent and young-adult suicide rates.[30] Panel A shows national urban and rural estimates of suicide rates and the percentage of all deaths from suicide for women and men, for ages 15 to 34 and for all ages. These estimates show that, overall, suicide rates among rural residents were much higher than those of urban residents—about three times as high. Women's rates were higher than men's, but the disadvantage faced by women was concentrated in rural areas. Furthermore, among rural populations, the excess suicide among women is larger among the young population than among the whole population. For rural women ages 15 to 34, fully 31 percent of all deaths were attributable to suicide. The rate of suicide for rural women in this age group, at 37.8 per 100,000, was 1.7 times the rate of rural men, 3.5 times the rate of urban women, and 4 times the rate of urban men. The 2001 *World Health Report* lists suicide as the leading cause of death in 1998 among rural women ages 15 to 34 in China (World Health Organization, 2001, Figure 2.5). Data from 1988, 1990, and 1992 (Panel B) suggest that the peak of rural young women's suicide rates occurs in the 20- to 24-year-old age range.

The most common technique is pesticide ingestion, which accounts for 34.3 to 66.6 percent of all suicides (Ji et al., 2001, pp. 3, 4; Phillips, Li, and Zhang, 2002). Ji and colleagues (2001) observe that this technique is extremely effective because rural health care systems are not equipped to handle pesticide poisoning. The ready availability of pesticides, and the inability of health systems to counteract their effects, may play a role in the excess suicide mortality for young women.[31] Contradictory evidence exists about the degree to which depression is a significant risk factor for suicide.

---

[30]Phillips, Li, and Zhang's (2002) estimates (Panel A) are based on mortality data for 1995-1999 provided by the Chinese Ministry of Health, adjusted according to estimates of unreported deaths, and projected to the corresponding population (pp. 835-836). The authors describe the estimates as "conservative." Ji's (1999) estimates (Panel B) were calculated from unpublished Chinese Ministry of Public Health data. These data were collected from each county of China, and therefore represent a national sample. Further details were unavailable (p. 1). There are a number of estimates using data from other sources showing variation in the overall level of suicide prevalence. However, patterns of high rural-urban ratios of suicide and high female-male ratios among rural populations emerge across different studies (see, e.g., Ji, Kleinman, and Becker, 2001; Yip, Callanan, and Yuen, 2000).

[31]Ji and colleagues (2001) point out that as many as 80 percent of female suicide attempts among Western women are unsuccessful attempts.

TABLE 8-11 Select Published Estimates of Suicide Rates in China for the 1980s and 1990s

Panel A: Mean Annual Rates of Suicide (1/100,000) and Percentage of All Deaths Due to Suicide, 1995-1999

Age	15-34		All Ages	
Population Group	Suicide Rate	% of all Deaths Due to Suicide	Suicide Rate	% of all Deaths Due to Suicide
Rural	30.3	20.4	27.1	4.0
Urban	10.2	10.3	8.3	1.5
Women	32.1	29.0	25.9	4.4
Men	20.0	12.1	20.7	2.9
Rural women	37.8	31.0	30.5	4.9
Rural men	22.8	13.1	23.9	3.3
Urban women	10.8	15.8	8.3	1.7
Urban men	9.5	7.4	8.3	1.3

Panel B: Rural Suicide Rates in 1988, 1990, and 1992 (1/100,000)

Age	15-19	20-24	25-29	30-34
Population Group				
Women				
1988	31.7	67.1	34.6	28.3
1990	23.3	47.6	37.3	25.9
1992	18.2	46.3	38.6	27.9
Men				
1988	14.1	38.2	23.6	22.8
1990	10.4	22.5	20.3	17.1
1992	9.8	28.4	23.0	19.8

SOURCES: Panel A: Section reproduced from Phillips, Li, and Zhang (2002a, Table 1). Panel B: Section reproduced from Ji (1999, Table 2).

Ji and colleagues' (2001) review suggests that serious depression is not a primary precipitant of suicide, while Phillips and colleagues' (2002b) national case-control study indicates that a high depression symptom score did significantly raise the risk of suicide. However, scholars agree that social stressors significantly raise the risk of suicide (Ji et al., 2001; Phillips et al., 2002b). Research on call-ins to mental health hotlines suggests that significant stressors, especially for women, include marital problems, pressures of extramarital or premarital affairs, family pressures, and education and employment pressures (Ji, 1999; Ji et al., 2001).

Trend data remain sketchy, but certain evidence suggests a decline in suicide rates. Ji's estimates for rural residents in the late 1980s and early 1990s (Tabel 8-11, Panel B) suggest that suicide rates are declining across time, as 1992 figures were somewhat lower for most age cohorts than 1988 figures. Consistent with this result, a World Health Organization report (2001, Figure 2.4) indicates that age-standardized suicide rates in China dropped by 17.2 percent in the most recent three years for which data were available. However, Phillips, Li, and Zhang (2002a) indicate that an earlier study using comparable Ministry of Health mortality data from 1987 suggests that both the level and the age pattern of suicide were stable, compared with their own results for 1995 to 1999.

Regardless of the trend, the scope of suicide in recent years has brought recognition of suicide as a major public health problem. The Ministry of Health, in collaboration with the World Health Organization, held a workshop on suicide prevention in March 2000 that took the first steps toward developing a national suicide prevention program (Phillips, Li, and Zhang, 2002a).

Some of the health problems described here—overnutrition, sexual health, and to some degree, smoking—are problems enabled by the rising wealth in China. Other problems, including persisting undernutrition faced by children and youth in poor rural areas and the high suicide rates of young people in these areas, especially women, reflect older issues such as poverty and the social pressures facing young women.

SUMMARY

The evidence presented here indicates that changes were taking place in the 1990s. Most significantly, youth were delaying transitions into adulthood across major domains of the life course. Figures 8-4a and 8-4b illustrate this point, combining rates of nonenrollment, employment, and marriage by age for females (8-4a) and males (8-4b) ages 11 to 29 in the 1989 and 1997 CHNS samples. These figures illustrate that cohorts coming of age in the latter year transitioned more slowly out of education, into work, and into marriage. Consistent with this story, fertility data also suggest a shift to later childbearing. These shifts can be characterized as favorable, from the perspectives of improving the educational composition of the population, reducing child labor, and promoting slower population growth.

However, improved standards of living and norms of social openness associated with market reforms have raised the significance of behavioral health issues, such as smoking and premarital sexual activity. Furthermore, while available evidence suggests that many favorable changes have been shared across social groups, some noteworthy social and economic inequalities continued to mark adolescents' lives. For example, youth in ur-

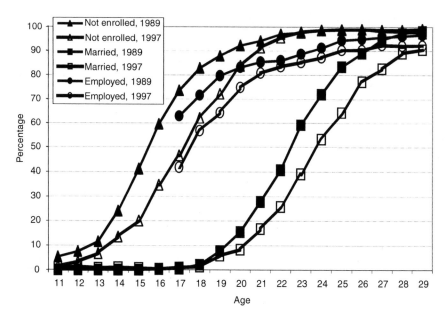

FIGURE 8-4a Nonenrollment, employment, and marriage, Chinese Health and Nutrition Survey, females, 1989 and 1997.

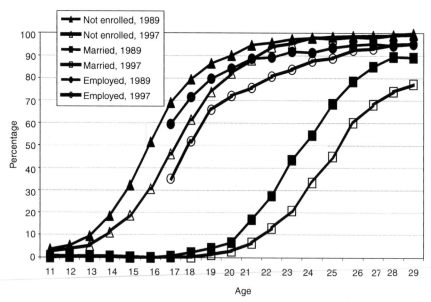

FIGURE 8-4b Nonenrollment, employment, and marriage, Chinese Health and Nutrition Survey, males, 1989 and 1997.

ban areas remained more likely to be in school, and thus to enjoy the benefits of education in a labor market that increasingly rewards credentials. The mirror image of this phenomenon is reflected in the elevated likelihood of rural youth to be in the labor force, in the high percentage of working youth employed in agricultural pursuits, and in the rise in youth migration into urban settings. Similar signs of disparity mark education and employment status along socioeconomic lines.

Urban-rural and socioeconomic splits are also glaringly evident in the health problems facing China's adolescents, with youth in some poor rural areas continuing to face basic health problems such as lack of adequate nutrition, while wealthier urban youth are beginning to face health problems associated with youth culture in more affluent settings. The lines of inequality are nowhere more painfully clear than in suicide rates, which are three times higher in the rural youth population, probably reflecting a combination of the poverty-related stressors that poor rural adolescents must cope with on a daily basis and their easy access to potent poisons. For reasons that remain murky, the toll is highest for young rural women.

DISCUSSION AND CONCLUSIONS

China's socialist past was characterized by an unusually high degree of policy involvement, using means that were sometimes harsh, to achieve state goals regarding education, job placement, marriage, fertility, and women's roles. China's more recent experience of rapid economic development has built on some of the hard-won achievements of these earlier policies to yield many patterns of adolescent transition that are favorable. Youth stay in school longer, and start work later, as time passes. The average age at marriage is high enough that marriage is unlikely to compete directly with educational opportunities, except at the highest levels of education. Low fertility rates, especially at young ages, suggest that women's childrearing responsibilities compete less with other opportunities than in many less developed countries. Strikingly, in the 1990s, many of these favorable patterns were markedly enhanced.

Yet, the institutional legacies of socialism are not always suited to addressing the current problems of adolescents. For example, the traditional system of family planning, oriented toward strict regulation of marital fertility, is working to offer a more service-oriented approach, and to address issues of nonmarital sexual activity among increasingly mobile youth.

Nor are the implications of market reforms exclusively favorable. Wealth and the opening of society have led to new concerns about adolescent welfare. Improved standards of living and norms of social openness associated with market reforms have raised the significance of overnutrition, sexual health, and to some degree, smoking as adolescent and young adult health problems. Among the new problems facing youth, AIDS has the potential to become a staggering social problem if not successfully addressed in a timely manner. In the area of work, adolescents enjoy much greater chances of achieving high incomes than in the past, but they also face a harshly competitive environment in which the rewards associated with work are more narrowly economic and the tenure of any job obtained is less secure. Further complicating the picture is evidence that, while opportunities have improved across social groups, socioeconomically disadvantaged youth face disproportionate barriers to successful transitions into adulthood.[32]

In short, successes in improving the lives of many adolescents have brought new challenges, as China's youth policy makers now serve populations that face increasingly divergent problems. Decision makers in education, labor, family planning, and health now need to adapt services to the needs of urban adolescents and impoverished young rural-urban migrants, while dealing effectively with the older problems facing the rural poor. Their degree of success in this endeavor will bear crucial ramifications for the future welfare of China's youth and adult populations.

REFERENCES

Adams, J., and Hannum, E. (2005, March). Trends in children's social welfare in China: Access to health insurance and education. *China Quarterly, 181,* 100-121.

Arnold, F., and Liu, Z. (1986). Sex preference, fertility, and family planning in China. *Population and Development Review, 12*(2), 221-246.

Banister, J. (1987). *China's changing population.* Stanford, CA: Stanford University Press.

Bian, Y. (2002). Chinese social stratification and social mobility. *Annual Review of Sociology, 28,* 91-116.

Bloom, G., and Gu, X.Y. (1997). Introduction to health-sector reform in China. *IDS Bulletin, 28*(1), 1-23.

Broaded, M.C. (1983). Higher education policy changes and stratification in China. *China Quarterly, 93,* 125-141.

Brown, D. (2002, July 9). *Survey finds China's AIDS awareness is lacking. Medicine scarce in India, conference is also told.* Available: http://www.thebody.com/cdc/news_updates_archive/july11_02/china_aids.html [accessed October 21, 2003].

Carter, C.A. (1997). The urban-rural income gap in China: Implications for global food markets. *American Journal of Agricultural Economics, 79,* 1410-1418.

---

[32]We note that our indicators may not fully represent the scope of disparities present in important dimensions of education and health care quality. The system of education is absorbing increasing proportions of children and youth, but it is also becoming increasingly stratified in quality as a direct result of economic and education policy shifts in the reform period. Similarly, the public health system is struggling to address persisting and new health problems of adolescents in a context where access to care is much more dependent on ability to pay than in the past.

Centers for Disease Control and Prevention. (2002, July 11). *Emerging epidemics in China and Russia. Press release.* Available: http://www.cdc.gov/od/oc/media/pressrel/r020711.htm [accessed August 11, 2002].

Chen, C. (2002). Fat intake and nutritional status of children in China. *American Journal of Clinical Nutrition, 72*(Suppl.), 1368-1372.

Cheng, K. (2003). China's education reform: Priorities and implications. In E. Hannum and A. Park (Eds.), *Education and reform in China.* Cambridge, MA: Harvard University Press

Cheng, T. (1999). Teenage smoking in China. *Journal of Adolescence, 22,* 607-620.

China Family Planning Association. (2001). *UNFPA/CFPA adolescent reproductive health pilot project final evaluation.* (UNFPA RH/FP project CPR/98/P01.) Available: http://www.unescobkk.org/ips/arh-web/arhnews/pdf/unfpa_cfpa.pdf [accessed October 13, 2002].

Coale, A.J., Feng, W., Riley, N.E., and Lin, F.D. (1991). Recent trends in fertility and nuptiality in China. *Science, 251*(4992), 389-393.

Communiqué on Promulgating Regulations on the Special Protection of Minor Workers. (1994). Available: http://www.molss.gov.cn/correlate/lbf1994498.htm [accessed June 5, 2002].

Croll, E. (2000). *Endangered daughters: Discrimination and development in Asia.* New York: Routledge.

De Brauw, A., and Rozelle, S. (2003). Returns to education in rural China. In E. Hannum and A. Park (Eds.), *Education and reform in China.* Cambridge, MA: Harvard University Press.

Gao, E., Tu, X., and Yuan, W. (1997). Shanghai premarital adolescent use of contraceptive methods and analysis of influencing factors. *Chinese Journal of Population Science, 9*(4), 375-388.

Gao, J., Tang, S., Tolhurst, R., and Rao, K. (2001). Changing access to health services in urban China: Implications for equity. *Health Policy and Planning, 16*(3), 302-312.

Goodkind, D., and West, L.A. (2002). China's floating population: Definitions, data and recent findings. *Urban Studies, 39*(12), 2237-2250.

Gu, B., Xie, Z., and Hardee, K. (1998). *The effect of family planning on women's lives: The case of the People's Republic of China.* Research Triangle Park, NC: Family Health International.

Gu, B.C. (2000, March). *Reorienting China's family planning program: An experiment on quality of care since 1995.* Paper presented at the annual meeting of the Population Association of America, Los Angeles, CA.

Gu, X.Y., Bloom, G., Tang, S.L., and Lucas, H. (1995). *Financing health services in poor rural China: A strategy for health-sector reform.* (Institute of Development Studies Working Paper No. 17.) Shanghai, China: Shanghai Medical University Collaborative Research Program.

Hannum, E. (1999a). Political change and the urban-rural gap in education in China, 1949-1990. *Comparative Education Review, 43*(2), 193-211.

Hannum, E. (1999b). Poverty and basic-level schooling in the People's Republic of China: Equity issues in the 1990s. *Prospects: The Quarterly Journal of Comparative Education, 29*(4), 561-577.

Hannum, E. (2002a). Educational stratification by ethnicity in China: Enrollment and attainment in the early reform years. *Demography, 39*(1), 95-117.

Hannum, E. (2002b). Market transition, educational disparities, and family strategies in rural China: New evidence on gender stratification and development. *Demography, 42*(2), 275-299.

Hannum, E. (2003). Poverty and basic education in rural China: Communities, households, and girls' and boys' enrollment. *Comparative Education Review, 47*(2), 141-159.

Hannum, E., and Park, A. (2002). Educating China's rural children in the 21st century. *Harvard China Review, 3*(2), 8-14.

Hesketh, T., Ding, Q.J., and Tomkins, A.M. (2001). Smoking among youths in China. *American Journal of Public Health, 91*(10), 1653-1655.

Hesketh, T., Ding, Q.J., and Tomkins, A.M. (2002). Disparities in economic development in Eastern China: Impact on nutritional status of adolescents. *Public Health Nutrition, 5*(2), 313-318.

Hsiao, W., Jamison, D.T., McGreevey, W.P., and Yip, W. (1997). *Financing health care: Issues and options for China.* (World Bank Report No. 17091.) Washington, DC: World Bank.

Ji, J. (1999, June). Committed suicide in the Chinese rural areas. *Updates on Global Mental and Social Health, 3*(1).

Ji, J., Kleinman, A., and Becker, A.E. (2001). Suicide in contemporary China: A review of China's distinctive suicide demographics in their sociocultural context. *Harvard Review of Psychiatry, 9*(1), 1-12.

Jiang, Z. (Ed.). (2000). *Data collection of the 1997 National Population and Reproductive Health Survey.* Beijing, China: China Population Publishing House.

Khan, A.R., and Riskin, C. (1998). Income and inequality in China: Composition, distribution and growth of household income, 1988 to 1995. *China Quarterly, 154,* 221-253.

Kwong, J. (1985). Changing political culture and changing curriculum: An analysis of language textbooks in the People's Republic of China. *Comparative Education, 21,* 197-208.

Li, X.M., Fang, X., and Stanton, B. (1996). Cigarette smoking among Chinese adolescents and its association with demographic characteristics, social activities, and problem behaviors. *Substance Use and Misuse, 31*(5), 545-563.

Li, X.M., Fang, X., and Stanton, B. (1999). Cigarette smoking among schoolboys in Beijing, China. *Journal of Adolescence, 22,* 621-625.

Liang, Z. (2001). The age of migration in China. *Population and Development Review, 27*(3), 499-524.

Lin, J. (1993). *Education in post-Mao China.* Westport, CT: Praeger.

Lin, J. (2003). Emergence of private schools in China: Context, characteristics, and implications. In E. Hannum and A. Park (Eds.), *Education and reform in China.* Cambridge, MA: Harvard University Press.

Lin, J.Y. (1988). The household responsibility system in China's agricultural reform: A theoretical and empirical study. *Economic Development and Cultural Change, 36,* S199-S204.

Liu, X., and Mills, A. (2002). Financing reforms of public health services in China: Lessons for other nations. *Social Science and Medicine, 54*(11), 1691-1698.

Lofstedt, J.-I. (1990). *Human resources in Chinese development: Needs and supply of competencies.* (IIEP Research Report No. 80.) Paris, France: International Institute for Educational Planning.

Luo, L., Wu, S.Z., Chen, X.Q., Li, M.X., and Pullum, T.W. (1995). Induced abortion among unmarried women in Sichuan Province, China. *Contraception, 51*(1), 59-63.

Maurer-Fazio, M. (2003). Education as a determinant of lay-off, re-employment, and earnings in China's transitional labor market. In E. Hannum and A. Park (Eds.), *Education and reform in China.* Cambridge, MA: Harvard University Press.

Ministry of Education. (1986). *People's Republic of China law on compulsory education.* Beijing, China: Ministry of Education.

Ministry of Education. (1999). *Action plan for revitalizing education for the 21st century.* Beijing, China: Ministry of Education.

Park, A., and Zhang, L.X. (2000). *Mother's education and child health in China's poor areas.* Ann Arbor, MI: University of Michigan Department of Economics.

Phillips, M.R., Li, X., and Zhang, Y. (2002a). Suicide rates in China, 1995-99. *Lancet, 359*, 835-840.

Phillips, M.R., Yang, G., Zhang, Y., Wang, L., Ji, H., and Zhou, M. (2002b). Risk factors for suicide in China: A national case-control psychological autopsy study. *Lancet, 360*, 1728-1736.

Popkin, B.M., and Udry, J.R. (1998). Adolescent obesity increases significantly in second and third generation U.S. immigrants: The National Longitudinal Study of Adolescent Health. *Journal of Nutrition, 128*(4), 701-706.

Poston, D.L., Jr., and Duan, C. (1999, March 25). *The floating population in Beijing, China: New evidence and insights from the 1997 census of Beijing's floating population.* Paper presented at the annual meeting of the Population Association of America, New York.

Powell, S.G. (1992). *Agricultural reform in China: From communes to commodity economy, 1978-1990.* New York: Manchester University Press.

Qi, Y., and Tang, W. (2000). Needs of Chinese youths for reproductive health. *China Population Today, 17*(4), 11-13.

Regulations on ending the use of child labor (in Chinese). (1991). Available: http://www.molss.gov.cn/correlate/gl9181.htm [accessed June 23, 2002].

Riley, N.E. (1994). Interwoven lives: Parents, marriage, and guanxi in China. *Journal of Marriage and the Family, 56*(4), 791-803.

Roberts, K. (2002). Female labor migrants to Shanghai: Temporary "floaters" or potential settlers? *International Migration Review, 36*(2), 492-520.

Rules and regulations related to the protection of children under 16 and the special employment protections of minors (in Chinese). (n.d.). Available: http://www.molss.gov.cn/column/ldbzfz/tgzc.htm [accessed June 15, 2002].

Short, S.E., and Zhai, F. (1998). Looking locally at China's one-child policy. *Studies in Family Planning, 29*(4), 373-387.

Simmons, R.S., Gu, B.C., Zhang, E.L., Xie, X.M., and Ward, S. (2000, March). *Initiating a quality of care transition in China.* Paper presented at the annual meeting of the Population Association of America, Los Angeles, CA.

Small survey of abortion shocked: Forty percent of abortions are among unmarried persons. (2001, March 12). In *Beijing Morning Post* (in Chinese). Available: http://www.cpirc.org.cn/new0312-1.htm [accessed June 10, 2002].

Some of Changsha's schools start a population and spiritual health curriculum. (2002, March 13). In *China Youth Post* (in Chinese). Available: http://www.cpirc.org.cn/new20010813-1.htm [accessed June 10, 2002].

Standing Committee of the Eighth National People's Congress (SCENPC). (1995). *Labor law of the People's Republic of China.* Available: http://ce.cei.gov.cn/frame_2.htm [accessed July 08, 2002].

State Council. (2000, October). Circular of the State Council on Policies and Measures Pertaining to the Development of the Western Region. Available: http://ce.cei.gov.cn/elaw/r_west.htm [accessed April 29, 2002].

Tien, H.Y. (Ed.). (1980). *Population theory in China.* New York: M.E. Sharpe.

Tsang, M.C. (2000). Education and national development in China since 1949: Oscillating policies and enduring dilemmas. Available: http://www.tc.columbia.edu/centers/coce/publications.htm [accessed May 20, 2002].

UNESCO. (1998). *World data on education.* Geneva, Switzerland: UNESCO; IBE Documentation and Information Unit.

UNESCO, Institute for Statistics. (2002). *World Education Indicators.* Geneva, Switzerland: UNESCO. Available: http://www.uis.unesco.org/en/stats/statistics/indicators/indic().htm [accessed May 20, 2004].

Unger, J.B., Yan, L., Chen, X., Jiang, H., Azen, S., Qian, G., Tan, S., Jie, G., Sun, P., Chunhong, L., Chou, C.-P., Zheng, H., and Johnson, C.A. (2001). Adolescent smoking in Wuhan, China: Baseline data from the Wuhan smoking prevention trial. *American Journal of Preventive Medicine, 21*(3), 162-169.

United Nations. (2002). *United Nations Common Database.* Marital status of population by sex, age group, urban, and rural (code 14880). Available: http://unstats.un.org [accessed March 12, 2005].

United Nations Millennium Indicators. (2002). *China country profiles.* Available: http://millenniumindicators.un.org/unsd/mi/mi.asp and http://millenniumindicators.un.org/unsd/mi/mi_results.asp?crID=156 [accessed August 17, 2002].

United Nations Theme Group on HIV/AIDS in China. (2002). *HIV/AIDS: China's titanic peril.* (Report prepared by UN Theme Group for the UN Country Team.) Available: http://www.casy.org/engdocs/China's%20Titanic%20Peril.pdf [accessed April 11, 2005].

U.S. Bureau of the Census. (2002). *International database. Age-specific fertility rates and selected derived measures, China 1990-2000.* Available: http://www.census.gov/ipc/www/idbnew.html [accessed August 5, 2004].

Wang, F. (2002). Rural migrants in Shanghai: Living under the shadow of socialism. *International Migration Review, 36*(2), 520-546.

Wang, F., and Yang, Q.H. (1996). Age at marriage and the first birth interval: The emerging change in sexual behavior among young couples in China. *Population and Development Review, 22*(2), 299-320.

Wang, Y., Popkin, B., and Zhai, F. (1998). The nutritional status and dietary pattern of Chinese adolescents, 1991 and 1993. *European Journal of Clinical Nutrition, 52*(12), 908-916.

World Bank. (1997). *Social crises in East Asia.* Available: http://www.worldbank.org/poverty/eacrisis/indicat/index.htm [accessed February 19, 2002].

World Health Organization. (2001). *Mental health: New understanding, new hope.* World Health Report 2001. Available: http://www.who.int/whr/2001 [accessed May 1, 2002].

Wu, J.Q., Gao, E. S., and Zhang, B. (2000). Analysis on menarche of Chinese reproductive-age women (in Chinese). *Reproduction and Contraception, 11*(1-2), 86-97.

Wu, W. (2002). Migrant housing in urban China: Choices and constraints. *Urban Affairs Review, 38*(1), 90-119.

Wu, Z.C., Gao, E.S., Ku, X.Y., Lu, S.Y., Wang, M.J., Hong, W.C., and Chow, L.P. (1992). Induced abortion among unmarried women in Shanghai, China. *International Family Planning Perspectives, 18*(2), 51-53, 65.

Xiao, B. (1996). Reproductive health in the People's Republic of China. *Advances in Contraception, 12*(4), 257-263.

Xie, Z. (2000). Population policy and the family planning programme. In X. Peng (Ed.), *The changing population of China* (pp. 51-63). Oxford, England: Blackwell.

Xu, X., and Whyte, M.K. (1990). Love matches and arranged marriages: A Chinese replication. *Journal of Marriage and the Family, 52*(3), 709-722.

Yang, G.H., Fan, L.X., Tan, J., Qi, G.M., Zhang, Y., Samet, J.M., Taylor, C.E., Becker, K., and Xu, J. (1999). Smoking in China: Findings of the 1996 National Prevalence Survey. *Journal of the American Medical Association, 282*(13), 1247-1253.

Yip, P.S., Callanan, C., and Yuen, H.P. (2000). Urban/rural and gender differentials in suicide rates: East and West. *Journal of Affective Disorders, 57*(1-3), 99-106.

Yu, H., Cao, S.H., and Lucas, H. (1997). Equity in the utilization of medical services: A survey of poor in rural China. *IDS Bulletin, 28*(1), 16-23.

Zeng, Y. (1989). Is the Chinese family planning program "Tightening Up?" *Population and Development Review, 15*(2), 333-337.

Zeng, Y. (2002). Marriage patterns in contemporary China. In X. Peng and Z. Guo (Eds.), *The changing population of China* (pp. 91-100). Oxford, England: Blackwell Publishers Ltd.

Zeng, Y., and Wu, D. (2000). Regional analysis of divorce in China since 1980. *Demography, 37*(2), 215-219.

Zhang, C. (2000). Evolution of Chinese population policies. In X. Yu and Z. Xie (Eds.), *China's population and development: Review and prospect* (pp. 1-26) (in Chinese). Beijing, China: People's Publishing House.

Zhang, J., and Zhao, Y. (2003). Returns to education in the 1990s. In E. Hannum and A. Park (Eds.), *Education and reform in China.* Cambridge, MA: Harvard University Press.

Zhang, W. (2003, July 11). *Pay special attention to adolescent sex and reproductive health and rights.* Speech by Zhang Weiqing, Minister of the State Population and Family Planning Commission, to mark World Population Day. Available: http://www.cpirc.org.cn/en/enews20030721.htm [accessed June 23, 2004].

Zhang, Z. (1997). Sex education vital for Chinese adolescents (in Chinese). *China Population Today, 14*(1), 13-14.

Zhao, W., and Zhou, X. (2003). Returns to education in China's transitional economy: Reassessment and reconceptualization. In E. Hannum and A. Park (Eds.), *Education and reform in China.* Cambridge, MA: Harvard University Press.

9

Growing Up in Pakistan: The Separate Experiences of Males and Females

Cynthia B. Lloyd and Monica J. Grant

This chapter examines gender differences in transitions to adulthood in Pakistan. The analysis is based on data from the 2001/2002 Adolescent and Youth Survey in Pakistan (AYSP), a nationally representative survey of young people ages 15 to 24. The survey covers key aspects of adolescents' lives, including the timing of several adult transitions and a detailed accounting of time use over the previous 24 hours. The results of the analysis confirm the fundamental importance of schooling to transitions to adulthood. Those without any schooling, which still include 15 percent of young men and 46 percent of young women, assume the work burdens of adults prematurely and are deprived of the opportunity for learning in an institutional setting outside the family. Those who do attend school eventually take up gender-stereotyped roles; however, they do so with some delay, allowing them to experience a longer transition to adulthood. For both males and females, there appears to be a large lag in years between the assumption of adult work roles, whether in the domestic setting or in the labor market, and the assumption of adult family roles as marked by the timing of first marriage. Recent further delays in the timing of first marriage for young women have been accompanied by a rise in the percentage working for pay during the later adolescent years; a similar trend is not apparent for young men. A multivariate analysis of some of the factors associated with variations in daily work hours among young people demonstrates the potential for change created by opportunities for higher levels of schooling, vocational training, and formal-sector jobs. The nature of current opportunities available to young people, however, appears to reinforce traditional gender-role stereotypes.

320

INTRODUCTION

In most parts of the developing world, adolescents and young adults face rapidly improving prospects for their future, as a result of economic development, modernization, and globalization. These changes have resulted in large increases in school participation and educational attainment among the young, which in turn have been associated with declines in child labor and delays in marriage and childbearing. Some of these changes are occurring as part of the natural process of development; others are occurring in response to the pressures and opportunities of the external environment that are affecting the economic, political, and cultural climates.

In Pakistan, however, primary school enrollment rates still fall far short of universal and have shown no improvement for males in the 1990s and only limited improvement for females from a relatively low base (Pakistan Federal Bureau of Statistics, 1998). As in much of the rest of the developing world, the age at marriage in Pakistan is rising for both males and females (Mensch, Singh, and Casterline, 2005, Chapter 5). Nonetheless, many adolescents, particularly females, continue to marry before the age of 18 despite the fact that the legal age for both sexes in Pakistan is 18. Furthermore, work among children under age 15 remains relatively common.

This chapter describes the transitions to adulthood of females and males in Pakistan, highlighting the implications of formal schooling for the timing and content of these transitions. Our analysis is based on the 2001/ 2002 AYSP, a nationally representative survey of young people ages 15 to 24 covering the key aspects of adolescents' lives, including the timing of specific transitions and a detailed accounting of time use (Sathar et al., 2003). The chapter begins with a brief review of pertinent literature and an introduction to the data. The results of the analysis are presented in two main sections. The first characterizes transitions to adulthood in terms of timing, sequencing, and duration. Here, we concentrate on three relatively easy-to-measure transitions in particular: the transition to paid work, the transition to marriage, and the departure from the natal home. The second section explores the transition to work in more depth with time use data on all types of work, including unpaid economic work and noneconomic household work. Because many young people in Pakistan, particularly females, assume adult work roles without entering the paid labor force, the transition to work is difficult to capture using conventional labor force data. A particular interest of this chapter is to map changes in social and economic mobility by age and to define the role of formal schooling in providing opportunities for mobility both directly and indirectly.

LITERATURE REVIEW

The developmental phase between childhood and adulthood is often labeled adolescence. This lifecycle phase, common to all societies, involves the acquisition of human and social capital, the consolidation of personal identity, and the emergence of a sense of personal efficacy (Mensch, Bruce, and Greene, 1998). It is a phase of life during which young people have many first-time experiences, including travel or residence away from home, paid work, sex, military service, unemployment, engagement, marriage, and birth. It is also a time during which young people emerge from dependency on their parents and other family members and acquire a growing scope for agency in their lives. Adolescence is now recognized in the International Convention on the Rights of the Child (ICRC) as a phase of "evolving capacities" requiring a balance of societal and familial protections, respect for rights, and opportunity for voice (United Nations General Assembly, 1989).

Although the ICRC defines legal adulthood as occurring by age 18, the developmental aspects of this phase of the lifecycle may continue past the teens and into the early to mid-20s. The social roles associated with adulthood include worker, spouse, parent, and household manager. By a certain age, society recognizes everyone as an adult, whether or not they have acquired any of these roles. If one or more of these roles is assumed during the teens, however, this does not necessarily mean that adulthood has been fully achieved if certain developmental tasks are not yet complete or if young people themselves have not had an opportunity to play a role in the decision-making process. Indeed, this shift in the locus of decision making over the course of the transition challenges current approaches to household allocation models, which tend to assume that married people regardless of age are decision makers, while unmarried young people who do not head their own households are not.

For the first part of the chapter, we build on an earlier U.S. literature that traces key transitions during adolescence and young adulthood, including exit from school, entrance into the labor market, and first marriage, as well as various indicators of mobility. Winsborough (1978) focused on trends over 30 years in the timing and duration of four transitions for young American males: exit from school, entrance into the labor market, entrance into the military, and first marriage. For each transition, he measured the age at which 25 percent, 50 percent, and 75 percent of each age cohort had made each transition, and he measured the duration of the transition as the mean years elapsed between the age at which the first 25 percent completed the transition and the age at which the first 75 percent completed the transition. He found a trend toward a later start to the transition, but at the same time a shortening of the duration of the transition both within and across categories.[1]

Rindfuss (1991), using both cross-sectional and longitudinal data, explored transitions during the "young adult years" from ages 18 to 30 for males and females. He observed that this phase of life is "dense" in demographic events, but with the possibility of much variability according to background characteristics such as sex, ethnicity, and socioeconomic status. Such demographic events could include, in addition to those analyzed by Winsborough, residential mobility and migration, unemployment, first sex, pregnancy, abortion, childbirth, and marital disruption. Furthermore, Rindfuss pointed out that "the density of events during the young adult years would be even more dramatic during periods of rapid social change because young adults typically are the engines of social change" (p. 499). Rindfuss provided a valuable perspective for thinking about transitions to adulthood in developing countries, where today's young people are often the first generation to go to school or progress far in school and the first to have opportunities for migration and formal-sector jobs. Rapid globalization requires rapid adaptation. Young people, if given the opportunity, are likely to be the first to respond by staying longer in school, migrating in search of jobs, finding better pay, and delaying marriage and childbearing. Rapid economic and social change can also challenge existing gender roles, including traditional pathways to adulthood.

There has been little opportunity to study transitions to adulthood in developing countries given the lack of longitudinal data on adolescents or retrospective life event calendars covering the adolescent years. Because of the rapidity of change across cohorts in the experience of the transition, it is inappropriate to use current age comparisons to simulate the transition (as done, e.g., by Filgueira, Filgueira, and Fuentes, 2001) or to rely on retrospective data from samples that are restricted to married couples.[2] We are aware of a series of six surveys in Asia focusing on the transitions to adulthood among all young people ages 15 to 24, and three of these—for Hong Kong (1986), Thailand (1994), and Nepal (2000)—have included questions on the timing of school exit, entry to work, and marriage and childbearing (Xenos, 1999). To our knowledge, however, a full treatment using all the key elements of the transitions to adulthood has not yet been published.

---

[1] For particular historical reasons in the United States, these results could be explained by changes in the timing of military service.

[2] For example, a series of marriage surveys conducted in four Asian countries in the late 1970s included retrospective data on the timing of key events in the transition; however, because the respondents were restricted to married women and their husbands, the samples of younger women are highly selective. These data can only provide baseline information on transitions to adulthood occurring during the 1950s and 1960s (e.g., Fricke, Syed, and Smith, 1986, for Pakistan).

We highlight two recent studies that have taken advantage of specially designed longitudinal data (Florez and Hogan, 1990, for Colombia) and of retrospective data on the timing of events (Echarri Cánovas and Perez Amador, 2001, for Mexico) in order to provide a context for the current study. Using longitudinal rural and urban surveys in Colombia to capture changes in the lives of young females ages 12 to 25 over the course of the demographic transition, Florez and Hogan describe the average number of person-years in each of five domains—school, wage work, plot work, living with husband, and living with children—and describe the diversity of combinations of activities. A key finding of their study was the increase in the time spent during these years in school or paid work relative to the past.

Echarri Cánovas and Perez Amador capture transitions for a group of young people ages 12 to 29 in Mexico using a national youth survey fielded in 2000 that covered the timing retrospectively of school leaving, first work, home leaving, first marriage or consensual union, and entry into parenthood. They found that work is likely to be the first transition, often predating school exit. Some 40 percent of both males and females took their first job before age 15. As a result, they conclude that job entry is often imposed by family circumstances at a premature age rather than freely chosen and, therefore, cannot necessarily be considered a marker of adult status.

In settings where schooling is not yet universal and where work is largely informal, lifecycle transitions may lack the precision associated with publicly recognized social statuses such as student and employee, making identification and measurement much more difficult. In such circumstances, much of the lives of young people remains invisible and unmeasured, particularly transitions to adulthood that involve the assumption of new roles, changes in the location of domestic and unpaid work, and changes in the time associated with work. Durrant (2000) provides a stark example of this problem using data from the 1991 living standards measurement survey in Pakistan, which show that 45 percent of females ages 10 to 19 are apparently doing "nothing." In such settings, time use data can provide an additional perspective on the association between age and all types of work.

In light of these circumstances, in the second part of the chapter we build on a literature exploring time use in the context of development—not just time spent in economic activity, but also time spent on noneconomic household work. While there is a rich literature on the determinants of child labor and schooling, little attention in the adolescent literature is devoted to other types of work, including unpaid work and domestic chores, which are less well measured in most surveys (for notable exceptions see Levison and Moe, 1998; Levison, Moe, and Knaul, 2001). Larson and Verma (1999) reviewed data on the time use of school-aged children (5 to 18) from around the world and categorized time use patterns according to country context into (1) nonindustrial unschooled, (2) transitional, and (3) postindustrial schooled populations. They found that in nonindustrial populations where most children and adolescents do not attend school, time in housework is considerable, starting at an early age, with girls by early adolescence often spending as much time on housework as adult females. By contrast, in postindustrial schooled populations, household work rarely exceeds one hour per day. Furthermore, their review of the literature suggests that girls spend significantly more time than boys on noneconomic domestic work, with their tasks more likely to be confined within the home. Among the unschooled, work for pay is particularly common for boys from poor families.

An increasing number of studies on household resource allocation, work participation, and agricultural production in developing countries include time use data (e.g., Brown and Haddad, 1995, with data for seven countries), but it is rare to find attention devoted to the changing patterns of time use by age and gender during the transition to adulthood. While the literature suggests that a gender disparity in time use emerges early in childhood (Larson and Verma, 1999; Mensch, Bruce, and Greene, 1998), rising enrollment rates and later ages of school leaving are likely to delay the social enforcement of these gender differences. A much more egalitarian pattern of time use is found among males and females who remain in school than among those who have left school (Ajayi et al., 1997; Arends-Kuenning and Amin, 2004). As a result, it is likely that the circumstances of current transitions to adulthood in terms of time allocation are shifting rapidly in developing countries as the proportion of time allocated to school attendance and school work increases—a trend that aggregated data are unlikely to reveal. For example, none of the data summarized by Larson and Verma (1999) are broken down by enrollment status.

DATA

The nationally representative AYSP was conducted by the Population Council and fielded from October 2001 to March 2002. The sample, drawn in collaboration with Pakistan's Federal Bureau of Statistics, is based on the sampling frame from the 1998 census. Using a two-step stratified sampling procedure, 254 primary sampling units (PSUs) were selected, with urban PSUs being overrepresented. Within each PSU, households were chosen at random after a preliminary listing. In each chosen household, a parent or knowledgeable informant was interviewed, as were all resident young people in the eligible age ranges of 15 to 24 years. A total of 6,812 household questionnaires were completed and 8,069 young people were interviewed. The questionnaires for young people included information on family background and personal characteristics, life event histories and time use profiles, detailed data on each transition, and information on decision making, mobility, and gender role attitudes. Data on community infrastructure and facilities were also collected.

The life event calendar asked each respondent to trace his or her life story, locating key changes in status related to school enrollment, grade, work status, residential location, living arrangements, marriage and engagement, and childbearing in relationship to each other and in calendar time going back to the age of five. The component of the life event calendar focusing on work experience was intended to ascertain the timing of both unpaid and paid work; however, given that many young people engage in multiple activities, some paid and others unpaid, we found that only paid work was recorded on the calendar. Thus, we use these data to identify the first entry into paid work and turn to the time use profile for a more complete picture of work roles over the course of the transition.

The time use component of the questionnaire collected data on the activities of each respondent in the previous 24 hours or, if currently enrolled, the most recent school day. Data were recorded in hourly increments from 6 am to midnight. Multiple activities could be recorded in each hour and, when that occurred, time was divided evenly by the number of activities reported. The grid is organized into 19 discrete activities grouped into categories including personal activities, school-related activities, domestic duties, work (both paid and unpaid), leisure/spare time activities, religious activities, in transit, and other activities.

Despite repeated attempts to interview all eligible adolescents while the field teams were on location, not all eligible young people were successfully interviewed. In the overwhelming majority of cases, the reason for the nonresponse was that adolescents could not be found in the home or nearby. Sixty-six percent of eligible males and 83 percent of females were successfully interviewed. Using data collected from knowledgeable informants in the households, we can compare interviewed and noninterviewed adolescents according to a few characteristics, including age, educational attainment, marital status, and household economic status (see Table 9-1). For both young men and young women, those who were not interviewed were slightly older than those who were. Other significant differences are apparent for males but not females. Males who were not interviewed have on average about a year less schooling than males who were interviewed, indicating that the survey underrepresented the less educated. On the other hand, a slightly higher proportion of young males who were not interviewed came from the richest quartile.[3]

Because our analysis focuses on the relationship between school enrollment and subsequent life-course transitions, we briefly examine patterns of

---

[3]Enrollment rates calculated from the household survey appear to be lower than rates calculated from the adolescent survey, even when comparisons are confined to those young people subsequently interviewed. This suggests that "knowledgeable" informants are not always as well informed as we assume.

TABLE 9-1 Characteristics of Interviewed and Noninterviewed Young People

	Males		Females	
Characteristic	Not Interviewed	Interviewed	Not Interviewed	Interviewed
Mean age	19.3^b	18.9^b	19.2^a	19.1^a
Ever married (%)	17.3	14.3	40.6	40.2
Mean grades completed	5.16^b	6.22^b	3.49	3.46
Poorest quartile (%)	20.4	21.4	19.1	23.0
Richest quartile (%)	23.3^a	29.3^a	23.4	26.1
N	1,697	3,328	1,006	4,741

^{a}Differences between Not Interviewed and Interviewed are statistically significant at 5% level.
^{b}Differences between Not Interviewed and Interviewed are statistically significant at 1% level.
SOURCE: 2001/2002 Adolescent and Youth Survey in Pakistan.

enrollment and grade attainment within our sample as reported by the young people (see Table 9-2). These estimates are weighted to adjust for the overrepresentation of urban PSUs in the sample. Looking at the youngest cohort first (ages 15 to 19), we see that a slight majority of females have ever attended school (54 percent), while the overwhelming majority of boys have attended (85 percent). There has been some improvement in enrollment relative to the older cohort (ages 20 to 24)—particularly for females, whose enrollment rates have risen over the past five years by 7 percentage points. Because of dropout during the primary years, these percentages are not maintained through primary completion. For the younger cohort, 40 percent of females and 70 percent of males completed primary school. There has been a slight improvement for females and virtually no change for males in the past five years.

TABLE 9-2 School Enrollment and Primary School Attainment by Age and Gender

Age and Gender	Percentage Ever Enrolled	Percentage Completing Primary
Ages 15 to 19		
Male	85	70
Female	54	40
Ages 20 to 24		
Male	82	69
Female	47	36

SOURCE: 2001/2002 Adolescent and Youth Survey in Pakistan.

THE TIMING, SEQUENCING, AND DURATION OF
TRANSITIONS TO ADULTHOOD

To characterize gender differences at various stages of the transition to adulthood, we divide adolescence and young adulthood into three phases: (1) early, ages 10 to 14; (2) middle, ages 15 to 19; and (3) late, ages 20 to 24. Although transitions may continue past the age of 24, we are constrained by our data to focus on persons under age 25. During the early phase of the transition, most young people in Pakistan experience puberty (Sathar et al., 2003), and many of those who start school complete their primary education. Work under the age of 15 is defined as child labor by various international labor conventions as well as by the International Convention on the Rights of the Child, and many countries, including Pakistan, have agreed to take steps to eliminate it. Thus economic work during this phase of life is discouraged and seen as jeopardizing schooling. During the middle phase of the transition, which encompasses the last phase of childhood as defined by the ICRC (when certain kinds of hazardous work continue to be discouraged and marriage is not yet legal in Pakistan) and the first few years after assuming the legal age of majority, young people begin to take up adult roles, including paid work, marriage, and departure from home. The last phase of the transition covered by our data captures further movement into the workplace and out of the natal home, steps usually linked to marriage for young women and often linked to work for young men.[4]

Figures 9-1 and 9-2 compare, for females and males respectively, the different transitions experienced by those who have never attended school and those who have ever attended. They are based on a life table analysis and depict transitions to first paid work, marriage, and leaving home starting at age 6 and ending at age 25. We are unable to look at timing of first work more broadly, including unpaid work, because little unpaid work was reported in the life event calendar despite efforts to define work broadly. Each figure is derived from the data collected in the life event calendar and depicted according to the three phases described above.[5]

Looking first at Figure 9-1, almost no females who ever entered school marry or leave home before age 15, and no more than 10 percent start paid work during this first phase of the transition. By contrast, slightly less than 30 percent of females who have never been to school have entered paid work before reaching age 15 and slightly less than 20 percent have married

---

[4]We do not include the timing of first birth in our analysis because it is so closely linked with first marriage; instead we consider the timing of first marriage as representing the transition to parenthood.

[5]All survey respondents contribute information to each year within the early phase of the transition. Information for the middle and late phases of the transition is more selective in that only those who have reached a particular age can contribute information to the life table construction for that age.

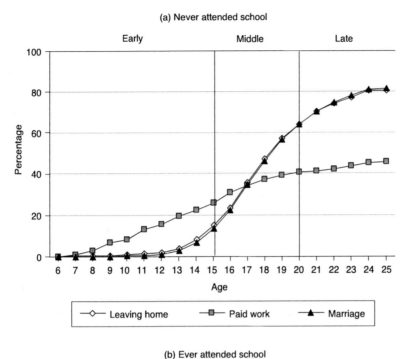

(a) Never attended school

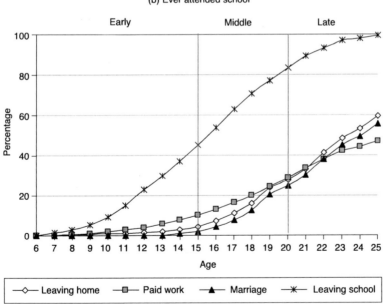

(b) Ever attended school

FIGURE 9-1 Comparison of transitions to adulthood: Females.
SOURCE: 2001/2002 Adolescent and Youth Survey in Pakistan.

and left home. For females who never attended school (Figure 9-1a), the transition to paid work flattens out during the middle phase of the transition and rises slowly to over 40 percent by age 25. The percentage of females who have ever worked for pay rises sharply among those who have ever attended school, ending up by age 25 at levels similar to those achieved by young females who never attended school. The transition to marriage, which coincides precisely with departure from home among females who never attended school, accelerates rapidly during the middle phase of the transition, and by age 20 more than 60 percent are married. By contrast, the percentage married among those who have ever been to school (Figure 9-1b) is only slightly above 20 percent by the age of 20, with a few leaving home before marriage. Also notable is a huge gap—roughly 8 to 9 years—between the age of school exit and the age of marriage for those who ever attended school.

Figure 9-2 depicts the same comparisons for young males. Among the minority of males who never attended school, 60 percent have entered paid work before age 15, with 30 percent having done so by age 10 (Figure 9-2a). Few males leave home during this first phase of the lifecycle transition. Marriage rates begin to rise during the middle phase of the transition, but reach only a little under 60 percent by our final point of observation. By contrast, entry into first paid work appears to be closely tied to school leaving among those who ever attended school, thus holding the prevalence of first work to about 25 percent by age 15, a rate that is still very high by international standards (Figure 9-2b). Few males leave home regardless of whether or not they ever attend school, and marriage among male school-goers is delayed much longer relative to those who never attended. About 35 percent of all males in our sample have married by age 25. Thus, for the majority there is a large gap of eight to ten years between entry into work and marriage.

We also explore the possibility of changes in the timing of the early and middle phases of the transitions within the past five years by comparing the experience of our two age cohorts (15 to 19 and 20 to 24). Because we found no evidence of changes in any of these transitions for young males, we present only the results for young females. Figures 9-3a and 9-3b show changes in the transition to first paid work and school exit (for those who ever attended school). For both categories of young females, we found evidence that the percent of females taking up paid work during the middle phase of the transition is greater among the younger cohort, and in both cases these changes are statistically significant.[6] Among those who ever

---

[6]Because the incidence of first work varies over time, the assumptions of a proportional hazards model are violated. When this time variance is controlled for in a Poisson regression, there is a significant difference between the two female age cohorts, such that the incidence rate ratio of the older to the younger cohort is 0.839 (P = 0.030) for those who never attended school and 0.767 (P = 0.004) for those who ever attended school.

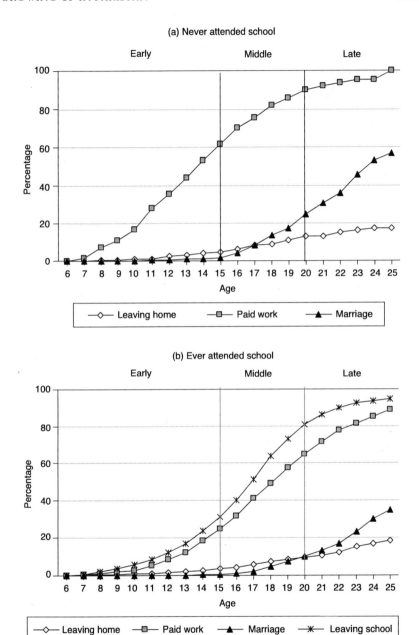

FIGURE 9-2 Comparison of transitions to adulthood: Males.
SOURCE: 2001/2002 Adolescent and Youth Survey in Pakistan.

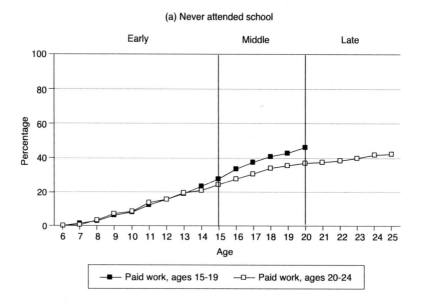

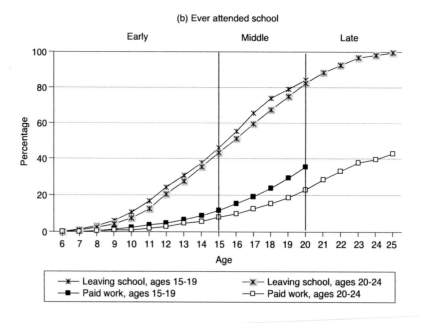

FIGURE 9-3 Changes in school and work transitions: Females.
SOURCE: 2001/2002 Adolescent and Youth Survey in Pakistan.

attended school, the rising prevalence of work is apparent even at earlier ages. We also see a hint of slightly higher dropout rates among females who have some schooling, perhaps in response to changes in job opportunities for those with some education.

Recent changes in transitions to marriage and home leaving during the early and middle phases of the transition are depicted for females in Figures 9-4a and 9-b. Whether or not females have ever attended school, there appears to be a tendency toward later ages of marriage and home leaving during the middle phase of the transition among the younger cohort. While leaving home and marrying for females tend to track closely together, we can see the beginnings of a separation between the two events in the younger cohort of females who have attended school, with some leaving home before getting married. This may be linked to the rapid rise in entry into paid work during this phase of the transition among the same cohort.

In Table 9-3, we present data on the first transition and indicate how the distribution of first transitions varies by phase of the transition and school enrollment status. We include "no transition" as a category in order to take note of those who have not yet embarked on any transition.[7] We include single transitions and joint[8] transitions when they are statistically important. These transitions include first paid work, first departure from home, first marriage, first paid work/marriage, first paid work/departure from home, and first paid work/school exit. For those never attending school, the majority of girls (68 percent) had not experienced any transition before age 15, while 50 percent of males had experienced a first transition into paid work. In the middle phase of the transition, three quarters of males have experienced a first transition to paid work. Females' experience during this phase of the lifecycle is more heterogeneous, divided roughly into thirds among those experiencing their first transition as paid work, the joint transition of leaving home and getting married, and no transition. Few marry without leaving home or leave home without simultaneously marrying. By age 25, 9 percent of males and 16 percent of females have experienced no transition.

If we look separately at those who ever attended school, it is not surprising that at any age school leaving is likely to be the most common first transition. Marriage and leaving home occur rarely while one is still a student. At each age, many more young females than males have dropped

---

[7]For transitions before the age of 15, data from the life event calendar for all respondents were included in the calculation. For transitions before age 20, life event calendar data were included for the 20 to 24 age group, all of whom had reached the age of 20. Finally, for transitions before age 25, only the experience of those aged 24 could be included.

[8]A joint transition occurs when two events are reported within the same time interval.

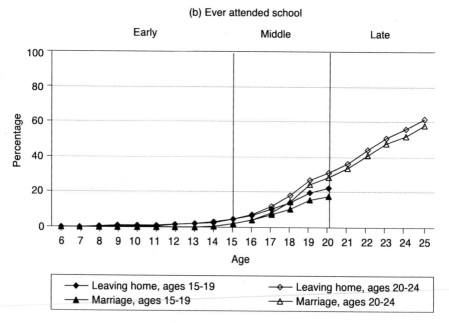

FIGURE 9-4 Changes in marriage and leaving home transitions: Females.
SOURCE: 2001/2002 Adolescent and Youth Survey in Pakistan.

TABLE 9-3 Distribution of First Transitions by the End of Selected Ages

Distributions	Age 14 Male	Age 14 Female	Age 19 Male	Age 19 Female	Age 24 Male	Age 24 Female
Those Who Never Attended School						
Paid work	50.4	22.1	75.4	27.9	85.0	20.0
Leaving parental home	1.7	1.8	1.5	2.9	0.0	3.3
Marriage	0.7	0.6	1.4	2.5	0.0	3.0
Paid work and leaving home	0.8	0.0	2.4	0.1	6.2	0.0
Leaving home and marriage	0.0	7.0	0.0	37.5	0.0	56.7
No transition	46.5	68.0	18.1	27.4	8.7	15.8
Other	0.0	0.5	1.2	1.7	0.0	1.3
N	535[a]	2,352[a]	218[b]	1,093[b]	32[c]	164[c]
Those Who Ever Attended School						
School leaving	18.0	38.4	41.3	69.0	46.7	77.0
Paid work	9.3	4.0	15.8	7.3	24.3	11.2
Leaving parental home	2.6	2.2	3.6	3.8	2.9	2.4
Marriage	0.3	0.0	1.6	0.2	1.3	0.4
School leaving and paid work	8.5	2.1	22.7	2.5	23.8	4.7
No transition	61.0	52.9	13.1	14.9	0.0	0.0
Other	0.3	0.3	2.0	2.3	1.0	4.2
N	2,724[a]	2,451[a]	1,003[b]	951[b]	133[c]	146[c]

[a]All respondents.
[b]Respondents ages 20-24.
[c]Respondents age 24.
SOURCE: 2001/2002 Adolescent and Youth Survey in Pakistan.

out of school. By age 20, however, 16 percent of young males and 7 percent of young females had entered paid work before leaving school and therefore pursued both activities jointly for a time. By age 25, 24 percent of young males and 11 percent of young females who had ever been to school started paid work before leaving school. Not surprisingly, many more males than females leave school and take up work simultaneously.

The rough duration of each of these three transitions can be measured as the difference between the age at which 25 percent have made the transition and the age at which 75 percent have made the transition (Winsborough, 1978). When transitions start late or at very different times and/or last a long time, a longer window of observation is required to capture each transition. Table 9-4, which shows the mean age at which each quartile of the transition is reached, demonstrates the difficulty of capturing transitions fully with a survey dedicated to only a decade of life between ages 15 and 24. For those who never attended school, we are able to observe the full transition to paid work for young males and to marriage and leaving home for young females; each transition lasts about six years. However, although a majority of males eventually marry, the completion of the marriage transition does not occur until well after age 25. Furthermore, not even a quarter of males have left home by age 24, given the tradition of bringing a new wife into the natal home. Additionally, while all females eventually take up noneconomic household work roles, only a minority ever take up paid work roles at any age. For females, our approach is unable to capture the timing of the work transition.

For those who ever attended school, only the school exit transition can be seen through to completion for both young males and females within our window of observation. The transition to paid work for males is also completed within this time frame, starting and ending later than the same transition among those who never attended school. School exit starts at a younger age for females than males: the first 25 percent of females have exited from school by age 11 as opposed to age 13 for males. On the other hand, the school exit process is slightly more prolonged for females: 6.4 years versus 5 years for males. Given the much later ages of marriage for young females who attend school, we cannot observe the full transition to marriage. The first 50 percent of young educated females have married by the age of 23; thus the transition to marriage is not complete by age 24.

An exploration of these life tables yields the following preliminary conclusions about the three adult transitions explored in this section. First, the lives of young males and females remain very different: For most young males, the first measured transition is to paid work; for most young females, it is to marriage and leaving home. As we will see below, however, this conclusion is misleading given the domestic work burden most females typically assume at a young age. Furthermore, some transitions occur prema-

TABLE 9-4 Age by Which 25 Percent, 50 Percent, and 75 Percent of Cohort Has Completed Each Transition and Duration of Transition

| | Mean Age at Life Table Quartile | | | | | | Duration | |
| | 25% | | 50% | | 75% | | Mean Years | |
Transition	Male	Female	Male	Female	Male	Female	Male	Female
Never Attended School								
First paid work	9.8	13.7	12.7	*	16.0	*	6.2	*
Leaving home	*	15.1	*	17.3	*	21.3	*	6.2
First marriage	19.0	15.2	22.6	17.4	*	21.2	*	6.0
Ever Attended School								
Leaving school	13.2	11.3	16.0	14.6	18.2	17.7	5.0	6.4
First paid work	14.0	18.2	17.1	*	20.6	*	6.6	*
Leaving home	*	18.3	*	22.3	*	*	*	*
First marriage	22.3	19.1	*	23.1	*	*	*	*

NOTE: * = Quartile was not reached by age 24.
SOURCE: 2001/2002 Adolescent and Youth Survey in Pakistan.

turely: the transition to paid work for those who never attended school—particularly for males—and transitions to marriage for females. Second, there are big lags in transitions: Young males take up paid work many years before they marry; young females who attend school marry many years after leaving school. As a result of such prolonged transitions, it is not clear when a young person becomes an "adult." Third, the transitions for those who attend school are very different from transitions for those who never attend. Those who attend school are allowed to complete childhood without taking up the burden of work (in the case of females and males) or marriage (in the case of females). Thus, subsequent transitions are already scripted at the time parents decide about school enrollment at the age of five or six—well before the adolescent years. Fourth, recent changes in the transition are notable for females. In particular, young females (ages 15 to 19) are more likely to enter paid work during the middle phase of the transition than were their older counterparts (20 to 24) during the same phase of the transition, whether or not they have ever attended school; they are also more likely to delay marriage whether or not they have been to school.

CHANGES IN TIME USE OVER THE TRANSITION TO ADULTHOOD

In a country such as Pakistan, where much work is informal or unpaid and domestic burdens are heavy, the transition to adult work roles is blurred. In this part of the analysis, we focus on changes over the transition in time spent in noneconomic household work (i.e., domestic duties) and time spent on economic activities or labor market work—whether paid work, unpaid work, or in some form of apprenticeship—drawing on the 24-hour recall data from the time use profile. Noneconomic household work includes domestic chores inside and outside the house, and the care of children, the sick, and the elderly. While little information on unpaid economic work was reported in the work section of the questionnaire or on the life event calendar, we picked up considerably more reporting of unpaid economic work in the time use profile, suggesting that it is often useful to use multiple research methodologies when collecting data on aspects of behavior that are known to be hard to measure. Tables 9-5 through 9-7 present descriptive data on time devoted to all types of work, including noneconomic household work broken down by type of work, age group,[9] sex, and current enrollment status. Table 9-5 shows the percentage engaged in each type of work, Table 9-6 shows the distribution of work time, and

---

[9]Age groups are 15 to 16, 17 to 19, 20 to 21, and 22 to 24. Because there is considerable age heaping at age 18, some who report themselves as 18 may in fact be younger or older. Because 18 is the legal age of majority in Pakistan, there may be some incentive for those who have assumed adult roles to report themselves as 18.

Table 9-7 shows the mean hours worked in each activity (including those who contribute no time to the activity).

Participation in some work is nearly universal for young females at all ages, with proportions ranging from 94 percent among 15- to 16-year-olds to 99 percent of 22- to 24-year-olds (Table 9-5). Participation in some kind of work rises with age primarily because of a rise in the percentage participating in paid work. Among young males the proportion reporting some type of work rises from 69 percent at ages 15 to 16 to 83 percent at ages 22 to 24. Fewer males in their 20s report participation in outside noneconomic household work. Males who stay in school into their 20s report much less participation in any type of work. The same is not true for the few young females who remain in school at later ages; their work participation increases with age.

The distribution of work by type does not change by age for females, whether or not they remain in school (Table 9-6). The same is not true for males. The main difference in the distribution of work between young females who stay in school and those who do not is that those currently enrolled spend nearly all their work time on noneconomic household work inside the house (91 percent), while young females out of school spend slightly more time on other activities (21 percent on other activities versus 79 percent on noneconomic household work inside the house). By contrast, the time allocation of young males shifts over the transition, with more time on paid work and less time on domestic chores and unpaid economic activities as they age through the transition. For young males, therefore, part of becoming an adult involves a shift from unpaid economic work for family to outside paid work. There appears to be no such transition for young females, the overwhelming majority of whom start working on non-economic household work as children and remain in that status as adults.

At all ages, young women's total work time exceeds men's, measured as mean hours worked per day (Table 9-7). For both sexes, mean hours worked per day rise with age, from 4.1 to 6.6 hours for young males and from 6.7 to 8.6 hours for young females starting with the 15 to 16 age group and ending with the 22 to 24 age group.[10] Thus at the end of the transition,

---

[10]In comparing the AYSP data on daily time spent in noneconomic household work for young females (15 to 19) with time use data on housework collected from female household members in the 1991 Pakistan Integrated Household Survey (PIHS), we find significantly greater time reported on domestic chores in the AYSP. Mean weekly hours for those reporting housework was 27 from the PIHS and 44 in the AYSP (by converting daily hours to weekly hours). We suspect this was because of the different reporting techniques; in the PIHS, females were asked how many times in the past seven days they performed 12 different household activities and, for each, how much time they spent; in the AYSP, respondents were asked to recall their activities in the previous 24-hour period. While in the AYSP all adolescents responded directly about their own activities, in the PIHS only 53 percent responded about their own activities, with slightly more time reported by self-reporters than when others responded on the adolescent girl's behalf (Durrant, 2003, personal communication; Sathar et al., 2003).

TABLE 9-5 Percentage Reporting Time on Each Category of Work Activity Recorded in Time Use Profile

Sex and School Status	Age	Noneconomic Household Work		Unpaid Work and Learning a Skill	Paid Work		Total Work	N
		Inside	Outside		Inside	Outside		
Male: Not in school	15-16	15.1	36.1	17.2	2.5	47.0	87.6	390
	17-19	15.4	32.2	15.1	2.6	49.4	85.1	899
	20-21	13.4	25.6	14.3	3.3	53.8	84.3	507
	22-24	17.2	24.0	10.3	3.3	59.0	86.3	643
	Total	15.4	29.4	14.1	2.9	52.4	85.7	2,439
Female: Not in school	15-16	97.4	19.7	9.9	9.8	10.1	98.9	946
	17-19	96.6	17.9	7.5	11.7	9.4	98.4	1,297
	20-21	98.4	16.2	6.6	11.2	7.3	99.1	865
	22-24	97.6	15.7	7.2	6.9	12.4	99.0	1,045
	Total	97.4	17.4	7.8	9.9	9.9	98.8	4,153
Male: In school	15-16	18.8	26.2	6.4	1.1	5.6	49.9	420
	17-19	12.9	22.9	7.2	0.3	6.0	43.5	294
	20-21	18.7	16.6	7.4	0.0	17.5	59.0	56
	22-24	6.6	3.0	2.3	2.2	12.6	25.7	50
	Total	16.1	23.3	6.5	0.8	6.9	47.1	820
Female: In school	15-16	74.2	3.1	2.9	0.9	0.0	75.5	276
	17-19	77.8	3.9	1.5	3.8	0.7	79.7	183
	20-21	64.3	13.5	0.0	3.5	4.8	67.2	36
	22-24	90.8	0.0	9.4	2.1	0.0	90.8	16
	Total	75.2	4.0	2.4	2.2	0.6	76.8	511

Male:							
All							
15-16	16.9	31.3	11.9	1.8	26.9	69.3	810
17-19	14.9	30.1	13.4	2.1	40.0	76.1	1,193
20-21	13.9	24.8	13.7	3.0	50.4	82.0	563
22-24	16.6	22.9	9.9	3.3	56.5	83.0	693
Total	15.6	28.0	12.3	2.4	41.9	76.8	3,259
Female:							
All							
15-16	92.6	16.2	8.4	7.9	8.0	94.1	1,222
17-19	94.5	16.4	6.9	10.8	8.4	96.4	1,480
20-21	97.3	16.1	6.3	11.0	7.2	98.0	901
22-24	97.5	15.6	7.2	6.8	12.3	98.9	1,061
Total	95.3	16.1	7.2	9.2	9.0	96.7	4,664

SOURCE: 2001/2002 Adolescent and Youth Survey in Pakistan.

TABLE 9-6 Percentage Distribution of Work Time by Type Recorded in Time Use Profile

Sex and School Status	Age	Noneconomic Household Work		Unpaid Work and Learning a Skill	Paid Work		N
		Inside	Outside		Inside	Outside	
Male: Not in school	15-16	5	17	17	3	57	390
	17-19	5	16	14	3	62	899
	20-21	4	12	13	5	66	507
	22-24	6	11	8	4	71	643
	Total	5	14	13	4	64	2,439
Female: Not in school	15-16	76	6	4	5	9	946
	17-19	78	6	3	6	7	1,297
	20-21	81	5	3	5	5	865
	22-24	80	5	2	3	10	1,045
	Total	79	5	3	5	8	4,153
Male: In school	15-16	24	44	15	2	15	420
	17-19	19	34	20	2	25	294
	20-21	24	16	15	0	45	56
	22-24	5	4	4	11	75	50
	Total	22	36	16	2	24	820
Female: In school	15-16	94	2	3	1	0	276
	17-19	91	3	1	3	2	183
	20-21	77	7	v0	5	12	36
	22-24	88	0	9	3	0	16
	Total	91	3	2	2	1	511

Male:						
All	15-16	8	21	17	3	51	810
	17-19	6	17	14	3	60	1,193
	20-21	5	12	14	4	65	563
	22-24	6	11	8	4	71	693
	Total	6	15	13	4	62	3,259
Female:						
All	15-16	77	6	4	5	8	1,222
	17-19	78	5	3	6	7	1,480
	20-21	81	5	3	5	5	901
	22-24	81	5	2	3	9	1,061
	Total	79	5	3	5	8	4,664

SOURCE: 2001/2002 Adolescent and Youth Survey in Pakistan.

TABLE 9-7 Mean Hours Worked per Day on Each Category of Work Activity Recorded in Time Use Profile

Sex and School Status	Age	Noneconomic Household Work		Unpaid Work and Learning a Skill	Paid Work		Total Work	N
		Inside	Outside		Inside	Outside		
Male: Not in school	15-16	0.4	1.2	1.2	0.2	3.9	6.9	390
	17-19	0.4	1.0	0.9	0.2	4.1	6.6	899
	20-21	0.3	0.8	0.9	0.3	4.2	6.4	507
	22-24	0.4	0.8	0.6	0.3	4.9	6.9	643
	Total	0.4	0.9	0.9	0.2	4.3	6.7	2,439
Female: Not in school	15-16	6.1	0.5	0.3	0.4	0.7	8.0	946
	17-19	6.2	0.4	0.3	0.5	0.6	7.9	1,297
	20-21	6.8	0.4	0.3	0.4	0.4	8.4	865
	22-24	6.9	0.4	0.2	0.3	0.8	8.6	1,045
	Total	6.5	0.4	0.3	0.4	0.6	8.2	4,153
Male: In school	15-16	0.3	0.5	0.2	0.0	0.2	1.1	420
	17-19	0.2	0.4	0.2	0.0	0.3	1.2	294
	20-21	0.4	0.3	0.3	0.0	0.8	1.8	56
	22-24	0.1	0.0	0.0	0.1	0.8	1.0	50
	Total	0.3	0.4	0.2	0.0	0.3	1.2	820
Female: In school	15-16	1.7	0.0	0.1	0.0	0.0	1.8	276
	17-19	2.0	0.1	0.0	0.1	0.0	2.2	183
	20-21	1.5	0.1	0.0	0.1	0.2	1.9	36
	22-24	3.0	0.0	0.3	0.1	0.0	3.4	16
	Total	1.8	0.1	0.0	0.0	0.0	2.0	511

Male:							
All							
15-16	0.32	0.86	0.69	0.13	2.10	4.10	810
17-19	0.33	0.90	0.77	0.15	3.26	5.41	1,193
20-21	0.28	0.73	0.81	0.27	3.93	6.02	563
22-24	0.38	0.72	0.52	0.30	4.67	6.59	693
Total	0.33	0.82	0.71	0.19	3.38	5.43	3,259
Female:							
All							
15-16	5.17	0.39	0.26	0.35	0.54	6.70	1,222
17-19	5.72	0.40	0.23	0.43	0.52	7.29	1,480
20-21	6.65	0.42	0.24	0.42	0.43	8.16	901
22-24	6.90	0.39	0.20	0.27	0.81	8.57	1,061
Total	6.04	0.40	0.23	0.37	0.58	7.61	4,664

SOURCE: 2001/2002 Adolescent and Youth Survey in Pakistan.

young males have achieved the work hours typical of young females at the beginning of the transition. Time spent working is radically different between those currently enrolled and those out of school. The school day appears to be roughly five hours regardless of level.[11] For young males, those in school report on average 5.5 fewer hours of work than those out of school. For young females, the difference is 6.2 hours. The main reason that work time grows with age for both males and females is that a rising proportion of the sample is out of school at each age. Thus, whether or not we see a close connection between the timing of school leaving and the timing of first paid work, school leaving is associated with an immediate assumption of work duties to fill the time previously consumed by school. Furthermore, for young females who work, time is largely spent inside the household, even if working for pay, whereas for males departure from school is associated with the assumption of external paid work.

REDUCED-FORM TIME USE REGRESSIONS

To identify some of the factors associated with changes in work time over the course of the transition to adulthood, we estimated reduced-form regression models of work time by work type, using individual, household, and community characteristics as righthand-side variables. We analyze unpaid economic work time, paid work time, and noneconomic household work separately using Tobit IV estimation to avoid the asymptotic bias of OLS in cases where there are a reasonable percentage of zero observations (see Table 9-8).[12] Given the tradeoffs between alternative uses of time, we expect that factors associated with increasing hours spent in one category of work time may be associated with reductions in another category. However, not all uses of time are considered in this analysis.

To explore how other factors affecting time use might vary by phase of the transition, we ran one model with three age dummies and then ran models separately for the younger age cohort representing the middle phase of the transition (15 to 19) and the older age cohort representing the late phase of the transition (20 to 24). The means of the variables used in the regressions are presented in Table 9-8, separately by sex and rural-urban residence status. At the individual and household levels, these variables include whether or not the mother is literate, whether or not the father is literate, the household socioeconomic status in quartiles, various measures

---

[11]This observation is based on the time use data of hours in school by current class attended.

[12]Although 8,069 respondents completed the survey, only 7,923 completed the entire time use profile. Therefore, Tables 9-5 through 9-14 are restricted to this subset of respondents.

TABLE 9-8 Descriptive Statistics for Estimation of Tobit Regressions of Time Use Determinants

Determinants	Male		Female	
	Rural	Urban	Rural	Urban
DEPENDENT VARIABLES				
Noneconomic household work, hours/day	1.43	0.51	6.91	5.18
Unpaid economic work and learning skills, hours/day	0.77	0.57	0.26	0.16
Paid work, hours/day	3.51	3.70	1.06	0.65
INDEPENDENT VARIABLES				
Age variables (15-16 omitted)				
17-19	36.28	38.75	31.26	33.31
20-21	15.98	18.34	19.31	19.06
22-24	21.12	20.78	23.97	22.51
Mother literate (yes = 1)	6.38	29.81	5.56	29.07
Father literate (yes = 1)	37.73	64.78	34.21	58.96
HOUSEHOLD SOCIOECONOMIC STATUS (LOW OMITTED)				
Low-mid	30.00	6.27	31.87	5.42
Mid-high	26.09	27.05	25.83	27.17
High	14.04	65.13	11.18	66.29
HOUSEHOLD COMPOSITION				
No. children 0-5	1.53	0.89	1.76	1.13
No. males 6-24	2.97	2.96	2.00	1.98
No. females 6-24	2.22	2.03	2.70	2.71
No. males 25-64	1.36	1.39	1.44	1.51
No. females 25-64	1.41	1.35	1.29	1.30
No. elderly 65+	0.32	0.22	0.34	0.24
COMMUNITY				
Government water supply (yes = 1)	14.66	75.52	16.01	73.98
Factory (yes = 1)	17.64	61.73	17.05	60.24
Vocational institute (yes = 1)	2.31	13.00	3.08	26.6
HIGHEST SCHOOL AVAILABLE (NONE OMITTED)				
Middle	16.95	7.46	17.78	9.9
Secondary	22.65	56.29	11.97	54.12
Higher secondary	10.97	28.92	5.57	28.03

SOURCE: 2001/2002 Adolescent and Youth Survey in Pakistan.

of household composition including the number of children under age five, the number of other males and other females ages 6 to 24, the number of other males and other females aged 25 to 64, the number of elderly adults (ages 65+), and, for rural households only, the number of acres of agricultural land.[13]

A key household variable in the analysis is a measure of the household's wealth or socioeconomic status. Following recent arguments that an asset index can serve as a reliable proxy for a household's socioeconomic status (Bollen, Glanville, and Stecklov, 2002; Filmer and Pritchett, 1999), we used 29 questions from the household survey that pertained to household possessions and amenities as the inputs to a principal components analysis. Following the lead of Filmer and Pritchett (1999), we scored the first component, which can reasonably be interpreted as a household's socioeconomic status, and divided it into quartiles of approximately equal size.[14]

In running these regressions, we were particularly interested in the associations between certain community variables and work time, especially variables affecting schooling and work opportunities as well as the availability of basic amenities such as water that would affect time allocation to noneconomic household work.[15] We include dichotomous variables representing whether or not there was a factory or vocational training institute (for the appropriate sex) within the community or within two kilometers of the community. We also include a series of dummy variables representing the highest level of school available (for the appropriate sex)

---

[13]Additional variables included but not shown are dummies for province, month of interview, and day of the week for which time use was reported. Other household variables that were tried and found not to be significant included whether or not the young person was a relative of the head and whether or not the household was female-headed. We did not include a variable representing whether or not the household was the young person's natal home. For females, this is synonymous with whether or not they are married—a status that we consider endogenous to intrahousehold decision making about resource allocation and time use within the household.

[14]We can see from Table 9-8 that the distribution of household socioeconomic status differs widely between rural and urban areas. This is not surprising, but raises questions about whether it might have been more appropriate to create specific rural and urban measures that could effectively differentiate between socioeconomic groups within each residential category separately.

[15]We had wanted to include some variables representing local wage rates for men and women. While these questions were asked in the community survey, many communities were not able to report a local wage for women, and while most reported a local wage for unskilled men, there was little variation in reported wages across communities. An alternative not yet pursued would be to use wages for those currently working to construct estimates at the community level.

within or close to the community.[16] The presence of government water supply was included as well. Although we recognize that the placement of community facilities may be endogenous to adolescent outcomes, we do not have historical data on community characteristics that would allow us to model these relationships completely. Thus we recognize that we are measuring associations, not causal relationships.

Tables 9-9 and 9-10 present the results for paid work, Tables 9-11 and 9-12 the results for unpaid economic work (including unpaid time spent learning a trade), and Tables 9-13 and 9-14 the results for work including noneconomic household chores inside and outside the household and care for children, the sick, and the elderly. The results for urban residence are presented in the first table of each pair, the results for rural residence in the second table. The numbers in the table are estimated parameters from the Tobit regressions. In the discussion of regression results below, we comment on the effects of each group of variables across all three categories of work time, pointing out differences in age effects when notable.

Mean daily hours in paid work rise significantly with age over the course of the transition for both young males and young females in urban areas and for young males in rural areas (Tables 9-9 and 9-10). This is likely to be linked with school leaving; most females in rural areas had already left school before our period of observation. Males and females ages 22 to 24 work for pay on average five to six more hours per day than their youngest counterparts (ages 15 and 16). Rural females in the oldest age group (22 to 24) experience some significant increase in time devoted to paid work, but much smaller in size (a little over an hour and a half). We see no change with age in time devoted to noneconomic household work for males, but a significant increase for females, with a greater increase in hours in urban than rural areas (Tables 9-13 and 9-14). This may be explained by the fact that hours spent on noneconomic household work are already high among the youngest rural females, ages 15 and 16, in our analysis. For males ages 22 to 24 we also see a significant decline of about two hours per day in time in unpaid economic work (Tables 9-11 and 9-12). So, while males' increase in paid work is partially offset by a decline in time spent on unpaid economic work as they proceed through the transition, females' paid work time, particularly in urban areas, increases along

---

[16]The community module of the questionnaire asked knowledgeable informants about the presence of various levels of schooling within the community. Unfortunately they were not asked whether a particular level of school also encompassed lower levels within it; such schools are called composite schools. Given the evidence from earlier research (Lavy, 1996) that the presence of a school of a higher level within a community encourages enrollment at lower levels because there is a greater chance that students can move on, it seemed plausible to assume that higher levels of schooling would encourage enrollment in that level and in lower levels.

TABLE 9-9 Results of Time Use Tobit Regressions: Paid Work, Urban[a]

Variables	Male			Female		
	Total	15-19	20-24	Total	15-19	20-24
	1,303	797	506	1,716	1,003	713
INDIVIDUAL						
Age dummy (15-16 omitted)						
17-19	3.909[b]	4.029[b]	n.a.	3.050[b]	3.027[b]	n.a.
20-21	4.276[b]	n.a.	n.a.	3.847[b]	n.a.	n.a.
22-24	6.464[b]	n.a.	2.126[c]	5.308[b]	n.a.	1.409
Mother literate (yes = 1)	4.925[b]	-6.604[b]	3.167[c]	0.006	-0.853	0.838
Father literate (yes = 1)	-1.816[c]	-1.602	-1.811[d]	-1.240	-2.823	0.990
HOUSEHOLD						
Household wealth quartile dummy (low omitted)						
Low-mid	2.719	2.503	3.776	1.428	-0.352	3.268
Mid-high	1.393	1.366	2.250	-1.100	-1.743	-0.521
High	0.832	0.204	2.091	-3.458	-3.444	-3.883
No. children 0-5	0.271	0.034	0.546[d]	-0.498[d]	-0.146	-0.394
No. males 6-24	0.106	-0.032	0.295	0.408	0.517[d]	0.218
No. females 6-24	-0.356	-0.559[d]	-0.031	0.150	-0.331	0.710[c]
No. males 25-64	-0.306	0.390	-0.827	-0.834	-0.447	1.255[d]
No. females 25-64	-0.174	-0.307	-0.238	-0.072	-1.343[c]	0.491
No. elderly 65+	-0.043	-0.038	-0.643	0.106	0.621	-0.657
No. agricultural acres	n.a.	n.a.	n.a.	n.a.	n.a.	n.a.

COMMUNITY					
Government water supply (yes = 1)	-0.098	-0.515	0.748	-1.040	-2.631^c	1.528
Factory (yes = 1)	-0.471	0.765	-1.313	1.098	0.679	1.869
Vocational institute (yes = 1)	-0.292	0.398	-1.505	-0.138	0.162	-0.550
Highest school available (none omitted)						
Middle	0.991	0.180	1.449	-2.640	-2.440	-4.597
Secondary	-0.701	-0.825	-0.681	-4.355^c	-5.165^b	-3.598
Higher secondary	0.495	0.867	-0.212	-4.224^d	-5.273^c	-3.757

[a]Controlling for province, month of interview, day of week, standard errors corrected for clustering on PSUs.
[b]Statistically significant at 1% level.
[c]Statistically significant at 5% level.
[d]Statistically significant at 10% level.
NOTE: n.a. = not applicable.
SOURCE: 2001/2002 Adolescent and Youth Survey in Pakistan.

TABLE 9-10 Results of Time Use Tobit Regressions: Paid Work, Rural[a]

Variables	Male			Female		
	Total	15-19	20-24	Total	15-19	20-24
	1,704	1,062	642	2,625	1,512	1,113
INDIVIDUAL						
Age dummy (15-16 omitted)						
17-19	2.305^c	2.426^c	n.a.	0.964	0.938	n.a.
20-21	4.494^b	n.a.	n.a.	0.400	n.a.	n.a.
22-24	5.588^b	n.a.	0.946	1.522^d	n.a.	1.147
Mother literate (yes = 1)	-1.472	-1.745	-1.269	6.684^b	8.057^b	-5.276
Father literate (yes = 1)	-3.710^b	4.956^b	-2.372^c	-1.673^c	-1.722^c	-1.330
HOUSEHOLD						
Household wealth quartile dummy (low omitted)						
Low-mid	-2.030^b	2.898^b	-0.889	1.801^b	-2.139^c	-1.303
Mid-high	-2.023^b	-2.536^c	-1.241	2.532^b	3.604^b	-1.424
High	-2.575^d	-2.000	-2.954^c	4.331^b	5.967^b	-2.325
No. children 0-5	0.088	0.094	0.154	-0.073	-0.284	0.079
No. males 6-24	0.615^b	0.683^b	0.534^c	-0.216	-0.125	-0.339
No. females 6-24	-0.364^d	-0.401	-0.314	0.337^c	0.290	0.424^d
No. males 25-64	0.125	-0.083	0.344	-0.434	-0.131	-0.783^d
No. females 25-64	-1.076^c	-0.626	1.631^b	0.875^c	1.115^c	0.657
No. elderly 65+	-0.304	-0.411	-0.205	-0.180	-0.034	-0.471
No. agricultural acres	-0.021	-0.039^c	-0.009	-0.015	-0.006	-0.025

COMMUNITY						
Government water supply (yes = 1)	-0.897	-2.116[d]	0.547	-1.062	-0.382	-1.691
Factory (yes = 1)	2.025[c]	2.478[c]	1.637[d]	3.071[b]	2.897[c]	3.361[b]
Vocational institute (yes = 1)	2.267	-1.096	7.048[b]	1.017	1.784	-0.469
Highest school available (none omitted)						
Middle	-0.802	-0.976	-0.845	-2.830[c]	-3.073[c]	-2.827[c]
Secondary	-1.810[d]	-2.061	-1.419	4.453[b]	3.752[b]	5.740[b]
Higher secondary	-0.009	0.458	-0.179	-2.487	-0.617	-4.780[c]

[a]Controlling for province, month of interview, day of week, standard errors corrected for clustering on PSUs.
[b]Statistically significant at 1% level.
[c]Statistically significant at 5% level.
[d]Statistically significant at 10% level.
NOTE: n.a. = not applicable.
SOURCE: 2001/2002 Adolescent and Youth Survey in Pakistan.

TABLE 9-11 Results of Time Use Tobit Regressions: Unpaid Economic Work, Urban[a]

Variables	Male			Female		
	Total	15-19	20-24	Total	15-19	20-24
	1,303	797	506	1,716	1,003	713
INDIVIDUAL						
Age dummy (15-16 omitted)						
17-19	-1.887	-2.016	n.a.	-0.560	-0.252	n.a.
20-21	-0.130	n.a.	n.a.	1.026	n.a.	n.a.
22-24	-2.552^b	n.a.	-2.791^b	-1.226	n.a.	-2.369
Mother literate (yes = 1)	0.107	0.599	-0.194	-2.199^b	-1.781	-3.079^b
Father literate (yes = 1)	-0.935	-1.347	0.764	-0.481	-0.920	-0.258
HOUSEHOLD						
Household wealth quartile dummy (low omitted)						
Low-mid	4.600^b	5.744^b	-0.717	1.431	1.021	1.582
Mid-high	0.712	3.007	-7.104	-0.114	-0.361	1.667
High	1.920	3.159	-4.331	0.957	0.077	3.343^b
No. children 0-5	0.311	0.369	0.460	0.116	0.447	-0.413
No. males 6-24	0.294	0.411	-0.027	0.453	0.645^b	-0.025
No. females 6-24	-0.059	-0.041	-0.101	0.061	0.309	0.033
No. males 25-64	0.865^b	0.729	1.320^c	-0.706^b	1.680^d	0.015
No. females 25-64	-1.265^b	2.820^d	-0.457	-0.389	-0.304	-0.379
No. elderly 65+	1.230	2.176^b	-0.184	0.075	-0.684	0.837
No. agricultural acres	n.a.	n.a.	n.a.	n.a.	n.a.	n.a.

COMMUNITY

Government water supply (yes = 1)	-2.445^c	-1.937	-3.661^c	-0.325	-0.885	0.505
Factory (yes = 1)	0.705	2.396^b	-2.521^b	1.476	1.817	1.443
Vocational institute (yes = 1)	0.750	1.229	-0.119	-0.738	-0.877	-1.374
Highest school available (none omitted)						
Middle	1.381	-2.533	7.054^c	3.233	1.352	5.505^c
Secondary	-2.207	-3.752	1.034	2.551	2.444	2.508
Higher secondary	-2.756	-2.957	-1.911	2.910	1.553	4.201

[a]Controlling for province, month of interview, day of week, standard errors corrected for clustering on PSUs.
[b]Statistically significant at 1% level.
[c]Statistically significant at 5% level.
[d]Statistically significant at 10% level.
NOTE: n.a. = not applicable.
SOURCE: 2001/2002 Adolescent and Youth Survey in Pakistan.

TABLE 9-12 Results of Time Use Tobit Regressions: Unpaid Economic Work, Rural[a]

Variables	Male			Female		
	Total	15-19	20-24	Total	15-19	20-24
INDIVIDUAL	1,704	1,062	642	2,625	1,512	1,113
Age dummy (15-16 omitted)						
17-19	0.532	0.397	n.a	-0.298	-0.313	n.a.
20-21	0.438	n.a.	n.a.	-0.944	n.a.	n.a.
22-24	-2.356[b]	n.a.	-2.938[b]	0.142	n.a.	1.048
Mother literate (yes = 1)	-3.162	-4.477[c]	0.212	1.816	1.953	2.041
Father literate (yes = 1)	0.051	-1.146	2.445[c]	-0.863	-0.587	-1.377
HOUSEHOLD						
Household wealth quartile dummy (low omitted)						
Low-mid	0.211	0.494	-0.275	0.317	0.730	-0.593
Mid-high	-0.253	-0.719	0.405	-1.283	-2.348[c]	-0.624
High	-0.071	0.823	-1.520	-2.142	-2.204	-3.074[c]
No. children 0-5	-0.018	-0.128	0.277	-0.166[b]	-0.215	-0.213
No. males 6-24	-0.735[b]	-0.669[c]	-0.902[b]	-0.170	-0.306	0.026
No. emales 6-24	0.265	0.298	0.398	0.116	0.047	0.376
No. males 25-64	0.718	0.754	0.608	-0.123	-0.406	0.106
No. females 25-64	0.064	0.149	0.150	0.500	0.388	0.409
No. elderly 65+	1.298	0.586	2.601[c]	-0.585	-0.789	-0.581
No. agricultural acres	0.010	0.011	0.006	0.011[c]	0.011	0.019[b]

COMMUNITY					
Government water supply (yes = 1)	-0.762	-1.585	0.543	-2.109[b]	-2.149[b]	-2.292[c]
Factory (yes = 1)	0.022	-0.004	1.059	-0.831	1.267	-3.660[d]
Vocational institute (yes = 1)	-2.925	-1.130	-6.941	2.901	-1.834	7.995[d]
Highest school available						
(none omitted)						
Middle	0.749	1.854	-1.831	-0.856	-2.468[b]	1.075
Secondary	1.227	1.743	0.390	-0.829	-0.480	-1.586
Higher secondary	3.291[b]	3.089[c]	3.707[c]	1.166	-0.940	2.381

[a]Controlling for province, month of interview, day of week, standard errors corrected for clustering on PSUs.
[b]Statistically significant at 1% level.
[c]Statistically significant at 5% level.
[d]Statistically significant at 10% level.
NOTE: n.a. = not applicable.
SOURCE: 2001/2002 Adolescent and Youth Survey in Pakistan.

358

TABLE 9-13 Results of Time Use Tobit Regressions: Noneconomic Household Work, Urban[a]

Variables	Male			Female		
	Total	15-19	20-24	Total	15-19	20-24
INDIVIDUAL	1,303	797	506	1,716	1,003	713
Age dummy (15-16 omitted)						
17-19	-0.363	-0.346	n.a.	1.083[b]	1.078[b]	n.a.
20-21	-0.459	n.a.	n.a.	2.392[b]	n.a.	n.a.
22-24	-0.404	n.a.	0.019	2.660[b]	n.a.	0.223
Mother literate (yes = 1)	0.287	-0.027	0.811	-1.026[c]	1.477[b]	-0.431
Father literate (yes = 1)	-0.247	-0.229	-0.513	-0.732[c]	-0.669	0.911[b]
HOUSEHOLD						
Household wealth quartile dummy (low omitted)						
Low-mid	-1.449	-0.588	-3.968[d]	-0.406	-0.051	-0.762
Mid-high	-0.177	0.325	-2.098	-0.971[d]	-0.594	-1.254[c]
High	-0.735	-0.339	-2.049	1.666[b]	-1.732[d]	-1.226[c]
No. children 0-5	-0.136	-0.177	-0.142	0.453[b]	0.296[c]	0.596[b]
No. males 6-24	-0.099	-0.022	-0.182	0.198[c]	0.188[d]	0.263
No. females 6-24	-0.128	-0.128	-0.111	-0.165[d]	-0.062	-0.275[d]
No. males 25-64	-0.110	-0.162	-0.009	0.249	0.229	0.219
No. females 25-64	0.263	0.399	-0.084	0.814[b]	0.713[b]	0.891[b]
No. elderly 65+	-0.197	-0.309	0.115	0.220	0.255	0.235
No. agricultural acres	n.a.	n.a.	n.a.	n.a.	n.a.	n.a.

COMMUNITY						
Government water supply (yes = 1)	-0.115	-0.279	0.449	-0.081	0.014	-0.368
Factory (yes = 1)	0.088	-0.068	0.356	0.119	0.207	-0.078
Vocational institute (yes = 1)	-0.030	0.016	-0.423	0.557	0.212	1.065[c]
Highest school available (none omitted)						
Middle	0.270	0.775	-0.709	0.691	0.416	1.060
Secondary	0.428	0.517	0.008	0.607	0.712	0.576
Higher secondary	0.123	0.212	-0.180	0.749	1.092	0.477

[a] Controlling for province, month of interview, day of week, standard errors corrected for clustering on PSUs.
[b] Statistically significant at 1% level.
[c] Statistically significant at 5% level.
[d] Statistically significant at 10% level.
NOTE: n.a. = not applicable.
SOURCE: 2001/2002 Adolescent and Youth Survey in Pakistan.

TABLE 9-14 Results of Time Use Tobit Regressions: Noneconomic Household Work, Rural[a]

Variables	Male			Female		
	Total	15-19	20-24	Total	15-19	20-24
INDIVIDUAL	1,704	1,062	642	2,625	1,512	1,113
Age dummy (15-16 omitted)						
17-19	0.009	-0.029	n.a.	0.416[b]	0.438[b]	n.a.
20-21	-0.695	n.a.	n.a.	1.057[c]	n.a.	n.a.
22-24	-0.588	n.a.	0.174	0.938[c]	n.a.	-0.167
Mother literate (yes = 1)	-0.807	-0.999	-0.241	-0.212	-0.181	-0.133
Father literate (yes = 1)	0.026	-0.382	0.761	-0.256	-0.320	-0.121
HOUSEHOLD						
Household wealth quartile dummy (low omitted)						
Low-mid	-0.007	0.208	-0.599	-0.173	-0.494[d]	0.242
Mid-high	-0.848[b]	-0.343	1.626[c]	-0.059	-0.369	0.399
High	1.641[c]	-0.966	2.567[c]	0.788[c]	1.205[c]	-0.457
No. children 0-5	-0.045	0.036	-0.148	0.327[c]	0.369[c]	0.304[c]
No. males 6-24	-0.176[d]	-0.193[d]	-0.191	0.115[d]	0.155[b]	0.047
No. females 6-24	0.039	0.130	-0.078	0.196[c]	-0.212[b]	-0.158[b]
No. males 25-64	0.148	0.136	0.046	-0.032	-0.183	0.153
No. females 25-64	0.140	-0.088	0.590[b]	0.489[c]	0.451[c]	0.556[c]
No. elderly 65+	0.232	0.350	0.091	0.245[b]	0.267[d]	0.169
No. agricultural acres	-0.005	-0.004	-0.009	-0.003	-0.004	0.000

COMMUNITY						
Government water supply (yes = 1)	-0.498	0.144	1.965^c	-0.049	-0.129	0.159
Factory (yes = 1)	-1.131^b	-1.191^d	-1.226^d	-0.469^d	-0.637^b	-0.162
Vocational institute (yes = 1)	-2.853^b	-2.464	3.451^c	-0.171	-0.284	-0.067
Highest school available						
(none omitted)						
Middle	-0.288	-0.489	0.251	0.357	0.107	0.638^d
Secondary	-0.444	-0.880	0.253	0.349	-0.227	1.084^b
Higher secondary	0.028	-0.209	-0.138	-0.300	-0.695^b	0.071

[a]Controlling for province, month of interview, day of week, standard errors corrected for clustering on PSUs.
[b]Statistically significant at 1% level.
[c]Statistically significant at 5% level.
[d]Statistically significant at 10% level.
NOTE: n.a. = not applicable.
SOURCE: 2001/2002 Adolescent and Youth Survey in Pakistan.

with time in noneconomic household work, suggesting that they work a "double shift." By contrast, for females in rural areas, work burdens are much heavier overall, but do not change much between ages 15 and 24.

Having literate parents (controlling for socioeconomic status) appears to be associated with a reduction in paid work time for rural females and for rural and urban males (Tables 9-9 and 9-10). Having a literate mother is relatively more beneficial than having a literate father for males in urban areas and for females in rural areas; having a literate father is beneficial for males in rural areas. Having literate parents is also associated with reduced time in noneconomic household work for young females in urban areas, with reductions in work time being associated with mother's literacy among younger females and with father's literacy among older females (Table 9-13).

Because of the way our household wealth quartiles were constructed, we see few statistically significant associations of household wealth with hours of work in urban areas. We see the biggest associations of household wealth in Table 9-10 with paid work in rural areas. For young males, the groups with higher socioeconomic status work about two hours less than the lowest socioeconomic group; for young females the time use differentials are much greater, with a gap exceeding four hours per day between the highest and lowest wealth group. These associations are most apparent for the youngest age group, where females in the wealthiest households work six fewer hours than those in the poorest. For young females, being in the highest quartile of the wealth distribution is associated with a small but statistically significant decline in noneconomic household work time in both urban (Table 9-13) and rural areas (Table 9-14).

Household composition is strongly associated with variations in paid work time among young males and females in rural areas (Table 9-10).[17] The signs of particular household composition variables nearly always have opposite effects for young males compared with young females, suggesting that rising household size reinforces the traditional gender division of labor. The presence of females of any age is associated with significant reductions in the paid work time of males but at the same time increases in the paid work time of young females; this suggests that the presence of more females in the household allows a division of labor between them, with some working at home and others working outside the home. The presence of other young males in the household is associated with an increase in the paid

---

[17]In a household decision-making model of the determinants of child outcomes, household composition variables can be seen as endogenous when parents are the prime decision makers. However, we are modeling the behavior of young people who are in a transition to adulthood. If we assume that young people have growing agency in their decision making about work roles relative to their parents, it is not unreasonable to see household composition variables as exogenous, rather than endogenous.

work time of young men. The presence of young children has a small negative association with paid work time for females in urban areas (Table 9-9). Household composition is a particularly important factor in young females' time spent on noneconomic household work in both urban and rural areas (Tables 9-13 and 9-14), and the sizes of the associations of different variables are similar. The presence of children, elderly, and young men is associated with increased time in females' noneconomic household work, and the presence of other females of any age is associated with a reduction in noneconomic household work, particularly so when older females are present. For young males, time in noneconomic household work, which is always small in any case, is rarely affected by household composition.

Because it is much easier to define a rural community than an urban one, we expected that our community variables would be more likely to show statistically significant associations with work time in rural areas. Although the community survey identified opportunities within a two-kilometer radius of each primary sampling unit, opportunities beyond two kilometers may still be accessible to urban residents, given the greater ease of transport. While we did find more associations in rural areas, we also found some relationships in urban areas. We found that the presence of a government source of water is significantly associated with a reduction of unpaid economic work time for males in urban areas and for females in rural areas. It is also significantly associated with a reduction in noneconomic household work time for males in rural areas (where there appears to be a gender division of labor, with males doing the outside domestic chores such as fetching water while females remain in the household).

The presence of a factory has a highly significant association with hours in paid work for both males and females in rural areas (Table 9-10), increasing paid work on average for males by two hours and for females by three hours. We see some compensating effects of a local factory in reducing noneconomic household work for young males and females, particularly young females (Table 9-14), and in reducing unpaid economic work for young females (Table 9-12).

The presence of a vocational institute for young males appears to be associated with increased paid work for males ages 20 to 24 in rural areas, which is compensated for by a significant reduction in time for noneconomic household work. On the other hand, the presence of a vocational institute for young rural females (these institutes are sex segregated) appears to be significantly associated with increased time in unpaid economic work, suggesting that the skills being acquired by young females are more likely to prepare them for unpaid than for paid work. The presence of a vocational school also appears to be associated with an increase in unpaid economic work for young urban females.

The presence of schools in the community that go beyond the primary level are strongly associated with a reduction in paid work for young females. In urban areas, the association is greatest when secondary or higher secondary is the highest level available within two kilometers and is significant only for the younger age group, who may still be enrolled in school and therefore have few hours available for paid work. At older ages, the presence of a middle school appears to be associated with an increase in time in unpaid economic work. In rural areas, however, the associations, which are greatest when middle or secondary is the highest level available, are apparent for young females of all ages, even those who would have long since left school. This result is counterintuitive, as one might expect higher levels of schooling to prepare females for paid work. Just the opposite appears to be true, however. Females in the poorest families are the most likely to do paid work in rural areas; females in the richest families are likely to be able to pursue an education, find a good match in the marriage market, and relieve themselves of any obligation to earn money for the family.

To summarize, workloads for young males and females remain relatively equal as long as they remain in school. Upon school exit, males for the most part take up paid work outside the home, while females take up noneconomic household work, primarily of the sort that can be done within the home. Our results demonstrate that opportunities at the community level for higher levels of schooling, for vocational training, and for jobs (in the form of factories) are strongly associated with time use patterns among young people, patterns that have implications for the timing of transitions to adulthood. Indeed, a recent rise in paid work for females suggests a possible response to changing employment opportunities. However, these growing opportunities do not seem to be altering certain strongly held norms against paid work for young females. For example, vocational training for females seems to be associated with an increase in unpaid economic work, whereas vocational training for males is associated with more time spent in paid work. Furthermore, the presence of higher level schools for females seems to be associated with a decline in paid work and a rise in unpaid economic work.

CONCLUSION

Pakistan is a country of contrasts caught in the conflicting tensions between global political and economic change on the one hand and severe financial duress because of a sluggish economy on the other. Although the past couple of decades have brought much social and economic change, many aspects of daily life remain unchanged. As a result there are growing contradictions between traditional values and ways of life and increasingly accepted global norms and external economic realities. The circumstances under which today's young people are assuming adult roles will have long-term implications for their future prospects and for those of their families, their communities, and the country as a whole.

Our results confirm the fundamental importance of schooling to transitions to adulthood in Pakistan. Without schooling, children in Pakistan are asked to assume the work burdens of adults prematurely and are deprived of the opportunity for learning in an institutional setting outside the family. Those who attend school eventually assume gender-stereotyped roles; however, they do so with some delay, which allows them to experience a longer transition to adulthood. For both males and females, there appears to be a substantial lag in years between the assumption of adult work roles and assumption of adult family roles as marked by the timing of the transition to marriage. For young males this is a lag between the timing of first paid work and marriage; in the case of young females it is the lag between school exit or (if never in school) the assumption of heavy domestic responsibilities and the timing of marriage and leaving home. Our data demonstrate the potential for change created by higher levels of schooling, vocational training, or formal-sector jobs. As Pakistan's demographic transition continues (Feeney and Alam, 2003; Sathar and Casterline, 1998), family sizes become smaller, and women's time becomes more flexible, greater educational and labor force opportunities should become available for young women.

REFERENCES

Ajayi, A., Clark, W., Erulkar, A., Hyde, K., Lloyd, C.B., Mensch, B.S., Ndeti, C., Ravitch, B., Masiga, E., and Gichaga, S. (1997). *Schooling and the experience of adolescents in Kenya.* New York and Nairobi, Kenya: Population Council and Government of Kenya, Ministry of Education.

Arends-Kuenning, M., and Amin, S. (2004). School incentive programs and children's activities: The case of Bangladesh. *Comparative Education Review, 48*(3), 295-317.

Bollen, K.A., Glanville, J.L., and Stecklov, G. (2002). Economic status proxies in studies of fertility in developing countries: Does the measure matter? *Population Studies, 56*(1), 81-96.

Brown, L.R., and Haddad, L. (1995). *Time allocation patterns and time burdens: A gendered analysis of seven countries.* Washington, DC: International Food Policy Research Institute.

Durrant, V.L. (2000). *Adolescent girls and boys in Pakistan: Opportunities and constraints in the transition to adulthood.* (Research Report No. 12.) Islamabad, Pakistan: Population Council.

Echarri Cánovas, C.J., and Perez Amador, J. (2001). *Becoming adults: Life course transitions in Mexican young people.* Paper presented at the International Union for the Scientific Study of the Population XXIV General Population Conference, Salvador, Brazil.

Feeney, G., and Alam, I. (2003). New estimates and projections of population growth in Pakistan. *Population and Development Review, 29*(3), 483-492.

Filgueira, C., Filgueira, F., and Fuentes, A. (2001). *Critical choices at a critical age: Youth emancipation paths and school attainment in Latin America.* (Latin American Research Network Working Paper No. R-432.) Washington, DC: Inter-American Development Bank.

Filmer, D., and Pritchett, L. (1999). The effect of household wealth on educational attainment: Evidence from 35 countries. *Population and Development Review, 25*(1), 85-120.

Florez, C.E., and Hogan, D.P. (1990). Demographic transition and life course change in Colombia. *Journal of Family History, 15*(1), 1-21.

Fricke, T.E., Syed, S.H., and Smith, P.C. (1986). Rural Punjabi social organization and marriage timing strategies in Pakistan. *Demography, 23*(4), 489-508.

Larson, R.W., and Verma, S. (1999). How children and adolescents spend time across the world: Work, play, and developmental opportunities. *Psychological Bulletin, 125*(6), 701-736.

Lavy, V. (1996). School supply constraints and children's educational outcomes in rural Ghana. *Journal of Development Economics, 51,* 291-314.

Levison, D., and Moe, K.S. (1998). Household work as a deterrent to schooling: An analysis of adolescent girls in Peru. *Journal of Developing Areas, 32*(3), 339-356.

Levison, D., Moe, K.S., and Knaul, F.M. (2001). Youth education and work in Mexico. *World Development, 29*(1), 167-188.

Mensch, B.S., Bruce, J., and Greene, M.E. (1998). *The uncharted passage: Girls' adolescence in the developing world.* New York: Population Council.

Mensch, B.S., Singh, S., and Casterline, J. (2005). Trends in the timing of first marriage among men and women in the developing world. Chapter 5 in National Research Council, C.B. Lloyd, J.R. Behrman, N.P. Stromquist, and B. Cohen, (Eds.), Panel on Transitions to Adulthood in Developing Countries, Committee on Population, *The changing transitions to adulthood in developing countries: Selected studies.* Washington, DC: The National Academies Press.

Pakistan Federal Bureau of Statistics. (1998). PIHS education sector performance in the 1990s: Analysis from the PIHS. *In Pakistan Integrated Household Survey.* Islamabad, Pakistan: Government of Pakistan.

Rindfuss, R.R. (1991). The young adult years: Diversity, structural change, and fertility. *Demography, 28*(4), 493-512.

Sathar, Z.A., and Casterline, J. (1998). The onset of fertility transition in Pakistan. *Population and Development Review, 24*(4), 773-796.

Sathar, Z.A., Lloyd, C.B., ul Haque, M., Diers, J.A., Faizunnissa, A., Grant, M., and Sultana, M. (2003). *Adolescents and youth in Pakistan 2001-02: A nationally representative survey.* Islamabad, Pakistan: Population Council.

United Nations General Assembly. (1989). *Convention on the Rights of the Child.* Available: http://www.unicef.org/crc/fulltext.htm [accessed July 2004].

Winsborough, H.H. (1978). Statistical histories of the life cycle of birth cohorts: The transition from schoolboy to adult male. In K.E. Taeuber, K.E. Bumpass, and J.A. Sweet (Eds.), *Social demography* (pp. 231-259). New York: Academic Press.

Xenos, P. (1999). *Events information and the life course framework in Young Adult Reproductive Health (YARH) survey studies of adolescent risk.* Paper prepared for the YARH Measurement Meeting, Focus on Youth. Centers for Disease Control and Prevention, Decatur, GA.

10

Multilevel Modeling of Influences on Transitions to Adulthood in Developing Countries with Special Reference to Cameroon

Barthélémy Kuate-Defo

Adolescence is a critical period in an individual's life. During this time many key social, economic, biological, developmental, and demographic events occur that set the stage for adult life. Not surprisingly, therefore, adolescents are widely recognized as a critical target group for reproductive health and other social policies and programs. Yet the growing interest in adolescents in the policy and programming arenas has drawn attention to the gaps in research regarding the status and situation of adolescents in developing countries and the transitions to adulthood that individuals experience.

One of the chronic methodological problems that has hampered a deep understanding of the transition from childhood to adulthood is the inadequacy of traditional statistical techniques for modeling hierarchy. Such techniques estimate models without taking into account the clustered structure of data. As a result they have fostered an impoverished conceptualization of relationships between exposure and response variables and have often discouraged the formulation of explicit multilevel models with hypotheses about effects occurring at each level and across levels. They have caused concerns about aggregation bias, misestimated precision, and the "unit of analysis" and "level of measurement" problems, concerns that are better addressed with multilevel approaches (Bryk and Raudenbush, 1992; Goldstein, 2003; Kuate-Defo, 2005a; Searle, Casella, and McCulloch, 1992; Snijders and Bosker, 1999). Building on a theoretical framework developed by the National Research Council (NRC)'s Panel on Transitions to Adulthood in Developing Countries, this chapter formulates and estimates multilevel models that identify the fixed and random effects of covariates at the appropriate units of analysis, level-specific contextual effects, and nested random influences in estimating the influences of competing factors on various transitional events.

Data from Cameroon are used to illustrate the features of this methodology and to test several assumptions of the theoretical framework of the NRC's Panel on Transitions to Adulthood in Developing Countries. Cameroon has special appeal because it is generally considered a microcosmic representation of tropical Africa due to its diversity. We use a multilevel modeling framework because individuals are bound by family, neighborhood, community, regional, national, and international factors that influence their individual or collective behaviors, so that treating these individuals as independent observations within a study may be quite misleading. Indeed, there is potentially some correlation among individuals interacting and behaving like others within their various contexts of life, which may remain even after all measured variables are taken into account in analyses. This study posits that this correlation is a consequence of developmental, normative or behavioral, structural or contextual factors that are related to various transitions to adulthood and are common to groups of individuals but that are unmeasured or unmeasurable. Correlated observations violate a standard assumption of independence in statistical analyses, resulting in understated standard errors and a greater likelihood of committing Type I errors and, in the case of nonlinear models such as survival models, estimated parameters that are both biased and inconsistent (Kuate-Defo, 2001).

The next section of this chapter considers the meaning of successful and healthy transitions to adulthood in the context of a developing country. The following section presents the logic and assumptions of multilevel modeling as well as data requirements. The data set, main relations considered and statistical methods are then described. The two final sections present the main empirical findings and discuss their implications.

SUCCESSFUL AND HEALTHY TRANSITIONS TO ADULTHOOD

Half of the population worldwide is now under age 25, with the largest ever generation of adolescents—1.2 billion people between the ages of 10 and 19—representing one fifth of the world's population (UNFPA, 2003a). Such growth puts untimely pressure on the limited and/or scarce resources that can prepare these young people for a better future. This is because more than 87 percent of them live in a developing world with changing and diverse socioeconomic, cultural, and epidemiological circumstances often made harsh by poverty. The impact of these circumstances on the options of adolescents and youth is apparent as they move through the lifecycle and are expected to assume adult roles. On the other hand, this large number of young people presents a unique opportunity for development and social growth in the developing world, notwithstanding variability in levels and areas of investment, fertility levels, dependency ratios, opportunity structures within the economy, socioeconomic situations of families, and level of development of communities and nations.

Adolescence is a critical stage in the development of gender roles and responsibilities. Individuals in this transitory period attempt to cope with many life options and choices, including those related to friendship, courtship, marriage, education, employment, reproductive life and health, family formation and childbearing, lifestyles, and nutrition. Within any society, these options and choices influence and determine the timing, sequencing, and readiness to experience events marking the passage from adolescence to adulthood as well as the well-being and quality of life at later ages.

Adulthood is characterized by a number of roles expected from people treated as adults. Role is a behavioral concept well established in social science and has special appeal within the multilevel framework, owing to the unique quality of the role concept as a link between the social and individual levels, because communities, households, families/extended families, and social groups are all structural contexts where individuals live and exercise their roles and responsibilities. The sequential pattern of those roles over the life cycle defines to some extent the adult life course. Adult life in all societies is more compartmentalized than the life of children because it is dominated to a greater extent by formalized expectations and obligations as expressed in the legal, social, cultural, and moral codes of conduct and behavior. These aspects of adult life are well captured by the concept of role and adult behavior.

To pinpoint the extent to which transitions are successful/unsuccessful or healthy/unhealthy for an adolescent within a given social context, one must come up with some role properties. Role properties, both positive and negative according to the legal, social, cultural, and moral codes of conduct and behavior, have relevance for understanding the changes in status of individuals as they experience events portraying specific transitions through their life course. As the life of an individual at any moment can be thought of as the array of roles that he or she enacts, so can the person's life course be conceptualized as a sequence of roles enacted. Throughout the life course, each person occupies a variety of roles involving opportunities and resource constraints as well as expectations and demands. Some of these roles are age dependent (e.g., being enrolled in school), while others are both age and sex dependent (e.g., being pregnant).

During the life course, attachment in the relatively uncompartmentalized life of the infant is seen as analogous to more diverse forms of social support in various adult role settings. The constructive aspects of adult roles embedded in experienced states are features of successful transitions, but have not been studied much in developing countries in part because the research emphasis has been on the demand and expectational attributes and therefore, the literature on successful transitions from adolescence to adulthood remains scarce. The constructive aspects of roles imply roles that offer opportunities to acquire new skills and abilities and use those already acquired. In this study, roles or events with positive properties will characterize successful transitions, in contrast to roles or events with negative properties. Furthermore, successful transitions can be associated with unhealthy events or health problems and in such cases, we treat the transition as unhealthy, whether it is successful or not. For example, in Cameroon, the legal age at marriage is 15 for girls and 18 for boys and the legal age at entry into the labor force is 15 for both sexes. This means that from a sociolegal point of view, transitions to employment, marriage, household headship, and marital childbearing are legal transitions in the Cameroon context if they occurred at or after age 15, except for marriage and fatherhood, which should occur only at or after age 18 for boys.

MULTILEVEL FRAMEWORK FOR THE STUDY OF TRANSITIONS TO ADULTHOOD: LOGIC, ASSUMPTIONS, AND DATA REQUIREMENTS

Many kinds of data in the social, biological, behavioral, biomedical and clinical sciences have a multilevel (or hierarchical, clustered or nested) structure and many designed surveys on human subjects also create data hierarchies. Young people from the same families (or households), communities, or higher level groupings tend to be more alike in terms of factors that are likely to be positively or negatively associated with their transition to adulthood than their peers chosen at random from the general population. We argue that multilevel modeling is the most appropriate methodology for testing the theoretical framework developed by the NRC's Panel on Transitions to Adulthood in Developing Countries. From a multilevel perspective, the panel's framework considers five units of analysis or levels of operation of influences for the study of changing transitions to adulthood: the global context, the national context, the community context, the individual, and the within-individual changes in the transition to adulthood. The panel's framework highlights the interlinkages and influences between context and individual behavior and is based on the main assumption that much of what happens to young people in developing countries and what constitutes their daily experience, are shaped by the contexts in which their lives are embedded. This chapter uses the multilevel framework to explicit test this panel's assumption that contexts matter in young people's transition to adulthood. We do so by separating the net influences of individual attributes from the fixed and random context-dependent effects using available data from Cameroon to document the significance of the fixed effects and random effects of both community context and province context, net of the fixed and random effects of individual-level and household-level covariates. Although not made explicit in the panel's framework, it is understood that how the effects of the global context, the national context and the community context operate will have different implications for young males and young females as well as for young people from different family backgrounds defined by such characteristics as socioeconomic status and ethnicity. We explicitly test this panel's conjecture by estimating separate models for young males and young females and by estimating the effects of ethnicity and the index of socioeconomic status at the household and community levels using illustrative data from Cameroon renown for its ethnic diversity. In order words, the panel's framework implicitly considers that young people differ for reasons that may be associated with the contexts they have been exposed to and this necessary differentiation may also be influenced by the characteristics of individuals so that once contexts are established and fixed for individuals, even if their establishment were effectively random, they will tend to become differentiated and this differentiation or variability implies that the context and those living in it both influence and are influenced by the context membership.

There is nothing methodologically and substantively wrong with aggregate analysis when the study focuses only on macro-level propositions once proper account is taken of the fact the reliability of an aggregated variable depends on the number of micro-level units in a macro-level unit and thus will be larger for the larger macro-units than for the smaller ones (Kuate-Defo, 2005a). In cases where the interest of the study centers on macro-micro propositions as articulated in the theoretical framework developed by the NRC panel, however, aggregation may result in gross errors and wrong conclusions. Such conclusions may be either due to the 'shift of meaning' in that a variable aggregated to the macro level refers to the macro-units and not directly to the micro-units (Snijders and Bosker, 1999), the ecological fallacy in that a correlation between macro-level variables cannot be used to make assertions about micro-level relationships (Robinson, 1950), the neglect of the original data structure especially when some kind of analysis of covariance is used (e.g., in a study of transition to adulthood, we may be interested among other things in assessing between-community differences in young people's transition to adulthood after correcting for innate individual differences), or due to the fact that aggregation prevents from examination the net effects of micro-level variables in the presence of other influential variables and nested random influences or the potential cross-level interaction effects of a specified micro-level variable (e.g., ethnic affiliation or gender) with a macro-level variable (e.g., urban place of residence). Multilevel statistical models are always needed if a multistage sampling design has been employed, and are used to examine the macro-micro relationships between variables at different levels of hierarchy.

With multistage samples typical of most surveys, the population of interest usually consists of sub-populations from which selection occurs. A common mistake in research is to ignore this sampling scheme and to overlook the fact that lower-level units were not sampled independently from each other but that instead they are dependent and nested observations: having selected a primary unit (e.g., a community) increases the chances of selection of secondary units (e.g., individuals or households) from that community. In multilevel analysis, such nested dependency of lower-level units within higher-level units is of focal interest and the underlying assumption is that units within an entity at a given level of observation share the same environment and resources. To ignore this relationship or the "unit of analysis" problem in testing the theoretical framework of the NRC panel—e.g., by using aggregate analysis or traditional regression techniques which recognize only the individual youth as the units of analysis and ignore their groupings within the community or other higher-level contexts nested in the national context for instance—amounts to overlooking the importance of context effects which are at its heart. For instance, young people within any one community share the same characteristics and may tend to be similar so that they provide rather less information than would have been the case if the same number of young people were drawn from different communities. Hence, for a meaningful study of transitions to adulthood and depending on available data, it is important to understand the factors associated with such variations from one young person to another within a family or household, from household to household within a community, and from community to community within a country, for example. One may draw wrong conclusions if either of these sources of variability is ignored. That is why it is illuminating to explicitly model the variability associated with each level of nesting, as documented in this study. One could then investigate the extent to which any of the explanatory variables at the individual/household level say, could explain between-community variation, or assess whether transition to adulthood rate differences between young males and young females vary from community to community within a province or from province to province within a country such as Cameroon.

One central issue in specifying context effects is the definition of an individual's geographical area which in turn is contingent upon the context being considered and the data requirements. There are no existing data or statistical methods that can fully test all the five levels of the theoretical framework of the NRC Panel on Transitions to Adulthood in Developing Countries, which we view as a generic framework from that standpoint, since past surveys including the Demographic and Health Surveys (DHS) have not been designed for doing such multilevel analysis. Nonetheless, because the most widely available and comparable data sources for developing countries remain the DHS-type surveys, which have multistage sampling designs, multilevel modeling is the most appropriate methodology for the analysis of such data to study transition to adulthood, given their complex patterns of variability. One cannot use such data without taking into account the clustering in complex sample design where the first-stage sampling unit is often a well-defined geographical unit and further stages of random selection are carried out until the eligible households are selected and individual respondents interviewed. Such sampling procedures only provide for clustered data and preclude the possibility that units are cross-classified (i.e., a young person belonging simultaneously to two or more contexts at the same level of observation, each of which being potentially an influential variable in that young person's life). Hence, we can articulate the multilevel models for clustered data, with a focus on nested/multilevel sources of variability. We do so by stacking DHS-type data from the individual (e.g., background information and individual characteristics), household (e.g., relationships to head of household, household amenities), and community (e.g., socioeconomic infrastructure and community endowment) questionnaires as well as macro-level data considered at higher levels (e.g., physical environment and climate), to create a clustered or hierarchical data file with appropriate units of analysis as illustrated in Kuate-Defo (2001), and that fully exploit information from these questionnaires that are relevant to a study of transition to adulthood. In order to stack these files together to build a clustered data file for multilevel modeling, a given individual must belong to one and only one household which in turn must belong to one and only one community which must belong to one and only one province, and so forth, in order to isolate "pure" context effects uncovered in our study. This stacking imposes that the hierarchical contexts (household, community, province) within which the life of an individual is embedded are invariant over the observation period in order for a given unit of analysis and level of observation to be valid for an individual in clustered data and for rigorous multilevel analysis to be doable since well-defined contextual units are required, otherwise the basic assumption of multilevel theory is violated. The identification of "pure" context effects necessary imposes that migrant respondents must be excluded from analyses because their inclusion would have as a prerequisite the availability of cross-classified data on the different age-specific contexts of residence and explanatory variables that may be time-varying in the life course of each individual; in this case, multilevel modeling of jointly clustered and cross-classified data would have to be available.

DATA AND RELATIONSHIPS BETWEEN EXPOSURE AND RESPSPONSE VARIABLES

Data Source

The data set used for application in this chapter comes from the 1998 Cameroon Demographic and Health Survey (or CDHS-98; Central Bureau of Population Studies, 1998) that collected cross-sectional and nationally representative information at the individual, household, community, and regional or provincial levels. The special feature of the CDHS-98 data most relevant for this study is the availability of duration data on mutually exclusive, cause-specific school termination reported by women ages 15 to 49 at the time of the survey. These data were retrieved from questions S111a ("Age stopped attending school") and V154 ("Reason stopped attending school"), which were asked to female respondents who attended school and obviously not to those with no schooling. We also adopt a gender perspective in this study by assessing the likelihood of investment in education on the transition opportunities of both female and male youth to adulthood within the socioeconomic context of Cameroon where statistically significant gender gaps in educational attainment still persists. The analyses therefore concern both female and male youths' experiences with specific events before their 25th birthday and characterizing their change of status to adult roles and responsibilities. Indeed, in the CDHS-98, 14.3 percent of female youth ages 15 to 19 years had no schooling, and 17.7 percent of female youth ages 20 to 24 years never started school; in contrast, only 5.6 percent of male youth ages 15 to 19 years had no schooling, and 4.5 percent of those ages 20 to 24 years never attended school. These data have been found to be of good quality (Fotso et al., 1999; Kuate-Defo, 2000).

The theoretical framework of the NRC's Panel on Transitions to Adulthood in Developing Countries assumes that the timing and sequencing of events and transitions experienced by young people during their life course are produced by the contexts in which they live. Thus, its main thrust is a nested structure of interlinkages of context effects in the presence of other explanatory and random influences on transition to adulthood. Dealing with cross-classified data on contexts for the same individual (which lends itself to viewing migration as a truly endogenous behavior), requires at least three things: (1) migration histories on the different places of residences of each individual and on changing individual, household, community, and national characteristics inherent in the life experiences of that individual; (2) relevant clustered and cross-classified multilevel data; and (3) multilevel models for clustered and cross-classified data with potentially endogenous variables. This implies that one would need for a study of transition within the nested contexts, both cross-classified contextual information on each individual and time-dependent-context-dependent explanatory variables in the life course of that individual. That would give rise to clustered cross-classified data and a multilevel modeling of such data could be undertaken. Given the limitations of existing data and the shortcomings of DHS-type data in particular regarding context-dependent migration histories and time-dependent-context-dependent explanatory variables, one cannot investigate transition to adulthood with the aim of testing the context effects without identifying one and only one context at each higher level per Level 1 (individual) unit. The identification of context is essential for clustered data used in multilevel modeling because the main premise of multilevel theories is that a context is well-defined and identifiable. Thus, analyses are based on all respondents irrespective of migration/residence history for relevant descriptive analyses, and migrant respondents are excluded from multilevel analyses because the CDHS-98, like other DHS surveys, only collect information on childhood place of residence, current residence, and lifetime place of residence. Clearly, we have adopted a more rigorous and conservative strategy to preserve our study from committing Type I errors or other inferential errors often encountered in aggregate and single-level studies and to detect "pure" contextual effects (e.g., associated with urban versus rural residence for community context), net of fixed and random influences of other measured and unmeasured factors. The data are therefore restricted to respondents who never migrated, for whom the childhood place of residence and current place of residence are the same, and to cases with no missing data on the dependent variables. In the CDHS-98, 47.2 percent and 63.8 percent of young males ages 15 to 19 years and 20 to 24 years ever migrated, respectively; 58.6 percent and 69.5 percent of young females ages 15 to 19 years and 20 to 24 years ever migrated—with the vast majority of girls migrating for marriage as shown in Kuate-Defo (2000), respectively. After all necessary exclusions, the samples used in various analyses are indicated in the respective tables of results (see Tables 10-2 to 10-6).

Table 10-1 specifying selected explanatory and response variables used in this study, is self-explanatory.

Response Variables

The Three Dichotomous Response Variables

In order to test the panel's conceptual framework, we identified measures of successful or unsuccessful transitions to adulthood that are avail-

TABLE 10-1 Definitions and Specifications of Variables Utilized in
Analyses: CDHS-98

Names

Dichotomous response variables
  Head of the household before age 25 (both male and female
    samples)
  Had sexually transmitted diseases during the last 12 months and
    before age 25 (both male and female samples)
  Had worked during the last 12 months and before age 25 (both
  male and female samples)

Polychotomous response variable
  Cause-specific school attrition before age 25 due to pregnancy
    and work
  The woman is still employed and married
  The woman is still married and school failure (females only)

Explanatory variables measured at the individual level or household level
  Age cohort (in years)
  Times to school attrition (duration in years)
  Gender
  Religion
  Ethnic affiliation

  Household wealth index

  Family structure

Explanatory variables measured at the community level
  Community development index

  Place of residence

Explanatory variables measured at the province level
  Main regions

SOURCE: Cameroon Demographic and Health Survey (1998).

Specifications

Dichotomous variable coded 1 if a respondent headed a household at
the survey date and by the 25th birthday, 0 otherwise.

Dichotomous variable coded 1 if a respondent age 24 or younger had
a sexually transmitted infection during the last 12 months,
0 otherwise.

Dichotomous variable coded 1 if a respondent age 24 or younger had
reported being employed during the last 12 months, 0 otherwise.

These causes of school dropout by the 25th birthday of women are
modeled within a competing risks framework. A series of multistate
life tables are constructed, followed by multilevel models for
competing events. The dependent variable is a categorical measure
of the six states (types of exits) of the female respondent: 1 if left
school due to work, 2 if left school due to marriage, 3 if left school
due to unwed pregnancy, 4 if left school due to failure, 5 if left
school for all other reasons, and 6 if still enrolled in school. The
detailed causes are listed in Table 10-2.

Coded 1 if 15-19, 0 if 20-24.

A series of 11 dummies for failure time <15, 15 to 24.

Coded 1 if male, 0 otherwise.

Coded 1 if Catholic, 2 if Protestant, 3 if Muslim or others.

Coded 1 if Pahouin-Beti, 2 if Douala-Bassa, 3 if Fulfulde-Fulani, and
4 if other ethnic groups.

Constructed using principal component analysis (PCA) on a set
of over 15 wealth items, and aggregating the deciles into three groups
coded 1 for the lowest 40%, 2 for the middle 40%, and 3 for the
highest 20%.

Coded 1 if respondent lives with biological or own parents,
0 otherwise.

Constructed employing PCA using more than 10 items capturing
various aspects of development per community and deciles
aggregated into three groups, and coded 1 for the lowest 40%, 2 for
the middle 40%, and 3 for the highest 20%.

Coded 1 if urban, 0 otherwise.

Coded 1 if forest, 2 if highlands, and 3 if Sudano-Sahelian.

able in the CDHS-98 and are consistent with the Cameroonian context: being a household head, being employed, being infected with an STI, and cause-specific school attrition marking transitions to adult roles.

Being household head. The DHS household questionnaire provides each household member's relationship to the head of the household. We use that information to find young people ages 15 to 24 who were heads of their household at the time of the CDHS-98. Being head of a household is considered a successful transition in Cameroon because it is viewed as taking adult responsibilities in managing one's life and usually as a prerequisite for other transitions such as from single to married states, especially for men. Orphans (i.e., those children under the age of 18 years who have lost one or both parents from any cause) have become an increasingly visible group since the rapid spread of HIV/AIDS in Africa, but our experience from the field in several African countries cautions against any claim that such group may be the one becoming necessarily heads of households of deceased parents, for there is a great level of familial and community solidarity still prevalent in Africa both as regards young and older people (Kuate-Defo, 2005b). In fact, many other children who are not orphans have been made vulnerable to wars and other shocks and of the 34 million orphans from any cause estimated in 2001, 11 million (less than one-third) were attributed to AIDS (Subbarao and Coury, 2004).

Contracting an STI in the last 12 months. For reproductive health problems, two questions were asked about sexually transmitted infections (STI):

1. During the last 12 months, have you had any sexually transmitted infections? (Yes, no, don't know.)
2. What sexually transmitted infections did you have? (STI included syphilis, gonorrhea, AIDS, genital wart, genital discharge, ulcer, other.)

Although a note in the questionnaire asked the interviewer to record all symptoms listed by a respondent, in the actual CDHS-98 data file, there is only one symptom (if any) per respondent in the last 12 months. But because of potential problems of misclassification in self-reports often by gender, we restrict the analyses to all STI symptoms and consider a response variable coded 1 if the respondent had any STI and 0 otherwise. This outcome is considered an unsuccessful and unhealthy transition to adult reproductive life.

Being employed in the last 12 months. In the CDHS-98, labor force participation in the last 12 months preceding the survey was measured by asking the following questions:

1. Besides your domestic work, are you currently employed? (Yes, no.)
2. As you know, some women/men have a job for which they are paid in money or nature, and others have a small business or work in the farm or in family business. Are you currently doing this type or any other type of job? (Yes, no.)
3. Have you done any work during the last 12 months? (Yes, no.)

We define a response variable coded 1 if the female or male respondent answered "yes" to these three questions and 0 otherwise. The CDHS-98, like DHS data in general, does not have information on the duration of employment. Therefore, this response variable captures only the prevalence of employment as some respondents may have moved in and out of employment status within the last 12 months. We consider entry into the labor market as a successful transition in Cameroon.

Cause-Specific School Attrition: School Leaving Due to Work, Marriage, Childbearing, or Failure

For cause-specific times to school attrition, besides the standard education questions found in all DHS, two very useful questions specific to the CDHS-98 alone were asked of female respondents:

1. At what age have you stopped going to school?
2. What is the main reason for you to stop attending school?

With this information, we define two response variables. First, we define an event-duration response variable coded 1 if a female respondent ages 15 to 24 years had left school at a given age since her first enrollment and 0 if she is still enrolled. Multilevel event-history analysis is used to estimate the effects of covariates on this age-dependent probability of leaving school. Next, we consider the self-reported causes of school leaving given exposure to the risk of doing so from the age at first enrollment within a competing risks analysis framework, focusing on key events marking transition to adulthood (i.e., work, marriage, unwed childbearing, and school graduation/failure). Leaving school to work or to get married is considered a successful transition to adult roles and responsibilities, whereas dropping out of school due to a pregnancy or grade failure is an unsuccessful transition.

Explanatory Variables and Expected Linkages
with Response Variables

Individuals live in an increasingly changing world, and the stabilizing or destabilizing effects are present in their lives as they attempt to make life course transitions through sequences of experiences of "stability" and "change." A study of transitions from adolescence to adulthood must acknowledge the simultaneous occurrence of stability and change in socioeconomic, political, community, and family contexts as well as individual life. In the context of globalization, however defined, a conceptually operational scheme for analyzing and interpreting the influences on and variability in experiences of life course transitions should ideally involve at least seven nested levels of influences: within-individual, individual, family/household, neighborhood/community, region/province, nation/country, and global levels. Some of these influences may be cross-leveled while others are level-specific. For these reasons, it is not feasible to develop a graphical representation of an operational framework that shows the various articulations of the level of operation of changing influences on various types of transitions while avoiding clutter and ensuring mutually exclusive classification categories. Therefore, we focus on main features of such an operational scheme and its aspects that will be tested in this study given the data at hand.

We examine three groups of determinants of transitions to adulthood among young people: (1) physiological influences (e.g., immune status and age at menarche); (2) demographic, socioeconomic, and sociocultural influences (e.g., age, sex, family structure, poverty and social class, ethnicity, religion); and (3) environmental influences (e.g., region and place of residence). Within the limits of the data at hand, we consider that those influences can be situated at the individual/family/household, community, and regional levels, which may entail different types of intervention targeted at young people.

Physiological Influences

Several physiological factors have been implicated in explanations of behaviors, risks, and events experienced during the life course. During childhood and adolescence, innate or acquired immunity or healthiness, menarche, and coinfection have been the most studied in relation to positive and negative behaviors and life events (Evans, Barer, and Marmor, 1994; Gray, Leridon, and Spira, 1993; National Research Council, 2001). Probably the most reliable information collected in most household surveys is female age at menarche. The age at menarche has been declining, a manifestation of better nutritional and hormonal microenvironments both in developed and developing countries (Rees, 1993). Menarche has been shown to occur generally later in life in developing countries, but earlier in urban than rural areas. This progressively earlier maturation and the progressively delayed mean age at marriage in many developing countries has greatly extended the length of time of exposure to premarital sexual intercourse and has made social, cultural, and religious norms and proscriptions about sexual conduct less effective than in the past (Narayan et al., 2001; UNFPA, 2003b). The extent to which age at menarche influences the risk of STI can be derived indirectly from the overwhelming evidence on close links between early sexual debut and increased risk of STI (Bang et al., 1989; Brabin, 2001; Cates, 1990; Committee on Adolescence, 1994). Because earlier menarche has been linked to earlier sexual debut (Kuate-Defo, 1998), early age at menarche may be at least indirectly associated with the STI risk.

There are no data on biological or physiological factors in the CDHS-98 that could be used. Information on age at menarche was collected only in the 1991 CDHS and none of the DHS has measured the general health status of youth. We posit that poor health reduces a youth's ability to live independently or to succeed in the educational, social, or professional domains of life; in fact, as shown in Table 10-2, 5 percent of young people aged 15 to 24 in 1998 in Cameroon reported that they had stopped school due to sickness. Such individual-specific unmeasured random influences will be captured in all fitted multilevel models at the individual level.

Demographic, Socioeconomic, and Cultural Influences

A number of studies have found that transitions to adulthood covary with age, gender, ethnicity and religion, family structure, and social class. This section reviews these factors in relation to transition to adulthood in the context of developing countries.

Age

In many cultures, the period of adolescence extends over many years. Previous developmental studies have consistently shown that it can be usefully subdivided into three developmental phases: (1) early adolescence, which encompasses the biological changes of puberty as well as sexual and psychological awakenings, extending roughly from ages 10 through 14; (2) middle adolescence, which is a time of increased autonomy and experimentation, covering ages 15 to 17 or so; and (3) late adolescence, for those who delay their entry into adult roles because of educational or social factors, which can stretch from age 18 into the early 20s (i.e., age 24 in this study). Each phase has a unique set of developmental challenges, opportunities, and risks. But there are limitations to taking a piecemeal approach to transitions to adulthood. Recently, researchers have started to examine why some adolescents in low-income contexts successfully navigate through environmental challenges, while others, similarly situated, adopt lifestyles that are at odds with successful transitions to adulthood (e.g., unprotected sexual behavior, premarital childbearing, school dropout due to failure).

Researchers have also sought to identify influences on these problems and patterns of resilience that protect teens and encourage them to succeed, and have emphasized the need to examine the "whole" youth—a concept that describes the assets as well as the deficits of individual adolescents—rather than isolating selected problem behaviors associated with adolescents in difficult circumstances (National Research Council and Institute of Medicine, 1999). Although this focus on the whole youth has been applauded, much more work needs to be done before the picture is clear about which combinations of factors, influences, contexts, and interventions will ultimately ensure healthy and successful transitions to adulthood, as we attempt to do in this study. For example, adolescents are less likely to be sexually active than their older counterparts, but are more likely to have asymptomatic infections than adults and to suffer long-term consequences such as chronic infection, spontaneous abortions, and infected offspring. Sexually active adolescents have also been shown to have the highest rates of gonorrhea, syphilis, and pelvic inflammatory disease of any age group, and the younger the teenager, the greater the risk of acquiring an STI (Cates, 1990). Studies on gonorrhea in selected Middle Eastern and African countries found infection levels were highest among the 15 to 19 age group (UNAIDS, 2001). Such disease-specific studies may underestimate the overall prevalence of STI among adults due to misclassification, unlike studies based on DHS-type questions.

Gender

Gender differences in exposure to and experience of various socioeconomic and demographic events across the life course are well established. In general, females are at a disadvantage compared to males in terms of educational attainment and employment opportunities, especially in developing countries (Jejeebhoy, 1995; UNFPA, 2003a), and they face higher risks of HIV/AIDS than males (UNAIDS, 2003). Most research has concentrated on females, partly because national fertility surveys interview only females and because of the historical interest in teenage pregnancy. However, studies that have included both males and females have consistently shown gender differences in the age at first sexual experience (Boutin, Lemardeley, and Gateff, 1987; Brabin, 2001; Brown et al., 2001; Committee on Adolescence, 1994; Kuate-Defo, 1998). In most societies, normative expectations about the appropriate age and circumstances of first intercourse vary by gender. Certain STIs have been shown to be more prevalent among males than females and vice versa, and therefore, may manifest gender differences in their prevalence. For example, in all developed countries with available data, chlamydia infections in women were shown to exceed those in men, and chlamydia prevalence is strongly correlated with younger age and heterosexual behaviors (Brabin, 2001; Cates, 1990; Holmes, 1994; National Research Council, 1997).

Ethnicity and Religion

Ethnicity and religion are two factors that carried a number of norms, practices, and prescriptions with much theoretical and empirical evidence on their influential role on individuals' behaviors (Bolin et al., 2003; Borjas, 1992; Kuate-Defo, 1998). Ethnic and religious affiliations are used as markers of cultural, normative, and moral values. Ethnic and religious differences may be explained by the fact that youth from some ethnic groups or religious faiths may be reacting to somewhat more proscriptive cultural, normative, and moral expectations regarding their behaviors. In Cameroon, people also carry a number of social norms and practices that influence behaviors (Fotso et al., 1999; Kuate-Defo, 1998; Podlewski, 1975). For example, we expect respondents from the Pahouni-Beti ethnic groups to report younger ages at first sexual intercourse than respondents from other ethnic affiliations in Cameroon because precocious sex and childbearing is encouraged, or at least not deterred, among the Pahouin-Beti (Kuate-Defo, 1998). In particular, because of differences in expectations regarding boys and girls across ethnic groups in Cameroon, we expect the ethnic influences to operate differently by gender.

Family Structure

In all societies, family is the most important setting for ensuring successful transitions to adulthood. Although not all adolescents growing up in poor or divorced families are destined to have problems, an extensive literature suggests that adolescents living in families experiencing economic hardship, divorce, or both are at increased risk for a range of health and behavioral problems, including school failure and high-risk behaviors (Binder and Woodruff, 2002; Bledsoe, 1994; Scarr and Weinberg, 1994). Parents who maintain strong emotional relationships with their children, display supportive attitudes, and practice loving and warm, yet firm and consistent, parenting can help their children and adolescents cope more successfully (Darling and Steinberg, 1992; Kuate-Defo, 1999). Family support is an important determinant of events in successful transitions to adulthood, both for its direct contribution and for its ability to moderate the effects of harmful influential factors during adolescence and young adulthood. Despite changes in family structure and composition over time, the family remains extremely important for adolescent development and readiness to transition to adult roles, and having a positive and warm relationship with parents remains one of the most important predictors of healthy and secure development during the adolescent years and later in life.

Socioeconomic Indexes at the Household and Community Levels

Among the many factors that influence young people's health, behaviors, development, and well-being are household wealth and amenities as well as socioeconomic conditions of the community (Binder and Woodruff, 2002; Bolin et al., 2003; Jensen and Nielsen, 1997). In terms of human capital, opportunities for advanced education and training and entry into the workforce are also closely linked to family income. Economic hardship—whether from low wages, sustained poverty or unemployment—is likely to diminish significantly the emotional well-being of parents, with direct and indirect effects on their children's health, education, and well-being. Changing societal and economic factors have threatened the stability of many families. Changes include increased divorce rates, increases in the number of single parents, increases in the rate of mothers' employment, and increases in the proportion of families living in poverty. Due to the economic crisis that has shaken Cameroon since the mid-1980s, one of the most profound changes in the last two decades is the increased proportion of adolescents living in or near poverty, with little or no access to education. These changes have transformed the nature of family life, and are likely to have influenced the experiences of adolescents.

Most of the social interactions of families and adolescence are embedded within neighborhood settings. In general, a neighborhood can be defined both spatially (as a geographic area) and functionally (as a set of social networks). Our field experience suggests that in most African societies and to the extent that community resources including recreational services are made available and accessible to the population, the benefit to youth is very likely because they reduce the risk of youth being bored. Lack of opportunity structures in disadvantaged communities means lack of employment opportunities, which translates into lack of financial resources (Bolin et al., 2003; Boserup, 1985; Warren and Lee, 2003). A missing factor in the lives of adolescents in disadvantaged communities is exposure to successful, upwardly mobile adults. Far too often, adults who become successful move out of the disadvantaged areas to higher income urban or suburban communities and make no attempt to promote a better environment for those left behind. Lacking this exposure, adolescents in disadvantaged neighborhoods may have limited opportunities to learn about strategies for identifying educational and career opportunities. Socioeconomic conditions (e.g., poverty and status of women) have also been shown to influence risks and patterns of STIs (Boutin et al., 1987; Cates, 1990). All STIs, including HIV/AIDS, thrive under crisis conditions, which coincide with limited access to the means of prevention, treatment, and care (UNAIDS, 2000, 2001). Financial and transportation barriers limit education and health care access for many poor teenagers, especially those living in worse-off or remote areas. Lack of access to such services often translates into lack of access to barrier contraceptive methods such as condoms or school-learned skills needed in the labor market.

We assess these potential influences of socioeconomic conditions by constructing socioeconomic indices (a household wealth index and a community development index) based on indicators built from weights derived from principal component analysis (PCA). This approach is of potentially broad application as nearly identical DHS have been carried out in developing countries. This method allows for comparison of differences in outcomes across socioeconomic groups. More generally, PCA is a statistical technique that linearly transforms an original set of observed variables into a substantially smaller, more coherent set of uncorrelated variables that captures most of the information by maximizing the variance accounted for in the original variables. Community is defined using sampling clusters grouped within administrative units. For the household wealth index, indicators include possessions (i.e., electricity, radio, TV, refrigerator, bicycle, motorcycle, car, oven, stove, and telephone), drinking water source, type of toilet facilities, and type of flooring material. The household wealth index includes components of parental assets and financial capacities. The variables of drinking water source, type of toilet facilities, and type of flooring material were recoded 0-1 in terms of access to clean water, to modern toilets, and to finished floors, respectively. For the community development index, we focus on electricity, telephone, and water source availability in the community. Using these indices, each household or community is assigned to categories labeled poorest (bottom 40 percent), middle (next 40 percent), and richest (top 20 percent).

ENVIRONMENTAL AND REGIONAL INFLUENCES

Environmental attributes consistently have been shown to influence human and adolescent behaviors in all aspects of life (National Research Council and Institute of Medicine, 1999; Podlewski, 1975; Warren and Lee, 2003). In most societies and in Cameroon in particular, girls typically are granted less autonomy and are subject to greater parental control. In low-income areas or rural/semirural areas, boys often spend more time hanging out on the streets. In rural settings in general, once a young woman has reached menarche and can have children, her mobility and opportunities may be restricted as her family fears she may be sexually victimized or have sexual intercourse, bringing dishonor to the family (Jejeebhoy, 1995; UNFPA, 2003a). On the other hand, urbanization resulting in large numbers of unskilled young people on the economic margin and only tenuously connected to their families, along with a ready market for sex, has led to large numbers of adolescents engaging in risky sexual behaviors in developing countries (MacPhail, Williams, and Campbell, 2002).

For the earliest part of the life course, life is relatively uncompartmentalized, and under normal circumstances, childhood place of residence is shared with biological parents. Place of residence has also been linked to opportunities for education and employment for young people (UNFPA, 2003a; Warren and Lee, 2003) and acquisition and transmission of disease and STIs, including HIV/AIDS (UNAIDS, 2003). In resource-constrained contexts typical of many developing countries, rural milieu is often associated with social norms and practices that perpetuate the low status of women and limited or no access to a number of opportunities offered by the social or institutional environments at the domestic, local, national, and international levels (Kuate-Defo, 1997). Thus, geographical location and access to services clearly play a role in access to information, which illuminates many decisions regarding life options and opportunities.

At the community and regional levels, norms, values, social roles, family and kin, community groups, and media play out as part of normative/behavioral influences on transitions. Climate, socioeconomic resources, and media contribute to structural and environmental influences on life course transitions. For adolescent and young adult behaviors, while many contextual studies have addressed the impact of family structure and peer group characteristics, few researchers have raised the level of explanation further, to examine, for instance, the influences of area and community contexts as we do in this study. The few studies that exist provide compelling evidence that those behaviors are shaped not just by individual-level characteristics, but also by the nature of the surrounding social context. Despite differences in sample, study design, and operational definition of "community," these studies all report significant contextual effects (National Research Council and Institute of Medicine, 1999). A community characterized by social disorganization and few economic resources seems to provide young people with little motivation to avoid behaviors that have potentially negative consequences on successful transitions to adulthood. Thus, the influences of region and place of residence on various outcomes considered in this study may operate differently for different age groups by gender.

FORMULATION AND ESTIMATION OF MODELS FOR TRANSITIONS TO ADULTHOOD

In this section, we present the statistical methods used to estimate the effects of influences on successful or unsuccessful transitions to adult roles, with applications to data from Cameroon.

Multilevel Logistic Regression Models for Dichotomous Response Variables

To assess the effects of factors associated with the probability of a young person being head of the household, being employed, or being infected with an STI during the last 12 months preceding the CDHS-98, we use multilevel logistic regression models for these three dichotomous response variables. Because our research endeavor implies isolating nested contextual effects along with fixed and random influences on these response variables, three levels of nesting are considered: individual (Level 1), community (Level 2), and province (Level 3), denoted by **i**, **j**, and **k**, respectively. This represents clustered data of individuals nested within communities and communities nested within provinces in Cameroon. The three-level logistic regression model is formulated in the most general form as follows:

$$Y_{ijk} = \beta_0 + \beta_1 Z_{1ijk} + \beta_2 Z_{2jk} + \beta_3 Z_{3k} + \eta_k + \vartheta_{jk} + \varepsilon_{ijk} \qquad (1)$$

where Y_{ijk} is the value of a young person **i** living in community **j** of province **k**, on the dependent variable **Y**. Y_{ijk} equals the logit or log-odds of being a household head at the interview date, or being employed within the last 12 months from the survey date, β_0 or having had an STI within the last 12 months from the survey date; the overall constant (intercept); Y_{ijk} the value of a young person **i** from community **j** belonging to province **k**, on individual-level vector of predictors Z_1; β_1 the vector of fixed and random effects of individual-level predictors Z_1; β_2 the vector of fixed and random effects of community-level predictors Z_2; and β_3 the vector of fixed and random effects of province-level predictors Z_3. This model also specifies nested sources of variability or nested random influences, denoted η_k, ϑ_{jk}, and ε_{ijk} for the province level, community level, and individual level, respectively. The main focus in the development of statistical techniques for mixed models was until the 1980s on random effects (i.e., random differences between entities in some classification system) (Baltagi, 1995; Clayton and Hills, 1993) more than on random coefficients (i.e., random effects of numerical variables) (Kreft and De Leeuw, 1998). The multilevel analysis formulated here is formed by these two streams coming together (Bryk and

Raudenbush, 1992; Goldstein, 2003; Searle et al., 1992; Snijders and Bosker, 1999) whereby the individual and the context in which his/her life is embedded, are modeled as nested random influences η_k, ϑ_{jk}, and for ε_{ijk}.

Multilevel Competing Risks Model for the Risk of Stopping School

One of the features of survival analysis is its ability to take into account censoring of exposure in the specification and estimation of effects of covariates on the response variable. The end of exposure to the risk of stopping school can occur for different censoring reasons. A concern is the appropriate categorization of school cessation by cause. We first consider a failure time model with one type of failure (i.e., whether a female youth left school any time before her 25th birthday) and then extend the model to allow for more than one type of failure by considering multiple causes/reasons of school cessation (i.e., in this study, exiting school due to work, marriage, childbearing, or grade failure) within a competing causes framework. In either case, the fitted models describe a young woman's decision at any time to stop school by her 25th birthday and for one of four possible reasons most relevant to transitions to adulthood in Cameroon (i.e., work, marriage, childbearing, and school failure).

Suppose that there are m observable causes (or failure types) of stopping school and that each young woman has an underlying failure time T that may be subject to censoring, and a covariate function $Z = \{z(u):u \geq 0\}$. Suppose also that when failure occurs, it may be one of m distinct types or causes denoted by $M \in \{1,2,...,m\}$. For the purpose of this study, at least two distinct issues arise in the analysis of such data: (1) the estimation of the relationship between the explanatory variables and the rate of occurrence of failure (or school cessation) of specific types (or for specific causes); and (2) the study of the interrelation between failure types (or causes of school cessation) under a specific set of study conditions. Issue 1 arose in the analysis of such data because the primary end point of investigation is the young girl's survival time (i.e., the time spent in school from the origin time of her first enrollment). Because the differential effects of attrition from school may depend markedly on cause of attrition, and because distinct causes of attrition may relate to different associated factors, our study argues that an analysis of overall survival time irrespective of cause of dropout (i.e., school cessation all causes combined) may be inadequate. Hence, we estimate models for both the overall hazard of school attrition as well as for cause-specific school dropout by age 25.

Issue 2 is also of interest in a number of situations. Knowledge of the interrelation between failure types would be valuable in defining the required strategies for successful transitions to adulthood by investing in youth. For example, there is a great deal of research on the links between school dropout and employment among young people (Jensen and Nielsen, 1997; Ravanera, Rajulton, and Burch, 1998; Warren and Lee, 2003). As several previous studies have shown (Arnold and Brockett, 1983; Cox, 1959; Heckman and Honoré, 1989; Kalbfleisch and Prentice, 1980; Tsiatis, 1975), the data of type we have at hand are not adequate to study the interrelation between failure types. Retrospective histories on various transitions and the timing and sequencing of episodes/spells of events would have allowed us to fully address dependent competing risks and correlated transitions at the individual level, as in Kuate-Defo (1995). Hence, we estimate a reduced-form model using a competing risks framework (Kalbfleisch and Prentice, 1980). The occurrence of a transition from the state of being in school since the age at first enrollment—marking the beginning of exposure to the risk of stopping school by her 25th birthday—to the state of being out of school for a given cause r removes the young woman from the risk of experiencing any other cause of stopping school at that exposure length. The competing risks framework characterizes each transition by a separate transition rate and hazard function. The split of the log likelihood into a sum of separate parts, one for each cause-specific rate, does not arise as a result of any assumption of independence of causes, but out of the way cause-specific school attrition rate parameters are defined in the data at hand. The rate for cause r is defined as the probability per unit of time (i.e., a year here) of failure due to cause r, conditional on the respondent having previously survived all causes of school attrition. In other words, the cause-specific hazard function is defined as the probability that a young female had transitioned from the state of "being in school" to "being out of school" due to cause r after $t + \Delta t$ years given that she was in school for at least t years. In a conventional hazard model, the hazard rate μ is defined to be a function of time and a set of individual-level, community-level, and province-level explanatory variables and written as:

$$\mu_r(t; Z_1, Z_2, Z_3) = \lim_{\Delta t \to 0} \frac{P(t \le T \prec t + \Delta t, R = r | T \ge t, Z_1, Z_2, Z_3)}{\Delta t} \quad r = 1, ..., m \quad (2)$$

where r is a given cause of stopping school marking a given transition; t is the number of years of school enrollment; and Z_1, Z_2, Z_3 are vectors of characteristics measured at the individual, community, and province levels, respectively. In other words, $\mu_r (t; Z_1, Z_2, Z_3)$ is the instantaneous rate of school leaving due to cause r at time t given, and in the presence of the other causes of school dropout. Because leaving school due to cause r must be a unique element of $\{1, 2, ..., m\}$, the overall hazard rate of school leaving is:

$$\mu(t; Z_1; Z_2; Z_3) = \sum_1^m \mu_r(t; Z_1, Z_2, Z_3) \quad (3)$$

Kalbfleisch and Prentice (1980) show that the likelihood function derived from equation 3 can be written entirely in terms of the cause-specific hazard functions and that these functions are identifiable, meaning, they can be estimated from school leaving data of the type we have at hand without further assumptions. Hence, following Heckman and Singer (1984) and Kuate-Defo (2001), and building from equations 2 and 3, the multilevel hazard function of failure of type r can be parameterized in a general and flexible way (without level-specific or cross-level interactions) and written as:

$$\mu_{rijk}(t|Z_{1ijk}(t); Z_{2jk}(t); Z_{3k}(t); \varepsilon_{ijk}; \vartheta_{jk}; \eta_k)$$

$$= \exp\left\{\left[Z_{1ijk}(t)\beta_1 + Z_{2jk}(t)\beta_2 + Z_{3k}(t)\beta_3\right]\right.$$

$$\left.+\psi\left[\frac{(t^\varphi - 1)}{\varphi}\right] + \delta\left[\frac{(t^\upsilon - 1)}{\upsilon}\right] + \varepsilon_{ijk}(t) + \vartheta_{jk}(t) + \eta_k(t)\right\}, \upsilon > \varphi \geq 0$$

(4)

where Z_1, Z_2, Z_3 are vectors of individual-level, community-level, and province-level characteristics, as in equation 1; here, their values are allowed to change over time. Duration dependence (not indexed for level-specific duration dependencies in order to avoid clutter and for simplicity of presentation) is captured by two terms,

$$\frac{t^\varphi - 1}{\varphi} \text{ and } \frac{t^\upsilon - 1}{\upsilon}.$$

This general formulation allows ε_{ijk}, ϑ_{jk}, η_k to be functions of time. By exponentiating the term in brackets, equation 4 ensures that the hazard function is positive, as required because it is a conditional density function. This general multilevel hazard formulation reduces to a multilevel power function hazard (multilevel Weibull distribution) when $\varphi = \delta = 0$, to a multilevel exponential hazard (multilevel Gompertz distribution) when $\varphi = 1$ and $\delta = 0$, to a multilevel log-quadratic hazard when $\varphi = 1$ and $\upsilon = 2$, and to a multilevel constant hazard (multilevel exponential distribution) when $\psi = \delta = 0$. This flexible specification makes it possible to test easily for multilevel constant, monotone increasing, or monotone decreasing hazards. Likewise, because the hazard is fully parametric, it is possible to extrapolate beyond the range of observations, although the usual caveats apply.

The overall hazard function from equation 4 is the sum of all the cause-specific hazard functions. The period of observation begins with a youth entering school and ends when that youth exits school or until the observation is right censored at the time of the interview. We use a discrete-time framework to estimate the models because of the annual nature of the data (i.e., age in years at school leaving). In practice, a discrete-time model specification is also useful because of the problem of ties. We fit multicategory (also called polychotomous) logit models by considering all pairs of categories composed of each of the four causes of school attrition of interest in this study (i.e., school leaving due to work, marriage, child-bearing, and failure) versus the baseline category "still enrolled in school," and describing the odds of duration response (or times to leaving school given enrollment) due to a particular cause (Agresti, 1990; Clayton and Hills, 1993; Kalbfleisch and Prentice, 1980). Let $\{\pi_1,...,\pi_R\}$ denote the duration response probabilities, satisfying $\sum_r \pi_r = 1$. The baseline-category logit models considered here are of the general form

$$\log\left(\frac{\pi_r}{\pi_R}\right), \ r = 1,...,R-1.$$

The estimated models consist of multilevel baseline-logit hazard equations, with separate parameters for each, that is, the effects of explanatory variables and unobserved heterogeneity vary according to the response category paired with the baseline. The relevant reduced-form multilevel competing risks models posit that the transition probability $\mu_r(t)$—that stopping school due to cause r occurs to the *i-th* individual from the *j-th* community of the *k-th* province at duration *t*-is a linear combination of the level-specific covariates, where the logit of a probability μ_r is the log-odds, defined as

$$\mathrm{logit}(\mu_r) = 1\mathrm{n}\left(\frac{\mu_r}{1-\mu_r}\right)$$

where ln (a) denotes the natural logarithm of the number a. We can define the odds of failure as if they followed a multilevel logistic pattern for age α, conditional on individual-specific (ε_{ijk}), community-specific (ϑ_{jk}), and province-specific (η_k) random influences assumed to operate multiplicatively on the baseline hazard. The model becomes:

$$\frac{q_{ijk}(\alpha)}{1-q_{ijk}(\alpha)} = \exp\left\{-\left([\beta_1 Z_{1ijk}(\alpha)][\beta_1 Z_{2jk}(\alpha)][\beta_3 Z_{3k}(\alpha)]\right)\varepsilon_{ijk}\vartheta_{jk}\eta_k\right\} \quad (5)$$

where $q_{ijk}(\alpha)$ is the probability of experiencing a transition of interest during the observation period in the individual life course by age α for the *i-th* individual from the *j-th* community of the *k-th* province in Cameroon. In this case, those who experience that transition are given a count of one year instead of the conventional exposure of half a year when a rate is computed in the (multistate) life table formulation, which forms the basis of our descriptive analyses (see Table 10-4). The only change from the hazard model formulated so far is that the conditional logit of the probability, instead of the logarithm of the rate, is expressed as a linear combination of the covariate effects. A comparison of the likelihood of the main-effects model with the likelihood of the fully saturated model reveals whether the main-effects model adequately fits the data. The substantive interpretation of the covariates does not depend on whether rates or probabilities are modeled. It follows from equation 5 that the discrete-time multilevel multinomial hazard model for the transition to a given state τ can be parameterized in a general formulation (without level-specific or cross-level interactions) and written as:

$$\frac{q_{ijk}^{\tau}(\alpha)}{1-q_{ijk}^{\tau}(\alpha)} = \exp\left\{-\left(\left[\beta_{1}^{\tau} Z_{1ijk}^{\tau}(\alpha)\right]\left[\beta_{2}^{\tau} Z_{2jk}^{\tau}(\alpha)\right]\left[\beta_{3}^{\tau} Z_{3k}^{\tau}(\alpha)\right]\right)\varepsilon_{ijk}^{\tau}\vartheta_{jk}^{\tau}\eta_{k}^{\tau}\right\} \quad (6)$$

The formulated model specifies nested random influences η_k, ϑ_{jk}, and ε_{ijk}, for the province, community, and individual levels, respectively.

Estimation of Models Formulated for Studying Transitions to Adulthood

After several trial runs of the models formulated above—including those allowing for covariance structure, cross-level effects, and interaction effects—the most stable and parsimonious models were those estimated as described below.

For the multilevel logistic regression models formulated for each dichotomous response variable, models were fitted separately for males and females as well as a pooled model for both sexes. An important question in this study is whether the effects of explanatory variables, structural contexts and random influences, vary by sex. To answer this question, we test for interactions with gender by providing a full set of parameter estimates that allows for separate effects and influences for men and women. In doing so, we provide formal tests of the theoretical framework of the NRC's Panel on Transitions to Adulthood in Developing Countries, which assumes that contexts matter over and above individual/household socioeconomic status and ethnicity and that the differences in influences on transitions to adulthood are also gender-dependent.

The multilevel survival models formulated above for school attrition outcomes have the advantage of being estimated with standard multilevel programs that have been designed to perform analysis with discrete data. The estimation is done jointly across time intervals, and this feature allows testing of multilevel survival models that are more general than the ones included in the proportional hazards model. In fact, one can test the hypothesis that the causal process of transition to adulthood may be different across time intervals during the life course to the extent that the values of covariates or of the estimated parameters differ by time interval (i.e., violation of the proportionality assumption). It is also worth noting that most computer programs used for estimating a logistic hazard model do not provide correct estimates of the baseline odds because the procedures usually assume that if the individuals are censored within an interval, they are censored right before the end of the interval. Other estimation procedures for discrete versions of a proportional hazards model, suggested, for example, by Kalbfleisch and Prentice (1980), involve likelihood functions that cannot be maximized easily with standard software. To produce more accurate estimates, we can incorporate a series of dummies capturing the duration structure of the hazard function during the observation period, while closely monitoring the full survival time of both censored and uncensored cases. With these methodological precautions taken into account, we have discrete survival times measured by 10 dummy variables (i.e., < 15 years as reference category, and 10 dummies for each of the ages 15 to 24 years) capturing the duration structure of school attrition. Like in the case involving multilevel logit models above, the multilevel survival analysis formulated here is designed to test the hypothesis of the theoretical framework of the NRC's Panel that contexts matter even after controlling for other influential measured and unmeasured factors of transitions to adulthood.

Parameter estimation in hierarchical nonlinear models such as the ones formulated in this chapter is more complicated than in hierarchical linear models, and a number of approximations have been proposed in the literature on multilevel nonlinear modeling (Kuate-Defo, 2001). Reviews of estimation methods were done by Rodríguez and Goldman (1995), Davidian and Giltinan (1995), and Goldstein (2003). The most frequently used estimation methods are based on a first-order or a second-order Taylor expansion of the link function. When the approximation is around the estimated fixed part of the model, this is called marginal quasi-likelihood (MQL), and when the approximation is around an estimate for the fixed plus the random parts of the model, it is called penalized or predictive quasi-likelihood (PQL) (Breslow and Clayton, 1993; Goldstein, 2003); both procedures are implemented in programs for multilevel modeling such as MLwiN. We estimate parameters using the MLwiN statistical software (Yang and Goldstein, 2003), given the stability of the algorithm, its statistical efficiency, the data set at hand, and the complexity of the fitted models in this study. Parameter estimates are computed by the PQL estimation procedure with second-order Taylor expansion. This procedure is computationally more demanding, but results in more reliable parameter estimates than the

MQL estimation procedure with first-order Taylor expansion that is used for model building (Goldstein, 2003; Rasbash et al., 2000). Convergence tolerance was set at 2, and the distributional assumption was the extra-binomial distribution of the residual for a youth i from community j of province k.

We also partition the nested random influences derived from equations (1) and (6) which capture the total variability of each outcome of interest, into three components: among individuals within communities (Level 1), σ^2; among communities within provinces (Level 2), τ_ϑ; and among provinces within Cameroon (Level 3), τ_η. The total variability for an outcome of interest is $\mathrm{var}(Y_{ijk}) = \sigma^2 + \tau_\vartheta + \tau_\eta$. In terms of multilevel modeling, this leads to a relation between the parameters in the fixed part and the parameters of the random part that takes account of the non-normal distribution of response variables specified in our models. Because our estimated models are based on logistic function and since the standard deviation of the residual (ε_{ijk}) is

$$\sqrt{\pi^2/3} = 1.81$$

for the logistic model, the fixed estimates for the logistic model will tend to be about 1.81 and the variance parameters of the random part of the model about $\pi^2/3 = 3.29$. This implies that for three-level models fitted with nested higher levels of random influences η_k and ϑ_{jk}, and following Commenges and Jacqmin (1994) and Snijders and Bosker (1999), we can estimate the proportion of variation associated with each context, that is, among communities within provinces, and among provinces within Cameroon as follows:

$$\rho_c = \frac{\tau_\vartheta}{3.29 + \tau_\vartheta + \tau_\eta} \quad \textit{is the proportion of variance among communities} \quad (7)$$
$$\textit{within provinces;}$$

$$\rho_p = \frac{\tau_\eta}{3.29 + \tau_\vartheta + \tau_\eta} \quad \textit{is the proportion of variance among provinces in} \quad (8)$$
$$\textit{Cameroon;}$$

The advantage of partitioning nested random contextual influences using this definition is that it can be directly extended to define the residual intraclass correlation coefficient that controls for the effects of explanatory variables (e.g., covariates at the individual/household or community levels, environment at the province level), which has special appeal in this study as we investigate the net multilevel effects of both fixed and random influences on transitions to adulthood (see Tables 10-5 and 10-6, Panel C).

RESULTS

Timing of School Leaving by Self-Reported Reasons

Table 10-2 shows the frequency distribution of self-reported causes of school dropout by all female respondents, ages 15 to 49 years in 1998 in Cameroon. The analyses are also stratified by age cohort and age at leaving school by cause, and allow us to shed some light on changes over time in causes of school attrition.

Of all 3,325 women irrespective of migration/residence history, nearly 98 percent of them (3,245 women) left school before their 25th birthday. Children in Cameroon normally start attending school at age 4 for pre-elementary school and 6 for elementary (or primary) school. The age pattern of school attrition indicates that the vast majority of young people leave school between 7 and 18 years of age.

The inability to pay school fees is the main cause of leaving school among women in Cameroon. Nearly 48 percent of all women ages 15 to 19 who dropped out did so because they could not afford to pay school fees. Younger generations tend to be more affected by the economic hardship than their older counterparts; nearly 51 percent of females ages 15 to 24 left school for this reason, compared with only 45 percent of females ages 25 to 49. Furthermore, when we consider the timing of stopping school by the 25th birthday for all females ages 15 to 49 years in 1998, we found a consistent cohort-dependent pattern of leaving school due to financial difficulties. There is a 6-percentage-point difference between girls (15 to 19 years) and adults (25 to 49 years): 52.5 percent for ages 15 to 19 left school for this reason, compared with only 49.5 percent for ages 20 to 24 and 46.1 percent for ages 25 to 49.

These findings are not surprising because since the mid-1980s, the government of Cameroon has substantially reduced its investment in education and stopped subsidizing private schools. These measures were enacted and have been implemented nationwide despite the increasing demand for education by the growing population of school-age children and adolescents, most of whom have impoverished parents. Also since the mid-1980s, the government has implemented a policy of imposing school fees in all public schools, which were previously free of charge. The policy has been so harsh that some families are sending their children to private schools (sometimes cost less than public schools) or only keep in school older siblings on whom they have already invested a lot financially for their education while younger siblings stop school or stay home to help in family work/farm or to sell carry-on/ready-to-eat meals, fruits and drinks at local markets or along the road at police checkpoints; our multivariate analyses below (see Table 10-5) substantiate these findings. As a consequence, large segments of the

TABLE 10-2 Cohort Differences in Self-Reported Reasons for Leaving
School by Female Respondents in Cameroon: Weighted Data, CDHS-98

Main Reason for Leaving School	All Female Respondents		All Female Respondents Ages 25-49 Years		Respondents Ages 15-49 Years At Interview Date	
	Number	%	Number	%	Number	%
Could not pay school fees	1,582	47.6	886	45.3	1,561	48.1
Got pregnant	396	11.9	243	12.4	392	12.1
Got married	327	9.8	237	12.1	324	10.0
Did not like school	211	6.4	104	5.3	211	6.5
Did not pass exams	192	5.8	122	6.2	187	5.8
To earn money/to work	155	4.7	96	4.9	137	4.3
Sickness	120	3.6	53	2.7	117	3.6
Family needed help	80	2.4	47	2.4	79	2.4
Graduated, enough	75	2.2	53	2.7	57	1.8
Take care of children	47	1.4	33	1.7	46	1.4
School not accessible/ too far	30	0.9	22	1.1	29	0.9
Other reasons	97	2.9	53	2.7	94	2.9
Don't know	13	0.4	8	0.5	13	0.4
Total	3,325	100.0	1,957	100.0	3,247	100.0

SOURCE: Cameroon Demographic and Health Survey (1998).

youth population and younger generations, especially in rural areas or from
economically worse-off segments of the population, are increasingly unable
to afford to attend school or to complete their education. Hence, although
"could not pay school fees" is not a specific category of the polychotomous
response variable in this study, the findings reported here highlight the
urgency with which investment in youth in Africa must start with investment in their education to complete at least the elementary school. This
investment should include government subsidies to public and private
schools in order to meet the second goal of the United Nations Millennium
Development Goals (MDG) of achieving universal primary education for
all school-age children, at least through the secondary schools.

Two other reasons for leaving school among young people, marriage
and childbearing, have been routinely cited in the literature, but with little
empirical evidence from self-reported reasons and from young people's
voices themselves. Among female respondents ages 15 to 49 who had left

Respondents Who Left School Before Their 25th Birthday

Respondents Ages 15-19 Years At Interview Date		Respondents Ages 20-24 Years At Interview Date		Respondents Ages 15-24 Years At Interview Date		Respondents Ages 25-49 Years At Interview Date	
Number	%	Number	%	Number	%	Number	%
321	52.5	375	49.5	696	50.9	865	46.1
60	9.8	93	12.3	153	11.2	239	12.7
36	5.9	54	7.1	90	6.6	234	12.5
46	7.5	62	8.2	108	7.9	103	5.5
25	4.1	45	5.9	70	5.1	117	6.2
28	4.6	31	4.1	59	4.3	78	4.2
28	4.6	38	5.0	67	4.9	50	2.7
24	3.9	10	1.3	33	2.4	46	2.5
6	1.0	15	2.0	21	1.5	36	1.9
6	1.0	8	1.1	14	1.0	32	1.7
7	1.1	2	0.3	9	0.7	20	1.1
21	3.4	24	3.2	44	3.2	50	2.7
3	0.5	1	0.1	4	0.3	7	0.4
611	100.0	758	100.0	1,368	100.0	1,877	100.0

school, childbearing and marriage account for about 12 percent and 10 percent of cases, respectively. Trends analysis shows the prevalence of pregnancy (12.4 percent compared with 11.2 percent) and marriage (12.1 percent compared with 6.6 percent) as reported reasons for leaving school to be higher among older (25 to 49 years) than younger (15 to 24 years) women. There is also a consistent cohort-dependent pattern in the timing of leaving school due to pregnancy and marriage by age 25. Nearly 13 percent of women ages 25 to 49 dropped out of school due to a pregnancy or marriage; 12.3 percent of women ages 20 to 24 who left school did so because of a pregnancy, and only 7.1 percent because of marriage. Among girls ages 15 to 19 who left school, 9.8 percent did so because of a pregnancy and only about 6 percent due to marriage. In the only other relevant study in Africa to our knowledge, conducted in Zimbabwe among girls ages 7 to 18, the proportion of those who reported they left school due to pregnancy was 4 percent and those who left school due to marriage was 2 percent (Jensen and Nielsen, 1997). Put together, these proportions are substantially lower than initially thought given the usually conjectured links among marriage, childbearing, and female education in Africa.

This empirical evidence from self-reports of women themselves is generalized across generations and clearly substantiates that economic hardship is by far the most important reason for limited educational opportunities for girls in Africa. The reason does not appear to be early marriage or childbearing, which may be the consequence of being out of school rather than the other way around. Or marriage may be an acceptable last resort for most of these girls, who may be faced with no other life options for securing their future, given that more than 50 percent of school dropouts among young females are attributed to lack of money to pay school fees.

The other reasons reported in CDHS-98 (Table 10-2) by approximately 5 percent of women who left school are "did not like school" (6.4 percent), "did not pass exams" (5.8 percent), and "to earn money/to work" (4.7 percent). The fact that more young people (7.5 percent for those ages 15 to 19 and 8.2 percent for those ages 20 to 24) than older women (only 5.5 percent for those ages 25 to 49) report having left school by age 25 because they did not like school may suggest that the quality of school has been deteriorating in recent years. This explanation is plausible given the limited government investment in school resources and infrastructures as well as the poor working conditions of teachers and their lack of motivation for training students, situations that have been reported regularly in the Cameroon media and in forums of public school teachers. Furthermore, school failure does not appear to explain the generational gap in liking school, given the fact that a greater proportion of older women reported that they dropped out of school by age 25 because they failed their exams.

Poor health accounts for nearly 4 percent of cases of women who left school, and up to about 5 percent of women who left school for that reason were less than 25. Other reasons less frequently reported include helping the family (2.4 percent of cases for all women, but up to 4 percent for girls ages 15 to 19). Only 2 percent of women ages 15 to 49 left school because they had graduated, an indication of dramatic unmet needs in school attendance and grade completion for women that is generalized in Cameroon and most likely in other African countries.

Descriptive Statistics of Samples Used in Multivariate Analyses

Table 10-3 shows, for each gender, the sample proportions of selected variables used in the analyses. The proportions of adolescents for each gender are quite similar (61.1 percent for girls and 58.2 percent for boys).

TABLE 10-3 Selected Samples and Frequency Distribution of Selected Variables: Weighted Data, CDHS-98

Selected Variables	Females Ages 15-24 (N = 1,210)	Males Ages 15-24 (N = 849)
Explanatory variables		
Age cohort (in years)		
15-19	61.1	58.2
20-24	38.9	41.8
Religion		
Catholic	36.7	36.6
Protestant	33.3	25.7
Muslim	22.6	25.4
Others	7.4	12.3
Ethnic affiliation		
Bamileke related	39.2	31.5
Pahouin-Beti related	15.9	18.6
Fulfulde-Fulani	33.9	41.1
Douala-Bassa	10.9	8.8
Respondent's education		
Some	76.8	88.4
None	23.2	11.6
Household wealth index		
Poorest 40%	33.7	43.3
Middle 40%	50.8	43.0
Richest 20%	15.5	13.7
Family structure		
Live with biological parents	50.3	56.6
Live alone with other people	49.7	43.4
Community development index		
Poorest 40%	29.2	41.0
Middle 40%	35.3	29.3
Richest 20%	35.4	29.7
Place of residence		
Rural	56.2	65.2
Urban	43.8	34.8
Main regions		
Forest	41.9	40.5
Highlands	25.2	19.4
Sudano-Sahelian	32.9	40.1
Events with undefined transitions to adult roles		
Times to school attrition	48.6	—

continued

TABLE 10-3 Continued

Selected Variables	Females Ages 15-24 (N = 1,210)	Males Ages 15-24 (N = 849)
Event marking successful transitions to adult roles		
Worked during the last 12 months	54.1	59.4
Head of household	6.4	18.6
Times to school attrition for work and still working	3.2	—
Times to school attrition for marriage and still married	3.0	—
Event marking unsuccessful transitions to adult roles		
Had an STI during the last 12 months	1.4	5.7
Times to school attrition due to unwed pregnancy	4.0	—
Times to school attrition due to failure	5.5	—

SOURCE: Cameroon Demographic and Health Survey (1998).

There are some differences in gender-specific sample proportions by religious affiliation (e.g., more girls than boys are Protestant), ethnic group (e.g., more girls are from the Bamileke-related ethnic groups), and main regions of residence (e.g., more boys in the Sudano-Sahelian regions). There are also more boys than girls who have some education (88.4 percent and 76.8 percent), live with biological parents (56.6 percent and 50.3 percent), live in rural areas (65.2 percent and 56.2 percent), or come from the poorest 40 percent of households (43.3 percent and 33.7 percent) and communities (41.0 percent and 29.2 percent).

The prevalence of household headship by age 25 is higher for boys (18.6 percent) than girls (6.4 percent), as expected. When work is broadly defined, as in the CDHS-98, to capture both outside and home-based work of young people, a sizeable proportion of youth are active (59.4 percent for boys and 54.1 percent for girls). There is also a higher prevalence of STI, among boys (5.7 percent) than girls (1.4 percent); such a gap may stem partly from the fact that young males have higher rates of premarital sex than girls and marry significantly later than young females may be more exposed to sexual activity associated with higher risks of STI than expected in stable unions. Finally, among girls who stopped going to school by age 25, the prevalence of the main reasons considered for the transitions to adulthood are 3.0 percent for transition to marriage never dissolved, 4.0 percent for unwed pregnancy, 3.2 percent for transition to employment, and 5.5 percent for grade failure. As noted above, the data at hand do not allow us to tease out the movements in and out of various states occupied during the life course.

Relative Risks of Factors Associated with Cause-Specific School Attrition

Table 10-4 presents the overall and cause-specific probabilities of school attrition, marking transitions of interest in this study. These probabilities are derived from multiple decrement life tables and are presented in the form of relative risks (RR) to ease interpretation, with the reference category having an RR of 1. Overall, young people who are in their teen years, who live with their parents, who live in urban areas, or who live in well-off households or communities are most likely to be significantly protected against risks of leaving school prematurely, especially due to work, marriage, childbearing, or grade failure. Furthermore, there are important ethnic and regional differences in risks of leaving school, especially due to marriage and childbearing: Pahouin-Beti and Douala-Bassa girls are most likely to leave school because of a pregnancy, but least likely to leave due to marriage; in contrast, Fulfulde-Fulani girls are most likely to abandon school for marriage and least likely to stop due to unwed pregnancy. Similarly, girls from the Sudano-Sahelian regions are most likely to drop out of school due to marriage, but least likely to quit due to an unwed pregnancy. These results are consistent with our previous findings in Cameroon (Kuate-Defo, 1998, 2000) and indicate that one cannot comprehend many biodemographic processes in Cameroon without considering the ethnic, regional, and contextual factors.

As expected, younger women (15 to 19 years) are less likely to stop schooling than their older counterparts (20 to 24 years), who are about twice as likely to leave school in general and three times as likely to do so because of marriage or childbearing. Girls who live with their biological parents have lower probabilities of stopping school earlier than their counterparts living with other people.

There are also statistically significant differences in the likelihood of school attrition according to the socioeconomic conditions of young people's families and the level of development of their communities. The higher the socioeconomic gradient of the household or community, the lower the probability is of leaving school, especially due to grade failure. Girls from the poorest households are more than three times as likely to drop out of school because of failure as their counterparts from the richest households, and more than twice as likely as those from the richest communities. Girls from families and communities with low socioeconomic standing (i.e., poorest 40 percent) consistently have the highest probabilities of quitting school. This is corroborated by the higher probability also found for girls of these groups who tend to report they "could not pay school

TABLE 10-4 Relative Risks from Multiple Decrement Life Tables Probabilities of Cause-Specific School Attrition for Cameroonian Young Females by Selected Explanatory Variables: Weighted Data, CDHS-98

	School Attrition	Cause-Specific School Attrition with Transition to Adult Roles			
		Work and Still Working	Marriage and Still Married	Unwed Pregnancy	Grade Failure
Individual-level explanatory variables					
Age cohort (in years)	$p < 0.0001$	$p < 0.0178$	$p < 0.0001$	$p < 0.0002$	$p < 0.0001$
15-19	1.00	1.00	1.00	1.00	1.00
20-24	1.78	2.30	3.09	2.63	2.81
Religion	$p < 0.0001$	$p < 0.5439$	$p < 0.0001$	$p < 0.7261$	$p < 0.2132$
Catholic	1.00	1.00	1.00	1.00	1.00
Protestant	1.07	1.18	2.05	0.73	1.43
Muslim	1.23	1.28	0.74	0.96	1.20
Others	1.06	1.02	3.80	1.03	1.15
Ethnic affiliation	$p < 0.0001$	$p < 0.0001$	$p < 0.0001$	$p < 0.0045$	$p < 0.0118$
Bamileke related	1.00	1.00	1.00	1.00	1.00
Pahouin-Beti related	0.91	0.59	0.35	2.28	0.76
Fulfulde-Fulani	1.12	2.28	3.27	0.35	0.88
Douala-Bassa	0.83	0.67	0.48	1.48	0.63
Household-level explanatory variables					
HWI	$p < 0.0001$	$p < 0.0005$	$p < 0.0019$	$p < 0.0002$	$p < 0.0001$
Poorest 40%	1.00	1.00	1.00	1.00	1.00
Middle 40%	0.90	0.67	0.70	1.25	0.80
Richest 20%	0.62	0.47	0.58	0.72	0.39
Family structure	$p < 0.0001$	$p < 0.0751$	$p < 0.0001$	$p < 0.0226$	$p < 0.0834$
Live with biological parents	0.67	0.77	0.06	0.70	0.48
Live alone or with other people	1.00	1.00	1.00	1.00	1.00

Community-level explanatory variables					
CDI	p < 0.0001	p < 0.0001	p < 0.0001	p < 0.0035	p < 0.0001
Poorest 40%	1.00	1.00	1.00	1.00	1.00
Middle 40%	0.92	0.54	0.59	0.92	0.70
Richest 20%	0.68	0.43	0.30	0.74	0.45
Place of residence	p < 0.0001	p < 0.0001	p < 0.0001	p < 0.0003	p < 0.0001
Rural	1.00	1.00	1.00	1.00	1.00
Urban	0.69	0.54	0.42	0.76	0.55
Province-level explanatory variables					
Main regions	p < 0.0001	p < 0.0003	p < 0.0001	p < 0.0020	p < 0.0029
Forest	1.00	1.00	1.00	1.00	1.00
Highlands	1.27	1.08	2.64	0.65	1.45
Sudano-Sahelian	1.26	2.25	5.39	0.26	0.95

SOURCE: Cameroon Demographic and Health Survey (1998).

fees" as the main reason for stopping school. For example, the probability of leaving school for marriage is more than three times higher for girls from the poorest communities than for their peers from the richest ones.

Religious and ethnic differences are also noticeable, but not uniform. In general, Muslim and Fulfulde-Fulani girls tend to quit school at higher rates than their counterparts from other religious or ethnic groups. This result is consistent with the fact that traditionally in Cameroon, young girls from these groups have the lowest levels of school attendance. In particular, the Fulfulde-Fulani girls are more than twice as likely to leave school due to work and three times as likely to drop out of school for marriage as Bamileke girls, whereas Pahouin-Beti and Douala-Bassa girls are more than nine times and six times as unlikely to leave school for marriage as Fulfulde-Fulani girls.

Finally, the place and region of residence have statistically significant impacts on school attrition. As expected, girls who live in rural areas have the highest probabilities of leaving school early during their life course; they are 1.4 times as likely to stop school earlier than their counterparts from urban areas. Their risk of stopping school for marriage is even higher: They are 2.36 times as likely to drop out of school prematurely due to marriage as urban girls. There are also important regional differences in school attrition, with the probability of school attrition due to marriage for girls from the Sudano-Sahelian regions (northern part of Cameroon) 5.39 times higher than the probability for girls from the forest regions (southern and eastern parts of Cameroon) and twice as high as the probability for girls from the highlands regions (western part of Cameroon). Also worth noting is that although girls from the forest regions have an overall lower probability of school dropout than their counterparts from the rest of the country, their risks of school dropout due to a pregnancy are 1.5 times and 3.8 times higher than the risks of girls from the highlands or the Sudano-Sahelian regions, respectively. This finding is consistent with the now well-established evidence from Cameroon that because of the practices of "trial marriage" and "testing of fecundity" often associated with the process of marriage among the populations of the forest regions (Kuate-Defo, 1998, 2000), girls from the forest regions are very likely to engage in premarital sexual activities that increase their risk of pregnancy. Cameroon law does not allow pregnant girls to continue attending school at least until delivery, and the risk of premarital childbearing among girls from the forest regions is the highest in the country (Fotso et al., 1999). These striking regional differences in school attrition by causes have important implications for policies and programs designed to promote girls' education in Cameroon. Clearly, different regions need to be targeted for changes in different practices, such as early marriage in the Sudano-Sahelian regions and early sexual debut and precocious/unwed childbearing among young people in the forest regions.

Tables 10-5 and 10-6 present the multilevel estimates of influences on the different transitions to adulthood considered given the data at hand. The results are presented with a focus on testing the conceptual framework developed by the NRC Panel on Transitions to Adulthood in Developing Countries by assessing: (1) the effects of socioeconomic status and ethnicity on transitions to adulthood; (2) the effects of (community and province) contexts on individual behavior which clarify the confusion often made by scholars between aggregate and individual effects (i.e., ecological fallacy); and (3) the nested sources of variability in such behavior.

Predictors of the Likelihood of Being Head of the Household, Employed, and Having an STI

Table 10-5 shows the estimated coefficients and standard errors (in parentheses) of the most parsimonious three-level logistic regression models for the dichotomous response variables considered in this study, namely whether the young person was head of the household at the time of the interview, was employed, or was infected with an STI during the 12 months preceding the survey date. Exponentiating these coefficients gives their corresponding odds ratios (OR). Because the sample being analyzed had on average fewer than two individuals per household, estimating models with a separate household level was numerically intractable. There was no covariance matrix structure for the random parameters of these models. Moreover, to accommodate sample sizes and robust estimation procedures utilized, we collapsed a number of categories of these covariates due to numerical problems encountered during the preliminary stage of the estimation of models. We consider statistically significant predictors with OR greater than unity as risk factors and those with OR less than unity as protective factors.

Young females, young people from the Douala-Bassa-related ethnic groups and to some extent young people from the Pahouin-Beti-related ethnic origins (p < 0.10), and adolescents (p < 0.10), have substantially lower odds of being head of the household than young males, young people with a Bamileke-related ethnic background, and young people ages 20 to 24. Separate analyses by gender indicate that the effects of ethnic affiliation and regional context on young people's likelihood of being head of the household vary by gender, as conjectured. Young men of Pahouin-Beti-related ethnic descent or from the Sudano-Sahelian regions are 2.5 times and 3.8 times as likely to be head of household as their counterparts of Bamileke-related ethnic descent or from the forest regions (p < 0.10), respectively. In contrast, young females from the Douala-Bassa-related ethnic

TABLE 10-5 Multilevel Logistic Estimates of Influences on the Probabilities of Being Head of Household, Employed, Infected with an STI Among Young People in Cameroon: CDHS–98

	Being Head of Household		
	Female	Male	Both Sexes
Panel A: Fixed part of the models			
Individual–level effects			
Constant	−3.167[a]	−2.413[a]	−2.945[a]
	(0.898)	(0.776)	(0.624)
Male gender	n.a.	n.a.	+0.724[a]
			(0.219)
Age cohort 15-19	−0.281	−0.365	−0.384
	(0.307)	(0.296)	(0.216)
Catholic	+0.607	−0.258	−0.084
	(0.573)	(0.371)	(0.289)
Protestant	+0.521	+0.129	+0.112
	(0.575)	(0.342)	(0.280)
Pahouin-Beti	+0.464	+0.932	+0.674
	(0.450)	(0.620)	(0.395)
Douala-Bassa	−1.451[b]	−1.197	−1.413[b]
	(0.704)	(0.991)	(0.625)
Household-level effects			
HWI poorest 40%	n.a.	n.a.	n.a.
Community-level effects			
CDI poorest 40%	+0.469	+0.329	+0.383
	(0.652)	(0.399)	(0.362)
Urban place of residence	−0.582	−0.621	−0.536
	(0.610)	(0.461)	(0.380)
Province-level effects			
Highlands regions	−0.080	+0.285	+0.094
	(0.777)	(0.912)	(0.751)
Sudano-Sahelian regions	+0.065	+1.322	+0.983
	(0.861)	(0.796)	(0.676)
Panel B: Random part of the models			
Individual-level	+0.778[a]	+0.969[a]	+0.923[a]
	(0.032)	(0.047)	(0.029)
Community-level	+0.892[b]	+0.001	+0.156
	(0.445)	(0.001)	(0.139)
Province-level	+0.367	+0.589	+0.545
	(0.367)	(0.368)	(0.316)
Panel C: Partitioning the nested contextual random influences			
Proportion of variance among communities within provinces (ρ_2)	0.196	0.001	0.039
Proportion of variance among provinces (ρ_3)	0.081	0.151	0.137
Panel D: Units per level			
Individual	1,210	849	2,059
Household	914	672	1,401
Community	76	76	76
Province	10	10	10

[a]p < 0.01.
[b]p < 0.05
NOTES: n.a. = not applicable; ne = no estimate.
SOURCE: Cameroon Demographic and Health Survey (1998).

Being Employed			Being Infected with an STI		
Female	Male	Both Sexes	Female	Male	Both Sexes
-0.400	-1.155[b]	-0.474	-4.808[a]	-2.587[b]	-3.202[a]
(0.387)	(0.411)	(0.277)	(1.385)	(0.922)	(0.796)
n.a.	n.a.	-0.299[b]	n.a.	n.a.	+1.413[a]
		(0.117)			(0.354)
+0.741[a]	+0.963[a]	+0.830[a]	+0.247	-1.625[a]	-0.758[b]
(0.141)	(0.173)	(0.106)	(0.586)	(0.598)	(0.390)
-0.127	-0.132	-0.135	+0.086	-0.572	0.706
(0.232)	(0.232)	(0.159)	(1.232)	(0.549)	-(0.503)
+0.171	+0.209	+0.171	+1.199	-0.032	+0.119
(0.231)	(0.230)	(0.160)	(1.138)	(0.543)	(0.477)
-0.417	+0.079	-0.290	+0.118	+0.250	-0.047
(0.235)	(0.314)	(0.183)	(0.767)	(0.568)	(0.454)
-0.771[a]	-0.104	-0.594[a]	n.e.	-0.095	-1.024[b]
(0.234)	(0.330)	(0.186)		(0.628)	(0.583)
+0.038	+0.099	+0.046	+0.266	-1.095	-0.292
(0.204)	(0.227)	(0.149)	(0.935)	(0.617)	(0.543)
+0.144	-0.068	-0.027	n.e.	+1.550[b]	+0.170
(0.255)	(0.262)	(0.175)		(0.759)	(0.590)
-0.901[a]	-0.575[b]	-0.813[a]	-0.358	+0.528	-0.255
(0.254)	(0.297)	(0.186)	(0.905)	(0.723)	(0.556)
-0.375	+0.066	-0.251	-0.220	-0.549	-0.943
(0.354)	(0.342)	(0.238)	(0.822)	(0.699)	(0.565)
-0.229	+0.371	-0.082	n.e.	-2.223[b]	-2.339[a]
(0.380)	(0.310)	(0.236)		(0.796)	(0.749)
+1.059[a]	+1.020[a]	+1.035[a]	+1.136[a]	+0.905[a]	1.021[a]
(0.043)	(0.051)	(0.032)	(0.046)	(0.044)	(0.032)
+0.001	+0.063	+0.001	+0.001	+0.001	+0.036
(0.001)	(0.078)	(0.001)	(0.001)	(0.001)	(0.209)
+0.104	+0.001	+0.033	+0.001	+0.001	+0.001
(0.075)	(0.001)	(0.028)	(0.001)	(0.001)	(0.001)
0.001	0.019	0.001	0.001	0.000	0.011
0.030	0.001	0.010	0.000	0.001	0.001
1,210	849	2,059	1,210	849	2,059
914	672	1,401	914	672	1,401
76	76	76	76	76	76
10	10	10	10	10	10

groups are more than four times as likely to live as a dependent in a household as their counterparts from Bamileke-related ethnic groups (p < 0.05). Significant random community (for females) and regional (for both sexes) influences are positively associated with females heading a household, controlling for the effects of nested explanatory factors and random influences at other levels, and account for 20 percent and 14 percent of the total variation across levels over and above significant ethnic differences, respectively.

Adolescents are 2.29 times (2.09 times for girls and 2.61 times for boys) as likely to report being employed in the last 12 months preceding the survey as young people ages 20 to 24. The likelihood of reporting being employed during the same reference period is substantially lower among young males than young females, among Douala-Bassa youth and to some degree their Pahouin-Beti peers (p < 0.10) than their Bamileke counterparts. Community context also matters significantly irrespective of gender, young people living in urban areas being less likely to work than their rural peers. These findings suggest that adolescents who declare being employed are most likely rural residents who are most prone to engage in apprenticeship, agricultural activities with their parents and relatives, and small commerce ventures, such as selling goods from family-owned agricultural production along the side of the road. This may explain in part why adolescent boys and girls are 2.6 times and 2.1 times as likely to report being employed in the recent past as their older counterparts, the former being also more likely to drop out of school for reasons such as 'could not pay school fees' or for "family needed help" than the latter (see Table 10-2, irrespective of their migration/residence history since all female respondents are analyzed therein).

Sexually transmitted infections are least likely among adolescents in general and female adolescents in particular and youth from the Douala-Bassa-related ethnic groups. Important contextual effects emerge from this study: young males from the poorest communities are most likely to have an STI, whereas their peers from the Sudano-Sahelian regions are least likely to be infected. These findings indicate that young males may be particularly vulnerable to reproductive health problems in poor neighborhoods where educational and other community resources are scarce or inexistent.

The female disadvantage in household headship and the fact that they are less likely than boys to report being infected with an STI, confirm our descriptive findings. Regarding employment, it is possible that by broadening the range of work (both home and outside work), some of the underreported work activities of the female population previously unaccounted for are being picked up in these data. These include agricultural work activities, which often represent the bulk of productive and economic activities of rural women, and working as housemaids, a vocation that is rarely considered as work for women in most household surveys in developing countries. Separate models for males and females substantiate that the effects of ethnic affiliation, place of residence, and region of the country vary significantly with the young person's gender, as most interaction parameters are statistically significant at the 1-percent level. These robust interactions between gender and other variables indicate that differences in cultural norms, practices, and expectations for boys versus girls inherent in ethnic groups in Cameroon—as well as community and regional differences for each gender in opportunity structures and life options—tend to perpetuate gender gaps in transitions to adulthood.

Factors Associated with Young People's Transition to Adulthood by Leaving School

Table 10-6 presents the estimated coefficients and standard errors (in parentheses) of the most complete, multilevel, discrete-time hazard models for the dichotomous duration response variable "age at leaving school" (first column of estimates in the table), as well as the multilevel, discrete-time, reduced-form, competing risks analysis for the duration response variable "cause-specific age at leaving school" (next four columns of estimates). As noted earlier, the study sample had on average fewer than two individuals per household so that estimating models with a household-level was not appropriate. No covariance matrix structure was found for the random parameters of these models. The final estimated models include explanatory variables whose estimates are shown in this table as well as 10 duration dummy variables (dummies not shown to conserve space, as the pattern of the duration structure is consistent with the age pattern of probabilities in Table 10-4, with no new insight worth noting). Estimated relative risks from these models are readily available by exponentiating the coefficients, with the baseline risk (or risk of the arbitrary reference category) equaling 1. In general, these multivariate analyses tend to confirm the significant effects of some exposure variables already identified in the multiple-decrement life tables results shown in Table 10-4. In essence, cohort membership, religious and ethnic affiliations, familial living arrangements, contextual community and regional factors, and community random influences (for pregnancy), are the main predictors of young people's hazards of leaving school as they transition to adult roles and responsibilities through employment, marriage, or childbearing. However, the significance of the urban-rural gap found in the overall hazard of stopping school cannot be explained by the causes of attrition analyzed here. Our preliminary analyses indicate that the rural disadvantage is partly ascribed to the

TABLE 10-6 Reduced-Form Multilevel Competing Risks Analysis Estimates of Influences on School Attrition and Cause-Specific School Attrition Among Young Women in Cameroon: CDHS-98

	School Attrition	Cause-Specific School Attrition Marking Successful or Unsuccessful Transitions to Adult Roles			
		Work	Marriage	Pregnancy	Failure
Panel A: Fixed part of the models					
Individual-level effects					
Constant	+3.564[a]	−2.707[a]	−1.073	−1.342[a]	−2.343[a]
	(0.461)	(0.710)	(0.615)	(0.624)	(0.625)
Age cohort 15–19	−2.516[a]	−1.030[a]	−1.300[a]	−1.083[a]	−0.994[a]
	(0.171)	(0.337)	(0.377)	(0.297)	(0.272)
Catholic	−0.464	+0.293	−0.557	−0.727	−0.012
	(0.272)	(0.443)	(0.353)	(0.418)	(0.358)
Protestant	−0.106	+0.349	−1.115[a]	−0.590	+0.209
	(0.277)	(0.435)	(0.376)	(0.414)	(0.354)
Pahouin-Beti	−0.205	−1.130[a]	−1.085[b]	+1.130[a]	+0.209
	(0.233)	(0.453)	(0.514)	(0.335)	(0.354)
Douala-Bassa	−0.276	−0.575	−0.120	+0.456	−0.228
	(0.223)	(0.403)	(0.456)	(0.347)	(0.316)
Household-level effects					
HWI poorest 40%	+0.292	+0.073	−0.281	−0.306	+0.050
	(0.295)	(0.386)	(0.358)	(0.398)	(0.315)
Live with own parents	−0.693[a]	+0.204	−2.095[a]	+0.057	−0.212
	(0.159)	(0.282)	(0.504)	(0.242)	(0.231)
Community-level effects					
CDI poorest 40%	−0.314	+0.377	+0.122	−0.278	+0.579
	(0.352)	(0.485)	(0.414)	(0.497)	(0.414)
Urban place of residence	−1.281[a]	−0.082	−0.646	−0.621	+0.458

	(0.321)	(0.526)	(0.446)	(0.445)	(0.426)
Province–level effects					
Highlands regions	+0.076	-0.795	+0.038	-0.469	-0.029
	(0.278)	(0.463)	(0.409)	(0.475)	(0.534)
Sudano-Sahelian regions	+1.105[a]	+0.502	+1.288[a]	-1.369	-0.427
	(0.339)	(0.458)	(0.428)	(0.812)	(0.604)
Panel B: Random part of the models					
Individual-level	+0.895[a]	+0.963[a]	+0.892[a]	+0.925[a]	+1.011[a]
	(0.037)	(0.040)	(0.037)	(0.038)	(0.042)
Community-level	+0.061	+0.177	+0.044	+0.414	+0.029
	(0.065)	(0.188)	(0.139)	(0.225)	(0.101)
Province-level	+0.001	+0.001	+0.001	+0.001	+0.237
	(0.001)	(0.001)	(0.001)	(0.001)	(0.176)
Panel C: Partitioning the nested contextual random influences					
Proportion of variance among communities within provinces (ρ_2)	0.018	0.051	0.013	0.111	0.008
Proportion of variance among provinces (ρ_3)	0.001	0.001	0.001	0.001	0.067
Panel D: Units per level					
Individual	824				824
Community	67				67
Province	10				10

[a]p < 0.01.
[b]p < 0.05.
SOURCE: Cameroon Demographic and Health Survey (1998).

poverty of rural inhabitants who are unable to pay school fees as well as geographic and cultural accessibilities of the school.

Teenagers irrespective of reasons for school attrition, youth living with their biological parents or in urban communities, and to some extent Catholic youth ($p < 0.10$) are unlikely to abandon school prematurely. The findings that young girls still living in the parental home are significantly unlikely to leave school and most unlikely to leave school due to marriage, imply that delayed marriage is a possible explanation for the continued school enrollment of girls living in the parental home. The relative advantage of Catholic girls is explained in part by the fact that they are less inclined to leave school due to marriage ($RR = 0.57$, $p < 0.10$) or premarital childbearing ($RR = 0.48$, $p < 0.10$). Moreover, Protestant girls are three times as unlikely to drop out of school due to marriage as girls from Muslim or other religious affiliations. Put together, these findings may indicate the protective effects of Christian moral codes of behavior, which may act as deterrents to precocious marriage or unwed childbearing (Kuate-Defo, 1998, 2000).

Significant contextual community and regional influences that vary by reason for leaving school are noticeable, so are community random influences on school dropout due to pregnancy, which account for 11 percent of the total variation across levels over and above significant influences of other covariates. Girls from the highlands regions tend to be unlikely to stop school due to work, while young girls from the Sudano-Sahelian regions (northern Cameroon) are most likely to drop out of school and most likely to successfully transition to marriage ($RR = 3.6$, $p < 0.01$), but are unlikely to report pregnancy as a reason for leaving school ($RR = 0.25$, $p < 0.10$). These findings are consistent with the overwhelming evidence of precocious marriages in northern Cameroon (Kuate-Defo, 1998, 2000), which tend to obviate exposure to premarital pregnancy while still in school.

Young girls from the Pahouin-Beti-related ethnic groups are singled out as the only ethnic groups with significant effects on girls' transitions to work, marriage, and childbearing. They are most unlikely to drop out of school due to work ($RR = 0.32$, $p < 0.01$) or because of marriage ($RR = 0.34$, $p < 0.05$), but are about three times as likely to stop school due to childbearing as other ethnic groups. The specificity of this finding among Pahouin-Beti girls may hinge on the fact that this sociocultural group tends to view premarital sexual activity leading to childbearing as "proof of fertility" and hence a normal component of the marriage process (Kuate-Defo, 1998). Therefore, in a national context where pregnant girls are expelled from school and may return only after delivery, these girls are most likely to leave school due to premarital pregnancy ($p < 0.10$).

CONCLUSION: KEY ISSUES

Implications for Analysis

Several major findings emerge from this study and lend support to the main assumptions underlying the theoretical framework developed by the NRC's Panel on Transitions to Adulthood in Developing Countries. More specifically, as that framework had conjectured, we found that there are similarities and differences that young people face in different contexts and regions of Cameroon, as well as differences between men and women and among different socioeconomic and cultural groups of young people as characterized by household or community socioeconomic status, religion and ethnicity, as they make their transition to adulthood. First, more than half of young people who leave school in Cameroon do so because they cannot pay school fees; only about 1 in 10 women under age 25 stop school because of marriage or childbearing; and poor health is reported as the main reason for leaving school by 5 percent of young females. Second, young people who live with their parents or in urban areas are most likely to pursue their studies and least likely to leave school. Third, this study provides compelling evidence that a meaningful study of biodemographic processes and transitions to adult roles cannot ignore ethnic and regional influences, which also covary with gender. Young people from the Douala-Bassa and Pahouin-Beti ethnic groups have substantially lower odds of being head of the household than their Bamileke counterparts; the likelihood of reporting being employed is substantially lower among Douala-Bassa and Pahouin-Beti youths than their Bamileke counterparts; young people from the Douala-Bassa ethnic groups and from the Sudano-Sahelian or the highland regions are most unlikely to report having had an STI; young females from the Sudano-Sahelian regions are most likely to stop school due to marriage and least likely to report pregnancy as a reason for leaving school; and young girls from the Pahouin-Beti ethnic groups are three times as likely to stop school due to pregnancy as Bamileke girls. The former are at significantly lower risks of stopping school to transition to work or marriage than the latter.

As hypothesized, ethnic influences operate differently by gender. Interaction parameters of ethnicity and place/region of residence with gender demonstrate that their effects are also gender dependent: Young men of Pahouin-Beti descent or from the Sudano-Sahelian regions are 2.5 times and 3.8 times as likely to be head of household as their counterparts of Bamileke descent or from the forest regions, while young females with a Douala-Bassa background are more than four times as likely to live as a household dependent as their counterparts from Bamileke ethnic groups. Young males are more than four times as likely to report having contracted a reproductive health STI as young females, and young males living in worse-off communities are five times as likely to report an STI as their peers from the richest communities. Our finding that the prevalence of STIs is significantly higher among boys than girls is also consistent with a recent multicountry study which found that more boys than girls have experienced STI symptoms in Argentina, Botswana, Peru, the Philippines, the Republic of Korea, and Thailand (Brown et al., 2001).

Studies of effects of parental structure on life course events during adolescence in developing countries remain scarce. Yet the proportion of children living in structures other than parental ones has increased in recent decades due to increased educational opportunities far away from the parental home and, to some extent, emergence of separation/divorce, greater prevalence of nonmarital childbearing, changing family relations, and economic crisis. Because of these changes, living conditions for some young people have changed substantially from the traditional parents-centered childrearing regime to a diversity of living arrangements in childhood, pre-adolescence, and adolescence. As a result, most young people in alternative situations live with one biological parent, a biological parent and a stepparent, grandparents, relatives, or unrelated guardians, or live independently.

Social scientists and biomedical researchers have been concerned about the implications of the increase in the proportion of children living in these alternative situations. One focus of research has been the long-range effects of such experiences on the health, education, behavior, and well-being of children. Our study finds that young people who are not living with their own parents are twice as likely to drop out of school as children who live with their biological parents (p < 0.01), are more than eight times as likely to marry earlier than their counterparts living in the parental home (p < 0.01), and to some extent have higher risks of stopping school due to a pregnancy than young people living with their parents. Our findings are consistent with those reported in various U.S. studies, which have shown that young people in alternative living arrangements without their own parents attain lower levels of education, have less chance of graduating from high school, marry earlier, become parents earlier, have sexual intercourse earlier, are more likely to have premarital births, and are more likely to divorce (for a review, see National Research Council and Institute of Medicine, 1999). Scarr and Weinberg (1994) also show that educational and occupational skills achievements of adolescents and young adults are greatly influenced by the social and familial environments. One of the distinctive, prevailing features of the African family is that individuals are encouraged to stay and live with parents and/or family members until they experience specific events marking a successful transition to adulthood, notably graduating from school and securing employment. Our findings here lend support to this African tradition, which is of great importance as long as it fosters successful transitions to adult roles among young people.

One of the most intriguing findings of this study is that more than half the girls who left school before age 25 reported they could not pay their school fees, and the situation tends to be worsening over time. Younger people tend to be more affected by the financial difficulties of their families at keeping them in school than their older counterparts, with almost 53 percent of females ages 15 to 19 years stopping school because their school fees was not paid, compared with only 49 percent of females ages 20 to 24 years and 46 percent for these ages 25 to 49 years; adolescent boys and girls ages 15-19 years are also 2.6 times and 2.1 times as likely to be employed in the recent past as their older counterparts ages 20-24 years. These findings may suggest an emerging phenomenon whereby parents may be attempting to rationalize their investment by selecting their children to remain in school given their scare financial resources on the basis of what they have already spent on their education and the likelihood of graduation for seeking employment so as to support the extended family, while keeping younger progeny out of school so that they can participate in the family's efforts to generate income through petit commerce and the like which often requires that young people walk along the roads and station at police checkpoints to sell handy cooked meals, fruits, and other consumable farm products in order to raise the family income needed to keep the most advanced and promising older child in schools. In addition, it is worth noting that in the total samples of young women and men in the CDHS-98, fully over 14 percent of females ages 15-19 years and 18 percent of females ages 20-24 years have never been to school, and over 5 percent of males ages 15-19 years and 4 percent of young males ages 20-24 years have no schooling. Obviously, if the main reason for stopping school is financial hardship among young respondents who ever attend school, it is most likely that those with no schooling are even more inclined because their parents could not afford to send them to school. In the 1980s and early 1990s, wages, the main source of income for most civil servants and their relatives, were slashed by nearly 70 percent by the government of Cameroon, part of a series of stern measures designed to deal with the rampant economic crisis. A series of social measures also were implemented, including charging fees to attend all public schools, some of which are now more expensive to attend than private schools. The combined effects of these measures and the enduring economic crisis in Cameroon, as in many African countries, may explain this situation, which has major implications for the development of Cameroon. Jensen and Nielsen (1997) also found that in Zimbabwe, inability to afford school fees ranked second (18 percent of cases) as the main reason for leaving school. Put together, these findings clearly call for an urgent need to invest in young people's future in Africa through education, particularly for girls. The international community should join efforts together at all levels focusing on the overall goal of the UN Millennium

Development Goals of overcoming poverty, especially in Africa where poverty lurks. Indeed, the UN Millennium Declaration stressed the special needs of Africa requiring that actions take place at the global and country levels.

Our study also shows that while the link between the socioeconomic conditions of families and school attendance is consistent with the standard human capital framework (Becker, 1964), other influential variables in the context of Cameroon are also important, such as ethnic groups, type of place of residence, region of the country, family structure, and child age. These findings imply that ethnic capital and social capital are important predictors of school attendance and transitions to adulthood in African settings, especially given the diversity of Cameroon, which has more than 200 ethnic groups. In addition, further research is needed to deepen our understanding of these other forms of capital on young people's transitions to adulthood because some evidence exists on these influential factors in other areas of the life course (e.g., Borjas, 1992).

This study's finding that more than half of girls stop schooling because they cannot pay school fees while barely 1 in 10 left school due to marriage is generalized across generations and place of residence. Furthermore, none of our multilevel analyses demonstrates statistically significant differences in school leaving due to marriage by place of residence. Put together, these findings call into question the widespread belief that in most African countries, girls stop going to school because of early marriage. Our proposition is that they often find that the only life option for securing their future is marriage, which has childbearing as one of its benefits. There is an urgent need to pay attention to these economics of schooling, marriage, and childbearing in order to clarify whether delayed marriage and/or childbearing has usually been concomitant with or followed by increased educational opportunities for girls, independent of other influential factors. Clearly, our findings indicate that the linkages between female schooling, marriage, and childbearing in Africa should be revisited, as pursued in Kuate-Defo (2005c).

Sexual initiation and relations and reproductive events free of infection are a genuine preoccupation in any reproductive health promotion program. Intervention programs targeted at adolescents and young people must assess the prevalence and biosocial determinants of STIs frequently encountered in the sites where the intervention is to be delivered. Yet the attention given to the health problems of adolescents and young people in designing and implementing national and/or large-scale intervention programs is still meager, in part because so little is known about the magnitude and patterns of health problems during these periods of life. The few studies that exist in a variety of settings in the developing world have documented high rates of morbidity among young people in both rural and urban populations (Bang et al., 1989; Brown et al., 2001; Fleming and Wasserheit, 1999; Holmes, 1994; Narayan et al., 2001).

In an effort to ensure healthy transitions of young people to adulthood in developing countries, it is crucial to have a deeper understanding of the socioepidemiological risk and protective factors of STIs among young people. Information concerning STI rates, including those for HIV, in the early years of sexual activity is of paramount importance in developing effective interventions to improve adolescent reproductive health and contribute to safe and healthy transitions to young adulthood. STIs, including HIV/AIDS, present a major public health problem in developing countries, and their drastic impact on morbidity and mortality across the lifespan has been widely recognized.

Our study has documented important age, gender, ethnic, socioeconomic, and contextual differences in the prevalence of STI symptoms among young people in Cameroon. The data at hand indicate that the prevalence of STIs is four times higher among boys than girls. Infection rates are highest among young people from rural areas, worse-off communities, and forest regions, where the prevalence of sterility remains notoriously high in the country (Kuate-Defo, 1997). However, the evidence regarding the accuracy of self-reported symptoms versus medical diagnoses is inconclusive in developing countries. Some studies have shown that women's self-reported symptoms understate the prevalent conditions compared with the medical diagnoses (Liu et al., 2003). This discrepancy has been ascribed to factors such as the fact that reproductive tract infections are sometimes asymptomatic and even when symptomatic, women's perceptions of the symptoms may not prompt her to seek treatment. Because of these cautionary notes and the possibility of misclassification, this study has focused analyses on all symptoms together as signs of STIs. Thus, although these estimates may understate or distort the scope and/or patterns of the problem of STIs among young people in Cameroon, the substantive finding that young males are significantly more likely to be infected with an STI than young girls is consistent with a recent multinational study conducted in developing countries by the World Health Organization (Brown, 2001). These findings provide a good yardstick that future research can use to deepen our understanding and improve the measurement of young people's perceptions of reproductive health problems, including STIs. Our field experience shows that information about these issues is generally poor among young people because their limited knowledge is often based on a mixture of facts, fictions, myths, and rumors.

Implications for Methodology

This study has situated the estimated influences on transitions to adulthood within a multilevel framework as the most appropriate and logical approach to formally test the theoretical framework of the NRC's Panel on

Transitions to Adulthood in Developing Countries. It has allowed a rigorous assessment of the robustness of estimated fixed effects and random effects at the individual, community, and province levels and helped to isolate the net effects of measured factors which are of primary interest in most applications and for engaging a decision-making dialogue with policy makers and planners concerned with young people's life experiences including the events charting their transitions to adulthood. We paid close attention to the assumptions required by multilevel models and theories and investigated the tenability of those assumptions in light of the available data and our best judgments based on accumulated data analytic experiences on a variety of topics for which data have clustered structures, so that specification assumptions must apply at each level of observation. While our general multilevel model formulated above allowed for the effects of covariates to be fixed or random at each level of hierarchy and for cross-level interactions, after trial runs and given the nature of the data, we were able to retrieve stable estimates for models that could only fit level-specific fixed and random effects of measured and unmeasured factors as shown in Tables 10-5 and 10-6. We found that these random effects are statistically significant in some models: significantly positive random community (for females) and regional (for both sexes) influences associated with females heading a household account for 20 percent and 14 percent, respectively, of the total nested variation, even after controlling for the influences of nested explanatory factors of other levels; community random influences on school dropout due to pregnancy account for 11 percent of the total variation across levels over and above the fixed and random effects of other influential factors. In particular, the between-individual variance is statistically significant in all models ($p < 0.01$), the between-community variance is statistically significant for girls only ($p < 0.05$) and for the transition out of school due to childbearing ($p < 0.10$), and the between-province variance is statistically significant for boys only ($p < 0.10$) in the model predicting being head of household. Notwithstanding their importance, the effects of several exposure variables considered in this study remain robust, including individual-level characteristics such as age, sex, ethnic affiliation, and contextual factors such as level of development of the community and region of residence. The multilevel approach employed here clearly shows significant correlations among individuals interacting and behaving likewise within their nested contexts of life and are robust to controls for all measured variables, and substantiates the shortcomings of aggregate analysis and single-level analysis that inherently ignore such nested correlations and often commit ecological fallacy for the former or Type I errors for the latter, among other inferential problems.

Overall, the presence of fixed and random effects of community-level and province-level factors identified does not change substantially the values for the individual-level parameters with the battery of multilevel nonlinear models applied here to explicitly handle the hierarchical or clustered structure of our data, while single-level modeling, which ignores the three levels of hierarchy (e.g., in the individual, household, community questionnaires of the DHS-type surveys), would have led us to commit the Type I errors by falsely rejecting the null hypothesis for some variables (results for single-level models not shown) because the standard errors of the associated parameters were underestimated. The estimated parameters suggest, for instance, that there may be more variation across communities and provinces in the likelihood of young males versus young females being head of household than standard single-level analyses would have implied. This study also demonstrates the significance of influential unmeasured variables affecting the various transitions of young people during their life course, independently of the significance of individual/household-level and contextual community-level and province-level covariates. A number of these unobserved influences may be unmeasurable in conventional qualitative or quantitative methods of inquiry, and often require triangulation research methodologies that combine qualitative and quantitative approaches to study biosocial events generally defining transitions during the life course. Most past surveys including the DHS-type surveys have not been designed with the goal of handling multilevel theories and sophisticated statistical models and therefore are not fully equipped to confront all methodological problems associated with causal inference. This study has employed a multilevel framework that locates the household, community, and provincial contexts that are invariant during the exposure length to the likelihood of making a transition to adulthood for a given individual given its characteristics, thereby illuminating some fundamental obstacles in the identification, specification, explanation, and insightfulness of multilevel contextual effect studies. A full implementation of the models formulated above, which will allow us to deal with all components of the theoretical framework developed by the NRC's Panel on Transitions to Adulthood in Developing Countries, will depend on the extent to which a multilevel survey design is used in collecting clustered data at the individual-level, including measures nested within individuals and higher levels of hierarchy (e.g., household, community, region, country). Our findings of significant variances at the individual, community, and province levels suggest that future efforts for data collection and investigation on influences on transitions to adulthood should go beyond existing research approaches in order to deepen our understanding of various nuances and manifestations of transitions to adulthood in developing countries.

Greater effort needs to be made to design surveys that actually measure some of the factors that we suggest might be important but at present are only inferred. For example, important changes have occurred in the last 15 years in the political and economic landscapes of many African countries. Introduction of political capital and social capital into such analyses may prove insightful in understanding some of these unobserved variations.

Although a number of theoretical perspectives are well advanced by now and the basic and advanced statistical methods for multilevel modeling in the literature are well known by methodologists, an area where much progress is needed concerns the design of multilevel surveys and data needs for empirical specification of models and testing of underlying theories and assumptions. Most past surveys have not been designed with the explicit aim of supporting multilevel modeling, and existing textbooks on multi-level modeling provide only scanty guidance as to the design of multilevel surveys, for instance, of children, families, and communities that are at the heart of most population investigations and policies. This makes it difficult to address the most important yet unresolved research issue in this area, namely the development of an understanding of the causal effects of postu-lated risk/protective factors of outcomes under investigation so that more effective intervention programs targeted at young people can be designed, implemented and evaluated. Our hope is for much progress in the near future.

ACKNOWLEDGMENTS

This work was supported by the Rockefeller Foundation's Interven-tion Research Grant RF 97045 #90 to the author; supplemental support was provided by the National Academies (Washington, DC) and the PRONUSTIC Research Laboratory at the Université de Montréal (Canada). We thank Barney Cohen, Jere Behrman, Nelly Stromquist, Cynthia Lloyd, and two anonymous referees for their discussions, sugges-tions, and comments.

REFERENCES

Agresti, A. (1990). *Categorical data analysis.* New York: Wiley.

Arnold, B.C., and Brockett, P.L. (1983). Identifiability for dependent multiple decrement/ competing risks model. *Scandinavian Actuarial Journal, 31,* 117-127.

Baltagi, B.H. (1995). *Econometric analysis of panel data.* Chichester, England: Wiley.

Bang, R.A., Bang, A.T., Baitule, M., Chaudhary, Y., Sarmukaddam, S., and Tale, O. (1989). High prevalence of gynecological diseases in rural Indian women. *Lancet, 8(29),* 85-88.

Becker, G. (1964). *Human capital: A theoretical and empirical analysis, with special reference to education.* New York: National Bureau of Economic Research.

Binder, M., and Woodruff, C. (2002). Inequality and intergenerational mobility in schooling: The case of Mexico. *Economic Development and Cultural Change, 50(2),* 249-267.

Bledsoe, C. (1994). Children are like young bamboo trees: Potentiality and reproduction in sub-Saharan Africa. In K. Lindahl-Kiessling and H. Landberg (Eds.), *Population, economic development, and the environment* (pp. 105-138). Oxford, England: Oxford University Press.

Bolin, K., Lindgren, B., Lindstrom, M., and Nystedt, P. (2003). Investments in social capital: Implications of social interactions for the production of health. *Social Science and Medicine, 56,* 2379-2390.

Borjas, G.J. (1992). Ethnic capital and intergenerational mobility. *Quarterly Journal of Economics, 107*(1), 123-150.

Boserup, E. (1985). Economic and demographic interrelations in sub-Saharan Africa. *Population and Development Review, 11*(3), 383-397.

Boutin, J.P., Lemardeley, P., and Gateff, C. (1987). Maladies sexuellement transmissibles et médicine de collectivité (sexually transmitted diseases and group medicine). *Médicine Tropicale, 47*(3), 307-320.

Brabin, L. (2001). Hormonal markers of susceptibility to sexually transmitted infections: Are we taking them seriously? *British Medical Journal, 323,* 394-395.

Breslow, N.E., and Clayton, D.G. (1993). Approximate inference in generalized linear mixed models. *Journal of the American Statistical Association, 88,* 9-25.

Brown, A., Jejeebhoy, S.J., Shah, I., Yount, K.M. (2001). *Sexual relations among young people in developing countries: Evidence from WHO case studies.* (WHO/RHR/01.8.) Geneva, Switzerland: Family and Community Health, Department of Reproductive Health and Research, World Health Organization.

Bryk, A., and Raudenbush, S. (1992). *Hierarchical linear models: Applications and data analysis.* Newbury Park, CA: Sage Publications.

Cates, W. (1990). The epidemiology and control of sexually transmitted diseases in adolescents. *Adolescent Medicine: State of the Art Reviews, 1,* 409-427.

Central Bureau of Population Studies. (1998). *Cameroon demographic and health survey (CDHS-98).* Calverton, MD: Macro International.

Clayton, D., and Hills, M. (1993). *Statistical models in epidemiology.* Oxford, England: Oxford University Press.

Commenges, D., and Jacqmin, H. (1994). The intraclass correlation coefficient: Distribution-free definition and test. *Biometrics, 50,* 517-526.

Committee on Adolescence, National Research Council. (1994). Sexually transmitted diseases. *Pediatrics, 94*(4), 568-572.

Cox, D.R. (1959). The analysis of exponentially distributed life-times with two types of failure. *Journal of Royal Statistical Society, 8*(21), 411-421.

Darling, N., and Steinberg, L. (1992). Parenting styles as context: An integrative model. *Psychological Bulletin, 113,* 487-496.

Davidian, M., and Giltinan, D.M. (1995). *Nonlinear models for repeated measurement data.* London, England: Chapman & Hall.

Evans, R.G., Barer, M.L., and Marmor, T.R. (1994). *Why are some people healthy and others not? The determinants of health of populations.* New York: Aldine De Gruyter.

Fleming, D.T., and Wasserheit, J. (1999). From epidemiological synergy to public health policy and practice: The contribution of other sexually transmitted diseases to sexual transmission of HIV infection. *Sexually Transmitted Infections, 75,* 3-17.

Fotso, M., Ndonou, R., Libité, P., Tsafack, M., Wakou, R., Ghapoutsa, A., Kamga, S., Kemgo, P., Fankam, M.K., and Kamdoum, A. (1999). Enquête démographique et de santé, Cameroun, 1998 (demographic investigation and health, Cameroon, 1998). Yaoundé: Bureau Central des Rencensements et des Études and Macro International (BCREP).

Goldstein, H. (2003). *Multilevel statistical methods,* 3rd ed. London, England: Arnold.

Gray, R., Leridon, H., and Spira, A. (Eds.). (1993). *Biomedical and demographic determinants of reproduction*. Oxford, England: Clarendon Press.

Heckman, J.J., and Honoré, B.E. (1989). The identifiability of the competing risks model. *Biometrika, 76*(2), 325-330.

Heckman, J.J., and Singer, B. (1984). A method for minimizing the impact of distributional assumptions in econometric models for duration data. *Econometrica, 52*, 271-320.

Holmes, K.K. (1994). Human ecology and behavior and sexually transmitted bacterial infections. *Proceedings of the National Academy of Sciences, 91*, 2448-2455.

Jejeebhoy, S.J. (1995). *Women's education, autonomy, and reproductive behaviour: Experiences from developing countries*. Oxford, England: Clarendon Press.

Jensen, P., and Nielsen, H.S. (1997). Child labour or school attendance? Evidence from Zimbabwe. *Journal of Population Economics, 10*, 407-424.

Kalbfleisch, J.D., and Prentice, R.L. (1980). *The statistical analysis of failure time data*. New York: John Wiley & Sons.

Kreft, I.G., and De Leeuw, J. (1998). *Introducing multilevel modeling*. London, England: Sage Publications.

Kuate-Defo, B. (1995). Epidemiology and control of infant and early childhood malaria: A competing risks analysis. *International Journal of Epidemiology, 24*, 204-217.

Kuate-Defo, B. (1997). Effects of socioeconomic disadvantage and women's status on women's health in Cameroon. *Social Science and Medicine, 44*, 1023-1042.

Kuate-Defo, B. (Ed.). (1998). *Sexuality and reproductive health during adolescence in Africa, with special reference to Cameroon*. Ottawa, Canada: University of Ottawa Press.

Kuate-Defo, B. (1999). *Family-level clustering of adolescent gender-specific risks of premarital reproductive activities*. Paper presented at the annual meeting of the Population Association of America, March 25-27, New York.

Kuate-Defo, B. (2000). L'Évolution de la nuptialité des adolescentes au Cameroun et ses déterminants (the evolution and determinants of the nuptiality of adolescents in Cameroon). *Population, 55*(6), 941-974.

Kuate-Defo, B. (2001). Modeling hierarchically clustered survival processes with applications to childhood mortality and maternal health. *Canadian Studies in Population (Special Issue on Longitudinal Methodology), 28*(2), 535-561.

Kuate-Defo, B. (2005a). Book review of D. Courgeau (Ed.), *Du Groupe à l'Individu: Synthèse Multiniveau*, Paris: INED, 2004, ix + 242 pages (translation). *European Journal of Population, 21*(1), 391-394.

Kuate-Defo, B. (2005b). Attributs sociodémographiques, comportement préventif, santé et capacité fonctionnelle des personnes âgées en milieu Africain (translation). *Cahiers Québécois de Démographie, 34*(1).

Kuate-Defo, B. (2005c). *Revisiting the interlinkages between female education, marriage, and childbearing in Africa with reference to Cameroon*. Unpublished manuscript, Department of Demography, University of Montreal.

Liu, H., Detels, R., Yin, Y., Li, X., and Visscher, B. (2003). Do STD clinics correctly diagnose STDs? An assessment of STD management in Hefei, China. *International Journal of STD & AIDS, 14*(10), 665-672.

MacPhail, C., Williams, B.G., and Campbell, C. (2002). Relative risk of HIV infection among young men and women in a South African township. *International Journal of STD and AIDS, 13*(5), 331-342.

Narayan, K.A., Srinivasa, D.K., Pelto, P.J., and Veerammal, S. (2001). Puberty rituals, reproductive knowledge and health of adolescent schoolgirls in South India. *Asia-Pacific Population Journal, 16*(2), 225-238.

National Research Council. (1997). *Reproductive health in developing countries: Expanding dimensions, building solutions*. A. Tsui, J. Wasserheit, and J. Haaga (Eds.), Panel on Reproductive Health, Committee on Population, Commission on Behavioral and Social Sciences and Education. Washington, DC: National Academy Press.

National Research Council. (2001). *Cells and surveys: Should biological measures be included in social science research?* Committee on Population, C.E.Finch, J.W.Vaupel, and K. Kinsella (Eds.), Commission on Behavioral and Social Sciences and Education. Washington, DC: National Academy Press.

National Research Council and Institute of Medicine. (1999). *Risks and opportunities: Synthesis of studies on adolescence*. Forum on Adolescence, M.D. Kipke (Ed.), Commission on Behavioral and Social Sciences and Education. Washington, DC: National Academy Press.

Podlewski, A. (1975). Cameroon. In J.C. Caldwell (Ed.), *Population, growth and socioeconomic change in West Africa* (pp. 543-646). New York: Columbia University Press.

Rasbash J., Browne, W.J., Goldstein, H., Yang, M., Plewis, I., Healy, M., Woodhouse, G., Draper, D., Langford, I., and Lewis, T. (2000). *A user's guide to MLwiN* (2nd ed.). London, England: Institute of Education.

Ravanera, Z., Rajulton, F., and Burch, T. (1998). Early life transitions of Canadian women: A cohort analysis of timing, sequences, and variations. *European Journal of Population, 14,* 179-204.

Rees, M. (1993). Menarche: When and where? *Lancet, 342,* 1375-1376.

Robinson, W.S. (1950). Ecological correlations and the behavior of individuals. *American Sociological Review, 15,* 351-357.

Rodríguez, G., and Goldman, N. (1995). An assessment of estimation procedures for multilevel models with binary responses. *Journal of the Royal Statistical Society, Ser. A, 158,* 73-89.

Scarr, S., and Weinberg, R.A. (1994). Educational and occupational achievements of adolescents and young adults in adoptive and biologically-related families. *Behavior Genetics, 24,* 301-325.

Searle, S., Casella, G., and McCulloch, C. (1992). *Variance components*. New York: John Wiley & Sons.

Snijders, T., and Bosker, R. (1999). *Multilevel analysis: An introduction to basic and advanced multilevel modeling*. Thousand Oaks, CA: Sage Publications.

Subbarao, K., and Coury, D. (2004). *Reaching out to Africa's orphans: A framework for public action*. Washington, DC: World Bank.

Tsiatis, A. (1975). A nonidentifiability aspect of the problem of competing risks. *Proceedings of the National Academy of Sciences, 72,* 20-22.

UNAIDS. (2000). *Consultation on STD interventions for preventing HIV: What is the evidence?* Geneva, Switzerland: WHO/UNAIDS.

UNAIDS. (2001). *Sexually transmitted infections: Policies and principles for prevention and care*. Geneva, Switzerland: WHO/UNAIDS.

UNAIDS. (2003). *AIDS epidemic update*. Geneva, Switzerland: WHO/UNAIDS.

UNFPA. (2003a). *State of the world population 2003*. New York: Author.

UNFPA. (2003b). *Preventing HIV infection, promoting reproductive health: UNFPA response 2003*. New York: Author.

Warren, J.R., and Lee, J. (2003). The impact of adolescent employment on high school dropout: Differences by individual and labor-market characteristics. *Social Science Research, 32,* 98-128.

Yang, M., and Goldstein, H. (2003). *Modeling survival data in MLwiN 1.20*. London, England: Center for Multilevel Modeling.

11

Assessing the Economic Returns to Investing in Youth in Developing Countries

James C. Knowles and Jere R. Behrman

Youth ages 10 to 24 constitute a large proportion of society and have many pressing health, education, economic, and social needs. Despite the critical value of youth to future well-being, countries may invest inappropriately in their healthy development. There may be gaps between current and socially desired levels of investment in youth such that social rates of returns to investments in youth are higher on the margin than for alternative uses of these resources. If so, the case may be strong for using public resources to close this gap.

Some evidence suggests that youth-focused interventions may be cost-effective in improving health, reducing poverty, and providing overall benefits to society. Compared to investments in child health and development, investments in youth often offer a shorter time lag between costs and benefits, thereby having higher benefit-cost ratios, all else equal, if even a relatively modest discount rate is used. Also, in countries in which there has been underinvestment in children, investments in youth may offer an opportunity to "catch up" in the area of human capital investments. Yet full economic analyses of the benefits and costs of investments in youth in developing countries are rare.

This chapter explores the economic case for investments in youth in developing countries by synthesizing the current knowledge of the economic costs and benefits of those investments, analyzing key gaps in the evidence, and identifying priority research needs.

MAJOR THEMES

The current cohort of youth in developing countries is the largest cohort ever, either in the past or predicted for the future, given the stage of the demographic transition which developing countries have experienced on average, though there are variations across countries and regions. This means that whatever investments are made in youth in developing countries have an important impact on a relatively large share of the population. It also means there may be large resource implications and large intergenerational transfers required to make substantial investments in youth.

Major changes have been occurring in the context for youth in developing countries:

• The world has become more integrated due to economic, technological, and cultural globalization.

• Developing countries in which hundreds of millions of youth live—particularly in Asia but also elsewhere—have experienced historically unprecedented economic growth, while smaller but still large numbers of youth, particularly in sub-Saharan Africa, Latin America, the Middle East/North Africa, and Central Asia, live in countries with limited economic growth or stagnation, often with high rates of youth unemployment.

• Human capital investments in the form of formal schooling and training have expanded rapidly, particularly for females, and have facilitated the exploitation of new technologies and new markets by those in whom such investments have been made.

• At the same time, severe fiscal constraints faced by most developing countries together with reappraisals of governmental roles have led to a growing share of the investments in youth, particularly in health and schooling, being financed directly by households rather than through governments.

• The health and nutritional environments have changed radically, with rapid transitions in each of these, so that on average there have been substantial improvements as reflected in increased life expectancies, with a shift from contagious diseases and malnutrition that impinge particularly on infants and children to chronic diseases that affect adults and particularly the aging—while at the same time new health problems, most notably HIV/AIDS, have spread rapidly and in some areas have become major threats.

• Cultural norms and legal changes, often related to globalization, have shifted to more emphasis on gender equalities, individualism, and materialism.

Therefore, it is necessary to rethink and to reevaluate the range of investments in youth in developing countries, inter alia, schooling, training, reproductive health, and investments in other aspects of health, including behavioral changes related to food consumption, physical activity, and substance use. The large cohort size means that there are pressures on resources that are likely to be squeezed due to the large numbers, therefore strengthening the need for the best evaluations possible for any use of scarce resources for investments in youth. The changed context means that the economic returns to different investments in youth probably have altered substantially.

This reappraisal of the economic returns to investing in youth in developing countries must incorporate certain critical features. These include:

- The inclusion of an appropriately wide range of such investments, including their costs and benefits, within a lifecycle context.
- The considerable lag in the effects and ultimate outcomes of many of these investments, implying that the choice of an appropriate discount rate may be of considerable importance.
- Consideration of these investments within the frameworks of standard policy concerns of efficiency and distribution and trade-offs between efficiency and distribution.
- Sensitivity to problems in making inferences from behavioral data given endogenous choices (selectivity), important unobserved variables, and other measurement and estimation problems.
- The likelihood that youth investments in one area impact investments and behavior in other areas. For example, reducing youth unemployment might strengthen the demand for schooling. Improving nutrition might improve school performance and reduce the health risks of a youthful pregnancy.
- Greater clarity regarding matters such as what are costs and what are transfers. The previous literature, for example, often confuses resource costs with transfers, such as welfare payments.

ORGANIZATION OF CHAPTER

Reassessing the economic benefits of investing in youth in developing countries requires frameworks for analysis to organize the existing fragmented and imperfect information. The next section presents such frameworks, then turns to problems of empirical inferences, and a basic framework for policy evaluation. Building on this foundation, the following sections turn to estimates of the rates of return to different investments, with an effort when possible (which is too infrequent) to distinguish between private and social rates of return and between females and males.

The strategy is to identify the time pattern of costs and benefits (requiring the translation of impacts into economic terms if they are not presented in those terms) over the lifecycle from a range of piecemeal estimates, and then to estimate the ratio of the discounted benefits to the discounted costs. The methodology used to measure costs and benefits is sufficiently flexible to incorporate, in a simple way, a wide range of effects of different investments. The robustness of these estimates is explored by relaxing different assumptions related to critical aspects of costs, benefits, and the discount rate. Such estimates are presented for a number of alternative investments in youth, including formal and nonformal schooling, reproductive health, school-based health interventions, and investments to reduce the consumption of tobacco. The final section presents a synthesis and conclusions, with emphasis on what are the highest return investments in youth, how these compare with other investments, and what are the highest priority research areas.

To implement this strategy, we combine the piecemeal information we have been able to find on the effects and costs of investments in youth in developing countries, together with information that permits translating the effects into benefits measured in monetary terms, in order to estimate benefit/cost ratios and internal rates of return. We start with a lifecycle perspective and consider the estimated costs at the time the investments are made and the subsequent effects over the lifecycle, based on the best estimates we have been able to find. For the benefits, we need the effects of investments in youth in areas such as schooling, unemployment, mortality and morbidity, teen pregnancies, and HIV/AIDS, and a way of associating a monetary value to each effect. We then calculate the present discounted values of the benefits and the costs, conditional on assumptions about the discount rate, and the internal rates of return to these investments. Because of the great uncertainties that underlie many of the estimates that we use, we present some alternative estimates based on alternative assumptions for key variables, such as the discount rate. In light of the considerations discussed below about policy motives, we would like to be able to make separate estimates of total benefits and costs and private benefits and costs in order to identify the extent to which there are efficiency reasons for using public resources to increase certain investments. Unfortunately, in most cases this distinction is difficult to make. However, we try to identify cases where the private and social benefits are likely to diverge.

THREE MAJOR CONCLUSIONS

First, there are large gaps in what we know with confidence about many aspects of rates of return to investments in youth in developing countries. Most studies are not sensitive to major estimation problems in assessing the determinants or the impacts of such investments. Most studies focus only on the impacts and do not consider the costs (including, possible distortionary costs), which also must be understood to assess the economic returns to such investments. In a number of cases, they further confuse resource costs with transfers. Often the impacts are in terms of some objective, such as improved health and nutrition, but not translated into economic benefits by assessing productivity effects or by using the resource cost of alternative means to attain the same effects. The majority of studies, moreover, do not consider whether the policies examined are likely to be the preferred policies for attaining the policy objective. For such reasons there is a considerable research agenda in order to inform policy makers and other interested parties about the economic returns to various investments in youth in different contexts in developing countries.

Second, nevertheless, the available evidence suggests there are some high-return investments in youth in developing countries and there are efficiency reasons for using public as well as private resources for such investments due to inadequacies in markets such as for capital, insurance, and information. Examples of such high-return investments include both supply-side and demand-side investments in formal schooling, investments in adult basic education and literacy targeted to adolescents, investments in some types of school health services (e.g., micronutrient supplementation), investments designed to reduce the consumption of tobacco, and possibly some types of reproductive health investments.

Third, what are relatively high rates of return for different investments in youth depends importantly on the context of such investments. Rates of return to schooling, for example, are likely to be much higher in dynamic contexts in which there are rapid changes in technologies and markets through greater integration into world markets. Many health and nutrition investments tend to yield higher returns in settings in which health and nutrition conditions are poor. The economic returns to reproductive health investments designed to reduce rates of HIV infection increase substantially with HIV prevalence in the targeted age groups.

FRAMEWORKS FOR ANALYSIS

Why Frameworks for Analysis Are Necessary

Good analysis of impacts of investments in youth has tripartite foundations: data, modeling, and estimation. These three dimensions are critically interrelated. Data, of course, are essential for empirical analysis, limit the extent to which analyses can be undertaken, and shape most of the estimation problems. If there were available data from well-designed and well-implemented experiments,[1] associations between observed investments in youth and observed outcomes would reveal the underlying causality directly. But for numerous reasons, including costs and ethical concerns, such experimental data are rarely available.[2]

Therefore, although there are likely to be high returns for some aspects of policy analysis to increase experimental data, most analysis will continue to be based on behavioral data. Such behavioral data can "speak for themselves" regarding associations between investments in youth and various outcomes. But they generally cannot "speak for themselves" with regard to what observed determinants—policies or otherwise—*cause* differences in investments in youth or to what extent observed investments in youth *cause* different outcomes. The problem is that most data result from a number of behavioral decisions taken by households, individuals, bureaucrats, policy makers, and others in light of a number of factors unobserved by analysts.[3] Good analysis of what causes household and individual investments in youth or of what effects such investments have is difficult, and requires a much more systematic approach than simply looking at associations among observed variables.

Analytical frameworks permit exploring systematically investments in youth, point to what data are needed for such explorations, facilitate the interpretation of empirical findings, and help to identify some of the probable estimation issues that should be addressed given the data used. The analytical frameworks provided by models are essential if the empirical estimates are based on behavioral data generated in the presence of unobservables such as innate ability and family connections. The problem, for example, is that youth with greater ability and motivation and better innate health may be more productive directly and may also benefit from higher levels of investments. Therefore, it may be difficult to sort out the effect of investments in youth per se as opposed to the fact that such investments are correlated with unobserved abilities, motivation, and innate health.

---

[1]Good experiments have random assignment between treatment and control groups, no attrition problems, and double-blind treatment.

[2]Data may be available from "natural experiments" in which, due to some fortuitous happenstance, all unobserved (by analysts) variables are the same in two groups. But though such natural experiments are a conceptual possibility, it is difficult to find two situations in which all unobserved variables are likely to be identical.

[3]Throughout this chapter "unobserved" means unobserved by analysts and policy makers—which, of course, depends on the data set, though there are some widely unobserved factors (e.g., innate ability, innate health, family connections, preferences). Such factors, although not observed by analysts, are observed (perhaps imperfectly with learning) by the individuals whose behaviors are being studied, and these individuals make decisions in part based on these factors. Many recent studies emphasize these unobserved factors and their importance in analysis of behavioral data.

For such reasons, empirical effects of investments in youth can be analyzed satisfactorily with nonexperimental data only within frameworks that incorporate well behaviors related to the phenomena of interest. To be interpretable, estimates based on behavioral data require some model of the underlying behaviors, though far too often in the literature the models used are not explicit. Those who are not clear about their framework of analysis may think they are revealing underlying truths unconstrained by such frameworks, but instead they are usually making implicit assumptions that may not be plausible upon examination.

Analytical Frameworks for the Determinants of Investments in Youth

Households and the individuals in them are the proximate sources of demands for many investments in youth (e.g., schooling, health, social capital, behaviors that lead to productive lives), given their predetermined assets (i.e., physical, financial, and human, including endowments[4]), production functions related to human resources, public and private services related to investments in youth (i.e., schools, health clinics), and current and expected prices for inputs used in investments in youth and for outcomes of the investments. Policies, of course, may enter directly or indirectly into this process through a number of channels, ranging from the accessibility and quality of public and private services to the functioning of capital markets for financing investments in youth to the functioning of markets in which these investments are expected to have returns. Becker's (1967) Woytinsky Lecture provides a simple framework for investments in human resources that captures many of the critical aspects of investments more broadly in youth and which has been widely appealed to in rationalizing empirical studies of the determinants of investments in youth.

In Becker's framework, human resource investment demands, under risk neutrality, reflect the equating of expected marginal private benefits and expected marginal private costs (both in present discounted terms) for investments in a given individual. The marginal private benefit curve depends importantly, inter alia, on expected private gains in productivity in all of the ways in which the human resource investment may have impacts. The marginal private benefit curve is downward sloping because of diminishing returns to investments in youth (given genetic and other endowments) and because, to the extent that investments in youth take time (e.g., schooling, training, and most other forms of education and social capital, as well as time and other resources devoted to search for better options in labor and other markets), greater investments imply greater lags in obtaining the returns and

---

[4]"Endowments" means characteristics that are given independent of behavioral decisions. Genetically determined innate ability and innate health robustness are examples.

a shorter postinvestment period in which to reap those returns. The marginal private cost may increase with investments in youth because of higher opportunity costs of more time devoted to such investments (especially for schooling and training) and because of increasing marginal private costs of borrowing on financial markets. The equilibrium human resource investment for an individual is where the marginal private benefits and the marginal private costs are equalized. This equilibrium human resource investment is associated with an equilibrium rate of return that equates the present discounted value of expected marginal private benefits with the present discounted value of expected marginal private costs. This simple stylized representation of human resource determinants is based on a dynamic perspective, with both benefits and costs not only in the present but also those that are expected in the future and with current period options conditional on past decisions. Thus it is consistent with placing investments in youth in a lifespan perspective, as has been emphasized from a number of perspectives.

The marginal private benefit and marginal private cost curves are likely to vary across youth because of variations in observed and unobserved individual, family, household, and community characteristics, the latter in part related to policies and to markets. Changes in any of these factors can shift these curves and thus the equilibrium investment levels. This simple framework systematizes six critical points for investigating dimensions of the determinants and the effects of investments in youth—and how these relate to policy choices.

First, the impacts of changes in policies may be hard to predict by policy makers and analysts. If households or other entities face a policy or a market change, they can adjust all of their behaviors in response, with cross-effects on other outcomes, not only on the outcome to which the policy is directed.

Second, aggregation to obtain macro-outcomes will average out random stochastic terms across individuals or households. But such aggregation does not average out systematic behavioral responses at the micro-level. Therefore associations among macro-variables can reveal, conditional on the overall context, what those associations are—but not causal effects of processes occurring at the micro-level.

Third, the marginal benefits and marginal costs of investments in a particular individual differ depending on the point of view from which they are evaluated: (1) There may be externalities or capital/insurance market imperfections so that the social returns differ from the private returns, and (2) there may be a difference between who makes the investment decision (e.g., parents) and in whom the investment is made (e.g., youth). The effectiveness of policies are likely to depend crucially on the perceived private effects by private decision makers, and these may differ from the social effects of interest to policy makers.

Fourth, investments in youth are determined by a number of individual, family, community, (actual or potential) employer, market, and policy characteristics, only a subset of which are observed in available data sets. To identify the impact of the observed characteristics on investments in youth, it is important to control for the correlated unobserved characteristics.[5]

Fifth, to identify the impact of investments in youth, it also is important to control for individual, family, community, market, and policy characteristics that determine the investments in youth and also have direct effects on outcomes of interest.

Sixth, empirically estimated determinants of, and effects of, investments in youth are relevant only for a given macroeconomic, market, policy, schooling, and regulatory environment in which there may be feedback both at the local level and at a broader level.

Empirical Issues: Measurement

To assess the rates of return to investments in youth, we need to (1) measure what we mean by investments in youth and by various outcomes that might be affected by investments, (2) estimate the impact of investments in youth on the latter measures, (3) assign a monetary value to these effects, and (4) measure the costs of these investments. These are not trivial tasks. This section considers some of the measurement difficulties.

Investments in Youth

In the case of schooling, which is an important example, most empirical studies represent human resource investments empirically by years of schooling or highest grade (level) of schooling completed. Though "years" and "grades" of schooling are often used as synonyms, they need not be the same if there is grade repetition, as is widespread in many parts of the developing countries (e.g., in much of Latin America). One of the major costs of schooling is the opportunity cost of time in school, which is greater if there is more grade repetition for a given schooling grade attainment. Putting aside the question of the time spent in school, there are other limitations of grades (years) of schooling as a measure of human resource investments. Probably most important is the implicit assumption that school quality is constant. But empirical measures indicate that school quality

---

[5]For example, suppose that schools with higher quality tend to be in areas in which expected rates of return from investments in youth tend to be greater, but only indicators of school quality and not expected rates of return are observed in the data. In this case, if there is not control for the unobserved expected rates of return in the analysis, the impact of school quality on such investments is likely to be overestimated because in the estimates school quality proxies in part for unobserved expected rates of return to these investments.

varies substantially, so it would be desirable in assessment of the impact of human resource investments in youth to represent not only the time (grades, years) that they spend in school, but also the quality of that schooling. If both the quantity and the quality of schooling should be included, but only the quantity is included, the likely result is to overstate the impact of time in school and to miss that there is likely to be an important quality-quantity trade-off.

Besides schooling (or education more broadly defined), there are many other investments in the human resources of youth. Such investments may be directed, for example, at improving health, nutrition, information, social capital, and habitual behaviors that lead to desirable outcomes. Similar problems exist in empirical measurement of these variables, as for education. For example, health is often measured by anthropometric indicators, respondent reports, or clinical reports on disease histories; respondent reports on capabilities for undertaking certain activities or tests for doing so; or respondents' self-assessment of health. Some of these indicators may be good measures of particular disease conditions, but that does not make them (or their inverse) necessarily good measures of what people mean by good health. For another example, social capital is often measured by participation in group activities, but this is at best an imperfect and endogenous indicator of whether one has social capital in the sense of being able to obtain information or resources at times of need.

Outcome Variables

Unfortunately there are many problems in measuring these outcomes.[6] For some outcomes that may be affected importantly by investments in youth, data usually used in the social science literature do not include direct measures—self-esteem and learning capacities are two examples. This may mean that important outcomes are missed when assessing the impact of investments in youth.

For some other outcomes there are, at best, imperfect indicators—representing health by health-related inputs (e.g., nutrients), reported disease conditions, curative health care, and preventative health measures (e.g., vaccinations). Some of these measurement problems may be systematic, moreover, resulting in biases in estimated impacts of investments in youth. If, for example, those who have less schooling report less sickness for the same health conditions than those with more schooling (perhaps because the degree of sickness viewed as normal is less with more schooling), impacts of schooling on actual sickness are likely to be underestimated.

---

[6]We limit our discussion here to microdata because the problems with the aggregate data are so severe (see Knowles and Behrman, 2005).

For some other measures of outcomes, conventions are used in the literature that may not be sensible. For example, economic gains from reducing mortality are represented at times by the present discounted value of foregone earnings of an individual (e.g., CGCED, 2002). For young individuals, such gains can be considerable. For measuring the purely economic benefits of survivors, however, this seems an overstatement of the economic costs of mortality because such individuals also would have consumed perhaps most or all of their earnings over their lifetime.[7] For another example, the economic gains from improving the earnings capacities of individuals are at times measured by the reduction of their demands on governmental social welfare systems for transfers (e.g., CGCED, 2002). But governmental transfers, though perhaps appropriately viewed as costs from a budgetary perspective, are not resource costs in the sense desirable to evaluate policies. There are likely to be some resource savings if social welfare programs are reduced because some resources are consumed in running and financing such programs. But such possible resource savings should not be confused with the amount of transfers involved (and the latter probably greatly exaggerate the true resource costs). For one last example, the gains from reducing crime are at times equated with the amount of losses that crime victims suffer due to crime. But, again, a significant component of the costs so calculated is the transfer from the victim to the criminal, particularly in thefts. The amount of such transfers, once again, is not likely to reflect well the true resource costs of crime. All three of these examples point to substantial difficulties in evaluating benefits and to questionable practices that have been used in some previous studies.

We intend to deal with these difficult questions by evaluating the benefits in terms of the least cost alternative way of obtaining the same objective, along lines implemented by Summers (1992, 1994) in a well-known study of the economic benefits of female schooling. This procedure gives, for hard-to-evaluate outcomes, what society is willing to pay for alternative ways of attaining the same gain—and thus, if the prices that are used in the evaluation reflect the true social marginal costs of resources, the true resource costs of such gains. Note that this method in principle includes both the direct resource cost gains and the indirect resource cost gains. To illustrate the latter, investments in youth that reduce crime may not only have gains from directly improving the safety of citizens, but from indirectly encouraging international tourism and international investments. This procedure accounts for what resources society would be willing to pay for alternative ways of reducing crime in light of all these gains.

---

[7]This measure of the economic value of life also implies that there is no value to the life of an individual who is not productive because, for example, of age or disability.

Even for the economic outcomes on which there long has been focus in evaluating the impact—particularly of schooling but also of training, health, and nutrition—there are often serious measurement problems. People with less schooling, for example, may remember income less well, may have more problems in assessing the value of their income because more is in kind or self-produced, and may be subject to greater variations in income because of greater fluctuations in employment. If such factors lead to a tendency to underreport their incomes, then all else equal, the returns to schooling will be overestimated due to these systematic errors.

Costs

There are often problems in measuring the costs of investments in youth. The direct budgetary expenditures for particular investments, for example, may be intermingled with many other expenditures in budgets, and therefore be difficult to identify. They also may be spread among various budgets at various levels of aggregation—for example, if health clinic staff salaries are paid by the Ministry of Health, but other recurrent expenditures are paid by local governments, as in the Philippines. Furthermore, there is frequently the problem that the budgetary expenditures do not reflect the true costs because of distortions in market prices, perhaps created by policies. For example, governments may mandate wage rates for some workers such as teachers that may differ from the true scarcity value of such individuals, and then introduce other distortions such as in benefits or job securities in order to attempt to attract enough qualified individuals to these positions. A major problem with evaluating costs, finally, pertains to the nongovernmental costs. Policy makers often ignore these because they are focused on governmental budgets. But the costs of a program to the private sector may be considerable. For example, many programs require considerable amounts of time from private individuals—time that has opportunity costs in the form of other uses. For another example, raising funds for governmental programs in itself may have large distortionary costs.

Measurement of Policies

Including policies among key variables for which there are measurement problems might seem strange. But there are serious measurement issues related to representing policies in empirical studies. For example, there is considerable emphasis on improved outcomes through policies that improve women's education. But the empirical foundation for these claims in substantial part relates associations between schooling attainment and desirable outcomes. Schooling attainment is *not* a policy variable, but behavioral outcomes that reflect schooling market interactions between household/individual demands for schooling and various aspects of schooling supply that generally are conditioned by policies.

Empirical Issues: Estimation of Effects of Investments in Youth

This chapter is concerned with assessing what we know about the rates of returns to investments in youth in developing countries. But obtaining good empirical estimates of the effects of investments in youth is not easy, in part because of the measurement problems discussed above and in part for other reasons to which we now turn. We first consider the possibility of empirical estimation through experiments and then through econometric methods using nonexperimental (behavioral) data.

Experimental Evaluation

To assess the impact of a particular change, such as increasing use of health clinics, the ideal approach generally is thought to be a double-blind experiment with random assignment to treatment and control groups for the policies of interest over a long enough time period to assess the effects of interest. Experiments have been conducted to evaluate a relatively small number of policies related to youth in developing countries. One example is the Mexican Programa de Educación, Salud y Alimentación, PROGRESA (Education, Health, and Nutrition Program), which was introduced as part of an effort to break the intergenerational transmission of poverty and which included an evaluation sample in which communities were randomly assigned to immediate versus delayed treatment. This design permitted evaluation of the impact of this program on a number of outcomes by comparing changes in treatment households with changes in control households (see Knowles and Behrman, 2003, Appendix A).[8]

But the possibilities for using such experiments for policy evaluation are limited. First, most such experiments cannot be double blind, with neither the subjects nor the evaluator knowing who received treatment (though some medical experiments can be if, for example, the placebo appears to human senses to be identical to the treatment). That those who are treated know they are treated may create better performance (i.e., the "Hawthorne effect"). That those who are not treated know they are not treated may create incentives to obtain treatment through migration, po-

---

[8]Angrist et al. (2002) analyze another example in which students were selected randomly from poor applicants to receive scholarships to attend private schools in urban Colombia. Miguel and Kremer (2002, 2004) analyze the impact of random assignment of deworming programs among schools in Kenya.

litical pressure, market purchases, or other means. Second, the argument often is made that new programs cannot easily be introduced at the same time throughout a country, so it may be effective in terms of evaluation, as was attempted with PROGRESA, to introduce them in a random set of treatment communities and only later in a random set of control communities. But if members of the control group know they will eventually be affected by the program and if they can transfer resources over time, they should immediately adjust their behavior to reflect their changed command over resources due to the expected eventual future direct program impact. If so, the comparison between the program and the treatment groups probably underestimates the program impact.[9] Third, many experiments cannot be conducted because they are unethical or too costly. Randomly imposing some human resources, particularly related to health and nutrition, but also to education, for example, is likely to be viewed as unethical. Even if some such possibilities are not viewed as unethical, they may be very costly in terms of resources or political costs. Consider the difficulties with the possibility of randomly assigning schooling among individuals in order to obtain better estimates of the effects of human resource investments in youth, as would be desirable for the present study. Fourth, even for the policies for which good experiments can be conducted at a reasonable (resource, ethical, and political) cost, they reveal only the gross changes induced by the experimental treatment conditional on a particular situation, not what would happen in somewhat different circumstances. That is, experiments basically are "black boxes" that reveal the total impact of some change, but do not reveal anything about the underlying structural relations that could be used to infer what the effects of other changes would be. Fifth, there may be insufficient time to observe effects of interest to policy makers. This is a particular problem for youth investments because many of the desired outcomes are expected to occur much later in life.

For such reasons, though it would be desirable to increase experimental evaluation of policies and to assure that the experiments undertaken are of high quality (e.g., with good baseline data and random assignment of treatment versus control groups), there are severe limits on what policies can be evaluated by experimental means. Nevertheless, the experimental design is an important benchmark against which other means of evaluation should

---

[9]Of course this is not a problem if members of the control group do not know that they eventually will be affected by the program, but such ignorance may be difficult to maintain because of interactions between members of the treatment and control groups and general information about the new program. In fact in some cases the administrators of the program may tell the control group directly that they will be included eventually in hopes of obtaining their agreement to serve in the control group and to enhance a sense of fair treatment.

be compared and judged to aid in understanding what probable biases may arise from nonexperimental evaluation.

Econometric Estimates of Impacts of Investments in Youth

Econometric or statistical methods are used to attempt to circumvent some data limitations. The basic point is that there are a number of reasons—including measurement errors in variables, right-side variables that reflect current or past choices, important variables that are not observed in data sets (e.g., innate ability, preferences), and selected samples (e.g., clinic health test results only from those who go to health clinics and have the tests)—why the stochastic term in relations being estimated often is not likely to be independent of the right-side variables. As a result, estimates are likely to be biased and therefore misleading unless special data and estimation procedures, grounded firmly in the analytical framework used for the analysis, are used to control for these problems.

Implications for Analysis of Endogenous Policies

Policies of all sorts—including those related to investments in youth—are not predetermined, but are made by individuals or groups of individuals with various objectives in mind, including accommodating to pressures from and needs of constituents. This means it may not be possible to evaluate the impact of governmental policies on various outcomes without controlling for the fact that governmental policies themselves are determined, implemented, and monitored as part of a larger set of behavioral decisions.[10] The failure to control for the determinants of governmental policies may cause substantial misestimates of their effectiveness. These misestimates, moreover, may either *over*estimate or *under*estimate policy effectiveness, depending on the nature of the governmental decision (Rosenzweig and Wolpin, 1986).

The basic intuition is clear from considering the simple example of evaluating the impact on youth health of special health programs from cross-sectional data from a number of communities. If the resources devoted to such special programs tend to be concentrated in communities that have greater political power, wealth, and more healthy youth net of the effects of the special health programs and of characteristics that are observed in the data, the association between youth health and resources devoted to special health programs without control for resource allocation among these special health programs in different communities *over*states the effectiveness of the programs. Those communities that receive more

---

[10]If programs are allocated randomly, this problem is avoided.

special health program resources would have had better youth health for other reasons that are correlated positively with the allocation of special health program resources (and vice versa). On the other hand, if the resources devoted to such special health programs tend to be concentrated in communities that have poorer health environments, greater poverty and less healthy youth net of the effects of the programs and of characteristics observed in the data, the association between youth health and resources devoted to special health programs without control for resource allocation among those programs in different communities *under*states the effectiveness of the programs. As a result, even if the programs are effective in improving youth health, the simple cross-sectional association between special health program resources in various communities and youth health *may* be negative (and, if positive, is an underestimate of the effectiveness of special health program resources). Therefore, it is essential to control for the determinants of program placement and intensity across recipients in order to evaluate the impact of programs with confidence.

Private Versus Social Returns, Efficiency, and Distribution

Often analyses of the impact of investments in youth are undertaken without consideration of the general rationale for policies. It is just presumed that policies that, say, through greater investments in youth increase some outcome such as subsequent health must be good. But such analyses may not provide much in the way of guidelines for choosing among policy alternatives. Therefore, it is useful to ask why policy interventions with respect to investments in youth might be desirable.

At a general level of abstraction, policy should be chosen in order to maximize social welfare. Of course, that begs the critical political economy question of how the social welfare function is determined. Even if that difficult question is put aside, the practical guidance offered by the injunction to maximize social welfare may seem quite limited. For that reason it is often useful to think separately of the two standard economic justifications for governmental policy interventions: (1) to increase efficiency/productivity and (2) to redistribute resources.[11] Policy justifications based on efficiency and on distribution are both firmly rooted in micro-dimensions of behaviors. Both of these standard economic motivations for policy are

---

[11]These two justifications include some other common concerns about policies, such as questions of access to and quality of services and sustainability of overall economic development and of particular programs, as discussed in Behrman and Knowles (1998b). The distributional justification includes, as a special case, poverty reduction, which is characterized by some as the overarching objective in contemporary development policy (e.g., van der Gaag and Tan, 1997).

concerned ultimately with the welfare of individuals as judged by those individuals.

Efficiency/Productivity

Resources are used efficiently in the economic sense if they are used to obtain the maximum product possible given the resources and available production technologies at a point of time, and over time, and if the composition of that product increases the welfare of members of society as much as possible given the resource and technological constraints and preferences, and the distribution of resource ownership. An investment (or expenditure) is efficient if the marginal *social* benefit of the last unit of that investment just equals its marginal *social* cost.[12] If the marginal social benefit of a particular investment is greater (less) than the marginal social cost, society is not investing enough (is investing too much) and would benefit from increasing (decreasing) the level of investment until the marginal social benefits and costs are equalized.

Although applying the above rule maximizes social gains, private maximizing behavior leads to investments (including those related to youth) at the level at which the marginal *private* benefit of the investment equals its marginal *private* cost under the assumption that, given the information available to them and the constraints they face, individuals act in what they perceive to be their best interests. Consider the possibility that private incentives for investments differ from social incentives for such investments, first with respect to the marginal benefits and then with respect to the marginal costs.

Why might marginal social benefits exceed marginal private benefits for investments in youth? The most frequent answers to this question include the following:

• There are externalities in the form of effects on others that are transferred "external to markets." Investments in education are thought to have not only private benefits to the person being educated, but, by adding to society's stock of knowledge, social benefits beyond the private benefits. Other relevant examples of externalities include being exposed to second-

---

[12]Three points should be noted: (1) Economic efficiency is not the same as engineering efficiency because of the incorporation of marginal benefits and marginal costs rather than focusing exclusively on technological efficiency. (2) These marginal conditions for efficiency may not hold if there are large discontinuities in production processes. In such cases choices may have to be made among a number of different alternatives, using an explicit welfare function to compare among the alternatives. (3) Because of uncertainty this discussion could be recast in terms of expected values, with concern about possible risk aversion (or something other than risk neutrality). But, for simplicity, we do not do so.

hand smoke, controlling contagious diseases such as HIV/AIDS, creating social capital, and developing incentives for legal rather than criminal behaviors.

• Information used to make schooling, health, and employment decisions may misrepresent the private rates of return to these investments because it is incomplete or incorrect. For example, youth may not know about contraceptives or about risks associated with sexually transmitted infections (STIs). The "public good" nature of information (i.e., that the marginal cost of providing information to another consumer is virtually zero) leads to underproduction of information from a social point of view by private markets because private providers cannot cover their costs if they price information at the social marginal cost as required for efficiency.

• The combination of uncertainty, risk aversion, and imperfect insurance markets may result in private incentives to underinvest in human, financial, and physical assets because, from a social point of view, the risks are pooled.

• The social discount rate may be lower than private discount rates because individuals value future outcomes more collectively than they do individually.

• Prices for outcomes affected by such investments may understate social gains, in part because of distortions due to policies (e.g., policy restrictions on salaries in the health and education sectors).

Why might marginal social costs be less than marginal private costs for investments in youth? Answers include the following:

• There may be capital market imperfections for some types of investments (e.g., social capital investments and human resource investments, in part because these forms of capital are not accepted as collateral) such that the marginal private costs for such investments exceed their true marginal social costs, which probably is more relevant for individuals from poorer families who cannot easily self-finance such investments.

• The sectors that provide some types of services (e.g., information, health care, schooling) may produce inefficiently because institutional arrangements do not induce efficient production of an efficient basket of commodities. School teachers and staff, for example, might be oriented toward rewards established by the Ministry of Education or union negotiations, not toward satisfying the demands of clients. Governmental health workers may be more interested in their private practices than in their public work.

• The sectors that provide services related to investments in youth may produce inefficiently because regulations preclude efficient production of an efficient basket of commodities. For example, regulations that limit hours during which schools are open, limit textbook choices, impose quality standards based on different conditions in other economies, or limit provision of services to public providers, all may result in much greater costs of attaining specific investments than would be possible with fewer regulations.[13]

What are the implications of differences in the marginal private and social benefits or costs? Simply, if there are such differences, private incentives for investments in youth differ from social incentives. In such circumstances, policies may increase efficiency by reducing the differences between the private and the social incentives or through other means that cause outcomes to be closer to the socially desirable outcomes.

Distribution

Distribution is a major policy motive distinct from efficiency. Distributional concerns, at least officially in pronouncements of governments and of international agencies, often focus on the command over resources of poorer members of society.[14] Society might want to assure, for example, that everyone has basic schooling, even at some efficiency cost (van der Gaag and Tan, 1997). Though distributional concerns are often characterized by focus on the distribution of income or other resources *among* households, there may also be important distributional considerations *within* households. Household decision makers are not likely to consider equally preferences of all household members in allocating household resources. For example, if women have preferences for using more resources to invest in children than do their husbands, these preferences may not be weighed equally as those of their husbands in decisions made by husbands. Moreover, even if some households as aggregates have sufficient resources to cover what society considers basic needs, certain types of individuals in households may not be allocated what society considers to be sufficient resources for their individual satisfaction of basic needs. A particularly germane example may be child labor. Such labor may contribute importantly to the resources and the welfare of the household decision makers, but may detract from improving the human resources of the child by, for

---

[13]This is not to say that all regulations are bad. In some contexts regulations may be the most efficient means of attaining a goal, particularly if there are certain types of information problems (e.g., those related to the quality of goods and services that cannot be easily discerned by consumers). But often regulations, no matter how good their intent might be, are not very effective policy tools.

[14]Many policies, whatever their official justification, however, distribute resources to middle- and upper class households. For some examples of human resource-related policies in Vietnam, see Behrman and Knowles (1998a, 1999).

example, exposing the child to health and other risks and limiting the education of the child. Thus there may be an important intergenerational distribution trade-off.

Policy Choices to Increase Efficiency and to Improve Distribution

If all other markets in the economy are operating efficiently and there are differences between marginal private and social incentives in a given market related to investments in youth, policies that induce investments at the socially efficient levels increase efficiency.[15] That still does not indicate what policies would be best to induce investments in youth at the socially desirable levels. There is a large set of possibilities, including governmental fiats, governmental provision of services at subsidized prices, price incentives in markets related to investments in youth, price incentives in other markets, and changing institutional arrangements in various markets. To choose among alternatives based on efficiency alone, there are two important considerations.

First, policies have costs. These costs include direct costs of implementing and monitoring policies and distortionary costs due to policies that may encourage socially inefficient behavior (including rent seeking by both public and private entities). Often policy makers focus only on the direct costs and ignore the distortionary costs because only the direct costs have obvious and visible direct ramifications for governmental budgets. In fact the costs may be sufficiently high that it is not desirable to try to offset some market failures by policies.[16] But, if it is desirable to do so, there is a case generally for making policy changes that are directed as specifically as possible to the inefficiency of concern because that tends to lessen the distortionary costs. An efficiency policy hierarchy can be defined in which alternative policies to attain the same improvement in efficiency are ranked according to their social marginal costs, including direct and distortionary

---

[15]If all other markets in the economy are not operating efficiently, then policies that narrow differences between private and social incentives in a particular market related to investments in youth do not necessarily increase efficiency. But, in the absence of specific information to the contrary, such as the existence of two counterbalancing distortions, a reasonable operating presumption is that lessening any one distortion between social and private incentives is likely to increase efficiency.

[16]If the policies involve public expenditures as do most policies, it is important to consider the cost of raising the necessary revenue to finance the policy. For example, it has been estimated that the distortionary cost ("deadweight loss") of raising a dollar of tax revenue in the United States ranges from $0.17 to $0.56, depending on the type of tax used (e.g., Ballard, Shoven, and Whalley, 1985; Feldstein, 1995). Estimates for some other countries range from $0.18 to $0.85, depending on the tax (van der Gaag and Tan, 1997). Harberger (1997) suggests using a shadow price of $1.20 to $1.25 for all fiscal flows on a project.

costs. This hierarchy indicates the preferential ordering of policies to deal with particular divergences between private and social incentives.[17]

Second, there are tremendous information problems regarding exactly what effects policies have, particularly in a rapidly changing world. This is an argument in favor of policies that are as transparent as possible, which generally means higher in the efficiency policy hierarchy with regard at least to distortionary costs because more direct policies are likely to be more transparent.[18] Information problems also provide an argument for price policies (taxes or subsidies) because if there are shifts in the underlying demand and supply relations, they are likely to be more visible in a more timely fashion to policy makers if they have impact on governmental budgets than if they only change the distortions faced by private entities, as tends to happen with quantitative policies.[19] Finally, information problems in the presence of heterogeneities across communities point to the possible desirability of decentralization and empowerment of users of social services in order to increase the efficacy of the provision of those services. However, such considerations must be balanced off against possible economies of scale, higher quality of staff, and possibly lower levels of corruption at more centralized levels, as well as intercommunity distributional concerns.

Thus, for efficiency/productivity reasons, particularly given that in the real world information is imperfect and changes are frequent, there is an argument generally for choosing policies as high as possible in the efficiency policy hierarchy defined by the extent of marginal direct and distortionary costs—and thereby using interventions that are focused as directly on the problem as possible. Note that this means that, for example, if there is a good efficiency reason for public support for investments in youth, that does not mean the best way to provide that support is through governmental provision of the relevant services. Higher in the efficiency policy hierarchy than direct governmental provision of such services, for example, may be subsidies or taxes that create incentives for the efficient provision of these services, whether

---

[17]For example, it is sometimes argued that female schooling should be subsidized because more schooled women have fewer children, which relieves budgetary pressures on subsidized schooling and health services. But in this case increasing female schooling through such subsidies would not obviously seem to be high in the efficiency policy hierarchy. Higher in the hierarchy might be the elimination of any public subsidies for education and health that are not warranted by the marginal social benefits exceeding the marginal private benefits.

[18]This is also an argument for considering an experimental approach to evaluating policy alternatives when possible; for example, rather than introducing a reform countrywide, introduce variants of reforms in randomly selected sites with careful monitoring of the results for both the experimental groups and the control groups.

[19]Nevertheless there are likely to be some cases, such as providing information regarding the quality of goods and services related to investments in youth, for which quantitative regulations may be higher in the efficiency policy hierarchy than price policies because of the nature of the information requirements.

the actual providers are public, private, or some mixture. On the other hand, policies that discriminate against one type of provider—for example, by making the availability of such subsidies dependent on whether the provider is public—are generally likely to be lower in the efficiency policy hierarchy than policies that do not have such conditions.

Now consider distribution. Generally subsidization of specific goods and services (and even less, the direct provision by governments of goods and services at subsidized prices) is *not* a very efficient way of lessening distributional problems. Because subsidies are designed to lower prices to consumers, they induce inefficient consumption behavior. Instead, it is generally more efficient (and thus less costly in terms of alternative resource uses) to redistribute income to consumers, allowing them to allocate the income in ways that lead to efficient patterns of consumption.[20] Nevertheless, there are cases in which subsidization of selected goods and services may be defensible to attain distributional objectives. For example, in cases where it is difficult (and therefore costly) to target the poor households or poor types of individuals within households, subsidizing certain goods and services that are mainly consumed by the poor may be relatively high in the efficiency policy hierarchy.

Rather than being concerned with the general command over resources of its poorer members, as noted above, society may deem it desirable that everyone enjoy basic services, including basic schooling, nutrition, and health care. Such an objective might be obtained through many means. But presumably it is desirable to assure that everyone has these basic options at as little cost in terms of productivity as possible, so, rather than ignoring efficiency considerations, it is desirable to choose policies as high as possible in the efficiency policy hierarchy and still assure that the basic service objectives are met. Thus, to obtain a given distributional objective, it is possible to define a distributional policy hierarchy in which policy alternatives that obtain that objective are ordered from lowest to highest marginal direct and indirect costs. Efficiency goals thus should play an important role in interaction with the pursuit of distributional goals, not as independent considerations.

Implications of Efficiency and Distributional Motives for Evaluating Benefits and Costs of Different Policies

There are important implications of the two policy goals—efficiency and distribution—for how the costs and benefits of policies should be valued:

---

[20]However, even redistributing income may lead to inefficiency because it can affect the work effort of those on both the tax-paying and tax-receiving sides.

• Whether particular policies are warranted or not depends on the social trade-off between efficiency and distribution.

• Transfers may be an important tool for attaining distributional ends, but they are not costs in the sense that in themselves they use resources. Related to transfers (as well as to other programs), however, generally are real resource costs related to program administration and distortions caused by programs.

• Just because there are large productivity gains relative to costs does NOT mean that a program warrants subsidies from the point of view of efficiency. From the point of view of efficiency, there is a reason for public policy support only if the social rate of return to a particular use of resources is greater than the private rate of return.

• With imperfect capital and insurance markets for the poor, there are likely to be some productivity and efficiency gains if the poor are beneficiaries of transfers.

• Measurement problems are great. These are particularly severe, for example, for the social welfare weights for marginal incomes for different members of society and for differences between social and private rates of returns due to market imperfections for the productivity and efficiency measures. But, despite such difficulties, it is important to attempt to undertake benefit/cost analysis with such considerations in mind—though, all too often, they are ignored.

Methodologies for Economic Evaluation of Investments in Youth

If one has reliable estimates of the effectiveness of a set of alternative investments in youth, how can one best evaluate them against the criteria of efficiency and distribution? Several methodologies are available.

Cost-effectiveness analysis (CEA) consists of ranking a set of related investments according to their cost per unit of effectiveness, where the measure of "effectiveness" is as clearly defined and narrow as practical. CEA has been widely used to evaluate alternative investments within a given sector. For example, cost per life saved or cost per disability-adjusted life year (DALY), are criteria that have been widely used in CEA evaluations of alternative investments in the health sector. However, CEA has several shortcomings in the context of evaluating alternative investments in youth. First, it requires a single effectiveness measure. This is impractical in the case of many youth investments because they involve such a wide range of possible outcomes. Second, CEA does not provide any basis for comparing investments in youth to alternative investments, such as investments in economic infrastructure or investments to improve governance. Third, although CEA addresses aspects of the efficiency motive for policies, it does not do so comprehensively (i.e., it does not address whether the objective used to measure "effectiveness" itself represents an efficient use of resources).[21]

Cost-benefit analysis (CBA) is an alternative methodology for evaluating investments that is designed to compare investments that may have several different outcomes. Because CBA values benefits in monetary terms, it obtains results (i.e., benefit/cost ratios or internal rates of return) that readily permit comparisons with alternative investments. If one has reliable estimates of effects, the problem is valuing them in monetary terms. This is often technically challenging and can be politically sensitive as well (e.g., assigning a monetary value to a human life). Although several approaches are used to do this in the literature, we focus on microestimates of direct productivity effects that can be measured in monetary terms on the one hand and, for the effects that cannot be easily translated into monetary terms, use the resource cost of the most cost-effective alternative to achieve the same effects on the other hand.[22, 23] Problems with this approach include that (1) it is partial equilibrium, and therefore market feedbacks, particularly within relatively closed economies, may be missed, and (2) information with which to assess private versus social rates of return, and therefore, the efficiency motive, is relatively rare. Nevertheless, this seems to be the best available methodology, so we adopt it in this chapter. In our estimates of benefits, we try to give appropriate attention to the lag between the investment and the expected effects, because with even a modest discount rate (e.g., 5 percent), the delay between investments and the resulting effects can have an important effect on benefit/cost ratios or internal rates of return. We also try to examine critically the case for public intervention with respect to each type of

---

[21]On the other hand, CEA can be, and often is, explicitly used to assess alternative means of attaining specific distributional goals, such as improving reproductive health outcomes for poor populations.

[22]An often-used alternative is to try to assess the impact on aggregate goals such as economic growth. In Knowles and Behrman (2003) we discuss this alternative, its strengths and limitations, and why we do not use it.

[23]This strategy is used by Summers (1992, 1994) to analyze the benefits and costs of investing in female education in Pakistan. He begins with estimates of effects of an additional year of women's schooling on lifetime earnings. Next he develops estimates of effects of an additional year of women's schooling on child mortality, fertility, and maternal mortality. He places a monetary value on these latter effects by using estimates of costs of producing similar effects using alternative cost-effective interventions (e.g., costs per child life saved through immunization). He compares these estimates (with some discounting to reflect the lagged nature of the effects) of "social benefits" to the cost of providing an extra year of schooling to women and concludes that investing in girls' education yields relatively high returns.

investment because most benefit/cost ratios by themselves do not shed any light on this issue.[24] Finally, we also try to examine the likely impact of investments on the poor as compared to the nonpoor and on women as compared to men, because distributional concerns are not usually incorporated directly into benefit/cost estimates.[25]

EFFECTS AND COSTS OF A RANGE OF BASIC INVESTMENTS IN YOUTH

Table 11-1 lists alternative investments in youth that are examined in Knowles and Behrman (2005). An important general point is that many estimates of effects of investments in youth are not persuasive because they are based on behavioral, not experimental, data and do not control for behavioral choices that led to the investments in youth nor for many measurement problems.

In surveying the literature on youth investments, we have found that there are a number of serious gaps in the information base that would support the kind of estimates we would like to present. In developing countries, there is little evaluation of the effectiveness of existing youth programs. Where reliable estimates of effectiveness exist, the measurement is often over too short a period of time to be useful or focused on only one or two effects of an investment (e.g., the productivity effects of investments in formal schooling). Without reliable information about the effectiveness of interventions, it is impossible to obtain reliable estimates of the benefits and thus of the benefit/cost ratios or the internal rates of return of various investments. The absence of reliable estimates of the full range of the hypothesized effects of investments frustrates efforts to obtain separate estimates of private and social benefits. Accordingly, the rationale for government intervention is absent or weak in the case of many of the possible investments in youth.

We summarize below the main findings of our review of the literature regarding the effects, costs, and cost effectiveness of various categories of investments in youth.

---

[24]To shed light on this issue, benefit/cost ratios or internal rates of return are needed from both private and social perspectives, but both rarely are presented in existing studies. For examples of attempts to reshape CBA to address the issue of the benefits and costs of public intervention, see Devarajan, Squire, and Suthiwart-Narueput (1997) and Behrman and Knowles (1998b).

[25]Of course, it is conceptually possible, but rarely done, to weight benefits differently for different groups.

TABLE 11-1 Alternative Investments in Youth Reviewed in Knowles and Behrman (2005)

School quality improvements	Vocational and technical	Child labor regulations
Scholarships	Adult basic education and literacy	Other employment regulations
Compulsory attendance laws	Military	(e.g., safety, minimum wage, maximum hours)
Reproductive health (RH)	School health investments	Other health investments
School-based RH education	School health policies	Tax on tobacco products
Social marketing of RH services	School-based health education	Ban on advertising tobacco
Youth-friendly RH services	School lunch/feeding	Antialcohol abuse programs
Linked services	School micronutrient supplements	Antidrug abuse programs
Peer counseling programs	School deworming programs	Mass media health programs
Mass media programs	School water and sanitization	Food supplements for pregnant women
Workplace/community outreach	School malaria treatment	Food fortification
Programs to delay marriage	School physical examinations	Road accident prevention
RH program development	School health insurance	Mental health programs
Community and other investments	Youth development programs	Microcredit for youth
Youth centers	Sports and recreation programs	Youth rehabilitation programs

Formal Schooling

There are reliable estimates for some countries of the cognitive achievement effects of both demand-side investments (scholarships) and supply-side investments (quality improvements) based on randomized experiments. However, there is no developing country evidence of the effects or cost effectiveness of investments to enforce compulsory school attendance laws. The effects of school quality investments and scholarships can differ significantly by income and gender. For example, investments that improve the quality of schooling mainly provide benefits to children already enrolled in school. Accordingly, such investments tend to benefit the better off more than the poor and boys more than girls in areas in which enrollments for boys are higher than for girls, particularly if the investments are made at the secondary level. In contrast, scholarships are often targeted to poor children or to girls in an effort to encourage them to enroll or remain in school. Cost estimates are provided in several studies. However, the cost estimates usually do not include estimates of distortionary and administrative costs, and in some cases they wrongly include transfers (e.g., scholarships) as if they are resource costs. Most of the countries for which reliable estimates of cognitive achievement effects are available are middle-income countries in Latin America (e.g., Mexico, Colombia), though a randomized experiment on evaluating alternative quality improvement investments is currently ongoing in Kenya.

Civilian and Military Training

Estimates are available of the cost of providing vocational/technical and adult basic education and literacy (ABEL) training in many countries. However, the cost estimates do not include distortionary costs, or even administrative costs in some cases. Reliable estimates of effects, in terms of cognitive achievement, are not available in any study that we have been able to locate. Most of the existing estimates do not address the problem of selectivity bias. In countries where female illiteracy rates are considerably higher than those of males, ABEL investments are likely to benefit more females than males. ABEL investments also tend to be effectively targeted to the poor. There are no studies that we have been able to find on the effects or costs of military training.

Work

There are no reliable estimates of the effectiveness of child labor regulations/laws and other employment regulations/laws in developing countries, nor is there any information on the costs of enforcing them. Some types of child labor (but clearly not all types) may enhance labor productivity, either through the acquisition of skills or through additional work experience. However, there are no reliable estimates of these possible negative productivity effects of child labor regulations/laws.

Reproductive Health

There are reliable estimates of effects of some investments (e.g., reproductive health education provided in schools). In some cases, these are obtained from randomized experiments. However, randomized experiments are rarely used to evaluate reproductive health investments in youth and are often too small to yield reliable results. Small quasi-experimental studies, which yield less reliable results, are much more common in the evaluation of reproductive health investments in youth. Other problems include the short time span over which effects are estimated in most studies and the reliance on intermediate outcome indicators (e.g., delayed sexual activity) rather than measures of health impact (e.g., HIV infections prevented). This is a significant problem because many reproductive health investments in youth are directed to low-risk populations (e.g., in-school adolescents) in which health impacts may be relatively small. Social benefits exceed private benefits for many investments in reproductive health because they involve the prevention or treatment of communicable diseases (e.g., HIV/AIDS prevention, STI diagnosis and treatment).

The biggest information gap in the reproductive health area is the lack of information on investment costs. There are almost no studies of reproductive health investments in youth that present cost estimates. The Honduras HIV prevention study (the results of which are used below) is an exception inasmuch as it provides estimates of both effects and costs. However, many of the "estimates" are based on the consensus views of Honduran and international experts, rather than on the results of carefully designed research. Another problem with the existing studies on reproductive health investments in youth is that they tend to focus on only one effect, such as HIV prevention, but not, for example, on teen pregnancy prevention. There is almost no information on either the cost or effectiveness of reproductive health policy development investments or on investments designed to delay age at marriage. In the case of highly active antiretroviral therapy (HAART) treatment of youth infected with HIV, the literature does not yet provide estimates of the potential health benefits or of the likely impact of HAART treatment on the secondary transmission of HIV.

School-Based Health Investments

There are reliable estimates of the costs and effects of some school-based investments, such as deworming and micronutrient supplements.

The available evidence suggests that both school-based deworming and micronutrient supplementation yield high returns in some settings (although there is apparent inconsistency in some of the findings of what appear to be carefully designed studies). There is somewhat less reliable information available on the costs and effects of school-based health education programs (other than those focused on reproductive health), school lunch and other feeding programs, and school water and sanitation investments. There is almost no information on the cost and effectiveness of investments in school health policy development, presumptive malaria treatment, periodical physical examinations, and school health insurance. An important distributional issue with respect to school-based health investments is that their benefits are mostly limited to children currently enrolled in school (who are predominantly from better off families and males in many countries).

Other Health Investments

There is reliable information on the effectiveness of tobacco taxes and bans on advertising, but there is little information on the cost of the investments required to implement these policies effectively. There is limited cost and effectiveness information for most of the remaining investments in this category (i.e., antidrug and antialcohol abuse programs, mass media interventions, food supplements for pregnant and lactating women, food fortification programs, road accident control programs). However, there is no information on either the cost or effectiveness of investments to improve the mental health of youth.

Community and Other Investments

There is very limited information on the cost and effectiveness of youth centers, but there is no information on the remaining investments in this category (i.e., youth development programs, micro-credit programs targeted to youth, youth rehabilitation programs, sports and recreation programs targeted to youth).

BENEFITS

Our literature review in Knowles and Behrman (2005) indicates that there is a wide range of possible effects from investments in youth. In order to carry out cost-benefit analysis of these investments, it is necessary to assign monetary values to their various possible effects. In some cases, it is possible to develop estimates of benefits directly in monetary terms that permit comparisons with costs and with other impacts that also are measured directly in monetary terms, such as the monetary value of enhanced labor productivity. We refer to benefits estimated in this way as "directly estimated" benefits, which are preferred, if possible. However, in cases where it is conceptually or practically difficult to value benefits directly in economic terms, we develop estimates based on the least amount of money society currently spends to secure the same effects, as discussed above. We refer to benefits estimated in this way as "indirectly estimated" benefits.[26] In using the indirect approach, the following caveats are noted:

- The effect(s) of the cost-effective alternative investment must be the same as the effect(s) for which a monetary value is sought. For example, if the cost per birth averted in a family planning program is used to value the effect of reduced fertility, it is important to adjust that cost for the other benefits that family planning programs provide, such as reduced maternal mortality and morbidity, reduced child mortality, ability to space births, and information.[27]
- It is important not to double count the value of effects that are directly and indirectly valued (van der Gaag and Tan, 1997). For example, if the value of enhanced labor productivity is used to value the benefits of increased education among all children, even those who may voluntarily not participate in the labor force (e.g., persons engaged full-time in housework), it is incorrect to include the value of improved health of children as an additional benefit (because this benefit should be reflected already in the enhanced productivity of more educated persons in housework).
- What is really needed for indirect estimation is the amount of money society spends on the margin to secure a given effect, that is, the marginal cost-effectiveness ratio rather than the average cost-effectiveness ratio. Unfortunately, there is little information currently available on marginal cost-effectiveness ratios (e.g., the marginal cost per DALY gained in immunization or family planning programs). However, in many programs, marginal cost-effectiveness ratios may differ substantially from average cost-effectiveness ratios.

In cases where a broad effect such as "increased education" is expected to be the primary effect of an investment (e.g., a targeted scholarship program), it is necessary to value each of its components either directly (the preferred approach) or indirectly (the second best approach). For example, in the case of "increased education," one of its components is enhanced

---

[26]When indirect estimates of benefits are used, care must be taken to find an alternative intervention with the same effects. Otherwise, the estimates have to be adjusted.

[27]Such adjustments have not been made in previous applications of this methodology (e.g., Summers, 1994; van der Gaag and Tan, 1997).

labor productivity. Because there is a substantial literature on relationships between increased education and enhanced labor productivity and on how to assign a monetary value to enhanced productivity, it is usually possible to value this component directly. However, other components of increased education (e.g., reduced teen pregnancy, reduced crime, reduced fertility) are more difficult to value directly, and an indirect valuation may be more practical.[28] Knowles and Behrman (2005) identify the components of such broad effects in order to facilitate such a two-step valuation process. This information is summarized in Annex A.

Knowles and Behrman (2005) also review the extensive literature relevant to valuing the benefits of the various hypothesized effects of investments in youth. It is convenient to group the various effects of investments in youth into the following categories: (1) directly monetizable effects, (2) effects that are difficult to monetize directly but that can be monetized indirectly, and (3) effects that are particularly difficult to monetize even indirectly. In the case of directly monetizable effects, such as "enhanced labor productivity," the review discusses only direct methods of valuation. In the case of effects that are more difficult to value directly, such as "increased education" or "improved health," the review discusses both direct approaches to valuing the effects (using the two-step procedure discussed above) and indirect methods based on the cost of cost-effective alternative investments currently used to obtain the same effects (the Summers method discussed above). In the case of effects that are inherently difficult to value in monetary terms, such as "enhanced social capital" or "enhanced self-esteem," the review provides only conjectures about how they might be valued. The main findings regarding the valuation of the effects of investments in youth are summarized below.

Directly Monetizable Effects of Investments in Youth

Enhanced Labor Productivity

An estimated percentage increase in labor productivity can be valued directly by multiplying it by the average wage.

Reduced Underutilization of Labor

There is often little information on activities of unemployed youth (i.e., the extent to which they may be engaged in housework or studying). This complicates efforts to place a monetary value on the increased labor utiliza-

---

[28]However, in the case of some of the hypothesized effects of increased education (e.g., increased self-esteem), even indirect valuation may be difficult.

tion benefits obtained from reducing youth unemployment (a broad effect).[29] However, where such information is available, the percentage increase in labor productivity that results from reduced unemployment can be multiplied by the average wage to obtain a direct estimate of this benefit.

Increased/Decreased Work Effort

There is often little information on the effect of investments in demand-side schooling (e.g., scholarships and other transfers) or the enforcement of child labor laws on adult and child work effort. However, when such information is available, this benefit (or cost) can be estimated directly by multiplying the reported change in work effort by the average wage.

Expanded Access to Risk-Pooling Services

Estimates of this benefit can usually be made from knowledge of the characteristics of the risk insured against (e.g., the risk of health care expenditure among youth), usually in combination with some rather strong assumptions.

Reduced Age at Which Children Achieve a Given Level of Schooling

In valuing the effects of a given schooling investment, it can be assumed that earlier completion of a given grade level results in a longer active period in which to recoup the benefits of enhanced productivity. Because this benefit occurs at the beginning of a person's active period, it is not as heavily discounted as some other education-related benefits.

Reduced Cost of Medical Care

There is some information on the cost of treating persons infected with HIV and other sexually transmitted infections. However, there is little information on the cost of medical care associated with unsafe abortions, or from female genital cutting. There is no problem in assigning a monetary value to the monetary component of this effect, because effects on the cost of medical care are usually expressed in terms of a percentage of an average level of spending on medical care. However, it is more difficult to assign a value to the opportunity cost of time and other indirect costs (e.g., transportation costs) involved in obtaining medical care.

---

[29]The most commonly used approach in the literature on youth investments is to assume that unemployed youth are not engaged in any productive activity. However, this is unlikely to be generally true.

Increased Tax Revenue

This is equivalent to a transfer. Hence, there is generally no benefit associated with the collection of increased tax revenue. However, in some cases (e.g., a tobacco tax), the tax revenue collected may have lower than usual distortionary costs because the tax may be offsetting in part or in whole some distortion, and in such cases this benefit should be valued, if possible.

Some possible approaches for indirectly valuing effects of investments in youth can be found in Table 11-2.

Effects That Are Particularly Difficult to Value Directly or Indirectly

Some examples of effects of investments in youth that are particularly difficult to value, whether directly or indirectly, include increased social capital, averted infertility, averted social exclusion, improved self-esteem, and enhanced national security (an effect of military training). For some of these effects (e.g., increased social capital, averted social exclusion), it is too difficult even to find a suitable measure of the effect. However, the difficulties involved in measuring and valuing these effects do not necessarily imply that they are less important than other effects of investments in youth.

BENEFITS AND COSTS OF INVESTMENTS IN YOUTH

Existing Cost/Benefit Analyses of Investments in Youth

There are only a few existing studies for developing countries in which the benefits and costs of investments in youth are calculated. Some of these studies are reviewed briefly in this section.

Bangladesh Food for Education (FFE) Program

The government-funded FFE program in Bangladesh provides grants of food (and more recently, cash) to households in designated poor localities on the condition that primary school-age children in the household are attending school. The annual FFE program expenditure needed to encourage an additional poor child to attend primary school was estimated to be $66.40, while the estimated annual expenditure for an additional very poor child to attend was estimated to be $95 (Ravallion and Wodon, 2000). Benefits in the form of additional per capita consumption enjoyed both by the child attending school and his/her family when the child reaches adulthood were estimated to be $69.90 for the poor child and $52.60 for the very poor child. After netting out the value of the food grains received under the program, which are a transfer (but without including any estimate of social or other private benefits or estimates of distortionary costs), the internal rate of return was estimated to be 8.11 for the very poor and 11.50 for the poor. The report concludes that the FFE program is cost-effective as an education program. However, it suggests that a cash stipend program might be more cost-effective because of the likelihood that it would involve lower administrative costs (a recommendation that has been adopted, as indicated above).

Colombia PACES School Voucher Program

The Programa de Ampliación de Cobertura de la Educación Secundaria (PACES) program provides vouchers to poor households that can be used to pay for children to attend private secondary schools. In municipalities in which the number of applicants exceeded the funds available, scholarship recipients were randomly selected through a lottery (Angrist et al., 2002). The total social cost of the program was estimated to be $43 annually per lottery winner, or $195 over a 3-year period (after adjusting for different rates of voucher take-up in each year of the program). This cost, however, does *not* include any distortionary costs incurred, for example, in raising revenues to finance this program or due to effects of the program on the behaviors of other household members (e.g., changing their labor supplies). The evaluation estimated that the additional 0.12 to 0.16 years of schooling completed by lottery winners would raise their annual incomes by about $36 to $48 per year (based on an estimated rate of return to schooling of 10 percent in Colombia and predicted average annual earnings of $3,000). Additionally, the estimated increase of 0.2 standard deviations in test scores among lottery winners was estimated to be the equivalent of about one full year of schooling (based on the mean test scores by grade of U.S. Hispanic students taking the same test), which if correct, would translate into an additional gain of about $300 in annual earnings. Clearly the estimated gain in earnings would exceed the program's cost as calculated in the study in any cost/benefit analysis, even if earnings gains are heavily discounted, distortionary costs are included, and social and other private benefits from improved cognitive achievement are ignored.

Increasing the Quality Versus the Quantity of Basic Schooling in Rural Pakistan

Increasing the quantity or quality of schooling an individual receives is likely to raise his or her cognitive skills. Increasing the quantity of schooling—by providing a primary education to children who otherwise would not go to school, or by providing a middle school education to children

TABLE 11-2 Possible Approaches for Indirectly Valuing Effects of
Investments in Youth

Effect
Reduced youth unemployment
Reduced child labor
Averted teen pregnancy
Averted HIV infection
Averted STIs (other than HIV/AIDS)
Averted TB infections
Improved health
Improved nutritional status
Improved mental health
Delayed marriage (females)
Averted drug/alcohol abuse
Averted physical and/or sexual abuse
Averted crime
Averted female genital cutting
Reduced fertility
Averted abortion
Reduced tobacco use
Reduced violence and civil conflict
Averted orphans

NOTE: STI = Sexually transmitted infection. DALY = Disability-adjusted life year.
SOURCE: Knowles and Behrman (2005).

Indirect Valuation Method

Cost of public works programs targeted to youth per job created.

Cost of scholarship programs per hour of reduced child labor.

Cost of family planning services targeted to youth per averted teen birth.

Cost of HIV/AIDS preventive programs targeted to high-risk populations. Alternatively, the estimated number of DALYs gained per averted HIV infection, multiplied by an estimate of the monetary benefits per DALY gained.

Cost per STI averted through cost-effective investments to prevent HIV/AIDS (e.g., cost of preventive interventions directed to high-risk populations).

Cost per DALY gained of cost-effective investments in health (e.g., immunization).

Cost per DALY gained of cost-effective investments in health (e.g., immunization).

Cost per unit of improved nutritional outcome (e.g., height-for-age, goiter rate, hemoglobin level, birthweight) of cost-effective nutrition investments (e.g., micronutrient supplements, food fortification).

No information available on the cost-effectiveness of alternative interventions designed to improve mental health. A less satisfactory interim solution might be to obtain an estimate of the average number of DALYs lost per case of mental illness and to value each DALY gained on the basis of cost-effective alternative investments in health (e.g., immunization).

Cost of scholarship programs for girls per year of delayed marriage.

No information available on the cost effectiveness of alternative interventions designed to avert drug/alcohol abuse. A less satisfactory interim solution might be to obtain an estimate of the average number of DALYs lost per case of drug/alcohol abuse and to value each DALY gained on the basis of alternative cost-effective investments in health (e.g., immunization).

No information available on the cost-effectiveness of alternative interventions designed to avert physical and/or sexual abuse. A less satisfactory interim solution might be to obtain an estimate of the average number of DALYs lost per case of physical and/or sexual abuse and to value each DALY gained on the basis of alternative cost-effective investments in health (e.g., immunization).

No information available on the cost-effectiveness of alternative interventions designed to avert crime in developing countries. In this case, direct estimates may need to be prepared. See Knowles and Behrman (2005).

If an estimate of the average number of DALYs lost per case of female genital cutting can be obtained, it would be possible to value each DALY gained on the basis of alternative cost-effective investments in health (e.g., immunization).

Cost of family planning services per birth averted (with adjustments for fact that family planning services have other effects, e.g., birth spacing, improved health).

Cost of family planning services per abortion averted (estimated crudely as the cost per pregnancy averted by family planning services divided by the proportion of pregnancies terminated by abortion).

Cost of enforcing an increase in the tobacco tax per 1 percentage reduction in tobacco use (can be used for any investment except investments designed to enforce an increase in the tobacco tax). Alternatively, an estimate of the number of DALYs gained, valuing each DALY gained on the basis of alternative cost-effective investments in health (e.g., immunization).

No reliable information available on the cost-effectiveness of alternative interventions designed to reduce violence and civil conflict.

Cost of cost-effective interventions (e.g., professionally assisted deliveries) designed to avert maternal deaths (which produce orphans).

who otherwise would leave school upon the completion of primary school—entails substantial costs. Similarly, improving the quality of schools has costs. However, in the case of quality improvement, there is little or no change in the opportunity cost of student time—a large component of the total cost of schooling.

Behrman, Ross, and Sabot (2005) developed a conceptual framework for evaluating the rates of return to increases in the quantity versus the quality of schooling. They collected most of the necessary data for rural Pakistan, and made estimates with methods that control for the key behavioral choices and for unobserved determinants of education. They found that increasing the quantity and improving the quality of schooling are alternative means of increasing the productivity and earnings of the labor force.[30] Their estimates are that the "social" rate of return to enabling the graduate of a low-quality primary school to complete middle school, 2.8 percent, is low compared to improving school quality, 13.0 percent, or providing access to a low-quality primary school, 18.2 percent.[31] The relatively high rate of return to improving quality reflects the absence of any additional opportunity cost to the students and the absence of higher capital costs for students already enrolled in school. In this context, it appears that productivity and equity concerns both point toward expanding primary schools, even if they are of lower quality. Additionally, because few boys now lack access to basic schooling, girls will benefit disproportionately.

This study again points to some of the difficulties in undertaking such evaluations. Even with the special data collected for the study, for example, it was not possible to identify with confidence the relative importance of the various components of teacher quality (i.e., the relative importance of factors such as teacher experience, teacher schooling, teacher training). This study also limits the measurement of the effects of changes in schooling to the private value of labor market outcomes, and provides no information on possible efficiency reasons for interventions. Furthermore, as in the other studies reviewed in this section, there is no attention to some possibly important distortionary costs, such as those incurred to raise governmental revenues.

---

[30]Alderman et al. (1996) found that higher cognitive skills lead to higher wages in rural Pakistan, presumably because more skilled workers are more productive. Because they are more skilled, graduates of even low-quality primary schools earn more than uneducated workers. In like manner, graduates of high-quality primary schools and graduates of middle schools who attended low-quality primary schools earn more than students who complete only low-quality primary schools.

[31]These "social" rates of return are similar to many estimates of schooling returns (e.g., see Psacharopoulos, 1994) in that they include both the private and public costs, but only the direct private productivity benefits—which is why we put "social" in parentheses.

Estimates of the Benefits and Costs of Investments in Youth

In this section, estimates are presented of the benefits and costs of some investments for which a sufficient amount of information is available to permit the preparation of estimates of investment effects, costs, and benefits. These estimates attempt to incorporate the direct and indirect effects of investments, using the method presented in Annex B. Before proceeding, attention is drawn to the fact that the estimates presented are quite specific to a particular country or context. They do not represent generally applicable estimates of the returns to the above investments. Additionally, as will become apparent in the discussion that follows, the estimated benefit/cost ratios (and internal rates of return) are quite sensitive to the particular assumptions used.

Scholarship Program

The effect of the investment on increased education is estimated on the basis of results obtained in the PACES voucher program (Colombia), which awarded scholarships to poor children (some of whom were selected randomly from among applicants via a lottery) to attend private secondary schools (Angrist et al., 2002; also see discussion above). The estimated effect of the scholarships was 0.12 additional grades of schooling completed by each lottery winner (as compared to lottery losers, all of whom had also applied to the program). In addition, each lottery winner performed 0.2 standard deviations higher on standardized achievement tests, a difference that was estimated to be equivalent to having completed approximately one additional grade of schooling.[32] There was almost certainly an effect of the investment on the average age at which secondary school was completed, because repetition rates were significantly lower among lottery winners and because 8th grade completion rates among lottery winners were about 10 percentage points higher (with age held constant). But the average age at which a given grade was completed was not reported, possibly because most of the sample children were still in secondary school at the time of the evaluation. There was also some evidence that lottery winners were less likely to be married at the time of the survey (although the effect was less than 1 percent). No information was provided on the possible effect of the scholarships or on the means used to raise revenues for the program on adult work effort. However, lottery winners (school children) worked significantly fewer hours per week (about 1.2 fewer hours).

---

[32]In PROGRESA, by comparison, the estimated effect of scholarships on cognitive achievement was estimated to be the equivalent of 0.7 grades completed.

In calculating the benefits and costs of a scholarship program, the following assumptions were used:

- The total cost of the investment (i.e., during the three years in which the program operated before its effects were measured) is equal to $227.65 per scholarship recipient (consisting of $9.07 in additional resources consumed to provide education, $185.93 in reduced work effort of children receiving scholarships, and $32.65 for administrative and distortionary costs).[33]
- Each scholarship recipient completes 0.12 additional grades of schooling (i.e., the effect of the scholarship on higher test scores is initially assumed to be zero).
- The cost of the investment is distributed equally during three years (i.e., ages 13, 14, 15).
- Each additional year of secondary schooling completed results in a 10 percent increase in annual earnings, as compared to expected future average annual earnings of $3,000.
- Earnings are received continuously from age 16 until age 60.
- The investment reduces the average age of completing secondary school by 0.2 years per scholarship recipient, which is assumed to provide an additional 0.2 years of earnings at age 15.
- There is no effect of the investment on age at marriage or on the number of hours worked by adults.
- The discount rate is 5 percent per annum.

Because increased education is a broad effect, the following additional assumptions were made about the components of increased education:

- Each additional year of completed secondary schooling results in reduced fertility (i.e., 0.1 fewer births at age 35, averaged over males and females) and improved health (i.e., 1.0 DALY spread out evenly between ages 15 and 70).
- Each additional year of completed secondary schooling results in 1.2 fewer hours worked per week by scholarship recipients while enrolled in school.

---

[33]Education costs ($9.07) were estimated as the additional amount spent by households on schooling for lottery winners ($235.81) less the amount saved by the government in public school costs per lottery winner ($226.74). The cost of reduced work effort ($185.93) was estimated on the basis of the estimated 1.2 hours less per week worked by lottery winners, assuming 48 weeks worked per year and an average hourly wage of $0.71 (adjusted for the fact that voucher take-up rates declined over time). Distortionary and administrative costs (including the cost of raising the necessary fiscal revenue) were assumed to be 30 percent of the net change in public expenditure ($108.83, i.e., public outlays on scholarships of $335.58 less reduced public expenditure on secondary schooling of $226.74).

• There is no effect of increased education on any of the following: crime, violence and civil conflict, social exclusion, youth unemployment, teen pregnancies, HIV infection or STIs, drug/alcohol abuse, physical/sexual abuse, or mental health. Clearly, this assumption (necessitated by the absence of estimates of increased education on these hypothesized effects) renders it impossible to obtain separate estimates of the social and private benefits of this investment.

The benefits from reduced fertility, improved health, and reduced child work are assumed to be as follows:

• $50 per birth averted (indirectly estimated, based on the cost of 4 couple years of protection using contraceptives).
• $20 per DALY gained (indirectly estimated, based on the cost of cost-effective health investments targeted to youth).
• $0 (based on the assumption, for secondary students, that the benefits of any decrease in child labor are offset by the loss in benefits from reduced work experience).

Under these assumptions, the benefits discounted to age 13 are $3,152, while the costs (also discounted to age 13) are $953. The benefit/cost ratio is 3.31, while the internal rate of return is 25.6 percent. However, these estimates are quite sensitive to the discount rate used. For example, if a discount rate of 3 percent is used instead of 5 percent, the benefit/cost ratio increases from 3.31 to 4.41. The estimates are also very sensitive to the assumed productivity effect of an additional year of schooling. For example, if this effect is reduced from 0.10 to 0.08, the benefit/cost ratio decreases from 3.31 to 2.77.

The estimates are not sensitive to the inclusion of other components besides enhanced labor productivity in the broad effect of increased education. For example, if both the assumed fertility and health effects are reduced to zero, the benefit/cost ratio decreases only from 3.31 to 3.30. However, the estimates are sensitive to the assumed effect of the scholarship on the average age at which children complete school. If this effect is reduced to zero, the benefit/cost ratio declines from 3.31 to 2.68.

The preceding estimates assume that the effect of the scholarship on education is limited to the increase in the number of grades completed by scholarship recipients. If the effect is expanded to reflect the improved performance of scholarship recipients on standardized achievement tests (estimated to be the equivalent of an additional grade completed in the Colombia study), the benefit/cost ratio increases dramatically, from 3.31 to 25.63, while the internal rate of return increases from 25.6 percent to 93.9 percent.

Adult Basic Education and Literacy Program

Information on the effectiveness of investments in adult basic education and literacy in creating lasting cognitive achievement is not readily available. It is also unclear how appropriately and accurately costs are measured in the available evaluation literature. Accordingly, cost/benefit estimates are prepared for this type of investment using a wide range of assumptions in terms of cost and effectiveness. Estimates of the cost per trainee successfully completing an ABEL course range from $20.40 to $97.78 for four projects in three countries, Ghana (two projects), Bangladesh, and Senegal (World Bank, 2002b). This implies that a $1,000 investment in ABEL could produce from 10.23 to 49.02 successful trainees. However, these cost estimates apparently do not include the distortionary costs resulting from raising revenues to finance these programs, and thus are probably underestimates of the true costs. There is no information on the level of lasting cognitive achievement that successful trainees would acquire. An upper limit is probably the equivalent of four years of primary schooling. A lower limit is plausibly the equivalent of one year of primary schooling (although the possibility cannot be ruled out that in some mass campaign programs, less is acquired). The range of assumptions about cost and effectiveness creates a wide range of estimates about the cost effectiveness of ABEL, that is, from 10.2 years of primary school equivalency to 196.1 years of primary school equivalency per $1,000 investment (not including distortionary costs).

The cost/benefit estimates are made using the following assumptions:

• The training is provided to 18-year-olds and is assumed to be the equivalent of only one year of primary schooling completed.
• The effect of $1,200 invested in ABEL (including distortionary costs of 20 percent) is initially assumed to create only 10.23 years of primary school equivalency.
• Each additional year of primary school equivalency results in a 10 percent increase in annual earnings, as compared to average annual earnings of $1,400 in Colombia.[34]
• Earnings are received continuously from age 19 until age 60.
• The discount rate is 5 percent per annum.

---

[34]The estimate of average annual earnings among those without any formal schooling completed is calculated assuming annual earnings of $3,000 for those having completed 8 years of schooling (from the preceding example for Colombia) and a 10 percent rate of return on an additional year of schooling.

Because the increased education that is assumed to result from ABEL investments is a broad effect, the following additional assumptions were made about the components of increased education:

- Each additional year of primary school equivalency results in reduced fertility (i.e., 0.1 fewer births at age 35, averaged over males and females) and improved health (1.0 DALYs spread out evenly between ages 19 and 70).
- There is no effect of increased education on any of the following: violence and civil conflict, crime, social exclusion, youth unemployment, teen pregnancies, HIV infection or STIs, drug/alcohol abuse, physical/sexual abuse, or mental health. Clearly, this assumption (necessitated by the absence of estimates of increased education on these hypothesized effects) renders it impossible to obtain separate estimates of the social and private benefits of this investment.

The benefits from reduced fertility and improved health are assumed to be as follows:

- $50 per birth averted (indirectly estimated, based on the cost of 4 couple years of protection using contraceptives).
- $20 per DALY gained (indirectly estimated, based on the cost of cost-effective health investments targeted to youth).

Under these assumptions, the benefits discounted to age 18 are $23,880, while the costs (including distortionary costs) are $1,200. The benefit/cost ratio is 19.9, while the internal rate of return is 70 percent. However, these estimates are quite sensitive to the discount rate used. For example, if a discount rate of 3 percent is used instead of 5 percent, the benefit/cost ratio increases from 19.9 to 27.6. The estimates are also very sensitive to the assumed productivity effect of an additional year of primary school equivalency. For example, if this effect is reduced from 0.10 to 0.08, the benefit/cost ratio declines to 15.93. If, alternatively, the productivity effect of the ABEL training is assumed to be 0.10 initially but to diminish at 5 percent annually, the benefit/cost ratio declines to 11.55. If it is assumed to decline at 10 percent annually, the benefit/cost ratio falls to 8.14.

If instead of the lower limit of cost effectiveness that is used in preparing the above estimates (i.e., 10.2 successful trainees per $1,000 invested and one year of primary school equivalency per successful trainee), the upper limit is used (i.e., 196.1 trainees per $1,000 invested and four years of primary school equivalency per successful trainee), the benefit/cost ratio rises to an astoundingly high 1,764 (i.e., discounted benefits of $2,116,248 for each $1,200 invested), corresponding to an internal rate of return of 980 percent.

School-Based Reproductive Health Education Program to Prevent HIV/AIDS

Estimates of the effectiveness of this investment are based on estimates developed in the Honduras HIV/AIDS modeling work supported by the World Bank (2002a). It is important to emphasize at the outset that the benefits presented for this investment are limited to the effects of the investment on HIV prevention. No other effects were considered in the Honduras study. It was estimated that a school-based reproductive health education program targeted to adolescents (ages 10 to 19) would reach an estimated 60 percent of the targeted population and, among those reached, would reduce HIV incidence by 38 percent (the baseline annual HIV incidence among adolescents was estimated to be 0.001 in Honduras). Such a program was estimated to cost $10.44 per targeted adolescent (and $12.53, if an additional 20 percent in distortionary costs are included in the unit cost estimate to represent the cost of mobilizing the necessary tax revenue to finance the investment). Under these assumptions, the cost per averted HIV infection is $54,947, or 0.0182 new infections averted per $1,000 invested.

Two alternative estimates of the benefits of this investment are presented. The first estimate (referred to as the "aggregate" estimate) is based on the Commission on Macroeconomics and Health's (2001) estimate that averting an HIV infection in a developing country involves a gain of 34.6 DALYs 5 to 8 years after the infection is averted and the Commission's recommendation that each DALY should be valued at one to three times the level of annual earnings. Assuming that annual earnings are $1,000 and that the lower limit of the estimate of benefits is used (i.e., one times annual earnings), the aggregate estimate of benefits per averted HIV infection would be $34,600 (34.6 × $1,000 = $34,600). Such an estimate would include the benefits not only from improved health, but also from the other components of the broad effect of averting an HIV infection (e.g., reduced medical care costs). Under these assumptions, the benefit/cost ratio is 0.493, while the internal rate of return is undefined (because even undiscounted benefits are less than costs).[35] If a 3 percent discount rate is used instead of 5 percent, the benefit/cost ratio rises to 0.543. This relative insensitivity with respect to changes in the discount rate reflects the fact that the benefits of the investment are assumed to occur at a relatively young age (23).

---

[35]If each DALY gained from an averted HIV infection is valued at twice the level of national earnings ($2,000, instead of $1,000, and still less than the upper range of three times the level of national earnings estimated by the Commission on Macroeconomics and Health, 2001, the benefit/cost ratio rises to 0.987 (with an internal rate of return of 4.7 percent).

An alternative estimate of the benefits from averting one HIV infection (referred to below as the "disaggregated" estimate), which is a broad effect, is based on the following assumptions regarding the benefits of the components:

- It is assumed that any HIV infection is averted at age 18.
- In the case of improved health, it is assumed that each HIV infection averted results in a gain of 34.6 DALYs (but valued differently, as explained below) at age 23.
- Each DALY of improved health gained is valued according to the cost per DALY gained from alternative cost-effective health investments targeted to the same age group. An estimate of $20 per DALY gained is used for this purpose.
- In the case of secondary HIV infections, it is assumed (consistent with estimates in the Honduras HIV/AIDS modeling) that each infected adolescent infects 0.1 others between the age of infection (18) and the age of death (23).
- Each secondary infection averted is assumed to provide a benefit of $4,867 (based on the estimated discounted benefits of averting an HIV infection, using the disaggregated method).
- It is assumed that each averted HIV infection averts the annual medical costs of caring for an AIDS patient, assumed to be equal to 2.7 times the level of annual earnings ($2,700, assuming annual earnings of $1,000) during the last two years of life (i.e., at ages 21 and 22).
- There is no effect of an averted HIV infection on secondary tuberculosis infections, orphans' social exclusion, or education. This assumption (necessitated by the absence of estimates of averted HIV infection on these effects) renders it impossible to obtain separate estimates of the social and private benefits of this investment.

Using the disaggregated estimate of benefits, the estimated benefit/cost ratio is only 0.102, while the internal rate of return is again undefined (the estimated benefit/cost ratio increases to 0.109 with a discount rate of 3 percent). The estimated benefit/cost ratio is so low in this case because the estimated benefits of each averted HIV infection are only $4,867 in this case (compared to $34,600 when an averted HIV infection is valued using the aggregate method discussed above).[36]

---

[36]Estimates of the benefit/cost ratio were prepared for two other reproductive health investments targeted to Honduran youth (i.e., social marketing of reproductive health services designed to prevent HIV/AIDS and workplace/community outreach services designed to prevent HIV/AIDS). The estimated benefit/cost ratios were 0.199 and 0.249, respectively, with plausible ranges of 0.041 to 0.399 and 0.051 to 0.548, respectively.

The estimated benefit/cost ratios for this investment are directly proportional to the incidence of HIV infection in the targeted adolescent population. For example, if the incidence is 1 percent, instead of 0.1 percent, the benefit/cost ratio increases by a factor of 10, from 0.493 to 4.93 in the case of the benefits estimated using the aggregate method and from 0.102 to 1.02 in the case of benefits estimated using the disaggregated method.[37] The benefit/cost ratio would presumably be significantly higher in both cases if some of the other benefits of such an investment (e.g., STIs averted, teenage pregnancies averted) were considered.

In addition to the fact that the Honduras study neglects benefits other than the prevention of HIV infections, it is also conservative in assuming that the benefits of health education do not continue beyond a single year. A more realistic assumption might be that the HIV prevention effectiveness of health education declines at a fixed annual rate over time. However, an offsetting factor is that the incidence of HIV infection is likely to rise with age. In the absence of better information, it is not unreasonable to assume for illustration that these two factors offset one another. In this case, health education received at age 15 would have the same impact, in terms of HIV infections averted per $1,000 investment, at ages 18 to 29. Under these revised assumptions, the estimated benefit/cost ratio would increase to 4.59 in the case of benefits estimated using the aggregate method, and to 1.115 in the case of benefits estimated using the disaggregated method.

Iron Supplementation Administered to Secondary School Children

It has been estimated that iron supplements provided to school children increase their cognitive achievement by 5 to 25 percent (McGuire, 1996). The annual cost of iron supplements per school child has been estimated to be $0.10 (World Bank, 2002c). A conservative estimate of delivery costs per child is $0.05 (i.e., 50 percent of the cost of the supplements).

A direct estimate of the benefits and costs of iron supplements administered to school children is based on the following relatively conservative assumptions:

- Iron supplements are administered to children ages 13 to 15 for three years.
- The annual cost of the iron supplements is $0.15 per child ($0.18, including additional distortionary costs of 20 percent).

---

[37]The estimated benefit/cost ratios for the two other youth reproductive health investments referred to in the preceding footnote would also increase proportionately with increases in HIV incidence in the targeted youth population.

• The cost of the investment is spread out equally during three years (i.e., ages 13, 14, 15).

• The effect of iron supplementation at age 15 is to increase each child's cognitive achievement by the equivalent of 0.05 years of completed schooling.

• Each additional year of secondary schooling completed results in a 10 percent increase in annual earnings, as compared to average annual earnings of $200.

• Earnings are received continuously from age 16 until age 60.

• The discount rate is 5 percent per annum.

Because increased education is a broad effect, the following additional assumptions were made about the components of increased education:

• Each additional year of completed secondary schooling results in reduced fertility (i.e., 0.1 fewer births at age 35, averaged over males and females) and improved health (1.0 DALYs spread out evenly between ages 15 and 70).

• There is no effect of increased education on any of the following: crime, violence and civil conflict, social exclusion, youth unemployment, teen pregnancies, HIV infection or STIs, drug/alcohol abuse, physical/sexual abuse, or mental health. Clearly, this assumption (necessitated by the absence of estimates of increased education on these hypothesized effects) renders it impossible to obtain separate estimates of the social and private benefits of this investment.

The benefits from reduced fertility and improved health are assumed to be as follows:

• $50 per birth averted (indirectly estimated, based on the cost of 4 couple years of protection using contraceptives).

• $20 per DALY gained (indirectly estimated, based on the cost of cost-effective health investments targeted to youth).

Under the above assumptions, the benefit/cost ratio is estimated to be 32.1, while the internal rate of return is 88 percent. Using a discount rate of 3 percent, the benefit/cost ratio increases from 32.1 to 45.2. If the productivity effect of an additional year of schooling is assumed to be 8 percent, rather than 10 percent, the benefit/cost ratio declines to 25.8.

Tobacco Tax

Estimates of the cost per DALY gained from a tax on tobacco products (i.e., $5 to $17) are obtained from the World Bank (1999). An aggregate estimate of benefits per DALY is based on the recommendation of the Commission on Macroeconomics and Health (2001) that a DALY should be valued at one to three times the level of annual earnings.

An aggregate estimate of the benefits from a tobacco tax is based on the following conservative assumptions:

- An investment of $1,000 ($1,200, including additional distortionary costs of 20 percent) would produce a gain of 58.82 DALYs (i.e., the cost per DALY gained is assumed to be $17).
- There is a lag of 30 years between the investment and the resulting gain in DALYs.
- Annual earnings are $1,000.
- Each DALY gained is valued at one times annual earnings.

Under these assumptions, $1,200 invested in a tobacco tax today would yield discounted future benefits of $13,610. The benefit/cost ratio is therefore 11.34, and the internal rate of return is 13.9 percent. Given the long lag between costs and benefits, the benefit/cost ratio is quite sensitive to changes in the discount rate. For example, using a discount rate of 3 percent instead of 5 percent raises the benefit/cost ratio from 11.34 to 20.20. The estimated benefit/cost ratio is also quite sensitive to the length of the lag between costs and benefits. For example, increasing the lag from 30 to 40 years reduces the benefit from 11.34 to 6.96. Valuing each DALY at twice annual earnings ($2,000) raises the benefit/cost ratio from 11.34 to 22.68. Reducing the cost per DALY gained from $17 to $5 (its lower limit) increases the benefit/cost ratio from 11.34 to 38.56.

SYNTHESIS AND CONCLUSIONS

What Are Highest Return Investments?

Based on the very limited information available on the effects of investments in youth, it would appear that the investments in youth with the highest economic returns include: investments in formal schooling (i.e., supply-side investments in the quality of schooling, demand-side investments in targeted scholarship programs), investments in adult basic education and literacy targeted to adolescents, selected investments in school-based health services (e.g., micronutrient supplements), and investments designed to reduce the use of tobacco products (e.g., an increase in tobacco taxes). School-based reproductive health programs to prevent HIV/AIDS provide comparably high economic returns when annual HIV incidence among targeted youth rises to 1 to 2 percent or more or when their effects are assumed to last over a period longer than one year (although there is

TABLE 11-3 Estimated Benefit/Cost Ratios (BCRs) of Some Investments in Youth in Selected Countries

Investment	BCR (5% discount rate)	Plausible Range in BCRs
Scholarship program (Colombia)	3.31	2.77 to 25.63
Adult basic education and literacy program (Colombia)	19.9	8.14 to 1,764
School-based reproductive health program to prevent HIV/AIDS (Honduras)	0.493	0.102 to 4.59
Iron supplementation administered to secondary school children (low-income country)	32.1	25.8 to 45.2
Tobacco tax (middle-income country)	11.34	6.96 to 38.56

SOURCE: Estimates in text.

unfortunately no information in the literature that establishes that the effects of these investments continue for several years). The economic returns to school-based reproductive health programs designed to prevent HIV/AIDS would also be higher if they could be shown to yield other benefits, such as the prevention of adolescent pregnancies and other types of STIs.

Table 11-3 presents estimates of the benefit/cost ratios for selected investments in youth in particular countries or country settings for which there is sufficient information available to support the preparation of such estimates. The data and assumptions used to obtain the estimates reported in Table 11-3 are discussed above. What is most interesting in this table is not the estimates obtained under a single set of assumptions (column 2), but rather the wide range of estimates one obtains by using alternative, and perhaps equally plausible, sets of assumptions (column 3). In fact, for several of the investments, the plausible ranges in the estimates of benefit/cost ratios overlap, making it impossible to develop an unambiguous ranking of their economic returns. The appropriate conclusion to draw from Table 11-3 is that, even in cases where the information base is relatively strong, a high level of uncertainty remains regarding the economic returns to alternative investments in youth.

How Do Investments in Youth Compare with Other Investments?

Of course, one purpose of estimating benefit/cost ratios (and internal rates of return) for alternative investments in youth is to compare their economic returns to those of alternative investments. If the benefit/cost ratios are properly calculated and are greater than one, the investment is worth undertaking in an expected value sense. For investments for which

TABLE 11-4 Benefit/Cost Ratios for Selected Development Bank-Supported Investments

Project (Year)	Benefit/Cost Ratio
Hill Forest Development Project, Nepal (1983)	1.18
Irrigation Systems Improvement Project, Philippines (1977)	1.48
Livestock Development Project, Uruguay (1970)	1.59
Livestock and Agricultural Development Project, Paraguay (1979)	1.62
Cotton Processing and Marketing Project, Kenya (1979)	1.80

SOURCE: van der Gaag and Tan (1997).

they are less than one, they are not worth undertaking. Therefore in an important sense, the estimates summarized in Table 11-3 provide a basis for comparing the economic returns of investments in youth with those of other investments.

Table 11-4 lists the benefit/cost ratios of some development bank-supported investments in other sectors for purposes of comparison. These investments were made in the so-called "hard" sectors. When one compares the estimates in Table 11-4 with those in Table 11-3, the immediate impression is that at least some types of investments in youth are likely to compare quite favorably to investments in other sectors.

What Are Highest Priority Research Areas?

At a general level, the highest priority research areas that emanate from this review are those that are necessary to obtain better empirical estimates of the benefit/cost ratios and internal rates of return to the plethora of possible policies that might improve the development of youth in developing countries. We refer to these as research gaps and discuss them below. In addition, the findings reported in this review raise a number of key questions that are also discussed in this concluding subsection.

Four Critical Research Gaps

First, an important gap is the absence of reliable estimates of many hypothesized effects of investments in youth. In future research, high priority should be given to obtaining reliable estimates of the effects of those investments for which little, if any, information currently exists (e.g., the effects of ABEL, vocational and technical training, military training, reproductive health policy development, investments designed to avert drug and alcohol abuse and to improve mental health, youth centers, youth rehabilitation programs, sports and recreation programs targeted to youth). There is clearly a need for more, and larger, randomized experiments of longer duration than have been conducted in the past. Such experiments also need to collect data on a wider range of outcomes than in previous studies. One important contribution of this chapter and of the companion papers (Knowles and Behrman, 2003, 2005) may be to guide future researchers in terms of the data needed to make reliable and complete assessments of the effects of investments in youth. Due to the limitations of randomized experiments for some purposes (i.e., measuring effects that occur only after a considerable lapse of time), there is also a parallel need for more careful behavioral research on the effects of investments in youth than has been done in the past. Such research will require better data, that is, more longitudinal data sets, more carefully measured variables, and data on appropriate instruments.

Second, investments in youth are hypothesized to have a wide range of effects, but many of these are difficult to evaluate. It is not the problem of attaching monetary values to these hypothesized effects that currently constrains efforts to obtain estimates of their economic returns. Rather, it is the lack of reliable estimates of the effects of the investments. One solution to this problem that is explored in this review is the valuation of broad effects indirectly on the basis of the cost of least cost alternative investments that obtain the same broad effects. Although this approach to valuing broad effects may enable one to obtain estimates of benefit/cost ratios for many investments in youth, treating broad effects as a package makes it more difficult to distinguish social from private benefits (because the social effects that give rise to a possible divergence between the two may be packaged together with private effects as components of a single broad effect).

Third, partly in the short to medium term, due to the lack of reliable information on many of the hypothesized effects of investments in youth, there is a role for indirect valuation of the effects of investments in youth (particularly of broad effects, such as "increased education" or "improved health," that are difficult to value directly). We have suggested some possible approaches to developing indirect valuations of many of the hypothesized broad effects of investments in youth in this review and in the companion literature review (Knowles and Behrman, 2005). However, there is a critical need for more research in this area. What is needed are estimates of marginal cost-effectiveness ratios for a number of alternative investments because these best reflect the value that society currently attaches to securing a given outcome.

Fourth, cost estimates are not available for many types of investments in youth (e.g., in the reproductive health area). In addition, the definition of costs (and in some cases, even benefits) used in many studies is incomplete and/or incorrect. Administrative costs and distortionary costs (most often related to the cost of financing investments) frequently have been neglected, while transfers often have been treated as costs. More effort clearly needs to be devoted to the collection of accurate cost data.

Seven Key Remaining Questions

First, could better information be obtained with which to make estimates for some of the areas that we touch on above for which information is scarce? For example, mental health recently has become more widely recognized as a potentially important area for future health intervention. Estimates suggest that mental health problems account for a rapidly expanding share of poor health in the developing world. However, we have been able to find almost no information with which to compare investments in mental health with other investments. For another example, the rapid nutritional transition means that being overweight and obese rapidly is becoming a widespread problem for many youth in developing countries, but there is almost no information available with which to evaluate possible investments designed to address these problems.

Second, are there important policy areas that we have missed in the discussion above despite our effort at broad coverage? Might there be, for example, important legal changes that we have missed concerning, for example, minimum ages of marriage or property rights of youth?

Third, where are the returns from better quality data likely to be greatest? Across the board, given positive discount rates, the costs and returns early in any investment are particularly important. Although there is a general scarcity of information on the public costs of investments in youth, private costs—such as the opportunity cost of time of private citizens necessary to participate in the benefits of various investments—are often ignored.

Fourth, how can information be collected to assess better investments in light of the efficiency motive for policy? For such assessments, it is important to distinguish between private and social benefits and costs—but there is almost no information with which to assess these differences. Obtaining reliable estimates of both private and social benefits depends critically on the availability of reliable estimates of a full range of the effects of a given investment, not only of the private benefits associated with increased productivity.

Fifth, can evaluations better integrate the efficiency and the distributional motives for policies and the trade-offs between them? Although both are often recognized, the trade-offs are infrequently explored. This is clearly a fertile area for future research.

Sixth, how do such estimates need to be fine tuned for particular countries? Many of the assumptions regarding costs and benefits are likely to vary substantially across countries because of differential prices and institutions. How do they need to be fine tuned for distinctions by gender, race, and ethnicity?

Seventh, in the absence of complete information on the economic returns to alternative investments in youth, are there guidelines that development practitioners can follow in designing youth programs that would prioritize youth investments in specific contexts in the short to medium term? One such guideline might be to focus on interventions that address highly prevalent problems, such as micronutrient supplements in poorly nourished populations or reproductive health interventions targeted to populations at high risk. Thus, examining the country context carefully may provide useful and immediate guidance as to which investments in youth are likely to yield the highest economic returns. In addition, some investments may provide benefits much sooner than others. For example, effective adult basic education and literacy training may raise labor productivity almost immediately. Investments involving a long lag before benefits are experienced will be attractive only in cases where the expected benefits are very large (e.g., reducing tobacco consumption). Lastly, investments in youth differ importantly in their distributional and gender effects. Often these differences are apparent from a careful consideration of the country context. In cases where investments in youth are targeted to specific groups, it may be relatively easy to identify those providing the highest returns.

ANNEX A
THE COMPONENTS OF BROAD EFFECTS OF INVESTMENTS IN YOUTH

Annex Table A11-1 lists the various components of broad effects of investments in youth. Each column in the table refers to a given broad effect. A "+" in a particular column indicates that the broad effect corresponding to that column includes the component corresponding to that row of the table. For example, column 1 refers to the broad effect of "increased education." The table indicates that the components of this broad effect include "enhanced labor productivity," "averted youth unemployment," and "reduced child labor," among others. Note that some of the components themselves are broad effects (e.g., "averted youth unemployment," "reduced child labor").

ANNEX B
METHODOLOGY USED TO CALCULATE THE BENEFIT/COST RATIO AND THE INTERNAL RATE OF RETURN

This annex calculates benefit/cost ratios and internal rates of return for various investments in youth using EXCEL spreadsheets in an extension of

ANNEX TABLE A11-1 The Components of Broad Effects of Investments
in Youth

Components	Units
Enhanced labor productivity	%
Reduced underutilization of labor	%
Increased adult work effort	%
Increased social capital	Crime rate
Expanded access to risk-pooling services	1 insured person
Reduced age at which children achieve a given level of schooling	1 year
Reduced cost of medical care	%
Averted infertility	1 woman
Increased tax revenue	$
Increased education	1 year of schooling completed
Averted youth unemployment	1 youth
Reduced child labor	1 hour
Averted teen pregnancy	1 pregnancy
Averted HIV infection	1 infection
Averted STIs	1 infection
Averted TB infections	1 infection
Improved health	1 DALY
Improved nutritional status (height)	1 cm
Improved nutritional status (body mass)	% change in body mass index
Improved nutritional status (anemia)	1 anemic person
Improved nutritional status (iodine deficiency)	1 iodine-deficient person
Improved nutritional status (Vitamin A deficiency)	1 Vitamin A-deficient person
Improved nutritional status (birthweight)	1 kilo
Reduced obesity	1 obese person
Improved mental health	1 depressed person
Delayed marriage	1 year
Averted drug/alcohol abuse	1 person
Averted physical and/or sexual abuse	1 victim
Averted crime	1 criminal
Improved self-esteem	1 youth
Averted female genital cutting	1 victim
Reduced fertility	1 birth
Averted abortion	1 abortion
Reduced tobacco use	1 tobacco user
Reduced violence and civil conflict	1 death
Averted social exclusion	1 excluded person
Averted orphans	1 orphan

Broad Effects

Increased Education (1)	Averted Youth Unemployment (2)	Reduced Child Labor (3)	Averted Teen Pregnancy (4)	Averted HIV Infection (5)	Averted STIs (6)	Improved Health (7)	Improved Nutritional Status (Height) (8)	Improved Nutritional Status (Body Mass) (9)
+	+					+	+	+
	+							
				+		+	+	
					+			
		+	+	+				
+								
+								
+	+							
+		+			+			
+		+						
				+				
+		+	+	+	+		+	
							+	+
+							+	
+	+							
+		+						
	+							
							+	
+			+			+	+	
			+					
+								
+			+	+				
				+				

continued

ANNEX TABLE A11-1 Continued

Components	Units
Enhanced labor productivity	%
Reduced underutilization of labor	%
Increased adult work effort	%
Increased social capital	Crime rate
Expanded access to risk-pooling services	1 insured person
Reduced age at which children achieve a given level of schooling	1 year
Reduced cost of medical care	%
Averted infertility	1 woman
Increased tax revenue	$
Increased education	1 year of schooling completed
Averted youth unemployment	1 youth
Reduced child labor	1 hour
Averted teen pregnancy	1 pregnancy
Averted HIV infection	1 infection
Averted STIs	1 infection
Averted TB infections	1 infection
Improved health	1 DALY
Improved nutritional status (height)	1 cm
Improved nutritional status (body mass)	% change in body mass index
Improved nutritional status (anemia)	1 anemic person
Improved nutritional status (iodine deficiency)	1 iodine-deficient person
Improved nutritional status (Vitamin A deficiency)	1 Vitamin A-deficient person
Improved nutritional status (birthweight)	1 kilo
Reduced obesity	1 obese person
Improved mental health	1 depressed person
Delayed marriage	1 year
Averted drug/alcohol abuse	1 person
Averted physical and/or sexual abuse	1 victim
Averted crime	1 criminal
Improved self-esteem	1 youth
Averted female genital cutting	1 victim
Reduced fertility	1 birth
Averted abortion	1 abortion
Reduced tobacco use	1 tobacco user
Reduced violence and civil conflict	1 death
Averted social exclusion	1 excluded person
Averted orphans	1 orphan

Broad Effects

Improved Nutritional Status (Anemia)	Improved Nutritional Status (Iodine Deficiency)	Improved Nutritional Status (Vitamin A Deficiency)	Improved Nutritional Status (Birthweight)	Reduced Obesity	Improved Mental Health	Delayed Marriage	Averted Drug/Alcohol Abuse	Averted Physical and/or Sexual Abuse	Averted Crime
(10)	(11)	(12)	(13)	(14)	(15)	(16)	(17)	(18)	(19)
+	+	+			+		+		+
+	+	+	+	+	+				
+	+					+			
						+		+	
						+	+	+	
						+	+	+	
+	+	+	+	+	+		+		+
			+						
+									
								+	
	+			+			+		
						+	+		
					+		+	+	
			+						
+	+	+	+		+				

continued

ANNEX TABLE A11-1 Continued

Components	Units
Enhanced labor productivity	%
Reduced underutilization of labor	%
Increased adult work effort	%
Increased social capital	Crime rate
Expanded access to risk-pooling services	1 insured person
Reduced age at which children achieve a given level of schooling	1 year
Reduced cost of medical care	%
Averted infertility	1 woman
Increased tax revenue	$
Increased education	1 year of schooling completed
Averted youth unemployment	1 youth
Reduced child labor	1 hour
Averted teen pregnancy	1 pregnancy
Averted HIV infection	1 infection
Averted STIs	1 infection
Averted TB infections	1 infection
Improved health	1 DALY
Improved nutritional status (height)	1 cm
Improved nutritional status (body mass)	% change in body mass index
Improved nutritional status (anemia)	1 anemic person
Improved nutritional status (iodine deficiency)	1 iodine-deficient person
Improved nutritional status (Vitamin A deficiency)	1 Vitamin A-deficient person
Improved nutritional status (birthweight)	1 kilo
Reduced obesity	1 obese person
Improved mental health	1 depressed person
Delayed marriage	1 year
Averted drug/alcohol abuse	1 person
Averted physical and/or sexual abuse	1 victim
Averted crime	1 criminal
Improved self-esteem	1 youth
Averted female genital cutting	1 victim
Reduced fertility	1 birth
Averted abortion	1 abortion
Reduced tobacco use	1 tobacco user
Reduced violence and civil conflict	1 death
Averted social exclusion	1 excluded person
Averted orphans	1 orphan

SOURCE: Knowles and Behrman (2005).

Broad Effects

Improved Self-Esteem	Averted Female Genital Cutting	Reduced Fertility	Averted Abortion	Reduced Tobacco Use	Reduced Violence and Civil Conflict	Averted Social Exclusion	Averted Orphans
(20)	(21)	(22)	(23)	(24)	(25)	(26)	(27)
		+				+	
					+		
			+	+	+		
		+					
		+			+	+	+
+							
+	+	+	+	+	+	+	+
							+
							+
							+
							+
							+
							+
			+				
	+				+		
+							
+					+		
+					+		
+							
							+

a procedure previously used, for example, by Summers (1992, 1994). This procedure simplifies the process of doing the simulation experiments referred to above. The next section develops the methodology using matrix algebra notation so that interested readers can understand the details of the procedures. Some readers may wish to skim this section and proceed directly to the following section, which presents an illustration.

Methodology for Cost/Benefit Analysis

The objective is to estimate an $s \times 1$ vector of discounted benefits (B) corresponding to an $s \times 1$ vector of alternative investments[38] in youth (H), expressed in thousands of US$ (for concreteness). Then this vector can be used together with an $s \times 1$ vector (C) of the discounted costs, again corresponding to the $s \times 1$ vector of alternative investments in youth (H), in order to calculate an $s \times 1$ vector of cost/benefit ratios or an $s \times 1$ vector of internal rates of return, once again with one element for each of the corresponding alternative investments in youth (H).

The procedure we use begins with a matrix (spreadsheet) of discounted effects (E) with $m + n$ rows and s columns.[39] The first m rows refer to directly monetizable effects of a $1,000 investment in youth. The last n rows refer to the broad effects of the investment (i.e., effects that cannot be directly monetized). The s columns refer to s alternative investments that is, H_1, H_2, H_3 ,..., H_s. We partition the matrix of effects (E) into submatrices E_1, containing the first m rows of E, and E_2, containing the last n rows of E.[40]

We next define the broad effects translation matrix (T) with $m + n$ rows and n columns, each $(m + n) \times 1$ column of which lists first the m directly monetizable components of one of the n broad effects and then the n remaining components of one of the n broad effects. The elements in each column of matrix (T), that is, the components of each broad effect, are in fact discounted effects, while the last n rows of each column in matrix (T) are themselves discounted broad effects. We next partition the matrix (T)

---

[38]Alternatively, the procedures described here might be used to estimate the benefit/cost ratios of a set of related investments that would extend the coverage of a program to successively larger percentages of the program's target population. In this case, the cost-effectiveness of each successive investment might decline to reflect the increasing marginal cost of providing services to successively harder-to-reach subgroups of the target population.

[39]Because the effects of a given investment in youth are assumed to occur over the person's lifetime, the effects are discounted to a single age (e.g., 18 years).

[40]E and T (see next paragraph) are assumed to be fixed matrices for the alternatives that we explore. This requires the assumption that, for the range of investments considered, the marginal effects are constant. In the interest of simplification, our procedure also assumes there are no interactions among the various investments (although there are clearly cases where this is not true, i.e., where synergies exist).

conformably into submatrices T_1, containing the first m rows of (T) (corresponding to directly monetizable effects), and T_2 containing the last n rows of (T) (corresponding to broad effects). The matrix (T) embodies an important simplifying assumption, that is, that the components of each broad effect do not vary by intervention. Otherwise, the matrix (T) would be much larger (i.e., $(m + n) \times n \times s$ instead of only $(m + n) \times n$).

Lastly, we define an $(m + n) \times 1$ vector of benefits (Z) corresponding to one unit of each of the $m + n$ directly monetizable and broad effects.[41] We partition Z into Z_1, containing the first m elements of Z, and Z_2, containing the last n elements of Z. The first m elements of vector Z (Z_1)—the benefits associated with directly monetizable effects—are estimated directly. The last n elements of vector Z (Z_2)—the benefits associated with the broad effects—are calculated by transposing the rows and columns of the two submatrices in matrix T to obtain the $n \times m$ submatrix T_1' and the $n \times n$ submatrix T_2', and then postmultiplying T_1' by the $m \times 1$ vector Z_1 and adding it to the expression obtained by postmultiplying T_2' by the $n \times 1$ vector Z_2:

$$Z_2 = T_1' Z_1 + T_2' Z_2$$

Which implies:

$$Z_2 = (I - T_2')^{-1} T_1' Z_1$$

Where I is the $n \times n$ identity matrix (i.e., matrix with 1s on the diagonal and zeroes elsewhere). In some cases, we may want to use indirect estimates of the benefits of broad effects rather than estimating them directly (i.e., use indirect estimates for some elements of Z_2, rather than basing them on estimates of the corresponding elements of $(I - T_2')^{-1}T_1' Z_1$).

Under these assumptions, the $s \times 1$ vector of discounted benefits (B) corresponding to s alternative investments in youth (H) is given by:

$$B = (E_1' Z_1 + E_2' Z_2) H$$

The vector of discounted benefits (B) is compared to the vector of discounted costs (C), both of which are discounted to the same age (e.g., age 18, or the age at which a given investment is assumed to occur). The benefit/cost ratio (BCR) for a given investment s is defined as:

$$BCR_s = b_s / c_s$$

---

[41]The benefits are discounted back to the actual average age at which the investment is assumed to occur, which we assume to be age 18 in the absence of any reason to make an alternative assumption.

Where b_s refers to element s of B and c_s refers to element s of C.

The internal rate of return (IRR) for a given investment s (IRR_s) is calculated as the discount rate that makes $b_s = c_s$.

A separate set of matrices (spreadsheets) in principle should be used for different categories of countries (e.g., grouped according to their per capita income), for different genders, and for other groups (e.g., ethnic minorities) for which disaggregated analysis is needed. The limited availability of the necessary disaggregated estimates, however, limits the extent to which such disaggregation currently is possible.

A Hypothetical Illustration of the Methodology

We illustrate the methodology with a (relatively) simple, purely hypothetical example. For our example, we take the case of an investment (e.g., a scholarship program for girls) designed to increase the amount of schooling a girl has by one year. We assume that the target group of girls would have quit school at age 13 after completing six grades, in the absence of the investment, and that with an investment of $1,000, we are able to keep 10 girls age 13 in school until they complete seven years of schooling, at which point they will be age 14. The $1,000 investment consists of the following costs: $250 in distortionary costs to raise the revenues to finance this investment, $100 for the program's administrative costs, $300 in costs to accommodate the additional 10 girls in school (i.e., $30 per enrolled pupil), $250 of household investments, largely in the form of foregone earnings of the girls, and a discounted cost of $100 for the girls' children to continue their schooling beyond the grade at which they otherwise would have left school.

We assume that the effect of the hypothetical investment is to increase schooling among the 10 girls by a total of 10 school years (one completed school year per scholarship beneficiary) and that this increase in years of schooling completed results in a proportionate increase in education (as measured by cognitive achievement). However, increased education is a broad effect assumed to have the following components:

• Each girl's labor productivity increases by 10 percent from age 16 until retirement (assumed to occur at age 60).
• Completed fertility is reduced by one child (i.e., the average woman decides not to have a fifth child at age 36).
• Each girl's health improves by 0.05 DALYs per year, beginning at age 14 and continuing throughout her lifetime (which is assumed to be 70 years).
• The health of each of the girls' four children is assumed to improve by 0.05 DALYs beginning at her age 36 and continuing for the 18 years that her children are assumed to spend with her.

- Each of the girls' four children completes 0.5 years more schooling than they otherwise would have completed by the time each girl (woman) reaches age 40.
- The probability that the girls will be infected by HIV decreases by 0.01 from age 15 to 24.

Most of the above components of increased education are directly monetizable effects. However, the increased education that the girls' children are assumed to receive is a broad effect assumed to have the same components as the girls' own increased education (but with substantially longer lags). But, in the case of the girls' children, it is assumed that there is no effect of the investment on their own children's schooling or on their children's risk of contracting HIV. In addition, each HIV infection averted is assumed to be a broad effect with the following components (reflecting the additional assumptions that a girl, if infected with HIV, would be infected on average at age 20, that the infection would turn into AIDS at age 25, and that she would die as soon as she turns 27):

- The additional medical care necessary to treat a person with AIDS is averted at ages 25 and 26 (i.e., during the last two years of life).
- There is an improvement in health equivalent to 34.6 DALYs at age 27.

Annex Table B11-1 presents the assumed effects (including the components of broad effects) of this hypothetical investment over each girl's lifecycle.

There is only one effect in Annex Table B11-2, the broad effect of 10 girls receiving one additional year of schooling at age 14. Because the benefits are discounted to age 18, the effect of the investment is shifted forward to age 18, using the discount rate. The last three effects (i.e., the last three rows of the table) are broad (i.e., not directly monetizable) effects.

Annex Table B11-3 presents the broad effects translation matrix (T) for this hypothetical example. The numbers presented in this table are the cumulative sums of the annual effects presented in Annex Table B11-1 discounted to age 18.

The unit benefits associated with each of the assumed effects are assumed to be as follows:

Enhanced labor productivity. Each woman's full earnings are assumed to be $100 annually.
Reduced fertility. The value to society of averting each woman's fifth birth at age 36 is assumed to be $50 (based on the least cost alternative means of reducing fertility by one birth).
Improved health. The value to society of each DALY gained is assumed to be $10 (based on the assumed cost per DALY gained from the least cost alternative investment to improve health).

ANNEX TABLE B11-1 Assumed Timing of Lifecycle Effects for One
Girl in Hypothetical Girls' Scholarship Example

Age	Increased Education	Enhanced Labor Productivity	Reduced Fertility	Improved Health	Improved Health of Children
Discounted (to age 18) cumulative sum of effect	1.2155	2.0576	0.4155	1.1972	1.0200
Age 13	0	0	0	0	0
14	1	0	0	0.05	0
15	0	0	0	0.05	0
16	0	0.1	0	0.05	0
17	0	0.1	0	0.05	0
18	0	0.1	0	0.05	0
19	0	0.1	0	0.05	0
20	0	0.1	0	0.05	0
21	0	0.1	0	0.05	0
22	0	0.1	0	0.05	0
23	0	0.1	0	0.05	0
24	0	0.1	0	0.05	0
25	0	0.1	0	0.05	0
26	0	0.1	0	0.05	0
27	0	0.1	0	0.05	0
28-35	0	0.1	0	0.05	0
36	0	0.1	1	0.05	0.2
37	0	0.1	0	0.05	0.2
38	0	0.1	0	0.05	0.2
39	0	0.1	0	0.05	0.2
40	0	0.1	0	0.05	0.2
41-53	0	0.1	0	0.05	0.2
54-60	0	0.1	0	0.05	0
61-69	0	0	0	0.05	0
70	0	0	0	0.05	0

Increased Education of Children	Reduced Risk of HIV Infection	Improved Health (HIV)	Decreased Medical Care (HIV)	Discount Factor
0.6837	0.0939	22.3035	1.3875	
0	0	0	0	1.2763
0	0	0	0	1.2155
0	0.01	0	0	1.1576
0	0.01	0	0	1.1025
0	0.01	0	0	1.0500
0	0.01	0	0	1.0000
0	0.01	0	0	0.9524
0	0.01	0	0	0.9070
0	0.01	0	0	0.8638
0	0.01	0	0	0.8227
0	0.01	0	0	0.7835
0	0.01	0	0	0.7462
0	0	0	1.0	0.7107
0	0	0	1.0	0.6768
0	0	34.6	0	0.6446
0	0	0	0	—
0	0	0	0	0.4155
0	0	0	0	0.3957
0	0	0	0	0.3769
0	0	0	0	0.3589
2	0	0	0	0.3418
0	0	0	0	—
0	0	0	0	—
0	0	0	0	—
0	0	0	0	0.0791

ANNEX TABLE B11-2   Effects Matrix (E) for Hypothetical Scholarship Program for 10 Girls

Effects of Hypothetical Investment	Scholarship Program
Enhanced productivity	0.0000
Reduced fertility	0.0000
Improved health	0.0000
Improved health of children	0.0000
Decreased medical care expenditure	0.0000
Increased education	12.1551
Increased education of children	0.0000
Averted HIV infections	0.0000

SOURCE: See text.

ANNEX TABLE B11-3 Broad Effects Translation Matrix (T) of Hypothetical Scholarship Program for Girls

Components of Broad Effects	Broad Effects Increased Schooling	Increased Schooling of Children	Averted HIV Infections
Enhanced productivity	2.0576	2.0576	0
Reduced fertility	0.4155	0.4155	0
Improved health	1.1972	1.1972	22.3035
Improved health of children	1.0200	1.0200	0
Decreased medical care expenditure	0	0	1.3875
Increased schooling	0	0	0
Increased schooling of children	0.6837	0	0
Averted HIV infections	0.0939	0	0

SOURCE: See text.

Decreased medical care expenditure. The medical care expenditure for HIV-infected persons is assumed to be $270 annually during their last two years of life.

The full unit benefit vector (Z) for this hypothetical example is presented in Annex Table B11-4.

ANNEX TABLE B11-4 Benefit Vector (Z) for Hypothetical Example of Scholarship Program for Girls

Benefits	Elements of Vector Z
Enhanced productivity	100
Reduced fertility	50
Improved health	10
Improved health of children	10
Decreased medical care expenditure	270
Increased schooling[a]	475
Increased schooling of children[a]	249
Averted HIV infections[a]	597

[a]Elements obtained by solving the equation above for Z_2, i.e., $Z_2 = (I - T_2')^{-1} T_1' Z_1$.
SOURCE: See text.

REFERENCES

Alderman, H., Behrman, J.R., Ross, D., and Sabot, R. (1996). The returns to endogenous human capital in Pakistan's rural wage labor market. *Oxford Bulletin of Economics and Statistics, 58*(1), 29-55.

Angrist, J.D., Bettinger, E., Bloom, E., King, E., and Kremer, M. (2002). Vouchers for private schooling in Colombia: Evidence from a randomized natural experiment. *American Economic Review, 92*(5), 1535-1559.

Ballard, C., Shoven, J., and Whalley, J. (1985). General equilibrium computations of the marginal welfare costs of taxes in the United States. *American Economic Review, 75*(1), 128-138.

Becker, G.S. (1967). *Human capital and the personal distribution of income: An analytical approach (Woytinsky Lecture).* Ann Arbor, MI: University of Michigan. (Republished in *Human capital* [2nd ed.] pp. 97-117) 1975, New York: National Bureau of Economic Research.

Behrman, J.R., and Knowles, J.C. (1998a). *The distributional implications of government family planning and reproductive health services in Vietnam.* (Prepared for the Rockefeller Foundation). Philadelphia: University of Pennsylvania.

Behrman, J.R., and Knowles, J.C. (1998b). Population and reproductive health: An economic framework for policy evaluation. *Population and Development Review, 24*(4), 697-738.

Behrman, J.R., and Knowles, J.C. (1999). Household income and child schooling in Vietnam. *World Bank Economic Review, 13*(2), 211-256.

Behrman, J.R., Ross, D., and Sabot, R. (2005). Improving the quality versus increasing the quantity of schooling: Evidence from rural Pakistan. Pennsylvania Institute for Economic Research. (PIER Working Paper 02-022.) Available: http://www.econ.upenn.edu/Centers/pier/Archive/02-022.pdf [accessed September 2005].

Caribbean Group for Cooperation in Economic Development (CGCED). (2002, June). *Youth development in the Carribbean.* (Draft Report No. 24163-LAC.) Washington, DC: The World Bank.

Commission on Macroeconomics and Health. (2001). *Macroeconomics and health: Investing in health for economic development.* Geneva, Switzerland: World Health Organization.

Devarajan, S., Squire, L., and Suthiwart-Narueput, S. (1997). Beyond rate of return: Reorienting project appraisal. *World Bank Research Observer, 12*(1), 35-46.

Feldstein, M. (1995). *Tax avoidance and the deadweight loss of the income tax.* (NBER Working Paper No. 5055.) Cambridge, MA: National Bureau of Economic Research.

Harberger, A.C. (1997). New frontiers in project evaluation? A comment on Devarajan, Squire, and Suthiwart-Narueput. *World Bank Research Observer, 12*(1), 73-79.

Knowles, J.C., and Behrman, J.R. (2003). *Assessing the economic returns to investing in youth in developing countries.* (For World Bank Human Development Network.) Bangkok, Thailand/Philadelphia: University of Pennsylvania.

Knowles, J.C., and Behrman, J.R. (2005). *The economic returns to investing in youth in developing countries: A review of the literature.* (World Bank Human Development Network; Health, Nutrition and Population Discussion Paper.) Available: www.worldbank.org/hnp>publications>Discussion Papers [accessed June 2005].

McGuire, J.S. (1996). *The payoff from improving nutrition.* Unpublished manuscript, World Bank, Washington, DC.

Miguel, E., and Kremer, M. (2002). *Why don't people take their medicine: Experimental evidence from Kenya.* Unpublished manuscript, Harvard University and University of California, Berkeley.

Miguel, E., and Kremer, M. (2004). Worms: Identifying impacts on education and health in the presence of treatment externalities. *Econometrica, 72*(1), 159-217.

Psacharopoulos, G. (1994). Returns to investment in education: A global update. *World Development, 22*(9), 1325-1344.

Ravallion, M., and Wodon, Q. (2000). Does child labor displace schooling? Evidence from behavioral responses to an enrollment subsidy. *Economic Journal, 110*(462), 158-175.

Rosenzweig, M.R., and Wolpin, K.J. (1986). Evaluating the effects of optimally distributed public programs. *American Economic Review, 76*(3), 470-487.

Summers, L.H. (1992). Investing in all the people. *Pakistan Development Review, 31*(4), 367-406.

Summers, L.H. (1994). *Investing in all the people: Educating women in developing countries.* (Economic Development Institute Seminar Paper No. 45.) Washington, DC: World Bank.

van der Gaag, J., and Tan, J.P. (1997). *The benefits of early child development programs: An economic analysis.* Washington, DC: Author.

World Bank. (1999). *Curbing the epidemic: Governments and the economics of tobacco control.* Washington, DC: Author.

World Bank. (2002a). *Optimizing the allocation of resources among HIV prevention interventions in Honduras.* Washington, DC: Author.

World Bank. (2002b). *Review of World Bank supported projects in adult basic education and literacy, 1997-2002.* Washington, DC: Author.

World Bank. (2002c). *School health toolkit.* Washington, DC: Author.

Appendix

Contents

Growing Up Global: The Changing Transitions to Adulthood in Developing Countries

Citation:
National Research Council and Institute of Medicine. 2005. *Growing Up Global: The Changing Transitions to Adulthood in Developing Countries.* Panel on Transitions to Adulthood in Developing Countries. Cynthia B. Lloyd, ed. Committee on Population and Board on Children, Youth, and Families. Division of Behavioral and Social Sciences and Education. Washington, DC: The National Academies Press.

PART II: PREPARATION FOR ADULT ROLES

PART III: TRANSITION TO ADULT ROLES